A-Z
BRITISH CARS
1945-1980

A-Z
BRITISH CARS
1945-1980

BY GRAHAM ROBSON

Herridge & Sons

Published 2006 by Herridge & Sons Ltd
Lower Forda, Shebbear,
Devon EX21 5SY

ISBN 0-9541063-9-3
Printed in China

Acknowledgments
Most of the photographs reproduced came from the
collection of the late David Hodges. The publishers are
grateful to the author, Chris Rees and the Turner and
Tornado Registers of the Fairthorpe Sports Club for
other photographs supplied.

Foreword

As I grew up when Britain's post-war motor industry was struggling back to life, the amazing variety of cars which followed has always fascinated me. Some were successful and some were failures. Some were exciting and some were desperately dull. But there were millions of them, and many have survived to become modern classics.

Until the 1980s, when globalisation, legislation, and the sheer cost of getting new British cars on to the market had killed off most of the enterprise, there always seemed to be new cars to admire. Cars as diverse as the Jaguar XK120, the Mini, the Triumph TR2, the AC Cobra, the Ford Lotus-Cortina and the Rolls-Royce Silver Shadow always kept us interested.

With the encouragement of my publisher, I set out to list, describe and assess every true British production car – three-wheelers, four-wheelers and even six-wheelers - built in the UK from 1945 to 1980. Quite simply, we decided that an A-to-Z of everything was required. It was a colossal task, made only slightly easier because we decided to eliminate foreign cars built over here (like the Renault Dauphine and Citroen DS19), and we decided not to include several build-it-yourself kit cars whose manufacturers relied on the customers to do the assembly. Single prototypes have been ignored, though those machines which died after just a handful had been delivered have been included.

Laying out the corporate histories of Ford, BMC and the Rootes/Chrysler groupings was relatively easy compared with the demanding need to delve into the life and times of cars as rare as the Rodley, as strange as the Peel, and as esoteric as the Invicta. It meant that we eventually listed no fewer than 703 models, and are delighted to have found no fewer than 1100 pictures to add to all the facts. We hope that every distinctly different motor car has been illustrated.

My "Rules of Engagement" were that I would cover every car built between 1945 and 1980: where appropriate I have carried on an individual history until the very end of its career. With the Mini, incidentally, that covered a further twenty years!

It was necessary to standardise and summarise specifications, performance and production figures and prices, but these had to come from a variety of sources. Although introduction and withdrawal dates were usually known, and performance figures could be found in the many independent road tests which were carried out when the cars were on sale, in some cases it was not easy to find accurate production figures. If those quoted are slightly at variance with an owner's own assumptions, I hope he will understand the assessments which sometimes have had to be made.

Incidentally, we do not claim that no interesting British cars have been introduced since 1980, though we think that most cases of individual British enterprise were suppressed after that.

GRAHAM ROBSON
March 2006

AC

AC started making cars in 1908, leading an independent existence for the next seven decades. The first example of a long-lived, overhead-cam six-cylinder engine arrived in 1919.

Controlled from the 1930s by the Hurlock brothers, AC produced elegant sporting machines, including the two-seater 16/80 and 16/90 sports cars.

Post-war production restarted in 1947, with the traditional-type 2-Litre model, but with no modern designs on the horizon, AC looked likely to wither away. In the meantime, sub-contract work and the development first of an invalid carriage, then of the Petite three-wheeler, kept the company afloat. The Petite was not a great product, but made money. The transformation came in 1953, when AC agreed to put an AC-engined version of John Tojeiro's racing sports car into production. This was a completely different type of AC, and it served the company well to late 1960s.

Both the Ace and the Aceca were attractive: once available with the Bristol engine they had performance equal to their looks and handling. AC then stumbled, with the Greyhound, which was bigger, heavier, and a lot more expensive.

Rescue came in 1962 when the American enthusiast Carroll Shelby persuaded them to redesign the Ace, the result being the Ford-USA V8 engined Cobra. AC built many engine-less Cobras at Thames Ditton and shipped them to the USA for completion. Copies, clones and re-creations later sprung up all around the world. This sometimes forced AC to take legal action to preserve their image rights. Real Cobras, though, were re-born from the late 1970s, by British-based companies to whom AC (and Shelby American) ceded the design rights. In the late 1960s AC launched the 428, which combined a longer-wheelbase, de-tuned Cobra 427 chassis with hand-crafted bodies by Frua of Italy. These cars were expensive and sold slowly. Later, to replace the 428, the company took up a new design for a mid-engined two-seater, this being the AC3000ME.

By the mid-1980s the Thames Ditton management had lost interest in car production. For a short time AC was owned by Ford, but no new models ever made it to the market place. Modern (early 2000s) ACs were still based on improved derivatives of the original Cobras – and they, don't forget, were lineal descendants of the Ace of 1953. In half a century, AC's image had not moved far.

2-Litre 1946-58

AC 2-litre saloon, in two-door form.

SPECIFICATION
BODY STYLES: saloon, drophead, tourer
PRODUCTION: 1284
ENGINE & TRANSMISSION: 1991cc, 6cyl ohc, 4sp man, f/r
POWER: 74 (later 85) bhp @ 4500rpm
MAX SPEED (MPH): 80 (Buckland 86)
0-60MPH (SEC): 19.9
SUSPENSION & BRAKES: beam leaf front, leaf rear, drums f&r
LENGTH (IN)/WEIGHT (LB): 184/2800 (Buckland 2688)
LAUNCH PRICE: £1277 (Buckland £1098)

The company announced its post-war car, the 2-litre, in 1947. Although the specification, layout and feel were redolent of the 1930s, AC produced a modern style to hide the traditional engineering.

Much of the detail was new. The X-braced chassis frame, with beam front and rear axles, was fresh. The 17in wheels hid a Girling hydro-mechanical braking layout, and for the first time on an AC there were hydraulic dampers.

The splendid alloy block/iron head overhead-cam engine, almost into its fourth decade, used triple SU carbs and was mated to a Moss gearbox. The 2-litre's two-door saloon body was framed in wood with aluminium panels. A smart drophead coupé followed in 1949, a four-door saloon in 1953.

Over time there were improvements such as a power boost to 85bhp, all-round telescopic dampers, a full hydraulic braking system, and 16in wheels in 1951. The most startling innovation was the launch of the Buckland Tourer in 1949, an open-top five-seater with cutaway doors, This was lighter and more fashionable, but still no sports car.

The 2-Litre always struggled to gain an image. Once the Ace sports car appeared, it faded into the background. From 1954, only 42 cars were produced, the last in 1958. In spite of the rust-resistant bodywork there seem to be surprisingly few survivors, mainly as they are a source of replacement engines for more valuable Aces and pre-war cars.

Petite 1953-58

The Petite three-wheeler, on sale from 1953, was a singularly nasty little "marginal motoring" machine. It competed with similarly horrid three-wheelers from Bond and Reliant. It offered little except a low price, and the fact that the driver did not need a motor car driving licence.

Technically this simple Villiers-engined machine was light, though not refined, and economical, but very slow by comparison with any small family car. Like Bond and Reliant, it had a single front wheel and two rear wheels. In this case the engine and motorcycle-type

AC Petite three-wheeler

gearbox were in the tail, with the gearchange lever on the steering column. The steel and aluminium structure was of unit construction, with coil spring independent suspension at all three corners. Drive from engine to gearbox was by rubber belts; there was no reverse. Early cars had different-sized front and rear wheels (8in diameter front, 18in diameter rears). Mk II versions (with marginally larger engine) had 12in wheels all round.

Styling was slab-sided and covered up the front wheel: the Petite looked like a grown-up AC invalid carriage, a fixed-

roof two-seater with a bench seat. The doors were of the suicide variety, with a simple roll-back fabric roof panel. The trim and equipment were basic. Even at the launch price of £399, the Petite was cheap (the contemporary Ford Anglia cost £491), but it was neither comfortable nor pleasurable at more than 40mph. Apart from the motorcycle licence angle, and a lower annual road tax charge, the main attraction was in the claimed fuel economy of 60-70mpg. Although the Mk II Petite was slightly improved, this was really no substitute for proper motoring.

SPECIFICATION

BODY STYLES: saloon

PRODUCTION: c.4000

ENGINE & TRANSMISSION: 346cc/353cc, 1cyl ts, 3sp man, r/r

POWER: 8bhp @ 3500rpm

MAX SPEED (MPH): 40 (E)

0-60MPH (SEC): not possible

SUSPENSION & BRAKES: coil ifs, coil irs, drums f&r

LENGTH (IN)/WEIGHT (LB): 123/845

LAUNCH PRICE: £399

Ace 1953-63

Commercially, the Ace transformed AC's image and ensured its survival. Here was a new, modern product which looked smart and handled well. In AC-engined form it could beat 100mph; with more powerful Bristol engines it was formidable.

The genesis was John Tojeiro's Tojeiro-Bristol racing sports car. The chassis frame was welded from large diameter tubes, and carried a Barchetta-like aluminium body on a lightweight body frame, with all-independent suspension by transverse leaf springs at front and rear. It was rugged, nimble and clearly could be modified to take different power units.

AC bought up the design rights, productionised it, and inserted their

Prototype AC Ace.

An Ace at Le Mans.

own 85bhp version of the ancient overhead-camshaft AC engine, with a Moss gearbox. The Ace went on sale in mid-1954, but it always seemed expensive. The AC-engined Ace wasn't as fast as it looked, but the Michelin X radial tyres and soft independent-suspension chassis made up for a lot. The chassis had a balance that persuaded the driver he was a genius.

AC power was gradually pushed up (finally to 102bhp), but from 1956 AC was able to offer the option of a 1971cc Bristol engine: this was being used in Bristol and Frazer-Nash cars, and was a descendant of the BMW 328 unit of the late 1930s. Many Ace-Bristols had 125bhp, giving 117mph, but a few used race-prepared 130bhp units.

Along the way there were more improvements – overdrive from 1956, front-wheel disc brakes from 1957, and 15in wheels from 1959. By that time the Ace was at its peak, but high prices and sometimes doubtful quality always held it back. With AC and Bristol engine supplies under threat, AC then offered highly-tuned Ford Zephyr engines in the early 1960s, but only a handful were sold.

The Ace inspired two further models – the Aceca coupé, and the Cobra. By then its reputation had been sealed.

SPECIFICATION

BODY STYLES: sports car

PRODUCTION: 228/466/38

ENGINE & TRANSMISSION: 1991/1971/2553cc, 6cyl ohc/ohv/ohv, 4sp man (optional o/d), f/r

POWER: 85bhp @ 4500rpm -170bhp @ 5800rpm

MAX SPEED (MPH): (85bhp) 103, (125bhp) 117

0-60MPH (SEC): (85bhp) 11.4, (125bhp) 9.0

SUSPENSION & BRAKES: leaf ifs, leaf irs, drums f&r (later disc f)

LENGTH (IN)/WEIGHT (LB): 153/1685 –1845

LAUNCH PRICE: £1439

AC Ace.

Aceca 1955-63

Although the Ace was a productionised Tojeiro at first, the two-seater fastback coupé Aceca was entirely to AC's credit. From 1955 AC offered the new model, with graceful styling and looks not unlike those of the contemporary Aston Martin DB2/4, including what was actually an early example of the hatchback.

Mechanically, Ace and Aceca were very similar, though changes were introduced to make the rear end of the chassis more robust. Much of the new superstructure was in shaped wood, clothed in aluminiun; glass-fibre also featured in the structure hidden away. Although AC made no attempt to provide extra seats (that would follow, later, with the Greyhound), a third passenger could occasionally cram him or herself into the tail.

Although the AC engine was standard at first, the more powerful Bristol alternative suited the Aceca very well – half the production run having this breed of power. Heavier than the open-top Ace, and significantly more expensive, the Aceca was always an exclusive car. Today's Acecas have all needed much renovation to restore the wooden body framing, and because fashion still favours open-top cars they do not command prices as high as the Ace.

SPECIFICATION

BODY STYLES: sports coupé

PRODUCTION: 150/169/8

ENGINE & TRANSMISSION:
1991cc/1971cc/2553cc, 6cyl ohc/ohv/ohv, 4sp man, optional O/D, f/r

POWER: 85bhp @ 4500rpm -170bhp @ 5800rpm

MAX SPEED (MPH): (85bhp) 102, (125bhp) 115

0-60MPH (SEC): (85bhp) 13.4, (125bhp) 10.3

SUSPENSION & BRAKES: leaf ifs, leaf irs, drums f&r (later disc f)

LENGTH (IN)/WEIGHT (LB): 153/1840

LAUNCH PRICE: £1722

The AC Aceca

Greyhound 1959-63

Without the successful Aceca hatchback coupé, AC might have sold more Greyhounds. The fact is that the "almost four-seater" Greyhound was too large, too heavy, and not nearly as nimble as the two-seater Aceca. Only 83 cars were sold in four years.

Because the style was neat, if not sensational, it is easy to miss the statistics – the Greyhound was 15in longer than the Aceca, and 400lb heavier. AC engines were not normally considered for this bigger machine, which usually relied on Bristol power.

The Greyhound used an entirely different type of 100in wheelbase frame. There was rack-and-pinion steering, and the rear end had semi-trailing arms instead of the Ace/Aceca's wishbone layout. Coil springs were used instead of a transverse leaf at each end.

The Greyhound's greater bulk, and its less "pure" rear suspension, ensured that it would not handle as well as the two-seaters. All this, and the fact that the Greyhound was very expensive – it cost £2999 in 1960, when the Aceca-Bristol cost £2561 (and a 3.4-litre Jaguar

SPECIFICATION

BODY STYLES: sports coupé

PRODUCTION: 83

ENGINE & TRANSMISSION: 1971cc/2216cc, 6cyl ohv, 4sp man, optional O/D, f/r (other AC and Bristol engines to special order)

POWER: 105bhp @ 4750rpm/105bhp @ 4700rpm

MAX SPEED (MPH): 104

0-60MPH (SEC): 11.4

SUSPENSION & BRAKES: coil ifs, coil irs, disc f/drum r

LENGTH (IN)/WEIGHT (LB): 175/2240

LAUNCH PRICE: £2891

XK150 cost only £1666) – meant that it was difficult to sell.

Not everyone liked the Greyhound's handling: when it was fully loaded with four occupants, more than half the weight was over the rear wheels, whose suspension geometry/wheel movements were by no means ideal. Several testers (so this must be a consistent opinion) complained of "rear wheel steering".

Even so, the Greyhound had a rarified charm. By the time the Cobra arrived, its time was past - only 18 were built in 1962, and three more in 1963.

AC Greyhound.

Cobra 1962-68

The Cobra legend, it seems, is true. American race driver/entrepreneur Carroll Shelby shoe-horned a Ford-USA V8 into the Ace, travelled to AC, and convinced them about the project. Ford-USA agreed to supply engines, and suitably robust transmission and back axle casings were also inserted. Shelby convinced AC to supply partly completed cars to him in California, where he would fit the engines and transmissions. Deliveries began in mid-1961 and just 61 cars were completed by the end of the year.

The original 4.2-litre/260 cubic inch Cobra used a much-modified Ace chassis and a lightly-modified body style. Differences soon built up after the brawnier 4.7-litre/289 cubic inch engine took over, outboard rear brakes replaced inboard types, and rack-and-pinion steering was added. Except for flared wheel arches and a modified nose, the original body style remained.

What the Cobra offered was raw, red-blooded, unashamed performance, with a harsh ride and deafening exhaust note. Wheelspin was part of the deal, but no-one complained. From 1964 Shelby evolved special-bodied versions known as Daytona Cobras, which won the World Sports Car Championship in 1965.

A few 289s (or Mk IIs) were sold in Europe: a UK version went on sale in 1964 for £2454. The wheel then came full circle, for the AC 289 (which was really a coil sprung AC 427 with the 289 cu in engine) followed in 1966.

Although the last of all was built in 1968, this was not the end. Late in the 1970s Brian Angliss gained the rights to make up-dated cars called Mk IVs, and for the next two decades small numbers continued to be manufactured.

Ownership and rights changed hands several times after that, but re-engined cars still looking like the early Cobras were still made in the 2000s.

Thousands of lookalike replicas, with different frames, most with glass-fibre bodies, were produced.

AC Cobra 289 retained the lithe looks of the Ace.

SPECIFICATION

BODY STYLES: sports car

PRODUCTION: 1137, all Cobra types

ENGINE & TRANSMISSION:
4261/4727cc, ohv, 4sp man, f/r

POWER: 260bhp/300bhp @ 5800rpm

MAX SPEED (MPH): 138

0-60MPH (SEC): 5.5

SUSPENSION & BRAKES: leaf ifs, leaf irs (coils f/r on Mk III), discs f&r

LENGTH (IN)/WEIGHT (LB): 158/2100

LAUNCH PRICE: £2454

Cobra 427 1965-68

The Cobra 427.

To improve on the Cobra 289, Shelby persuaded Ford-USA to supply their larger and extraordinarily powerful 6998cc/427 cubic inch V8 engine. The result, from January 1965, was the Cobra Mk III, with a much-changed tube frame, and more precisely controlled coil spring suspension at each corner.

Every detail of the running gear and drive line had been beefed up, knock-off alloy wheels were bigger, brakes were larger, and the body style featured swollen wheelarches to cover the fatter tyres. An even larger front air intake was needed to get yet more air into the engine bay.

Everyone loved this monstrously fast, super-extrovert, over-the-top sports car, though few could actually afford to buy, insure and run it. Independent tests promised 0-100mph in little more than ten seconds, and a top speed of more than 160mph – scary, but also

quite extraordinary for the price asked.

Almost everything in the car, from tyres to transmissions to brakes – and elements of the chassis – could be treated as a consumable. Anyone who drove one, and did not admit to a raised heartbeat, clammy palms, and unstoppable smiles or even outright laughs, was not normal.

A few cars were produced with larger 7014cc/428 cubic inch V8 engines. These were refined road-car units of a type fitted to the Ford Galaxie saloons, and had "only" 345bhp. At first, amazingly, the 427 cost no more than the 289 in the USA – $5995. Officially it was never available in the UK, though a few cars were registered here.

By that time, though, the Cobra's time had been and gone, for most buyers seemed to want more luxury, space and creature comforts than the 427 could offer. Amazing, shocking, but true. The result was that sales fell away and the

last cars were produced in 1968.

Difficult to believe? Maybe, but the figures speak for themselves. AC built only seven cars in 1967, the last ten in 1968. A development, the plush Frua-styled 428, was never likely to fill the gap left by the Cobra.

SPECIFICATION

BODY STYLES: sports car

PRODUCTION: 413 in the 1960s. Production re-started late 1970s

ENGINE & TRANSMISSION: 6998/7014cc, V8cyl ohv, 4sp man, f/r

POWER: 480bhp @ 6000rpm/345bhp @ 4600rpm

MAX SPEED (MPH): (480bhp) 165

0-60MPH (SEC): (480bhp) 4.2

SUSPENSION & BRAKES: coil ifs, coil irs, discs f&r

LENGTH (IN)/WEIGHT (LB): 159/2354

LAUNCH PRICE: not officially sold in UK

428 1965-73

When the Cobra phenomenon was at its height, AC started work on a luxury development of the latest Mk III chassis. The result was the AC 428.

Although AC wanted only two-seater motoring, the new project had a six-inch longer wheelbase: the chosen engine was the "soft" 7014cc/428 cu in V8. Although very powerful, Ford had developed it to last indefinitely in large passenger cars. Like the parent company, AC matched it to a three-speed auto 'box. The AC 428 was meant to be a gentleman's carriage.

AC hired Frua, of Italy, to produce twin body styles – an elegant fastback coupé and an equally smart convertible. Both were luxuriously trimmed and well equipped. As Frua was already producing bodies for Maserati, it was easy to see similarities between the Italian and the British models.

AC would send rolling chassis to Italy, Frua added the trimmed and painted body shells, then returned the cars to Thames Ditton for completion. This always took time. When Italy's anarchic working practices and strike record were mixed in, AC 428 build quality was often doubtful, and deliveries were patchy.

Although the 428 was fast, it retained

The 428 used a stretched Cobra chassis.

most of the Cobra 427's handling quirks and little habits, including a rather squirmy tendency at the rear when the gas pedal was firmly floored. Much detail development was needed to make it match its competitors.

The 428 was expensive. In 1968 it cost £5573, compared with the Aston Martin DB6 (£4229), the Jensen Interceptor (£4460) and, worse, the Jaguar E-Type (£2225). This, the long-distance problem of ensuring body supplies, and continuing worries over quality, eventually saw sales drop away. The last car of only 81 428s was built in 1973.

SPECIFICATION

BODY STYLES: two-seater convertible and sports coupé

PRODUCTION: 81

ENGINE & TRANSMISSION: 7014cc, V8 cyl ohv, 3sp auto, f/r

POWER: 345bhp @ 4600rpm

MAX SPEED (MPH): 139

0-60MPH (SEC): 5.9

SUSPENSION & BRAKES: coil ifs, coil irs, discs f&r

LENGTH (IN)/WEIGHT (LB): 176/3115

LAUNCH PRICE: £4250

AC 428 was styled by Frua.

3000ME 1979-84

The mid-engined AC 3000ME.

This ill-fated mid-engined project held only one record – that it took no less than six years to go from public launch to first deliveries. Having bought the basic design of a one-off called the Diablo, AC completely misjudged the time it would need to get it ready for sale. Year after year prototypes were shown at motor shows, the price kept going up, and by 1979 (when deliveries started) the AC-buying public had virtually lost interest.

The platform chassis was made of pressed and fabricated sheet steel, with a transversely-mounted Ford V6 engine behind the seats, driving through an AC/Hewland gearbox. The rolling chassis, which had all-independent suspension and four-wheel disc brakes, plus cast alloy wheels, was covered by a rather chunky fixed-head body, built from glass-fibre.

There was some luggage space ahead of the passengers' feet, and a little behind the engine, but on the whole this was a small and rather self-indulgent car.

Although it was brisk (120mph, for instance, was no better than a mass-produced 2-litre sports car of the period), this was not an outstanding car in any way, for the handling was still not right (a rear weight bias didn't help), and few could warm to the style.

It was also expensive: when first on sale, for £12,432, a Morgan Plus 8 cost half that, and a Lotus Elite/Eclat (prettier and better-engineered) sold for similar money.

Sales petered out in 1984. The rights were then sold to a Scottish enterprise, which tried to re-engineer it with an Alfa Romeo V6 engine, but this too failed, and it was rarely seen in public.

SPECIFICATION

BODY STYLES: sports coupé

PRODUCTION: 82 produced by AC

ENGINE & TRANSMISSION: 2994cc, V6cyl ohv, 5sp man, m/r

POWER: 138bhp @ 5000rpm

MAX SPEED (MPH): 120

0-60MPH (SEC): 8.5

SUSPENSION & BRAKES: coil ifs, coil irs, discs f&r

LENGTH (IN)/WEIGHT (LB): 157/2483

LAUNCH PRICE: £12,432

Chunky two-seater bodywork was made of glass-fibre.

ALLARD

It was the massive post-war demand for cars – any cars – after the Second World War which helped bring the Allard motor car into existence. Engineer and motorsport enthusiast Sydney Allard had already built a dozen Ford-based Allard Specials in the 1930s. His family business had been frantically busy with military transport maintenance and repairs during the war years, so in 1945 he was encouraged to look ahead.

Because they were Ford dealers, the Allard family decided to build up a model range which used newly-designed chassis frames, but with a mass of Ford V8 running gear and components, allied to lightweight body shells which would be brought in from small businesses in the London area.

A notional range (not all of which existed, except in artists' impressions) was launched in 1946, and sales soon built up. Right from the start there were J1 two-seaters, K1 touring two-seaters, L-Type four-seater tourers, and M-Type drophead coupés, with a P-Type saloon promised for the future. With a quaint divided-axle type of independent front suspension, the cars handled very strangely at times, but everyone seemed to forgive them. Assembly was

Chassis of a typical pre-war Allard Special, with V8 engine.

by hand, and deliveries rarely exceeded 300 cars a year, but Sydney Allard was always optimistic about the future.

By the early '50s, not only had Allard developed a special new tubular-framed chassis, but fierce J2 and J2X sports cars arrived, alternative, powerful Cadillac V8 engines had become available, and Allard even entered cars in the Le Mans 24 Hour sports car race. By then the cars handled better than the originals too!

The problem, as with all such marques, was that prices were high, while build quality was only average, and once post-war shortages had ceased, demand fell away. Not even victory in the 1952 Monte Carlo rally for Sydney Allard himself could stop the decline, The all-new and much smaller Palm Beach range might have succeeded if only it had been a lot cheaper, but cars like the Triumph TR2 and the Austin-Healey 100 soon saw it off. The weird little Allard Clipper micro-car of 1954 was a complete flop.

Production declined to "Special Order" status by 1956, and finally petered out altogether in 1959. Sydney Allard himself continued with the modification of Ford cars, but Allard no longer made machines of its own.

J1 1946-47

Taking over from the Allard Specials of the 1930s, the J1 was a starkly trimmed and equipped two-seater, which ran on a 100in wheelbase, featured the divided-axle independent front suspension for which the early cars would become famous, and ushered in the basic post-war style

SPECIFICATION

BODY STYLES: sports car

PRODUCTION: 12

ENGINE & TRANSMISSION: 3622/3917cc, V8 sv, 3sp man, f/r

POWER: 85bhp @ 3800rpm/100bhp @ 3500rpm

MAX SPEED (MPH): 85 (E)

0-60MPH (SEC): not measured

SUSPENSION & BRAKES: transverse leaf ifs, transverse leaf rear, drums f&r

LENGTH (IN)/WEIGHT (LB): 149/2240

LAUNCH PRICE: £1125

Rare Allard J1 was a short-chassis two-seater.

which all the big V8-engined Allards would share.

Little known, and not advertised, the J1 was effectively a competition car which Sydney Allard wanted to see used to get his cars' names known more widely. For that reason, the ground clearance was quite high, the front

wings were removable, and there were few creature comforts.

Allard didn't mind that, and made sure that these cars – there were only to be 12 of them – went to buyers who would rally them. Very rare at the time, even rarer today, they are among the starkest and most evil of all Allards.

K1 1946-48

The first of the real series-production Allards (if you could ever describe a car built by hand, from hand-beaten body panels on a wooden body skeleton, in this way) was the K1 tourer. Built on a longer wheelbase than the J1 – at 106in – this was a purposeful two-seater open tourer, with the waterfall grille and the often bow-legged stance to the front wheels which would become so familiar on other models over the years.

Raucously quick – 0-60mph in only 13 seconds was rapid by mid-1940s

Allard K1 on the Furka Pass.

SPECIFICATION

BODY STYLES: sports tourer

PRODUCTION: 151

ENGINE & TRANSMISSION: 3622/3917cc, V8 sv, 3sp man, f/r

POWER: 85bhp @ 3800rpm/100bhp @ 3500rpm

MAX SPEED (MPH): 86/90

0-60MPH (SEC): 13

SUSPENSION & BRAKES: transverse leaf ifs, transverse leaf rear, drums f&r

LENGTH (IN)/WEIGHT (LB): 168/2632

LAUNCH PRICE: £1151

standards – it offered real performance with almost no refinement. Character, though – oh yes, bags of it. Maybe the front suspension geometry looked grotesque (lots of positive camber when being cornered hard), and maybe the build quality (quality?) was iffy, but this was an early post-war man's car, built to do a man's job.

Theoretically, K1s were available only with sidevalve Ford-UK or Ford-Canada Mercury V8s, but even in the 1940s other more modern types of V8s tended to be fitted by subsequent owners. Nowadays, as long as the cars have survived, no-one seems to mind.

L-Type 1946-48

Third in line of the post-war Allard pedigree, the L sports tourer was really a K1 with a stretched (by six inches) wheelbase, and an extra two seats squeezed into the longer passenger compartment. For Allard, and with minimal tooling, it was easy to mix-and-

The four-seater Allard L1.

SPECIFICATION

BODY STYLES: sports tourer

PRODUCTION: 191

ENGINE & TRANSMISSION: 3622/3917cc, V8 sv, 3sp man, f/r

POWER: 85bhp @ 3800rpm/100bhp @ 3500rpm

MAX SPEED (MPH): 85 (E)

0-60MPH (SEC): not measured

SUSPENSION & BRAKES: transverse leaf ifs, transverse leaf rear, drums f&r

LENGTH (IN)/WEIGHT (LB): 182/2968

LAUNCH PRICE: £1259

match specifications like this.

Compared with the K1, the front end style was the same, the changes being aft of the front seats. The penalty was a longer car, which weighed three hundredweight (336lb/152kg) more. It was still useful for club motorsport at the time, though elephantine by later standards – and still expensive, of course.

Not the most desirable of all early Allards, but still appealing because it was so rare.

M1 1947-50

Work this one out for yourselves – usual post-war Allard chassis, the longest of the wheelbases (112in), the same choice of engines, the same front-end style, but this time a full four-seater drophead coupé body style. Because it was the most complicated

Allard M1 was a civilised drophead coupé.

body style to engineer, it was late becoming available, but once there it took most of the sales.

The M1, in fact, was the best-selling of all soft-top Allards (the P1 saloon shaded it, though – 559 against 500), and appealed to more people than the more starkly-trimmed sports tourers. A

Ford Pilot-type three-speed steering-column gearchange didn't do much for the character, but it seemed to be wanted in some export markets.

Even in later years, Allard couldn't develop a straight replacement for the M1. They tried, but the M2X was a complete flop.

SPECIFICATION

BODY STYLES: drophead coupé

PRODUCTION: 500

ENGINE & TRANSMISSION: 3622/3917cc, V8 sv, 3sp man, f/r

POWER: 85bhp @ 3800rpm/100bhp @ 3500rpm

MAX SPEED (MPH): 82

0-60MPH (SEC): 15.2

SUSPENSION & BRAKES: transverse leaf ifs (later coil ifs), transverse leaf rear, drums f&r

LENGTH (IN)/WEIGHT (LB): 189/2884

LAUNCH PRICE: £1125

P1 1949-51

Allard's original saloon – P1 – was not only its best-seller, but one of its most successful too, for Sydney Allard himself used a P1 to win the Monte Carlo Rally in 1952. No other driver, before or since, has won this event in a car of his own manufacture.

The P1 was the fourth derivative of the original sweep of Allard models (and the last to go on sale), all of them sharing the

A P1 Allard hard at work on the Col de Braus on the way to Monte Carlo.

same basic mechanical layout. Logically enough P1, the four-seater saloon, used the longest of the three wheelbases (112in), but had an updated type of front suspension, still with a divided axle geometry but with coil springs instead of a transverse leaf. The body style, and panelling up to the passenger bulkhead, was like that of the M1 DHC and the L-Type sports tourer, and there were the usual engine choices. Only two doors were provided, and a three-speed steering-column change was standard. Although Allard used aluminium

panelling to try to keep the weight within check, this was a heavy beast which rarely beat 16mpg.

Maybe these cars would never have sold so well if there had not been a huge post-war shortage of supply for, at £1277, the P1 cost exactly the same as the original Jaguar Mk VII saloon. No contest, you might say – yet Allard sold 559 cars, the most of any individual model. Even so, Sydney's Monte victory came too late to save the P1, which was already moribund. The P2 Monte Carlo, which followed, was a commercial failure.

SPECIFICATION

BODY STYLES: saloon

PRODUCTION: 559

ENGINE & TRANSMISSION: 3622/3917cc, V8 sv, 3sp man, f/r

POWER: 85bhp @ 3800rpm/100bhp @ 3500rpm

MAX SPEED (MPH): 85 (E)

0-60MPH (SEC): not measured

SUSPENSION & BRAKES: coil ifs, transverse leaf rear, drums f&r

LENGTH (IN)/WEIGHT (LB): 186/3024

LAUNCH PRICE: £1277

J2/J2X 1950-52

Here were the first of Allard's really fierce sports two-seaters, in which performance was everything, creature comforts came well down the list of priorities, and (relatively) light weight was always sought. The majority were exported.

The original J2 had a narrow body with two seats, cycle-type front wings and absolutely no weather protection. Like the P1, it had divided axle/coil spring front suspension, but also had De Dion rear suspension by coil springs, all packed into a 100in wheelbase. Brakes were big drums, there being no disc brake alternative at the time.

Wire spoke wheels were usually specified, and though it was possible to order this car with the usual Ford/Mercury sidevalve V8s, many J2s were built with modern, overhead-valve, 5.4-litre Cadillac V8s instead. A three-speed gearbox was quite enough to cope with such truck-loads of torque.

In 1950 the first J2s were faster in a straight line than all but ultra-rare Ferraris, though their roadholding was unruly. To rectify this somewhat, Allard evolved the J2X, which appeared in 1951. This car had a new and sturdy multi-tubular chassis frame (hence the "X") and the heavy engines were

Allard J2 on show in 1950.

mounted seven inches further back in the frame. In spite of the handling and braking deficiencies, J2Xs won many races, especially in North America.

A J2X could be rated as: Excitement 100 per cent, Character 100 per cent, Refinement Nil – which meant that this car appealed to those who wanted nothing less than an adrenalin rush every time they fired up the engine.

So what if they were not built very well? And does it matter if you get wet every time it rains? Then, and later, they were every red-blooded man's dream, and today their value in the classic car market is extremely high.

SPECIFICATION

BODY STYLES: sports car

PRODUCTION: 90 J2, 83 J2X

ENGINE & TRANSMISSION: 4375cc/5420cc, V8 sv/V8 ohv, 3sp man, f/r

POWER: 120bhp @ 3800 rpm/172bhp @ 4000rpm

MAX SPEED (MPH): (172bhp) 111

0-60MPH (SEC): 7.4

SUSPENSION & BRAKES: coil ifs, DD coil rear, drums f&r

LENGTH (IN)/WEIGHT (LB): 148/2016

LAUNCH PRICE: (J2) £1277, (J2X) £1713

Three J2s racing at Pebble Beach in the 1950s. The car partially obscured by trees is a Crosley Hotshot.

K2 1950-51

As its name suggests, K2 was a successor to the K1 two-seater sports car, up-dated in many ways, and technically really a half-way house from the original to the final tubular-frame Allards.

Under the skin, the K2 used the coil

Allard K2 two-seater.

SPECIFICATION

BODY STYLES: sports tourer

PRODUCTION: 119

ENGINE & TRANSMISSION: 3622/3917cc, V8 sv, 3sp man, f/r

POWER: 85bhp @ 3800 rpm/140bhp @ 3500rpm

MAX SPEED (MPH): (3.9-litre) 101

0-60MPH (SEC): (3.9-litre) 11.6

SUSPENSION & BRAKES: coil ifs, transverse leaf rear, drums f&r

LENGTH (IN)/WEIGHT (LB): 168/2464

LAUNCH PRICE: £1277

spring front end of the P1 saloon, but retained a 106in wheelbase and the original type of pressed chassis side-members, while the choice of V8 engines was not changed.

There were some, but not startling, changes to body style, with a more full-width front end and an opening boot, and all cars had a floor gearchange to control Ford's three-speed gearbox, whose ratios still left a yawning gap between second and third gears. By this time the J2/J2X had become Allard's performance-leader, so K2s were seen as fast tourers. As post-war shortages eased, demand for this type of big, crude Allard eased. Even so, the company did well to sell 119 cars in two years.

Classic values? Think one-third of J2/J2X levels, and you wouldn't be far wrong.

M2X 1951-53

By now you can almost work out an Allard's specification from its title. This car, therefore, took over from the M1 in 1951. It used the new-type tubular chassis as premiered on the J2X, but in 112in-wheelbase form, and was a four-seater drophead coupé. Engine choices, the basic specification, and equipment levels could all be

M2X Allard was a drophead version of the P1 saloon on a new chassis.

SPECIFICATION

BODY STYLES: drophead coupé

PRODUCTION: 25

ENGINE & TRANSMISSION: 3622/3917cc, V8 sv, 3sp man, f/r

POWER: 85bhp @ 3800rpm/100bhp @ 3500rpm

MAX SPEED (MPH): (85bhp) 86

0-60MPH (SEC): (85bhp) 15.7

SUSPENSION & BRAKES: coil ifs, transverse leaf rear, drums f&r

LENGTH (IN)/WEIGHT (LB): 190/3136

LAUNCH PRICE: £1790

related to the P1 saloon, ie sidevalve V8 and three speeds.

Styling was much like the P1 saloon, though in drop-top guise, but this was the first Allard to use what we might

call an A-shape front grille motif.

This was all too late for a market which had moved on. A Jaguar XK120 cost no more – which would you have? Only 25 were ever sold.

K3 1952-53

Though Allard once again played mix-and-match with all its proven, and modern, chassis engineering for the K3 of 1952, it also introduced a new and far more pleasing sports car style. If only it could have been sold at a more attractive price, everything might have been well – but in the end just 62 were produced.

The K3's basis was the 100in tubular X-Type chassis frame of the latest J2X, complete with coil spring front end, and

K3 Allard got a new look.

SPECIFICATION

BODY STYLES: sports tourer

PRODUCTION YEARS: 62

ENGINE & TRANSMISSION: 3622/3917cc, V8 sv, 3sp man, f/r

POWER: 85bhp @ 3800rpm/100bhp @ 3500rpm

MAX SPEED (MPH): 85 (E)

0-60MPH (SEC): not measured

SUSPENSION & BRAKES: coil ifs, DD coil rear, drums f&r

LENGTH (IN)/WEIGHT (LB): 177/2604

LAUNCH PRICE: £1713

De Dion rear suspension by coil springs, plus the usual choice of engines. The body style, though, was completely new (some pressings, but not all, would be shared with the Palm Beach), and although larger had very similar proportions to the later Austin-Healey 100. The grille was a simple oval aperture. It was a wide car, with a bench seat which could seat three abreast, the gearchange was between door and seat

(left or right, depending on wheel position), and there were twin fuel tanks in the rear wings. Acknowledged to be aimed at export markets (the USA in particular) it would sometimes be sold without an engine – so that some K3s received Cadillac V8s and automatic transmission!

Not as fast, or as extrovert, as the J2X to which it was related, the K3 has rather slipped off the radar in modern times.

P2 Monte Carlo/Safari 1952

By 1952, Allard was getting desperate. In spite of the Monte victory, sales were slumping. The P2, therefore, was a massive shuffle of available resources. Under the skin was the latest

SPECIFICATION

BODY STYLES: saloon, (Safari) estate

PRODUCTION: 11 MC, 10 Safari

ENGINE & TRANSMISSION: 3622cc/3917cc, V8 sv, 3sp man, f/r

POWER: 85bhp @ 3800rpm/100bhp @ 3500rpm

MAX SPEED (MPH): 85 (E)

0-60MPH (SEC): not measured

SUSPENSION & BRAKES: coil ifs, DD coil rear, drums f&r

LENGTH (IN)/WEIGHT (LB): 192/3248

LAUNCH PRICE: £2568/£1946

P2 Monte Carlo saloon at Earls Court in 1952.

112in-wheelbase X-type chassis, with a multi-tube layout and coil spring De Dion rear suspension.

Two body styles were available. The Monte Carlo was a two-door saloon, while the Safari was a massive three-door woody estate car. For the saloon, think of a new style, but with the same basic P1 profiles around a roomier cabin (and some shared inner panels). At the front, and like the M2X, there was an "A" (for Allard) motif to the grille, and the entire front end – wings, bonnet and front shroud – tilted up for access. (Aston Martin had already done this, and the E-Type would follow).

Any number of engines could be fitted, but Ford's venerable sidevalve V8 was the standard, though by now inadequate, unit, as was its three-speed gearbox. As on the K3, the gear lever was outboard of the seats.

The Safari estate car shared the same chassis and the same front end, but had a nostalgically constructed woody station-wagon cabin. Surprisingly, it was priced a long way below the Monte Carlo saloon.

Both these cars were commercial flops, for only 11 saloons and 10 station wagons were built. Time, and motoring standards, it seems, had moved on, but Allard had not.

PALM BEACH 1952-1959

The second-generation Allard was completely different from the original types – smaller, lighter, and originally based around Ford Consul and Zephyr power units. Unhappily, it came all too late – for the new Triumph TR2 and Austin-Healey 100 sports cars were faster, more powerful and a lot cheaper.

The basic chassis layout was technically like larger X-Type Allards, but differed in having a much shorter wheelbase and narrower track. Divided-axle front suspension, and coil spring/radius arm location of the back axle, looked familiar too. Engines and related three-speed gearboxes were from Ford Consul (4-cylinder) and Zephyr (6-cylinder), both in standard form, though the gear change was converted from steering column (Ford) to centre floor (Allard).

Neat and simple bodywork had a visual family resemblance to the K3. Featuring aluminium skin panels, it provided

1952 prototype Palm Beach, rejected by Sidney Allard.

The Mark II Palm Beach.

SPECIFICATION

BODY STYLES: sports car

PRODUCTION: 8 21C, 61 21Z, 7 Mk II

ENGINE & TRANSMISSION:
1508cc/2262cc/3442cc, 4cyl/6cyl ohv/6cyl 2ohc, 4sp man, f/r

POWER: 47bhp @ 4400rpm/68bhp @ 4000rpm/210bhp @ 5500rpm

MAX SPEED (MPH): (68bhp) 85, (210bhp) 120mph

0-60MPH (SEC): (68bhp) 16.9, (210bhp) 9.6

SUSPENSION & BRAKES: coil ifs, coil rear, drums f&r

LENGTH (IN)/WEIGHT (LB): 156/1850 - 2856

LAUNCH PRICE: £1246/£1347 (£2409 with 3442cc)

three-abreast seating and a useful boot. Disc or wire-spoke wheels (13in diameter) and the promise of tuned engines were all mentioned, but it didn't help. Road tests showed that even the Zephyr-engined car was much slower than the competition, so it flopped. In fact only eight examples of the Consul-engined version were ever sold.

By 1954 Allard's Palm Beach era was all over, except that there was a re-style for the Mark II which provided more sensuous lines. Only seven such cars were sold, with various engines including, would you believe, an XK140 power unit.

Only two Mark II Palm Beach coupés were made.

Clipper 3-wheeler 1954-55

Described by micro-car experts as "weird by any standards", the Clipper three-wheeler was a complete change for Allard, and evolved from a design by David Gottlieb (whose company was known as Powerdrive). Based on a simple chassis fabricated from channel and square box-section steel tubing, it had its air-cooled Villiers two-stroke engine in the tail, where it drove just one wheel (at the nearside) through a Burman motorcycle gearbox, a primary belt and a secondary chain.

Suspension of the single front wheel was by a trailing arm and André rubber blocks in compression, the rear suspension being similar but with shorter arms. Brakes were from the Morris Minor.

Allard Clipper.

SPECIFICATION

BODY STYLES: coupé

PRODUCTION: 22

ENGINE & TRANSMISSION: 346cc, 2cyl ts, 3sp man, r/r

POWER: 8bhp @ 4000rpm

MAX SPEED (MPH): 40 (E)

0-60MPH (SEC): not possible

SUSPENSION & BRAKES: rubber ifs, rubber irs, drums f&r

LENGTH (IN)/WEIGHT (LB): 121/672

LAUNCH PRICE: £268

The 52in-wide bench seat lived inside a coupé body shell, being made from glass-fibre (still a novelty in the British industry in those days) by Hordern-Richmond of Haddenham in Oxfordshire, the shape being likened to "a pair of eggs given a styling job by Chevrolet". The only door was on the left side. The gear lever was on the right side of the seat, and rather tenuously linked to the gearbox on the other corner of the chassis. Weather-protective side curtains were available, but only as extras. The boot lid folded down, and the space could double as a dickey seat. In theory an extra passenger could sit in there, not necessarily in comfort.

The overall effect was bizarre, and the appeal non-existent. Although Allard claimed only a 40mph top speed, they also claimed 70mpg on petroil mixture. However, a combination of awful styling, engine noise, cooling problems and crude equipment meant that it did not sell.

Amazingly, one or two Clippers have survived to be wondered at, and also as a dreadful warning to anyone else.

ALVIS

Once established in the 1920s, Alvis of Coventry soon built up a reputation. By the end of the 1930s they were making some of Britain's finest, fastest and most exclusive cars, which could rival Bentley on performance and even image grounds. To increase sales, however, Alvis introduced the "middle-class" 1.8-litre 12/70 in 1937.

By 1945 the company had changed considerably. The original factory had been blitzed, and a new plant nearby was concentrating on making aircraft engines, so a reshuffle was needed. To get car sales under way, the company revised the 12/70's chassis and coachwork, calling it the TA14, and sold no other model until 1950. Roadsters with bodies by Panelcraft were limited-production aberrations.

The first (and only) true post-war Alvis chassis, coded TA21 at first, made its debut in 1950, and would be the basis of all private cars built by the company until the end in 1967.

All were powered by a brand-new, though conventional, in-line six-cylinder engine. Early models were traditional in style, but from 1955 the first of the Graber-styled coupés went on the market.

Alvis kept on improving engine power and chassis specification, so the last of the line – the TF21 – was a fast, powerful and exclusive machine. It's worth remembering that the original TA21 had 90bhp, the last no less than 150bhp.

In the meantime, Alec Issigonis had been hired to design a new car, but this was cancelled, and the Great Man went back to BMC. Alvis then continued to prosper by building aircraft and helicopter engines and military vehicles. The slow-selling cars were in danger even before an agreed takeover by Rover in 1965, the last car being produced in mid-1967.

TA14 1946-50

Pure late-1930s in its design and in its appearance, the TA14 model was a modified 1939 12/70, but it kept Alvis's pot boiling for five post-war years. Notably, the post-war car had a four-inch wider body and a two-inch longer wheelbase than the 12/70.

Revealed to the public gaze in November 1946, it featured a widened box-section chassis frame with leaf-sprung beam axles front and rear, along with Marles steering and mechanically-operated brakes.

The pushrod engine had just one SU carburettor, and was backed by an all-synchromesh gearbox. Though the pre-war model had had 17in wire wheels, the TA14 wore 16in steel disc wheels

Three different body styles were available – a four-door four-light saloon from Mulliners of Birmingham, and two different dropheads, one by Carbodies (built just across the road!),

Alvis TA14 saloon, nicely made but still resolutely pre-war in character.

Dignified rear view of the TA14. The car sat quite low on the road.

and one by Tickford. All, naturally, shared the same front end, with a traditional vertical radiator and exposed headlamps.

Inside the cabin there was wood, leather and real carpets, for this was a true upper middle class car. No rush, no fireworks, and certainly no extrovert behaviour. The TA14 was a car for gentlemen, and of course for ladies too. Progress was always in a dignified and seemly manner, with sure handling and relaxed cruising; most post-war Alvises would be like that.

SPECIFICATION

BODY STYLES: saloon, drophead

PRODUCTION: 3311

ENGINE & TRANSMISSION: 1892cc, 4cyl ohv, 4sp man, f/r

POWER: 65bhp @ 4000rpm

MAX SPEED (MPH): 74

0-60MPH (SEC): 22.2

SUSPENSION & BRAKES: leaf front, leaf rear, drums f&r

LENGTH (IN)/WEIGHT (LB): 175/3136

LAUNCH PRICE: £893

TB14 1950

In 1948, in what now seems a self-indulgent move, Alvis commissioned AP Metalcraft of Coventry (who also built bodies for Healey) to develop a new two-seater sports car body on the TA14 chassis. This was a strictly limited deal, for only 100 such machines were produced, all of them during calendar year 1950. A prototype had been shown at the end of 1949.

Based on the TA14's chassis, the TB14 used a twin-SU version of the engine giving 68bhp, but much of the other running gear remained unchanged. AP Metalcraft's two-seater body was

Alvis TB14 came as a bit of a surprise to the traditionalists.

SPECIFICATION

BODY STYLES: sports car

PRODUCTION: 100

ENGINE & TRANSMISSION: 1892cc, 4cyl ohv, 4sp man, f/r

POWER: 68bhp @ 4000 rpm

MAX SPEED (MPH): 80

0-60MPH (SEC): 19.0

SUSPENSION & BRAKES: leaf beam front, leaf rear, drums f&r

LENGTH (IN)/WEIGHT (LB): 174/2730

LAUNCH PRICE: £1276

somewhat bulbous, with an appallingly ugly front grille, behind which were the headlights. Although there was much aluminium in its body construction, the car was still heavy – heavy enough to damp down its performance.

Along the sides the wing line dipped across the cutaway doors, the windscreen could be folded flat, and the doors were of the rear-hinged suicide variety. The TB14 was flat out at 80mph, and had the character of a middle-aged lady trying to embrace modern music – and failing.

Priced at £1276, the car was never likely to be a big seller (this was, after all, Jaguar XK120 territory), but Alvis managed to sell all the 100 TB14s made before they introduced the larger TB21.

TA21 1950-53

Five years after the war ended, Alvis finally produced its only new chassis design of the period, clothing it in a traditionally-styled body which had strong links with the old TA14 (and a modified version of its four-door cabin). This was the 3-Litre which, in further developed chassis form, and with a new Graber-influenced style, would persist until 1967.

The new longer-wheelbase chassis frame featured coil spring independent front suspension and used a brand-new short-stroke 3-litre six-cylinder engine – a sturdy design with seven crankshaft bearings, which produced 90bhp with a single Solex carburettor. Hydraulic instead of mechanical brakes were an advance. Although the body style by

Alvis TA21, the first of the Three Litres, in handsome drophead guise.

Mulliners was updated a little – the headlamps were partly recessed (Bentley Mk VI-style) – this was still a car with 1930s character.

Exactly as wide in the body as the old TA14, there was just the same amount of space in the cabin since the wheelbase "stretch" was all around the engine. As with TA14, the front doors were rear-

The TA21 dropead's hood could be set in the de ville position.

SPECIFICATION

BODY STYLES: saloon, drophead coupé

PRODUCTION: 1316

ENGINE & TRANSMISSION: 2993cc, 6cyl ohv, 4sp man, f/r

POWER: 90bhp @ 4000rpm

MAX SPEED (MPH): 86

0-60MPH (SEC): 19.8

SUSPENSION & BRAKES: coil ifs, leaf rear, drums f&r

LENGTH (IN)/WEIGHT (LB): 182/3190

LAUNCH PRICE: £1598

hinged. The two-door Tickford drophead was particularly smart. There were no Carbodies dropheads on this model, by the way.

It is a pity that this car looked so old-fashioned, for it handled very well and positively exuded class. The TA21 was also expensive, so Alvis rarely produced more than 600 cars in a year. It is well thought of today, but the rather more powerful TC21s and 21/100s are considered more desirable.

TB21 1951

Easy to work this one out. Using the longer-wheelbase, more powerful TA21 chassis instead of the one from the TA14, Alvis asked AP Metalcraft to restyle their TA21 body to produce a new roadster.

By extending the nose, and choosing a traditional Alvis grille instead of the TB14's monstrosity, Panelcraft produced a more acceptable style. The basic proportions, along with the cutaway doors, hinged at the rear, and the fold-flat screen, were retained.

The TB21 looked rather more like an Alvis than the TB14. This is the 1950 prototype.

SPECIFICATION

BODY STYLES: sports car

PRODUCTION : 31

ENGINE & TRANSMISSION: 2993cc, 6cyl ohv, 4sp man, f/r

POWER: 90bhp @ 4000rpm

MAX SPEED (MPH): 95

0-60MPH (SEC): not measured

SUSPENSION & BRAKES: coil ifs, leaf rear, drums f&r

LENGTH (IN)/WEIGHT (LB): 177/2830

LAUNCH PRICE: £1598

Having some 90bhp (TB21) instead of 68bhp (TB14), this was a considerably quicker car, with a torquey and turbine-smooth engine, which could reach 95mph. The problems, as ever, were so-so build quality and a very high price. At £1598, this sports tourer was more expensive than Jaguar's XK120 – which explains why Alvis built only 31 of them, all in 1951.

TC21 & TC21/100 "Grey Lady" 1953-55

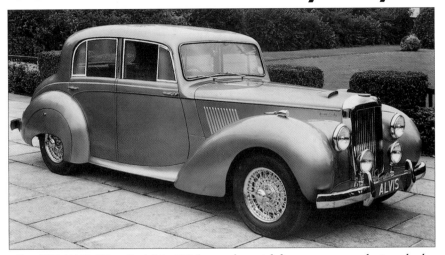

SPECIFICATION

BODY STYLES: saloon, drophead coupé

PRODUCTION: 757

ENGINE & TRANSMISSION: 2993 cc, 6cyl ohv, 4sp man, f/r

POWER: 100bhp @ 4000rpm

MAX SPEED (MPH): 100

0-60MPH (SEC): 16.5

SUSPENSION & BRAKES: coil ifs, leaf rear, drums f&r

LENGTH (IN)/WEIGHT (LB): 182/3346

LAUNCH PRICE: £1822

Alvis TC21/100 "Grey Lady" in 1954, complete with bonnet scoops and wire wheels.

The TC21 and in particular the TC21/100 represented a valiant effort to spice up the TA21's image while remaining in character. From the autumn of 1953, the outwardly staid-looking 3-litre got a twin-SU 100bhp engine, while the more specialised TC21/100 got air scoops in the bonnet and wire-spoke wheels to give it a more sporty image. As ever with Alvis, though, it's safer to say most rather than all cars, as customers often made specific requests. As before, four-door saloon or two-door (Tickford) drophead coupé coachwork was available. Both types now had concealed hinges in the doors, a recognition point.

Road tests suggested a 100mph maximum, but this might have been with a breathed-on factory-prepared car – 95mph was more repeatable, and still quite creditable for a 1954 model.

This was a nice car, especially in DHC form, but increasingly old-fashioned, and expensive. Deliveries dropped away in 1955, not only because the body style was old, but because Mulliners had been taken over by Standard-Triumph (and was concentrating on them) – hence the arrival of the Graber model. Today's survivors are well-loved, especially restored dropheads.

A TC21 on the Tulip Rally in 1954, driven by Banks/Porter.

TC108G 1955-58

TC108G was styled by Graber, bodied by Willowbrook.

SPECIFICATION

BODY STYLES: saloon

PRODUCTION: 37

ENGINE & TRANSMISSION: 2993cc, 6cyl ohv, 4sp man, f/r

POWER: 104bhp @ 4000rpm

MAX SPEED (MPH): 102

0-60MPH (SEC): 13.5

SUSPENSION & BRAKES: coil ifs, leaf rear, drum f/r

LENGTH (IN)/WEIGHT (LB): 189/3285

LAUNCH PRICE: £2776

When Standard took control of Mulliners in Birmingham, and David Brown bought up Tickford, Alvis's regular body supplies came under threat. Swiss coachbuilder Graber had produced a smart, ultra-modern style on the TC21, so Alvis bought the rights to replicate this. The result, in 1955, was the TC108G.

The chassis was updated TC21/100, with a touch more power, but except for the traditional grille the smooth full-width body was all new. At this stage only a two-door four-seater was available. The aerodynamic performance must have better, for 100mph was easily beaten.

Bodies came from Willowbrook of Loughborough (whose ususal business was building bus rather than car bodies), where aluminium and steel panelling was laboriously tacked and welded together on an ash structural skeleton, but costs were high and progress was slow. Only 37 cars were built before the deal was terminated and the better TD21 took over.

TD21 1958-63

From 1958 Alvis turned TC108/G into TD21 by hiring Park Ward to build their bodies. Although the external styling was little changed, Park Ward had raised the rear roof line to increase the cabin space, and a convertible was now also available. The bodies were a mix of wooden framing, steel and aluminium

TD21 drophead offered four seats, just.

SPECIFICATION

BODY STYLES: saloon, drophead coupé

PRODUCTION: 1073

ENGINE & TRANSMISSION: 2993cc, 6cyl ohv, 4sp man, o/d or auto (5sp from 1962), f/r

POWER: 115bhp @ 4000rpm

MAX SPEED (MPH): 104

0-60MPH (SEC): 13.9

SUSPENSION & BRAKES: coil ifs, leaf rear, drum f/r at first, disc f/drum r from 1959 (later, disc f/r)

LENGTH (IN)/WEIGHT (LB): 189/3450

LAUNCH PRICE: £2827

panelling, and some alloy castings. The equipment level is excellent – Park Ward's huge Bentley/Rolls-Royce experience fed to the Alvis – so look for much wood, thick carpets and real leather. The fascia/instrument layout was totally new.

Mechanically, the immediate development was the adoption of a four-speed Austin/Austin-Healey type of four-speed gearbox, and the option of Borg Warner automatic transmission. Improvements

followed, with 115bhp and front disc brakes from late 1959 and an optional overdrive from late 1960, though this disappeared after two years. From January 1962 the TD21 became Series II, where four-wheel Dunlop discs were made standard, and from October 1962 a ZF five-speed manual gearbox followed. The short-stroke engine was happy to rev, and its ability to sustain high-speed cruising made the TD21 an effective mile-eater.

TE21 1963-66

For TE21, think TD21 but with more toys and further improved equipment. The TE21 took over from the TD21 in October 1963, and would run through to 1966. Four headlamps (paired, vertically) replaced the original two headlamps, and the front end/front wing sheet metal was changed to suit, but otherwise there were no external styling changes. At the same time there

SPECIFICATION

BODY STYLES: saloon, drophead coupé

PRODUCTION: 352

ENGINE & TRANSMISSION: 2993cc, 6cyl ohv, 5sp man or auto, f/r

POWER: 130bhp @ 4000rpm

MAX SPEED (MPH): 107

0-60MPH (SEC): 12.5

SUSPENSION & BRAKES: coil ifs, leaf rear, discs f&r

LENGTH (IN)/WEIGHT (LB): 189/3450

LAUNCH PRICE: £2774

The second TE21 built shows off its twin-headlamp arrangement.

was a slight regrouping of the interior controls and equipment.

Mechanically, the big change was to the engine, which was made to produce 130bhp (improved cylinder head, improved exhaust manifolding) and offered close to 110mph. Four-wheel disc brakes and a five-speed ZF manual transmission remained. Power-assisted steering (long awaited by Alvis buyers)

became optional in October 1964.

The new front-end style suited the car very well, while the extra power helped to balance the considerable weight and bulk. The car was still expensive, but the cognoscenti put up with that. Today's values reflect its desirability.

This model was replaced by the TF21 in 1966, but it was still available (theoretically) to special order in 1967.

TF21 1966-67

This was the last, and (many agree) the best, of the Graber-styled, Park Ward-bodied 3-litre Alvises. Launched in March 1966, the TF21 featured a triple-SU 150bhp version of the now 15 year old engine. This output was about as much as the unit could be expected to withstand reliably. There was also a revised fascia, now placing all

SPECIFICATION

BODY STYLES: saloon, drophead coupé

PRODUCTION: 106

ENGINE & TRANSMISSION: 2993cc, 6cyl ohv, 5sp man or auto, f/r

POWER: 150bhp @ 4750rpm

MAX SPEED (MPH): 120

0-60MPH (SEC): 9.9

SUSPENSION & BRAKES: coil ifs, leaf rear, discs f&r

LENGTH (IN)/WEIGHT (LB): 189/3450

LAUNCH PRICE: £3225

The TF21, sadly the last Alvis model, had 150bhp and a 120mph top speed.

the instruments in front of the driver.

Otherwise there were no style changes – the vertical-paired four-headlamp arrangement was still much admired – but there were some chassis changes under the skin, including variable rate coil springs and new damper settings.

Power-assisted steering was still an optional extra, for £121.

Top speed was now up to 120mph, which was a good way to bring Alvis private car assembly to a climax – and an end – for the last of these elegant cars was produced in mid-1967.

ARKLEY

Once the Austin-Healey Sprite (but not the MG Midget) had dropped out of production, John Britten Garages of Arkley (north of London), who were recognised sports car motor traders, offered a cheap-and-cheerful rebodying exercise on the BMC car's platform, running gear, and some of its inner panels. John Britten himself invented the project, and asked Lenham to provide GRP body moulds to his design.

Since there were plenty of rusty old Sprites and Midgets around in the 1970s and early 1980s, this enterprise prospered, especially as the car could be supplied as a kit or as a complete machine. Even so, there was no long term strategy to establish Arkley as a permanent marque, and no successor to the S and SS Types seems to have been developed.

Although the garage business continued, especially in the thriving "classic car" era, when demand for this car died away so did the Arkley marque.

S and SS 1970-85

The basis of this neat and very appealing little two-seater sports car was the ubiquitous Austin-Healey Sprite/MG Midget model, of which hundreds of thousands would be made from 1958 to 1980.

To build it, it was first necessary to strip out much of the existing car (retaining the structural elements: platform, front bulkhead, doors and much of the bodywork) and then to add on the special Arkley pieces.

There were two basic types – the S having steel wheels, the SS having wider-rim alloy wheels – but all used the same cute style of glass-fibre (GRP) body shell, including a new lift-up front end (hingeing at the extreme front end) with semi-goggle-eye headlamps and with almost a Morgan-like tail which included an exposed spare wheel.

The centre section was based on using post-1966 Sprite or Midget doors, which had wind-up windows, together with the fold-away soft top and windscreen from the 1275cc

Sprite or Midget models.

The running gear was whatever engine and transmission were fitted to the chosen donor car. Thus the engine might be a 948cc, 1098cc or 1275cc BMC A series unit, or the 1493cc engine fitted to 1975-79 Midgets and the Spitfire 1500. Although a few cars were built on the very early quarter-elliptic-spring rear axle installation, as used on the Frogeye Sprite, the vast majority had the later conventional

half-elliptic-spring rear end. As with the donor cars, the ride was always quite hard and the steering exhilaratingly direct.

Because BMC fascia, instruments, doors, cockpit furniture and seating were all re-used, these cars looked much more "professional" than they actually were. Yet they provided a stylish and distinctive alternative to the BMC models, kept some of them alive, and gave lots of fun.

SPECIFICATION

BODY STYLES: sports car

PRODUCTION: c.900

ENGINE & TRANSMISSION: 948cc/1098cc/1275cc/1493cc, 4cyl ohv, 4sp man, f/r

POWER: 43bhp @ 5200rpm to 65bhp @ 5500rpm

MAX SPEED (MPH): (with 65bhp/1275cc) 95

0-60MPH (SEC): (with 65bhp/1275cc) 13.4

SUSPENSION & BRAKES: coil ifs, leaf rear, drums f&r (or disc f/drum r)

LENGTH (IN)/WEIGHT (LB): 138/1456

LAUNCH PRICE: £1018 as complete car

Arkley SS.

ARMSTRONG-SIDDELEY

Armstrong-Siddeley of Coventry emerged in 1919 as the result of a merger between Armstrong-Whitworth of Newcastle-upon-Tyne and Siddeley-Deasy of Coventry.

The first Armstrong-Siddeley car was produced in 1919, and before long the marque had established itself as a manufacturer of solid, well-built, elegant but mostly staid models for a middle-class market.

In the 1930s the company adopted and produced the Wilson preselector transmission in big numbers, and also became an important aero engine manufacturer. As for its cars, Armstrong-Siddeley's typical sales profile embraced retired colonels, country squires, and ladies whose husbands might already have a Rolls-Royce of their own.

From 1945 the company first concentrated on building a whole series of slightly different models all based on the same chassis frame – there being very strong technical similarities between Hurricane, Lancaster, Typhoon, Whitley and 18hp Limousine models. The names came from famous World War Two aircraft, and most of the models had bodies crafted within the big factory at Parkside, Coventry.

The launch of the elegant Sapphire range of 1952 was a big step forward (the engine, in particular, was technically admirable) but in the meantime the company's aircraft gas turbine and rocket engines were becoming notable, profitable, and tending to take over the business. Before the car division was marginalised, though, the company had time to launch the 234/236 family, which was neither elegant nor successful.

Contract activities included allowing Humber to re-design the Sapphire engine to use in its own Super Snipes, while from 1959 to 1962 the Parkside works also embraced assembly of the Rootes Group's Sunbeam Alpine sports car.

With the 234/236 dropped, and with the earlier abandonment of a proposed new car which had been designed (under contract) by W O Bentley's consultancy business, the company allowed the private car business to fade away, with profitable jet engine manufacture taking its place instead.

The last Armstrong-Siddeley-badged cars were built in November 1960.

The finest of pre-war Armstrong-Siddeleys was the 5-litre Siddeley Special.

Lancaster 16/18hp 1946-52

One of the motor industry's first new designs post-war was the Lancaster.

Armstrong-Siddeley amazed everyone by launching a new range of models immediately after the Allies had clinched victory in Europe in the Second World War. Work started years earlier had been completed even while the fighting continued.

For the post-war models there was to be an all-new chassis, complete with a new torsion bar independent front suspension and the choice of preselector or manual transmission. The engine and the pre-selector gearbox were well-proven, the rest (including the four-speed gearbox from the Rootes

Group) being brand new to Armstrong-Siddeley. At first the engine was a developed version of the company's late-1930s 2-litre unit, a quite conventional 70bhp overhead-valve six-cylinder design which delivered top speeds of at least 75mph. The chassis was fitted with hydro-mechanical brakes (hydraulic operation of front brakes, mechanical by rods and cables at the rear) and disc wheels – bolt-on wire wheels were optional but rarely specified.

Between 1945 and 1950 five new body styles would eventually be announced on this same chassis, each with the same front-end shape but with its own unique type of cabin, and each bearing a different name. The Lancaster, therefore, was a four-door six-light saloon. The steel and aluminium body, built up on a wooden body skeleton, was produced by Mulliners of Birmingham, and a slide-back sunshine roof was standard. As in the other models, there was an abundance of wood, leather and careful trimming in the cabin, most tastefully executed.

From mid-1949 a 2309cc version of the engine took over. Visually almost identical, it was significantly more torquey than its predecessor and carried on to the end of this range's run in 1954. Production continued steadily until the winter of 1951/52, after which the Lancaster was replaced by the more razor-edged six-light Whitley.

Like the other models in the family, a few of these cars have survived, and they are well respected for their quality. They were very well built and in flavour retain the quiet, understated dignity that had long been a hallmark of the marque.

Hurricane/Typhoon 16/18hp 1946-49/1946-53

Mechanically the Hurricane and Typhoon models were the same as the Lancaster saloon, but both carried their own unique type of coachwork. When changes including the upgrade of the engine to 2.3 litres were brought in, they were applied across the range.

The Hurricane carried an elegant two-door four-seater drophead coupé, while the Typhoon was a two-door four-seater fixed-head coupé which shared the same passenger doors, rear quarters and almost all the structural part of the coachwork. The doors, incidentally, were hinged at the rear – it was only in later years that the phrase "suicide doors" was applied to this arrangement, because of their tendency to flip wide open if inadvertently unlatched when the car was in motion. The bodies of both types were based on a complex amalgam of steel, cast aluminium and a wooden (ash) skeleton frame, with steel or aluminium outer skin panels. This made them rot-prone in later life. Mechanically, however, the cars have proved exceptionally durable.

Although 1701 Typhoon fixed-heads would be sold in four years, at the end of 1949 this model was the first of the entire range to be dropped. The Hurricane, however, carried on steadily until mid-1953.

SPECIFICATION
BODY STYLES: (Typhoon) coupé, (Hurricane) drophead coupé
PRODUCTION: 1701/2606
ENGINE & TRANSMISSION: 1991/2309cc, 6cyl ohv, 4sp man or pre-sel, f/r
POWER: 70bhp @ 4200rpm/75bhp @ 4200rpm
MAX SPEED (MPH): (70bhp) 75
0-60MPH (SEC): (70bhp) 29.7
SUSPENSION & BRAKES: tor ifs, leaf rear, drums f&r
LENGTH (IN)/WEIGHT (LB): 186/2968
LAUNCH PRICE: £1214 (Typhoon), £1151 (Hurricane)

The Hurricane was the drophead of the range and is the most desirable today.

Whitley 1950-54

Announced in late 1949, the Whitley was also a saloon model and was therefore in competition with the Lancaster, though the two types were rather different, for the Whitley body was more close coupled, and had a longer boot and tail. The Whitley's body was made in the Parkside works – it was the first saloon to be produced in-house after the end of the War.

Compared with the Lancaster, its cabin had more razor-edged styling, and it was built in four-light and, from 1953, six-light versions. The six-light took over from the Lancaster, which meant that the company no longer had to rely on Mulliners for body supplies.

The Whitley was the last of this well-made and understatedy elegant series to be built, production ceasing in the spring of 1954.

The Whitley had semi razor edge treatment at the rear. This is a four-light.

SPECIFICATION

BODY STYLES: saloon, export-only station coupé and commercials

PRODUCTION : 2582

ENGINE & TRANSMISSION: 2309cc, 6cyl ohv, 4sp man or pre-s, f/r

POWER: 75bhp @ 4200rpm

MAX SPEED (MPH): 80

0-60MPH (SEC): 19.0

SUSPENSION & BRAKES: tor ifs, leaf rear, drums f&r

LENGTH (IN)/WEIGHT (LB): 185/3115

LAUNCH PRICE: £1247

Limousine 18hp 1950-54

The 2.3-litre Limousine was the final body derivative to be launched on the original post-war chassis. Not only was the body style unique, but it was mounted on a much-lengthened wheelbase – 122in instead of 115in.

SPECIFICATION

BODY STYLES: limousine, landaulette, and one special

PRODUCTION: 125

ENGINE & TRANSMISSION: 2309cc, 6cyl ohv, 4sp man or pre-s, f/r

POWER: 75bhp @ 4200rpm

MAX SPEED (MPH): 75 (E)

0-60MPH (SEC): not measured

SUSPENSION & BRAKES: tor ifs, leaf rear, drums f&r

LENGTH (IN)/WEIGHT (LB): 195/3920

LAUNCH PRICE: £1758

Armstrong-Siddeley Limousine.

Although the front end was shared with other 18hp types, the rest of the body was different.

Produced as a formal six-light limousine, it was not nearly as rakish as other types, for it had larger and higher doors and a higher roof line. With the foldaway jump seats occupied, the Limousine could carry five people in the rear compartment and two up front ahead of the division.

No fewer than 125 were produced, but few of them now remain, treasured by Armstrong-Siddeley fans as real rarities.

Sapphire 3.4-Litre/346/Limousine 1952-58

The second new post-war chassis did not appear until 1952, this being the powerful and attractive Sapphire range of saloons, which would carry on until the very last Armstrong-Siddeley was built in November 1960.

With a new frame, a new body shell and a new engine this was a major investment for Armstrong-Siddeley, who hoped to take on Jaguar and its Mark VII saloon.

Unhappily, because the company's prices were much higher than those of Jaguar, this target was never reached.

The Sapphire's new box-section chassis had cruciform cross-bracing and featured coil spring ifs and full hydraulic brakes. Power-assisted steering was optional on later models. The new engine incorporated overhead valve gear, hemispherical combustion chambers and cross-flow

Sapphire six-light saloon.

breathing. It proved to be very tuneable. Single-carb 125bhp and twin-carb 150bhp versions were available.

Some years later (from 1958) Humber announced its own version of the engine, powering the Super Snipe/Imperial range; the two units looked similar but many details including castings were different.

Sapphire transmissions came in three varieties. Some cars had manual synchromesh gearboxes from Humber, some had pre-selector 'boxes, and (from 1955) some were fitted with the Rolls-Royce-type Hydramatic transmission.

The bodies were almost entirely made from steel panels and were assembled in-house. There was a little structural wood. Right from the start the cars were available in four- and six-light styles, the two sharing the same cabin size and proportions. Internal fittings were well up to earlier 16hp/18hp standards.

From 1955 there was a Limousine on a 19in-longer wheelbase. The extra space was devoted to enlarging rear passenger accommodation. The styling was similar but aft of the screen most of the panelling was changed, and the roof was higher. Sapphires rusted badly, which is why few of these impressive machines survive.

SPECIFICATION

BODY STYLES: saloon, limousine, specials

PRODUCTION: 8187 Sapphires, all types, 381 limousines

ENGINE & TRANSMISSION: 3435cc, 6cyl ohv, 4sp man, pre-select or auto, f/r

POWER: 125bhp @ 4200rpm/150bhp @ 5000rpm

MAX SPEED (MPH): (150bhp) 100

0-60MPH (SEC): 13.0

SUSPENSION & BRAKES: coil ifs, leaf rear, drums f&r

LENGTH (IN)/WEIGHT (LB): 193/3472 (Limo: 212/4032)

LAUNCH PRICE: £1728 (Limo £2866)

Sapphire four-light saloon.

Sapphire 234 1955-58

The Sapphire 234 had a four-cylinder version of the 346 engine.

SPECIFICATION

BODY STYLES: saloon

PRODUCTION: 803

ENGINE & TRANSMISSION: 2290cc, 4cyl ohv, 4sp man, o/d, f/r

POWER: 120bhp @ 5000rpm

MAX SPEED (MPH): 97

0-60MPH (SEC): 15.5

SUSPENSION & BRAKES: coil ifs, leaf rear, drums f&r

LENGTH (IN)/WEIGHT (LB): 180/2912

LAUNCH PRICE: £1599

Here was the direct replacement for the 16hp/18hp, but it could not be developed until the Sapphire was up and running. The company evolved a programme based on a common chassis and body style which was to be powered by two entirely different engines. None of the car's chassis and suspension was shared either with the old 18hp or with the Sapphire ranges. The 234 effectively had two-thirds of the Sapphire's advanced power unit while the 236 had the old-type six-cylinder engine and was much less powerful. Both were commercial failures, because of their awkward styling, their price – and because of the new Jaguar 2.4.

An all-synchromesh four-speed gearbox was standard, with optional overdrive. A pre-selector transmission was not available. The 234's four-cylinder version of the Sapphire engine was very powerful but rather rough and unrefined.

The steel body shell (with some light-alloy skin panels) was new, with a lofty roof line said to have been specified by a director who wanted to wear his hat in comfort! In later life body rust was a big problem, so most of these cars have disappeared. A pity, as the 234 was quite an interesting device.

Sapphire 236 1955-58

Although this was an amalgam of the new body with the old-type six-cylinder engine, it was a happier combination than the 234. The engine might have been less powerful (although it produced 85bhp, which was 10bhp more than the last of the 18hp types) but it was smooth, refined, and more in the Armstrong-Siddeley tradition. Even so, customers had the same reservations about the styling as with the 234, and this restricted sales to just 603 cars.

Like the 234, the 236 came with a four-speed manual gearbox, optional Laycock overdrive, or optional Manumatic two-pedal control (which was not popular). The pre-selector transmission was not available. With its solid frame and body, perhaps the 236 was a little underpowered, but no one ever doubted its pedigree or the level of its equipment.

In many ways this was the better of the two models in the range – though the public did not seem to agree.

SPECIFICATION

BODY STYLES: saloon

PRODUCTION: 603

ENGINE & TRANSMISSION: 2309cc, 6cyl ohv, 4sp man, o/d or semi-auto, f/r

POWER: 85bhp @ 4400rpm

MAX SPEED (MPH): 85 (E)

0-60MPH (SEC): not measured

SUSPENSION & BRAKES: coil ifs, leaf rear, drums f&r

LENGTH (IN)/WEIGHT (LB): 180/2968

LAUNCH PRICE: £1657

Star Sapphire 1958-60

The 4-litre Star Sapphire left the stage in 1960.

From 1958 the Star Sapphire took over from original Sapphire/346 types. Although it looked much the same as before, energetic facelifting of the cabin and tail meant that few unaltered panels remained aft of the screen.

All cars now had six-light styling, the engine had been standardised at 3990cc/165bhp, Borg Warner DG automatic transmission was standard (no

manual or pre-selector option was offered) and front-wheel discs brakes finally became available. Oddly enough, when a Star Sapphire limousine was finally launched, in 1960, it came with manual transmission as standard and automatic as an option!

The last Star Sapphire, in fact the last-ever Armstrong-Siddeley, left the factory in November 1960.

SPECIFICATION

BODY STYLES: saloon, limousine

PRODUCTION: 902 saloons and 77 limousines

ENGINE & TRANSMISSION: 3990cc, 6cyl ohv, 4sp man, or auto, f/r

POWER: 165bhp @ 4250rpm (140bhp for limousine only)

MAX SPEED (MPH): 100

0-60MPH (SEC): 14.8

SUSPENSION & BRAKES: coil ifs, leaf rear, disc f, drum r

LENGTH (IN)/WEIGHT (LB): 194/3920

LAUNCH PRICE: £2646/(Limo) £3150

ARNOLT-BRISTOL

1954-61

This car was inspired by S H "Wacky" Arnolt, who was vice-president of the Italian coachbuilders, Bertone, in 1953. Having seen the new short-wheelbase Bristol 404 chassis, he persuaded Bristol to allow Bertone to rebody this running gear, and market it in the USA as an Arnolt-Bristol.

Starting in 1954, this was an amicable agreement which pottered on, at no great pace, until 1961. Chassis were sent to Milan, Italy, bodies were added there, and completed cars were shipped to the USA, where they were marketed from Arnolt's other business in Chicago.

In fact the Arnolt-Bristol combined the short-wheelbase 404 chassis with a 130bhp (Type BS1) sports-racing Bristol engine and Bristol 403 gearbox and brakes. The style was sinuous and much more akin to, say, a Jaguar D-Type or XKSS than to any current Bristol. Having supplied all the running gear, the British company had no more to do with the completion of the job.

Limited series production ended in 1961, though it is believed that the last of all was constructed, from spare parts, in 1964.

The fixed-head version of the Arnolt-Bristol, bodied by Bertone.

SPECIFICATION

BODY STYLES: sports car, sports coupé

PRODUCTION: 3 coupés, 139 sports

ENGINE & TRANSMISSION: 1971cc, 6cyl ohv, 4sp man, f/r

POWER: 130bhp @ 5500rpm

MAX SPEED (MPH): 107

0-60MPH (SEC): 10.1

SUSPENSION & BRAKES: leaf ifs, tor rear, drums f&r

LENGTH (IN)/WEIGHT (LB): 167/1988

LAUNCH PRICE: not officially sold in UK

Arnolt-Bristol sports.

ASTON MARTIN

Aston Martin had already enjoyed a chequered history – and several different ownerships – before tractor-building industrialist David Brown bought the company in 1947. In the same year Brown also bought up the Lagonda concern.

The first Aston Martins had been produced in 1922: all pre-war types were small, light sports models. Under the previous management, a post-war model (which became the DB1) had already been designed, but it was only David Brown's backing which made production possible.

The rebirth of Aston Martin was paralleled by that of Lagonda. Happily it was the Lagonda six-cylinder twin-cam engine (which had been inspired by W O Bentley during the Second World War) that would power future Aston Martins in the 1950s. For the first post-war decade, car assembly was at Feltham, close to Heathrow Airport.

Aston Martin was a loss-making enterprise throughout the 1945-70 period, making only a handful of cars every week, but David Brown had expected this to be so. Always exquisitely designed, and substantially hand-built, the DB2, DB2/4 and DB Mk III models were fast and nimble. This was

a period when the company was encouraged to go motor racing – they won the Le Mans 24 Hour Race and the World Sports Car Championship in 1959.

Having taken over the Tickford body making business in the 1950s, David Brown soon moved all Aston Martin and Lagonda assembly into the Tickford factory at Newport Pagnell, and this would become Aston Martin's home until the 1990s.

From the late 1950s, the DB4 and all its successors became larger, heavier and more GT than sports coupé. A brand-new V8 engine, first previewed in 1967, completed that transformation. However, even though the cars had become super-fast, and very expensive, the business had still not become profitable.

David Brown eventually sold out to Company Developments in 1972, and after several other changes of ownership Aston Martin finally became a Ford subsidiary in 1987. After that, production soared, new assembly plants were opened near Banbury, and at Gaydon, and in the 21st century the company was transformed.

Two-Litre Sports (DB1) 1948-50

By any standards an interim model, the Two-Litre Sports (retrospectively known as the DB1, DB signifying David Brown) used the new multi-tube frame and high-output four-cylinder engine that engineer Claude Hill had designed for the previous management. It was never meant to go into series production, was hand-built at almost every stage, and was priced accordingly.

The chassis frame was derived from that of a pre-war Aston Martin prototype known as the Atom. It was built up of slim square-section tubes and extensively

Aston Martin Two Litre Sports, also known as the DB1.

SPECIFICATION

BODY STYLES: drophead coupé

PRODUCTION: 15

ENGINE & TRANSMISSION: 1970cc, 4cyl ohv, 4sp man, f/r

POWER: 90bhp @ 4750rpm

MAX SPEED (MPH): 100 (E)

0-60MPH (SEC): not measured

SUSPENSION & BRAKES: coil ifs, coil rear, drums f&r

LENGTH (IN)/WEIGHT (LB): 176/2520

LAUNCH PRICE: £2332

cross-braced. This, with the coil spring front suspension, and the rear axle located by coil springs and radius arms, was the signature for a whole new type of Aston Martin. The engine, however, a pushrod ohv 2-litre, really belonged to the past and would not be used on any future model. On this car the spare wheel was mounted in a pocket in the front wing.

A special-bodied prototype won the (Belgian) Spa Touring Car race of 1948, but cars delivered to customers had a

smart, though bulky, four-seater drophead coupé body style which was produced in-house at Feltham. Looking back, it is surprising that the Two-Litre Sports was larger than the six-cylinder DB2 which followed.

Although the car was commercially unsuccessful, the engineering elements of the chassis frame, and the styling theme of the nose, would be seen again on the DB2 which followed. Today a DB1 is a real rarity, and desirable because of that.

DB2 1950-53

SPECIFICATION

BODY STYLES: coupé, drophead coupé

PRODUCTION: 411

ENGINE & TRANSMISSION: 2580cc, 6cyl 2ohc, 4sp man, f/r

POWER: 105bhp @ 5000rpm

MAX SPEED (MPH): 116

0-60MPH (SEC): 11.2

SUSPENSION & BRAKES: coil ifs, coil rear, drums f&r

LENGTH (IN)/WEIGHT (LB): 163/2464

LAUNCH PRICE: £1920

Early DB2s had this form of grille, with vertical bars.

Raced in prototype form in 1949, then first delivered as a road car in 1950, the DB2 was really the first true "David Brown" Aston Martin. Its chassis and running gear were the basis of road cars produced to 1959, its style persisting in modified form throughout the 1950s.

The DB2's multi-tube frame was a shorter-wheelbase evolution of the DB1's design. During development, several important changes were made to stiffen it up and make it more durable, and during this period the rear axle location was also modified.

Two of the three lightweight Le Mans prototypes used DB1 engines (which were obsolescent), but one used the new Lagonda twin overhead camshaft six-cylinder unit designed by W O Bentley.

The grille was soon revised, as here. This works car ran at Le Mans in 1951.

This, in 105bhp form, was the engine chosen to power the DB2 production car, while an uprated "Vantage" version,

The Sims/Walton DB2 on the 1958 RAC Rally. The same car won the rally in 1956.

with 116bhp, soon became optional.

It seems extraordinary that for a car of this thoroughbred type a steering-column gear change was available, along with a floor-change alternative; many of the column-change survivors were converted in later years.

The body was a sleek two-seater fastback (though not a hatchback) mainly clothed in aluminium, which set the template for many other later Aston Martins. The screen was still in two pieces, and seating was by split bench.

The original grille, with vertical slats in the centre section, was displaced by a face-lifted version (and horizontal slats) in 1951, by which time a smart two-seater drophead version by Tickford was also on sale.

The much-improved DB2/4 took over in 1953.

DB2/4 & DB2/4 Mk II 1953-57

The DB2/4 had a full hatchback and rear seats.

Three years on from the launch of the DB2, the DB2/4 arrived with a raft of improvements. The new car was more powerful and the body (by Mulliners of Birmingham) was better-trimmed, better-equipped and more versatile.

This time around, the roof line of the coupé was more hump-backed, with a hatchback lid at the rear (this was certainly the first fitted to a British car), the windscreen was one-piece, and the cabin had been re-shuffled so that 2+2 seating was available. The rear of the chassis frame was modified to make space for a rear seat pan and for a larger fuel tank. A centre-floor gear change was now standard. As

before, a most attractive Tickford two-seater drophead coupé was available.

After only one year the engine was enlarged to 2922cc (this being the standard size for the remainder of the family's production run), which meant that power went up to 140bhp. Then, from 1955, the DB2/4 Mk II featured a third body alternative – a notchback saloon with more squared-up tail, this being Tickford's modification of the drophead style.

Eventually an even more powerful engine, with 165bhp, became available. The DB2/4 family was supplanted by the DB Mk III in 1957.

SPECIFICATION

BODY STYLES: saloon, hardtop coupé, drophead coupé

PRODUCTION: DB2/4, 565, DB2/4 MkII, 199

ENGINE & TRANSMISSION: 2580cc/2922cc, 6cyl 2ohc, 4sp man, f/r

POWER: 125bhp @ 5000rpm/140bhp @ 5000rpm

MAX SPEED (MPH): (140bhp) 119

0-60MPH (SEC): (140bhp) 10.5

SUSPENSION & BRAKES: coil ifs, coil rear, drums f&r

LENGTH (IN)/WEIGHT (LB): 169/2690

LAUNCH PRICE: £2622

DB Mk III 1957-59

This was the final flowering of the original DB2 line, with chassis changes, a further boost to the choice of engines, and style changes to match. Recognisably the same as earlier types, but distinctive, this was the last of the compact Aston Martins, for the DB4 which took over was much larger and heavier.

This time the standard 2.9-litre engine produced 162bhp, though no less than 178bhp was optional. Behind it, not only

The DB Mark III had a revised nose and grille.

was there a hydraulically-operated clutch, and Laycock overdrive available as an option, but Borg-Warner automatic transmission (only with the 162bhp engine) could also be specified. At the same time, the chassis was modified to accept Girling front-wheel disc brakes, making this the first road-going Aston Martin so equipped.

Bodies (now all built by Tickford, rather than Mulliners) had a modified front-end style, complete with a more curvaceous grille aperture, and less angular panelwork to suit. As before, the hatchback feature of the coupé was continued, and three different body types were still available.

Although this model and its predecessors were very much liked and were the dream cars of many enthusiasts, sales were always limited by their high selling price. In 1957 a Mk III cost £3076 – which was 60 per cent more than the £1920 asked for an early DB2. This represented a rise of 60 per cent in only seven years, yet according to David Brown he was still losing money on every car sold.

The last DB Mk IIIs were produced in 1959, and there was no successor, for when the DB4 arrived it was an entirely different type of car.

DB4 1958-63

Launched in 1958, the DB4 inaugurated a family of models which lasted more than 12 years. Every car in the DB4 to DB6 Mk II range used the same basic pressed steel platform chassis, though there were several different wheelbases, and all used a version of the new straight-six all-alloy twin-cam engine designed by Tadek Marek.

The original DB4 ran on a 98-inch wheelbase and had a 240bhp 3670cc engine. Front suspension was by coil springs and wishbones, the rear axle being sprung on coils and located by radius arms and a Watts linkage. Rack-and-pinion steering was standard, as were four-wheel disc brakes.

The body style and design, credited to Touring of Milan, followed the "Superleggera" construction method, where the skin was built up on a network

Touring of Milan's styling of the DB4 was sensational.

of lightweight shaped steel tubes which accurately defined every profile. Although platforms, engines and transmissions were bought in from other David Brown companies, the bodies were manufactured at Newport Pagnell.

Five different "Series" of DB4s were produced in five years, each more appealing than the last. From 1960/61, Second Series had overdrive as an option, while Third Series (1961) had detail improvements. Fourth Series (1961) introduced the DB4 drophead coupé as an option, along with cowled headlamps as on the DB4GT (see below) and more power options, while Fifth Series (1962) was made roomier in the cabin. A few late cars had automatic transmission. A desirable option was the 266bhp Vantage engine, giving a 148mph top speed.

DB4 drophead coupé was introduced in 1961.

DB4 GT 1959-63

Introduced in 1959, and made only in limited numbers for four years, the DB4 GT was, effectively, a short-wheelbase DB4 coupé mainly intended for competition, with a more powerful engine and only two seats.

Compared with the DB4, the style of the GT was very similar, though all

DB4 GT had a shorter wheelbase than the DB4 and power was increased to 302bhp.

SPECIFICATION

BODY STYLES: sports coupé

PRODUCTION: 81

ENGINE & TRANSMISSION: 3670cc, 6cyl 2ohc, 4sp man, f/r

POWER: 302bhp @ 6000rpm

MAX SPEED (MPH): 152

0-60MPH (SEC): 6.4

SUSPENSION & BRAKES: coil ifs, coil rear, discs f&r

LENGTH (IN)/WEIGHT (LB): 172/2800

LAUNCH PRICE: £4534

cars had the cowled-headlamp nose. The wheelbase was shortened by five inches, all the shrinkage being in the doors and cabin area, and the engine was super-tuned to 302bhp against the DB4 Vantage's 266bhp, using triple Weber carburettors in place of the SUs. There was more light alloy in the body than in the standard DB4's, so the

unladen weight came down by a considerable 200lb.

Because of its high price – £4534 in 1959, compared with £3755 for the regular DB4 – sales of the DB4 GT were very limited. These cars soon became real icons among Aston Martin enthusiasts, their value increasing rapidly in later years.

DB4 GT Zagato 1960-63

The ultimate derivative of the DB4 family came along in 1960. Combining the short-wheelbase chassis of the DB4 GT with an ultra-powerful 314bhp version of the 3670cc engine, which had a twin-plug cylinder head, and a sensuous new ultra-light alloy two-seater coupé body by Zagato of Italy, Aston Martin offered its fastest-ever six-cylinder model.

These bodies were not only very light

DB4 GT Zagato had yet more power, at 314bhp, and was lighter than the GT.

SPECIFICATION

BODY STYLES: sports coupé

PRODUCTION: 19 at first, 4 in 1990s

ENGINE & TRANSMISSION: 3670cc, 6cyl 2ohc, 4sp man, f/r

POWER: 314bhp @ 6000rpm

MAX SPEED (MPH): 153

0-60MPH (SEC): 6.1

SUSPENSION & BRAKES: coil ifs, coil rear, discs f&r

LENGTH (IN)/WEIGHT (LB): 168/2700

LAUNCH PRICE: £5470

(the whole car weighed 100lb less than the DB4GT and 300lb less than the conventional DB4), but they were also therefore very fragile, and were intended mainly for motor racing. Front and rear bumpers were not normally supplied, though these were eventually made available.

Because these cars were very expensive

– £5470 in 1962 – and very specialised, they were also extremely rare. Only 19 were originally built, though four more "Second Sanction" machines were eventually produced by an officially-approved Aston Martin specialist in the 1990s. With a top speed of around 155mph, they became, and remained, the most desirable of all Aston Martins.

DB5 1963-65

The DB5, effectively, was the Sixth Series DB4, for in all ways it was a logical progression from the last of those types. Famous in later years as the James Bond car (a specially-equipped version appeared in the film *Goldfinger* and more recently in *Goldeneye*), the DB5 was a better car than any conventional DB4, and sold even faster in its two-year life.

Although visually nearly identical to the last of the DB4s, and running on the same 98in-wheelbase platform, the DB5 had a much improved drive line. Not only was the engine enlarged to 3995cc, giving 282bhp, but from 1964 a 325bhp version was available as an option.

No fewer than four different gearboxes were available – the original David Brown

DB5 drophead coupé.

four-speed unit, the same 'box with overdrive, a ZF five-speed gearbox, or Borg Warner automatic transmission. In fact the DB gearbox was soon abandoned as the ZF alternative was more effective and therefore more popular.

As with the previous range, fixed-head coupés and dropheads were sold, there also being a removable hardtop option for the drophead. A few estate cars were also produced, but these were conversions by the Harold Radford coachbuilding concern.

The Volante drophead coupé which arrived in the autumn of 1965 was effectively a DB5 convertible, but within a year that particular car had been upgraded to DB6 Volante status. Simply because they offered open-air motoring, Volante values in later years were colossally high.

The weight of the DB5, incidentally, had crept up by about 200lb over the original DB4 – and there was more to come. As with the DB6 (below), the DB5 became, and remained, one of the most popular of all classic Aston Martins, and deservedly so.

DB5 of 1963.

SPECIFICATION

BODY STYLES: saloon, drophead coupé

PRODUCTION: 1063

ENGINE & TRANSMISSION: 3995cc, 6cyl 2ohc, 4sp, o/d, 5sp man or auto, f/r

POWER: 282bhp @ 5500rpm/325bhp @ 5500rpm

MAX SPEED (MPH): (282bhp) 141

0-60MPH (SEC): (282bhp) 8.1

SUSPENSION & BRAKES: coil ifs, coil rear, discs f&r

LENGTH (IN)/WEIGHT (LB): 180/3200

LAUNCH PRICE: £4249

DB6 & Volante 1965-70

Structurally and visually (though not in its drive line) here was the biggest carve-up in the history of the DB4 – DB6 Mk II family. Compared with the DB5, which it replaced in the autumn of 1965, the DB6 had a longer wheelbase (by 3.75in) to allow for a more spacious cabin and more genuine four-seater accommodation.

Aft of the windscreen (and even that was bigger) the body shell was largely new, for the roof was higher, the cabin was more voluminous, and there was a pronounced swept-up spoiler shaped into the new boot lid.

Aston Martin DB6 had a longer wheelbase than the DB5.

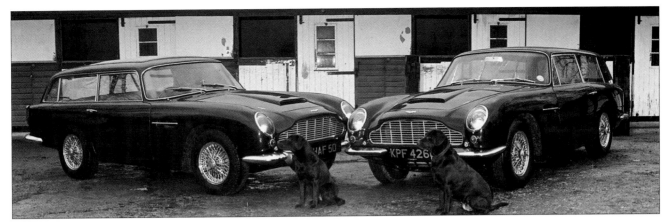

DB5 (left) and DB6 estate cars.

At the same time, the Superleggera method of construction was dropped, the DB6 having a more conventional type of steel and aluminium body assembly.

When the DB6 was launched, a Volante drophead coupé was also announced, though the first sanction of these cars were effectively carry-over DB5 types on the shorter 98-inch wheelbase. The definitive DB6 Volante, on the longer wheelbase, came along at the end of 1966. Once again, a few estate cars were produced by Radford to very special order.

Mechanically, and compared with the DB5, there were few innovations; the old DB manual transmission had been dropped, and increasing numbers of automatics were being sold. Engines were still 282bhp or 325bhp (both figures were a little exaggerated), and power-assisted steering was available from late 1966.

From late 1969 the DB6 became Mk II, with flared wheel arches, plus DBS wheels and tyres. Although AE-Brico fuel injection was available on the Mk II as an extra, it was not a success, and in later years most surviving cars tended to be converted back to carburettors.

Heavier than ever, and more bulky, the DB6s were later seen as less desirable than DB5 types, though the open-air Volante will always be valuable.

The Volante's tail retained a boot lid spoiler

SPECIFICATION

BODY STYLES: saloon, drophead coupé, estate

PRODUCTION: 1755, of which 423 were Mk IIs

ENGINE & TRANSMISSION: 3995cc, 6cyl 2ohc, 5sp man or auto, f/r

POWER: 282bhp @ 5500rpm/325bhp @ 5500rpm

MAX SPEED (MPH): (325bhp) 148

0-60MPH (SEC): (325bhp) 6.5

SUSPENSION & BRAKES: coil ifs, coil rear, discs f&r

LENGTH (IN)/WEIGHT (LB): 182/3250

LAUNCH PRICE: £4998

DBS-6 1967-73

Announced in 1967, the DBS was only the fourth new-generation Aston Martin to be built since 1945. Larger, wider and heavier than the last of the DB6s, it was always meant to be powered by a new V8 engine (see DBS-V8, below), but the original interim machine used the last of the Marek six-cylinder engines instead.

The DBS did not replace the DB6 (the two cars carried on, together, until early 1971) for it was a different type of car. Based on the old DB6 platform chassis, it had a one-inch longer wheelbase, but it had 4.5-inch wider wheel tracks. Front suspension was familiar (coil springs and wishbones) but the De Dion rear end was new. In spite of the increased weight (3760lb), power-assisted steering was still an optional extra. The running gear was very similar to the DB6, with either 282bhp or 325bhp from the 3995cc engine, and with ZF manual or Borg Warner automatic transmission.

The new body – wider and more angular than the DB6 – covered an almost-four-seater cabin, where leg room was very similar to the DB6, but the seats were all wider than before. Four headlamps and a very horizontal grille motif were features. In the last year of the DBS's life a two-headlamp nose took over from the original.

No traces of the old Superleggera-style construction remained, this being a conventional body shell, skinned in light-alloy but with much steel out of sight. At this time there was no provision for any alternative body style.

Until fitted with the new V8 engine,

The DBS-6 began life with a four-headlamp nose.

SPECIFICATION

BODY STYLES: saloon

PRODUCTION: 899

ENGINE & TRANSMISSION: 3995cc, 6cyl 2ohc, 5sp man or auto, f/r

POWER: 282bhp @ 5500rpm/325bhp @ 5500rpm

MAX SPEED (MPH): (325bhp) 148

0-60MPH (SEC): (325bhp) 8.6

SUSPENSION & BRAKES: coil ifs, DD coil rear, discs f&r

LENGTH (IN)/WEIGHT (LB): 181/3760

LAUNCH PRICE: £5500

DBS styling was sleek and modern.

the DBS was underpowered, needing all the 325bhp to provide adequate performance. Yet it proved a useful interim model (899 cars produced) before the DBS-V8 came on stream; the last 70 of those cars, incidentally, were merely known as Aston Martin Vantage models – though this model was often confused with others which followed.

DBS-V8 1969-72

The V8-engined version of the DBS was introduced in late 1969, went on sale in 1970, and in further developed form was to remain a staple model at Aston Martin until 1989, when it was replaced by the Virage. The early version, fitted with Bosch mechanical fuel injection, was built only until 1973 (by which time the name had also been changed).

Based on the DBS-6 (above), the new

The DBS-V8 was introduced in 1969.

SPECIFICATION

BODY STYLES: saloon

PRODUCTION: 2666 all DBS-V8 types produced by 1989

ENGINE & TRANSMISSION: 5340cc, V8 2ohc, 5sp man or auto, f/r

POWER: not quoted (estimated 345bhp)

MAX SPEED (MPH): 162

0-60MPH (SEC): 6.0

SUSPENSION & BRAKES: coil ifs, DD coil rear, discs f&r

LENGTH (IN)/WEIGHT (LB): 181/3800

LAUNCH PRICE: £6897

model used a new light-alloy V8 power unit of 5340cc. Aston Martin no longer quoted peak power ratings, so we may only guess at that 1969 output: it was probably about 345bhp, with a colossally high torque figure, maybe 400lb ft at 4500rpm.

This 90-degree V8 had twin overhead camshafts for each bank of cylinders. Although it was bulky, the engine was beautifully detailed, and over time it

proved to be very durable. Both manual and automatic transmission were available, the automatic 'box being Chrysler's latest Torqueflite three-speed unit. Air conditioning, still optional at first, was standardised in late 1971.

On this model adjustable rear dampers (from Armstrong) were standard, as was power-assisted steering (at last), the result being a car easier to drive hard than any other Aston Martin of the previous decade. Fitted with the fuel-injected engine, its top speed was more than 160mph, which made this the DBS-V8 fully a match in performance for any Ferrari or Maserati which was then on the market.

Faced with a continuously loss-making

business, Sir David Brown sold out to Company Developments in February 1972. Under the new management, from April 1972 the nose of the car was restyled – it had two 7in instead of four paired 5¾in headlamps – and it was renamed, officially, as Aston Martin V8.

Injected DBS V8 engine, with twin overhead cams for each bank of cylinders.

Then, from mid-1973, the Bosch injection system was discarded in favour of four downdraught twin-choke Weber carburettors (and a larger bonnet scoop to clear them!). This was when the last link with the DBS-V8 was lost.

Crash testing a DBS.

V8 1972-89

Officially, the DBS-V8 became simply V8 in May 1972, when new management (Company Developments) wanted to shrug off the David Brown connection. The name change was headlined by a twin (rather than four) headlamp nose and a slightly longer front end. Then, as later, the vast majority of cars were fitted with automatic transmission.

In the next 17 years, significant changes were made to the design (though a mid-1980s example was always demonstrably similar to the 1972 type), but these never changed the British Bulldog character of the machine, and the same alloy-skinned style was preserved throughout. A Weber-carburetted engine took over from fuel injection in August 1973 (there was a larger bonnet bulge to clear the carburettors). Due to financial problems, no cars were built from December 1974 to mid-1975.

Series 4 cars (the "Oscar India" series) went on sale in 1978, with 304bhp, a slimmed-down bonnet bulge and integral rear spoiler, with much wood veneer on dashboard. The Volante drophead coupé appeared in June 1978. Much later, from January 1986, the Series 5 car appeared, equipped with Weber-Marelli fuel injection instead of carburettors. The last car was built in December 1989, after which the Virage took over.

Aston Martin V8.

The days of light and agile Astons was long gone, but these cars – coupé and (Volante) drophead coupés – were amazingly nimble. Power steering, power brakes and exellent handling balance all helped, but it was always wise not to worry too much about fuel consumption, servicing costs and depreciation. By definition this was always going to be a slow-selling exclusive car, as it wasn't really a four-seater and it wasn't really a sports car. Aston Martin, too, realised that the drophead car's soft top and a 150mph top speed did not tie up together, so the company recommended owners to stay below 130mph unless the top was furled!

The V8 was nevertheless a well-built Aston Martin which evolved a following of its own. A high proportion of the cars

built have survived, have been restored, and are a part of the thriving club scene.

SPECIFICATION

BODY STYLES: sports coupé, drophead

PRODUCTION: 2666 all V8 coupés including earlier DBS-V8, 562 Volantes, all types

ENGINE & TRANSMISSION: 5340cc, V8 2ohc, 5sp man, or auto, f/r

POWER: not quoted (unofficially 320bhp @ 5000rpm/304bhp @ 5500rpm)

MAX SPEED (MPH): 155 (E)

0-60MPH (SEC): 6.0

SUSPENSION & BRAKES: coil ifs, DD coil rear, discs f/r

LENGTH (IN)/WEIGHT (LB): 184/4001

LAUNCH PRICE: (Coupé) £8457, (Volante) £33,864

Vantage 1977-89

Directly developed from the V8, the Vantage was a much more powerful derivative which looked the same, handled the same – but went a good deal faster. Although Aston Martin never published its peak output figures in those days, we now know just how powerful the 5.3-litre V8 actually was : later examples, built from 1986 on, could produce up to 432bhp.

Introduced in February 1977, the Vantage saloon was a 380bhp version of the contemporary V8, with a blanked-off front grille, stiffened suspension,

The Aston Martin Vantage of 1977.

SPECIFICATION

BODY STYLES: saloon, drophead

PRODUCTION: see V8 above

ENGINE & TRANSMISSION: 5340cc, V8cyl 2ohc, 5sp man, f/r

POWER: not quoted (unofficially 380bhp @ 6000rpm/400bhp @ 6000rpm/432bhp @ 6000rpm)

MAX SPEED (MPH): 170 (E)

0-60MPH (SEC): 5.4

SUSPENSION & BRAKES: coil ifs, coil DD rear, discs f&r

LENGTH (IN)/WEIGHT (LB): 184/4001

LAUNCH PRICE: £20,000

fatter tyres, and (theoretically, at least) only manual transmission. From then until 1989, the visual and equipment changes made usually mirrored those produced for "ordinary" V8s.

An integral rear spoiler appeared in 1988 and 400bhp engines became standard from late 1986. However, fuel injection never featured on this car. For the last three years, too, there was a Vantage Volante version, this being a

drophead coupé (the style was near identical to that of the V8 Volante), with the soft top re-engineered to cope with the 160mph-plus top speed.

Compared with the ordinary V8, the Vantage was much more accelerative, much more extrovert, and much more expensive to run. Think of a V8 with added "wow" factor, and you will have it right. The last car of this series was produced in 1989.

Lagonda 1974-76

Way back in the late 1960s, stylist William Towns produced the DBS two-door shape which would sell for many years. At the same time he also

SPECIFICATION

BODY STYLES: saloon

PRODUCTION: 7

ENGINE & TRANSMISSION: 5340cc, V8cyl 2ohc, 5sp man, or auto, f/r

POWER: not quoted

MAX SPEED (MPH): 149 (E)

0-60MPH (SEC): not measured

SUSPENSION & BRAKES: coil ifs, coil DD rear, discs f&r

LENGTH (IN)/WEIGHT (LB): 194/4410

LAUNCH PRICE: £14,040

The 1974 Aston Martin Lagonda had four doors. Only seven cars were made.

drew up designs for a longer-wheelbase version with four doors.

Nothing transpired until 1974, when a four-door car called the Aston Martin Lagonda was introduced. In every way except its bulk (it weighed 400lb more than the two-door type), this car felt, drove, sounded and handled like the regular V8.

Running on a twelve-inch longer version of the Aston Martin V8 platform, the Lagonda retained the same V8 engine, transmission, steering, braking, and front and rear suspension as the two-door car.

The body, though retaining many V8 panels under the skin, particularly at the front end, was a rather ungainly four-door saloon, with an awkward Lagonda-type front end.

Perhaps the looks did not help, perhaps the selling price – £14,040 when launched – was another factor, while the company's state of suspended animation in the first half of 1975 must have done nothing for the Lagonda's prospects.

Whatever the reason, the fact is that only seven of these cars (two with manual transmission) were ever produced, the last in June 1976.

Lagonda 1976-90

The second-generation Aston Martin Lagonda, which was revealed in October 1976 but was not in series production until late 1978, was very different from the first car – and much more successful. Though equipped with controversial sharp-edged four-door saloon styling, it sold steadily for more than a decade, underpinning Aston Martin's very existence at times when the V8's sales had almost dried up.

The basic chassis engineering – massively powerful V8 engine, automatic transmission, four-wheel disc brakes, De Dion rear suspension, power-assisted steering and all – was that of the contemporary two-door V8, but the structure was almost totally different. The rear suspension featured self-levelling dampers, and manual transmission was not available.

The steel platform chassis was different from that of the V8 not only in its wheelbase length – 114.5 inches instead of 103 inches – but also in constructional detail. The super-structure itself (basically in steel, though with aluminium skins) was immensely long, sharp-edged, with a much overhanging (though slim) nose, four passenger doors and space for four occupants. Main headlamps were four rectangular pop-up units hidden under flaps during daylight.

The prototype had a mass of electronic instruments and controls in a futuristic display, but these were mostly abandoned before true series production began at the end of 1978. By that time the fascia looked positively conventional, though still angular in

The startling Aston Martin Lagonda, styled by William Towns.

theme, with many digital read-outs. The possibilities for electronic malfunction seemed to be endless, yet somehow Aston Martin made them all work, most of the time.

The Weber-carburetted engine was less highly tuned than in the V8 (the power output was not quoted though unofficially estimated at 280bhp), but the top speed was a rather impressive 145mph. In terms of sales this Lagonda was not very successful at home but it sold well overseas, particularly in the Middle East.

BBS wheels became standard from September 1983, and an uprated Weber-Marelli injected 300bhp engine was fitted from January 1986. The Series 4 type of 1987 featured not only a restyle with rounded-edge body styling and six rectangular headlamps permanently exposed, but also a conventional-looking wood-trimmed fascia/instrument layout, along with yet another multi-spoked style of alloy wheel. The last Lagonda was produced in January 1990.

The Lagonda was first shown with this digital electronic dashboard.

SPECIFICATION

BODY STYLES: saloon

PRODUCTION: 645

ENGINE & TRANSMISSION: 5340cc, V8 2ohc, auto, f/r

POWER: 280bhp @ 5000rpm/300bhp @ 5000rpm/305bhp @ 5500rpm

MAX SPEED (MPH): 143/145

0-60MPH (SEC): 8.8/8.4

SUSPENSION & BRAKES: coil ifs, coil DD rear, discs f&r

LENGTH (IN)/WEIGHT (LB): 208/4459-4662

LAUNCH PRICE: £24,570 at launch, £32,620 early 1979, £95,000 Series 4

ASTRA

This was a totally obscure small car firm, which sprung up in the mid-1950s to take advantage of a market for cheap-and-cheerful economy cars. Built at Hampton Hill in Middlesex, it was controlled by British Anzani, a motorcycle engine specialist which had once produced noted engines for fine car makers such as Frazer Nash, but all that was already a long time ago.

By this time British Anzani was producing two-stroke engines for the motorcycle trade, and wanted to cash in on the economy car market.

Given the evidence of what we now know, they need not have bothered, for after the complete failure of the Utility there were no further attempts to produce an Astra four-wheeler.

Utility 1956-60

Here was another of those cheap and nasty little machines which Britain could only have produced at a time of fuel shortages and economic gloom. Few people, for sure, ever took it seriously.

The Utility had originally been marketed as the Jarc Little Horse with an Excelsior engine, but as an Anzani-engined Astra it was previewed in August 1956. Apart from being the cheapest four-wheeler on the UK market – it cost £348 when an Austin A30 was priced at £540, and a BMW Isetta at £439 – it had almost no virtues.

The chassis featured channel-section side members with a steel floor welded to them, and the twin-cylinder air-cooled two-stroke Anzani engine was mounted in the tail, where it drove a motorcycle-type Albion gearbox, with a reverse gear, by chain. Amazingly, there was coil spring independent suspension (by swing axles) at front and rear, but this appeared to be the Astra's single advanced feature.

The only body available was an aluminium-panelled van with woody-

Astra Utility of 1956.

type rear corners which Astra described as a Utility (Australians, who knew all about Utes, which were something else entirely, must have been amused). There were two seats with tubular frames, hammock-style, and a loading floor behind them. There was also a a lift-up tailgate. The style, if it could be called a style, featured flat sides with insets for the panels behind the doors. The fuel tank was mounted up front where visual clues suggested the engine should be.

The Autocar drove one (the only one?) in 1956, and suggested that it had "merit" – which was nice of them – but they also found that the ride was hard, and that this marginal machine had a tendency to wander away from the

straight line under all conditions: "The castor action was inadequate. With a passenger and a load of 130lb on the platform, the wandering tendency increased. There was considerable oversteer…"

The only merit seemed to be a cruising speed of 45mph (57mph was the fastest speed seen), and the promise of up to 60mpg using two-stroke petroil fuel. That formidable historian Michael Sedgwick wonders if any Utilities were ever sold, even in the kit form at which they eventually became available.

Even if none survive, they will surely never be missed. Later, incidentally, the chassis was re-used, in the equally dreadful Gill Getabout.

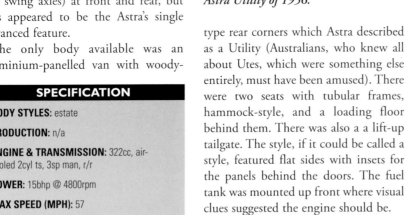

SPECIFICATION

BODY STYLES: estate

PRODUCTION: n/a

ENGINE & TRANSMISSION: 322cc, air-cooled 2cyl ts, 3sp man, r/r

POWER: 15bhp @ 4800rpm

MAX SPEED (MPH): 57

0-60MPH (SEC): not possible

SUSPENSION & BRAKES: coil ifs, coil irs, drums f&r

LENGTH (IN)/WEIGHT (LB): n/a/710

LAUNCH PRICE: £348

AUSTIN

In the late 1930s Austin had fought neck-and-neck with Morris for market leadership. Both makes offered traditional engineering, neither offered startling styling, and both sold cars at very low prices.

After that irrepressible tycoon, Leonard Lord, arrived at Austin in 1938, Longbridge changed, rapidly. First of all, Lord pushed through the launch of new 8hp, 10hp and 12hp models, along with a range of trucks. During the War, Longbridge built huge numbers of aircraft, trucks and cars for military use. Then, in the late 1940s, a period of massive expansion began again.

New A125, A40, A70, A90 and A30 ranges followed in quick succession, and by 1950 Austin was building nearly 170,000 vehicles a year. Then, in 1951/52, came the momentous merger with Nuffield, this being when the British Motor Corporation (BMC) was founded. Len Lord soon became chairman of BMC and he made sure that Austin was always the dominant partner. Selling the cars was never a problem — but making them definitely was, as labour relations were often abysmal, and Longbridge was regularly wracked by self-defeating strikes.

In the 1950s Austin inspired the birth of many new BMC cars, and from 1958 (with the new-generation A40) a design partnership was forged with Pininfarina. The B-Series Farina range was typical of this partnership.

From 1959, however, Austin gradually adopted front wheel drive for its new products — Mini, 1100, and 1800 — all of which were then cloned with other badges up front. Though the Mini never made much money, it captured the hearts of the British — and more than five million would be built in the next forty years. The Farina-styled cars, on the other hand, especially the big-engined ranges, were perhaps less memorable but they did good business.

Even in the mid-to-late 1960s, when BMC first absorbed Pressed Steel and then Jaguar, Austin was still the dominant marque and UK market leader. Once BMH/BMC merged with Leyland to form British Leyland, Austin became Austin-Morris, the volume-selling business, continuing to make the most cars but also continuing to cause most of the management headaches too.

Although British Leyland abandoned most other marques in the 1970s, Austin would survive until the end of the 1980s, when the Rover badge took over instead.

Herbert Austin at the wheel of the original 1922 Austin Seven.

8hp 1945-47

Introduced in February 1939, this was Austin's new entry-level car, effectively a replacement for the legendary Seven/Big Seven range. Apart from its 900cc sidevalve engine and gearbox, which came from the Big Seven, it was all new. Only 20,000 were built before the onset of war meant that production was tailed off. This was one of the trio of cars re-introduced immediately after the guns fell silent.

Under Lord Austin, but not under Len Lord, Austin had always been a very conservative business. This, therefore, was the first Austin to make tentative steps towards modernity and thus towards unit

construction. Because Longbridge's body shops still needed to be modernised, the new 8 had a pressed-steel platform chassis, which was really only part way towards the monocoques already adopted by Morris and Vauxhall.

The basic styling themes were shared with the new 10 and the new 12 which would soon follow. Conventional when they first appeared in 1939, these cars looked distinctly old-fashioned by 1945, yet the 8 would sell strongly until 1947, when it and the 10 were both displaced by the A40 Devon. Technically, here was a classic 1930s-type Austin, with beam axle

SPECIFICATION

BODY STYLES: saloon

PRODUCTION: 33,000 post-war, 20,000 in 1939

ENGINE & TRANSMISSION: 900cc, 4cyl sv, 4sp man, f/r

POWER: 23bhp @ 4000rpm

MAX SPEED (MPH): 56

0-60MPH (SEC): not possible

SUSPENSION & BRAKES: beam leaf front, leaf rear, drums f&r

LENGTH (IN)/WEIGHT (LB): 149/1701

LAUNCH PRICE: £326

front and rear suspension, a bouncy ride, very mediocre roadholding, a sidevalve engine, and a gearbox with a long and willowy change-speed lever.

The principal merit was the cars' reliabilty and durability, these having long been the traditional virtues of the Austin. Of three body styles, only the four-door saloon reappeared after in 1945.

Performance, and character? Plenty of old-style 1930s character, for sure, but if you were in a hurry you would surely never have bought an Austin 8. Forty mph, all day, was the sensible limit – which explains why the brakes were poor but didn't need to be any better.

The 1945 Austin 8 – only the four-door saloon was available.

10hp 1945-47

Amazingly, Austin's new-generation 10 appeared just three months after the new 8 – but this miracle was explained by the two cars sharing many features, including the new-style pressed-steel chassis platform, the basic suspension and all other chassis layouts. Although the 10 had a five-inch longer wheelbase and wider wheel tracks, much of the rest of the car came out of the same parts bins (and off the same drawing boards) as the 8, and there were very close similarities in the appearance of the two models..

Very few pre-war 10s were built, but assembly continued throughout the war and more than 40,000 "Tilly"

The New
AUSTIN TEN

With a sparkling performance and a superb appearance, motoring finds its newest thrill in this masterpiece amongst light cars.

Easy to look at and even easier to ride in, this new Ten provides the roomiest accommodation for four persons and affords wide-angle vision.

For economy and dependability it is every inch an Austin—for all-round satisfaction it stands alone.

The Austin 10, close cousin of the 8.

SPECIFICATION

BODY STYLES: saloon

PRODUCTION: 49,000 post-war

ENGINE & TRANSMISSION: 1125cc, 4cyl sv, 4sp man, f/r

POWER: 28bhp @ 4000rpm

MAX SPEED (MPH): 60

0-60MPH (SEC): not measured

SUSPENSION & BRAKES: beam leaf front, leaf rear, drums f&r

LENGTH (IN)/WEIGHT (LB): 158/1975

LAUNCH PRICE: £397

types (military versions, many of them pick-ups) followed before 1945. No sooner had peace broken out than civilian 10 models (four-door saloons only) began to appear. Technically there was nothing to get excited about, for the sidevalve four-cylinder engine dated from 1932, so owners then and now had to get used to the idea of 45-50mph cruising at best, and a maiden aunt character.

It tells us much about post-war demand for new cars – any cars – that this was Austin's best seller until the

new-generation A40 Devon came on the scene.

To place them in their historical and social context, these Austins had a quaint, gentle, roses-round-the-door, suburban-England ambience, for they could not be hurried, they were distinctly old-fashioned, and yet they quintessentially represented pre-war Britain in so many ways. If Len Lord hadn't needed time to get the A40 ready, he would surely have been a bit embarrasssed about this dear old 10 by the time 1947 came along.

12/16hp 1945-49

The 12 was the third new-style Austin to be launched in 1939, and the post-war 16 version previewed in 1944 was the first-ever Austin car to use an overhead-valve engine. Like the 8 and 10 already described, the 12 was another new model rushed through by Len Lord to update Austin's image at the end of the 1930s.

The 12s mechanical link with the past was its old-style 1535cc sidevalve engine (which had been around since 1933) and the related four-speed gearbox, but all the rest – the separate chassis, the beam axle suspension and rod-operated brakes – was new.

And so was the four-door saloon body style, which looked like that of the new

An Austin 12 .

10 but was totally different, being much larger, bulkier and more spacious. Production didn't get going in 1939 (public launch was on 1 September 1939, just two days before war broke out), but the 12 was then the first of the post-war Austins to be revealed. That was when it was joined by the new 16, which had a 2199cc overhead-valve four-cylinder engine.

Final fettling of an Austin 16 in the factory.

Related to the new six-cylinder Austin truck engine, the 2.2-litre four would later be enlarged for use in the Austin A90, the Champ 4x4 and (more famously) in the Austin-Healey 100/4. Vans and taxicabs also used this almost unburstable power unit, which proved to be surprisingly tuneable.

Although the 12 was quite sluggish (it was underpowered, no question about that), the new 16hp was a much more lively proposition, with a top speed of around 75mph. Two definite advances were that a heater, and a radio, were both optional, which was rare in the UK in 1945.

Both models were quite expensive by 1945 standards and the lower powered 12 suffered relatively poor sales. The 12 and the 16 were superseded by the new-generation A70 Hampshire.

SPECIFICATION

BODY STYLES: saloon, estate

PRODUCTION: 8698 12hp, 35,434 16hp

ENGINE & TRANSMISSION: 1535cc/2199cc, 4cyl sv/ohv, 4sp man, f/r

POWER: 42bhp @ 4000rpm/67bhp @ 3800rpm

MAX SPEED (MPH): 63/75

0-60MPH (SEC): not measured/25.1

SUSPENSION & BRAKES: Beam leaf front, leaf rear, drums f&r

LENGTH (IN)/WEIGHT (LB): 171/2643, 171/2995

LAUNCH PRICE: £531/£569

A40 Dorset/A40 Devon 1947-52

These twins were Austin's first all-new post-war models, designed with mass production and export appeal in mind. Although chairman Leonard Lord still made a resounding success of this model – and because it replaced the old 8hp, 10hp and 12hp models it brought much-needed rationalisation to Longbridge – technically it was a real mish-mash of new and old-fashioned features.

The overhead-valve engine was all-new (it was the forerunner of the legendary B-Series which followed), as were the coil spring independent front suspension and the new styling, but this car reverted to

separate-chassis construction when all Austin's main rivals were manufacturing monocoques, and at launch it still had hydro-mechanical brakes (ie hydraulic at the front, mechanical at the rear). Before the end of production a steering-column gearchange and full hydraulic brakes had been adopted. Although the price was right these cars didn't handle well, and they were not put together that well at Longbridge, for they rusted very readily

Dorsets had two-door saloon bodies (at one time, too, it had been proposed that there be a narrower A35, but that never happened), while the Devon used the

Austin A40 Devon.

SPECIFICATION

BODY STYLES: saloon, estate, commercials

PRODUCTION: 15,939 Dorsets, 273,958 Devons, 26,587 Countryman estates produced

ENGINE & TRANSMISSION: 1200 cc, 4cyl ohv, 4sp man, f/r

POWER: 40 bhp @ 4300rpm

MAX SPEED (MPH): 67

0-60MPH (SEC): 34.8

SUSPENSION & BRAKES: coil ifs, leaf rear, drums f&r

LENGTH (IN)/WEIGHT (LB): 153/2100

LAUNCH PRICE: £403

The two-door A40 Dorset was discontinued in 1949.

The A40 Countryman was a highly practical vehicle.

same silhouette but had four doors. Len Lord hoped to take the USA by storm with this car, but the Americans found it too slow and small to interest them.

The Brits and those from Empire countries simply lapped them up, though, and at peak Longbridge was churning out 2000 A40s every week. Until overtaken by the A30/A35, and then by the Mini in the 1960s, no other Austin had ever sold so well, so it must have had its merits.

An A40 pick-up in British Petroleum livery.

A110/A125 Sheerline 1947-54

Traditionally, Austin had always produced one very large model, even if only in small numbers, looking to mop up taxi, private hire, business and the middle-class mayoral markets. In the 1930s there had been 20s and even, in 1938-1939 only, a 28.

Now, for post-war austerity Britain, Austin developed the massive Sheerline and the closely-related A135 Princess, announcing them in February 1947. Amazingly, these were Austin's very first all-new post-war models. Sheerline bodies were assembled at Longbridge, while the larger, glossier and much more expensive A135 Princess (described below) was bodied by Vanden Plas in North London.

Apart from inheriting a modified version of Austin's ohv six-cylinder truck engine (which had been new in 1939, and whose four-cylinder derivatives were used in the 16 and later in the A70 and A90), the rest of the A110 and A125 was new. There was a rock-solid long-

The imposing A125 Sheerline. One could not claim they skimped on the headlamps.

wheelbase chassis with box-section side members, partly razor-edged styling which positively cribbed the theme of the Bentley Mk VI (though the headlamps were still exposed to the headwind), lashings of rear seat space, coil spring independent front suspension, and enough wood, leather and other up-market trim to keep company bosses and municipal grandees happy. Most Sheerlines were four-door saloons but a few ultra-long-wheelbase types had six-

Sheerline limousine on the long-wheelbase chassis.

A gas turbine-powered Sheerline on test.

light limousine bodies instead.

The new car's "Sheerline" name was a good title, though with those exposed headlamps it was all rather meaningless. The first 12 cars were A110s, with 110bhp 3.5-litre engines, but this was not enough, so more power was immediately made available: 125bhp and 4 litres turned the definitive models into A125s and made them fast enough. A top speed of 80mpht with 70mph as a cruising speed, was accept-able in those days, but it was always best not to talk about fuel consumption (14mpg and worse).

Not even the most creative account-ant could have made this model profitable, for only 9000 were sold in nine years, but Austin persevered with it. The genuinely well-specified Princess lived on much longer, until 1968. Just a few Sheerlines survived into the 2000s, but as curiosities rather than valued antiques.

A120/135 Princess I,II,III 1947-56

Austin bought up the London-based Vanden Plas coachbuilding business in 1946, allowing them to press ahead with projects like the new Princess, which was effectively the Sheerline in a more tasteful, better-equipped and prettier party frock.

The Princess used the same rolling chassis and running gear as the Sheerline, though with the engines in a slightly higher state of tune. Everything about the running gear, the box-section chassis, the big truck-derived engines, the floppy coil spring independent front suspension, and the elephantine handling, were as also found in the Sheerline. There were, in fact, just 32 of the original A120 120bhp 3.5-litre cars, which were then supplanted by the A135 135bhp 4-litre model.

The bodies, by Vanden Plas, were built

A135 Princess had faired-in headlamps and smoother styling than the Sheerline.

by traditional methods, and by hand, with ash frames reinforced in certain areas by alloy castings (VDP had learnt a lot during the war, when fabricating aircraft pieces), while the aluminium skin panels were mainly pressed by Austin at Longbridge. Lots of wood and leather, along with square instruments, adorned the interior.

The style, though similar in its basic proportions to the Sheerline, was at once more elegant, more finely detailed, and more costly to produce. Faired headlamps and spatted rear wheels were a feature, as was the higher selling price. Princess II took over in 1950, with restyled rear door window shapes (there was also a long-wheelbase limousine version from that moment), while Princess III arrived in 1953, with a more tasteful front grille and revised front-end lines.

This was a very slow-selling but quite prestigious model. In 1947/48 an early Princess cost £2102 compared with £1277 for a Sheerline. This, no doubt, explains why only 1913 Princesses were built up to 1956 – only 200 cars a year.

The Princess' dash is a period piece.

Princess 4-Litre Limousine 1952-57

After five years of producing four-light A135 Princess saloons, Austin's Vanden Plas subsidiary produced its very first unique-style six-light limousine in 1952. Though the limousine would never be a fast seller, it ran and ran, the last of all being produced in 1968. Not without change, mind you – the Austin became a Princess in 1957, and a Vanden Plas in 1960.

Original cars used the longer-wheelbase version of the A135 Princess chassis, but GM/Rolls-Royce-type Hydramatic transmission became optional in 1956, along with optional power-assisted steering.

Complete with its division, and its hand-crafted wooden-framed coachwork, the 215in-long body was well proportioned, and elegant for its purpose. Many a business, funeral director or local

Princess 4-litre limousine.

authority would buy these machines instead of investing in a Daimler or a Rolls-Royce, for they had all the presence while being much cheaper.

Because of their solid separate chassis and light alloy body panels a surprising number have survived. They are still in demand as wedding cars.

A Princess 4-litre landaulette built for a Royal Tour in 1953.

A70 Hampshire 1948-50

Although Austin historians will forget all about this model if you promise to do the same, it still managed to sell more than 35,000 examples in only two years. Technically, like the closely-related A90 Atlantic, it was a great disappointment, for the handling was awful, the steering-column gear change abysmal, and even the styling was unsuccessful.

This, though, was a car mainly exported and aimed at selling into the Standard Vanguard market. Although it obviously had the same influences as the A40 Devon, it was larger and heavier, so there were few shared components in the chassis and the body.

The engine was lifted from the old 16hp saloon, which the Hampshire replaced, and most of the oily bits were shared with the A90 Atlantic (described below) and the A70 Hereford which followed. The style of the four-door saloon was somewhat like that of the A40 Devon, but the cabin was not very roomy.

Financially the Hampshire cannot have been a success, for it was only made for two years – 1948 to 1950. Yet this car had a pressed-steel body, and capital costs had to be amortised, so what happened? The restyled A70 Hereford happened, that's what.

Rust-prone like most early-post war Austins, these cars had virtually disappeared by the new century.

Austin A70 Hampshire, imperfect but an 80mph car.

The semi-woody Hampshire Countryman.

A Hampshire tackles a hill climb during the 1949 Monte Carlo Rally.

SPECIFICATION

BODY STYLES: saloon, estate, commercials

PRODUCTION: 34,360 saloons, 901 estates

ENGINE & TRANSMISSION: 2199cc, 4cyl ohv, 4sp man, f/r

POWER: 64 bhp @ 3800 rpm

MAX SPEED (MPH): 82

0-60MPH (SEC): 21.5

SUSPENSION & BRAKES: coil ifs, leaf rear, drums f&r

LENGTH (IN)/WEIGHT (LB): 163/2688

LAUNCH PRICE: £608

A90 Atlantic 1948-52

W hat on earth was Leonard Lord thinking of? Could he really have expected the weirdly-styled A90 Atlantic ever to take the USA market by storm? He could, apparently, but he was proved wrong.

The A90, in summary, had a great engine but awful everything else. The chassis was that of the A70 Hampshire, with the same too-soft suspension, and the same terrible four-on-the column gearchange, yet it was blessed with the torquey 88bhp 2660cc engine which would eventually be bequeathed to the excellent Austin-Healey 100/4.

The body style – well, what can one say? Unlike any other Austin, before or since, it had a "Cyclops" front lighting treatment, a three-piece windscreen, flush body sides, covered rear wheels, only two passenger doors and a divided bench front seat. Two "flying A" (for Austin) badges – one behind each headlamp – made good aiming points, which was just as well, since the handling was poor.

A90 2.6-litre Atlantic saloon had a fabric roof covering..

This Atlantic completed 11,850 miles at 70mph at Indianapolis in 1949.

The dashboard of the Atlantic featured a rev counter and two ashtrays.

SPECIFICATION

BODY STYLES: saloon, drophead

PRODUCTION: 7981

ENGINE & TRANSMISSION: 2660cc, 4cyl ohv, 4sp man, f/r

POWER: 88 bhp @ 4000rpm

MAX SPEED (MPH): 91

0-60MPH (SEC): 16.6

SUSPENSION & BRAKES: coil ifs, leaf rear, drums f&r

LENGTH (IN)/WEIGHT (LB): 177/2698

LAUNCH PRICE: £953

Early cars were sold only as convertibles, power operation for the soft top being an option, while a hardtop alternative was available a year later. It didn't help. Production stuttered to a halt in 1952, two whole years before the A90 Westminster replacement could be made ready.

The A90 Atlantic was such an extraordinary car that a few simply had to be preserved for latter-day car nuts to inspect. Even today, they say, the A90 still causes quite a stir.

An Atlantic on the Monte Carlo Rally in the early 1950s.

A40 Somerset 1952-54

A ustin provided the A40 chassis with a new and more rotund body style in February 1952, calling the new model the Somerset. Although mechanically very like the late-model A40 Devon (steering-column gearchange and all), this was a more spacious, more pleasing machine, especially as a nice two-door

convertible (bodywork by Carbodies of Coventry) was an offering.

All other Somersets were four-door saloons with bench front seats, and shared very similar styling to the A70 Hereford which had appeared earlier – the passenger doors, apparently, were the same as those of the Hereford.

On the market for just three summers, the Somerset sold very well, and was a commercial success. Even though the car's handling qualities were no great shakes in any department, the Somerset was a sound and serviceable product. Surviving dropheads are very rare and are well regarded.

SPECIFICATION

BODY STYLES: saloon, drophead

PRODUCTION: 173,306, of which 7243 were convertibles

ENGINE & TRANSMISSION: 1200cc, 4cyl ohv, 4sp man, f/r

POWER: 42bhp @ 4300rpm

MAX SPEED (MPH): 69

0-60MPH (SEC): 31.6

SUSPENSION & BRAKES: coil ifs, leaf rear, drums f&r

LENGTH (IN)/WEIGHT (LB): 159/2156

LAUNCH PRICE: £728

The attractive A40 Somerset convertible was built by Carbodies of Coventry.

A40 Somersets in the factory.

A40 Sports 1950-53

Although Leonard Lord wasn't really interested in sports cars and sports motoring, he allowed the A40 Sports to go ahead in 1950. The rolling chassis, complete with a 46bhp version of the 1200cc engine, was built at Longbridge, but Jensen Motors (which had styled the car) produced the two-door four-seater convertible body at its West Bromwich factory.

Although the Sports looked very like the enormous Jensen Interceptor of the period, it did not share its character.

The twin-carburettor A40 Sports, with body styled and built by Jensen.

Angela Palfrey's A40 Sports during the final test of the 1956 RAC Rally at Blackpool.

Like the Devon and later Somerset family cars, the Sports was hampered by the same floppy chassis, and (from late 1951) a steering-column gear change, so it was not very sporting. An A40 Sports was flat out at 78mph, which did not frighten its competitors.

Yet this model had its attractions and 4011 were sold. When Donald Healey sold the idea of the Austin-Healey 100 to Leonard Lord the A40 Sports was discontinued.

The A40 Sports's crew after their "Round the World in Thirty days" adventure in 1951.

A70 Hereford 1950-54

As with the second-generation A40, the revised and rebodied A70, named the Hereford, improved on the Hampshire. Only two years after the A70 chassis had appeared, the Hereford body was put on it. The new model was more bulbous, arguably more handsome, and demonstrably more saleable than before.

With a longer wheelbase and wider track than the original, the handling was somewhat improved, but the non-supportive bench front seat, along with a column change, still held it back.

Sensible product planning meant that the door pressings could later be shared with the A40 Somerset, and there was some component sharing, too, between the A70 drophead coupé, made by Carbodies, and the slightly smaller A40 drophead. Estate cars (rare) were either all-steel or decked out as woodies.

Not a sensational car (but, in the early 1950s, how many British cars were?), it sold steadily and well, until replaced by the new monocoque A90 Westminster in 1954. Today it is a popular model among Austin "Counties" enthusiasts.

Hereford drophead.

A Hereford on the 1952 RAC Rally.

The A70 Hereford was successor to the Hampshire.

Hereford Countryman.

Hereford pick-up, a useful machine

A30/A35 1951-62

Here was Austin's first post-war baby car. Although the company had itched to replaced the Austin Seven, it took ages to raise the capital to prepare a new monocoque structure, a new engine and transmission – in fact everything, for there were no carryover or shared parts in this machine.

Though new, almost all the running gear was scaled-down A40. The A30's A-Series engine became legendary and would live until the 1990s. Along with the gearbox and the axle, A-series engines would be fitted to later cars as diverse as the Morris Minor, Austin A40 Farina, Austin-Healey Sprite and MG Midget.

Obsessed with the old Austin Seven, Austin not only gave the new A30 a similar footprint, but tried to impose the old name on the public too. That misfired (it wasn't "Seven" anythings, after all), so the new car simply became known as A30 instead. The cabin was cramped for a four-seater, the narrow track led to rather "topply" roadholding,

A four-door Austin A30 awaits the public at the 1953 motor show.

and equipment was minimal (a heater was still extra!) but there was plenty of potential. With work, The A30 proved it could be a successful little racing saloon too!

Most versions sold well, and after five years the A30 became A35, with a bigger engine and better gearbox with remote-control change. A new pick-up version failed, but only because HM Government applied Purchase Tax to what Austin thought was really a commercial vehicle.

From late 1959 the A35 was dropped in favour of the new Mini, though the Countryman estate persisted to 1962, and vans until 1968. The A30 and A35 were not inspiring machines but they enjoyed huge commercial success and they still have a keen following today.

A35, recognisable from the front by the chrome band round the grille.

A one-off A30 tourer. Note the sporty cutaway doors.

Only about 500 of the quirky A35 pick-ups were built.

SPECIFICATION

BODY STYLES: saloon, estate, pick-up, light commercial

PRODUCTION: 527,000, including commercials

ENGINE & TRANSMISSION: 803cc/948cc, 4cyl ohv, 4sp man, f/r

POWER: 30bhp @ 4800rpm/34bhp @ 4750rpm

MAX SPEED (MPH): 63/72

0-60MPH (SEC): Not measured/30.0

SUSPENSION & BRAKES: coil ifs, leaf rear, drums f&r

LENGTH (IN)/WEIGHT (LB): 137/1484

LAUNCH PRICE: £507/£541

The popular and willing A30 Countryman was all-metal, unlike the part-woody Hampshire and Hereford estates.

Champf 1952-55

What a tangled birth and career… Originally the Champ was a late-WW2 military 4x4 project, which the British Army might have used to replace the famous Jeep. Nuffield designed it, and Austin might have provided the 16hp/A70-type 2.2-litre engine, but after the war everything stalled.

Finally, Austin was contracted to build the car which, in military form, had a 2.8-litre Rolls-Royce B40 engine, and was christened "Champ". Much heavier than the Jeep, and not by any means as versatile, it had a cruciform chassis frame with torsion bar all-independent suspension, five-speed transmission (with which, in theory,

The four wheel drive Austin Champ.

one could go backwards just as fast as forwards!) and a bulbous four-seater open-top shell. The Champ could go almost anywhere, though at considerable expense, as the fuel consumption was heavy.

Part of the deal was that Austin could market a civilian version, which they did by fitting a detuned 75bhp version of the 2.6-litre A90/Austin-Healey 100 engine as a lower-cost alternative, but this wasn't a lasting success. The Army preferred the Land Rover, which the British public did too, as the price of Solihull's best was much lower.

Civilian sales of new Champs were in the hundreds, though many ex-military versions were purchased at disposal

sales. Like early-type Land-Rovers, they still have their adherents among military vehicle enthusiasts.

A Champ at work.

SPECIFICATION

BODY STYLES: open utility

PRODUCTION: 13,000, mostly for military use

ENGINE & TRANSMISSION: 2660cc/2838cc, 4cyl ohv/ioe, 5sp man, f/4

POWER: 75bhp @ 3750rpm/80bhp @ 3750rpm

MAX SPEED (MPH): 65 (E)

0-60MPH (SEC): not measured

SUSPENSION & BRAKES: tor ifs, tor irs, drums f&r

LENGTH (IN)/WEIGHT (LB): 144/3470

LAUNCH PRICE: £750/£1100

Princess IV/Limousine 1956-59

When the Princess IV took over from the Princess III in 1956, sales slumped alarmingly. Although the new car did not look as impressive as expected, this has puzzled historians for, under the skin, the rolling chassis of the

SPECIFICATION

BODY STYLES: saloon, limousine

PRODUCTION: 200

ENGINE & TRANSMISSION: 3993cc, 6cyl ohv, 4sp auto, f/r

POWER: 150bhp @ 4100rpm

MAX SPEED (MPH): 99

0-60MPH (SEC): 16.1

SUSPENSION & BRAKES: coil ifs, leaf rear, drums f&r

LENGTH (IN)/WEIGHT (LB): 201/4590

LAUNCH PRICE: £3376

Austin Princess IV, a very bulky car.

latest car was much like that of its predecessor. The latest model had a slightly longer wheelbase than before, power-assisted steering, Hydramatic transmission and power brakes. The 4-litre D-Series engine now had 150bhp

instead of 135bhp, propelling this huge car to 100mph. The clientele – private hire, businesses, dignitaries – shunned it. It struggled on for less than three years, during which time Vanden Plas built just 200 examples. Do any survive?

A40/A50/A55 Cambridge 1954-58

As with the A30, this was "take a deep breath" time for Austin. Not only was a new-generation of medium-sized cars to be introduced, but they would be the first to use chassisless (monocoque) construction, to use the new-fangled corporate B-Series engine, and to use entirely different styling themes.

New from end to end, this was Austin's second monocoque design (the A30 had been the first), and it featured what was nicknamed "cow-hips" styling at the rear. Longer in the wheelbase than the obsolete A40 Somerset, though using that car's IFS, the A50 Cambridge was a more roomy, better-packaged car. Body options were quirky: four-door saloons were joined by vans and pick-ups, but there were no estate cars, and two-door saloons were strangled after birth.

The first cars were A40s with 1.2 litres, or A50s with 1.5 litres, both with steering-column gearchange, soft coil-sprung front suspension and rather basic trim and furnishings. From early 1957 the A40 was dropped, while the A50 became A55, with a longer, more droopy tail enclosing a much bigger boot, more power and eventually an optional centre-floor gearchange.

This was also the time to try out transmission options (Manumatic two-pedal control and Borg Warner overdrive were both made available), though Joe Public wisely shunned the unreliable Manumatic system.

The A40 Cambridge of 1954 represented a big step forward in Austin styling.

The A55 Cambridge had a longer tail and a larger rear screen.

In the end, with nearly 300,000 of all types produced, the accountants were happy, though the discerning public were always dismissive. Austin (BMC by this time, of course) was delighted, and in 1959 the company was happy to move on to another Farina-styled range. Many of these cars have survived and examples regularly appear at old-car events, though no-one could call them memorable.

The Cambridge pick-up and van stayed in production until 1971.

SPECIFICATION

BODY STYLES: saloon, light commercials

PRODUCTION: 299,500, including commercials

ENGINE & TRANSMISSION: 1200cc/1489cc, 4cyl ohv, 4sp man, overdrive or semi-auto, f/r

POWER: 42bhp @ 4500rpm/50bhp @ 4400rpm/51bhp @ 4250rpm

MAX SPEED (MPH): 70/74

0-60MPH (SEC): not measured/28.8

SUSPENSION & BRAKES: coil ifs, leaf rear, drums f&r

LENGTH (IN)/WEIGHT (LB): 162/2248

LAUNCH PRICE: £650/£678

A90/A95/A105 Westminster 1954-59

Here was one of the new BMC's biggest investment gambles, for the A90 had not only a new monocoque but a brand-new six-cylinder engine too. The body, for sure, may have looked like a long-wheelbase A50 Cambridge, but only the doors were shared, in a structure which was wider and more solid than the smaller car.

The new C-Series engine, a long and heavy overhead-valve six, was central to this design (it would eventually go into many other BMC models, including the Austin-Healey 3000 and Wolseley's 6/90 police cars), but the rest of the chassis was conventional in the extreme, with modified A70/A90 front suspension and – you guessed it – a steering-column gearchange.

Although replacing the A70 Hereford and the A90 Atlantic, the Westminster looked entirely different and was much more modern in concept. Not rust-proof, of course, and certainly not agile, but much quicker.

In the same re-styling manoeuvre as with the A50s of the period, A90 became A95 in 1956, with a longer wheelbase/ longer tail style, and automatic transmission became available; by this time the A105 (with 102bhp) had joined in too. From 1958 there was an optional floor gearchange – a real improvement. The range was eventually supplanted by the new-generation A99 in mid-1959.

For collectors, the original short-wheelbase/cow-hipped A105s of 1956, and the specially-trimmed A105 Vanden Plas (500 made) are the most desirable.

The A90 Westminster first appeared in 1954.

A105 had more power and decoration.

A95, showing the 1956 range restyle.

The restyled A105.

The A90's six-cylinder C-Series engine.

A105 Countryman, 1957, dripping with goodies.

Painted metal dash of the A90.

SPECIFICATION

BODY STYLES: saloon, estate

PRODUCTION: 60,367

ENGINE & TRANSMISSION: 2639 cc, 6cyl ohv, 4sp man, o/d, or auto, f/r

POWER: 85bhp @ 4000rpm/92bhp @ 4500rpm/102bhp @ 4600rpm

MAX SPEED (MPH): 86/90/96

0-60MPH (SEC): 18.9/19.8/15.4

SUSPENSION & BRAKES: coil ifs, leaf rear, drums f&r

LENGTH (IN)/WEIGHT (LB): 181/2975

LAUNCH PRICE: £792

Gipsy 1958-68

According to legend, Sir Leonard Lord was jealous of the Land-Rover, and was quite convinced that Austin could do better. The Gipsy, launched in 1958, was a valiant effort which failed on three counts – one was to use steel (not aluminium) bodywork, one was to use an unproven type of rubber-in-shear independent suspension, and the third was that it simply wasn't a Land-Rover.

Learning from the too-heavy, too-costly Champ (but not carrying over any parts), Austin's Gipsy was a good

Gipsy with windscreen folded flat.

SPECIFICATION

BODY STYLES: utility, estate

PRODUCTION: 21,208

ENGINE & TRANSMISSION: 2199cc, 4cyl ohv/2178cc, 4cyl diesel, 4sp man, f/r

POWER: 62bhp @ 4100rpm/72bhp @ 4100rpm/diesel 55bhp @ 3500rpm

MAX SPEED (MPH): 63/68/60

0-60MPH (SEC): not measured

SUSPENSION & BRAKES: rubber ifs (some beam leaf front), rubber irs (some leaf rear), drums f&r

LENGTH (IN)/WEIGHT (LB): 139/2688 or 160/2890

LAUNCH PRICE: £650

effort, however. Based on a solid box-section chassis, there were two wheelbase lengths, A70-type petrol or diesel engines (Austin taxis used both, even though the private car lines had abandoned them), and various bodies including "utes", vans and station wagons. The ground clearance was generous (but on undulating going the independent suspension wasn't ideal), the ride hard, and the versatility considerable, but as far as the clientele was concerned it simply wasn't a Land-Rover.

The government bought thousands for emergency Civil Defence uses (they were never needed) but otherwise sales dragged. Later models reverted to a conventional leaf-spring, solid-axle suspension, and there was even a rear wheel drive pick-up version. Given time, and careful study of the catalogue before ordering, there was a Gipsy for almost every off-road or rugged job.

Production had almost dried up by the late 1960s, and ended completely when British Leyland was formed. Survivors? Not many – most have rotted away.

The Gipsy was Austin's second attempt at a four wheel drive vehicle.

A40 Farina 1958-67

Compared with any previous Austin, the new-generation A40 of October 1958 was sensationally styled. Not only was it the first to be shaped by Farina of Italy, but it was also certainly the best and most pure of his designs for BMC.

Originally launched as a square-back saloon with a fixed rear window glass (the full estate version, which had the same profile, followed a year later), it had been meant as an A35 replacement but just grew and grew during development. The A35, therefore, carried on, and the Farina car became the A40.

The structure was all-new, and very attractively styled, with wider track and a longer wheelbase, but all the original underpinnings – that is to say the engine, the transmission, the rear axle, the hydro-mechanical braking and the suspension – were modified versions of A35 equipment.

Original types had lift-up (not wind-up) door windows, and felt a touch under-powered. From autumn 1961 the

Mark I Austin A40 "Farina", 1958.

Mk II version had more power (37bhp instead of 34bhp), a longer wheelbase, better handling, fully hydraulic brakes, a revised front end and a new fascia style.

This interim model lasted only a year. From autumn 1962, the A40 embraced BMC's new 1.1-litre 48bhp A-Series engine, which pushed up the top speed to nearly 80mph. Less heralded, but a

great improvement linked to the 1.1-litre engine, was the baulk-ring gearbox.

There was one more fascia re-style in 1964, but otherwise the A40 sailed serenely on until the end of 1967. With 364,064 sold, it was a major commercial success, and everyone seemed to like it. Much-modified versions even shone in rallies and production-car races.

The dashboard of a 1966 A40, with a wood finish.

In 1959 the A40 became available as a Countryman, with a split tailgate.

The Mark II A40 had a longer wheelbase and a new grille.

SPECIFICATION

BODY STYLES: saloon, estate

PRODUCTION: 364,064

ENGINE & TRANSMISSION: 948cc/1098cc, 4cyl ohv, 4sp man, f/r

POWER: 34bhp @ 4750rpm/37bhp @ 5000rpm/48bhp @ 5100rpm

MAX SPEED (MPH): 72/75/79

0-60MPH (SEC): 35.6/27.1/23.9

SUSPENSION & BRAKES: coil ifs, leaf rear, drums f&r

LENGTH (IN)/WEIGHT (LB): 144/1680

LAUNCH PRICE: £639

The Sprinzel/Turner A40 on the Col de Turini in the 1961 Monte Carlo Rally.

A55/A60 Cambridge (Farina) 1959-69

Here was BMC's badge-engineering at its most prolific. Not only this Austin A55 but four other marques shared a brand-new body, engine and running gear. The A55 version was the best-selling B-Series Farina, but it was actually launched after the related Wolseley 15/60.

The theme was straightforward: one new monocoque, to be built as a four-door saloon or five-door estate car, was to replace all the old and disparate Austin, Morris, MG, Riley and Wolseley types. The new-type A55 Cambridge replaced the 1954-59 generation, using the same basic 1489cc B-Series engine and gearbox choices (steering-column or floor gearchange), but in a sharply-styled (by Farina) body. From The saloon became available in January 1959, and the five-door "Countryman" followed in September 1960.

Michael Sedgwick once described these cars as "dull, worthy and indestructible" to which we add badly built, poor-handling, and lacking in performance. Austin/BMC agreed, and from autumn 1961 turned these cars into A60s.

Improvement then came on many fronts – longer wheelbase, wider track, better roadholding, modified styling, and better mechanicals. This time the petrol engine was 1622cc (and, though rarely seen, there was also to be a 1489cc diesel), allied to the option of automatic transmission. All in all, the A60 was what the A55 always should have been.

The 1959 A55 Cambridge, styled by Farina.

The middle classes, especially older people, bought them in huge numbers.

Technically, little changed after 1961, though assembly was moved from Longbridge to Cowley in 1965.

The A60 even outlived the British Leyland merger until early 1969. Today the simply-engineered A60 has a small but devoted following: some remarkably well-loved ones still survive.

The A55 estate was commendably spacious and a tireless day-in-day-out workhorse.

SPECIFICATION

BODY STYLES: saloon, estate

PRODUCTION: 426,500

ENGINE & TRANSMISSION: 1489cc/1622cc, 4cyl ohv/1489cc diesel, 4sp man or auto, f/r

POWER: 52bhp @ 4350rpm/61bhp @ 4500rpm/diesel 40bhp @ 4000rpm

MAX SPEED (MPH): 78/81/68

0-60MPH (SEC): 23.0/21/4/34.3

SUSPENSION & BRAKES: coil ifs, leaf rear, drums f&r

LENGTH (IN)/WEIGHT (LB): 175/2473

LAUNCH PRICE: £802

The A60 Cambridge arrived in 1961. Reduced tailfins and a wider track gave a much happier appearance.

A99/A110 Westminster 1959-68

Here was the basis of BMC's third (commercially successful) foray into badge engineering. From summer 1959 there was a new Austin A99, a Wolseley 6/99 and – soon – a Vanden Plas Princess 3-litre. One new monocoque shell had replaced four old-type platforms.

Clever, certainly, and financially astute, if not technically inspiring. Austin's A99 was the paradigm from which others evolved. With styling influenced by Farina, here was a big new four-door saloon (the 108in-wheelbase machine weighed 3305lb), totally conventional in layout, with the 2.9-litre C-Series up front. There was the choice of a new three-speed manual gearbox with steering-column change and Borg Warner overdrive as standard, or an optional automatic transmission. Front-wheel disc brakes were a real advance on these cars, but otherwise the A99 was swamped by the impact of the Mini, which arrived at the same time.

From the autumn of 1961 the A99 grew up to become the A110. As in the case of the A55 to A60 transformation, many small improvements added up well – 120bhp instead of 103bhp, floor gearchange, a slightly longer wheelbase and improved handling. Within a matter of months power-assisted

A99 Westminster of 1959. Engine capacity was 2.9 litres.

steering became optional.

There was more to come. From May 1964 the A110 became Mk II with some style changes, smaller road wheels, a new four-speed gearbox with overdrive optional, not standard, and telescopic rear dampers instead of lever arm units.

The A110 Westminster, 1961, with power increased to 120bhp.

The A110 did not break any records but it went on selling until 1968, when the ill-fated Austin 3-Litre took over.

SPECIFICATION

BODY STYLES: saloon

PRODUCTION: 41,250

ENGINE & TRANSMISSION: 2912cc, 6cyl ohv, 3sp, 4sp man, o/d or auto, f/r

POWER: 103bhp @ 4500rpm/120bhp @ 4750rpm

MAX SPEED (MPH): 98/102

0-60MPH (SEC): 14.4/13.3

SUSPENSION & BRAKES: coil ifs, leaf rear, disc f/drum r

LENGTH (IN)/WEIGHT (LB): 188/3305 - 3470

LAUNCH PRICE: £1149

An A110 on the Monte Carlo Rally in 1962, driven by Daily Express motoring writer Robert Glenton.

1100/1300 1963-74

Austin 1100 appeared in 1963, a year after the Morris version.

BMC's second transverse-engined front wheel drive car, the 1100 and 1300 series, was a big success. Vast numbers were sold, and the project was extremely profitable. The combination of Issigonis's innovative engineering, Farina styling and great packaging could hardly fail – and it did not.

To put this ADO16 design firmly in context, the whole range (there would be six different badges up front) was engineered by Austin at Longbridge, but the Morris 1100 came first. The Austin version, always made at Longbridge, arrived a year later, in the autumn of 1963.

Although the Mini's already famous mechanical package – transverse A-Series engine with gearbox in sump and front-wheel drive – was retained, everything else was new. The 1100 was longer at 147in instead of 120in, it had a bigger cabin, disc front brakes were standard equipment, and suspension was by newly-developed Hydrolastic units. These combined rubber cones at each end of the car, interconnected by liquid tubes at high pressure, and provided a floaty ride.

Better than the Mini in so many ways – more spacious, more elegant, more comfortably appointed – the 1100 also handled well and was priced right. Optional AP automatic transmission came in 1965, the Countryman estate car followed in 1966, and the design was retouched in late 1967 as Mk II.

Mk IIs were available with 1098cc or 1275cc engines, all-synchromesh gearboxes came in 1968, and the 70bhp 1300GT followed in 1969. From 1968 there was even an automatic-only "Austin America" model solely for sale in the USA.

The last of all these well-loved types were built in 1974, displaced by the awful Austin Allegro.

SPECIFICATION

BODY STYLES: saloon, estate

PRODUCTION: 1,119,800

ENGINE & TRANSMISSION: 1098/1275 cc, 4cyl ohv, 4sp man or auto, f/f

POWER: 48bhp @ 5100rpm/58bhp @ 5250rpm/70bhp @ 6000rpm

MAX SPEED (MPH): 78/88/93

0-60MPH (SEC): 27.2/17.3/15.6

SUSPENSION & BRAKES: Hydro ifs, Hydro irs, disc f/drum r

LENGTH (IN)/WEIGHT (LB): 147/1780

LAUNCH PRICE: £593

The 1300 model arrived in 1967.

1800 1964-75

The third-generation front wheel drive BMC car was the Austin 1800 of 1964, which soon spawned off Morris and Wolseley derivatives. Although the 1800 layout was just like that of the 1100 – technically, in fact, the 1100 writ large – there were absolutely no shared parts, and no sign of Farina styling either.

In a much larger car – 164in/2645lb compared with the 1100's 147in/1780lb – with what seems like a vast passenger cabin, Austin used a transverse 1798cc B-Series engine and a more robust gearbox-in-sump layout. Suspension was by Hydrolastic, as in the 1100, while the rounded styling of the four-door saloon was Longbridge-inspired and definitely "Plain-Jane". The interior, too, was plain,

Austin 1800, 1964, largest of Issigonis's front wheel drive creations.

with a very utilitarian fascia style – but at least the gearchange was on the floor.

Big, with a rock-solid structure, and dependable, but rather stodgy to drive, it would serve well until 1975. Amazingly, it lived in harness with the A60 until 1969, though the one was originally supposed to replace the other. Power-assisted steering became optional in 1967 (good thing too, the original needed it), AP automatic transmission was optional in the little-changed Mk IIs from 1968, and the more sparkling 96bhp 1800S model arrived in 1969. All in all, it was a case of great chassis, shame about the looks and lack of charisma.

In 1972, Austin launched the six-cylinder 2200, with an engine derived from that of the four-cylinder Maxi; this was the model which displaced the 1800S. In 1975 the range's successor was the wedge-styled Princess.

The Mark II Austin 1800, 1968, had a power increase to 85bhp.

SPECIFICATION

BODY STYLES: saloon

PRODUCTION TOTAL: 210,000 produced

ENGINE & TRANSMISSION: 1798cc, 4cyl ohv, 4sp man or auto, f/f

POWER: 80bhp @ 5000rpm/86bhp @ 5300rpm/96bhp @ 5700rpm

MAX SPEED (MPH): 90/93/99

0-60MPH (SEC): 17.1/16/3/13.7

SUSPENSION & BRAKES: Hydro ifs, Hydro irs, disc f/drum r

LENGTH (IN)/WEIGHT (LB): 164/2645

LAUNCH PRICE: £769

Paddy Hopkirk took second place in the 1968 London-Sydney Marathon.

3-Litre 1967-71

Austin 3-litre replaced the Westminster but never caught on.

Austin's ADO61 project, which was engineered by Charles Griffin's team, not by Issigonis, was a great idea which went wrong. In a fit of rationalisation, BMC commanded him to develop a replacement for the A99/A110 cars, still with a front engine and rear-wheel drive, but to evolve it around the front-drive 1800's hull, cabin, doors and general proportions. Excuse me? Was someone smoking something exotic when that decision was made?

The result was a barrelful of compromises, and too much complication in the suspension, for the design to be a success. The A110's engine was completely re-designed (MG's MGC would share it, but there were no other

users), and drove through an up-dated A110 gearbox (with Laycock overdrive this time) to a chassis-mounted differential and self-levelling independent rear suspension. Servo-assisted front discs and power-assisted steering were good, but the handling was stodgy, as was the engine itself.

Styling was a problem. Original cars, announced months before deliveries could begin, had rectangular headlamps, though production models had prettier pairs of circular lamps instead. Even so, the result was an angular beast which few people loved.

The 3-Litre never caught on. Less than 10,000 were built before British Leyland pulled the plug early in 1971. By the 1980s there were few

survivors, and anyone who has managed to preserve a 3-Litre into the new century deserves a medal – or counselling.

SPECIFICATION

BODY STYLES: saloon

PRODUCTION: 9992

ENGINE & TRANSMISSION: 2912cc, 6cyl ohv, 4sp man, o/d or auto, f/r

POWER: 124bhp @ 4500rpm

MAX SPEED (MPH): 100

0-60MPH (SEC): 15.7

SUSPENSION & BRAKES: Hydro ifs, Hydro irs, disc f/drum r

LENGTH (IN)/WEIGHT (LB): 186/3290

LAUNCH PRICE: £1418

Maxi 1969-81

The Maxi was Austin's last trump before the fog of British Leyland fell on Longbridge. This car, the fourth use of Issigonis's celebrated transverse-engine/front-wheel drive scheme, was new from end to end and cost a fortune to tool up.

Not only was it Austin and British Leyland's first-ever hatchback, but it also featured a new breed of engine, the overhead-camshaft 1485cc E-Series, and a new five-speed gearbox.

In size pitched half way between

The Austin Maxi of 1969.

SPECIFICATION

BODY STYLES: hatchback

PRODUCTION: 472,098

ENGINE & TRANSMISSION: 1485cc/1748cc, 4cyl ohc, 5sp man or auto, f/f

POWER: 74bhp @ 5500rpm/84bhp @ 5500rpm/91bhp @ 5250rpm

MAX SPEED (MPH): 86/89/97

0-60MPH (SEC): 16.6/15.8/13.2

SUSPENSION & BRAKES: Hydro ifs, Hydro irs, disc f/drum r

LENGTH (IN)/WEIGHT (LB): 158/2160

LAUNCH PRICE: £979

1100/1300 and 1800 dimensions, what became known as the Maxi shared doors with the 1800 but nothing else. At 158in long and weighing 2160lb, it was usefully larger than the 1100, and much lighter than the 1800. Like those cars, too, it featured Hydrolastic suspension and had front-wheel disc brakes.

Announced in 1969, one year after British Leyland had been formed, the Maxi got off to a bad start, for it had a very plain interior style, a poor cable-operated gearchange, and very doubtful build quality.

Within two years, British Leyland had sorted the gearchange quality (with rod control), re-designed the interior, provided a more muscular 1748cc engine, and brought an AP automatic transmission option to market in 1972. The only version which fell by the wayside was a proposed four-door saloon, which was killed off at the tooling stage.

Throughout the 1970s the Maxi was ever-present but not loved. Its engines were used in other products (the Allegro for instance), but nothing could restore its sparkle. 1500s disappeared in 1979, and the last 1750 was produced in 1981. Today? A number of well-kept examples remain, but they have little value.

Sprite 1971

British Leyland boss Lord Stokes apparently objected to paying a royalty to Donald Healey for the use of his name on the Sprite sports car, so that

SPECIFICATION

BODY STYLES: sports car

PRODUCTION: 1022

ENGINE & TRANSMISSION: 1275cc, 4cyl ohv, 4sp man, f/r

POWER: 65bhp @ 6000rpm

MAX SPEED (MPH): 94

0-60MPH (SEC): 14.6

SUSPENSION & BRAKES: coil ifs, leaf rear, disc f/drum r

LENGTH (IN)/WEIGHT (LB): 135/1525

LAUNCH PRICE: £924

Austin Sprite.

deal ended in 1970. In 1971, a car called the Austin Sprite was sold instead, this being totally identical except for the badge on the nose and the steering wheel.

Ridiculous, and the clientele obviously agreed, for only 1022 such cars were sold.

2200 1972-75

The simplistic way to describe this car is as a re-engined front wheel drive 1800 with one-and-a-half Maxi power units! The engine transplant was of a six-cylinder overhead-camshaft engine (coded E6), which shared many of its components with the four-cylinder Maxi engine (E4), and was manufactured on the same machine tooling. This new engine, fed by twin SU carburettors, was both smooth and powerful, producing 110bhp and endowing this sturdy (over-

Austin 2200 of 1972 had a six-cylinder engine.

SPECIFICATION

BODY STYLES: saloon

PRODUCTION: 20,865 Austin and Morris 2200s

ENGINE & TRANSMISSION: 2227cc, 6cyl ohc, 4sp man, or auto, f/f

POWER: 110bhp @ 5250rpm

MAX SPEED (MPH): 104

0-60MPH (SEC): 13.1

SUSPENSION & BRAKES: Hydro ifs, hydro irs, disc f/rum r

LENGTH (IN)/WEIGHT (LB): 167/2620

LAUNCH PRICE: £1325

engineered, some say) body/chassis unit with the performance it had always deserved.

The engine was mated to the same manual or automatic gearbox options as the 1800, power-assisted rack-and-pinion steering was still optional, the handbrake was placed between the seats, and there was a padded-spoke steering wheel. The fascia, complete with circular instruments (not the strip-speedometer of old) was flanked by face-level ventilation eyeballs.

This model immediately replaced the four-cylinder 1800S, and was a good if not inspiring top-of-the-range saloon. It would hold the line until British Leyland was ready to launch yet another front wheel drive car, the 18-22 range (see below), one of whose engines was the same power unit.

Here was an understated but quite rapid saloon which was never truly appreciated because of its close relationship to the lumpen 1800.

Allegro 1973-82

This replacement for the much-loved 1100/1300 range might just have been British Leyland's biggest mistake at Austin Morris. Except arguably in its handling and its packaging, it was worse

The Austin Allegro 1750 Sport, one of a bewildering range of Allegro models.

SPECIFICATION

BODY STYLES: saloon, estate

PRODUCTION: 642,350

ENGINE & TRANSMISSION: 998cc/1098cc/1275cc, 4cyl ohv/1485cc/1748cc, 4cyl ohc, 4sp man, 5sp man or auto, f/f

POWER: 44bhp @ 5250rpm - 90bhp @ 5500rpm

MAX SPEED (MPH): (E) 79 — 100

0-60MPH (SEC): not measured – 11.0

SUSPENSION & BRAKES: Hydragas ifs, Hydragas irs, disc f/drum r

LENGTH (IN)/WEIGHT (LB): 152/1794 - 2011

LAUNCH PRICE: £974

in every respect than the cars it replaced – it looked dumpy, it was often badly-built, and it had little positive character.

Underneath the Allegro's all-new unit-construction body/chassis unit, sold as two-door or four-door saloons, or (from May 1975) as a three-door estate car, was a range of cars with what we might call standard Austin layout – transverse

engine, transmission in the sump, front-wheel drive. There were two different types of engine, and the new-fangled Hydragas suspension. The only badge-engineered derivative, by the way, would be the Vanden Plas 1500 of 1974. Compared with Hydrolastic, The Allegro's Hydragas system relied on high-pressure gas instead of the rubber convolutes of the earlier type, along with the usual simple type of ride levelling.

The smaller engines were A-Series, with four-speed manual gearboxes, while Maxi-style overhead-camshaft 1485cc and 1748cc E-Series engines had five-speeders. Depending on the year and the edition, automatic transmission was available with all types of engine.

The cabin was more spacious than that of the 1100/1300, but no more tasteful, especially for the first two years, when a strange "Quartic" steering wheel (rectangular with the corners smoothed off) was fitted. It was only after media and customer ridicule that a conventional circular wheel was fitted.

Well-built Allegros might have sold better if only the style had not been so lumpy, with a relatively high bonnet line (the E-Series engine was tall, and had to be cleared). There were so many derivatives that even the product planners must have needed a sedative at times, the most enterprising being the TC/HL, which had 90bhp and a 100mph top speed. Allegro became Allegro II for 1976 (more leg room and a cosmetic job), then Allegro III from late 1979 (more cosmetic changes).

1100s were dropped after 1980, with 1.0-litre engines taking over instead. The rest of the range struggled on to 1982 – the better Maestro of 1983 effectively being the replacement.

Amazingly, some of these cars have survived, and there is even a one-make club where owners can gather together for mutual comfort. It takes all sorts…

Early Allegros had this "Quartic" steering wheel, much ridiculed.

Allegro 1750HL, 1979.

18-22 Series (ADO 71 type) 1975

British Leyland's replacement for the long-running 1800/2200 range appeared in March 1975. At any other time, and if British Leyland had not been tottering close to receivership, with awful labour relations problems in the background, this would have been hailed as an excellent car, for the styling was crisp, the cabin spacious, and the engineering technically elegant.

Even larger than the 1800/2200 range which it replaced, the new car used the latest BL Hydragas suspension (see the Allegro entry, above), but was otherwise a recognisable update of the well-established Issigonis/Austin theme of the 1960s.

Although it looked as if it should be a hatchback (the designers and styling engineers had wanted that but had been over-ruled by management), this was a conventional four-door saloon, with a big cabin, soft and comfortable suspension, and well-balanced front wheel drive handling.

SPECIFICATION

BODY STYLES: saloon

PRODUCTION: 19,000 including Morris and Wolseley versions

ENGINE & TRANSMISSION: 1798cc,4cyl ohv/2227cc, 6cyl ohc, 4sp man, or auto, f/f

POWER: 82bhp @ 5200rpm/110bhp @ 5250rpm

MAX SPEED (MPH): 96/104

0-60MPH (SEC): 14.9/13.5

SUSPENSION & BRAKES: Hydragas ifs, Hydragas irs, disc f/drum r

LENGTH (IN)/WEIGHT (LB): 175/2557 - 2600

LAUNCH PRICE: £2117/£2424

The engines – four-cylinder B-Series and six-cylinder E6-Series – were closely similar to the old 1800/2200 types, while power-assisted steering was optional on 1800s and standard on the 2200.

Recognition points? Austins had trapezoidal headlamps, while Morris versions had four circular lamps, as did the rare Wolseley of the period. All these cars were replaced in September 1975 by the newly-minted Princess range.

Austin 2200HL, 1975.

Mini Metro 1980-1990

All manner of banners were hung on this model, which had been in the making for some years. Placarded as BL's Make or Break car, the Mini Metro was a direct replacement for the Mini Clubman and 1275GT, and would also cut a mighty swathe through the classic Mini's market too.

In the 1980s Metros like this soon spawned MG versions (one of them turbocharged), and from 1990 the car would be re-badged as a Rover and given new engines.

In marketing terms (and to give this car its official early title), the Austin Mini Metro was effectively a larger, modernised, hatchback iteration of the classic Mini, though with Allegro/18-22-style Hydragas suspension units. Although much was made of the engine changes at launch time, the transversely-mounted engine/ transmission units were still A-Series,

A flock of Mini Metros on a hillside.

and were little more than slightly up-dated versions of the Mini Clubman installations.

Compared with the Mini/Mini Clubman, the Mini Metro had a more spacious cabin – it was 14 inches longer overall, with a longer wheelbase – and was originally sold as a three-door hatchback; an estate car was never available.

Automatic transmission (on 1275cc cars only) was optional from mid-1981, a 72bhp Vanden Plas version appeared in mid-1982, and the five-door hatchback was made progressively

available from late 1984. Thereafter, a bewildering number of model names, trim packs and special editions were put on sale, but the basic package, performance and chassis were not altered.

Because BL (and their successors) sold more than one and a half million Metros, it definitely qualified as a "Make" rather than a "Break" model. BL never intended it to be a sporty performance hatchback, which was a relief to the clientele, whose age profile gradually rose throughout the life of the car.

SPECIFICATION

BODY STYLES: hatchback, commercials

PRODUCTION: 1,518,932

ENGINE & TRANSMISSION: 998cc/1275cc, 4cyl ohv, 4sp man, or auto, f/f

POWER: 41bhp @ 5400rpm/63bhp @ 5600rpm/73bhp @ 6000rpm

MAX SPEED (MPH): 84/94/103

0-60MPH (SEC): 18.9/13.5/11.8

SUSPENSION & BRAKES: Hydragas ifs, Hydragas irs, disc f/drum r

LENGTH (IN)/WEIGHT (LB): 134/1675-1828

LAUNCH PRICE: £3095

AUSTIN-HEALEY

Donald Healey was already famous before he promoted the first car to bear his name, first as a trials and rally driver (he won the Monte Carlo rally in 1931 in an Invicta), then as the technical director of the still-independent Triumph. He went on to set up the Healey concern (see later entry) at Warwick in 1945.

In 1951 he and his son Geoffrey laid out the design of the Healey 100, which used Austin A90 components. Austin's abrasive chief Leonard Lord then saw the prototype, adopted it, re-named it Austin-Healey 100, and put it into production at Longbridge; the first 19 cars were actually put together, though, at Warwick.

For the next 17 years Healey did most of the engineering development work, but except for the specialised 100S types, all the cars were built by BMC, at Longbridge until 1957 and at the MG factory at Abingdon thereafter.

Over the years the layout of the original 100 evolved steadily. The longer-wheelbase, six-cylinder 100-Six arrived in 1956, the larger-engined 3000 in 1959, and the much-modified Mk III in 1964. The layout was retained, and each was descended from a previous type, but by the end most of the original details had changed.

Healey also designed the original, small "Frogeye" Sprite, using Austin and Morris running gear, which was launched at Abingdon in 1958. From 1961 it was re-styled, and gained an MG Midget-badged clone. Throughout the 1960s, company politics ensured that the Sprite gradually became subservient to the Midget.

The last-ever Austin-Healey Sprite was built in 1970, though there was an Austin Sprite in 1971 only, and the Midget, further developed, carried on until 1979. The Healey name was revived on the Jensen-Healey of 1972-76.

100 1953-56

Originally intended to be built by Healey at Warwick, with a body supplied by Tickford, all 100s except the first 19 production cars were re-badged and assembled at the Austin factory at Longbridge.

The structure was advanced for the period, with the inner steel panels of the shell welded to a sturdy box-section (with cruciform) chassis frame on manufacture, effectively making this a monocoque. The main chassis side members ran under the line of the rear axle. The body/chassis unit was completed, painted and trimmed by Jensen before being completed at Longbridge. Except for early cars (which used many aluminium skin panels),

Austin-Healey 100. At the wheel is the car's owner, celebrated Le Mans Bentley driver S C H "Sammy" Davis.

almost all the structure was in pressed steel, the unladen weight increasing by about 135lb between 1953 and 1956. The windscreen could be folded flat.

Engine, transmission, rear axle and front suspension were all lifted, then modified, from the unsuccessful Austin A90 Atlantic. On original (BN1) models

One of the two 100s entered for Le Mans in 1953..

SPECIFICATION

BODY STYLES: sports car

PRODUCTION: 14,634

ENGINE & TRANSMISSION: 2660cc, 4cyl ohv, 3sp or 4sp man, o/d, f/r

POWER: 90bhp @ 4000rpm/110bhp @ 5000rpm

MAX SPEED (MPH): (90bhp) 103

0-60MPH (SEC): (90bhp) 10.3

SUSPENSION & BRAKES: coil ifs, leaf rear, drums f&r

LENGTH (IN)/WEIGHT (LB): 151/2150

LAUNCH PRICE: £1064

the gearbox was modified to provide only three forward gears, with overdrive on top and second gears as standard. Because the A90 gearbox had originally been laid out for steering column change, the conversion to a centre-floor change was a little awkward. Centre-lock wire-spoke wheels were standard

The second version, BN2, appeared in late 1955, this car having a new C-Series 4-speed gearbox, still backed by Laycock overdrive; at the same time larger brakes were fitted.

There was one important derivative of both these cars – the 100M, where "M" really stood for "Modified" or "Le Mans". Researchers now agree that at least 1159 such cars were produced, mostly as kits added to cars after initial

The 2.6-litre four-cylinder engine was first seen in the Austin A90 Atlantic.

An unhappy event for an entrant in the 1954 Tulip Rally.

assembly. In the 100M, the engine was tuned up to produce 110bhp, and had stiffened front suspension which included an anti-roll bar. A louvred bonnet panel, and a leather strap across it, were also included.

The genuine 100M is the most desirable of these types, but all are seen as the most nimble and the most pure of the Big Healey family. The four-cylinder 100 was replaced by the new six-cylinder 100-Six in autumn 1956.

100S 1955

To make the Austin-Healey more suitable for motor racing, BMC agreed that Healey should build a limited series of specialised cars called 100S (S for "Sebring"). Although based on the 100 BN1 layout, these cars were lighter and much more powerful. Their development was inspired by Healey's own "Special Test Cars", which had been raced, or used in record attempts in the USA, during 1953 and 1954.

The A90-based engine, still of 2660cc, had a new light-alloy cylinder head casting and produced 132bhp, which was nearly 50 per cent more than the standard unit. This was matched by a C-Series (BN2-type) gearbox, though without overdrive. An engine oil cooler was fitted, a 20-gallon fuel tank was standard, the suspension was beefed up, and Dunlop disc brakes were fitted at front and rear.

Jensen produced light alloy panels for the entire skin of the body shell, and to keep down the weight there was no provision for bumpers, glass windscreen, side curtains or a hood. The front grille aperture was oval in shape, and smaller than standard, while a low, full-width, plastic windscreen was provided. Most cars were delivered in a smart white-over-blue duotone colour scheme. Compared with the standard 100, the

Austin-Healey 100S outside the factory in 1954. Note the smaller grille.

weight saving was approximately 200lb.

Healey retained a handful of these cars for their own use, the others being delivered to hand-picked motor sport customers. Only six went to British customers, the balance of the limited production of 50 going overseas.

Most cars were used in motor sport when young, but in later years the survivors (most of the 50-off run, it seems) have become prized. Although too starkly trimmed and equipped for everyday road use, they have always been extremely desirable to collectors.

SPECIFICATION	
BODY STYLES: sports car	
PRODUCTION: 50	
ENGINE & TRANSMISSION: 2660cc, 4cyl ohv, 4sp man, f/r	
POWER: 132bhp @ 4700rpm	
MAX SPEED (MPH): 119	
0-60MPH (SEC): 7.8	
SUSPENSION & BRAKES: coil ifs, leaf rear, discs f&r	
LENGTH (IN)/WEIGHT (LB): 148/1924	
LAUNCH PRICE: special order	

100-Six 1956-59

Introduced in late 1956 to replace the successful four-cylinder 100 BN2, the 100-Six BN4 was a major redesign intended to further BMC's marketing strategy.

Not only was the new version powered by BMC's latest 2.6-litre six-cylinder engine, but the body had been stretched by two inches to allow rather cramped 2+2 seating to be provided.

The new car was different in so many small but significant ways. The slightly longer shell now had a fixed windscreen, and the front-end style had been altered to provide an air scoop in the bonnet. Before long, a smart lift-off hardtop became optional, though the take-up of this item was always limited. According to the price list, disc wheels were not

The Austin-Healey 100-Six, 1956.

100-Six with hardtop fitted.

standardised, though wire-spoke wheels were an optional extra.

The 102bhp engine was matched to the same gearbox as used in the BN2, but this time overdrive transmission was an optional extra. Because the BN4 was considerably heavier (by 270lb) than the BN2, and because the engine was by

no means as sporty – despite its healthy-sounding growl – the original BN4 felt slower than the model it replaced.

In the next three years there were many improvements. From late 1957, final assembly was moved from Longbridge to Abingdon, and at about the same time a more powerful engine – 117bhp instead of 102bhp – took over. Then, from the spring of 1958, the BN6 derivative appeared, this model retaining the BN4 structure but returning to a two-seater cabin once again.

Both types continued, side-by-side, until mid-1959, when they were replaced by the 3000 model.

SPECIFICATION

BODY STYLES: sports car

PRODUCTION: 14,436 including 4,150 two-seater BN6

ENGINE & TRANSMISSION: 2639cc, 6cyl ohv, 4sp man, o/d, f/r

POWER: 102bhp @ 4600rpm/117bhp @ 4750rpm

MAX SPEED (MPH): 103/111

0-60MPH (SEC): 12.9/11.2

SUSPENSION & BRAKES: coil ifs, leaf rear, drums f&r

LENGTH (IN)/WEIGHT (LB): 158/2435

LAUNCH PRICE: £1144

3000 Mk I/II/III 1959-68

From mid-1959, the original 3000 (restrospectively called Mk I) took over from the 100-Six, this model then continuing, with progressive changes and improvements, until the last of all was built in the winter of 1967-68.

The original 3000 looked exactly like the last 100-Six, though the engine was now a 124bhp 2922cc six-cylinder unit, and front-wheel disc brakes (by Girling) were now standardised. As before, wire wheels, overdrive and the lift-off hardtop were all optional, as were two-seater or 2+2

Austin-Healey 3000 Mark I.

seating arrangements.

Early in 1961 the 3000 became Mk II, complete with a 132bhp engine which was fuelled by three SU carburettors. These proved to be fussy to keep in balance.

Visually the there was a change, the Mk II being the first Big Healey to have vertical grille bars. Halfway through the short run of this version, a new gearbox casing and remote-control centre change were adopted, a big improvement on the earlier type. Very few two-seaters, incidentally, were now being made.

The two-seater 3000 shown here is rarer than the 2+2..

Austin-Healey 3000 Mark II Convertible gained a wrap-round windscreen.

In the summer of 1962 the 3000 Mk II Convertible arrived, heralding a number of significant revisions. Not only did this model get wind-up door windows, a curved windscreen and a neat foldaway hood, but it also went back to having two instead of three SU carburettors and produced 131bhp. only 1bhp less than the triple-SU Mk II. Only 2+2 seating was now available.

The last change came in the spring of 1964, when the 3000 became Mk III. This car featured a re-designed interior with a wooden fascia and relocated

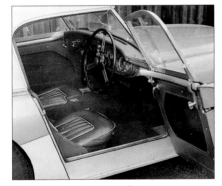

Interior of the 3000 Mk I.

Pat Moss driving a works 3000 to second place in the 1961 RAC Rally, early on in the 3000's splendid rally career.

Donald Morley climbs into his 3000 during the 1960 RAC Rally.

instruments, while the engine was further tuned (still with twin SU carburettors) to produce 148bhp. Original Phase I cars (just 1390 of them) had the usual rear suspension, but Phase II cars, built to the end, had re-profiled chassis members (which allowed rear axle movement to be increased), and radius/trailing arms took the place of the Panhard rod axle location.

Works competition versions of these cars, complete with aluminium-panelled bodies, four-wheel disc brakes and lusty 210bhp aluminium-headed engines, were the best of all the world's rally cars in the early to mid-1960s.

Series production of Mk IIIs ended before Christmas in 1967, though one further car was produced in March 1968, after which the Big Healey was finally laid to rest. BMC/British Leyland liked to think that the MGC took its place, but there was really no comparison.

Here was a genuine case of a car getting better every time it was revised. The Mk IIIs, especially when loaded with optional extras, are still the most desirable.

SPECIFICATION

BODY STYLES: sports car

PRODUCTION: 13,650/5450/6113/17,712

ENGINE & TRANSMISSION: 2912cc, 6cyl ohv, 4sp man, o/d, f/r

POWER: 124bhp @ 4600rpm/132bhp @ 4750rpm/131bhp @ 4750/148bhp @ 5250 rpm

MAX SPEED (MPH): 114–121

0-60MPH (SEC): 11.4–9.8

SUSPENSION & BRAKES: coil ifs, leaf rear, disc f/drum r

LENGTH (IN)/WEIGHT (LB): 158/2460

LAUNCH PRICE: £1168

Another first on the Convertible was wind-up windows.

The Mark III had a wooden dash.

Businesslike cockpit of a works 3000.

Even on the Mark III the exhaust was still perilously low-slung.

One of the last works 3000s.

Sprite (Frogeye) 1958-61

Donald Healey's small engineering team developed the new two-seater Sprite sports car for BMC, though each and every car was assembled at the MG factory at Abingdon. Using an all-new steel monocoque shell, the Sprite picked up modified engine, transmission, front suspension, steering gear and brakes from the parts bin – mainly Austin A35, but with some Morris Minor components.

The rear end of the original car was provided with trailing cantilever quarter-elliptic leaf springs, and radius arms for location, while the entire front end of the body was hinged at the passenger bulkhead, to lift up for superb engine bay access. Although Healey had originally hoped to provide flip-up headlamps, the production car had fixed, rather protruding lamps – hence the nickname "Frogeye" (or "Bugeye" in certain markets). Even so, the front-end style was controversial, and a thriving cottage industry grew up, supplying new and more shapely bonnets in GRP. On this car there was no external access to the capacious boot area, which had to be reached from the passenger compartment.

The specification was simple but effective and appealing. Although the 948cc engine produced only 43bhp, the

1958 Austin-Healey Sprite.

top speed was 86mph and the acceleration spirited. The handling was very sporting (the ride was bumpy and oversteer was a feature of the early cars), and the cockpit was small and snug, if not entirely waterproof in poor weather. Rubber mats on the floor were typical of the cost constraints which were clearly applied.

The character of the Sprite was so appealing, and it was priced so keenly (£669 in the UK in 1958 when – say – an MGA cost almost 50% more at £996), that it was a great commercial success. It was only because BMC saw the need to restyle it, and produce an MG Midget "clone" from the result,

that it had a life of less than three years.

Because it was the original Sprite, and because it had a unique style, this has always been one of the most desirable of Sprites for latter-day collectors. Many survivors have been modified to make them faster.

Cockpit of the Sprite was sparsely furnished.

SPECIFICATION

BODY STYLES: sports car

PRODUCTION TOTAL: 48,987

ENGINE & TRANSMISSION: 948cc, 4cyl ohv, 4sp man, f/r

POWER: 43bhp @ 5200rpm

MAX SPEED (MPH): 86

0-60MPH (SEC): 20.5

SUSPENSION & BRAKES: coil ifs, leaf rear, drums f&r

LENGTH (IN)/WEIGHT (LB): 137/1328

LAUNCH PRICE: £669

The Sprite may not have been fast but it gave plenty of fun.

Sprite Mk II/III/IV 1961-70

During the 1960s the Sprite was regularly improved. Although the same basic hull and structure were retained throughout, its engine became larger and more powerful, its suspension was refined, and its equipment was uprated. In all cases, though, it ran parallel with the near-identical MG Midget, the two cars being assembled on the same production lines at Abingdon.

The Mk II Sprite appeared in mid-1961. Compared with the original "Frogeye" (this being a feature which was lost for ever), clever re-styling provided a conventional nose, with headlamps at the front of the wings and a conventional tail with an opening boot lid. At first the engine was a 46bhp version of the same 948cc power unit, but from the autumn of 1962 it gave way to a 56bhp 1098cc A-Series engine, and front-wheel disc brakes were standardised. All these revisionss were mirrored by the identical MG Midgets of the day.

Further big changes followed in the spring of 1964. The Sprite became Mk III, complete with a revised rear structure and conventional half-elliptic leaf spring rear suspension (the radius arms were abandoned at that time. This made the handling less nervous, though still firm and sporting in character. The engine's output was improved further, to 59bhp. The big equipment change was the provision of wind-up windows

Sprite Mk II, with hood and sidescreens removed.

The Sprite III arrived in 1964 with wind-up windows.

Sprite IV had 1275cc and a permanently attached hood.

in the doors, along with a deeper windscreen and a revised instrument panel.

The Sprite Mk IV of 1966 took that improvement a stage further by adopting a larger 1275cc A-Series engine of 65bhp, and by providing a more sophisticated fold-back soft-top. This was a genuine 95mph car, and because the engine was so tuneable it was also used with great success in motorsport.

British Leyland's royalty agreement with Donald Healey concluded at the end of 1970, so the Austin-Healey brand was then dropped. For 1971 only, an Austin Sprite was sold (only 1022 such cars were produced), though all subsequent cars were MG Midgets, which ran on until 1979.

Although Midgets have always held the marketing and image edge over the equivalent Sprites, the Austin-Healeys remain collectable: thriving one-make clubs make this a long-term probability.

SPECIFICATION

BODY STYLES: sports car

PRODUCTION: 20,450/25,905/21,768

ENGINE & TRANSMISSION:
948cc/1098cc/1275cc, 4cyl ohv, 4sp man, f/r

POWER: 46bhp @ 5500rpm/56bhp @ 5500/59bhp @ 5750rpm/65bhp @ 6000rpm

MAX SPEED (MPH): 86 – 94

0-60MPH (SEC): 20.0 – 14.6

SUSPENSION & BRAKES: coil ifs, leaf rear, drums f&r (disc f/drum r from 1962)

LENGTH (IN)/WEIGHT (LB): 138/1525

LAUNCH PRICE: £670

BEDFORD

For Bedford, read Vauxhall, as this unique machine was no more than a re-badged derivative of the Vauxhall Viva HA range. The Bedford connection lies in the fact that Vauxhall's owners since 1925, General Motors Corporation, had set up the Bedford truck brand, logically choosing the Bedford badge because the Vauxhall factory was in Bedfordshire.

The Beagle, in fact, was the only Vauxhall ever to be re-badged as a Bedford. All other details of the Vauxhall/Bedford marque and models are more rightly described in the Vauxhall section.

Beagle 1964-73

Once GM had taken control of Vauxhall, it set about popularising the brand, inspiring more and yet more mass-production models, and turning the marque into the obvious British competitor to Ford. Even so, it was not until 1963 that the very first small Vauxhall, the Viva, was introduced.

Although there was some cross-pollination with the Opel Kadett of the period (Opel was another GM-owned brand and floor pans, engines and transmissions were closely related) Vauxhall set out to market the Viva only as a slab-sided two-seater saloon. Before long, however, Bedford revealed a Viva-related panel van, and it was from the van that an estate car called the Bedford Beagle was developed. This, though unashamedly van-derived, was always built by a favoured coachbuilder, Martin Walter.

Although Martin Walter trimmed it to small-car standards, like the van from which it had evolved the Beagle suffered from a hard ride, somewhat skittish handling, a rear axle that pattered up and down when given half a chance, and

Bedford Beagle.

a tendency to oversteer. Even so, and to misuse a modern advertising catch line, the beagle did "exactly what it said on the tin", for it was a cheap and cheerful estate car/load carrier which had no up-market pretensions.

As the Viva private car was up-engined,

so was the Beagle (and the van from which it was derived). By the time the 1256cc engine of the third-generation Viva had been fitted, the Beagle was a genuine 80mph machine. But a classic car? Perhaps as a collector's piece for a Vauxhall fanatic.

SPECIFICATION

BODY STYLES: estate

PRODUCTION: 309,538, all HA private and commercial types

ENGINE & TRANSMISSION:
1057cc/1159cc/1256cc, 4cyl ohv, 4sp man, f/r

POWER: 40bhp @ 5200rpm/45bhp @ 4600rpm/49bhp @ 5100rpm

MAX SPEED (MPH): (1057cc)73

0-60MPH (SEC): (1057cc) 29.1

SUSPENSION & BRAKES: leaf ifs, leaf rear, drums f&r

LENGTH (IN)/WEIGHT (LB): 150/1680

LAUNCH PRICE: £620

Although it does not strictly belong in this book, no review of motoring in Britain would be complete without the Bedford Dormobile, here in the 4-berth version built by Martin Walter.

BENTLEY

Everyone, surely, knows that the first Bentley was made in 1919, the first deliveries followed in 1921, that the company lost its independence – to Rolls-Royce – in 1931. Rolls-Royce then changed every part of Bentley and transformed the marque into a sportier version of Rolls-Royce itself. By the end of the 1930s, Bentley was outselling Rolls-Royce, this situation persisting up to the mid-1960s.

Up to 1939, when war broke out, Rolls-Royce and Bentley never produced complete cars, but supplied complete driveable chassis to specialist coachbuilders to body. Until then, chassis assembly had been centred at Derby, but from 1945 the company made two hugely important commercial decisions. One was that there would be rationalised designs (of Bentleys and Rolls-Royces), where cars would henceforth be produced at a modern ex-aero engine factory at Crewe, the other being that for the first time the company would begin to build complete cars around a "standard steel" four-door saloon body.

This established a routine which carried on for the next generation. Most Bentleys would be four-door saloons, some chassis would be supplied to special coachbuilders and (from 1952) there would also be a series of "Continentals", with special coachwork.

Bentley's all-new Mk VI appeared in 1946, would evolve into the R-Type in 1952, and would not be replaced by the larger, more ostentatious S-Series until 1955. This Bentley then carried on for ten successful years, inheriting a brand-new V8 engine in 1959. A series of impressive Continentals were built from 1952.

Bentley and Rolls-Royce had been coming ever closer together, and from 1965 the new monocoque Bentley T and Rolls-Royce Silver Shadow models were virtually the same, so Bentley sales dropped accordingly. This trend was not reversed until the 1980s, when the first of the turbocharged Bentleys was put on sale.

Bentley and Rolls-Royce continued at Crewe, in harness, until 1998, when the two marques were separated once again and sold off. Bentley became a subsidiary of VW (Rolls-Royce went to BMW), and new VW-based models followed in the early 2000s.

Mk VI 1946-52

The Mk VI of 1946 was the first "standardised" Bentley model to be revealed. Its new chassis and six-cylinder engine were also the basis of the Rolls-Royce Silver Dawn and Silver Wraith.

The Mk V Bentley model of 1939-40 (stillborn because of the War) had previewed much of the new chassis engineering, though the Mk VI's engine layout (with overhead inlet and side exhaust valves) had not been seen on the Mk V. As ever with these cars, the peak power output was never published, merely acknowledged as "sufficient"!

Bentley Mark VI standard steel saloon in 1947.

SPECIFICATION

BODY STYLES: saloon, coachbuilts

PRODUCTION: 5201

ENGINE & TRANSMISSION: 4257cc/4566cc, 6cyl ioe, 4sp man, f/r

POWER: not quoted

MAX SPEED (MPH): 100

0-60MPH (SEC): 15.2

SUSPENSION & BRAKES: coil ifs, leaf rear, drums f&r

LENGTH (IN)/WEIGHT (LB): 192/4004, (1952 only) 200/4060

LAUNCH PRICE: £2997

The engine itself was backed by a four-speed synchromesh transmission. On right hand drive cars the change-speed lever was on the floor to the right and ahead of the driver's seat; on left hand drive cars a steering column change was provided instead.

The cruciform-braced chassis frame supported coil spring independent front suspension, and a transmission-driven friction servo still boosted the brakes in the traditional Rolls-Royce way. A control on the steering wheel boss

The Mark VI engine as first launched in 1946. The disc on the side of the gearbox is the clutch for the gearbox-driven brake servo.

altered the hardness of the rear springing to suit road and load conditions. A feature of the new design was centralised chassis lubrication, which involved a maze of pipes sending oil to suspension and steering joints (this system can be a major headache at restoration time).

Fitted with rear-hinged "suicide" front doors, a hangover from pre-war days, the body shell was supplied complete by Pressed Steel at Cowley, near Oxford, though Bentley painted and trimmed it before carrying out final assembly at Crewe. Real wood, picnic tables, leather upholstery, a sliding sunroof and deep-pile carpets were of course all present.

For the Mk VI's final model year, 1951-52, the engine was enlarged from 4257cc to 4566cc, giving a useful power increase and a genuine 100mph top speed. In late 1952 the Mk VI was replaced by the R-Type, which was a further improved version.

Popular when new, and well-loved in later life, Mk VIs have needed much work on their bodies to stop them rusting away, but the mechanicals are pretty unburstable. These cars, unlike most of their era, have the perfor-mance and stamina to deal with modern motoring.

Various coachbuilders clothed the Mark VI. This is a 1946 foursome coupé typical of the period.

This 1949 coupé by James Young was one of the more extreme coachbuilt styles.

H J Mulliner's Lightweight Coupé of 1951.

Fascia of the Mulliner-bodied car, classically restrained.

Later Mark VIs gained rear wheel spats.

Mike Couper's Mark VI in Monte Carlo.

R-Type 1952-55

The R-Type, launched in late 1952, was effectively an improved Mk VI, with the latest 4566cc engine, and with a long-tail version of the Mk VI shell to provide more boot space, which had been lacking on the Mk VI. There was the option of Rolls-Royce/GM Hydramatic automatic transmission, which featured a fluid coupling (not a torque converter) and four forward ratios. Such were the demands of export markets that the first UK-market R-Type automatic was not delivered until October 1953.

With no more than development changes – a higher compression-ratio engine from April 1953, and a fully-welded chassis frame from late 1953, for instance – the R-Type continued, visually unaltered, until the spring of 1955, when it was replaced by the S-Series saloon.

Front and rear views of the Bentley R-Type, showing its enlarged boot.

SPECIFICATION

BODY STYLES: saloon, coachbuilts

PRODUCTION: 2320

ENGINE & TRANSMISSION: 4566cc, 6cyl ioe, 4sp man or auto, f/r

POWER: not quoted

MAX SPEED (MPH): 101

0-60MPH (SEC): 13.8

SUSPENSION & BRAKES: coil ifs, leaf rear, drums f&r

LENGTH (IN)/WEIGHT (LB): 200/4060

LAUNCH PRICE: £4824

R-Type Continental 1952-55

Although the R-Type Continental was introduced in 1952, neither the name nor the philosophy of super-fast Bentleys was new. Rolls-Royce had built a series of Phantom II Continentals in the 1930s, while Bentley had dabbled with wind-cheating body shells (the Embiricos car, and the Corniche) immediately before the War.

With this post-war project, Bentley aimed to give the Mk VI/R-Type chassis extra-special performance by using a sleek and lightweight body. This was achieved when the coachbuilder, H J

The Bentley R-Type Continental was effective as well as glamorous.

The fastback styling of the Continental has seldom been bettered.

SPECIFICATION

BODY STYLES: coupé, coachbuilts

PRODUCTION: 208

ENGINE & TRANSMISSION: 4566cc/4887cc, 6cyl ioe, 4sp man or auto, f/r

POWER: not quoted

MAX SPEED (MPH): 115

0-60MPH (SEC): 13.5

SUSPENSION & BRAKES: coil ifs, leaf rear, drums f&r

LENGTH (IN)/WEIGHT (LB): 207/3700

LAUNCH PRICE: £7608

Mulliner, evolved a stunning two-door four-seater coupé style.

The chassis had the 4566cc engine with a higher compression ratio and a free-flow exhaust system. The back axle ratio was raised to allow an expected (and duly delivered) higher top speed. To keep up with increasing weight, the engine was enlarged to 4887cc in May 1954, the last 82 cars produced being so equipped.

Hydramatic transmission became an option in April 1954, and just 36 R-Type Continentals were fitted with it.

All but a handful of the 208 R-Type Continentals were equipped with the H J Mulliner body, which featured a long and smooth fastback cabin, a 1.5-inch lower roof line, and a lowered radiator shell. Much of the body shell was of aluminium, individual front seats were

Pininfarina designed this coupé on the Continental chassis.

fitted, most of the wood was stripped out and equipment was slimmed down, with the result that early cars were 300lb lighter than the saloon. Over the years, though, as more and more equipment was demanded, weight crept up again.

When new, the Continental cost £7608, which made it Britain's most

expensive car. It was also one of the fastest, and there was always a small, but definite, queue of millionaires ready to buy one. Then, as now, these cars were seen as magnificent Magic Carpets.

All but 15 cars used the standard HJM body, and of those 15 Park Ward provided just four drophead coupés.

S1 1955-59

It was almost as though the directors had given orders: "Make it different, but just the same as before". Though the Bentley S (later known as the S1) had a new and longer-wheelbase chassis than before, with an all-new but bulky body shell (still built by Pressed Steel), it used the same engine and transmission combination as the old R-Type, though now in 4.9-litre form. All in, it weighed 420lb more than before. The Rolls-Royce equivalent this time was the Silver Cloud, which unlike the Dawn had the same power output as the Bentley.

The massive all-welded chassis frame and coil spring independent suspension

The styling of the standard Bentley S1 saloon was beautifully balanced.

were as expected, though not the clever "Z-bar" location of the rear axle. Drum brakes were still assisted by the transmission-mounted friction servo, and the ride seemed to be even smoother than before. Hydramatic automatic transmission was standard, though the R-Type manual gearbox could be specified..

The body (rust-prone, unfortunately) now had front-hinged doors, was graceful, dignified, much larger than before, but was acknowledged to look rather retro. Bentley didn't mind that, nor did the clientele, who still bought more of them than Rolls-Royce Silver Clouds.

Regular development changes followed. Power-assisted steering and air-conditioning options came along in 1956, engines were more powerful from late 1957, when a longer-wheelbase (by four inches) body style also arrived. After that, though, Crewe began to prepare for the S2, which would have a brand-new V8 engine.

Much-loved by the classic fraternity, the S1 is not as fast as the S2 and S3 types but it is more economical and its engine is easier to work on.

SPECIFICATION

BODY STYLES: saloon, coachbuilts

PRODUCTION: 3107

ENGINE & TRANSMISSION: 4887cc, 6cyl ioe, 4sp man or auto, f/r

POWER: not quoted

MAX SPEED (MPH): 101

0-60MPH (SEC): 14.2

SUSPENSION & BRAKES: coil ifs, leaf rear, drums f&r

LENGTH (IN)/WEIGHT (LB): 212/4480

LAUNCH PRICE: £4669

S1 Continental 1955-59

Carrying on where it had left off with the R-Types, Bentley soon produced Continental versions of the new S-Series chassis. This time around, however, the engines tended to be in exactly the same state of tune as those of the saloons, so the difference in performance was not as marked.

Because almost all S1 Continentals had

SPECIFICATION

BODY STYLES: coupé, drophead coupé, coachbuilts

PRODUCTION: 431

ENGINE & TRANSMISSION: 4887cc, 6cyl ioe, 4sp man or auto, f/r

POWER: not quoted

MAX SPEED (MPH): 119

0-60MPH (SEC): 12.9

SUSPENSION & BRAKES: coil ifs, leaf rear, drums f&r

LENGTH (IN)/WEIGHT (LB): 212/4255

LAUNCH PRICE: £7164

The Park Ward Bentley Continental S1 drophead.

automatic transmission (a very few had a manual gearbox, to special order), and because technical development marched in parallel with the saloons, all the interest was in the wide choice of light-alloy coachbuilt bodies which were on offer. H J Mulliner offered two-door coupés rather like the old R-Type style, while Park Ward offered both coupé and convertible bodies; before long James Young added a coupé to this list.

Then, in late 1957, H J Mulliner announced the first ever four-door Continental, the Flying Spur saloon, this enterprise soon being matched by James Young and by Hooper.

More than 400 such special S1s were produced in less than four years. Many of them – the majority, probably – have survived to become much admired and revered icons of the classic car movement, with prices to suit.

S2 & S3 1959-62/1962-65

The light-alloy ohv V8 engine which would power all Bentley and Rolls-Royce cars for the next forty years appeared in 1959. In the case of Bentley, this allowed the S1 to be uprated to S2 by the fitment of the (unofficially-rated) 200bhp 6230cc power plant.

Unless one raised the bonnet to look into the engine bay, visually there was little to distinguish the S2 from the earlier six-cylinder car, for standard and longer-wheelbase saloons received no re-styling. The new engine was 30lb lighter than the old six, which meant that no changes needed to be made to the suspension. Although it was no longer, the V8 was much wider, so access to some parts for service was a nightmare. Gentlemen, though, never talked about that.

Automatic transmission and power-steering were both now standard, and the old-style central chassis lubrication had been abandoned. Air-conditioning was still optional, though the massive "works" had been relocated.

After only three years S2 was turned into S3 in October 1962. The big change was at the front, where four (paired) headlamps were specified, the entire front end (including the radiator shell) being subtly re-shaped and lowered to suit. Other detail changes included extra leg room in the back seat, reduced power-steering effort, and (unofficially) a 15bhp power increase..

This was the period in which equivalent-model Bentley sales finally slipped behind those of Rolls-Royce, and it was also the start of a run-down of separate-chassis Bentley designs. The last S3 saloon was produced in August 1965, after which the monocoque T-Series took over.

Bentley S2 saloon of 1959 had unchanged looks and a V8 engine.

SPECIFICATION

BODY STYLES: saloon, coachbuilts

PRODUCTION: 1922/1318

ENGINE & TRANSMISSION: 6230cc, V8cyl ohv, auto, f/r

POWER: not quoted

MAX SPEED (MPH): 113

0-60MPH (SEC): 11.5

SUSPENSION & BRAKES: coil ifs, leaf rear, drums f&r

LENGTH (IN)/WEIGHT (LB): 212/4225

LAUNCH PRICE: £5661

S3 had a restyled front end with twin headlamps and a lower bonnet line.

S2 & S3 Continental 1959-65

The S-Series Continental pedigree marched on in parallel with that of the saloons, which means that the first V8-engined S2s arrived before the end of 1959, and the more powerful S3s from late 1962. Because the manual

SPECIFICATION

BODY STYLES: saloon, coupé, drophead coupé, coachbuilts

PRODUCTION : 388 S2, 312 S3s

ENGINE & TRANSMISSION: 6230cc, V8cyl ohv, auto, f/r

POWER: not quoted

MAX SPEED (MPH): 113

0-60MPH (SEC): 12.1

SUSPENSION & BRAKES: coil ifs, leaf rear, drums f&r

LENGTH (IN)/WEIGHT (LB): 212/4225

LAUNCH PRICE: £7857

Bentley Continental S2 drophead of 1960 by Park Ward.

transmission option had finally been dropped, the Continental's running gear was now virtually the same as that of the equivalent production saloon.

In styling terms, the most significant novelty was the stunning Park Ward design of 1959, which featured a long and flowing shape with a high, straight-through wing crown line. Not only was this style to be available in two-door drophead or fixed-head coupé versions, but a few special-bodied Rolls-Royce S3s were also built using the same basic body shell. As far as the Rolls-Royce

S2 Continental by James Young.

Fixed-head S3 version of the Park Ward Continental, with twin headlamps.

H J Mulliner S2 Continental two-door.

company's captive coachbuilding industry was concerned, nothing was ever totally logical, totally simple, or without exceptions! When S2 turned into S3, each and every one of the Continental body styles on offer was modified to accept a four-headlamp nose. It is worth noting that Park Ward had been a Rolls-Royce subsidiary since the late 1930s, H J Mulliner became a subsidiary in 1959, and that those two businesses were progressively merged after 1961. The tendency, thereafter, was not to let the two businesses compete with one another. Significantly, sales were higher than ever before – sometimes at the rate of more than 100 cars a year.

These S2s and S3s were the very last of the coachbuilt, separate-chassis Bentleys.

T1 1965-77

When the third post-war generation of Bentleys and Rolls-Royces arrived in 1965, the changeover was virtually complete. Apart from using the still-modern 6230cc V8 engine, and its automatic transmission, every single component was new.

The Rolls-Royce Silver Shadow version of this car went on to become the best-selling car of that marque: it was only marketing pressures which gradually pushed the Bentley T-Series equivalent back into the shadows.

Central to the theme was a brand new four-door saloon body, produced, as ever, by Pressed Steel. The only difference between the brands was the radiator and badging, for mechanically and in their equipment they were identical.

Backing the V8 engine was automatic transmission – Hydramatic on UK-market cars at first but only until 1968, when it was replaced by the GM400 installation. Independent front and rear suspension – at the rear by semi-trailing arms and coil springs – also involved self-levelling dampers. Power steering was standard, as were disc brakes on all four wheels. The steering, brakes and self-levelling suspension were supplied with high-pressure hydraulic power from pumps and accumulators on the engine.

Bentley T1 saloon.

Behind the four-headlamp nose, the styling was simple, but inside the cabin there was wall to wall leather, deep-pile carpets and wood, all shaped, cosseted and assembled by hand at the Crewe factory.

In twelve years, any number of development changes kept the T-Series (T1, as it later became known) up to date. Originally the suspension was very soft and the steering woolly, so much effort went into chassis changes. A larger 6750cc V8 engine was fitted in 1970, compliant front suspension in 1972, and there was a suspension upgrade in 1974. Front-end self-levelling, on the other hand, was abandoned in 1969. Amazingly, air-conditioning was still optional at first, but it became standard in 1969.

The next important change came in 1977, when T1 gave way to T2, which looked virtually the same but had rack-and-pinion steering, a new fascia style and two-level air-conditioning.

Silver Shadows outsold T1s by ten-to-one. Within twenty years, though, both had lost most of their value, and many had rusted very badly.

SPECIFICATION

BODY STYLES: saloon, coachbuilts

PRODUCTION: 1712

ENGINE & TRANSMISSION: 6230cc/6750cc, V8cyl ohv, auto, f/r

POWER: not quoted

MAX SPEED (MPH): 115

0-60MPH (SEC): 10.9

SUSPENSION & BRAKES: coil ifs, coil irs, discs f&r

LENGTH (IN)/WEIGHT (LB): 204/4659

LAUNCH PRICE: £6496

T1 2-door H J Mulliner Coupé/Convertible 1966-71

Within months of the launch of the Bentley T-Series (and equivalent Rolls-Royce Silver Shadow), the first of the special two-door models had appeared. Although these cars retained the same platform and all the high-tech running gear, they had brand new, two-door four-seater bodies which were produced by H J Mulliner in London.

Above the platform level every panel was different, and the result looked very graceful. At first only a two-door "saloon" (some people called it a coupé) was

Bentley T1 Corniche convertible.

available, but an elegant drophead coupé derivative appeared before the end of 1967. Although some aluminium skin panels were used, these were never meant to be lightweight GT machines – in fact the fixed-head version weighed 300lb more than the four-door, and the drophead coupé even more than that.

Originally these cars carried no special model name, but from 1971 they were somewhat modified, took up the enlarged engine, and became known as the Corniche. Such Bentley-badged cars then carried on selling steadily until the mid-1990s, becoming known as Continentals from 1984.

Faced with such high technology, and a monocoque structure, James Young could no longer compete, though they somehow managed to build 15 two-door saloons in 1965/66. That, though, was their swansong as special body manufacturers.

T1 coupé, 1969.

SPECIFICATION

BODY STYLES: saloon, drophead coupé

PRODUCTION: 579

ENGINE & TRANSMISSION: 6230cc/6750cc, V8cyl ohv, auto, f/r

POWER: not quoted

MAX SPEED (MPH): 115 (E)/120

0-60MPH (SEC): not measured/9.6

SUSPENSION & BRAKES: coil ifs, coil irs, discs f&r

LENGTH (IN)/WEIGHT (LB): 204/4978

LAUNCH PRICE: £9789

Corniche 1971-84

By the 1970s, the balance between Bentley and Rolls-Royce sales had swung completely. Bentley was very much the minor player in this partnership.

SPECIFICATION

BODY STYLES: saloon, drophead coupé

PRODUCTION: 140

ENGINE & TRANSMISSION: 6750cc, V8cyl ohv, auto, f/r

POWER: not quoted

MAX SPEED (MPH): 120

0-60MPH (SEC): 9.6

SUSPENSION & BRAKES: coil ifs, coil irs, discs f&r

LENGTH (IN)/WEIGHT (LB): 205/4930

LAUNCH PRICE: £12,829/£13,410

Bentley Corniche, 1979.

Accordingly, it is enough to say that the Bentley Corniche was always identical with the Rolls-Royce Corniche, which is fully described later in the text.

Sales of the Bentley Corniche were very restricted. Only 63 saloons and 77 drophead coupés were produced in thirteen years – a total of 140 cars,

amazingly few compared with sales of nearly 4500 Rolls-Royce badged Corniches in the same period.

From 1984, however, Bentley's renaissance was about to begin, so the near-moribund Bentley Corniche was renamed Bentley Continental, and sales rebounded.

T2 1977-80

As with the Corniche, so with the second type of T-Series, the Bentley-based version of the Rolls-Royce Silver Shadow made up a very small percentage of sales from Crewe at this period.

SPECIFICATION

BODY STYLES: saloon

PRODUCTION: 568

ENGINE & TRANSMISSION: 6750cc, V8cyl ohv, auto, f/r

POWER: not quoted

MAX SPEED (MPH): 119

0-60MPH (SEC): 9.4

SUSPENSION & BRAKES: coil ifs, coil irs, discs f&r

LENGTH (IN)/WEIGHT (LB): 205/4930

LAUNCH PRICE: £22,809

Bentley T2 saloon.

Except in its badging, the Bentley T2 was identical to the Rolls-Royce Silver Shadow of the same period (see the appropriate Rolls-Royce entry). In late 1980 it would be replaced by the Mulsanne model.

Mulsanne 1980-87

When the new-generation Bentley and Rolls-Royce saloons appeared in late 1980, Rolls-Royce was by far the dominant brand. The new Bentley – the Mulsanne – was identical to the new Rolls-Royce Silver Spirit in every way except for the radiator shell and badges. Even the prices were identical.

Because the Mulsanne was virtually ignored for years, it sold very slowly, and only 529 such cars were produced, including 47 with the four-inch longer wheelbase, in seven years. The renaissance, however, would begin in 1982, when the Mulsanne Turbo (the first "blower" Bentley since 1930!) was launched.

For all technical details, including up-dates, see the Rolls-Royce Silver Spirit entry.

SPECIFICATION

BODY STYLES: saloon

PRODUCTION: 529

ENGINE & TRANSMISSION: 6750cc, V8cyl ohv, auto, f/r

POWER: not quoted – unofficially estimated at 200bhp @ 4000rpm

MAX SPEED (MPH): 119

0-60MPH (SEC): 10.0

SUSPENSION & BRAKES: coil ifs, coil irs, discs f&r

LENGTH (IN)/WEIGHT (LB): 207/4950

LAUNCH PRICE: £49,629

Bentley Mulsanne.

BERKELEY

This just might be the unluckiest new-car project of this classic period. Although Berkeley cars were built down to a price, and were lacking in refinement in some ways, they had advanced constructional features, front-wheel drive, handled well, and delivered a remarkable amount of performance from simple British motorcycle power trains. Inspired by that inventive engineer, Lawrie Bond, these were resourceful little sports cars which delivered at least as much as they promised.

Berkeley of Biggleswade, though, came out of nowhere, struggled to build up a dealership and client base, and always had to operate as a subsidiary of Charles Panter's caravan manufacturing enterprise. When the caravan business hit trouble, limited demand for the most powerful four-seaters meant that the Berkeley car business was dragged down with it, and all production ended just as the promising Tojeiro-designed Bandit model (the first Berkeley to use a car, as opposed to motorcycle, engine) was ready to go on sale.

B60/B65 1956-58

Once vividly described by another historian as an "engaging miniature", Berkeley's original sports car was a tribute to consultant engineer Lawrie Bond's imagination, and to Berkeley's bravery in taking it on. Although it was a neat and conventional-looking little two-seater sports car, it used a motorcycle engine driving the front wheels. It pre-dated the BMC Mini by three years, and thus at the time it was Britain's only front wheel drive four-wheeler.

The parent company was skilled in the use both of GRP and aluminium pressings and extrusions, which possibly explains why the basis was a platform hull made mainly in GRP, but with sheet aluminium stiffening, to which the nicely styled two-seater shell was bonded on assembly. Unlike some GRP-bodied microcars of the period, passenger doors were provided. The headlamps were cowled behind Perspex panels.

The air-cooled two-stroke twin-cylinder motorcycle engine/gearbox

Berkeley B65.

assembly was transversely mounted ahead of the line of the front wheels. Power was provided either by Anzani (for the B60 model) or Excelsior (for the B65), and drive from the Albion three-speed gearbox was by chain to the Bond-designed spur gear final drive casing, with shaft drive from there to each front wheel. Gear changing was by a steering column mounted quadrant. Late models got a four-speed gearbox, with a floor (quadrant) change on the B65.

Front suspension was by coil springs and wishbones, allied to a Burman steering box, while independent rear suspension was by surprisingly well controlled swing axles and coil springs.

The neat body was tiny – the whole car was only 123in long – but nicely detailed. Although the car was packaged as (and meant to be) a two-seater, there was a removable GRP tonneau panel behind the seats which exposed a moulded space sufficient to accept two willing children.

Rough-and-ready, but capable, the B60 and B65 models introduced ex-motorcycle people to the sports car habit, but the cars were really very slow. The B90 which followed was better. Quite a number of these machines survive.

SPECIFICATION

BODY STYLES: sports car

PRODUCTION: c.2000, all four-wheeler Berkeleys

ENGINE & TRANSMISSION: 322cc/328cc, 2cyl ts, 3sp (later 4sp) man, f/f

POWER: 15bhp @ 5000rpm/18bhp @ 5250rpm

MAX SPEED (MPH): 65

0-60MPH (SEC): 38.3

SUSPENSION & BRAKES: coil ifs, coil irs, drums f&r

LENGTH (IN)/WEIGHT (LB): 123/700

LAUNCH PRICE: £575

B90 1957-59

The B90 arrived in 1957 as a direct response to those who wanted more performance than early Berkeleys. In many ways this was a simple engine transplant process: in place of the previous twin-cylinder engines Berkeley fitted a transverse three-cylinder two-stroke Excelsior unit producing 30bhp

Berkeley B90 Foursome.

SPECIFICATION

BODY STYLES: sports car, sports coupé

PRODUCTION: see B60/B65 above

ENGINE & TRANSMISSION: 492cc, 3cyl ts, 4sp man, f/f

POWER: 30bhp @ 5500rpm

MAX SPEED (MPH): 80

0-60MPH (SEC): 21.8

SUSPENSION & BRAKES: coil ifs, coil irs, drums f&r

LENGTH (IN)/WEIGHT (LB): (2-seat) 123/850, (2+2 seat) 131/925

LAUNCH PRICE: £650/£728

and giving a top speed of 80mph. A four-speed 'box became standard, with a quadrant centre-floor change, and the doors were lengthened to improve cockpit access.

Except in refinement, but certainly in performance and nimble roadholding, the B90 was the equal of the new Austin-Healey Sprite and slightly cheaper, at £650 compared with £689.

The lack of refinement and of pedigree, though, always told against it.

To widen the car's appeal Berkeley also introduced a slightly longer "Foursome" version of the B90 with 2+2 seating, and there was an optional hardtop.

The B90 was overshadowed by the larger-engined B95/B105 which followed, and it was dropped within two years.

B95/B105 1959-61

This was the Big One, the most powerful of all front wheel drive Berkeleys, since instead of the relatively humble two-stroke motors Berkeley now installed brawny four-stroke motorcycle twins from Royal Enfield.

Announced in spring 1959, the B95 and B105 soon took over completely

SPECIFICATION

BODY STYLES: sports car

PRODUCTION: see B60/B65

ENGINE & TRANSMISSION: 692cc, 2cyl ohv, 4sp man, f/f

POWER: 40bhp @ 5500rpm/50bhp @ 6250rpm

MAX SPEED (MPH): (B95) 83

0-60MPH (SEC): (B95) 17.2

SUSPENSION & BRAKES: coil ifs, coil irs, drums f&r

LENGTH (IN)/WEIGHT (LB): (2-seater)125/885, (2+2-seater) 131/950

LAUNCH PRICE: £628

Berkeley B95/105.

from earlier four-wheeler types, but were not built in big numbers. By that time, most Berkeley sales were of the T60 three-wheeler.

To install the more bulky Royal Enfield Super Meteor (B95) or Constellation (B105) twins, the front end was re-shaped, with a big rectangular grille to channel cooling air, the headlamps now

being exposed. As before, final drive was by chain. A longer-wheelbase 2+2 hardtop version was also available.

This was really an engine transplant too far, as the vertical twins were too loud, too rough-running and not nearly as refined as were Berkeley's obvious competitors. Only a limited number were sold, and a few have survived..

T60 three-wheeler 1959-60

Here was a rare example of a three-wheeler developing from an existing four-wheeler car, rather than the other way around. The T60, in fact, was little more than a single rear wheel conversion of the already-popular B60 two-seater. It looked good and sold very well, becoming Berkeley's best-selling model, with 1850 sold in just over a year.

SPECIFICATION
BODY STYLES: tourer, saloon
PRODUCTION: 1850
ENGINE & TRANSMISSION: 328cc, 2cyl ts, 4sp man, f/f
POWER: 18bhp @ 5250rpm
MAX SPEED (MPH): 60
0-60MPH (SEC): Not available
SUSPENSION & BRAKES: coil ifs, coil irs, drums f&r
LENGTH (IN)/WEIGHT (LB): 124/763
LAUNCH PRICE: £400

Berkeley T60 three-wheeler.

From the nose to the rear of the doors the T60 was nearly identical to the B60 and it was still front wheel drive. Aft of the cockpit the bodywork was swept in to enclose a single wheel which was suspended by an Armstrong coil spring/damper unit and a trailing arm.

Road testers found that the T60 was amazingly stable and all agreed that this was more like a sports car than mere marginal motoring. Like the Morgan three-wheelers of old, the sturdy three-wheel layout, with two wheels up front, gave the car an impressive platform. It was Berkeley's last fling; the parent company's problems dragged it down.

Bandit 1960

OK, so this car never actually went on sale, but it was in fact launched before Berkeley was forced into liquidation – and it showed how the Berkeley brand was meant to evolve in the 1960s. But could Berkeley have survived with the Bandit selling for £798 against the £632 asked for a contemporary Austin-Healey Frogeye Sprite?

SPECIFICATION
BODY STYLES: sports car
PRODUCTION: only prototypes produced
ENGINE & TRANSMISSION: 997cc, 4cyl ohv, 4sp man, f/r
POWER: 39bhp @ 5000rpm
MAX SPEED (MPH): 80 (E)
0-60MPH (SEC): not measured
SUSPENSION & BRAKES: coil ifs, coil irs, disc f/drum r
LENGTH (IN)/WEIGHT (LB): 143/1450
LAUNCH PRICE: £798

Berkeley Bandit prototype.

Breaking with every Berkeley tradition, this new model was not only designed by John Tojeiro, but also used a car-type engine and had rear-wheel drive. It had a pressed steel platform chassis to which the GRP floor and undertray were riveted on assembly. The GRP body was neat and clearly competed with the Sprite, being of similar size and weight.

Much of the running gear was modern Dagenham, with an Anglia 105E engine, its matching gearbox and final drive unit,

and rear drum brakes. Berkeley devised its own type of MacPherson strut front suspension and swing-axle rear, combining it all with Triumph Herald rack-and-pinion steering and a Girling front disc brake installation.

Berkeley proposed to add bubble and fastback hardtop derivatives, and even suggested that the high-output Coventry-Climax FWA engine could be available.

This was not to be, as Berkeley collapsed before series production could begin.

BOND

Bond was born when that inventive engineer, Lawrie Bond, sold his ideas of a minimal-motoring three-wheeler project to Sharps Commercials of Preston in Lancashire. Bond provided the original concept and the first detail designs, but all future work was to Sharps engineers' credit.

On sale from 1949, original Minicars had aircraft-like stressed-skin construction, there being no separate chassis. The bodies were made almost entirely from sheet aluminium. One feature was that there was no reverse gear: from 1951 (and Mk C) this was no handicap, as the front wheel could be turned through 90 degrees in each direction, the car then turning in its own length.

Over the years, though, the Minicar evolved strongly, first by gaining rear suspension and larger engines, then with new styles and finally, from 1958, getting a separate chassis structure. Three-wheeler sales were then at their height, after which Bond moved up into building Equipe sports coupés,

first based on Triumph Herald/Spitfire running gear, then on Triumph Vitesse chassis, both with a mixed steel and GRP body shell. Although production numbers were quite limited, these cars were more profitable and enhanced the marque's image. In the meantime, a replacement for the three-wheelers (of which 24,484 had been sold since 1949), the GRP-bodied and much more ambitious Imp-engined 875 had been a commercial failure.

The Bond business was then absorbed by Reliant in 1969, in an agreed takeover which simplified Bond's parent company structure. Although Reliant ran down the marketing of the Triumph-engined machines, and soon closed down the factory in Preston, they encouraged the birth of the Reliant Regal-based Bug, which was latterly built at the Reliant factory at Tamworth in the Midlands. Because this too was a commercial failure, the Bond marque then died out, the last of all being produced in 1974.

Minicar Mk A & B 1949-51/1951-52

Bond's original Minicar, Mark A as it subsequently became known, was a curiously minimal machine but with advanced engineering. Built down to a price, it was a two-seater tourer with a reinforced aluminium body, an open top, a bench seat, exposed headlamps – and a Perspex windscreen which gradually went opaque!

The air-cooled Villiers engine, motor-cycle type gearbox and front wheel support were up front, as one, an assembly that turned as the steering (by cable and bobbin!) was operated. There was no rear suspension, and cable/rod-operated brakes worked only on the rear

An early Bond Minicar ahead of a Mark F.

SPECIFICATION

BODY STYLES: drophead, light commercials

PRODUCTION: approx 2000 and 3000

ENGINE & TRANSMISSION: 122cc/197cc, 1cyl ts, 3sp man, f/f

POWER: 5bhp @ 4400rpm/8bhp @ 4400rpm

MAX SPEED (MPH): 43/50

0-60MPH (SEC): not possible

SUSPENSION & BRAKES: coil ifs, none/coil irs, drums r

LENGTH (IN)/WEIGHT (LB): 111/308 – 111/364

LAUNCH PRICE: £199/£263 with 197cc/Mark B £356

wheels. The gearchange was operated by a lever behind the steering column.

Though a simple rack-and-pinion steering soon replaced the crude cable and bobbin mechanism, this was truly marginal motoring, and a cruising speed of 30-35mph felt quite enough. With no rear suspension, very simple seats, no heater and sketchy weather protection, driving was never much of a pleasure.

From 1950, De Luxe Mk As had the

197cc Villiers engine, an electric wind-screen wiper, a glass windscreen, the latest rack-and-pinion steering and a hydraulic front shock absorber. Luxury – and up to 40 a week were being sold. The 1951 Mk B had coil spring independent rear suspension in addition to the above, all as standard, this being when the first commercial types were launched, but before long it was overtaken by the newly-styled Mk C.

Minicar Mk C & D 1952-56/1956-57

This was the first Bond to have a styled body, rather than one which merely surrounded the running gear and the cabin. Here was a neat two/three-seater with headlamps recessed into faired wings (which looked as if they covered wheels but did not), and with a single door on the nearside. A cast aluminium bulkhead added much-needed stiffness, and a front brake was standard. There was still no reverse gear, but a new type of worm-and-sector steering allowed the front wheel to be turned 90 degrees left or right – a 180-degree sweep which enabled the car to turn in its own length. The 1956 Mk D had a modified grille, an improved Villiers engine and (from 1957) four speeds and 12v electrics. The "Family" version of this range even squeezed a rear seat in.

SPECIFICATION

BODY STYLES: drophead, hardtop coupé, light commercials

PRODUCTION: 6700/ n/a

ENGINE & TRANSMISSION: 197cc, 1cyl ts, 3sp man (Mark D 4sp man), f/f

POWER: 8bhp @ 4400rpm

MAX SPEED (MPH): 49/51

0-60MPH (SEC): not possible

SUSPENSION & BRAKES: coil ifs, rubber irs, drums f&r

LENGTH (IN)/WEIGHT (LB): 118/460

LAUNCH PRICE: £269/£279

Bond Minicar Mk C.

Minicar Mk E, F & G 1958-59/1959-61/1961-66

The third and last style of Minicar arrived in 1958, almost completely different in engineering, though not in character. First, there was a new steel box-section chassis frame which was riveted to the underside of the new-style aluminium body, which itself was longer and more sleekly detailed, with

SPECIFICATION

BODY STYLES: saloon, drophead, light commercials

PRODUCTION: c.1800/7000/3250

ENGINE & TRANSMISSION: 197cc/246cc/249cc, 1cyl/2cyl ts, 4sp man, f/f

POWER: 8bhp @ 4400rpm/12bhp @ 4500rpm/15bhp @ 5500rpm

MAX SPEED (MPH): 50/55/60

0-60MPH (SEC): not available

SUSPENSION & BRAKES: rubber/coil ifs, rubber/coil irs, drums f&r

LENGTH (IN)/WEIGHT (LB): 132/660 - 826

LAUNCH PRICE: (E) n/a /(F) £380/(G) £395

Minicar Mk G saloon.

flush sides, and a wide-mouth grille. Now, for the first time, there were doors on both sides of the body, while a glass-fibre roof option to make this car a Coupé was also available. The track was wider than on previous Minicars, so the Mk E handled better than before.

The Mk F of 1959 added the option of a squarer-shaped GRP-topped roof, this being the Minicar's first-ever saloon. At the same time the larger

246cc Villiers engine was standardised, restoring the top speed to around 55mph, and there was an optional reverse gear. Soon, nearly 100 such Bonds were being built every week.

The third (and last) version of this range arrived in 1961, the Mk G having a more roomy cabin, not only with the windscreen/bulkhead moved forward, but with the saloon roof incorporating an Anglia-like reversed-slope style of rear window. Compared with the Mk F, this was a more practical type of "almost-four-seater".

Other new features included wind-up door windows, coil spring rear suspension, hydraulic brakes and 10in road wheels.

Later there was more innovation, a tiny estate car body style being added, and eventually (from 1963) the use of a smoother-running 249cc twin-cylinder engine which produced nearly 15bhp (though the older engine was still fitted to stripped-out Tourer models).

Sales fell away sharply in the mid-1960s, the last of all being produced in 1966. The Mk G's replacement, though not a car of the same type, was the Hillman Imp-engined 875.

875 1965-70

Although it succeeded the last of the motorcycle-engined Minicars at Preston, the new 875 was totally different in every way, for it was powered by the modern Hillman Imp overhead-cam engine and its related gearbox, which lived in the tail of the four-seater saloon structure. It was, in any case, a larger and more ambitiously specified product. Because it represented a direct challenge to the contemporary Reliant Regal, it is easy to see why it did not long survive the Reliant takeover of Bond.

The 875's main body shell, in the form of a two-door four-seater saloon, was in reinforced glassfibre. At the rear, the entire engine (a low-compression version), transmission, rear suspension, cross-member, brakes and wheels were those of the Hillman Imp. At the front, a coil spring/damper unit suspended the single front wheel on a forward-facing link. Somehow or other, this assembly was brought in at just under the 8cwt (896lb) unladen weight limit needed for

Bond 875: a three-wheeler with a Hillman Imp engine.

it to qualify for a reduced rate of annual road tax.

Weight reduction meant that the trim and fittings were spartan, and sound-deadening was very limited, the entire car being definitely in the "marginal" category.

Performance, on the other hand, was sparkling (0-60mph took 17.4sec, quite remarkably better than any previous Bond three-wheeler), and also much better than the Imp from which the power pack was borrowed.

No less than 72 per cent of the unladen weight was over the rear wheels, which meant that there could be considerably front-end wander in crosswinds. Serious understeer, particularly in the wet, was a

another of the 875's characteristics.

Testers found this the "fastest thing on three wheels since the Super Aero Morgan of 1930", but sharply criticised the trim, fittings and build quality. These latter shortcomimgs, and the fact that the 875 cost more than a BMC Mini, meant that it sold slowly.

From 1968, a facelift included a restyled nose with rectangular head-lamps and a much larger front grille, but little change to the running gear. Sales always disappointed, so following the takeover by Reliant the last 875 of all was built in February 1970.

No one, surely, looked on this machine as a classic, though a number have survived into the new century.

SPECIFICATION

BODY STYLES: saloon, light commercials

PRODUCTION: 3431

ENGINE & TRANSMISSION: 875cc, 4cyl ohc, 4sp man, r/r

POWER: 34bhp @ 4700rpm

MAX SPEED (MPH): 81

0-60MPH (SEC): 17.4

SUSPENSION & BRAKES: coil ifs, coil irs, drums f&r

LENGTH (IN)/WEIGHT (LB): 116/800

LAUNCH PRICE: £497

Equipe GT/GT4S 1963-70

The 1964 Equipe GT4S featured a four-headlamp nose, replacing a two-lamp design.

Bond's first real motor car – real, that is, in having four wheels and a water-cooled engine – appeared in 1963. Taking advantage of their dealer-to-manufacturer relationship with Standard-Triumph, Bond's parent company gained approval to build a new four-seater sports coupé around the Herald chassis. This would receive the factory warranty, and the car would even be sold through Triumph dealerships.

The first Equipe, in fact, had a mix-and-match specification, for the all independent suspension Herald-based chassis used a 63bhp Spitfire engine and Spitfire disc front brakes. The body shell used the steel floorpan, passenger bulkhead, windscreen and doors, plus much of the glass, from the Herald, the rest of the body being of GRP, styled and moulded by Bond.

Original types were called Equipe GT. They had a simple two-headlamp nose and a sloping tail but no opening boot lid. From late 1964 the Equipe GT4S arrived to take over from the GT, this having a restyled nose which incorporated four headlamps in pods lifted from the Triumph 2000, more rear-seat headroom, a sawn-off rear-end

style and an opening boot lid.

Behaviour and specification were always much like the Heralds of the day. The 67bhp Spitfire II engine took over from 1965, centre-lock wire wheels were optional from mid-1965, and the 75bhp 1.3-litre engine took over in 1967. After that the Equipe 2-litre GT took most of Bond's attention, so the 4S merely soldiered on to 1970.

Much of the body was rot-proof (though not the Triumph-sourced steel parts, of course), so a number of GTs and GT4Ss have survived. Because the cars were based on readily available Herald and Spitfire units, restoration is not as problematical as it might be.

SPECIFICATION

BODY STYLES: coupé

PRODUCTION: 2956

ENGINE & TRANSMISSION: 1147cc/1296cc, 4cyl ohv, 4sp man, f/r

POWER: 63bhp @ 5750rpm/67bhp @ 6000rpm/75bhp @ 6000rpm

MAX SPEED (MPH): 82/91/95 (E)

0-60MPH (SEC): 17.6/20.0/not measured

SUSPENSION & BRAKES: coil ifs, leaf irs, disc f/drum r

LENGTH (IN)/WEIGHT (LB): 155/1625 - 1834

LAUNCH PRICE: £822

Equipe GT, 1963.

Equipe 2-Litre 1967-70

Like its little brother the GT4S, the Equipe 2-Litre could not have existed without approval from the Triumph factory, or without wholesale use of Triumph components.

The Equipe used the Vitesse rolling chassis with its six-cylinder engine and transmission. For the first 12 months the cars had 95bhp and the Vitesse's swing-axle rear suspension, but from late 1968 the Vitesse 2-litre Mk II provided 104bhp and a better wishbone rear suspension.

Much of the body's internal structure was Herald/Vitesse-based, but with a longer and freshly reshaped two-door coupé GRP body. When the Mk II chassis arrived, Bond also introduced a convertible version of this model, which looked well.

Sales were always restricted by the price (Vitesse pricing was below that of the equivalent Bond), but the 2-Litre remained in production well after the takeover of Bond by Reliant.

SPECIFICATION

BODY STYLES: coupé, drophead

PRODUCTION: 1432

ENGINE & TRANSMISSION: 1998cc, 6cyl ohv, 4sp man, o/d, f/r

POWER: 95bhp @ 5000rpm/104bhp @ 5300rpm

MAX SPEED (MPH): 102

0-60MPH (SEC): 10.7

SUSPENSION & BRAKES: coil ifs, leaf irs, disc f/drum r

LENGTH (IN)/WEIGHT (LB): 166/2016

LAUNCH PRICE: £1096

The Bond Equipe 2-litre convertible.

Bug 1970-74

Seriously trendy, but never likely to appeal to the very people at which it was aimed, the Bug was a Reliant under another name. Having bought Bond in 1969, Reliant decided to create a new Bond in its own image, which explains why this was a three-wheeler with a single front wheel, using many elements of the Reliant Regal/Rebel family. The chassis was a modified version of the Regal 3/30

Bond Bug.

SPECIFICATION

BODY STYLES: coupé

PRODUCTION: 2270

ENGINE & TRANSMISSION: 700cc/748cc, 4cyl ohv, 4sp man,f/r

POWER: 29 or 31bhp @ 5000rpm/35bhp @ 5500rpm

MAX SPEED (MPH): (700cc) 75

0-60MPH (SEC): (700cc) 23.2

SUSPENSION & BRAKES: coil ifs, coil rear, drums f&r

LENGTH (IN)/WEIGHT (LB): 110/868

LAUNCH PRICE: £629

layout, with a truncated rear and different rear suspension.

The acutely wedge-shaped glassfibre body hid a front-mounted engine which drove the rear wheels, yet there was a lift-up nose which did away with the need for doors. To echo the trendy image, the Bug was available in only one colour, Bug Tangerine. This was a stubby little car – wheelbase 77in, overall length only 110in – and had only two seats, though the performance was brisk, roughly equal to a

Mini's. The handling, however, was another story, for when pressed the Bug felt as if it might to tip over. Road testers discovered that a tipping rear wheel, which destroyed traction, was a self-limiting feature, but those who inverted a Bug found that they could not get out of the cabin as the only way out was by lifting the roof.

At £629 in 1970 it was no bargain – an 850 Mini cost £620 at the time – and it was all over by 1974.

BRISTOL

After the Second World War, the Bristol Aeroplane Co. set out to diversify its business, establishing a motor car operation. By taking what were called post-war reparations from Germany (along with the services of a senior engineer, Fritz Fiedler) Bristol was able to adopt, then improve upon, much of the late-1930s BMW car. Starting from premises at Filton Airfield, a series of hand-built saloons was launched .

The BMW 328 cross-pushrod engine would form the heart of the first generation of Bristols. It was remarkably tuneable, and would be supplied to sports car companies as diverse as AC, Frazer-Nash and Cooper. In the 1950s it also became a successful race-car unit.

In the beginning, Bristol was in harness with the Aldington family and Frazer-Nash, but this deal soon foundered, and the aircraft company subsidiary eventually became independent. By 1960 Bristol had sold out their interests to Sir George White and motor trader Tony Crook. After Sir George retired in 1973, Crook took sole control, and would then retain personal (and rather secretive) direction of the brand until the start of the twenty-first century.

Bristol never made the mistake of widening its range too much, so it was rare to see more than two models on the market at the same time. Engineering evolution was slow, but steady and deliberate. The original 400-type chassis was retained until 1961, when the first of the V8-engined types coincided with a different front suspension. That chassis was so successful, and so carefully developed, that a version of it would still be in use more than forty years later.

Until the arrival of the first Chrysler-engined model (the 407), Bristol always manufactured its own engines and transmissions, and in the majority of cases it also built its own bodies. Early styles owed much to the BMW heritage which had been absorbed in 1945, but some wind-tunnel testing certainly helped shape later cars. By the 1960s, though, Bristol had evolved its own style, which would alter only slowly in the next twenty years.

Decades after our period closed, Bristol was still in private ownership, still making very limited numbers of cars every year (Tony Crook would never say how many), and still selling them all from a single Crook-owned outlet in West London.

400 1946-50

The launch of the new Bristol was forecast for 1946, but a Motor Show debut was delayed until January 1947. The original car, which was called the 400, established a pedigree which would evolve slowly in the decades which followed.

Sometimes glibly described as an Anglicised BMW, which it most certainly was not, the 400 clearly drew inspiration from the BMW 326's chassis. It had a further-developed

The handsome 2-litre Bristol 400.

SPECIFICATION

BODY STYLES: saloon, drophead, coachbuilt specials

PRODUCTION: 475

ENGINE & TRANSMISSION: 1971cc, 6cyl ohv, 4sp man, f/r

POWER: 80bhp @ 4500rpm (some cars with 85bhp)

MAX SPEED (MPH): 94

0-60MPH (SEC): 14.7

SUSPENSION & BRAKES: leaf ifs, tor rear, drums f&r

LENGTH (IN)/WEIGHT (LB): 170/2464

LAUNCH PRICE: £2374

version of the cross-pushrod BMW 328 engine, and owed something to the 327 in its two-door four-seater styling. Manufacture, however, was entirely at Bristol, or using components supplied by British suppliers.

The 400's base was a sturdy box-section chassis frame, in which the floor members also contributed to overall strength. Independent front suspension

was by wishbones and a transverse leaf spring, while the rear axle was suspended on longitudinal torsion bars and located by radius arms and an A-bracket. Rack-and-pinion steering, almost universal today, caused a real stir at the time, for this pre-dated the Morris Minor and other cars which boasted about it. Lubrication of the suspension joints was by an Enots one-shot pedal-operated installation.

The engine produced 80bhp (though more powerful versions were already being prepared for other models, and for supply to other brands), the gearbox being Bristol's own. The body, so reminiscent of the BMW 327 Autenreith coupé, had been assessed in Bristol's own wind tunnel. It was built on an ash frame with most internal panels in steel, though the opening panels were in light alloy. An HMV radio was standard – a very rare fitting at the time. Just two of the cars built were fitted with convertible bodywork.

The 400, the original Bristol, was built to very high standards, and many have survived. By 1940s standards its roadholding was outstanding and its performance exhilarating. As the first of the marque, it is highly prized today.

The 400 has its spare on the tail and sliding door windows.

401 1949-53

The second-generation Bristol was really the company's second thoughts on what a close-coupled four-seater coupé should look like, though built on the same chassis frame. Technically there were few changes to the running gear, except that the latest 85bhp engine was usually fitted. Over the years, two different sets of gear

Bristol 401, 1949.

SPECIFICATION

BODY STYLES: saloon, coachbuilts

PRODUCTION: 605

ENGINE & TRANSMISSION: 1971cc, 6cyl ohv, 4sp man, f/r

POWER: 80bhp @ 4200rpm/85bhp @ 4500rpm

MAX SPEED (MPH): 97

0-60MPH (SEC): 15.1

SUSPENSION & BRAKES: leaf ifs, tor rear, drums f&r

LENGTH (IN)/WEIGHT (LB): 192/2700

LAUNCH PRICE: £3214

ratios were used, though there was still no servo assistance for the rather heavy drum brakes.

The new car, called 401, featured a modified version of a body style by Touring of Milan, who provided not only the shape but also their own patented Superleggera type of body shell structure, where a lattice of lightweight steel tubes formed the base for the mounting of the skin panels. As before there was a mixture of steel and aluminium panelling, for structural wood no longer existed in this new model.

Although it was still not quite a 100mph car, the 401 was definitely faster – and therefore more aerodynamically efficient – than the 400. Many observers also found this uniquely styled saloon extremely attractive.

Although the 403 which followed was faster, the 401 was (and still is) much liked as a thoroughbred car. Long in the nose, with much more glass area than the 400, it was a pleasing-looking shape. In fact, more 401s were produced than any other type of six-cylinder Bristol.

A 401 tackling a driving test at Blackpool on the 1952 RAC Rally.

402 1949-50

To quote Bristol authority Charles Oxley, "Many reasons have been advanced for the 402's inability to generate sales, the most common being that its dashboard shook, that its doors flew open on corners, and that its hood mechanism was far too complicated."

Although all these comments were true, there must have been other factors involved, especially as the price was exactly the same as that of the 401 saloon. In truth, the 402 was a two-door two-seater model based on the complete rolling chassis of a 401. The front end of the body style was precisely like that of the 401, but the cabin and tail were unique.

Compared with the 401, though, the cabin was much shortened, and the rear

The 402 had a strikingly long tail.

The front end was pure 401.

Well-equipped dash of the 402.

SPECIFICATION

BODY STYLES: drophead, coachbuilts

PRODUCTION: 21

ENGINE & TRANSMISSION: 1971cc, 6cyl ohv, 4sp man, f/r

POWER: 85bhp @ 4500rpm

MAX SPEED (MPH): 95 (E)

0-60MPH (SEC): not measured

SUSPENSION & BRAKES: leaf ifs, tor rear, drums f&r

LENGTH (IN)/WEIGHT (LB): 190/2632

LAUNCH PRICE: £3214

end, though smooth, seemed almost endless. Unlike the 401, the body contained a fair amount of wood in its framing. Erecting or furling the soft-top was indeed complex (Oxley lists an 11-stage procedure!), but this cannot have deterred customers. Another so-called authority called the 402 "a bit of a Hollywood special", which sounds unkind.

The fact is that the 402 was a marketing failure (it was virtually ignored in the British motoring press). Not even a few specially-built examples by Farina could rescue it, and very few examples now remain.

403 1953-55

Who was it who unkindly called the 403 a "401 with more bells and whistles"? That is a cruel but mainly accurate way of describing a successful model, only in production for two years, which sold as well as any previous Bristol model.

Structurally, technically and visually, the 403 was the same basic motor car as the 401, though with certain important changes. The most significant was the adoption of the Type 100A engine, which had an improved cylinder head, larger inlet valves, and a different camshaft. With 100bhp instead of the 401's 85bhp, this guaranteed a top speed of more than 100mph, making the 403 the first Bristol to achieve the magic figure.

Matching this was the latest type of Bristol gearbox, which had a freewheel

This Bristol 403 is on its way to Dover on a "Marble Arch to Arc de Triomphe in Five Hours" stunt.

on first gear (a few late-model 401 had this feature too), along with Alfin brake drums (all wheels at first, fronts only in

due course), an anti-roll bar for the front suspension, and many other smaller development changes.

This team of Bristol 450s came first, second and third in class at Le Mans in 1954.

SPECIFICATION

BODY STYLES: saloon

PRODUCTION: 275

ENGINE & TRANSMISSION: 1971cc, 6cyl ohv, 4sp man, f/r

POWER: 100bhp @ 5000rpm

MAX SPEED (MPH): 104

0-60MPH (SEC): 13.4

SUSPENSION & BRAKES: leaf ifs, tor rear, drums f&r

LENGTH (IN)/WEIGHT (LB): 192/2788

LAUNCH PRICE: £2976

404 1953-55

What started as a private-enterprise project by Bristol engineer Jack Channer eventually turned into a short-wheelbase derivative of the 405 saloon, which was really its parent. Even so, it was the 404 coupé which was announced first (late in 1953), the larger 405 following a full year later. Compared with the current 403 chassis, that of the 404 had a much shorter wheelbase – 96in instead of 114in – which meant that there was only enough

The new Bristol 404 sits alongside a 403 in 1953.

space for a two-seater cabin. Although all the elements of the existing chassis were retained, much of the 404's structure was newly engineered. The now-familiar 1971cc engine was available in 105bhp or 125bhp forms – the latter representing a 56 per cent improvement over the original power unit of the 400, an increase which had been achieved in just eight years. To keep this power in check, there were larger 12-inch front brake drums.

For the Bristol evolved its own body style, which featured a stubby cabin, a short tail with embryo fins, and a long snout which included a plain air intake said to be modelled on the shape of that used in the Brabazon airliner. The body, which was completely different from earlier Bristol efforts, was a handbuilt creation including structural steel, wood and some aluminium panels. The later 405 would share the front end, which included mounting the spare wheel in the recess of the left-side front wing, with battery and other electrical gear in a similar recess on the right.

The 404's problem was not only that it offered much less cabin space than previous Bristols, but that it was priced at £3543 (when a Jaguar XK120 fixed-head of the period cost just £1616, and an Aston Martin DB2/4 £2622). Not only that, but the drophead coupé promised on announcement never appeared. Even then, there might have been more demand if Bristol had provided any form of external access to the luggage compartment, but not so!

Bristol sold only 51 of these cars in two years and then dropped it. Perversely, the 404 became on of the most prized of all Bristols as the classic movement spread and matured.

SPECIFICATION

BODY STYLES: sports coupé, coachbuilts

PRODUCTION: 51

ENGINE & TRANSMISSION: 1971cc, 6cyl ohv, 4sp man, f/r

POWER: 105bhp @ 5000rpm/125bhp @ 5500rpm

MAX SPEED (MPH): (105bhp) 115 (E)

0-60MPH (SEC): not measured

SUSPENSION & BRAKES: leaf ifs, tor rear, drums f&r

LENGTH (IN)/WEIGHT (LB): 171/2290

LAUNCH PRICE: £3543

405 1954-58

If the 404 from which its front end style was derived was a failure, the larger, more versatile 405 which followed a year later was a resounding success. This, the very first four-door saloon to carry the Bristol badge, was also the last, as every succeeding model would be a two-door machine.

Technically, the 405 rolling chassis was an up-dated version of the 403 unit, with which it shared the same 114in wheelbase, though the engine was boosted slightly, to 105bhp (and similar to the lower-powered of the two types used in the short-lived 404). Here was a smart new 100mph sports saloon with Bristol's usual exemplary build quality and equipment level. The cabin was spacious enough for four adults and, need it be said, it came complete with exterior access to the boot!

The 405 was the first Bristol to be equipped with Laycock overdrive, which made high-speed cruising on good roads

The 1954 405 saloon, powered by a 105bhp version of the 2-litre engine.

(there were few in Britain at the time!) much more of a pleasure. Overdrive would also be used on the next model (the 406), but not thereafter, when automatic transmission was standardised.

The body exhibited many similarities to that of the 404, for the front end was virtually identical, and the vestigial rear fins were also similar. However, the cabin was completely different, and of course much more "touring".

As with the 404, bodies were constructed from a carefully integrated mix of wood, steel and aluminium pressings. At the time this was hailed as advance, but in later years, as rot set in, an old 405 would become a nightmare to restore.

There were two types of body – the four-door saloon built by the factory, and the two-door drophead coupé built for Bristol by Abbotts of Farnham.

SPECIFICATION

BODY STYLES: saloon, drophead

PRODUCTION: 297 saloons, 43 dropheads

ENGINE & TRANSMISSION: 1971cc, 6cyl ohv, 4sp man, o/d, f/r

POWER: 105bhp @ 5000rpm

MAX SPEED (MPH): 103 (E)

0-60MPH (SEC): not measured

SUSPENSION & BRAKES: leaf ifs, tor rear, drums f&r

LENGTH (IN)/WEIGHT (LB): 1889/2712

LAUNCH PRICE: £3189

405 had a wraparound rear screen.

406 1958-61

Three years after the 405 went on sale it was replaced by the 406, which used the same basic 114in chassis but had an entirely different body style. Not only did it revert to a two-door saloon layout, but a convertible was not available. The engine was enlarged (for the first and only time in this long-running series), and Bristol contracted out the production of its bodies.

It was not all-change time at Filton, but it signalled that changes could be and would always be made when it looked

For the 1958 Bristol 406 the engine was enlarged to 2.2 litres.

right to do so. Mechanically the main innovation in the 406 was that the engine capacity was increased to 2216cc, which delivered the same 105bhp as the 405 but with more torque than before.

Although the overdrive gearbox was retained, Bristol adopted a hypoid-bevel back axle (earlier types had used a spiral-bevel axle), and sideways location of the rear axle was now by a Watts linkage and a single fore-aft radius arm. Not only that, but four-wheel Dunlop disc brakes (with a Lockheed vacuum servo) were also adopted.

The body, built for Bristol by Jones Brothers of Willesden in north-west London, was a rather chunky two-door

four-seater with a similar front end to the 405's. It was harmonious and had sleek detailing. In progressively modified form this style would form the basis of all other four-seater Bristols covered in this volume. With more steel than before, the 406 was quite a bit heavier than the 405 had ever been. It was also considerbaly more expensive than its predecessor..

Because engine development had not kept up with the increase in weight, the 406 was actually slower than the 405 – which may explain why no official road tests were ever carried out by independent magazines. Even so, the 406 is important because of the way it formed the basis for later V8-engined models.

SPECIFICATION

BODY STYLES: saloon

PRODUCTION: 178

ENGINE & TRANSMISSION: 2216cc, 6cyl ohv, 4sp man, o/d, f/r

POWER: 105bhp @ 4700rpm

MAX SPEED (MPH): 100 (E)

0-60MPH (SEC): not measured

SUSPENSION & BRAKES: Leaf ifs, tor rear, discs f&r

LENGTH (IN)/WEIGHT (LB): 196/3010

LAUNCH PRICE: £4494

406 Zagato 1960-61

Here was an indulgence that Bristol could afford, for it took no part in building the bodies fitted to this version of the 406. In fact the 406 Zagato took shape by sending a number of 406 rolling chassis out to Italy to be bodied by the Italian specialist.

According to contemporary publicity, Zagato was to build normal-wheelbase saloons and special short-wheelbase coupés. As far as is known, only one coupé was built, the balance being rather jaggedly-detailed two-door saloons.

Zagato customers could specify which of the various 2.2-litre engines they required, the most powerful being the 130bhp unit known to be fitted in the single coupé.

Visually, the saloons looked awkward, which explains why they failed to find more than half a dozen customers, and

Zagato-bodied 406, 1960.

while the coupé was sinuously styled, its long nose and short tail made it look a bit unbalanced. These Zagato cars are

valuable today because of their rarity, but conventional Bristols were, and are, more graceful.

BODY STYLES: sports saloon, sports coupé

PRODUCTION: 7, of which
one coupé

ENGINE & TRANSMISSION: 2216cc, 6cyl
ohv, 4sp man , o/d, f/r

POWER: 130bhp @ 5750rpm

MAX SPEED (MPH): 120 (E)

0-60MPH (SEC): not measured

SUSPENSION & BRAKES: leaf ifs, tor rear,
discs f&r

LENGTH (IN)/WEIGHT (LB): 185/2469

LAUNCH PRICE: £4800

This 406 coupé was shown on the Zagato stand at Earls Court in 1960.

407 1961-63

By Bristol standards, the 407 was a complete re-think, the first of a new family. Not all new of course – the chassis platform and much of the 406's body were carried forward – but there was a new engine and new transmission to turn the Bristol into a 120mph-plus machine. In view of this, keeping the price rise to only £48 more than the 406 was something of a miracle.

The ageing Bristol six-cylinder engine had finally reached the limit of its development, and Bristol turned to Chrysler of Canada for its 250bhp 5130cc V8, matching it with Chrysler's own Torqueflite three-speed automatic transmission (Bristol's own nicely-detailed four-speed manual gearbox could not cope with the torque). Not only that, but under the engine was coil spring independent front suspension – a

The 407 was the first Bristol to have a V8 engine, a 5.1-litre V8.

novelty, for all previous Bristols had used a transverse leaf spring layout.

Commercially, too, there had been a major change. Although the style was similar to that of the 406, part of the body was now to be produced by Park Royal Vehicles of Acton, in West London. As ever, Bristol would paint, trim and finish off the car before delivering it to the customer.

What were the visual clues to distinguish the 407 from the 406? These were very limited – a flatter bonnet profile, modifications to the front air intake, no number plate recess in the tail, and very little else.

Inside the car, of course, fixtures and fittings were of the usual very high quality – some say that a Bristol was built as well, and as carefully, as a Rolls-Royce – these including the automatic transmission gear-change quadrant on the steering column. The driver had extra manual control buttons for the transmission on the fascia too.

This was the very first of a whole line of Bristols which would evolve on logical lines in the next 15 years. All of them are well loved, and deservedly so. They are durable and exclusive, and they have a habit of becoming part of the family.

BODY STYLES: saloon

PRODUCTION: 300

ENGINE & TRANSMISSION: 5130cc, V8cyl
ohv, auto, f/r

POWER: 250bhp @ 4400rpm

MAX SPEED (MPH): 122

0-60MPH (SEC): 9.9

SUSPENSION & BRAKES: coil ifs, tor rear,
discs f&r

LENGTH (IN)/WEIGHT (LB): 199/3585

LAUNCH PRICE: £4848

408 1963-65

Really a 407 Mk 2 (but don't ever say this within the hearing of the owner), the 408 was a logical development of the original Chrysler-engined 407. Visually the way to pick one from the other was by the new four-headlamp nose, which included a rather square front radiator grille, a flatter roof line, and chrome strips along the flanks.

Mechanically there were only development changes, though later types, unofficially described as 408 Mk 2s – just 15 of them – had a very marginally larger Chrysler engine. Automatic transmission was standard, and to the disgruntlement of some there was still no manual option. Whatever their complaints, they could not deny

the Bristol's vigorous performance. One chassis novelty was that electrically-controlled Armstrong Selectaride adjustable dampers were now fitted to the rear suspension.

For some strange reason, the 408 was never as well regarded as the 407 had been, but it is still a great and dignified sporting car.

The 408 had a wider grille and quad headlights.

SPECIFICATION

BODY STYLES: saloon

PRODUCTION: 66/15

ENGINE & TRANSMISSION: 5130cc/5211cc, V8cyl ohv, auto, f/r

POWER: 250bhp @ 4400rpm

MAX SPEED (MPH): 121 (E)

0-60MPH (SEC): not measured

SUSPENSION & BRAKES: coil ifs, tor rear, discs f&r

LENGTH (IN)/WEIGHT (LB): 199/3585

LAUNCH PRICE: £4459

409 1965-67

Amazingly, Bristol soon ousted the 408 in favour of the 409, which was once again only a development of the 408, and therefore of the 407. With new model numbers following each other in such rapid succession, the company ran the risk of being accused of a Detroit "Model Year Change" policy.

SPECIFICATION

BODY STYLES: saloon

PRODUCTION: not known

ENGINE & TRANSMISSION: 5211cc, V8cyl ohv, auto, f/r

POWER: 250bhp @ 4400rpm

MAX SPEED (MPH): 121 (E)

0-60MPH (SEC): not measured

SUSPENSION & BRAKES: coil ifs, tor rear, discs f&r

LENGTH (IN)/WEIGHT (LB): 199/3527

LAUNCH PRICE: £4849

Bristol 409 .

As far as the machinery was concerned there were few innovations, for the 5211cc V8 engine was retained throughout. Bristol claimed a slight weight reduction, due to the use of an alloy-

cased transmission (which had been fitted to 408 Mk 2s as well), though no change to peak output or performance.

Mechanical novelties included moving the engine back in the chassis to improve weight distribution, specifying Girling instead of Dunlop disc brakes, a pre-engaged engine starter, an alternator, and fitting Marles steering. Power-assisted steering, by ZF of Germany, would follow after the first year.

Once again, still an under-estimated car – and one which Bristol were only making in small numbers. By this time, Bristol themselves were reluctant to admit to the very limited rate at which they were building cars.

410 1967-69

More development changes, none of them revolutionary, brought about the 410, which took over from the old 409 in the autumn of 1967. Along the way, too, the UK retail price rose by £824.

Except that the chrome highlighting strips along the flanks were slightly re-shaped, and a new style of 15in road wheel was adopted, the new looked much like the old, for the 114in. chassis and the basic two-door body shell were the same as before.

Once again this was a Bristol with the 250bhp 5.2-litre Chrysler engine, and a matching TorqueFlite transmission, though the gear-change lever and its quadrant had now been positioned atop the transmission tunnel.

Restoration fanatics may also want to know that this was the point at which Bristol adopted acrylic paintwork instead of the previous cellulose. A minor point? Not to concours experts, it isn't.

Another great Bristol – very rare then, even more rare today.

Bristol 410 had more side chrome.

SPECIFICATION	
BODY STYLES: saloon	
PRODUCTION: not known	
ENGINE & TRANSMISSION: 5211 cc, V8cyl ohv, auto, f/r	
POWER: 250bhp @ 4400rpm	
MAX SPEED (MPH): 130	
0-60MPH (SEC): 8.8	
SUSPENSION & BRAKES: coil ifs, tor rear, discs f&r	
LENGTH (IN)/WEIGHT (LB): 199/3527	
LAUNCH PRICE: £5673	

411 1969-76

Yet another re-jig of a well-established design led to the 411 taking over from the 410 at the end of 1969. This time round, though, the same model number would persist for a long period – in fact for seven years, until 1976. Once again Bristol brought in a considerable price increase, to no less than £6997 at launch, but few potential owners complained.

The company had clearly decided that the 407-410 style was so good that it needed little attention for the 411. A careful look at the archives shows that there would be no fewer than five Series, each of which had minor decorative differences from the last, but all types kept the same proportions and two-door saloon packaging. Compared with the 410, for instance, the first 411s had less brightwork on the flanks.

A 1973 411 alongside a 405.

SPECIFICATION

BODY STYLES: saloon

PRODUCTION: 600

ENGINE & TRANSMISSION: 6277cc/6556cc, V8cyl ohv, auto, f/r

POWER: 335bhp @ 5200rpm/264bhp @ 4800rpm

MAX SPEED (MPH): (335bhp) 138

0-60MPH (SEC): (335bhp) 7.0

SUSPENSION & BRAKES: coil ifs, tor rear, discs f&r

LENGTH (IN)/WEIGHT (LB): 193/3726

LAUNCH PRICE: £6997

Series IV 411.

Technically, the big change was that the original 411 was equipped with a larger 6277cc Chrysler engine in place of the previous 5211cc unit. Cubic capacity was further inflated to 6556cc from October 1973.

On the 411 too, a limited-slip differential became standard; on previous models it had been optional. Inside the cabin, the noticeable change was the use of a smaller steering wheel (not the 17-inch wheel of old).

The 411 was considerably faster than previous Bristols, with a top speed approaching 140mph – and the car now felt as if it could give a Ferrari a run for its money on the open road.

Series 2 types (introduced in 1970) featured self-levelling suspension, and Series 3s had a much-changed front end, with a new grille and four 7in diameter headlamps. Series 4 cars benefited from the larger engine (already mentioned), while the final Series 5 (1975), gained cruise control to the transmission along with various new styling details.

This took the car well into the 1970s period. When its successor, the Type 412, appeared, it would finally break the mould. To traditionalists, the mid-period 411 was probably the best of all these Bristols – but all of them were great, hand-built, machines.

412 1975-80

In May 1975, Zagato provided the styling for the first radically new Bristol body since the 404 of 1953. Badged the 412, the car still used the Bristol chassis frame, Chrysler engine and related running gear, but there was a very angular close-coupled two-door four-seater body with rectangular headlamps. Though there was little mechanical novelty, the styling caught the pundits' attention. Originally sold as a convertible, the 412

SPECIFICATION

BODY STYLES: saloon, drophead

PRODUCTION: not known

ENGINE & TRANSMISSION: 6556cc/5898cc, V8cyl ohv, auto, f/r

POWER: not quoted/172bhp @ 4000rpm

MAX SPEED (MPH): 140/ (E) 135

0-60MPH (SEC): 7.4/not measured

SUSPENSION & BRAKES: coil ifs, tor rear, discs f&r

LENGTH (IN)/WEIGHT (LB): 195/3780

LAUNCH PRICE: £14,584

Bristol 412.

featured a massive roll-over bar behind the front seats, providing crash protection and torsional stiffness. Within months the convertible gave way to a "Convertible Saloon" (really a hardtop), with a large electrically-heated glass window. The entire roof section could be removed and replaced by the folding hood.

From 1977, the 412 became the 412 Series 2, with a smaller V8 of 5898cc, this being the latest Chrysler engine to have full and up-to-date exhaust emission features. This car then carried on, selling gently until 1980, when it was replaced by the Beaufighter, which was really a 412 Series 3.

Beaufighter (412 S3)/Beaufort 1980-92

Announced in 1980, and enjoying a twelve year production life, the Beaufighter was the third and final iteration of the Zagato-styled 412 convertible-saloon type of Bristol. Proprietor Anthony Crook was entering his "military aircraft" naming phase at this time, for the car was

SPECIFICATION

BODY STYLES: saloon, drophead

PRODUCTION: not known

ENGINE & TRANSMISSION: 5898cc, V8cyl ohv, auto, f/r

POWER: not quoted

MAX SPEED (MPH): 140

0-60MPH (SEC): 6.7

SUSPENSION & BRAKES: coil ifs, tor rear, drums f&r

LENGTH (IN)/WEIGHT (LB): 195/3850

LAUNCH PRICE: £37,999

The turbocharged Beaufighter convertible.

clearly just a development of the 412.

Except that the nose had an array of four rectangular headlamps instead of the two lamps of 412s, the angular Zagato looks were not changed, and the facility to convert saloon to convertible, or back again, had been replaced by a fixed roof where a roof panel could be tilted or removed completely.

The engine was now equipped with a Rotomaster turbocharging system, which (Bristol said) increased peak power by 30 per cent, though they never revealed what that meant in actual figures.

A little-known derivative was the Beaufort, which kept the same chassis but had no fixed roll-over bar.

603 1976-82

The 603, new in October 1976, was a two-door saloon with fastback styling, totally different from the 412 with which it shared a chassis and Chrysler-derived running gear. It was a more spacious car than the 412, with four circular headlamps in a style rather akin to the earlier 411. The "603" name apparently commemorated the passage of 603 years since Bristol had received its first-ever Royal charter as a city!

SPECIFICATION

BODY STYLES: saloon

PRODUCTION: not known

ENGINE & TRANSMISSION: 5211cc/5898cc, V8cyl ohv, auto, f/r

POWER: not quoted

MAX SPEED (MPH): 120/140 (E)

0-60MPH (SEC): not measured/8.6

SUSPENSION & BRAKES: coil ifs, tor rear, discs f&r

LENGTH (IN)/WEIGHT (LB): 193/3931

LAUNCH PRICE: £19,360/£19,661

Bristol 603.

Mechanically, the innovation was in there being a choice of Chrysler V8s, which, at Bristol, seemed to be getting smaller as the years passed. Engines of 5211cc or 5898cc could be fitted, according to the individual customer's requirements.

The chassis was pure evolutionary Bristol, including the mounting of the spare wheel within the bodywork behind the nearside front wheelarch. The smaller engine was not available for 1978, when the car was given standard air-conditioning and dubbed 603 S2.

Up-to-date features included mechanical cruise control, electrically-adjustable front seats, and self-levelling rear suspension.

This car, like all such Bristols, was for the affluent few. It was trimmed and equipped after the fashion of a latterday gentleman's club, and it was fast, quiet and discreet in everything that it attempted.

Though the production run looks short, this is because it was replaced in 1982 by the Brigand and Britannia models, which were both evolutions of the same fastback style.

BRITANNIA

GT 1957-60

This project was initiated by Acland Geddes and Murray Beecroft in 1957. Like many such small enterprises, the goal was to sell cars in North America; like almost all such projects, too, this aim foundered, as did the company.

With chassis engineering by John Tojeiro, and with Raymond Mays-tuned Ford Zephyr six-cylinder engine and Jaguar four-speed overdrive gearbox, it should certainly have delivered. Independent front suspension was by coil springs and wishbones, with an independent rear end using low-mounted diagonal-pivot swing axles.

Britannia GT.

Cars were to be built at Ashwell, in Hertfordshire, and forecast production was five cars a month. Although Tojeiro became technical director, the factory, as a production unit, never really swung into action.

SPECIFICATION

BODY STYLES: sports coupé

PRODUCTION: 6

ENGINE & TRANSMISSION: 2553cc, 6cyl ohv, 4sp man, o/d, f/r

POWER: 150bhp @ 5000rpm

MAX SPEED (MPH): 125 (E)

0-60MPH (SEC): 9.0 (E)

SUSPENSION & BRAKES: coil ifs, coil irs, discs f&r

LENGTH (IN)/WEIGHT (LB): 156/2184

LAUNCH PRICE: £2400

This was a classic case of how not to run a business, and the Official Receiver stepped in during December 1960.

BUCKLER

Sports 1949-62

Derek Buckler really founded the British kit car industry. Starting from modest premises in Reading, he introduced the well-engineered and carefully-built Mark V space frame chassis (there was actually no MkI – IV series, by the way!), inviting customers to find and fit their own Ford Prefect E93A or E493A-type 1172cc engines, gearboxes, mechanical braking systems, and suspension units. The first cars were available with starkly-equipped two-seater aluminium bodies with cycle-type

A Buckler Mark V doing what Bucklers do.

SPECIFICATION

BODY STYLES: sports car

PRODUCTION: c.400

ENGINE & TRANSMISSION: 1172cc, 4cyl sv, 3sp man, f/r

POWER: 30bhp @ 4000rpm/36bhp @ 4400rpm

MAX SPEED (MPH): 75

0-60MPH (SEC): 21.8

SUSPENSION & BRAKES: beam leaf front (optional leaf irs), leaf rear, drums f&r

LENGTH (IN)/WEIGHT (LB): 120/not quoted

LAUNCH PRICE: c. £450 - £500

wings. They were versatile machines used for trials, rallies, hill climbs, sprints and other events.

Before long, Buckler was also offering a close-ratio three-speed gearbox, divided-axle independent front suspension (by LMB), and other features to improve the existing Buckler chassis. By the mid-1950s a complete kit was available for around £450 (Purchase Tax not being payable on kits).

Mark after Mark evolved during the

1950s, all using the gradually updated space-frame two-seater chassis which would serve Buckler so well. Various open two-seater styles were made available, originally in light alloy, and produced by coachbuilders local to the Reading (later Crowthorne) premises; later shells, particularly the Mistral shell provided by Microplas, were in GRP.

By the end of the 1950s, Buckler sales had all but dried up, though special orders could still be satisfied.

CATERHAM

During the 1960s, Graham Nearn's garage business, Caterham Cars (of Caterham in Surrey) became the biggest retailer of Lotus Sevens, and eventually became the UK's sole distributor. When Lotus tired of making the Seven in the early 1970s, it agreed to sell the rights and all the existing manufacturing facilities to Nearn so that production of the cars could continue.

This change officially took place in June 1973, assembly was speedily moved to Caterham, and from 1974 the first Caterham Super Sevens (the Lotus Seven S3 reborn and re-developed) went on sale. For the next three decades Caterham concentrated on making this Seven more versatile, faster, and better in almost every way, such that the car entered the new century as saleable as it had been in 1974.

Along the way Caterham had moved Seven assembly to a new and more modern building in Dartford, and had once dabbled with making a more modern-looking car, but it was the much-developed ex-Lotus Seven S3 which kept the company afloat all those years. The Nearn family finally sold the Caterham business to a venture capital concern in 2005.

Super Seven 1974 to date

Original Caterham Super Sevens were basically the same as Lotus Super Seven S3s (described below), the first cars being delivered with 126bhp 1558cc "Big Valve" Lotus twin-cam engines. Extra stiffening was built into the chassis, but otherwise the cars were visually and technically the same.

Alternative engines to the Lotus Twin-Cam followed, mainly Ford Cortina and Capri pushrod overhead-valve types, but Vegantune also gained a contract to supply their own breed of twin-cam units. Chassis and running gear changes centred around the rear axle, for when Ford Escort Mk II supplies threatened to dry up, Caterham switched to British Leyland (Morris Marina/Ital) units instead. By 1980, too, Ford Corsair 2000E gearboxes were no longer available, so the Escort (Mk II) Sport

gearbox came to be fitted instead.

This process continued – and still continues – so except for the existing basic tubular chassis and stark two-seater body there was really no such thing as a settled specification for the Caterham. Over the years (and well beyond our period) further development included a revised chassis which allowed a larger cockpit, De Dion suspension (from 1984), and a host of different, non-Ford, engines, including Rover K-Series and 16-valve twin-cam Vauxhall 2-Litre.

All Super Sevens, whether low or high powered, standard or race-car equipped, had magnificent handling and steering, and were guaranteed to bring a smile to any driver who did not mind the minimalist trim and weather protection. Not for nothing was this car sometimes described as "a motorcycle on four

wheels". Production, which had been about four cars a week in the early days, gradually increased, so that Caterham came to outstrip Morgan's build rate.

SPECIFICATION

BODY STYLES: sports car

PRODUCTION: ongoing

ENGINE & TRANSMISSION: 1558cc, 4cyl 2ohc, 4sp man, f/r

POWER: 126bhp @ 6500rpm

MAX SPEED (MPH): 114

0-60MPH (SEC): 6.2

SUSPENSION & BRAKES: coil ifs, coil rear, disc f/drum r

LENGTH (IN)/WEIGHT (LB): 131/1162

LAUNCH PRICE: £2196 (as kit)

NOTE: In 1970s, other Ford engines – 72bhp/1298cc, 84bhp/1599cc, and tuned versions – were also available, along with 130bhp/1598cc Vegantune Twin-Cams.

Caterham Super Seven Twin Cam of 1979.

CHRYSLER

Chrysler of Detroit, which had controlled the Rootes Group since 1967, took the softly-softly approach to marketing change. In 1970 the new Avenger was badged as a Hillman (or as a Sunbeam, or even a Plymouth, in certain overseas markets).

Chrysler also owned Simca of France, and from 1975 unveiled its first true jointly-engineered project, which was badged as a Simca in France and (eventually) as a Chrysler Alpine when manufactured in the UK.

In the meantime, from late 1976 the Avenger was mildly facelifted and re-badged as a Chrysler. Only a year later, the Chrysler Sunbeam (a short-wheelbase hatchback derivative of the Avenger) joined in.

Chrysler-Europe, however, was in almost continuous financial turmoil by this time, and was happy to sell out to Peugeot in 1978. Peugeot maintained the status quo for a full season, then from summer 1979 it abruptly renamed every current car "Talbot", and the European Chrysler identity disappeared completely.

Avenger 1976-79

Introduced in September 1976, the Chrysler Avenger was no more and no less than a mildly facelifted Hillman Avenger. Mechanically there were no important revisions from the 1976 Hillman models, for this was almost entirely a cosmetic update.

As before, there were three body styles – two-door saloon, four-door saloon and five-door estate car. For the Chrysler, the

Chrysler Avenger GL, 1978.

SPECIFICATION

BODY STYLES: saloon, estate

PRODUCTION: 150,413

ENGINE & TRANSMISSION: 1295cc/1598cc, 4cyl ohv, 4sp man, or auto, f/r

POWER: 59bhp @ 5000rpm/69bhp @ 4800rpm/80bhp @ 5400rpm

MAX SPEED (MPH): 90/94/95

0-60MPH (SEC): 17.5/13.7/13.6

SUSPENSION & BRAKES: coil ifs, coil rear, disc f/drum r

LENGTH (IN)/WEIGHT (LB): 163/18789-2013

LAUNCH PRICE: £1755

front end was rounded off, with larger, rectangular headlamps, while at the rear there were horizontal tail lamp clusters.

All cars had a new-style fascia and instrument display, new steering wheel and seat styles, and there were trim packs including De Luxe, Super and GLS and GT. The 1.6-litre 80bhp engine, with a single Zenith-Stromberg carburettor, was only available with the four-door saloon GLS trim pack and the two-door GT. The

GLS also had a vinyl roof covering and Rostyle road wheels.

A 1300 GT was re-introduced briefly in 1977, but all GTs had disappeared by summer 1978.

As before, Avengers were thoroughly practical cars, and some were quite lively too. Starting in the late summer of 1979, already-built but unsold cars were re-badged as Talbots, and by January 1980 that process was complete.

Alpine 1975-79

This new front wheel drive hatchback was a massive joint project between Chrysler-UK and Chrysler-France (which had previously been Simca). Here was a totally new five-door fastback hatchback, which used a modified and updated version of the transverse engine and transmission, as well as the front-suspension installation, from the Simca 1100 family car.

The Alpine is often thought of as

French, but it was British in many engineering details, and British manufacture began in 1976.

The monocoque body shell was crisply styled, with a huge rear hatchback door and the usual flexible layout of rear seat and luggage accommodation. Two versions of the high-revving engine were offered, the 1294cc unit only being available with LS and GL trim. The GLS version (1442cc only) had electric

window lifts and (from 1977) a rear window wipe/wash fitting, plus higher-specification trim and fittings.

Like other British Chryslers of this period, from the late summer of 1979 this car was re-badged as a Talbot. As Chrysler-UK's first hatchback it proved to be very versatile, and it sold well on that basis. Even so, it has never built up any collectors' appeal, and almost all these cars have long since disappeared.

SPECIFICATION

BODY STYLES: hatchback

PRODUCTION: 108,405

ENGINE & TRANSMISSION: 1294cc/1442cc, 4cyl ohv, 4sp man, f/f

POWER: 68bhp @ 5600rpm/85bhp @ 5600rpm

MAX SPEED (MPH): 90/100

0-60MPH (SEC): 16.9/12.9

SUSPENSION & BRAKES: tor ifs, coil irs, disc f/drum r

LENGTH (IN)/WEIGHT (LB): 167/2314

LAUNCH PRICE: £2164

Chrysler Alpine S.

Sunbeam 1977-79

Amazingly, this short-wheelbase three-door hatchback derivative of the Avenger came more than seven years after that car had been introduced. Yet another famous Rootes name, Sunbeam, was revived, not as a marque but as a model line. Intended to fill a marketing gap below the Chrysler Avenger (it was smaller, lighter, and had an extra small-engined option), the Sunbeam was developed in a tearing hurry.

The chassis platform (with the wheelbase shortened by three inches), front and rear suspension, steering, braking and inner panels of the front end were all lifted from the latest Avenger, as were the 1295cc and 1598cc engines and transmissions. The only mechanical novelty was the entry-level Sunbeam 1.0LS and 1.0GL, which featured an enlarged 928cc Hillman Imp

Chrysler Sunbeam LS, 1977.

engine, this time mounted in the front, vertically, and with a 42bhp output. This version of the Sunbeam, in retrospect, was underpowered and rather too slow for modern traffic conditions (thank goodness there was no attempt to link it with an optional automatic transmission). It did not sell at all well, though other Sunbeams were quicker, engine for engine, than the equivalent Avengers.

Much of the fascia, instrumentation and steering wheel detailing was shared with the Avenger and with the Alpine, for these cars were all being styled and product-planned at the same time. The body itself had unique and crisply styled skin lines, featured much more glass than the Avenger and had a large glass lift-up tailgate, while the rear seats could be folded forward to increase the load

area. Like the Avenger, the handling was neat but not sporty, though the 80bhp 1498cc engined car could reach 100mph.

As a Chrysler, this car only had a two-year career which started in July 1977. Like other British Chryslers of this period, from the late summer of 1979 the Sunbeam was re-badged as a Talbot, and no other important technical or visual changes would be made thereafter.

Although the Sunbeam Lotus and Sunbeam 1600Ti – one of them featuring a twin overhead camshaft Lotus engine – were first shown in 1979 wearing a Chrysler badge, by the time they actually went on sale all but the very first cars were badged as Talbot models. For all details, therefore, see the Talbot entry.

SPECIFICATION

BODY STYLES: hatchback

PRODUCTION: 104,547

ENGINE & TRANSMISSION: 928cc, 4cyl ohc/1295cc/1598cc, 4cyl ohv, 4sp man, or auto, f/r

POWER: 42bhp @ 5000rpm/59bhp @ 5000rpm/69bhp @ 4800rpm/80bhp @ 5400rpm

MAX SPEED (MPH): 77/92/95

0-60MPH (SEC): 24.3/14.8/12.9

SUSPENSION & BRAKES: coil ifs, coil rear, disc f/drum r

LENGTH (IN)/WEIGHT (LB): 151/1757-1953

LAUNCH PRICE: £2324

CLAN

Paul Haussauer, founder, design engineer, entrepreneur and manager of this business, had been a development engineer on the Europa and other Lotus models in the 1960s. He thought he could do as good a job on his own, so he searched around for inspiration, and a site.

After settling on the Sunbeam Imp Sport's hardware for his new product, a rear-engined sports coupé called the Clan Crusader, he set up shop in Washington New Town (Nissan would later choose the same location, though on a much larger scale!), not far from Sunderland.

Not only were there some compelling financial and personnel advantages in choosing this site, and in marketing

the Crusader as a partly-assembled (tax free) kit car, but the cars seemed well built and soon built up a demand and a reputation. Unhappily, when new EU legislation imposed VAT on all cars, including semi-assembled ones, demand for the Crusader collapsed, and by the end of 1973 the business had to close down.

No more was heard of the North East-based Clan company, though attempts to restart the project in the Middle East, and even in Northern Ireland, briefly flared up. Haussauer himself dabbled with restarting the project in 1984, this time with Alfa Romeo flat-four engines instead of the Imp Sport power unit, but that, too, died.

Crusader 1971-74

By using all the experience he had gained when working at Lotus in the 1960s, Paul Haussauer developed the Crusader around a GRP (glass-fibre) monocoque, rather like cars such as the Lotus Elite and the Rochdale Olympic of the period.

Although the sharp-edged style of the rear-engined two-seater coupé was his own, the entire running gear and mechanical components were lifted from the contemporary Sunbeam Imp Sport/Stiletto.

The body was a fixed-head two-seater, with recessed but fixed rectangular headlamps, a very sharply detailed nose, and a neat though simply equipped cabin. Under the Crusader's skin, Imp Sport/Stiletto suspension,

steering and brakes were used up front, with the same car's tail-mounted engine (leaning sharply over to the right of the engine bay), four-speed transaxle and coil spring semi-trailing arm independent rear suspension all in the rear.

Like the Ginetta G15, with which there were some similarities in engineering philosophy, the Crusader was small, light and very nimble, yet at an initial price of £1399 for a kit it was expensive (for comparison, the Stiletto donor car cost only £902 at this time). Properly-built Crusaders (the quality depended much on the diligence and competence of the owner who completed the car at home) were comfortable, well-sprung and surprisingly rapid little cars.

Once treated to engine tune-ups (all of which were available from Rootes or Chrysler specialists) they could be formidable little performers.

SPECIFICATION

BODY STYLES: sports coupé

PRODUCTION: 315

ENGINE & TRANSMISSION: 875cc, 4cyl ohc, 4sp man, r/r

POWER: 51bhp @ 6100rpm

MAX SPEED (MPH): 100

0-60MPH (SEC): 12.5

SUSPENSION & BRAKES: coil ifs, coil irs, drums f&r

LENGTH (IN)/WEIGHT (LB): 152/1278

LAUNCH PRICE: £1399

The rear-engined Clan Crusader, based around Hillman Imp Sport mechanicals.

CONNAUGHT

Connaught was a small and perennially under-financed concern, based at Send in Surrey, which made a few charming Lea-Francis engined sports cars before the main protagonists (Rodney Clark and Kenneth McAlpine) got sucked into the motor racing scene.

First with A-Type F2 single-seaters and then, from 1954, with Alta-engined B-Type F1 cars, Connaughts often put up a brave show, but they were rarely powerful enough to beat the might of Ferrari and Maserati. There was one famous exception, however, when Tony Brooks won the Syracuse GP In 1955.

Once the tiny company got involved in motor racing, this was a full-time task, so there was no attempt to replicate the original L2 roadgoing sports car. The lighter and faster L3 model, which supposedly followed, was a rare as a Unicorn's tooth.

Connaught, in any case, fell into financial difficulties in 1957 and had to close its doors. No revival was possible.

L2 1949-51

Connaught's first and, as it transpired, last foray into building a road car was the L2, which was based on the 14hp Lea-Francis. As originally raced in British regional sports car events, the Connaught L2 was built on the Lea-Francis chassis, a rigid affair with box-section side members and a mixture of tubular or channel-section cross members.

Not only was the tunable Lea-Francis engine screwed up to produce no less than 102bhp (a remarkably efficient figure for the late 1940s), but that car's running gear components were also used, including a beam-axle front end with leading quarter-elliptic springs. The brakes were of the hydro-mechanical type.

The body, by Connaught themselves, was built as light as possible, featuring a somewhat TR2-like nose (though it was four years ahead of that seminal design), two cutaway doors and a full-width windscreen. The cockpit had two racing-type bucket seats and few creature comforts.

The entire front end of the body was hinged at the nose, and could be swung upwards and forwards (E-Type-style – again pre-dating a more famous layout by many years) for access to the engine bay.

If the L2 had been more of a success, Connaught would have updated the chassis with a torsion bar independent front suspension, but this never seems to have been done.

Along with the L3 (does any single example remain?), only 27 such road cars were ever made. Today they are real rarities.

SPECIFICATION

BODY STYLES: sports car

PRODUCTION: 27

ENGINE & TRANSMISSION: 1767cc, 4cyl ohv, 4sp man, f/r

POWER: 102bhp @ 6000rpm

MAX SPEED (MPH): 100

0-60MPH (SEC): approx 14.0

SUSPENSION & BRAKES: leaf beam front, leaf rear, drums f&r

LENGTH (IN)/WEIGHT (LB): 147/2464

LAUNCH PRICE: £1350

Connaught L2.

CORONET

This shapely little three-abreast machine, looking more like a sports car than the marginal-motoring roadster it really was, was born from the wreckage of the Powerdrive project (see Powerdrive). It was backed by Blue Star Garages and eventually between 250 and 500 examples were sold. This sales figure, by any standards, made it one of the more successful machines in its particular British sub-class.

Coronet Cars Ltd was set up at Denham in Buckinghamshire, not far from Fairthorpe, though the two were not commercially related. The only product was the slightly redeveloped and re-bodied Powerdrive Roadster,

now powered by Excelsior rather than British Anzani engines. This time, though, extremely smart GRP body shells came from Whitson, whose links with the motor industry would also encompass shells for the Peerless/Warwick sports coupé, and for the 2CV-based Citroen Bijou.

The Coronet looked much smarter with the hood furled and stowed, and according to some judges was the prettiest of such machines, though the use of a noisy motorcycle-type two-stroke engine was always a major handicap.

It was a good effort, though never profitable to its sponsors, and a few of the cars deservedly survived.

Coronet 1957-60

Coronet three-wheeler.

SPECIFICATION

BODY STYLES: drophead

PRODUCTION: between 250 and 500

ENGINE & TRANSMISSION: 328cc, 2cyl ts, 3sp man, r/r

POWER: 18bhp @ 5000rpm

MAX SPEED (MPH): 55 (E)

0-60MPH (SEC): not possible

SUSPENSION & BRAKES: coil ifs, coil irs, drums f&r

LENGTH (IN)/WEIGHT (LB): 0812

LAUNCH PRICE: £450

Another product of the versatile David Gottlieb, the Coronet had the same basic rolling chassis as the Powerdrive (described below), though it was re-engined and provided with a very smart glass-fibre body which almost entitled it to be described as a three-seater sports car. The Coronet was roomy too, for the wheelbase was 95 inches. But like the Powerdrive it was by definition crude, noisy and slow, with the result that it never attracted enough customers. Its price, at £450, also militated against it.

COSTIN

Frank Costin was a gifted aerodynamicist and stress engineer who had already contributed to Marcos chassis engineering, as well as to Vanwall and Lotus aerodynamic styling. His brother Mike was a founding partner of Cosworth. Branching out on his own, Frank Costin conceived the Amigo car which bore his name.

Amigo 1970-71

The exotic-looking Costin Amigo.

Technically advanced, the Amigo featured a wooden monocoque chassis (earlier Marcos road cars had used the same type of construction) topped by a GRP body shaped by Frank Costin's experience in aerodynamics. Long in the wheelbase, slim, with a fixed coupé roof,

SPECIFICATION

BODY STYLES: sports coupé

PRODUCTION: 8

ENGINE & TRANSMISSION: 1975cc, 4cyl ohc, 4sp man, o/d, f/r

POWER: 96bhp @ 5800rpm

MAX SPEED (MPH): 134 (E)

0-60MPH (SEC): not measured

SUSPENSION & BRAKES: coil ifs, Hydro-pneumatic rear, disc f, drum r

LENGTH (IN)/WEIGHT (LB): 163/1568

LAUNCH PRICE: £2781

the Amigo was a two-seater, whose recessed rear window would later be emulated by Jaguar and the XJ-S.

Costin believed in cheating the wind of its ability to generate drag, so features like a flush-mounted windscreen, a minimal front air intake, and a cabin air-intake bulge which doubled as a door hinge cover, were all included. Such was Costin's attention to this coupé shell that in standard tune the 96bhp engine was claimed to deliver a top speed of 134mph.

The Amigo was powered by the overhead-cam Vauxhall Victor FD engine and gearbox. Overdrive was standard. Many chassis components – including the front suspension, steering, brakes and rear axle – were also lifted from the Vauxhall parts bin. One interesting feature was the use of Koni hydro-pneumatic units in the rear suspension, replacing coil springs and

providing self-levelling too.

There were to be two versions – the VS, which would have a standard-tune Vauxhall engine, and the CS, which was to have the same engine tuned considerably by Brian Hart's engine business – and the cars were to be assembled in North Wales.

Sadly, Costin's technical bravery was not matched by his commercial or production abilities. Priced at an astronomical £2781 (at a time when the Jaguar E-Type fixed-head coupé cost only £2465), and with no established pedigree behind it, the Amigo project was almost bound to fail. Even though it looked good, was well-equipped, was fast and handled well, it stood no commercial chance. Although two prototypes had already been built when it was previewed in September 1970, a total of only eight were produced before the enterprise folded.

DAIMLER

By 1945 Daimler, based in Coventry, was one of the most prestigious British car-makers. Originally building German cars under licence, Daimler was independent in the 1900s, then taken over by BSA in 1910. In the 1920s and 1930s a series of magnificent machines ensured Royal Family patronage, and the company produced a range of graceful and dignified middle-class machines. By this time it was also building bus chassis, and had absorbed Lanchester to produce smaller middle-class cars.

After building thousands of scout cars and armoured cars during the war, Daimler started up again with one pre-war type (the DB18), and the enormous DE27 and DE36 saloons.

Under Sir Bernard Docker's chairmanship (with his notorious and extravagant wife, Lady Norah Docker, interfering in all directions), Daimler then thrashed around in search of a post-war theme. Conspicuous consumption, and a series of ludicrously over-the-top Motor Show specials did not help the image, and a "works" motorsport effort was short-lived.

At least the Consort and Conquest series sold well, and made some economic sense, but the Regency and Regina types did not. The 104 was promising, but it wasn't enough to save the Dockers from being sacked.

Daimler then regrouped, introduced the Majestic, the SP250 sports car and the Majestic Major, before selling out to Jaguar, who needed factory space rather than new models. Under Sir William Lyons the business was revived, and Daimler-badged

Jaguars (such as the Mk 2-based 2½ litre, and the 420-based Sovereign) sold very well indeed. The Mk X-based DS420 was a fine weddings, funerals and business limousine that lasted into the 1990s.

By the end of the 1960s new Daimlers were really no more than badge-engineered Jaguars. That situation persisted for the rest of the century, after which the marque went into hibernation for a while, only to be revived a few years later.

Classic Daimlers are well liked – the pure Daimler (as opposed to Jaguar-Daimlers) best of all – and almost every model has survived in small numbers.

A magnificent pre-war Daimler: the low-chassis Double-Six sports.

DB18 1938-50

Introduced in 1938, the DB18 was Daimler's "entry-level" saloon, and it sold in considerable numbers. This was the obvious model to bring back into production in 1945, the announcement of its revival coming in September. As with many other such cars, however, not all pre-war versions were revived, and there was no no sign of the pre-war sports saloon or four-door cabriolet.

Daimler DB18 drophead.

SPECIFICATION

BODY STYLES: saloon, drophead coupé

PRODUCTION: 3365 post-war

ENGINE & TRANSMISSION: 2522 cc, 6cyl ohv, 4sp pre-sel, f/r

POWER: 70bhp @ 4200rpm

MAX SPEED (MPH): 72

0-60MPH (SEC): 28.3

SUSPENSION & BRAKES: coil ifs, leaf rear, drums f&r

LENGTH (IN)/WEIGHT (LB): 180/3472

LAUNCH PRICE: £1183

Instead, the DB18 was available as a smart four-door six-light saloon or as a two-door drophead coupé. Mulliners of Birmingham produced the saloon shell for Daimler (the style dating from 1936), while Tickford produced the more expensive drophead coupé.

Daimler might have considered the DB18 to be an interim post-war model, but they sold no fewer than 3365

examples. re-introducing the marque to the middle-class market.

The chassis was both robust and conventional (though it swept under the line of the rear axle, which limited rebound movement), with coil spring independent front suspension. The Girling braking system was strictly mechanical, with rod actuation, there was automatic chassis lubrication, and a

DWS jacking system was built in.

New in the 1930s, the overhead-valve six-cylinder engine had powered Daimler's military scout cars and was all the more rugged for that experience. As usual at this time, it was backed by Daimler's unique pre-selector gearbox with fluid flywheel, gear changing being effected by depressing the "clutch" pedal), and the rear axle was of the worm type (not spiral-bevel or hypoid).

In later life, the Mulliners saloon body would prove a nightmare for restorers, for there was wood, aluminium and pressed steel in the structure, which were prone to all manner of corrosion or rot. Even so, these were graceful if not fast cars, 60mph being a sensible cruising speed. They still have their followers. The Consort which followed was an evolution of the DB18 theme.

DB18 Special Sports 1948-53

Although Daimler was outwardly a very conventional, slightly stuffy business, it occasionally allowed itself a marketing indulgence: the DB18 Special Sports was one of those cars. Built originally in 1938-39 as the Dolphin drophead coupé, after the war the chassis was treated to a more sinuously shaped Barker four-seater body.

Although some would say that it was too heavy at 3584lb to be a "sports'" machine, it had 85bhp – which was more than any other Daimler of this engine size – and could reach 84mph, a rousing pace for the late 1940s. A 0-60mph time of 23.3 seconds sounds pedestrian today, but was impressive in its day.

The pre-selector transmission was a

Daimler DB18 Special Sports. This car, one of six Hooper-bodied Special Sports built, was ordered by King George VI.

joy, particularly for those who understood all its little quirks – especially that on this model third ratio was arranged to be direct drive, and fourth a definite overdrive. An underslung worm-drive rear axle was retained to the end, this model being the very last to use Dr Lanchester's final drive, which was famed for its silence..

Quite overshadowed by the Barker drophead coupé were the 108 chassis fitted with Hooper coachwork, nearly all of them being in the Empress saloon style. The Empress theme proved to be popular, and would re-appear on later Daimlers with longer wheelbases and more powerful engines.

Under the skin, the rolling chassis and running gear were all evolutions of the DB18, while the Barker body was mainly of seasoned ash, with aluminium panels, except for the wings, which were in steel to provide greater strength. The seating arrangement was quirky – two in the front, with a third seat mounted transversely behind them.

Good leather, a walnut dash and fine carpets all helped justify the high asking price of £2560. Even though sales were slow, they did not flag until the early 1950s, at which point Daimler prepared to introduce the Conquest family and made the chassis of the Special Sports obsolete.

SPECIFICATION

BODY STYLES: drophead coupé, coachbuilts

PRODUCTION: 608

ENGINE & TRANSMISSION: 2522cc, 6cyl ohv, 4sp pre-sel, f/r

POWER: 85bhp @ 4200rpm

MAX SPEED (MPH): 84

0-60MPH (SEC): 23.3

SUSPENSION & BRAKES: coil ifs, leaf rear, drums f&r

LENGTH (IN)/WEIGHT (LB): 180/3584

LAUNCH PRICE: £2560

Consort 1949-53

Like many of its rivals, Daimler needed several post-war years to get an all-new model ready, so they filled the gap by cleverly devising an interim update of a pre-war design instead.

The Consort saloon (there was no drophead coupé, by the way – this market niche being left to the Special Sports) was originally launched in late 1949 as a parallel model to the DB18, but would replace it completely in 1950. In many ways it was no more than a tastefully updated DB18. The front end of the Mulliners coachwork featured part-recessed headlamps and a curved radiator grille but the basic six-light passenger cabin was not changed.

Under the skin, the running gear was much as before, though the wheels were now plain discs with 5in rims, and the braking system was by Girling's currently fashionable hydro-mechanical system (hydraulic, that is, at the front wheels only). The most important modernisation was to the rear axle, which was no longer worm-driven but now had a modern hypoid-bevel drive instead.

The Consort's character was much like that of the ousted DB18, as was the performance, though the more wind-cheating front end allowed the top speed to rise to 78mph. Compared with the DB18's 1945 price, the

SPECIFICATION

BODY STYLES: saloon, coachbuilts

PRODUCTION: 4250

ENGINE & TRANSMISSION: 2522cc, 6cyl ohv, 4sp pre-sel, f/r

POWER: 70bhp @ 4200rpm

MAX SPEED (MPH): 78

0-60MPH (SEC): 26.7

SUSPENSION & BRAKES: coil ifs, leaf rear, drums f&r

LENGTH (IN)/WEIGHT (LB): 180/3360

LAUNCH PRICE: £1977

Daimler Consort had faired-in headlamps.

Consort was now an expensive car, at £1977, though by 1951 the price had dropped to £1624

Like the DB18 the Consort sold well, and until it was superseded by the Conquest the production figure of 4250 examples was a record for a Daimler private car.

DE27 1946-51

When war broke out in 1939 Daimler had a brace of 4-litre and 4.6-litre chassis on the market, but both were technically obsolescent and neither was revived in 1945. Instead, the company developed a related pair of massive new chassis with Girling-type coil spring independent front suspension. One, the DE27, had a wheelbase of 138in, while the other (DE36 Straight Eight) stretched to no less than 147in. Daimler was aiming to attract Royal,

SPECIFICATION

BODY STYLES: saloon, limousine, coachbuilts

PRODUCTION: 255

ENGINE & TRANSMISSION: 4095cc, 6cyl ohv, 4sp pre-sel, f/r

POWER: 110bhp @ 3600rpm

MAX SPEED (MPH): 79

0-60MPH (SEC): 29.0

SUSPENSION & BRAKES: coil ifs, leaf rear, drums f&r

LENGTH (IN)/WEIGHT (LB): 213/5572

LAUNCH PRICE: £1400 (chassis only) + body costs

The six-cylinder DE27 limousine.

aristocratic and big business patronage.

The box-section chassis had a hypoid-bevel rear axle (Daimler's first) and, as expected, a fluid flywheel with pre-selector gearbox, but the engine was new – or new to Daimler private cars. During the war Daimler had built a successful armoured car with a four main bearing 4095cc six. It produced 100bhp in military form and 110bhp in the DE27. Brakes were hydro-mechanical, with Clayton Dewandre servo assistance, but there was none to the steering, so a

chauffeur had to be at peak fitness.

The bodies were large, stately and hand-built, available either as Barker saloons or as limousines. Chassis were also supplied to other coachbuilders, some of them being bodied as ambulances. Very spacious inside, some bodies had seating for eight and were used by private hire companies for many years.

Big, heavy, complex, and with bodies for which parts cannot be found, any surviving DE27 has to be a labour of love for its latter-day owner.

DE36 Straight Eight 1946-53

If you thought the DE27 was big, consider the DE36 Straight Eight, for the wheelbase was 147 inches and the overall length of Daimler's own limousine body was no less than 18ft 6in.

This, the sister car to the DE27, had a longer-wheelbase version of the chassis to accept even larger formal coachwork. It could weigh up to three tonnes, so the new straight-eight engine was absolutely necessary. A total of 205 chassis were bodied in seven years, all of them wearing sumptuous bodies, some for owner-driving, but many for chauffeurs to steer. The British Royal Family bought several.

The easy way to describe this chassis is as "DE27 plus nine inches", and the engine as "DE27 plus two cylinders", the technical relationship being very close. The engines had the same bore, stroke, valve gear and other details. Although the engine produced 150bhp, all of that was needed to produce acceptable

Daimler DE36 had an eight-cylinder engine.

performance; the cars' huge frontal area meant that few achieved even 80mph.

Bodies came from all around the British coachbuilding industry, with Hooper and Freestone & Webb prominent. More than one of the notorious Lady Docker "Motor Show specials" used this chassis. Never, with fuel consumption of 10mpg, a car

for the private individual, the DE36 was a costly indulgence for the rich and notable. Some have survived, to be used, but sparingly, by 21st-century owners.

A "Docker Daimler" by Hooper from 1952. These extravaganzas created a lot of publicity and drew crowds at motor shows.

SPECIFICATION
BODY STYLES: saloon, limousine, landaulette, drophead, coachbuilts
PRODUCTION: 205
ENGINE & TRANSMISSION: 5460cc, 8cyl ohv, 4sp pre-sel, f/r
POWER: 150bhp @ 3600rpm
MAX SPEED (MPH): 83
0-60MPH (SEC): 21.4
SUSPENSION & BRAKES: coil ifs, leaf rear, drums f&r
LENGTH (IN)/WEIGHT (LB): 222/5910
LAUNCH PRICE: £1700 (chassis only)

Regency 1951-54

Daimler's second all-new post-war model (the DE27/DE36 types had been first) came along in 1951. Its box-section chassis frame (with a cruciform centre section) and overhead-valve six-cylinder engine would provide the engineering base for many later Daimler models including the Regina, the 104 and the Majestic ranges. Even the styling (though not the structure or panels themselves) would inspire some of those cars, and the smaller Conquest too.

The 114in chassis frame was swept up

and over the line of the back axle (the old DB18 and Consort chassis was underslung), and featured Girling-type independent front suspension by coil springs and leading arms, and automatic chassis lubrication. Brakes were Girling hydro-mechanical, and steering was cam-and-roller, by Marles.

The engine was a six-cylinder version of the four already seen in the Lanchester LJ200 Fourteen model, sharing the same bore, stroke, valve gear and the same production machinery. Transmission, as ever, was by the well-

known Daimler fluid flywheel/pre-selector combination.

The Regency, though, was never intended to be a series-production model, as the initial price of £2335 confirmed. Barker provided the four-door six-light coachbuilt bodies – Barker actually being a subsidiary operating within the Daimler complex at the Radford factory in Coventry.

Only a year later the saloon was joined by a very smart convertible coupé which looked rather like the Special Sports, though not sharing that body. Hooper also carried forward its razor-edge Empress style, first seen on the DB18, which needed only slight modification to fit. The last cars had an enlarged 3468cc engine.

The first Regency was more of a coat-trailing exercise than a serious long-term model range as Daimler was fully occupied with developing the successful Conquest at the time. It was superseded by the more ambitious "production" Regency II in 1954.

Hooper-bodied versions of the original, though rather rare these days, are still much admired.

Daimler Regency saloon, 1951.

SPECIFICATION

BODY STYLES: saloon, drophead, sports saloon

PRODUCTION TOTAL: 51

ENGINE & TRANSMISSION: 2952cc/3468cc, 6cyl ohv, 4sp pre-sel, f/r

POWER: 90bhp @ 4100rpm/100bhp @ 4400rpm/107bhp @ 4000rpm

MAX SPEED (MPH): 78 (E)/83

0-60MPH (SEC): not measured/19.1

SUSPENSION & BRAKES: coil ifs, leaf rear, drums f&r

LENGTH (IN)/WEIGHT (LB): 191/3808

LAUNCH PRICE: £2335

Regency II 1954-56

Three years after introducing the first Regency, Daimler tried again. Although the latest car was visually similar to the 1951 model, Daimler claimed improvements all round and added larger and more powerful engines, all without increasing the price.

The new Regency's chassis was the same as before – with a 114in wheelbase, Girling-type independent front suspension and automatic chassis lubrication. Fully hydraulic Girling brakes with 12in drums were now fitted on the 4½-litre chassis, though the 3½-litre retained the older hydro-

Regency II Sportsman saloon.

SPECIFICATION

BODY STYLES: saloon, coachbuilts

PRODUCTION: 153/66

ENGINE & TRANSMISSION: 3468cc/4617cc, 6cyl ohv, 4sp pre-sel, f/r

POWER: 107bhp @ 4000rpm/140bhp @ 4400rpm/127bhp @ 3600rpm

MAX SPEED (MPH): (140bhp) 95 (E)

0-60MPH (SEC): not measured

SUSPENSION & BRAKES: coil ifs, leaf rear, drums f&r

LENGTH (IN)/WEIGHT (LB): 196/4312

LAUNCH PRICE: £2325

mechanical system. Both engines were descended from the original Regency six and drove via a fluid flywheel and four-speed pre-selector transmission; on the 4½-litre this transmission had a direct third gear and an overdrive top.

The six-light four-door body style was based on that of the first Regency, though it had a five-inch longer tail and a larger boot. According to Daimler it was also 2.5 inches lower. This was the

standard body, there being two other body options: the razor-edge Hooper Empress saloon and the H J Mulliner Sportsman, which had a four-light body and a wrap-around rear window.

Once again, though, this was a medium-large Daimler with a short career, for Regency II would become the "104" in 1955, a car which looked similar but which had considerably more performance.

Conquest 1953-56

This was one of Daimler's largest early-1950s investments and did much to plunge the company into financial turmoil in the years which followed. The style of the Conquest looked similar to the Regency ,but there was no common engineering, or common panels, as the body was produced by the Pressed Steel Company at Cowley – another first for Daimler.

Although the Conquest was a direct replacement for the Consort, there were no carryover parts, for the Conquest had a new shorter-wheelbase cruciform-based chassis frame, new torsion bar front suspension, and a new short-stroke six-cylinder engine which had some affinity with the original Regency power unit. The Conquest's chassis and body evolved from the export version of the Lanchester Leda/LJ201 model, which had been on the market since 1950-51.

Much of the running gear had the traditional flavour – including the usual fluid flywheel/pre-selector transmission and Girling hydro-mechanical braking. Inside the car there was the customery Daimler combination of polished wood, leather seating and fine carpets. Characteristically for a Daimler,, the Conquest also had quite a lofty, airy cabin with plenty of hat room and only a minimal transmission tunnel hump. If smoothness, comfort and a restrained air

Daimler Conquest.

of quality were your requirements, the Conquest would suit you well.

The handling was good if not outstanding but this Conquest was not a fast car – 75bhp from 2.4 litres, with an iron head and single Zenith carburettor, was no big deal, even in 1953, but there was potential locked away, as the related Century saloon and Roadster model soon made clear. Once the Century came along the following year the original Conquest was speedily overshadowed.

As for the name Conquest, this apparently came about when the sales force realised that its basic price would be £1066. 1066 – Battle of Hastings – Norman Conquest. Sales started well, but drooped in 1956 (a government credit squeeze didn't help), so in spite of

a price reduction the basic Conquest failed to survive the summer.

Rust was the problem with these all-steel bodies, but some well-loved examples are still around to this day.

SPECIFICATION

BODY STYLES: saloon

PRODUCTION: 9620 including Century

ENGINE & TRANSMISSION: 2433cc, 6cyl ohv, 4sp pre-sel, or auto, f/r

POWER: 75bhp @ 4000rpm

MAX SPEED (MPH): 82

0-60MPH (SEC): 24.3

SUSPENSION & BRAKES: tor ifs, leaf rear, drums f&r

LENGTH (IN)/WEIGHT (LB): 177/3136

LAUNCH PRICE: £1511

Conquest Century 1954-58

Within a year of the original Conquest going on sale, Daimler announced the Conquest Century, the "Century" part referring to the power output of the 2.4-litre engine, which had been pushed up from 75bhp to 100bhp with the help of a light-alloy cylinder head, twin SU carburettors, larger valves and a different camshaft profile.

Although that represented a one-third boost in power, much of the engineering of the Conquest itself was carried over unchanged. The brakes were enlarged, and a rev-counter was added to the fascia display, while an

The 100bhp Conquest Century.

extra four inches of rear seat space was created by moving the seats backwards: this change was also made to later examples of the Conquest saloon.

Soon afterwards, in June 1954, Daimler also introduced the Century Drophead Coupé, which had been previewed months earlier and for which the new chassis was treated to a coachbuilt two-door drophead body by Carbodies with a power-operated soft-top. There was no rev-counter in this version of the car. Even though it was attractively priced - £1737 in 1954 – the drophead sold only slowly, and it was abandoned in mid-1955 after 234 had been built.

By mid-1956 the Century was not selling well, and prices had to be reduced by £198. Later that year Borg Warner fully automatic transmission became optional, and from September 1957 it was standardised, the pre-selector box finally being relinquished. Daimler abandoned the medium-size saloon market in 1958. The Conquest is a well-remembered car, especially as brief attempts to race and rally with a works team were, at least, credible.

Cyril Corbishley drove this Conquest Century into 64th place in the 1954 Alpine Rally. Here he is at the Vipiteno control.

SPECIFICATION

BODY STYLES: saloon, drophead coupé

PRODUCTION: see Conquest above

ENGINE & TRANSMISSION: 2433cc, 6cyl ohv, 4sp pre-sel or auto, f/r

POWER: 100bhp @ 4400rpm

MAX SPEED (MPH): 87

0-60MPH (SEC): 16.3

SUSPENSION & BRAKES: tor ifs, leaf rear, drums f&r

LENGTH (IN)/WEIGHT (LB): 177/3080

LAUNCH PRICE: £1661

Century Roadster/Sports DHC 1953-57

Daimler tried hard with the Conquest Roadster, but they could not get their clientele interested in a sports car, for the company had no pedigree to back it. Sports cars, the customers thought, did not have Daimler badges or pre-selector transmissions. Not even a revamp in 1955, when the body was made more civilised, could save the day.

Built on the basis of what would be the Conquest Century chassis – complete with an alloy-headed 100bhp engine – the original Roadster had a two-seater body with detachable side-screens and a wrap-around screen. Carbodies built the bodies around a lower radiator shell, cast-alloy body framing and aluminium panels, Daimler set the price at £1673

The 1953 Daimler Century Roadster.

(when a 2.6-litre Austin-Healey 100 cost £1064), *The Motor* recorded a top speed of 101mph – and the orders simply never came in.

Not even the launch in 1954 of a fixed-head coupé derivative, with wind-up windows, could help (only two or three were made), so in autumn 1955 Daimler tried again. This time the body was thoroughly re-engineered, with a raised waistline, wind-up windows (so the fixed-head work had been worthwhile, after all…), and a third seat mounted sideways behind the two front seats.

That didn't help either, so after only 54 such cars had been produced the three-seater was abandoned in 1957. Interesting but rare today, it is the later, rather than the earlier, variety which has most merit.

Century Sports drophead had wind-up windows.

SPECIFICATION

BODY STYLES: sports car, sports drophead coupé

PRODUCTION: 65/54

ENGINE & TRANSMISSION: 2433cc, 6cyl ohv, 4sp pre-sel, f/r

POWER: 100bhp @ 4600rpm

MAX SPEED (MPH): 101

0-60MPH (SEC): 14.5

SUSPENSION & BRAKES: tor ifs, leaf rear, drums f&r

LENGTH (IN)/WEIGHT (LB): 178/2688

LAUNCH PRICE: £1673

DK400/Regina 1955-60

At the same time as Daimler introduced the Regency II, it also previewed the new DK400 Regina. Though much of what was in the Regina was shared with the Regency II, Regina was a specialised machine, always produced with limousine coachwork. It took over in the market place from the early post-war DE27.

The Regina had a colossally long 130in-wheelbase version of the Regency II chassis and shared its suspension, steering and 4½-litre engine. On this car, though, there was no overdrive transmission

Daimler DK400 limousine.

SPECIFICATION

BODY STYLES: limousine, specials

PRODUCTION: 132

ENGINE & TRANSMISSION: 4617cc, 6cyl ohv, 4sp pre-sel, f/r

POWER: 127bhp @ 3600rpm/167bhp @ 4000rpm

MAX SPEED (MPH): 88 (E)/94

0-60MPH (SEC): not measured/16.3

SUSPENSION & BRAKES: coil ifs, leaf rear, drums f&r

LENGTH (IN)/WEIGHT (LB): 217/4964

LAUNCH PRICE: (Hooper) £6213, (Carbodies) £3958

(fourth ratio in the pre-selector gearbox was direct drive).

The first cars used the familiar semi-razor-edge Hooper limousine style, but from the autumn of 1955 Daimler produced its own derivative of the Regency II, a craftsman-built limousine body shell of composite construction, made by Carbodies of Coventry, which was longer (the larger rear quarter windows gave the game away), higher and bulkier. This one was much cheaper, at £3958.

From this point the Regina name was dropped, though the DK400 title was retained. A year later the Carbodies

exterior style was changed considerably, this time to incorporate a straight-through wing crown line, though the overall size of the cabin (which included 61 inches across the rear seat) was not affected. Some of these cars were later fitted with three occasional seats, and later cars also got a more powerful version of the 4½-litre engine.

Daimler/Carbodies and Hooper built most bodies, but there were all manner of specials. Slow-selling, but very prestigious, this was Daimler's top-of-the-line limo until the DR450 took over for the 1960s.

Fascinating today, but horrifyingly expensive to run and to restore.

104 1955-59

Because Daimler needed to recoup its initial investment in the Regency, it modified it persistently, and from late 1955 it was transformed into the 104. 104? Apparently this was the maximum speed achieved by a prototype.

The entire 104 motor car – body shell, chassis and running gear – was a lineal descendant of the Regency II, retaining the same 114in wheelbase and the same initial choice of 3½-litre or 4½-litre six-cylinder engines. The chassis frame was treated to a more robust cruciform member, and vacuum-servo assistance to the brakes was standard.

Engines were significantly more powerful than before – 137bhp from the 3½-litre and 167bhp from the 4½-litre, both due to using an aluminium cylinder head, though the 4½-litre was only price-listed for the 1956 model year. As ever, a pre-selector transmission was standard, though for the 104 the overall gearing had been raised to provided more relaxed high-speed cruising.

Two versions were provided, the so-called Ladies' Model showing the notorious Lady Docker's influence. All 104s were built, equipped and finished as well as ever (now with power-assisted window lifts), but the list of extra equipment in the Ladies' Model included a travelling rug, a sheepskin rear compartment floor mat, an umbrella, lightweight suitcases, a picnic case and an ice flask, plus a well-equipped vanity case in a

Daimler 104 of 1956 was an improved Regency.

drawer under the fascia. As the brochure proclaimed, "No other production car is equipped with such a galaxy of especially feminine features".

This was the first and only Ladies' Model derivative of any Daimler, or any British car, for that matter, and the first Daimler saloon to record 100mph on test. In October the basic 104 cost £2672, the Ladies' Model £2983 – a £311 premium – and few of the latter were sold.

Daimler reduced all prices in 1956, which meant that 104 motoring then began at £2260. From late 1956, Borg Warner automatic transmission became an optional extra, and by mid-1957 it had been standardised. The 104s was listed alongside the new Majestic for months, but only until dealers had cleared their existing orders.

Do any Ladies' Models still remain complete with all their special kit? If so, they are the rarest and most desirable of all 1950s Daimlers.

SPECIFICATION

BODY STYLES: saloon, specials

PRODUCTION: 459

ENGINE & TRANSMISSION: 3468 cc/4617cc, 6cyl ohv, 4sp pre-sel, or auto, f/r

POWER: 137bhp @ 4400rpm/167bhp @ 4000rpm.

MAX SPEED (MPH): 100/not measured

0-60MPH (SEC): 15.4/not measured

SUSPENSION & BRAKES: coil ifs, leaf rear, drums f&r

LENGTH (IN)/WEIGHT (LB): 196/4144

LAUNCH PRICE: £2672

Majestic 1958-62

Three years on, with the 104 model dying on its feet, Daimler made yet another change to this long-established 114in chassis and six-light saloon body. The result, which would take the range into the 1960s and the era of Jaguar ownership, was the Majestic.

This time around, to envisage the Majestic, think of the 104 but with a larger engine, disc brakes and a smoothed out body. The body style changes made a real difference – along the flanks both door pressings were altered to eliminate

the previous model's impression of a falling wing line, while at the front the radiator and the bonnet line had been dropped by two inches; there were no cooling grilles in the nose, though extra driving lamps remained. Daimler claimed that the rear cabin was five inches wider due to the changes.

Under the skin, the solid box-section chassis, complete with Girling-type independent front suspension, was much as before, though for the first time in many years automatic chassis

lubrication was no longer fitted. The big change, though, was that the familiar overhead-valve six-cylinder engine had grown to 3794cc (the cylinder bore had been increased), and now produced 135bhp (net), 147bhp (gross). It was linked to a Borg Warner three-speed automatic gearbox, and the traditional pre-selector transmission was no longer available.

The Majestic was the first Daimler to be equipped with disc brakes – all round, by Dunlop, with assistance from a Lockheed vacuum servo. The Majestic was soon joined by the V8-engined Majestic Major in October 1959, the facia was re-styled in March 1960, and power-assisted steering was optional from October 1960. The Majestic, however, was the first Daimler model to be culled by Jaguar after the takeover, and the faithful old six-cylinder engine died with it.

The Majestic was the best of the Regency-based six-cylinder cars, no question; the sales figures back this up.

Daimler Majestic, 1958.

SPECIFICATION

BODY STYLES: saloon

PRODUCTION TOTAL: 940

ENGINE & TRANSMISSION: 3794cc, 6cyl ohv, auto, f/r

POWER: 135bhp @ 4400rpm

MAX SPEED (MPH): 101

0-60MPH (SEC): 15.3

SUSPENSION & BRAKES: coil ifs, leaf rear, discs f&r

LENGTH (IN)/WEIGHT (LB): 196/3900

LAUNCH PRICE: £2495

Majestic Major 1960-68

As one pseudo-rapper journalist once said, this really was "Da Big Mutha" – a re-engined hot-rod if ever there was one. Once the Docker management regime had been dismantled, a new technical chief, Edward Turner, was installed, his first priority being to design not one but two brand new engines. The smaller 2½-litre type was first fitted to the SP250 sports car, while the much larger 4½-litre unit went into the Majestic Major.

This, a further developed Majestic, was a wonderful beast, and far too capable for most of the private hire companies who bought it. Road tests showed that it could reach 120mph and

The Majestic Major is identified by the V8 motifs alongside the grille.

SPECIFICATION

BODY STYLES: saloon

PRODUCTION: 1180

ENGINE & TRANSMISSION: 4561cc, V8cyl ohv, auto, f/r

POWER: 220bhp @ 5500rpm

MAX SPEED (MPH): 119

0-60MPH (SEC): 10.3

SUSPENSION & BRAKES: coil ifs, leaf rear, discs f&r

LENGTH (IN)/WEIGHT (LB): 202/4228

LAUNCH PRICE: £2995

feel totally poised in the process.

Visually there was little to distinguish the Major from the Majestic, for the wheelbase, body style, proportions and equipment were all much the same. In the nose, air intakes made a return, carrying a V8 motif. Only the brakes needed upgrading to deal with the extra performance, for the rest of the chassis was still well-balanced. Series production did not begin until late 1960, by which time power-assisted steering was optionally available; it became standard in late 1964.

The V8 engine was really big brother to the SP250 (though the two shared no components), with aluminium cylinder heads and twin SU carburettors. For the Major it produced a storming 220bhp, with 283lb ft of torque at 3200rpm, and drove via a Borg Warner automatic gearbox..

All Majors were saloons, for the ultra-long-wheelbase DR450 (which arrived in 1961) would look after the limousine market. Nor, since Hooper had gone out of business, were there any special-bodied types. Jaguar kept the Major going for eight seasons. A magnificent dinosaur, now very rarely seen.

DR450 Limousine 1961-68

Simply developed — if you were as experienced and resourceful as Daimler had always been – the DR450 Limousine was really a Majestic Major in which the passenger cabin had been gracefully stretched by a massive 24 inches, and a division inserted between front and rear compartments.

The wheelbase was back up to 138 inches (longer, even, than the colossal Straight Eight of the late 1940s), but

supported all the existing running gear of the Majestic Major saloon. Front and rear bodywork were also lifted from the saloon, but the passenger cabin was much larger, with longer rear doors and larger rear quarter windows.

Although the new limousine could carry five or six people in the rear compartment (and often did), it could still cruise at 100mph. The original selling price of £3557 was only about

one third of the Rolls-Royce Phantom V level – for a car which looked good, was much faster, and was very familiar to all Daimler dealers. No wonder Jaguar was happy to keep it until 1968, when the Jaguar Mk X-inspired DS420 took over instead.

A total of 864 were produced in eight years, but few now remain, for rust eventually took a terrible toll of the bodies.

The DR450 limousine was an extended Majestic Major capable of 114mph.

SPECIFICATION
BODY STYLE: limousine
PRODUCTION: 864
ENGINE & TRANSMISSION: 4561 cc, V8cyl ohv, auto, f/r
POWER: 220bhp @ 5500rpm
MAX SPEED (MPH): 114
0-60MPH (SEC): 11.3
SUSPENSION & BRAKES: coil ifs, leaf rear, discs f&r
LENGTH (IN)/WEIGHT (LB): 226/4564
LAUNCH PRICE: £3557

SP250 1959-64

If ever a new car was out of character with the existing brand, Daimler's SP250 was it. Not only had Daimler never before built a popular-priced two-seater, but they had never attempted to produce cars with glass-fibre (GRP) bodywork. If engineer Edward Turner had not produced a magnificent new V8 engine to power it, there would have been no excuse even to exhibit a prototype.

The new car, originally called Dart until Dodge of the USA complained about the use their own trade mark, was built around a 92in-wheelbase chassis and suspension unashamedly copied from that of the Triumph TR3A, as was the gearbox. The 90-degree 2548cc V8 engine, which benefited from its designer's Triumph motorcycle engine experience, was a beautiful, high-revving masterpiece. The engine was backed by a Triumph-like gearbox with

Daimler SP250 sports of 1959 had a glassfibre body.

a stubby centre change (Daimler had not built manual transmissions since the 1920s!), and everything was kept in check by Girling disc brakes on all four wheels. Disc or wire-spoke wheels were both available. Automatic transmission

was optional from early 1961, but overdrive never figured.

The GRP body, built by Daimler itself, was a two-seater with a gawky but interesting style and prominent fins. Wind-up windows were fitted and the fascia also took its layout from the TR3A. A lift-off hardtop was optional from October 1960.

Early cars had bodies which were not stiff enough or refined enough (there was enough flex for doors to fly open at times). B-spec cars from 1961 were more solid, and had an adjustable-length steering column. C-spec cars (from April 1963) had a heater as standard.

A quick car (it could beat 120mph), the SP250 was neither cheap enough (it cost £1395 when a TR3A cost only £991), nor sturdy enough to attract many buyers. Jaguar persevered with it until 1964, then killed it off. Because the bodies and chassis were fairly rot-proof, many have survived, and the quirky looks are now viewed with great affection.

Unmistakable nose of the SP250.

SP250 dash echoed the TR3's.

SPECIFICATION

BODY STYLES: sports car

PRODUCTION: 2650

ENGINE & TRANSMISSION: 2548cc, V8cyl ohv, 4sp man or auto, f/r

POWER: 140bhp @ 5800rpm

MAX SPEED (MPH): 121

0-60MPH (SEC): 10.2

SUSPENSION & BRAKES: coil ifs, leaf rear, discs f&r

LENGTH (IN)/WEIGHT (LB): 161/2090

LAUNCH PRICE: £1395

2½-litre/V8 250 1962-69

This was the first "post-Jaguar" Daimler model to have any Jaguar influence. It was effectively a re-engined Jaguar Mk 2 saloon, but with the SP250-type V8 engine. Mk IIs were normally sold with a twin-cam straight six unit, but Jaguar found to their joy that the wide V8 could also squeeze into the engine bay.

When originally launched in late 1962, the new car featured a Daimler-style fluted radiator shell, but no panel changes. It was called the 2¹/-litre and was available only with Borg Warner automatic transmission. Four-wheel disc

SPECIFICATION

BODY STYLES: saloon

PRODUCTION: 17,620

ENGINE & TRANSMISSION: 2548cc, V8cyl ohv, 4sp man, o/d or auto, f/r

POWER: 140bhp @ 5800rpm

MAX SPEED (MPH): 112

0-60MPH (SEC): 13.8

SUSPENSION & BRAKES: coil ifs, leaf rear, discs f&r

LENGTH (IN)/WEIGHT (LB): 181/3046

LAUNCH PRICE: £1786

Daimler 2¹/₂ Litre saloon of 1963.

brakes were standard, power-assisted steering was optional, and with 140bhp available the car could reach 112mph – competitive with the 2.4-litre Jaguar Mk 2 but not with any other Mk 2s.

Interior trim was up to Jaguar Mk 2 standards and included the use of a split-bench front seat since the automatic transmission gearchange control was on the steering column.

Assembly was always at the Jaguar plant at Allesley, this being the first Daimler to be built on that site. The new car became a Daimler best-seller at once. More changes followed. From February 1967 a Jaguar manual transmission, with or

The 1968 V8 250.

without overdrive, became available, and from August 1967 the car was given styling and equipment changes including reclining front seats, at which point it was renamed V8 250. Assembly continued even after Jaguar's XJ6 had been announced, the last true Daimler-engined Daimler therefore being built during 1969.

Daimler owners might cosset their cars more than Jaguar owners, but even so not a great many of these unit-construction Daimlers survived the dreaded tin-worm.

Sovereign 1966-69

SPECIFICATION

BODY STYLES: saloon

PRODUCTION: 5700

ENGINE & TRANSMISSION: 4235cc, 6cyl 2ohc, 4sp man, o/d or auto, f/r

POWER: 245bhp @ 5400rpm

MAX SPEED (MPH): 123

0-60MPH (SEC): 9.9

SUSPENSION & BRAKES: coil ifs, coil irs, discs f&r

LENGTH (IN)/WEIGHT (LB): 188/3440

LAUNCH PRICE: £2121

Daimler Sovereign of 1967.

By the late 1960s, Jaguar's marketing men were ruthlessly re-shaping the Daimler brand, and were busy badge-engineering Jaguars wherever possible.

The new Daimler Sovereign launched in 1966, therefore, was a re-grilled and re-badged derivative of the Jaguar 420 of the period (described below).

DS420 Limousine 1968-92

Although it took Jaguar seven years to come up with a replacement for the magnificent Daimler DR450 limousine, the result was worth it. The imposing DS420 limousine (there were also a few landaulette versions) was in production – and selling steadily – for no less than 24 years.

Starting from the basis of a lengthened Jaguar 420G platform, underframe and inner panels, along with all that car's chassis and running gear, Jaguar and Daimler devised a large but graceful limousine, for which Motor Panels of Coventry built the steel shell, which incorporated some alloy panels. Accordingly, this was the first-ever monocoque Daimler-badged limousine.

Vanden Plas trimmed, painted and

completed the cars in their North London premises. Such co-operation would not have been possible if Jaguar had not joined hands with BMC, who already owned Vanden Plas, in 1966. At the same time, VDP's work on the DS420 meant that production of the old Austin 4-Litre Limousine was finally discontinued.

Complete with its noble Daimler-style front grille, the new limousine was colossal by any standards – at 227in long, it often weighed up to 5000lb by the time extra equipment had been added. All cars used Jaguar's celebrated 4.2-litre XK twin-cam engine, while automatic transmission, power-assisted steering, four-wheel independent suspension and four-wheel disc brakes were all standard. Most cars had air conditioning, which became a

standard fitment in later years.

Every company which had previously bought real Daimler limousines bought

SPECIFICATION

BODY STYLES: limousine, landaulette, specials

PRODUCTION: 4206

ENGINE & TRANSMISSION: 4235cc, 6cyl 2ohc, auto, f/r

POWER: 245bhp @ 5500rpm

MAX SPEED (MPH): 105 (E)

0-60MPH (SEC): not measured

SUSPENSION & BRAKES: coil ifs, coil irs, discs f&r

LENGTH (IN)/WEIGHT (LB): 226/4706

LAUNCH PRICE: £4424

the new breed of Daimler, and no one was disappointed. Over the years there were no significant styling changes, and precious few mechanical innovations (except to meet the latest safety and emission standards), though GM400 transmission took over from Borg Warner in the 1980s. Once Vanden Plas's factory had closed down, assembly then took place at Jaguar's Allesley plant, where it pottered on until 1992, many years after the 420G donor platform had breathed its last. By any standards, this had become the best-selling Daimler limousine of all time. Quite a number survive.

Daimler DS420 limousine.

Sovereign (XJ6-type) SI & SII 1969-79

If Ford or the Rootes Group had done this, there would have been howls of indignation about badge engineering. In this case, though, the fact that the second-generation Sovereign was no more than a slightly dolled-up Jaguar XJ6 didn't raise too many hackles. In the next decade the Sovereign would faithfully track everything being done to the XJ6, including style and engineering changes. (See the Jaguar XJ6 entry.)

The Sovereign, in fact, was endowed with everything that was good about the XJ6, together with a Daimler front grille and slight differences in trim and equipment. However, the Sovereign was not introduced until a full year after the XJ6 had gone on sale. The customer had to pay more for the

Daimler Sovereign SI was introduced in 1969.

Daimler badge – in October 1969 a 4.2-litre overdrive version cost £2714, compared with £2475 for the equivalent Jaguar.

An amazing number of people thought this premium was worth paying. Were they justified?

Sovereign SII arrived in 1974.

SPECIFICATION

BODY STYLES: saloon

PRODUCTION: 45,413

ENGINE & TRANSMISSION:
2792cc/3442cc/4235cc, 6cyl 2ohc, 4sp man, o/d or auto, f/r

POWER: 140hp @ 5150rpm/160bhp @ 5000rpm/173bhp @ 4750rpm

MAX SPEED (MPH): 117-124

0-60MPH (SEC): 11.0-8.8

SUSPENSION & BRAKES: coil ifs, coil irs, discs f&r

LENGTH (IN)/WEIGHT (LB): 190/3388 - 3708

LAUNCH PRICE: £2356

The Sovereign SII Vanden Plas was the most lavishly equipped model.

Double Six SI & SII 1972-79

SPECIFICATION

BODY STYLES: saloon

PRODUCTION: 5040, SI and SII

ENGINE & TRANSMISSION: 5343cc, V12cyl ohc, auto, f/r

POWER: 265bhp @ 5850rpm/285bhp @ 5850rpm

MAX SPEED (MPH): 146/147

0-60MPH (SEC): 7.4/7.3

SUSPENSION & BRAKES: coil ifs, coil irs, discs f&r

LENGTH (IN)/WEIGHT (LB): 190-195/3881-4116

LAUNCH PRICE: £3849/£4812

Double Six SII.

Double Six SI.

By the early 1970s the Daimler brand had become completely subservient to that of its owner, Jaguar. Accordingly, the V12-engined Double Six, whose name was a revival of a legendary 1920s vintage family of 12-cylinder sleeve-valve Daimlers, was little more than a re-grilled and re-badged version of the desirable and impressively fast Jaguar XJ12. Like that car, the Double Six SI evolved into the SII model at the end of 1973, and the latter was replaced by the subtly restyled SIII in early 1979.

For all technical details, analysis, and notes on production changes, readers should see the Jaguar XJ12/XJ5.3 entries.

Sovereign Coupé/Double Six Coupé 1975-77

Announced prematurely in October 1973, but not available until spring 1975, these two-door cars were the

SPECIFICATION

BODY STYLES: two-door coupé

PRODUCTION : 1598/399

ENGINE & TRANSMISSION: 4235cc, 6cyl 2ohc/5343cc V12cyl ohc, 4sp man, o/d or auto (V12 only auto), f/r

POWER: 173bhp @ 4750rpm/285bhp @ 5750rpm

MAX SPEED (MPH): 124/148

0-60MPH (SEC): 8.8/7.6

SUSPENSION & BRAKES: coil ifs, coil irs, discs f&r

LENGTH (IN)/WEIGHT (LB): 190/3724-3885

LAUNCH PRICE: £5590/£6959

1975 Double Six Coupé.

absolute equivalents of the Jaguar XJ6C and XJ5.3C, with carburetted six-cylinder and fuel-injected V12 cylinder engines respectively. Technically, and visually in all respects except for grille and badging, the Daimlers were the same as the Jaguars.

Like the Jaguars, they sold only slowly, and were dropped in the autumn of 1977.

For all details, see the Jaguar XJ6C/XJ5.3C entries.

Sovereign SIII 1979-87

When the Jaguar XJ6 was facelifted in 1979, with styling advice from Pininfarina, to become the SIII, the equivalent Daimler Sovereign received the same changes and updates, including the use of a five-speed manual gearbox and the 205bhp fuel-injected XK engine.

Daimler Sovereign SIII.

SPECIFICATION

BODY STYLES: saloon

PRODUCTION: 29,354

ENGINE & TRANSMISSION: 4235cc, 6cyl 2ohc, 5sp man, or auto, f/r

POWER: 205bhp @ 5000rpm

MAX SPEED (MPH): 127

0-60MPH (SEC): 10.0

SUSPENSION & BRAKES: coil ifs, coil irs, discs f&r

LENGTH (IN)/WEIGHT (LB): 195/3875

LAUNCH PRICE: £12,983

Except for the grille and badging, and a few minor items of equipment and fittings, in all other details the Daimler was identical with the Jaguar. For all technical details, please see the Jaguar XJ6 Series III entry.

Double Six SIII 1979-92

Like the Sovereign, the Double Six was updated from SII to SIII in 1979 to match the changes being made to the Jaguar XJ12 of the period. In all respects except for grille, badging and a few items of cabin equipment, the Daimler was identical with the Jaguar,

Double Six SIII saloon.

SPECIFICATION

BODY STYLES: saloon

PRODUCTION: 11,568

ENGINE & TRANSMISSION: 5343cc, V12cyl ohc, auto, f/r

POWER: 299bhp @ 5500rpm

MAX SPEED (MPH): 150

0-60MPH (SEC): 8.1

SUSPENSION & BRAKES: coil ifs, coil irs, discs f&r

LENGTH (IN)/WEIGHT (LB): 195/4234

LAUNCH PRICE: £15,689

and carried on in production until 1992, which was long after the six-cylinder cars had been replaced by the late-1980s XJ40 range of models.

For all details, please see the Jaguar XJ12 SIII entry.

DAVRIAN

Structural engineer Adrian Evans's Davrian dream was sparked by his first sight of the Hillman Imp in 1963. After building a special based on the Imp floorpan and running gear in 1965, he formed Davrian Developments in 1967, and began selling similar rear-engined kit cars from premises in Clapham, south-west London.

As with most such enterprises, cars could be supplied as body shell, as a kit comprising shell with suspension and steering gear, or as a complete kit, all being based around the Imp running gear. For really serious customers, Davrian could supply cars with 998cc Rally Imp engines, in which case the top speed was well over 100mph.

Once VAT replaced Purchase Tax and had to be paid on all types of car, whether kit-built or not, Davrian also began selling complete cars, but because prices were higher sales dropped away. Although most cars had Imp-based running gear, the Mk 7 and Mk 8 types allowed various other engines to be fitted, whether in-line or transversely-mounted, these models becoming more and more bespoke and less and less production-line. These cars were usually called Darrians.

Following the rapid decline in sales in the mid-1970s (and with the Imp about to drop out of production), Davrian moved to rural Wales, where production was split between two tiny sites – one in Llwyngroes, the other in Pontyfendigaid. Davrian then carried on a hand-to-mouth existence until finally collapsing into receivership in 1983. The remnants of the project were then sold to Corry Cars of Northern Ireland, though the result – the Corry Cultra – was also a commercial failure. Having lost out with Davrian, Adrian Evans then turned to making glassfibre two-wheel or four-wheel horse-drawn competition vehicles, and never tried to return to the motor-manufacturing business.

Imp 1967-83

Evolved from Evans's very first specials, the Davrian Imp "production" car featured a chassis-less but very shapely two-seater two-door fixed-head coupé body. This, like the Lotus Elite and the Rochdale Olympic sports coupés which had preceded it, was actually a glassfibre monocoque, with a certain amount of steel framing added for reinforcement and to support the entire "chassis" of the rear-engined Hillman Imp/Imp Sport.

Up front, therefore, there was the de-cambered coil spring swing axle suspension of the Imp. Although a few cars had drum brakes, many used the front-wheel discs which found their way on to a number of Hillman Imp race cars. At the rear, the entire Imp engine, transmission and semi trailing arm rear suspension set-up was adopted, this all being supported by a sturdy (not to say crude) steel tubular framework.

Davrians were very simply equipped, but because they used the well-liked Imp chassis and running gear, they were found to have remarkably good roadholding and great traction. They were also so light that they were remarkably fast, and they achieved great things in British club sport, both in circuit racing and to a lesser extent in rallies.

These were individually specified cars, usually built to order, and there was really no such thing as a standard Davrian. Once the non-Imp engine packages began to be used, and the Darrian name was adopted instead, the fog really descended. These days, virtually no one uses Davrians on the road, but a number still pop up in circuit racing, sprints and hill-climbs.

SPECIFICATION

BODY STYLES: sports coupé

PRODUCTION: 200 built by 1972, total production not known

ENGINE & TRANSMISSION: 875cc/998cc, 4cyl ohc, 4sp man, r/r

POWER: 37bhp @ 4800rpm/60bhp @ 6200rpm

MAX SPEED (MPH): (37bhp) 90 (E)

0-60MPH (SEC): (37bhp) 17.0 (E)

SUSPENSION & BRAKES: coil ifs, coil irs, disc f/drum r

LENGTH (IN)/WEIGHT (LB): not quoted/1120

LAUNCH PRICE: £350 for body shell, £1400 as complete kit

Davrian Imp.

DELLOW

Dellow Mk I, II, III and V 1949-57

The Mk V Dellow had coil-spring front supension.

KC Delingpole and R B Lowe of Alvechurch, near Birmingham, owned a small garage business, built themselves a Ford-based trials special, and found a demand for replicas from like-minded customers. In less than ten years they sold almost 500 Dellows.

The basis of the design was a simple tubular chassis frame, but all the main mechanical components were of Ford Ten or Prefect E493A (later Prefect 100E) origin, including engine, three-speed gearbox, back axle, much of the suspension, the transverse leaf springs, and the road wheels.

As a grown-up trials special the body was in light alloy on a tubular framework. Weather protection was very sketchy, though a hood was available to special order. Trials-orientated features included a big 15-gallon fuel tank, and twin spare wheels, both of which were in the extreme tail. The handbrake, mounted outside the body on the right, actuated the front brakes when pushed forward, the rears when pulled back! Footbrake operation was mechanical.

There was really no such thing as a standard Dellow, so some cars had larger Ford Consul engines, some were supercharged, and others had bodywork modifications.

Later Dellows were Mk Vs, where the transverse leaf spring front suspension was discarded in favour of vertical coil springs. A new Mk VI Dellow, announced in 1956, had a full-width glass-fibre body, but does not seem to have gone into production. The last traditional type was built in 1957, and the company then closed down.

Because they had rot-resistant frames and bodies, many of the Dellows built have survived the century and find a new life in the modern-day breed of classic runs and trials.

An early Dellow with transverse-leaf front springing.

SPECIFICATION

BODY STYLES: sports car

PRODUCTION TOTAL: approx 500

ENGINE & TRANSMISSION: 1172cc, 4cyl sv, 3sp man, f/r

POWER: 30bhp @ 4000rpm/37bhp @ 4500rpm

MAX SPEED (MPH): (30bhp) 69

0-60MPH (SEC): (30bhp) 20.3

SUSPENSION & BRAKES: leaf beam front, leaf rear (coil front and rear on late-model cars), drums f&r

LENGTH (IN)/WEIGHT (LB): 136/1344

LAUNCH PRICE: £570

DUTTON

Tim Dutton-Woolley served five years as a toolmaker's apprentice before making himself a two-seater special using his rusty Austin-Healey Sprite. Friends persuaded him to build replicas of the car, so the move into building up Dutton sports cars was almost inevitable.

Although Dutton claimed to be the largest specialist sports car builder in the UK, its products were not that often seen on the roads. Dutton claim to have made 8000 kits of all types, sometimes at the rate of more than 20 kits per week.

First based in Sussex, Dutton was founded in 1969, the company's first product being the spaceframe chassis P1, looking somewhat like the Lotus Seven. Only nine of those

cars were produced, but once the much-revised B-Series/Malaga range appeared sales took off.

Before the end of the 1970s Dutton had moved to larger premises, had evolved the two-seater style yet further into the Phaeton range (mostly with Ford engines from that point), and had also shown the Sierra off-roader. Phaetons evolved into Series 2 and Series 3 during the 1980s, along with an even more retro version known as the Melos, but demand gradually fell away, until the marque folded in 1991. Tim Dutton-Woolley had already sold out, and dropped out of the motoring scene. Attempts to relaunch the brand failed. Were the claimed production figures for real?

P1 1970-71

Dutton's first own-brand machine was the P1 (guess what – this meant Project 1), and was based on the same basic layout, though with totally different engineering, as the contemporary Lotus Seven.

A simple multi-tube frame with coil-spring front suspension was clothed in a neat GRP two-seater body style, with flowing front wings and separate head-

Dutton P1.

SPECIFICATION

BODY STYLES: sports car

PRODUCTION: 9

ENGINE & TRANSMISSION:
948cc/1098cc/1275cc, 4cyl ohv, 4sp man, f/r

POWER: 43bhp @ 5200rpm/56bhp @ 5500rpm/65bhp @ 6000rpm

MAX SPEED (MPH): not measured

0-60MPH (SEC): not measured

SUSPENSION & BRAKES: coil ifs, coil rear, disc f/drum r

LENGTH (IN)/WEIGHT (LB): not quoted

LAUNCH PRICE: £190 as chassis/body kit

lamps, but no doors as the body sides were cut away to allow access to the seats. There was a practical little luggage boot in the body moulding behind the seats.

Dutton never quoted a top speed, which was wise, as the drag coefficient must have been awful.

Motive power was any of the various BMC A-Series engine and gearbox

combinations normally found in the Austin-Healey Sprite or MG Midget, the customer usually providing those from donor cars.

Refinement and creature comforts were non-existent, for this Lotus Seven-like car was all about motoring fun and performance, which Duttons seemed to provide.

B-Series/B-Plus/Malaga 1972-78

With this car, Dutton got into series. First there was the B-Series, of which more than 240 were produced, and when the name became Malaga the total run exceeded 700.

The B-Series was a lineal successor to the P1, with a similar multi-tube chassis frame which used the special-

builder's friend, square-section tubing. An astonishing choice of engines was offered (though the first batch all had 1296cc Triumph Spitfire power). There was Spitfire-type coil spring and wishbone front suspension and until 1973 cars were fitted with a modified version of the Spitfire swing-axle

independent rear suspension.

Styling was similar to the P1, with long, sweeping wings, a letter-box engine air intake and cutaway body sides which meant that doors were unnecessary. There was a sturdy roll hoop behind the cockpit. To match the rectangular front grille, the headlamps mounted above it and to each side were also rectangular in shape.

From 1973 the B became B-Plus, with a beam rear axle (usually Ford Escort or Cortina type), while a number of cars

SPECIFICATION

BODY STYLES: sports car

PRODUCTION: c.700, all types

ENGINE & TRANSMISSION: Ford Kent/BMC A-Series/Triumph Spitfire, to customers choice – 4cyl ohv, 4sp man, f/r. Malaga used 2994cc, V6, ohv).

POWER: 4cyl –43bhp (A-Series) to 88bhp (Ford Cortina GT). V6 –138bhp (Ford Capri)

MAX SPEED (MPH): (with approx 88bhp) 95

0-60MPH (SEC): (with approx 88bhp) 9.4

SUSPENSION & BRAKES: coil ifs, leaf irs (coil beam rear from B-Plus, 1974), disc f/drum r

LENGTH (IN)/WEIGHT (LB): 139/1120lb

LAUNCH PRICE: Dependent on completeness of kit, and engine – but £295 for complete trimmed & wired body/chassis unit. As an example: £724 complete with Ford 1600GT engine.

Dutton B series 1974.

were fitted with Ford Capri-type V6 engines and known as Malagas. Cars with wide beam axles also had wider bodywork and more cockpit space.

The character of the B-Series/Malaga was similar to that of the Lotus and Caterham Sevens – fast, noisy, extro-vert, sporty and fun, but devoid of refinement and creature comforts.

No one seemed to care about these privations, however, and according to Dutton the cars sold just as fast as they could be made. But where are they now?

Phaeton 1978-83

The Phaeton of 1978 was the next derivative of the established B-Plus model, and although it had different styling and even a sturdy front bumper, it still had the same basic layout.

From this point, all Duttons theoretically used Ford Escort or Cortina engines and gearboxes, although if a customer decided otherwise, this was the sort of car that he could modify to personal choice.

The square-tube chassis frame was

SPECIFICATION

BODY STYLES: sports car

PRODUCTION: not known

ENGINE & TRANSMISSION: Wide choice of Ford Escort/Cortina, 4cyl ohv, 4sp man, f/r

POWER: up to 88bhp

MAX SPEED (MPH): not quoted/not measured

0-60MPH (SEC): not quoted/not measured

SUSPENSION & BRAKES: coil ifs, coil; beam rear, disc f/drum r

LENGTH (IN)/WEIGHT (LB): 139/1120

Dutton Phaeton.

revised to make it stiffer (and easier to make), and no matter what engine and transmission were chosen all cars were fitted with Triumph Spitfire/GT6 coil spring independent front suspension, and all of them used Ford-based rear axles, which were properly located.

Similar in character to the B-Plus/Malaga, the Phaeton had a squarer and forward leaning grille, larger and semi-recessed headlamps, and chunkier front wings which hid more of the suspension hardware than before.

The formula seemed to work, for Phaetons were sold in large numbers (or so Dutton claimed) during the 1960s, the model progressing to Series 2 and then Series 3.

ELVA

Frank Nicholls started by building a low-cost sports racing car for his own use, apparently christening it Elva after the French phrase "Elle va" (she goes). From 1958 he set up Elva Engineering Co. Ltd at Bexhill to start selling road-going Courier sports cars. At the same time he also indulged himself with the design and building of budget-price single-seaters, later adding more exotic racing sports cars.

Originally export-only machines, the Couriers did not appear on the UK market, or in the kit form in which many people bought them, until 1960. Demand for Couriers so far exceeded Nicholls's ability to produce them that the business almost had to close down at the end of 1961.

After this, Nicholls sold out to Trojan Ltd of Croydon, which was a more established business, and several more derivatives (some with MGA/MGB and a few with Ford Cortina GT power units) were built. Trojan then became bound up with McLaren, and sold on the rights of the Courier to Ken Sheppard Customised Sports Cars at Shenley, north of London, where the last Courier (and therefore the last Elva) was built in 1968.

Courier 1958-69

All Couriers followed the same basic line, which is to say that they had a simple ladder-type tubular steel chassis frame, which was topped off by a smart but rather crudely-finished GRP sports car body style. Elva always built their own independent front suspension, but the back axle was first a BMC unit or in some cases from Ford.

Couriers had a nose style which resembled the Lotus Elite in some ways, later the MGB in others. Early cars had divided screens, but later cars used MGB screens and curved surrounds. Most were open two-seaters, but later there were fastback coupés (nice), or rather ugly types with Ford Anglia 105E-style reverse-slope rear windows.

Early cars used MGA engines of 1489cc, but as the BMC engine grew at Abingdon, so did the kits, and by 1962 the MGB's 1798cc engine was

Elva Courier had neat lines and usually MGA or MGB engines.

the normal wear: all these engines drove through BMC B-Series gear-boxes. A few cars were fitted with Ford Cortina GT engines and transmissions. Rear suspension became independent when the Mk IV arrived in the mid-1960s.

It is never wise to insist that all Couriers of a particular model used such-and-such components since many of these cars were sold as kits, to which the owners added hardware that perhaps the Courier's designer had not originally contemplated!

Fashionable when new, and cheap, in later years these cars were virtually forgotten and ignored.

Courier Mk III.

Courier Mk IV.

SPECIFICATION

BODY STYLES: sports car, sports coupé

PRODUCTION: approx. 500

ENGINE & TRANSMISSION:
1489cc/1588cc/1622cc/1798cc, + Ford 1498cc, 4cyl ohv, 4sp man, f/r

POWER: 72bhp @ 5000rpm-95bhp @ 5400rpm/78bhp @ 5200rpm

MAX SPEED (MPH): 98-110 (E)

0-60MPH (SEC): 12.7-9.5 (E)

SUSPENSION & BRAKES: coil ifs, coil rear (coil irs on final 1.8-litre cars), disc f/drum r

LENGTH (IN)/WEIGHT (LB): 152/1554

LAUNCH PRICE: £725

The Courier Mk IV GT Coupé was particularly nicely styled.

ENFIELD

Before the Energy Crisis struck in 1973, there was really no incentive to produce super-economy cars. Then, as later, no-one could make electric cars popular if they had to rely on power storage by lead-acid batteries. One-off prototypes were sometimes produced, and companies like Ford (with the Comuta) built project cars to garner publicity, but the results were always the same.

Enfield, an international group of companies with interests in marine engineering and industrial power units, thought they could do better, and backed what they called the Enfield 465 in 1969. The company they supported was owned by Greek shipping tycoon John Goulandris, the car being engineered by ex-Apollo space shot engineer Konstantine

Adraktas. Factory premises were set up at, of all places, Cowes on the Isle of Wight – never known as the centre of automotive excellence – and towards the end of the project structures were produced on Syrus before completion at Cowes.

Enfield Automotive found it impossible to drum up much demand from private customers, but eventually sold 61 of the re-titled Enfield 8000 to the British Electrical Council, which was obviously promoting its product! Private sales, placarded at £2808, were always difficult to achieve – and in the end only 42 such machines were ever delivered.

The last vehicles, we are told, were delivered in 1975/76, though production had been discontinued some time earlier.

8000 1969-76

The electrically-powered Enfield 8000 always fell into the "high hopes" category, though technically it was interesting. In appearance it was a rather stumpy two-seater coupé. Prototypes were fitted with sliding doors (milk-delivery style), though conventional doors were used on production cars. Power came from a massed bank of lead-acid batteries stored up front, ahead of the passengers' feet. The batteries alone weighed a shocking 680lb and could only produce up to 8bhp from motors driving the live rear axle via spur gears. The driving range, naturally, was pitiful, but the batteries could at least be recharged overnight by plugging the car in to the mains.

The structure was based around a chassis frame made of square-section steel tube with coil spring independent front suspension but a live (in more senses than one!) rear axle. This set-up was allied to rack-and-pinion steering from the Hillman Imp and conventional hydraulic braking. The body was mainly made from aluminium panels.

The styling was odd and the interior was spartan in the extreme, but the sliding doors were extremely practical. On the one hand there were two nicely shaped seats of the Microcell sports variety, but then the driver faced a very Plain-Jane dash. A clutch was not needed as the car started when the "go"

Enfield 8000 was battery-powered.

pedal was pressed, so this was a two-pedal machine.

In summary, here was an extremely slow car (30mph was a good cruising speed) which handled remarkably well. Because the car was eerily quiet in motion, and engine braking was non-existent, driving the Enfield was almost an out-of-body experience.

No one (not even the British Electrical Council) seems to have found these cars enjoyable, so most were dumped before the end of the 1980s. A few have survived to this day, all the time proving that naiveté about low emissions and alternative energies lives on.

SPECIFICATION

BODY STYLES: saloon

PRODUCTION: 103

ENGINE & TRANSMISSION: 12-volt lead/acid batteries and electric motor, these attached to driven rear road wheels by spur gears.

POWER: 7-8bhp

MAX SPEED (MPH): 37

0-60MPH (SEC): not possible

SUSPENSION & BRAKES: coil ifs, coils rear, drums f&r

LENGTH (IN)/WEIGHT (LB): 112/2150

LAUNCH PRICE: (1969 prototype) £550, (production car) £2808

FAIRTHORPE

World War Two flying hero Air Vice-Marshall Donald "Pathfinder" Bennett, who had established the legendary Pathfinder force, an élite bombing squadron of the RAF, started post-war life by founding an airline which connected the UK to South America. In 1954, though, he set up Fairthorpe Ltd, and began building glassfibre-bodied cars at Chalfont St Peter, Buckinghamshire. For the first ten years at least, all Fairthorpes had various types of simple chassis frame, bought-in mechanical components, and body shells that Bennett's business produced on the premises. Fairthorpe was never large enough, or foolish enough, to design its own running gear, eventually becoming a regular user of engines from Triumph or Ford UK.

After progressing rapidly via rear-engined Atom to front-engined Atomota, Fairthorpe then launched the Electron and Electron Minor sports cars, which provided the company's bread-and-butter for the next decade.

Factory moves, first to Gerrards Cross and then to Denham, allowed the company to keep on producing new models of limited interest (such as the Electrina, Zeta and Rockette), though most sales continued to be of Triumph-engined Electron Minors. From the late 1960s the Air Vice Marshall stepped back to allow his inventive engineer son, Torix Bennett, to develop new cars, the TX-GT/S/SS family, which featured a technically brave type of independent suspension.

Although Fairthorpe survived several economic storms, including the Energy Crisis of 1973, the last of its rather rough-and-ready machines was produced in 1978. There were no successors, and Torix Bennett's talents were therefore lost to the motor industry.

Atom 1954-57

The original Fairthorpe, the Atom, was an awkwardly-styled two-seater mini-car which Fairthorpe hoped would tap into the tiny market for super-economy cars then dominated by Bond and Reliant. Donald Bennett's company had no previous experience of car-building, and it showed in the crude detailing of this machine.

Based on a central steel backbone frame, the Atom had its air-cooled motorcycle engine in the tail, linked to a three-speed Albion motorcycle gearbox, and final drive was by chain. Initially there was no differential. Fairthorpe listed four engines of ascending fierceness, three from BSA and one (322cc) from British Anzani.

Fairthorpe Atom, 1954.

SPECIFICATION

BODY STYLES: sports coupé

PRODUCTION: 44

ENGINE & TRANSMISSION: 250cc/350cc, 1 cyl ohv, 322cc, 2-cyl rotary valve, 646cc, 2cyl ohv, 3sp man, r/r

POWER: 11/17/15/35bhp

MAX SPEED (MPH): (35bhp) 75

0-60MPH (SEC): not measured

SUSPENSION & BRAKES: coil ifs, coil irs, drums f&r

LENGTH (IN)/WEIGHT (LB): 132/940

LAUNCH PRICE: 250cc – £250.17.0 +tax, 350cc – £274.17.0+tax, 650 – £315.14.0+tax

In a bold move, the big BSA 646cc Golden Flash engine was fitted to one car and propelled it up to a worrying 75mph, accompanied by some fairly excessive vibration. There were also experiments with a diesel engine, but the results were so frightening that it was swiftly removed.

Perhaps surprisingly in such a basic machine, the suspension was independent all round, by coil springs and wishbones at the front, and coil springs and swing axles at the rear, with hydraulic brakes and Ford-sized 5.20 x 13 wheels. The body shell, of glassfibre, had two passenger doors with sliding sidescreens, but the fit and finish in and around the cabin were pretty poor.

Nimble enough – a "sporty bubble" as once described – the Atom was advertised by Fairthorpe as "The Road Holder", and could produce enviable operating economy, but because of its crudeness it never really found the market at which it had been aimed. In three years (learning years, one might say), Fairthorpe sold only 44 of them – then turned to producing the Atomota, which was entirely different.

This was by no means a great car, but every motor manufacturer has had to start somewhere and the less fortunate ones never went any further. One or two Atoms are still in existence.

Atomota 1957-60

Don't be fooled by the similar name to the original Atom, for the Atomota was a completely different Fairthorpe. Firstly it had a front-mounted engine, which at least helped with the cooling problems experienced on the Atom. Secondly it had an entirely different steel chassis (based on

Fairthorpe Atomota was beginning to look more like a car.

SPECIFICATION

BODY STYLES: sports coupé

PRODUCTION: not known

ENGINE & TRANSMISSION: 646cc, 2cyl ohv, 4sp man, f/r

POWER: 35bhp @ 5750rpm

MAX SPEED (MPH): 75

0-60MPH (SEC): not measured

SUSPENSION & BRAKES: coil ifs, coil irs, drums f&r

LENGTH (IN)/WEIGHT (LB): 129/945

LAUNCH PRICE: £640

that of the prototype Electron Minor). The body was a glassfibre fastback coupé, and drive was to the rear wheels. The Atomota was much more expensive than the Atom, which might explain why Fairthorpe could only sell a few of them.

This time the big air-cooled BSA vertical twin-cylinder engine was somehow linked to a Standard 10 synchromesh gearbox, thence via a propeller shaft to a hypoid-bevel final

drive. Front suspension, by coil springs and wishbones, was like that of the Atom, but the coil spring rear suspension now had trailing wishbones.

The body had a sloping tail which effectively made it into a coupé, but it was, like the Atom, a gawky creation, and the Atomota did not sell. Fairthorpe's finances, by this time, were being underpinned by the new Electron family of sports cars, which was probably just as well.

Electron 1956-65

Compared with the first Fairthorpe, the Atom, the new Electron was a positively svelte front-engined two-seater sports car. As first seen in 1956, it joined the growing band of specialists who saw the new lightweight overhead-cam Coventry-Climax FWA engine as a sure way to fame and fortune. Unhappily, though, this engine was expensive (over £300 in 1956), which meant that Fairthorpe had to charge no

Fairthorpe Electron, 1956, had a Coventry-Climax engine.

SPECIFICATION

BODY STYLES: sports car

PRODUCTION: approx 20

ENGINE & TRANSMISSION: 1098cc, 4cyl ohc, 4sp man, f/r

POWER: 84bhp @ 6500rpm/93bhp @ 6900rpm

MAX SPEED (MPH): 110 (E)

0-60MPH (SEC): not measured

SUSPENSION & BRAKES: coil ifs, coil rear, drums f&r

LENGTH (IN)/WEIGHT (LB): 132/1204

LAUNCH PRICE: £1050

less than £1050 for a 1.1-litre engined car. This improved in late 1958 when the car became available as a kit, and hence without Purchase Tax, for £734.

The Electron had basically the same chassis as the gawky front-engined Atomota (which, chronologically, followed the Electron), but because it used the exquisite 71bhp (or even 83bhp) Climax sports car engine, it was an entirely different proposition. The handling was well up to the straight-line performance, which was a good thing as Fairthorpe claimed that

this crudely-built and detailed two-seater could reach 112mph with the more powerful engine. The prototype and press car wore a proprietary Microplas Mistral GRP body. Later Electrons used a shell made in-house and looked more like the car's little brother, the Electron Minor.

Worth preserving? Only for the Coventry-Climax engine (for which the description "hen's teeth" began to apply in later years), and for curiosity value. Only two are known to survive with their original motors.

Electron Minor 1957-73

Here was the car which set Fairthorpe on to the modest but profitable path which it maintained during the 1960s. Based throughout a 15-year career on Standard-Triumph engines and transmissions, the Electron Minor outsold every other Fairthorpe by a huge margin.

Fairthorpe had learned quite a lot, no question, from the high-powered Electron and from the Atomota project, for this was a much more sales-friendly project. The original Minor, described in *The Autocar* in March 1958, was powered by a 38bhp version of the Standard Ten engine, and priced at a reasonable £750.

Using Standard-Triumph running gear (including wheels and tyres) was one way to get prices down, as was the use of live-axle rear suspension. The Standard 10 back axle was well located by two

The Electron Minor underwent various front-end restyles over the years.

bottom "A" brackets and single top links. Overdrive (as available on the equivalent Standard) was optional. First cars even used the long and willowy Standard Ten gear lever and the fascia instruments from that car.

Stubbier than the original Electron, the Minor had a simple but effective chassis and a GRP body shell. On the first cars, at least, there were no bumpers at front or rear. Fit and finish of most components, plus equipment levels, were well below the standard of, say, the contemporary Austin-Healey Sprite, but at a price of £450 in kit form this didn't really matter. On the road, the car's light weight and well-located suspension made it lively and chuckable. It did well for Fairthorpe, although sales slowed with the growing competition from

mass-produced sports cars such as the Sprite/Midget and Triumph Spitfire.

The main body tub remained largely unchanged throughout production, although a bewildering number of new bonnets were fitted over the years. Technical development marched ahead alongside that of the Triumph Spitfire. The 1147cc engine arrived in 1963, the 1296cc unit from 1969, and Spitfire-type front discs appeared in 1966. Options included a hardtop, and coil spring independent rear suspension based on the Triumph Herald set-up was fitted to some later examples. The MkVI (two made) version used a Triumph GT6 chassis. Built-up or kit cars were both available. The arrival of VAT in 1973 effectively killed off a what was by then a very old model.

SPECIFICATION

BODY STYLES: sports car

PRODUCTION: approx 500

ENGINE & TRANSMISSION:
948cc/1147cc/1296cc, 4cyl ohv, 4sp man, o/d, f/r

POWER: 38bhp @ 5000rpm/63bhp @ 5750rpm/75 bhp @ 6000rpm

MAX SPEED (MPH): 75-90 (E)

0-60MPH (SEC): (38bhp) 17.9

SUSPENSION & BRAKES: coil ifs, coil rear (coil irs on some models), drums f&r, disc f/drum r with 1.3-litre engine.

LENGTH (IN)/WEIGHT (LB): 132/1288

LAUNCH PRICE: £720

Electrina 1961-63

To get the flavour of the Electrina, think Electron Minor but with independent rear suspension, a modified nose and a 2+2-seater fastback coupé derivative of the body. Without stretching the wheelbase, which they did not do, Fairthorpe could not provide a big cabin, but at least the Electrina was more pleasing to the eye than the ugly Atomota which it

replaced. Not that it sold any better, for only about 20 Electrinas ever found customers, even at £799.

By this time the Triumph engine was in 48bhp Herald Coupé tune, and Fairthorpe claimed an 85-90mph top speed. Such speeds, by all accounts, sounded very busy in this shell, for little effort had been made to reduce in-cabin sound levels.

As with the Electron Minor, bumpers were not normally fitted, but at least they were available as extras. One also had to pay extra for a heater, which was a normal practice at the time, and even for a spare wheel, which by contrast seems unnecessarily mean.

Not surprisingly, therefore, most customers turned their backs on this Ugly Duckling.

SPECIFICATION

BODY STYLES: saloon

PRODUCTION: approx 20

ENGINE & TRANSMISSION: 948cc, 4cyl ohv, 4sp man, f/r

POWER: 48bhp @ 4500rpm

MAX SPEED (MPH): 85-90 (E)

0-60MPH (SEC): not measured

SUSPENSION & BRAKES: coil ifs, coil irs, drums f&r

LENGTH (IN)/WEIGHT (LB): 147/945

LAUNCH PRICE: £799

Fairthorpe Electrina.

Zeta 1960-65

As the 1950s turned into the 1960s, Fairthorpe played mix-and-match with whatever proprietary engines were available. With a claimed 137bhp in full-house Raymond Mays tune, the hefty Ford Zodiac six-cylinder engine, with six Amal carbs, turned the strengthened and lengthened (by nearly six inches) Electron Minor chassis into a tyre-stripping machine, though at a

SPECIFICATION

BODY STYLES: sports car

PRODUCTION: 5

ENGINE & TRANSMISSION: 2553cc, 6cyl ohv, 4sp man, f/r

POWER: 137bhp @ 5500rpm

MAX SPEED (MPH): 117

0-60MPH (SEC): 7.9

SUSPENSION & BRAKES: coil ifs, coil irs, disc f/drum r

LENGTH (IN)/WEIGHT (LB): 140/1834

LAUNCH PRICE: £1482

Fairthorpe Zeta had a six-cylinder 2.5-litre Ford Zodiac engine.

list price (fully-assembled) of £1482 it never stood a chance. Not even at £868 for a kit did Fairthorpe find it easy to convince the clientele that the quality and prospects were up to the straight-line performance – and even the offer of fitting a standard 85bhp Ford engine didn't help.

Yet they tried, by fitting Triumph TR3

suspension and back axle and using Girling front-wheel disc brakes to keep everything else in check. Really, though, this was a tune-up too far, so Fairthorpe decided to withdraw it after only a short and unsuccessful career. A mere five Zetas are said to have been made, and only three chassis are known to survive.

Rockette 1963-67

More mix-and-match from Fairthorpe, the short-lived Rockette effectively being a Zeta with a Triumph Vitesse 1600 engine and overdrive gearbox instead of the original tuned Ford Zodiac kit, and simpler rear suspension.

Visually the two cars looked much the same (early cars had a central "Cyclops-

eye" extra headlamp, but Fairthorpe soon thought better of that), which is to say that both were two-seater sports cars, with an oval front grille and no bumpers. The Rockette had a stretched Electron Minor chassis with tight-turning Triumph Herald/Vitesse coil spring independent front suspension. There was a beam axle at the rear,

sprung on coils and located as on the Electron Minor, plus Herald rack-and-pinion steering and Girling front-wheel disc brakes.

The Vitesse engine, in standard 70bhp tune, was backed by the close-ratio Vitesse gearbox, and overdrive was a £70 extra. This produced a lively car which could nudge 100mph and sprint up to 80mph in only 26.4 seconds.

Unhappily, Fairthorpe always let itself down with poor quality. *The Autocar* commented in its 1963 test, "It can be hurled into corners with considerable satisfaction and virtually no qualms", but then also pointed out, "the

The Rockette used the Triumph Vitesse 1600cc "six".

SPECIFICATION

BODY STYLES: sports car

PRODUCTION: approx 25

ENGINE & TRANSMISSION: 1596cc, 6cyl ohv, 4sp man, o/d, f/r

POWER: 70bhp @ 5000rpm

MAX SPEED (MPH): 99

0-60MPH (SEC): 13.7

SUSPENSION & BRAKES: coil ifs, coil rear, disc f/drum f&r

LENGTH (IN)/WEIGHT (LB): 147/1576

LAUNCH PRICE: £998 (£625 in kit form)

standard of fit and finish provided by the works was disappointing", which, in those diplomatic days, was serious criticism.

Like the Zeta, no-one really wanted this one, even as a £625 kit car, so Fairthorpe sold only very few in its four years. Hardly worth the effort, really?

TX-GT 1967-73

For the first time since the 1950s, Fairthorpe produced a new chassis – or rather Torix Bennett was allowed to play about with a Triumph GT6 backbone frame, to which he grafted his own ingenious type of transversely crossed link independent rear suspension.

Look at a diagram of the rear suspension and wonder how it can work – but it does, and a lot better than the dodgy Triumph swing axle which had been discarded to make space for it. The GT6 engine up front, was originally of 95bhp but went to

104bhp from late 1968, and with optional overdrive this was certainly a 110mph car.

To GT6 front suspension and steering, Fairthorpe then added a very rakish two-seater fastback coupé body in GRP, which contained such details as a Vauxhall Viva front screen, MGB GT rear window, and headlamps from a Renault 12. Much of the rest of the car was sourced from Triumph, who had a long-term relationship with Fairthorpe. The interior was well-

equipped with instruments, but the interior finish was down to the usual iffy Fairthorpe levels.

Pity about the style, for a real industrial designer could surely have made more of these fastback proportions and detailing. And, at an initial price of £1362 (or, for a kit, £954) that is what this machine needed. The TX-S and SS types were very closely related – and even more expensive. Just one or two survive – and the suspension still works!

SPECIFICATION

BODY STYLES: sports coupé

PRODUCTION: 7

ENGINE & TRANSMISSION: 1998cc, 6cyl ohv, 4sp man, o/d, f/r

POWER: 95bhp/104bhp @ 5300rpm

MAX SPEED (MPH): 111 (E)

0-60MPH (SEC): 9.5 (E)

SUSPENSION & BRAKES: coil ifs, coil irs, disc f/drum r

LENGTH (IN)/WEIGHT (LB): 144/1792

LAUNCH PRICE: (complete) £1362, (Kit) £954

Fairthorpe TX-GT, 1967.

TX-S/TX-SS 1968-76

Evolved still further from the TX-GT, these cars had slightly restyled bodies (the rear quarter window was longer), though the chassis, layout and general proportions were maintained.

Under the skin, Torix Bennett's special

Fairthorpe TX-SS.

SPECIFICATION

BODY STYLES: sports coupé

PRODUCTION: 4 TX-S and 6 TX-SS

ENGINE & TRANSMISSION: 1296cc, 4cyl ohv, 1998cc/2495cc, 6cyl ohv, 4sp man, o/d, f/r

POWER: 75bhp @ 6000rpm/112bhp @ 5300rpm/140bhp @ 6000rpm

MAX SPEED (MPH): not quoted/115 (E)/130 (E)

0-60MPH (SEC): not quoted/8.8 (E)/7.4 (E)

SUSPENSION & BRAKES: coil ifs, coil irs, disc f/drum r

LENGTH (IN)/WEIGHT (LB): 144/1736

LAUNCH PRICE: TX-S (Complete) £1578, (Kit) £1198: TX-SS (Complete) £1683), (Kit) £1286

rear suspension was a feature, but the novelties were up front. On the TX-S the original cars had 112bhp from 1998cc, though a very few late models went down-market with a Spitfire 1296cc four-cylinder engine. The TX-SS gained its title by always using a fuel-injected version of the largest Triumph TR6 engine – but because this was Fairthorpe

they used a special TJ Installation rather than the standard Lucas kit.

The Torix rear end was dropped in 1971 (but available to special order) and was replaced by the upgraded Triumph GT6 Mk2 set up.

As with the TX-GT, too expensive, too out-of-the-ordinary, and not well-enough built to attract many buyers.

TX Tripper 1970-76

Torix Bennett, they say, thought up the Tripper while in hospital recovering from a stomach ulcer – in which case one has to ask what sort of medication he was on at the time.

On to an unmodified Triumph GT6 chassis (or, a few times, a TX-type frame and suspension as described above), Fairthorpe dropped a weird open-topped two-seater buggy style of GRP body which had cutaway door access but no

SPECIFICATION

BODY STYLES: sports car

PRODUCTION: c.20

ENGINE & TRANSMISSION: 1296cc/2498cc, 4cyl/6cyl ohv, 4sp man, f/r

POWER: 75bhp @ 6000rpm/132bhp @ 5450rpm

MAX SPEED (MPH): 85 (E)/112

0-60MPH (SEC): not measured/8.0

SUSPENSION & BRAKES: coil ifs, leaf irs or coil irs, disc f/drum r

LENGTH (IN)/WEIGHT (LB): 146/1120 - 1568

LAUNCH PRICE: £1151/£1412

Fairthorpe TX Tripper.

doors and definitely no weather protection. There was, though, a token roll cage behind the seats which didn't seem to reassure anyone.

The first prototype was powered by a Triumph 1.3-litre four, but fuel-injected Triumph straight-six types were also available. Those who drove the Tripper suggested that some development and

proving would have been an advantage, for it was clear that it had had very little of that.

Amazingly, there were a few sales in the early 1970s – 20 complete cars, they say – but if ever there was a specialist motor car which deserved to die, this was it. When the last Tripper was produced, Fairthorpe finally closed its doors.

FALCON

Essex-based Falcon Shells started trading in 1958, first by selling GRP two-seater shells. They then moved on to providing shells and tubular frames, into which customers were expected to insert their own Ford 100E mechanical components.

Moving gradually up-market, Falcon also supplied multi-tube chassis frames based on Len Terry's engineering skills, and at one time even provided four-seater saloon shells. By the early 1960s their offerings were able to embrace several different engines. All this time, incidentally, the company paid the rent by working in the GRP industry, with items as ambitious as boat hulls and hoppers for farming use.

The 515, introduced in 1963, was really the only Falcon which could be called a complete car, and was really the hobby project of managing director M A E Mosely. Built around the basis of a multi-tubular steel chassis frame, with a very smart fixed-head coupé shell, it could have had a great future if only the costs could have been kept within bounds.

Customers, however, objected to paying £1055 for a complete car (or even £845 for a kit which they had to complete for themselves), so the project died after little more than a year. Falcon therefore withdrew from the automotive market, and never made any attempt to get involved again.

Falcon had built their business on glassfibre bodyshells, like this 1960 Caribbean, for home-built specials.

515 1963-64

Drawing on all their previous experience with both chassis and GRP bodies, Falcon commissioned Tom Rohonyi (a Brazilian stylist) to shape a new coupé for them. Meant to compete in what could loosely be called the MGA market, but with a fixed roof, and at a higher price, the new 515 was a brave attempt that ultimately failed.

The basis of the design was a complex multi-tubular frame, welded up of square-section and round-section steel tubing, where the sills were substantially high to provide beam strength. This frame was bonded to a sleek GRP shell. Progress Chassis, who built the frame, had a very good reputation, so its

Falcon 515, 1963.

integrity was never in doubt.

Front suspension was independent by coil springs and wishbones, and the rear (Ford Cortina) axle was suspended by coil spring/damper units and radius arms. Triumph Herald rack-and-pinion steering, with a Ford front disc/rear drum braking installation, promised competence. Power was by a 1498cc Ford Cortina engine and its related four-speed gearbox; Falcon tuned the engine mildly by fitting twin SU carburettors.

The style was attractive, if derivative, for the front was reminiscent of recent Ferrari road cars. Centre-lock wire wheels were fitted, and this looked like a car which ought to achieve 100mph. No road test was ever published, though, and demand was negligible. Twenty-five cars were reputedly built, but are there are any survivors?

SPECIFICATION

BODY STYLES: sports coupé

PRODUCTION: 25

ENGINE & TRANSMISSION: 1498cc, 4cyl ohv, 4sp man, f/r

POWER: 70bhp @ 4600rpm

MAX SPEED (MPH): 100 (E)

0-60MPH (SEC): not quoted

SUSPENSION & BRAKES: coil ifs, coil rear, disc f/drum r

LENGTH (IN)/WEIGHT (LB): 150/1260

LAUNCH PRICE: £1055 (£845 as kit)

FORD

Founded in the USA in 1903, Ford started building cars in Britain, originally from kits, at Trafford Park, near Manchester, in 1911. The Dagenham plant in Essex was commissioned in 1931, and would be Ford-UK's only private-car assembly plant until 1963. From that point a second assembly plant, at Halewood (on the outskirts of Liverpool), was added.

In the 1930s, Ford grew rapidly by making tens of thousands of sidevalve-engined 8hp and 10hp cars, plus a limited number of V8 machines. After the Second World War, the company for many years had only these two model ranges on sale. Even so, there was so much demand that more expansion followed, using these old models (they were called Anglia/Prefect, and V8 Pilot). The first all-new post-war model range was the Consul/Zephyr family of 1950 – these cars being the first Ford-UK models to use an overhead-valve engine, independent front suspension and unit construction bodywork. Three years later this range was followed by the new-style Anglia/Prefect 100E – but still with sidevalve engines.

Further massive expansion followed with the launch of the all-new Anglia 105E in 1959, the Classic in 1961, the original Cortina in 1962, the Corsair in 1963, and eventually the (Halewood-built) Escort in 1968. Once the Capri had been added to the range, the Ford brand was on its way to gaining UK market leadership; this was achieved in the 1970s, and was never again ceded during the remaining years of the twentieth century.

Along the way Ford became involved in motorsport, which led to niche cars like the GT40 being built, and to specialised meant-for-competition saloons being put on sale like the Lotus-Cortina, Escort Twin-Cam and the Escort Mexico.

Ford's first car designed for Europe was the Model Y, introduced in 1932. It enjoyed great success in Britain.

Anglia E04A 1939-48

The first of Ford-UK's legendary small cars was the 8hp Model Y, built at Dagenham from 1932. The Anglia Model E4A, launched in 1939 immediately after the outbreak of war, was a direct descendant – and the first to carry the name of Anglia. Like the Model Y, it had a simple separate chassis frame, a beam axle with a transverse leaf spring and radius arms at each end, and torque tube transmission. It used a four-cylinder sidevalve engine with thermo-syphon cooling, and a three-speed gearbox. There was no synchromesh on first gear, and the

Ford Anglia EO4A had begun life in 1939.

brakes were mechanically operated. The sit-up-and-beg two-door saloon body style featured separate headlamps and a rather square prow.

There was no heater as standard, the whole car being built rigidly down to a price: the Anglia was of course Britain's cheapest car at the time.

Compared with the 1939 model, the 1945/46 E04A had larger (10in) drum brakes, but no other frills. Cheap and cheerful (but with the larger, Prefect-style, 1172cc engine for some overseas markets, hence the name "Export Anglia"), this car had a hard, bouncy ride, a raucous engine, no concessions to comfort, and was not at all stable in cross-winds, but in the days when few cars were cheap it sold just as fast as Ford could make it.

The successor to this model, launched in 1948, was the Anglia E494A, really the same machine but with some visual and technical changes. Amazingly, both types built up a considerable following in the decades that followed – and mechanical parts are still available.

SPECIFICATION

BODY STYLES: saloon, light commercials

PRODUCTION: 55,807

ENGINE & TRANSMISSION: 933cc/1172cc, S4 sv, 3sp man, f/r

POWER: 23bhp @ 4000rpm/30bhp @ 4000rpm

MAX SPEED (MPH): 57/60 (E)

0-60MPH (SEC): not available

SUSPENSION & BRAKES: leaf beam front, leaf rear, drums f&r

LENGTH (IN)/WEIGHT (LB): 152/1649

LAUNCH PRICE: £293

Anglia E494A 1948-53

Anglia E494A arrived in 1948.

SPECIFICATION

BODY STYLES: saloon, light commercials

PRODUCTION: 108,778

ENGINE & TRANSMISSION: 933cc/1172cc, S4 sv, 3sp man, f/r

POWER: 23bhp @ 4000rpm/30bhp @ 4000rpm

MAX SPEED (MPH): 57/60 (E)

0-60MPH (SEC): not available

SUSPENSION & BRAKES: leaf beam front, leaf rear, drums f&r

LENGTH (IN)/WEIGHT (LB): 152/1649

LAUNCH PRICE: £310

As Ford guru David Burgess-Wise once commented, "Possibly the only time that the motor industry has reintroduced the model-before-last as a new design, the 1949 Anglia was almost identical in appearance to the 1937 [8hp] Model Y…"

This facelifted Anglia, in fact, had a new and more rounded nose, but retained the protruding boot compartment of the E04A (which the 1937 Model Y had never had). Technically identical to the E04A, and therefore obsolete by any other post-war standards, the E494A carried on serenely for another five years – and even then the story was not quite over…

A 1950 Anglia with Martin Walter "Utilecon" body.

Prefect E93A 1938-49

The Ford 10hp Model C saloon of 1934 was an obvious extension of the original 8hp Model Y theme, and was the first car to use the now-legendary sidevalve 1172cc engine. Model C gave way to the longer-wheelbase 7W in 1937, and to the very first E93A Prefect in

SPECIFICATION

BODY STYLES: saloon, light commercials

PRODUCTION: 158,007

ENGINE & TRANSMISSION: 1172cc, S4 sv, 3sp man, f/r

POWER: 30bhp @ 4000rpm

MAX SPEED (MPH): 60

0-60MPH (SEC): not available

SUSPENSION & BRAKES: leaf beam front, leaf rear, drums f&r

LENGTH (IN)/WEIGHT (LB): 156/1754

LAUNCH PRICE: £352

Prefect E93A.

1938. It was this car which Ford revived in 1945.

Although it shared the same basic chassis and running gear as the Anglia, the Prefect of course used the larger 1172cc engine, and had a four-door body shell with a slightly more commodious cabin. Pre-war Prefects were built in some variety, but post-1945 cars were only built as four-door saloons.

Once again, although the engineering and in particular the suspension and roadholding were somewhat prehistoric, this was a very hardy and long-lasting dinosaur which sold, and sold, and sold…

Prefect E493A 1948-53

Announced at the first post-war Earls Court Motor Show (October 1948), the E493E was an up-dated E93A, with almost exactly the same mechanical

The Prefect gained faired-in headlamps and a new grille in 1949.

SPECIFICATION

BODY STYLES: saloon, light commercials

PRODUCTION: 192,229

ENGINE & TRANSMISSION: 1172cc, S4 sv, 3sp man, f/r

POWER: 30bhp @ 4000rpm

MAX SPEED (MPH): 60

0-60MPH (SEC): not available

SUSPENSION & BRAKES: leaf beam front, leaf rear, drums f&r

LENGTH (IN)/WEIGHT (LB): 156/1754

LAUNCH PRICE: £371

specification and the same passenger cabin, which was better equipped than the Anglia's.

The big change, though, was the new front end style, where the headlamps were built into the front wings – this being the first time Ford UK had provided such a feature.

V8 Pilot 1947-51

Ford V8s of one sort or another had been on sale in the UK since 1932, the first Dagenham-built variety being announced in 1935. The chassis faithfully followed Ford-USA's ideas, with transverse leaf springs and beam axles front and rear.

Various derivatives, some built in Europe, followed, so when Ford-UK was ready to launch a "new" post-war V8 in 1947, it could mix-and-match from available tooling and facilities. In fact the Pilot used a lightly-modified version

The V8 Pilot was a tough, heavily-built car.

SPECIFICATION

BODY STYLES: saloon, estate, commercials

PRODUCTION: 22,155

ENGINE & TRANSMISSION: 2525cc/3622cc, V8 sv, 3sp man, f/r

POWER: 65bhp @ 4000rpm/85bhhp @ 3500rpm

MAX SPEED (MPH): (85bhp) 78

0-60MPH (SEC): (85bhp) 20.2

SUSPENSION & BRAKES: beam leaf front, leaf rear, drums f&r

LENGTH (IN)/WEIGHT (LB): 175/3192

LAUNCH PRICE: £748

of the flathead V8-62 of 1936.

Although the V8 was another very basic Ford power unit – cast iron block and heads and side valves – it was unburstable, torquey, and potentially quite tuneable. As ever on Fords of that era, it had a three-speed gearbox (with a steering-column gearchange), hydro-mechanical brakes, and agricultural handling.

A few were built with a 2525cc engine, but almost all had the 85bhp 3622cc V8. This engine was supplied to other

manufacturers, including Allard. In spite of their bulk, Pilots were surprisingly fast cars.

V8 Pilot "woody" shooting brake.

Consul Mk I 1951-56

Ford-UK's first true post-war model finally broke free from the company's old set-in-stone standards. Along with the closely-related six-cylinder Zephyr, the Consul provided a whole series of "firsts" – the first Ford-UK unit-construction car, the first with a short-stroke overhead-valve engine, the first with MacPherson strut independent front suspension, and the first with hydraulic brakes. Add the use of small-diameter (13in) wheels and a smooth, modern body style, and the extent of the revolution becomes obvious.

In 1951 the new Ford Consul made everything else in the car park look very dated.

SPECIFICATION

BODY STYLES: saloon, drophead, estate

PRODUCTION: 231,481

ENGINE & TRANSMISSION: 1508cc, S4 ohv, 3sp man, f/r

POWER: 47bhp @ 4400rpm

MAX SPEED (MPH): 73

0-60MPH (SEC): 27.2

SUSPENSION & BRAKES: coil ifs, leaf rear, drums f&r

LENGTH (IN)/WEIGHT (LB): 166/2436

LAUNCH PRICE: £663

While the Zephyr had a longer wheel-base to fit its longer engine, the Consul shared the same structure and basic body style. Consuls had 1508cc and 47bhp, with a surprisingly precise column change, but were afflicted by bench front seats and very soft front suspension. For the first one to two years they had too-plain fascia/instrument panels, but by 1952 this problem had been solved.

Shrugging off post-war austerity, Ford was also able to offer different versions. A two-door convertible (by Carbodies of Coventry) went on sale in 1953, and an estate car followed from Abbots of Farnham in 1954/55 – though Ford saw this as a conversion rather than a dedicated alternative.

A very successful, very simple machine, the Consul wasn't fast, nor particularly economical, but it was hugely successful. There were would be better and equally successful Consuls in future years.

Zephyr/Zodiac Mk I 1951-56

Big brother to the Consul, the original Zephyr shared the same basic structure, but at the front end the wheelbase was stretched by four inches to accommodate the new six-cylinder engine, which was essentially a Consul unit plus two cylinders. Maybe a long straight-six instead of a V6 would not satisfy today's packaging purists, but it made economic and tooling sense – and proved to be highly tuneable.

Almost everything else about the Zephyr was shared with the Consul – basic layout, passenger cabin, three-speed gearbox, bench front seat, soft McPherson strut suspension and all – though the front-end style was different, and of course there was much more performance. Pundits found it fashionable to complain about poor traction, citing a lack of weight over the

Ford Zephyr photographed in 1952 beside the world's first jet airliner, the De Havilland Comet.

The Zodiac sported two-tone paint, whitewall tyres and spot/fog lamps.

SPECIFICATION

BODY STYLES: saloon, drophead, estate

PRODUCTION: 175,311 produced, of which 22,634 Zodiacs

ENGINE & TRANSMISSION: 2262cc, S6 ohv, 3sp man, o/d, f/r

POWER: 68bhp @ 4000rpm

MAX SPEED (MPH): 80

0-60MPH (SEC): 20.2

SUSPENSION & BRAKES: coil ifs, leaf rear, drums f&r

LENGTH (IN)/WEIGHT (LB): 172/2602

LAUNCH PRICE: £842

rear axle, but better-spec tyres helped enormously, and since the cars soon built up a race and rally record Ford-UK was not at all worried.

As with the Consul, Ford marketed a convertible from 1953 (the soft-top had electro-hydraulic operation up to the "de Ville" position), and there were some estate car conversions from Abbot in later years.

The Zodiac, a jazzed-up and better equipped Zephyr, came on the scene in 1953/54 (and, incidentally, pre-dated the Vauxhall Cresta, which aped the concept). All the bells and whistles included two-tone paintwork, exterior rear view mirrors, whitewall tyres, extra driving lamps, leather upholstery, a heater as standard, and a radio as a factory-installed option. There was no Zodiac convertible option – that would come on the Mk II.

This range was a great commercial success; the Mk II which followed in 1956 would go on to do even better.

The two-door Zephyr convertible had a power hood.

Like the Pilot, the Zephyr was a tough car. Here Sidney Allard hurls his wrecked example through the driving tests at Hastings in the 1955 RAC Rally.

Popular 103E 1953-59

If they could milk a proven formula, Ford believed in keeping it going. Accordingly, when the all-new Anglia 100E arrived in October 1953, the ancient Anglia E494A was stripped out, making it even cheaper to manufacture and sell, and became the Popular.

Mechanically, the "new" Popular was exactly the same as the "old" Anglia E494A with a 30bhp 1172cc engine

SPECIFICATION

BODY STYLES: saloon

PRODUCTION TOTAL: 155,340 produced

ENGINE & TRANSMISSION: 1172cc, S4 sv, 3sp man, f/r

POWER: 30bhp @ 4000rpm

MAX SPEED (MPH): 60

0-60MPH (SEC): not available

SUSPENSION & BRAKES: beam leaf front, leaf rear, drums f&r

LENGTH (IN)/WEIGHT (LB): 152/1624

LAUNCH PRICE: £391

Last of the "sit-up-and-beg" Fords was the Popular, which was made until 1959.

and a three-speed gearbox. Even so, it had a plastic-coated felt floor covering, a single wiper, silver-painted bumpers, smaller headlamps, a brutally plain painted dashboard, no parcel shelf, no interior light and no ashtrays.

Basic motoring? For sure, but at £391 Ford could, and did, advertise it as Britain's cheapest car. It sold so well that Ford had to move assembly from

Dagenham to a Briggs factory, also in Dagenham, from summer 1955, and the last cars of all were not produced until 1959. Every other British car maker would no doubt be jealous of the sales figures.

Some of these cars have been preserved – rather like old Labradors, people can pat them with affection as they get older.

Anglia/Prefect 100E 1953-59

Even eight years after the end of World War Two, the 100E range was only Ford's second all-new range of private cars. Except for the famous names and the use of an 1172cc engine there were no links with the past – for even the engine itself was new.

Though more Anglicised than the still-modern Consul/Zephyr series, these machines followed the same basic layout, with rather boxy unit-construction bodies, MacPherson strut independent front suspension, a three-speed gearbox, and hydraulic braking. All that was novel enough, but these were also the first Anglia/Prefect cars with 13in road wheels and conventional half-elliptic leaf spring rear suspension.

The 1172cc engine shared the same bore and stroke as the old unit (tooling

The new generation: the Anglia 100E of 1954 . But it still had a sidevalve engine.

considerations had much to do with this), but was totally new. It still had side valves, but now with pump (not thermo-syphon) cooling, and produced 36bhp instead of 30bhp.

While the basic body shell and cabin dimensions were the same for both types, Anglias had two doors, while Prefects

had four doors and subtly better trim and fittings.

Over the years the range expanded. Two-door estate cars (Escort and Squire) arrived in 1955, and Ford unwisely offered Newtondrive two-pedal control in 1957 and 1958, but this was a complete failure. Fascia panels were re-styled from 1955, De Luxe versions with more trim appeared at the same time, while both cars got enlarged rear windows and (Anglia only) a new grille in October 1957.

Here was nother major commercial success, helped by the Anglia's performance in racing and rallying. Need one say that when the range was replaced by yet another Anglia (the 105E) a Popular version of the 100E persisted for a while?

SPECIFICATION

BODY STYLES: saloon, light commercials

PRODUCTION: 601,496, including Prefect

ENGINE & TRANSMISSION: 1172cc, S4 sv, 3sp man or semi-auto, f/r

POWER: 36bhp @ 4500rpm

MAX SPEED (MPH): 70

0-60MPH (SEC): 29.4

SUSPENSION & BRAKES: coil ifs, leaf rear, drums f&r

LENGTH (IN)/WEIGHT (LB): 150/1708

LAUNCH PRICE: £571

Anglia De Luxe, 1957, with new grille.

Escort/Squire Estate 1956-61

The original Ford Escort was not a saloon but the Anglia 100E estate car. The Escort was the less lavishly equipped version. The more up-market model, trimmed and equipped like the contemporary Prefect 100E, was badged Squire, and initially suffered from having wooden rubbing strakes along the flanks, though these were withdrawn amid customer scorn in October 1957.

These estate cars outlived the saloons, for as one combined model, under the Escort name, they were built until 1961.

Ford Squire had Prefect grille and wood strakes.

The Escort was the budget version of the estate.

Popular 100E 1959-62

When the sidevalve Anglia 100E was replaced by the all-new overhead-valve Anglia 105E at the end of 1959, the old car was kept going by renaming it, slightly downgrading the spec, reducing the price, and calling it the Popular. This trick had worked in 1953, and it would work again.

The Popular 100E was little more

Ford Popular 100E replaced the old upright model in 1959.

than a re-badged Anglia 100E, and once again it was to be Britain's cheapest real four-wheeler car for some time. A week earlier the Anglia 100E had cost £539, then the Anglia 105E arrived, at £589. The Popular 100E was only £494.

Recognition ponts were stacked circular rear lights and a slightly stripped-out cabin with fixed quarter-lights and no ashtrays, sun visors or interior light. To ease the austerity there was a De Luxe for £515, in which most of those fixtures had been reinstated.

Consul Mk II 1956-62

With the new Consul/Zephyr/Zodiac range of 1956, Ford-UK began its march towards larger cars, which would eventually leave a big gap down to the Anglia/Prefect range. Like the Mk I models, the Mk II types shared the same basic structure, cabin dimensions and suspension/steering, the

Consul being the one with the four-cylinder engine and the shorter wheelbase.

Still influenced by Ford-USA styling trends, the new cars had a sharper profile, and were wider than before. Built on an all-new unit-construction monocoque, the Consul Mk II had a four-inch longer

wheelbase than the Mk I, and was eight inches longer overall. Because the new car was also considerably heavier, by nearly 100lb, Ford enlarged the engine to 1703cc, with 59bhp.

This time around, the Consul became a complete family in the first few months, for there was also a Carbodies-built convertible and a five-door Abbot estate car.

Development changes over time included a De Luxe model from October 1957, a lower-roofline facelift from February 1959, which also included cosmetic changes inside and out, and finally the option of front-wheel disc brakes from September 1960. Front discs

Mark II Consul, 1956, was a bigger car than its predecessor.

actually became standard in May 1961, and (with Ford's own approval) dealers retro-fitted disc brake kits to many older cars.

All in all, and because it was a better balanced and better thought-out car than the original, this was a very successful machine. Structural rust has put paid to all but a few.

Consul Mk II Convertible.

SPECIFICATION

BODY STYLES: saloon, drophead, estate

PRODUCTION: see Zephyr/Zodiac, below

ENGINE & TRANSMISSION: 1703cc, S4 ohv, 3sp man, o/d, f/r

POWER: 59bhp @ 4400rpm

MAX SPEED (MPH): 80

0-60MPH (SEC): 23.2

SUSPENSION & BRAKES: coil ifs, leaf rear, drums f&r (later disc f/drum r)

LENGTH (IN)/WEIGHT (LB): 172/2520

LAUNCH PRICE: £781

Zephyr/Zodiac MK II 1956-62

Along with the Consul Mk II, the Zephyr/Zodiac models were completely revamped in early 1956. Sharing the same passenger cabin as the Consul, the new six-cylinder cars had a three-inch longer wheelbase than the Mk I, and the engine had been increased to 2553cc, producing 85bhp. This was a remarkable unit, capable of being tuned to twice that output. There was the usual three-speed column-shift gearbox, with

SPECIFICATION

BODY STYLES: saloon, drophead, estate, (export) commercials

PRODUCTION TOTAL: 682,400, all Consul/Zephyr/Zodiac II produced

ENGINE & TRANSMISSION: 2553cc, S6 ohv, 3sp man, o/d or auto, f/r

POWER: 85bhp @ 4400rpm

MAX SPEED (MPH): 88

0-60MPH (SEC): 17.1

SUSPENSION & BRAKES: coil ifs, leaf rear, drums f&r (later disc f, drum r)

LENGTH (IN)/WEIGHT (LB): 179/2688

LAUNCH PRICE: £871

Ford Zephyr Mk II, 1956.

optional overdrive or (from late 1956) a Borg Warner automatic 'box.

The Zephyr convertible arrived soon after launch, and within a year a Zodiac convertible. Naturally there was an Abbot estate car conversion too.

Changes mirrored those made to the Consul Mk II: there were trim improvements in late 1957 (a new Zephyr grille replacing the original egg-crate variety), the low-line roof facelift from early 1959, and servoed front disc brakes became optional from September 1960

and standard from May 1961.

Socially these might not have been the classiest mid-size cars on the block, but they were much the best selling, for they almost completely obliterated what BMC (Austin and Wolseley) and, to a lesser extent, Vauxhall, had on sale. Once drivers learned how to deal with the sometimes dodgy traction (Ford always penny-pinched on tyres at this stage), a Zephyr was a fast way of going anywhere. And how do we know? The police bought them in thousands.

Zephyr estate car, bodied by Abbot.

Zodiac "low-line".

Zodiac convertible.

Zephyr convertible..

Zephyr 4 Mk III 1962-66

In a deliberate marketing move, Ford made the third-generation Zephyrs and Zodiacs even larger than the Mk IIs had been, and even more transatlantic in their styling. The Consul name was dropped, the entry-level type now being described as a Zephyr 4.

The wheelbase had stretched yet again – at 107in it was seven inches longer than the very first Consul of 1951 – and for the first time it was shared with the six-cylinder-engined cars. The cabin was even more spacious than before, and the weight had crept up by another 55lb. The basic chassis layout was retained, as

Ford Zephyr 4 Mk III arrived in 1962.

SPECIFICATION

BODY STYLES: saloon, estate

PRODUCTION: 106,810

ENGINE & TRANSMISSION: 1703cc, S4 ohv, 4sp man, o/d or auto, f/r

POWER: 68bhp @ 4800rpm

MAX SPEED (MPH): 84

0-60MPH (SEC): 19.6

SUSPENSION & BRAKES: coil ifs, leaf rear, disc f/drum r

LENGTH (IN)/WEIGHT (LB): 180/2576

LAUNCH PRICE: £847

was the 1703cc engine, though now it produced 68bhp. Front wheel discs, servo-assisted, were standard.

The four-speed all-synchro manual gearbox was brand new (and shared with the parallel Zephyr 6/Zodiac Mk IIIs), but was still lumbered with a column shift. As on the last of the Mk IIs, Borg Warner overdrive or a Borg Warner automatic gearbox were both optional.

Saloons and estate cars (from October 1962) were both on offer, though there was no convertible derivative. There was

one significant improvement, in the form of a more spacious rear seat package from late 1962 (including a wider rear track axle), and upgrading to Zephyr 6 trim standards. A floor gear-change was optional from late 1963. The overdrive option disappeared from summer 1965.

A best seller in its class, this was not a car for enthusiasts, but it was great for fleets as part of the carefully graded Ford line-up of models. Handling was soft, and character was distinctly lacking.

Zephyr 6/Zodiac Mk III 1962-66

The six-cylinder versions of the Mk III were at once more characterful and more appealing than the Zephyr 4 (ex-Consul) derivative. Although these cars shared their wheelbase and basic body shell with the Zephyr 4, they had distinctly different noses – the Zodiac's having a prominent prow and four headlamps – and different passenger cabins.

The Zephyr 6 had the same four-light "greenhouse" as the Zephyr 4, while the Zodiac had a unique "greenhouse" with a different rear cabin profile and a rear quarter window behind that. A five-door estate car derivative was available on both types from late 1962 – all of them (including the Zephyr 4 version) using Zodiac rear doors and having lift-up glassfibre tailgates.

As on the Zephyr 4, the suspension and running gear were an evolution of Mk II types, though the 2553cc engine's output was up again, to 98bhp (Zephyr 6) and 109bhp (Zodiac). There was also the new four-speed all-synchromesh

Zephyr 6 Mk III had a full-width grille.

gearbox with optional overdrive, or optional automatic transmission. The Zodiac could just beat 100mph, making it the first Ford car to breach that barrier.

Development changes included the rear seat packaging changes of late 1962 (see Zephyr 4, above) and enhanced interior trim with fake wood veneer fascias from late 1963, when a floor gearchange also became optional.

In January 1965 Ford announced the Zodiac Executive, the first of its "E" cars – there would be several more in future years – which added radio, auxiliary lamps, seat belts, driving mirrors, and new trim and colour schemes.

Handling and performance? Not at all bad, though the suspension was still too soft. Zephyr 6s starred in TV's *Z Cars*, and works Mk IIIs raced and rallied with brief honour in 1962. These were glitzy motors, certainly, but they have been well liked by the classic fans and are still to be seen on the nostalgia circuit.

SPECIFICATION

BODY STYLES: saloon, estate

PRODUCTION: 185,089

ENGINE & TRANSMISSION: 2553cc, S6 ohv, 4sp man, o/d or auto, f/r

POWER: 98bhp @ 4800rpm/109bhp @4800rpm

MAX SPEED (MPH): 95 (E)/ 101

0-60MPH (SEC): not measured/13.4

SUSPENSION & BRAKES: coil ifs, leaf rear, disc f/drum r

LENGTH (IN)/WEIGHT (LB): 180/2744-2800

LAUNCH PRICE: £929/£1071

Mk III Zodiac sported twin headlamps.

Zodiac estate car.

A Zodiac mixes it with a Mercedes and a Mini in a saloon car race in the 1960s.

Anglia 105E/Super 123E 1959-67/1962-67

This was one of Ford's most important new models of the period, principally because it was the first to use the brand new (and highly over-square) small four-cylinder overhead-valve engine. Once again this was a massive investment, involving not only the new engine but also a new

unit-construction shell and a slick little floor-change four-speed gearbox into the bargain.

A direct replacement for the Anglia 100E (which continued, renamed, as the Popular 100E for three years), the 105E was a two-door saloon which featured the now-fabled reverse-slope

rear window. Pious reasons given by Ford-UK for its use were unconvincing – this style had already been seen on Ford models (Lincoln and Mercury) on the other side of the Atlantic – though one benefit was the enlarged boot lid. This time round there was no four-door model, though a three-door estate came on stream from September 1961.

The chassis – MacPherson struts at the front, leaf-spring axle location at the rear – was conventional Ford, but the engine was a little jewel, the first of many in a family which became known by its "Kent" code name. It was the base unit for many race engines, and the power unit of the Lotus-Cortina (see below) was developed from it. The transmission was another little jewel which would have a long life.

The 1198cc-engined Anglia Super, which had the all-synchromesh gearbox of the Cortina, arrived in late 1962. The more torquey 50bhp engine made all the difference, turning the Anglia into an 82mph car, a pace undreamed of at Ford ten years earlier.

Anglia assembly was moved from Dagenham to Halewood in 1963, and before the end of the Anglia's eight-year career more than one million were

Anglias were handy on the track. Here Anita Taylor leads two well-known racers, Jack Sears in the Cortina and Sir John Whitmore in the Mini at the rear.

Anglia Super 123E.

Anglia estate car.

produced – another milestone for Ford.

Once you got used to the strange styling (which would not be used on the replacement Escort), this was an appealing car – it handled well, was cheap to run, and was surprisingly sporty. The measure of this is that a one-model enthusiast's club was set up, and thrives to this day.

Anglia 105E undergoing testing.

SPECIFICATION

BODY STYLES: saloon, estate, light commercials

PRODUCTION: 1,083,960, all types

ENGINE & TRANSMISSION: 997cc/1198cc, S4 ohv, 4sp man, f/r

POWER: 39bhp @ 5000rpm/50bhp @ 4900rpm

MAX SPEED (MPH): 76/82

0-60MPH (SEC): 26.9/21.6

SUSPENSION & BRAKES: coil ifs, leaf rear, drums f&r

LENGTH (IN)/WEIGHT (LB): 154/1679

LAUNCH PRICE: £589/£599

Prefect 107E 1959-61

Only weeks after the 105E Anglia had been launched, Ford installed the new overhead-valve engine and its gearbox in the old-type Prefect four-door saloon body. Visual changes included two-tone bodywork, but apart from the use of the last Prefect 100E De Luxe's trim and equipment there were no other clues

This, in every way, was an interim model, meant only to provide four-door motoring until the Consul Classic came along, It was dropped within two years.

Overhead valves at last: the Prefect 107E of 1959.

SPECIFICATION

BODY STYLES: saloon

PRODUCTION: 38,154

ENGINE & TRANSMISSION: 997cc, S4 ohv, 4sp man, f/r

POWER: 39bhp @ 5000rpm

MAX SPEED (MPH): 73

0-60MPH (SEC): 27.2

SUSPENSION & BRAKES: coil ifs, leaf rear, drums f&r

LENGTH (IN)/WEIGHT (LB): 154/1764

LAUNCH PRICE: £622

Consul Classic 1961-63

Here was a real oddity – a medium-sized model intended to bridge the gap between the Anglia 105E and Zephyr/Zodiac ranges which was in production for little more than two years and which was rendered obsolete by the Cortina well before then.

Although the Classic (officially "Consul Classic", by the way) had a brand new monocoque, and little mechanically in common with the Anglia 105E, it was effectively the second iteration of that car. In fact the original engine was a longer-stroke 54bhp 1340cc version of the Anglia's unit, and the gearbox was exactly the same (though in this case there was a column-shift option), while there were similarities in the MacPherson

Ford Consul Classic, 1961.

SPECIFICATION

BODY STYLES: saloon

PRODUCTION: 109,045

ENGINE & TRANSMISSION: 1340cc/1498cc, S4 ohv, 4sp man, f/r

POWER: 54bhp @ 4900rpm/60bhp @ 4600rpm

MAX SPEED (MPH): 79/81

0-60MPH (SEC): 21.8/20.1

SUSPENSION & BRAKES: coil ifs, leaf rear, disc f/drum r

LENGTH (IN)/WEIGHT (LB): 171/1995-2080

LAUNCH PRICE: £767

strut front suspension. Front-wheel disc brakes were standard.

The body – built in two-door or four-door forms – had the briefly fashionable reverse slope rear window, whose principal benefit was to provide a vast luggage boot, and Ford sold the car in base or De Luxe guise.

Even in a short career there was time for one major change. In summer 1962 the short-lived 1340cc three-main-bearing engine was discontinued, replaced by an enlarged 60bhp 1498cc five-main-bearing version, which it would soon share with the new Cortina.

Even then, there was little time for this model to settle down, for the last example was produced in the summer of

1963. All of them, incidentally, could suffer from wayward handling in side winds. This was never a memorable car, but it did at least give rise to the Consul Capri coupé which lived on for another year. Fortunately, too, this was the very last of Ford's reverse-slope rear window models.

A Consul Classic prototype was driven 23,000 test miles through Africa.

Consul Capri & Capri GT 1961-64

Introduced a few months after the Consul Classic, the Consul Capri (this was not, by the way, the "Car You Always Promised Yourself") was effectively a bubble-top coupé derivative of the two-door Classic, and rode on that car's platform.

From the nose back to the screen, and along the flanks and tail, the Capri shared its panels and packaging with the Classic. The cabin, though, was a 2+2 seater, with a truncated roof, all very much in the "personal car" mode (this was a US-inspired title for such cars).

Technically the Capri was much like the Classic, which is to say that the first

Ford Consul Capri, 1961.

Capri GT could nudge 100mph.

cars used the three-bearing 1340cc engine, which was replaced by the five-bearing 1498cc engine from mid-1962. The steering-column change option still existed, but few seem to have been made.

Then, from early 1963, the Capri GT was launched, with a 78bhp 1498cc engine in which a Weber carburettor and camshaft development by the then-new Cosworth concern played a big part. This car also had a remote-control floor change (like the Cortina GT), a supplementary instrument panel which included a rev-counter, and the servo-assisted brakes which the other Classics and Capris always lacked.

The Capri GT was a quick and quite nimble car, but its transatlantic front styling put off many potential customers. Even so, it lived on to mid-1964, a full year after the last Classic saloon.

SPECIFICATION

BODY STYLES: coupé

PRODUCTION: 18,716

ENGINE & TRANSMISSION: 1340cc/1498cc, S4 ohv, 4sp man, f/r

POWER: 54bhp @ 4900rpm/60bhp @ 4600/78bhp @ 5200rpm

MAX SPEED (MPH): 81/ 83 (E)/95

0-60MPH (SEC): 21.3/not measured/13.7

SUSPENSION & BRAKES: coil ifs, leaf rear, disc f/drum r

LENGTH (IN)/WEIGHT (LB): 171/2055-2163

LAUNCH PRICE: £916

Cortina Mk I 1962-66

In 1962 the Cortina was the most important new car Ford had ever announced, for it was the first to offer so much space at such little cost, and with so much dead weight saved. Further, it was the first of many Fords for which US-style product planning (different engines, different trim packages) would take effect.

The 98in-wheelbase monocoque was new, and much lighter than previous Fords. Always intended to be built in two-door, four-door and five-door estate types, it was also meant to accept 1198cc and 1498cc engines, manual gearboxes with centre-floor or steering-column change, and automatic transmission. It was also to be offered in several different trim levels.

All these would be launched in the first year, along with the charismatic 78bhp 1498cc Cortina GT, which came complete with a remote-control gear change and front-wheel disc brakes. Other Cortinas retained all-drum brakes to the end.

The base model four-door Cortina Mk I, with painted grille.

The ever-stubborn Ford marketing men insisted that this was a Consul Cortina at first, but no one took any notice, so the Consul badging and naming was dropped after two years. Early cars had rather plain fascia styling, but this was up-dated more than once in four years. The big trim/packaging change came in October 1964, with another brand-new fascia style, face level ventilation by swivelling "eyeballs", and air outlets in the rear quarters; at the same time the grille was widened to make a recognition point.

The first Cortina Supers came along in January 1963, the very successful Cortina GT in March 1963, and there was a Borg Warner automatic transmission option on non-GT 1498cc examples from January 1964. From late 1964, Cortina GTs got extra radius arm location to the rear axle. During

Stirling Moss in his custom Cortina.

Cortina GT, 1963, had a 78bhp engine.

The estate featured fake wood side trim.

Cortina Super.

SPECIFICATION

BODY STYLES: saloon, estate

PRODUCTION: 1,010,090

ENGINE & TRANSMISSION: 1198cc/1498cc, S4 ohv, 4sp man or auto, f/r

POWER: 50bhp @ 4900rpm/62bhp @ 4700/78bhp @ 5200rpm

MAX SPEED (MPH): 75/80/94

0-60MPH (SEC): 25.4/19.8/13.9

SUSPENSION & BRAKES: coil ifs, leaf rear, drums f&r (later disc f/drum r)

LENGTH (IN)/WEIGHT (LB): 168/1750

LAUNCH PRICE: £639 - £749

the life of the car, front-wheel disc brakes were standardised, and the steering-column change was dropped.

Every Cortina, but especially the Cortina GT, handled much better than previous Fords, though Ford tried to spoil everything by specifying narrow-tread cross-ply tyres. The combination of low price, low maintenance costs and the spacious cabin, however plainly furnished, made the Cortina hugely attractive to fleets. Before long it had become a real icon, and had even established a new market sector called the "Cortina class". There would be

four further generations of Cortina before 1982, all of which sold in enormous numbers.

Roger Clark won the 1965 Scottish Rally in this Cortina GT.

Lotus Cortina MkI 1963-66

The result of a "why don't we...?" conversation between Ford's Walter Hayes and Colin Chapman of Lotus, the Lotus-Cortina was a homologation special, meant for motor sport. Ford supplied the stripped-out two-door body shells to Lotus, and assembly was at Cheshunt, north of London.

At first the Lotus-Cortina was almost entirely different from the ordinary two-door Cortinas, with aluminium body skin panels (doors, bonnet and bootlid), a Lotus-designed twin-cam engine, close-ratio gears, alloy trans-mission and axle casings, and a complex rear axle location with coil springs over dampers, radius arms and an A-frame locating the rear axle. The ride and handling were very firm, helped by the 5.5in rims.

Special instruments and special seating all added to the mystique, which was topped off by a lowered ride height, front quarter bumpers, and a special green-on-white paint job; no other colours were available.

Serious unreliability problems led to

Lotus Cortina Mk I.

many development changes. From mid-1964 alloy panels and castings disappeared back into the options catalogue, and at the same time a wider set of gear ratios was standardised. The updated wide-grille body, with Aeroflow ventilation, arrived in October 1964.

From June 1965 the coil spring/A-frame type of rear suspension was abandoned, replaced by Cortina GT-type leaf springs and radius arms. Finally, from autumn 1965, yet another set of gearbox ratios (the Corsair 2000E set) was adopted.

Although a fast and always charismatic car which won bucket-loads of touring car races (and, in leaf-spring guise, rallies too), the Lotus-Cortina had a troubled career as a road car. Reliability problems were endemic (particularly the A-frame rear axle, which persistently

leaked oil). But new-car and later classic-car owners forgave it everything. In later years most early snags had been ironed out, and early-type cars have become very desirable.

SPECIFICATION

BODY STYLES: saloon

PRODUCTION: 2894

ENGINE & TRANSMISSION: 1558cc, S4 2ohc, 4sp man, f/r

POWER: 105bhp @ 5500 rpm/115bhp @ 6000rpm

MAX SPEED (MPH): (105bhp) 106

0-60MPH (SEC): (105bhp) 9.9

SUSPENSION & BRAKES: coil ifs, coil (later leaf) rear, disc f/drum r

LENGTH (IN)/WEIGHT (LB): 168/1820

LAUNCH PRICE: £1100

Jim Clark lifts a wheel in a Lotus Cortina.

Corsair & GT 1963-70

Billed originally as a replacement for the (Consul) Classic, the (Consul) Corsair used a stretched Cortina Mk I GT floor pan, along with many of that car's inner structural panels, steering, suspension and brakes, all topped off by a sharp-nosed body style with a more spacious cabin. At first assembled at Ford's new factory at Halewood, the Corsair had a 101in wheelbase.

Original cars came in a choice of two-door or four-door saloon styles, along with 60bhp or 78bhp Cortina GT four-cylinder engines. Steering-column or remote-control floor gearchanges were available with the 60bhp unit, and a remote-control floor change for the 78bhp Corsair GT, Borg Warner automatic transmission was optional with the 60bhp engine.

Only two years later the Corsair was updated. The original straight-four engines were dumped in favour of the new corporate V4 engine, in 77bhp/1.7-litre and 88bhp/2.0-litre (GT) form. In due course these engines would also be used in Zephyrs, Capris and Transit

Corsair V4 GT four-door.

vans. At the same time, larger front discs, Aeroflow ventilation and improvements to the handling all added up to significant second thoughts. A five-door estate car version of the 2-litre model (actually an authorised conversion by Abbot of Farnham) was added in March 1966. About this time, too, reclining front seats became available on GTs.

The 2.0 GT was replaced by the 2000E in 1967, but an 88bhp Corsair 2000 carried on. Corsair assembly was moved from Halewood to Dagenham in 1969, and the last car was produced in June 1970.

Criticised at the time for a rather transatlantic look, flavour and character, the Corsair nevertheless became a major commercial success for Ford. The better equipped and more powerful versions were almost as nimble as the Cortina

Corsair two-door.

GT, but somehow never became icons. The Corsair 2000E (see the entry below) was a different story.

SPECIFICATION

BODY STYLES: saloon, estate

PRODUCTION: 331,095, all types, of which only 940 estate cars

ENGINE & TRANSMISSION: 1498cc/1663cc/1996cc, S4/V4/V4, ohv, 4sp man or auto, f/r

POWER: 60bhp @ 4600rpm/78bhp @ 5200/77bhp @ 4750rpm/88bhp @ 4850rpm

MAX SPEED (MPH): 86-95

0-60MPH (SEC): 17.8-14.3

SUSPENSION & BRAKES: coil ifs, leaf rear, disc f/drum r

LENGTH (IN)/WEIGHT (LB): 177/1950 - 2194

LAUNCH PRICE: £653

Corsair 2000E 1967-70

Ford's second-ever "E" car (the Zodiac Executive had been first, in 1965), the Corsair 2000E was only on sale for three and a half years but it made many friends. Succeeding the V4 GT in January 1967, it was better specified, faster, better trimmed and better equipped.

All production-line 2000Es were four-door saloons (if you see others, they were private conversions), with 97bhp versions of the 2.0-litre V4

engine and – important, this – a new set of gear ratios (this became known as the 2000E 'box). There was no automatic transmission option. Radial ply tyres were standard, as was a vinyl roof covering and a much upgraded interior which included reclining front seats and a walnut veneer fascia. For 1968 further changes included bucket-style rear seats, and a clock on the fascia.

Although it wasn't a competition car,

the 2000E felt and behaved like a sports saloon. With a top speed of nearly 100mph, brisk acceleration and very sporty gear ratios, along with radial-tyre handling (which was still a relatively new experience on mass-market cars in the mid-1960s, don't forget) and its up-market equipment, the 2000E was an appealing package. Ford learned from this, and went on to produce other cars in the same mould in the 1970s.

Corsair 2000E.

GT40 1966-68

The fabulous GT40 started life in 1964 as a pure-bred racing sports car, its objective to win the Le Mans 24 Hour race. Two years later, and after myriad changes, it did just that. Apart from works race and development cars, Ford Advanced Vehicles also built 91 production GT40s, of which 35 were "road specification" race cars (a loose description, for each car was different) and just seven true Mk III road cars.

True road cars, built only in 1967 and 1968, looked basically the same as earlier types, but had centre-lock wire-spoke wheels and a modified, four-headlamp, front-end style. Like every GT40, they were based on a mid-engined layout, the tubular frame being in steel with GRP skin panels, with a Ford-USA engine behind the two-seater cabin, driving the rear wheels through a ZF five-speed transaxle. Massive disc brakes were fitted to all four wheels. For this application, the Mustang-derived V8 was de-tuned to a claimed 335bhp (though even less power – 306bhp – was also quoted for this machine)

The GT40 which won at Le Mans in 1968 in practice before the race.

Ford GT40 Mk III, an all-time classic.

Though the Mk III was a de-tuned race car, the cockpit was fully trimmed, with adjustable seats. Unlike the pure race cars, the gear change was in the centre, between the seats, Aeroflow ventilation (essential in this poorly-ventilated coupé) was standard.

Amazingly, both left- and right-hand-drive specifications were available, and two heat-resistant luggage lockers were fitted in the tail, one at each side of the exhaust system.

Although Ford said they were serious about selling such road cars (twenty sets of components were apparently laid down), it proved almost impossible to sell them, for the combination of supercar horsepower, cramped accommodation and a noisy cabin environment was not totally seductive.

The clutch in these cars had a limited life, and at 40 inches tall GT40s were all but invisible in heavy traffic, yet they

were surprisingly practical for open road use. The few people who owned them found them incredibly fast, satisfying and charismatic to drive. No one ever lets a GT40 rot away (though the tub could, indeed, do that), with the result that many cars are still in existence.

Zephyr/Zodiac/Executive Mk IV 1966-72

Was this one of Ford-UK's biggest mistakes? Egged on by a British-based but American-born technical chief, Ford developed the Mk IVs to be bigger, heavier, more transatlantic and less wieldy than any previous car in the Zephyr/Zodiac family. They were larger than the Mk IIIs (which had also been a lot bigger than the Mk IIs), with an ultra-long bonnet and a spacious cabin but a rather truncated tail. Zodiacs had four headlamps, other types two. Almost every major component was new, including independent rear suspension and a new Ford automatic transmission.

The platform had a 115in wheelbase (eight inches longer than the Mk III) with MacPherson strut front suspension and semi-trailing link independent rear. All this, with four-wheel disc brakes (servoed on V6 cars) and (originally on the Executive) power steering available, made for a complex car. The packaging of the tail was tight, so the spare wheel was mounted ahead of the engine.

Ford Zephyr 4 Mk IV, 1966.

All models used the new range of "Essex" V4 and V6 engines (2.0 and 2.5 litre in Zephyrs, 3.0 litre in Zodiacs). A four-speed manual gearbox with column change was standard, while floor change, overdrive and Ford-USA Type C4 automatic transmission were options.

In October 1966 the Zodiac Executive arrived, with automatic transmission, power-assisted steering and enhanced trim/equipment. At the same time an estate car (by Abbot) appeared.

Changes included grille and trim enhancements from late 1967, plus radial tyres, and standard power steering on Zodiacs. The Borg Warner Type 35 auto 'box replaced Ford's C4, but C4 re-appeared on 3-litre types in late 1968.

Though nearly 150,000 cars were produced, this was due to Ford's marketing machine, for the cars were turkeys. The handling was poor, with much understeer, then snap-oversteer when the independent rear suspension threw in the towel, ultra-low-geared steering unless power-assisted, and a very transatlantic character.

Mk IV Zephyr 6 de Luxe.

SPECIFICATION

BODY STYLES: saloon, estate

PRODUCTION: 149,263

ENGINE & TRANSMISSION:
1996cc/2495cc/2994cc, V4/V6/V6, ohv, 4sp man, o/d or auto, f/r

POWER: 88bhp @ 4750rpm/112bhp @4750rpm/136bhp @ 4750rpm

MAX SPEED (MPH): 95/96/103

0-60MPH (SEC): 17.7/14/6/11.0

SUSPENSION & BRAKES: coil ifs, coil irs, disc f/disc r

LENGTH (IN)/WEIGHT (LB): 185/2828-2912

LAUNCH PRICE: £933

Zodiac estate car.

Mk IV Zodiac Executive.

Cortina Mk II 1966-70

This was the second Cortina, and Ford sold even more of it than the first. As before, the car was light, economical and, because of the wide range of specifications, likely to appeal to most buyers. Businesses running fleets had a field day.

Technically it was the mixture as before, but with extra choices. The Cortina Mk I's platform and suspension were carried forward, changed only by using wider wheel tracks, though this time they were covered by a smoother, somewhat blander body, which was built

in two-door and four-door saloon and five-door estate car types, with several different trim levels.

In the UK, pushrod four-cylinder engines eventually spanned 54bhp to 88bhp (there was even a puny 1.1-litre unit for some export territories), manual

SPECIFICATION

BODY STYLES: saloon, estate

PRODUCTION: 1,023,837, all types

ENGINE & TRANSMISSION:
1297cc/1498cc/1599cc, S4 ohv, 4sp man or auto, f/r

POWER: Seven ratings - 54bhp @ 5000rpm through to 88bhp @ 5400 rpm

MAX SPEED (MPH): 81-98

0-60MPH (SEC): 21.4-13.1

SUSPENSION & BRAKES: coil ifs, leaf rear, disc f/drum r

LENGTH (IN)/WEIGHT (LB): 168/1900-1994

LAUNCH PRICE: £669

Cortina Mk II GT four-door.

or automatic transmission was on offer, as were steering-column or centre-floor shifts (except on the GT, where the floor change was standard). All models got front-wheel disc brakes as standard .

In the first year, 1.3- and 1.5-litre engines used the original-type cylinder

Interior of the Cortina Mk II GT, with instrument pod in the top of the dash.

heads, but from October 1967 the new cross-flow (Ford called it "Bowl-in-Piston") cylinder head engine took over instead, in 1.3- and 1.6-litre guise. At this time further changes included a remote-control gearshift for Super models (already standard on GTs), plus standard radial tyres on GTs.

The remote shift was standardised on all cars a year later, while reclining front seats became optional, and what Ford called a mid-life facelift saw changes to the instrument panel and to the seating. It was enough to see the Cortina bow out as a UK best-seller – just as it had been for some years.

As with the Mk I, this was a car for almost everyman, and many have survived into the new century. Two special versions – 1600E and Lotus-Cortina – are separately described.

Mk II estate.

Cortina 1600E 1967-70

After what was one of the shortest development periods on record, the Cortina 1600E went on to become one of Ford's greatest 1960s successes. Just one mock-up was enough to convince the company's marketing men that the 1600E project would fill the gap between the Cortina GT and the Lotus-Cortina, which it did – perfectly.

In summary, the 1600E used Cortina GT running gear, slightly modified Lotus-Cortina suspension settings, and a glittering array of extra equipment including a full-width wooden fascia, plushy seats, 5.5-inch wide Rostyle

Cortina 1600E, top of the range.

wheels, fat radial-ply tyres, extra driving lamps and other goodies. Automatic transmission was never available, however. All this, plus a vinyl roof covering and special colour schemes and trim materials, made the 1600E unique among other Cortinas. Mainly a home market car, it was only meant to be a four-door saloon, but some two-door types were made for export. No estate cars were ever officially built.

Even in only a three-year life there was time for modification. For 1969 the new corporate Cortina single selector rail gearbox was adopted, there was a new wood veneer fascia panel, and other trim updates. When the Cortina II died in summer 1970, the 1600E had to die with it – and there was no replacement – not, that is, until the Cortina (Mk III) 2000E came along in 1973.

With a top speed of nearly 100mph and sporty handling, this was a car which soon earned itself a very particular image of its own – one which it never lost in later life, for a dedicated one-make club sprung up to service it in retirement.

SPECIFICATION

BODY STYLES: saloon

PRODUCTION: 55,833

ENGINE & TRANSMISSION: 1599cc, S4 ohv, 4sp man, f/r

POWER: 88bhp @ 5400rpm

MAX SPEED (MPH): 98

0-60MPH (SEC): 13.1

SUSPENSION & BRAKES: coil ifs, leaf rear, disc f/drum r

LENGTH (IN)/WEIGHT (LB): 168/2064

LAUNCH PRICE: £982

Cortina Lotus Mk II 1967-70

Here is a conundrum – how is it that the Lotus-Cortina Mk II was always a much better road car than the original Mk I, but has always been worth much less as a classic car? The answer, presumably, is that Jim Clark and Sir John Whitmore never raced a Mk II, so the motorsport image could never be the same.

Although the original Lotus-Cortina dropped out of production in September 1966, the new-shape Mk II did not appear for another six months. Apart from the fact that it had the shape of the new-type Cortina II two-door saloon, the most significant change was that it was always assembled at Ford's own Dagenham factory, and was available in a full range of body colours; striping, if any, was applied by the Ford dealer before delivery took place. Compared with the original car, too, it was a bit

Cortina Lotus Mk II, with green side flashes as on the Mk I.

SPECIFICATION

BODY STYLES: saloon

PRODUCTION: 4032

ENGINE & TRANSMISSION: 1558cc, S4 2ohc, 4sp man, f/r

POWER: 109bhp @ 6000rpm

MAX SPEED (MPH): 105

0-60MPH (SEC): 9.9

SUSPENSION & BRAKES: coil ifs, leaf rear, disc f/drum r

LENGTH (IN)/WEIGHT (LB): 168/2027

LAUNCH PRICE: £1068

more powerful with an output of 109bhp instead of 105bhp.

Like the last of the Mk Is, the Mk II was basically a Cortina GT with a Lotus-Ford twin-cam engine, for there were no aluminium panels, no light-alloy transmission casings, and certainly no unique rear suspension. Apart from the fact that it rode subtly lower and stiffer than the GT, and had 5.5-inch wheels (not Rostyles, by the way, only 1600Es had those), its chassis – suspension, steering, brakes and all – was shared with the GT.

By 1968 the Lotus-Cortina had officially become the Cortina Twin Cam, and had badging to prove this, but no one – customers, dealers or specialist press – took any notice of that, for to everyone who cared about motoring it remained Lotus-Cortina to the end in the summer of 1970. Like all Cortinas of the period, in the autumn of 1968 this car gained a different style of fascia, the single-rail gear shift, and a centre-floor mounted handbrake.

Like the Mk I, this was a great car to drive and enjoy. Because Ford's quality control was more rigorous than that of Lotus had been on Mk Is, it was also a much more reliable and enjoyable car to own. In later life, though, it was overshadowed by the Escort Twin-Cam, and in "classic" life by the Lotus-Cortina Mk I. A pity, for this was, and is, a splendid car.

Escort 1100/1300/GT 1968-74

Ford's new Escort went on sale in January 1968 as a direct replacement for the long-running Anglia. For the next thirty years the Escort became the backbone of the company's sales. It was the first British Ford to be truly European, for it was engineered in conjunction with Ford-Germany, and was assembled at Halewood and at Saarlouis in Germany.

Along with the latest Cortina Mk II, the Escort was the first Ford to use the legendary Kent crossflow engine. Apart from this, everything about the Escort was new – new platform, new all-synchromesh gearbox and new axle. This was also the first Ford road car to use rack-and-pinion steering.

Technically, the only innovation in the platform was the lack of a front anti-roll bar in the MacPherson strut assembly at first (though this was phased in within a year). Engines were either 1098cc, 1298cc or 1298cc GT-tune, the 72bhp GT being matched to closer-ratio gears and disc brakes on the front wheels. Automatic transmission became available on 1100s and 1300s, but soon disappeared from 1100s.

Two-door saloons arrived first, with rectangular headlamps on Supers and GTs, the other cars having circular lamps. Three-door estate cars were added within months; these all had front-wheel disc brakes.

Ford Escort Mk I.

Changes and permutations followed rapidly, as four-door saloons were added from late 1969 and engines became slightly more powerful from late 1970. Later in the cars' career Ford also introduced the Escort Sport and the 1300E models. The last of the original Mk Is was produced towards the end of 1974, this car having comfortably outsold the Cortina Mk II of the period and, of course, the previous Anglia.

Like the original Cortina, the Escort was designed to be every car for everyone – but lower down the price scale. With three engine tunes, three different body shells, and several trim levels, there was something for every taste and budget. Except on cars with no disc brakes (early 1100s, really) the package was easily able to deal with available performance, and the handling was surprisingly good. Specialised versions like the Twin Cam became true collectors' cars.

Escort de Luxe, 1968.

Escort 1300 XL estate car, 1972.

Escort Mk I GT two-door,

SPECIFICATION

BODY STYLES: saloon, estate, light commercials

PRODUCTION: 1,082,472

ENGINE & TRANSMISSION: 1098cc/1298cc, S4 ohv, 4sp man or auto, f/r

POWER: 48bhp @ 6000rpm/57bhp @ 5500rpm/72bhp @ 6000rpm

MAX SPEED (MPH): 79/83/94

0-60MPH (SEC): 22.3/20.6/13.1

SUSPENSION & BRAKES: coil ifs, leaf rear, drums f&r (disc f/drum r with 72bhp, and in estate cars)

LENGTH (IN)/WEIGHT (LB): 157/1641

LAUNCH PRICE: £666

Escort Twin Cam 1968-71

Invented by Ford Motorsport at Boreham, the Escort Twin Cam was intended as a homologation special to allow Ford to win World Championship rallies. Basically consisting of a two-door Escort shell into which the latest Lotus-Cortina Mk II running gear had been fitted, the car was built at Halewood.

The two-door body shell was stiffened to make it more durable, given slightly flared front arches to clear the bigger tyres, and modified only to make room for Lotus-Cortina components – there was only just enough engine bay space for the engine, which was mounted askew. The twin overhead camshaft Lotus-Ford engine, Cortina gearbox, lowered and stiffened suspension, servo-assisted front disc brakes, wide rims and radial tyres were all standard. The battery was in the boot.

British-built cars were right-hand drive (a few lhd cars were built in other countries from CKD packs) and all but the last few were white, with rather basic black trim. Rectangular headlamps at first, but circular units from mid-1969.

Built to be a readily-prepared competition car, the road-going Twin Cam was a bit rough and ready, with a hard ride and a tendency to oversteer when pressed. Even so, a characterful car and, at the time, Ford's fastest-accelerating road machine. One either loved or hated the very idea of such a car. Few road cars remained standard, for the majority soon became full-blown race or rally machines. For that reason they are very valuable today.

SPECIFICATION

BODY STYLES: saloon

PRODUCTION: 1263

ENGINE & TRANSMISSION: 1558 cc, S4 2ohc, 4sp man, f/r

POWER: 110bhp @ 6000rpm

MAX SPEED (MPH): 113

0-60MPH (SEC): 9.9

SUSPENSION & BRAKES: coil ifs, leaf rear, disc f/drum r

LENGTH (IN)/WEIGHT (LB): 157/1730

LAUNCH PRICE: £1171

Ford Escort Mk I Twin Cam used the Lotus engine.

Escort RS1600 1970-74

The easy – and accurate – way to describe the RS1600 is as a re-engined Twin-Cam. The new car's power unit was the 16-valve twin overhead camshaft BDA (which Cosworth had evolved for Ford), still based on the pushrod Kent engine's bottom end, but entirely different in detail. The RS1600 was assembled at Halewood during 1970, but from the end of that year assembly was moved to a newly-converted facility, AVO, at Aveley in Essex. Like the Twin Cam, these were basic competition machines, most of which were turned into race or rally cars. Late-model engines could be enlarged to 2.0 litres, and gave up to 280bhp in race tune.

Unlike Twin Cams, RS1600s were always available in a range of colours, and could be bought with right-hand or left-hand drive. All had circular headlamps. From autumn 1972 they got an engine with a light-alloy cylinder block. At the same time, trim and equipment improvements were phased in. The new Escort Mk II floorpan arrived in late 1973, though you would never know unless told.

Once again, a great road car if you liked high-revving, rather thrashy noises from up front – but the whole point was what this car could become, not what it was. Road cars were dropped at the end of 1974, but new competition cars were still being built up years later.

Escort RS1600 had a 120bhp 16-valve Cosworth motor.

Escort Mexico 1970-74

The Mexico, a car developed in a real hurry after works Escorts won the London-Mexico World Cup rally in May 1970, was launched in December 1970, and was always built at Aveley in Essex.

Mechanically it was no more and no less than a re-engined Twin Cam or RS1600, this time with an 86bhp 1.6-litre overhead-valve Kent engine as used in Cortinas and Capris of the period. Much simpler, much less powerful but much easier to maintain, this was the Escort "fun car" for someone who could not afford the 16-valve RS1600 along-side which it was built.

Identical in styling to the RS1600 (only the badging and striping were different), it was not a competition car

The Escort Mexico recalled the Escorts which triumphed in the 1970 London-Mexico World Cup Rally.

One of the 1970 World Cup Rally Escorts, car number 14, driven by Zasada and Wachowski. These cars were 1850GT "specials" with enlarged ohv Kent engines producing 140bhp.

in waiting, and became the best-selling product of the short-lived AVO factory.

Given the same trim and packaging updates at the end of 1972 as the RS1600, and the new floorpan in late 1973, it was popular to the very end, and was joined by the Escort RS2000 from mid-1973.

In character it was like other hot Escorts, even though not nearly as powerful or as fast. Well loved then, and still popular in later life, the Mexico was the model which introduced many young people to the whole idea of the "Fast Ford".

Escort RS2000 Mk I 1973-74

Third and last of the Mk I Escort RS Models, the RS2000 was as fast as the RS1600, but with a much simpler 2-litre overhead-camshaft Pinto engine. Some early types were assembled in Germany, but most came from the special AVO factory in Essex between mid-1973 and the end of 1974.

RS2000s shared the same stiffened two-door saloon monocoque and suspension as the Mexico/RS1600 types, but the 100bhp Pinto engine (exactly as used in Capris and Cortinas of the day) was matched to a new-generation four-speed gearbox.

Trim and fittings were different and more up-market, with an easily recognisable striping layout. In spite of requests, no other body derivatives were ever put on sale, but a few "specials" have been created in later years by private owners.

In many ways these were the most desirable of the Mk I RS types – their successors, the beaky-nose Mk IIs, being even more successful.

Escort Mk I RS2000 was powered by the Ford sohc 2-litre Pinto unit.

SPECIFICATION	
BODY STYLES: saloon	
PRODUCTION: 4324	
ENGINE & TRANSMISSION: 1993cc, S4 ohc, 4sp man, f/r	
POWER: 100bhp @ 5750rpm	
MAX SPEED (MPH): 108	
0-60MPH (SEC): 9.0	
SUSPENSION & BRAKES: coil ifs, beam leaf rear, disc f/drum r	
LENGTH (IN)/WEIGHT (LB): 160/1978	
LAUNCH PRICE: £1568	

Capri 1300/1600 1969-74

The Car You Always Promised Yourself was launched in January 1969. Simply engineered, it used a derivative of the Cortina/Corsair platform with similar suspension, brakes (discs at the front) and running gear, and several different engine and transmission options. It was wrapped in a smart 2+2 coupé body with a small boot and rectangular headlamps. Like the Escort, it was built on two sites – in the UK at Halewood, and in Germany at Cologne.

Rack-and-pinion steering was a novelty (the Cortina/Corsair still used a recirculating-ball unit), as was the number of trim and dress-up packs

The Capri 1600GT could touch 100mph.

available. With X, L, R. XL and XLR specs to choose from, it was essential to read the catalogue before thinking of an order.

Right from the start, a big choice of engines was planned, those used in Britain being British-built, those in Germany (not available in the UK) being German V4s and V6s at first. Entry-level UK Capris used 1298cc or 1598cc Kent engines in four power outputs. A four-speed all-synchromesh manual gearbox was standard, and automatic transmission was optional on 1.6-litre models.

A mid-life upgrade in autumn 1972 included the introduction of the ohc 1593cc Pinto engine instead of the 1600GT power unit, and a front-end

facelift which included larger head-lamps. Inside there was a new fascia layout which would be carried forward to the Capri II.

Although some derivatives were not successful (the 1300GT disappeared in October 1971, and the combination of some odd trim packs, XR for instance, was discouraged), the Capri I sold very well indeed.

Trendies are prone to saying that they always despised the Capri I, yet many of them bought at least one in its five-year life.

The 1.3- and 1.6-litre versions were "starter" Capris, lighter and better-handling than any other version, which hit the spot with many customers and which could be insured and main-tained at family car prices.

SPECIFICATION

BODY STYLES: coupé

PRODUCTION: 374,700, all UK-built Mk I Capris

ENGINE & TRANSMISSION: 1298cc/1599cc, S4 ohv, 1593cc, S4 ohc, 4sp man or auto, f/r

POWER: 52bhp @ 5000rpm/64bhp @ 6000rpm/64bhp @ 4800rpm/82bhp @ 5400rpm

MAX SPEED (MPH): 86 (E)-100

0-60MPH (SEC): 20.0 (E)-12.7

SUSPENSION & BRAKES: coil ifs, leaf rear, disc f/drum r

LENGTH (IN)/WEIGHT (LB): 168/1940 - 2030

LAUNCH PRICE: £890

Mk I Capri 1600. It sertainly seemed to attract the girls!

Capri 2000GT/3000GT 1969-74

At the top end of the range, the larger-engined Capris looked almost identical to the small-engined types but were faster and more sporting. At first, in 1969, the 2000GT used the 1996cc V4 engine, which produced 93bhp. Maybe this wasn't smooth but it was torquey and reliable – and guaranteed 106mph.

Before the end of the year, the 3000GT appeared, this having the impressive 2994cc V6 Essex engine and 128bhp, bigger brakes and more rubber on the road. The same trim packs were available, and automatic transmission (increasingly popular as time passed) was always

The Capri 3000, with six-cylinder power, was effortlessly fast. This is a 3000GXL.

available. At once the 3000GT became the sports-car baiter of the moment.

The better trimmed and equipped 3000E appeared in March 1970, and all 3-litre types were improved from October 1971, with a more powerful engine (138bhp) and better internal gearbox ratios. A top speed of 113mph, sometimes up to 120mph, was available, but the rather nose-heavy and under-steery handling balance limited pace on some roads.

In October 1972 another facelift included dropping the 3000E in favour of the 3000GXL, fitting four circular headlamps on the 3000GXL, bigger headlamps on all others, a bonnet bulge and the new fascia style. Surprisingly, the V4 engine was retained.

At the end of the 3-litre's life the RS3100 appeared, this being a limited-production homologation special intended for use in motor racing.

Larger-engined Capris reinforced the car's reputation because of their value-for-money and visceral performance. Sadly, most have succumbed to a hard life and/or corrosion.

For ultimate performance, you could order the Comanche V8 Capri from Jeff Uren.

SPECIFICATION	
BODY STYLES: coupé	
PRODUCTION: see Capri 1300/1600	
ENGINE & TRANSMISSION: 1996cc/2994cc, V4/V6 ohv, 4sp man or auto, f/r	
POWER: 93bhp @ 5500rpm/128bhp @ 4750rpm/138bhp @ 4750rpm.	
MAX SPEED (MPH): 106/113	
0-60MPH (SEC): 10.6/10.3	
SUSPENSION & BRAKES: coil ifs, leaf rear, disc f/drum r	
LENGTH (IN)/WEIGHT (LB): 168/2115/2380	
LAUNCH PRICE: £1088/£1291	

Cortina Mk III 1970-76

Except for the use of some existing engines and transmissions, the third-generation Cortina was totally different from the Cortina II, for it had a new platform, new styling, and new suspension. In addition, rack-and-pinion steering was adopted for the first time on a Cortina. In effect, the new Cortina also took over from the last of the Corsairs too.

The new structure was built around a 101.5in wheelbase – similar to that of the old Corsair model, but having nothing in common with it.

The basic engineering was also used in the new-generation Taunus from Ford-Germany, though the external style of that Taunus was quite different.

SPECIFICATION	
BODY STYLES: saloon, estate	
PRODUCTION: 1,126,559, all types	
ENGINE & TRANSMISSION: 1298cc/1599cc/1593cc/1993cc, S4 ohv/ohv/ohc/ohc, 4sp man or auto, f/r	
POWER: 50bhp @ 5000rpm -98bhp @ 5500rpm	
MAX SPEED (MPH): 84-105	
0-60MPH (SEC): 18.1-10.7	
SUSPENSION & BRAKES: coil ifs, coil rear, disc f/drum r	
LENGTH (IN)/WEIGHT (LB): 168/2083-2346	
LAUNCH PRICE: £914	

Ford Cortina Mk III, the classic "Coke-bottle" shape, in 1971 2000 GXL guise.

Wishbone independent front suspension with coil spring/radius arm location of the rear axle were both Cortina novelties – the front suspension, in fact, also being due for use in the new Granada which would be launched in 1972.

The Ford-UK body, available in two-door and four-door saloon and five-door estate configurations, featured the then fashionable "Coke-bottle" profile of the wing crown line over the rear wheelarch. The styling was transatlantic in many ways, especially in the flamboyant fascia design with its deeply cowled dials.

The first Mk III Cortinas came with a choice of four four-cylinder engines – two overhead-valve Kent and two of the new overhead-camshaft Pinto – along with all the usual Ford choice of transmissions and no fewer than four different trim/equipment packs, which included a four-headlamp nose on GXL models.

As ever, Ford meant this Cortina to be all things to all customers. Although build quality was only mediocre at first, this range gradually made its mark, and it would sell strongly for six years, with a welcome mid-life facelift in 1973 which included a much more suitable (more European, somehow) fascia style.

Ford's own-brand automatic transmission would take over from the Borg Warner installation in 1972, and there was a Cortina 2000E derivative from 1973. A further uplift followed in the autumn of 1975, which added more features, some of which had previously been optional extras.

For the first time, this was a mainstream Cortina which could reach 100mph in 2-litre form and which had surprisingly good and well-balanced handling. Unhappily it was just as prone to corrosion (and depreciation) as previous types, and very few survived to become classic cars.

The lightly made-over 1976 base model Cortina Mk III two-door.

Cortina 2000E 1973-76

The Cortina 1600E of 1967-70 had been such an unexpected and low-budget success, that Ford was happy to try again with the next-generation car. Three years after the launch of the Mk III (not, please note, at once), the 2000E arrived. Timed to appear at the same time as the other mid-term facelift Mk III Cortinas, it was the top-of-the-range model and it sold steadily for three years.

Mechanically and structurally, the 2000E was exactly like all other 2-litre engined Cortinas (but not the GTs), which is to say that it had a 98bhp 1993cc overhead-camshaft Pinto engine with a choice of manual or automatic transmissions. Unlike the 1600E of old, the 2000E did not come with different suspension or wheels. Available only as a four-door saloon (and, from late 1974, a five-door estate car), it was purely a top-of-the-line trim and equipment enhancement, though this was done sensitively and well.

On to the 2000GT package Ford added a vinyl roof and the latest

SPECIFICATION

BODY STYLES: saloon, estate

PRODUCTION: see Cortina Mk III

ENGINE & TRANSMISSION: 1993cc, S4 ohc, 4sp man, or auto, f/r

POWER: 98bhp @ 5500rpm

MAX SPEED (MPH): 102

0-60MPH (SEC): 10.6

SUSPENSION & BRAKES: coil ifs, coil rear, disc f/drum r

LENGTH (IN)/WEIGHT (LB): 168/2346

LAUNCH PRICE: £1638

Top of the Mk III Cortina range was the 2000E, here in estate car form in 1974.

sculpted steel wheels. All cars had rectangular headlamps, a distinctive grille and a special badge on the vinyl-clad rear quarters behind the doors. Inside, the new and more satisfactory fascia/instrument panel was set in polished teak, there were deep pile carpets (which hid much extra sound-deadening material), a centre console, and both the clock and a push-button radio were standard equipment. Yet at that time seat belts, a laminated windscreen and metallic paintwork were all still optional extras.

Selling at £1638, the 2000E's price had to be compared with £1403 for the 2000XL and £1437 for the 2000GT, but there were plenty of customers. However, by the autumn of 1975, when the VFM package was applied, the price had rocketed to £2456, and there was more price inflation to come. All in all, the 2000E was the best of the Mk III breed.

Capri RS3100 1973-74

This short-lived and unsuccessful model would never have been put on sale if Ford had not needed a new homologation special with which to go motor racing in 1974. To take advantage of the regulations, Ford needed a Capri with an engine larger than 3 litres, and with more aerodynamic downforce. The result was the Capri RS3100, built at Halewood in the winter of 1973-74, just before the original-shape Capri went out of production. Based very closely on the Capri 3000GT, the RS3100 also picked up chassis features from the German-built Capri RS2600 like its alloy wheels, front quarter bumpers and ventilated front disc brakes, while it also had a 3093cc version of the V6 engine. There was no automatic transmission option. The big rear spoiler really did push down the back end at high speeds.

According to the rules, Ford needed to build 1000 cars, swore they had done so, but did not: the facts are not complete, but 200-250 is nearer the truth. As the RS3100 was announced in November 1973, in the depths of the Energy Crisis, it proved very hard to sell, and the last cars were not registered for months after the Capri II had been introduced.

Although very few survive, most of them are kept in absolutely immaculate condition, and are the best performing and best balanced of all such Capris.

SPECIFICATION

BODY STYLES: coupé

PRODUCTION: c.200

ENGINE & TRANSMISSION: 3093cc, V6 ohv, 4sp man, f/r

POWER: 148bhp @ 5000rpm

MAX SPEED (MPH): 123

0-60MPH (SEC): 7.2

SUSPENSION & BRAKES: coil ifs, leaf rear, disc f/drum r

LENGTH (IN)/WEIGHT (LB): 168/2315

LAUNCH PRICE: £2450

Capri RS3100.

Capri II (four-cylinder) 1974-76

Five years on, in March 1974, the second-generation Capri used the same platform and basic engine/drive line/suspension layout as the original type, though with an entirely new body superstructure, style and theme. Not only was the style more curvaceous, and the cabin more roomy, but there was a hatchback, and the rear seats could be folded forward to provide more stowage space.

There were three engine options, the smallest being the older-type overhead-valve Kent, the others being overhead-camshaft Pinto types. Automatic transmission was an option with Pinto engines. All cars had the fascia and instrument layout introduced on late-model Capri Is, there being L, XL and GT trim packs at first.

Evolution continued, with a top-of-the-range Ghia trim spec (which included a wooden fascia) on 1993cc cars from May 1974. S models replaced GT models from late 1975, 1300GT and 1600GT types being dropped at the same time. From mid-1975 the special edition all-black "Midnight Capri" with Pinto engines, gold-painted alloy wheels, sports steering wheel and more, became popular.

Capri IIs were more versatile, and more ride-comfortable than the Capri I

had been, and they were subtly more family-friendly than before. Certainly they had become "almost four-seater" sports saloons.

In production terms, Ford-of-Europe rationalisation then set in, with Capri II

assembly henceforth concentrated in Germany from October 1976.

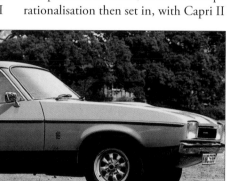

Ford Capri II 1600GL.

SPECIFICATION

BODY STYLES: hatchback coupé

PRODUCTION: 403,612, all types, all engines, UK and Germany

ENGINE & TRANSMISSION: 1298cc, 4 cyl ohv/1593cc/1993cc, S4 ohc, 4sp man, or auto, f/r

POWER: 50bhp @ 5000rpm/57bhp @ 5000rpm/72bhp @ 5200rpm/88bhp @ 5700rpm/98bhp @ 5200rpm

MAX SPEED (MPH): 86-106

0-60MPH (SEC): 18.8-10.4

SUSPENSION & BRAKES: coil ifs, leaf rear, disc f/drum r

LENGTH (IN)/WEIGHT (LB): 171/2178-2348

LAUNCH PRICE: £1336

Capri II (V6) 1974-76

In parallel with the four-cylinder models, the V6-engined Capris progressed from Series I to II in March 1974, taking on the same new hatchback body with its more spacious cabin. The 2994cc V6 engine was the same as before, backed by manual or optional automatic transmission.

The original 3000GT was joined by an up-market Ghia derivative (better trim and equipment) from May 1974, this car having optional power-assisted steering. Automatic transmission was becoming more popular, and by the end of the 1970s the majority of 3-litres would be so equipped.

From June 1975 there was the all-black "Midnight" limited edition 3000S (see 1600/2000 types, above), this becoming a mainstream model in 1976. From autumn 1975, the 3000GT was discontinued, the 3000S taking its place in the line; at the same time, the 3000 Ghia got power-assisted steering as standard equipment.

From April 1976, automatic transmission was no longer available on 3000S types but became standard on the 3000 Ghia. This kind of complication was typical of Ford product planning of the period. Then, as with the four-cylinder types, assembly was progress-

ively concentrated in Germany, the last British-built Capri 3000 being produced at Halewood in September 1976.

Compared with the 3-litre engined Capri I, the 3-litre Capri IIs were smoother, more refined, more driveable, and certainly less overtly sporty than before – but became popular for that very reason.

An increasing proportion were produced with automatic transmission, power steering and some of the "comfort" options in what was a complicated range. These are the derivatives which survived into the 2000s, as collectors' cars in one-make clubs.

Capri II 3.0 Ghia. All Capri Ghias had a vinyl roof and alloy wheels.

SPECIFICATION

BODY STYLES: hatchback coupé

PRODUCTION: see Capri II above

ENGINE & TRANSMISSION: 2994cc, V6 ohv, 4sp man, or auto, f/r

POWER: 138bhp @ 5000rpm

MAX SPEED (MPH): 117

0-60MPH (SEC): 9.0

SUSPENSION & BRAKES: coil ifs, leaf rear, disc f/drum r

LENGTH (IN)/WEIGHT (LB): 171/2580

LAUNCH PRICE: £1932

Escort Mk II 1975-80

The second-generation Escort ran from January 1975 to the summer of 1980. British assembly was at Halewood but millions of Escorts were built in Germany and other countries. Along with the Cortina III and IV, these were Britain's fastest-selling cars.

The Escort Mk II used the same chassis platform as the late-model Escort Mk I (MacPherson strut front end, live axle rear, rack-and-pinion steering), with a new and rather more slab-sided body shell. There were three types of Kent engine, these being the first Escorts to have a mainstream 1598cc engine option, which was very successful.

It was built in two-door and four-door saloon, three-door estate car (and light van) versions. Trim packs were carefully graded – base, L, GL and Ghia at first – with 1300 and 1600 Sport versions too.

An auto 'box was optional on non-Sport 1298cc and 1598cc types.

Then from mid-1975 the stripped-to-the-bone Popular and Popular Plus models appeared, replacing 1100 Base models, and for the next five years there was a continuous shift between models, spec levels and options, with a mid-term facelift (involving such things as new square headlamps) from late 1978. Specifications were gradually improved – so, as an example, a car which had an optional radio in 1975 would have it as standard by 1980.

All cars shared the same basic type of fascia/instrument panel, though Sport models had more instruments and special steering wheels. Lower-spec cars had four-wheel drum brakes, but higher-spec ones (and all cars from the late 1970s) had front-wheel discs.

None of these cars was exciting to drive but they sold hugely – they were available, reliable, handled well and didn't cost a lot to maintain.

SPECIFICATION

BODY STYLES: saloon, estate, commercials

PRODUCTION: 960,007 UK-built

ENGINE & TRANSMISSION:
1097cc/1298cc/1598cc, S4 ohv, 4sp man, or auto, f/r

POWER: 41bhp @ 5300rpm/48bhp @ 5500rpm/57bhp @ 5500rpm/70bhp @ 5500rpm/84bhp @ 5500rpm

MAX SPEED (MPH): 79-100

0-60MPH (SEC): 20.8-10.3

SUSPENSION & BRAKES: coil ifs, leaf rear, drums f&r or disc f/drum r

LENGTH (IN)/WEIGHT (LB): 171/1844 - 1987

LAUNCH PRICE: £1299

Ford Escort Mk II 1.6GL.

Escort RS1800 1975-77

Although Ford sold three different types of Mk II RS models, only one of them, the RS1800, was built in the UK; others were assembled in Germany. This car, spiritual successor to the Mk I RS1600, was built in tiny numbers,

effectively by re-engining near-complete 1600 Sport or RS Mexico types.

RS1800s were all two-door cars, with a slightly reinforced version of the Mk II body shell. All the running gear was an updated version of RS1600 machinery,

this time with a single-carburettor 1835cc light-alloy block 16-valve BDA engine, little more powerful than before but rather more torquey. Externally, badges, striping and a transverse rear spoiler gave the game away, while interior trim was the same as

SPECIFICATION

BODY STYLES: saloon

PRODUCTION: not known

ENGINE & TRANSMISSION: 1835cc, S4 2ohc, 4sp man, f/r

POWER: 115bhp @ 6000rpm

MAX SPEED (MPH): 111

0-60MPH (SEC): 9.0

SUSPENSION & BRAKES: coil ifs, leaf rear, disc f/drum r

LENGTH (IN)/WEIGHT (LB): 157/2015

LAUNCH PRICE: £2825

in German-built RS Mexicos and RS2000 Mk IIs.

The first cars were hand-assembled at Halewood, the remainder in a corner of the redundant AVO building at Aveley.

Few cars remained standard for long, most of them being re-prepared for racing or rallying. This makes the surprisingly civilised road cars very rare and very desirable.

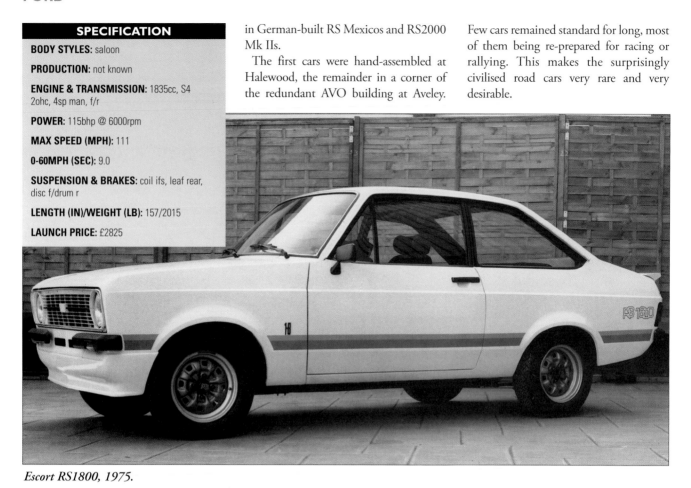

Escort RS1800, 1975.

Escort RS Mexico MK II 1976-80

Enthusiasts are grateful that this car existed since Escort RS1800s were made from part-complete Mexicos, but otherwise the Mexico had little to make it special. Using the same two-door body as other Escorts of the late 1970s, the RS Mexico had a 95bhp 1593cc Pinto engine which gave it a 106mph top speed, but the model was too close

SPECIFICATION

BODY STYLES: saloon

PRODUCTION: 1442

ENGINE & TRANSMISSION: 1593cc, S4 ohc, 4sp man, f/r

POWER: 95bhp @ 5750rpm

MAX SPEED (MPH): 106 (E)

0-60MPH (SEC): 11.1

SUSPENSION & BRAKES: coil ifs, leaf rear, disc f/drum r

LENGTH (IN)/WEIGHT (LB): 157/1990

Escort Mk II RS Mexico, 1976.

to the RS2000 Mk II in price and never took off. It was certainly not as successful as the 1970-74 Mk I Mexico had been.

Much of the interior – seating, trim and instrumentation – was like that of

the Escort 1600 Sport (which made spare parts easier to find in later years). This was an appealing but simple little car, which was quite overshadowed by the larger-engined RS2000. Assembly was always at Saarlouis, in Germany.

Escort RS 2000 MKII 1976-80

By any standards, and by a wide margin, the RS2000 Mk II was the most successful rear wheel drive Escort RS model of the 1970s.

Its chassis – MacPherson strut front suspension, rack-and-pinion steering, leaf spring rear suspension and the braking installation – was shared completely with the RS Mexico and the RS1800. The two USPs (Unique Selling Propositions) were the use of a 110bhp 1993cc Pinto engine, and the special "beaky-nose" front-end which incorporated four circular headlamps.

As with other Mk II RS Escorts, European manufacture was always at Saarlouis in Germany. In Europe, this model was only ever sold as a two-door saloon.

(Note for collectors of oddities: in South Africa and Australia, some types had conventional "flat-front" styling, and in Australia the RS2000 was also available as a four-door saloon!)

This road car was found to be as fast and capable as the RS1800, and faster than the old-type RS1600 and RS2000. It was also a remarkably refined, well-trimmed and robust

Escort RS2000, 1976.

machine which handled very well and which appealed to thousands of RS enthusiasts.

Early cars were available in only one trim specification, but from late 1978 there were two types, the "Base" and the more lavishly equipped "Custom", although both models shared the same unchanged mechanical package. Ford's number crunchers were delighted with the performance of this model – just look at the sales figures – and so were the customers.

A well liked classic today.

SPECIFICATION
BODY STYLES: saloon
PRODUCTION: 25,638
ENGINE & TRANSMISSION: 1993cc, S4 ohc, 4sp man, f/r
POWER: 110bhp @ 5500rpm
MAX SPEED (MPH): 109
0-60MPH (SEC): 8.6
SUSPENSION & BRAKES: coil ifs, leaf rear, disc f/drum r
LENGTH (IN)/WEIGHT (LB): 163/2075
LAUNCH PRICE: £2857

Cortina Mk IV 1976-79

In Britain the fourth-generation Cortina took over smoothly from the Mk III in the autumn of 1976, though a near identical looking car, the Ford Taunus, had been on sale in Germany since early 1976 (that car, by the way, had a different line-up of engines). The Mk IV, in fact, was the first of the Ford-of-Europe Cortinas, where duplicated factories produced similar cars; before the end of the run, some Cortina Mk IVs were actually being assembled outside Britain.

The basic platform, engine, transmission, suspension and steering had been lifted from the last of the Mk IIIs, but all Mk IVs were to have disc front brakes. The much more angular new body style had 15 per cent more glass area. In many ways this was a much

Ford Cortina Mk IV GL models had sports wheels as standard.

more European-looking car than the Mk III, for all traces of the coke-bottle shape had disappeared.

In common with the new-for-1976 Ford-Germany Taunus, the Mk IV/V Cortina would last for six seasons, and more than one million would be sold. As ever, there were two-door and four-door saloons, plus a five-door estate car.

British Cortinas were immediately available with four different four-cylinder engines (one was an old-style 50bhp Kent unit, dropped for 1979), manual or automatic transmission, and a bewildering cocktail of Base, L, GL, Ghia and S (for Sporting) trim and equipment packs. Cars supplied to S pack specification were really Ghias with fatter wheels and tyres, a rev-counter, extra driving lamps and stiffer suspension, for instance.

This range sold very strongly for just three years before being replaced in October 1979 by what Ford initially called "Cortina 80", but everyone else would know as the Mk V. Like earlier Cortinas, there were so many different derivatives of the Mk IV that it was, and drove like, whatever the customers wanted it to be.

Although rust protection had advanced markedly during the 1970s, these cars were still consumables, and few were worthy of being preserved in future years.

SPECIFICATION

BODY STYLES: saloon, estate

PRODUCTION: 1,131,850 all Mk IV and Mk V

ENGINE & TRANSMISSION: 1298cc, S4 ohv/ 1593cc/1993cc, S4 ohc, 4sp man, or auto, f/r

POWER: 50bhp @ 5000rpm/57bhp @ 5500rpm/59bhp @ 4500rpm/72bhp @ 5000rpm/98bhp @ 5200rpm.

MAX SPEED (MPH): 88 (E)-100

0-60MPH (SEC): not measured-11.0

SUSPENSION & BRAKES: coil ifs, coil rear, disc f/drum r

LENGTH (IN)/WEIGHT (LB): 170/2128-2307

LAUNCH PRICE: £1950

Cortina Mk IV 2300 1977-79

Although vee-engined Ford-of-Germany Taunuses had been on sale since 1964, the first of the British V6-engined Cortinas did not appear until September 1977. Only on sale for two years in the Cortina Mk IV body shell, this car was available in 2300GL, 2300S and 2300 Ghia versions as a four-door saloon or five-door estate car.

Trim and furnishings were at the same level as the equivalent 2000 models,

SPECIFICATION

BODY STYLES: saloon, estate

PRODUCTION: see Cortina Mk IV above

ENGINE & TRANSMISSION: 2293cc, V6 ohv, 4sp man, or auto, f/r

POWER: 108bhp @ 5000rpm

MAX SPEED (MPH): 103

0-60MPH (SEC): 10.5

SUSPENSION & BRAKES: coil ifs, coil rear, disc f/drum r

LENGTH (IN)/WEIGHT (LB): 170/2507

LAUNCH PRICE: £3901

Cortina Mk IV 2.3S model, 1977.

though in this 108bhp installation S-level spring and damper settings were standardised, as was power-assisted steering. Automatic transmission was available on the GL and the Ghia, but not the S.

In fact this car was little faster than the 2000, and because it was 64lb heavier at the front end the handling was not quite as well balanced. For comparison, when it was announced the 2000GL cost £3452, whereas the 2300GL cost £3901. Even so, it was a car which appealed to many fleet managers, who could stretch their Cortina coverage over a wider number of managers.

Like other Mk IVs, this type of Cortina gave way to the Mk V in the autumn of 1979, when an improved version would be carried forward.

Cortina Mk V 1979-82

Although the Cortina Mk V looked superficially like the Mk IV, it was different in many ways. According to Ford's parts lists, every external body panel, all the glass, and most related details had been changed in one way or another. The roof pressing was much flatter than before, tail lamps were much enlarged, and every engine had been made more powerful and/or more fuel-efficient. By this time, inertia reel seat belts and laminated windscreen glass were standard on all derivatives.

Once again, this Cortina shared its basic platform with that of the Mk IV and the Mk III. There was a choice of four-door saloon or five-door estate car (plus a two-door saloon with the

Cortina Mk V 1.6L, 1981.

SPECIFICATION

BODY STYLES: saloon, estate

PRODUCTION: 1,131,850, all Mk IV and Mk V

ENGINE & TRANSMISSION: 1298cc, S4 ohv/1593cc/1993cc, S4 ohc, 4sp man, or auto, f/r

POWER: 61bhp @ 6000rpm/76bhp @ 5500rpm/93bhp @ 58900rpm/102bhp @ 5400rpm

MAX SPEED (MPH): (E) 88-103

0-60MPH (SEC): Not measured-10.3

SUSPENSION & BRAKES: coil ifs, coil rear, disc f/drum r

LENGTH (IN)/WEIGHT (LB): 170/2128 - 2274

LAUNCH PRICE: £3346

1298cc engine), and four-cylinder engine power outputs now spanned 61bhp to 102bhp.

The usual range of Base, L, GL, and Ghia trim packs was available, there being no fewer than 20 different Mk V derivatives at first. This time there was no "S" model on its own, but an "S" pack (firmer suspension, alloy road wheels, wider radial ply tyres and other details) was available instead. On 2000 models this cost an extra £153.

In the final year there were two special editions, Carousel and Crusader. There were only 6000 Carousels, and the Crusader provided the majority of production in the closing months of the car's life. Mechanically these cars were not changed, but had different and enhanced trim and equipment packages.

The last Cortina was produced at Dagenham on 22 July 1982, its replacement being the very different Sierra. The Mk V, like other Cortinas, had wanted to be something for everyone, and the sales figures prove that this approach worked. Though it was never super-fast, super-agile or super-cheap, it was a simple car to maintain. Very few, however, seem to have survived.

Cortina Mk V 2300 1979-82

The 2293cc V6-engined version of the Cortina Mk V was, logically enough, a progression of the Mk IV V6-engined car, with all the Mk V style changes, and with 116bhp. This was enough to deliver a top speed of well over 100mph, and (except for the Lotus-Cortinas of the 1960s) it was the fastest Cortina of all time. GL and Ghia Specifications were both available, as was the "S" pack already mentioned in the main Cortina Mk V entry above.

The last 2300 was produced in July 1982.

Cortina Mk V 2.3 Ghia estate.

SPECIFICATION

BODY STYLES: saloon, estate

PRODUCTION : 1,131,850, all Mk IV and Mk V

ENGINE & TRANSMISSION: 2293cc, V6 ohv, 4sp man, or auto, f/r

POWER: 116bhp @ 5500rpm

MAX SPEED (MPH): 103

0-60MPH (SEC): 10.5

SUSPENSION & BRAKES: coil ifs, coil rear, disc f/drum r

LENGTH (IN)/WEIGHT (LB): 170/2472

LAUNCH PRICE: £5243

Consul/Granada (Mk I) 1972-77

To every Ford-watcher's relief, the Consul/Granada of 1972 was a much better car than the Zephyr/Zodiac Mk IV which it replaced. Though some of the old Zodiac's running gear – V4 and V6 engines, plus manual gearboxes – was carried over, the rest of the car was new. In particular, the style was more restrained (the bonnet was shorter), the cabin package was better, and the independent rear suspension was quite transformed.

Announced in March 1972, and built in Britain and Germany (where the engine line-up was quite different), the new four-door saloon was sold as a Consul with 1996cc V4, 2495cc V6 or 2994cc V6 (GT only) engines, or as a Granada with 2495cc or 2994cc V6 engines. As ever with Ford there were several different trim packs (Base, L and GT Consuls, Base and GXL Granadas), a choice of four-speed floor-change manual or Ford C4 automatic transmission, and a comprehensive options list. At first there were only four-door saloons, but a five-door estate car (V6 engines only) was added from September 1972.

All cars had wishbone front suspension much the same as the Cortina III layout, with optional power-assistance for the rack-and-pinion steering on V6-engined cars. From April 1973, PAS became standard on Granadas and the 2495cc Granada was dropped.

Ford Consul GT of 1972 had the 138bhp 3-litre engine.

The 1972 2.5-litre Consul L estate.

For 1974 there was a revised fascia and instrument panel, and the top-of-the-range, automatic-transmission 2994cc Granada Ghia was introduced in March 1974. From September 1974 a reshuffle saw the old-type V4 engine dropped in favour of the 1993cc overhead-camshaft Pinto engine. Within a year, names and specifications were reshuffled so that the Consul name disappeared and all engine options were covered by the Granada badge.

From the spring of 1976, automatic transmission was standardised on all GL

SPECIFICATION

BODY STYLES: saloon, coupé, estate

PRODUCTION: 123,368 UK-built

ENGINE & TRANSMISSION: 1993cc, S4 ohc/1996cc, V4 ohv/2495/2994cc, V6cyl ohv, 4sp man, or auto, f/r

POWER: 75bhp @ 5000rpm -138bhp @ 5000rpm

MAX SPEED (MPH): 90-113

0-60MPH (SEC): not measured- 9.1

SUSPENSION & BRAKES: coil ifs, coil irs, discs f&r

LENGTH (IN)/WEIGHT (LB): 184/2673-3073

LAUNCH PRICE: £1255

Granada Ghia saloon, 1974.

The German-built Granada Ghia Coupé attracted many favourable comments. This 2-litre model was dropped in 1976, leaving only the 3-litre available in Britain.

and Ghia-specified types (a manual option remained), and a two-door fastback coupé (built in Germany, though) joined the range.

This was typical of Ford's flamboyant new-model thinking in the mid-1970s. After September 1976 all Consul and Granada models were assembled at a Ford-of-Germany factory.

The Mk I cars were simple, robust and spacious, providing efficient service in a wide range of roles, from taxi through police car to executive express.

Consul/Granada (Mk II) 1977-85

Introduced in late 1977, the Mk II Granada used the original Granada platform and running gear, but with different engines, a smart new crisp-edged style, and an overall improvement in build quality. As on the original types, all-independent suspension and four-wheel disc brakes were standard. These cars were available in four-door saloon and five-door estate car form. The saloon was capacious and well-equipped, the estate car being positively cavernous.

From this date, all Granadas were manufactured in Germany. For the UK market there was a different line-up of engines made up of a 1993cc Pinto and three different versions of the German Cologne V6 engine, in 2293cc and 2792cc form. The flagship model used a fuel-injected 160bhp V6. At the same time (but rarely seen) there was a diesel alternative, a 2112cc Peugeot engine which produced a mere 63bhp. Automatic transmission was optional on all petrol-engined derivatives.

As ever, there were several trim packs – L, GL, S and Ghia – the "S" (for

Granada Mk II 2000L.

Sporting) denoting a car which had firmer suspension and crisper handling. 2.3-litre cars were boosted from 108bhp to 114bhp at the end of 1979, and the enlarged 69bhp 2498cc Peugeot diesel engine came on stream at the end of 1982.

Production figures show just how successful this range was, though most sales were of the less powerful, less luxuriously equipped versions. This model retired in favour of the new-type Granada/Scorpio hatchbacks in 1985.

SPECIFICATION

BODY STYLES: saloon, estate

PRODUCTION: 639,440 Europe-wide

ENGINE & TRANSMISSION: 1993cc, 4cyl ohc/2293cc/2792cc V6 cyl, ohv/2112cc/2498cc 4cyl diesel, 4sp man, 5sp man or auto, f/r

POWER: 63bhp@4500rpm-160bhp@5700rpm

MAX SPEED (MPH): 85-117

0-60MPH (SEC): 27.2-8.9

SUSPENSION & BRAKES: coil ifs, coil irs, discs f&r

LENGTH (IN)/WEIGHT (LB): 182/2735-3009

LAUNCH PRICE: £4144-£5863

Granada Mk II 2.8 Ghia.

Mk II Ghia estate.

Fiesta 1976-83

Launched in 1976, and planned to be assembled in Spain, Germany and at Dagenham, the new Fiesta was the first of a whole range of transverse-engined front wheel drive hatchbacks which Ford would launch in future years. Apart from the fact that the three-main-bearing Valencia engines were re-designed versions of the Kent overhead-valve power unit, the entire car was new. Introduction and sale of the British-built Fiestas came in February 1977.

Fiestas had a unit-construction shell, with a steel platform, MacPherson strut front suspension, rack-and-pinion steering, and a simple dead axle beam at the rear. Front disc brakes were standard on all types. The 957cc or 1117cc engines drove through an all-indirect four-speed gearbox, there

Ford Fiesta GL.

being no alternative transmissions in view at the time. All cars had the same three-door hatchback style with rectangular headlamps. There were Base, L, S and Ghia trim and equipment packs; Ghias had alloy road wheels.

A 66bhp 1298cc-engined version, trimmed as an S or a Ghia, joined the range from late 1977, and an even larger-engined type was built in Germany for export to North America.

As usual with Ford, Fiestas received regular trim and equipment updates, though entry-level Popular and Popular Plus models joined from December 1980. After several special editions had also been put on sale, in September 1983 the entire range was given a major

Fiesta Supersport.

facelift, with a different front-end style, new engines and new transmissions.

Smaller than the Escort (of which a front wheel drive type appeared in late 1980), the Fiesta sold in huge numbers all round the world. Small, compact, and with good handling, it would give rise to several new-generation models over the decades which followed.

SPECIFICATION

BODY STYLES: hatchback

PRODUCTION: 1,750,000

ENGINE & TRANSMISSION:
957cc/1117cc/1298cc, S4 ohv, 4sp man, f/f

POWER: 40bhp @ 5500rpm/53bhp @ 6000rpm/57bhp @ 5700rpm/66bhp @ 5600rpm

MAX SPEED (MPH): 79-94

0-60MPH (SEC): 19.0-13.7

SUSPENSION & BRAKES: coil ifs, coil beam rear, disc f/drum r

LENGTH (IN)/WEIGHT (LB): 141/1635-1764

LAUNCH PRICE: £1856

Escort Mk III 1980-86

Compared with the Mk II, the third-generation Escort of September 1980 was almost entirely new. It was the first Escort to use a transverse-engine front wheel drive layout, the first to be based on a hatchback body style, and (from April 1984) the first to have a diesel-engined option.

British-made Mk IIIs were built at Halewood on Merseyside, German ones at Saarlouis, and over the years both factories would occasionally supply each

other's markets with particular derivatives. Based on a conventional unit-construction shell with sharp-edged styling, the Mk III was available in three-door or five-door hatchback and three-door estate car forms at first. MacPherson strut front suspension, rack and pinion steering and coil spring/strut independent rear suspension featured on all types, as did front-wheel disc brakes.

Originally there was a choice of 1117cc ohv and 1296cc and 1596cc ohc (CVH)

engines, all cars sharing the same type of four-speed Fiesta-type manual 'box. The higher-output XR3 model is described separately. There were Base, L, GL and Ghia trim levels, in fact 23 separate models from the outset.

Over the years the specification evolved, with a mid-term trim and equipment "freshener" in early 1983, before the range was facelifted to Mk IV form in February 1986. A four-door notchback saloon, the Orion, appeared in September 1983, there was an entry-level Popular model (1117cc only) from April 1984, the original 54bhp 1608cc diesel engine appeared in April 1984 (L and GL), and the up-market XR3i-based Cabriolet from mid-1984. A five-speed manual gearbox was standard on 1600s from April 1982, optional on 1300s from January 1983, and automatic transmission (1600 only) was optional from November 1982.

This was typical of Ford's covering-all-bases product planning of the period. Each and every one of these cars handled well, was cheap and simple to maintain, and sold in very big numbers. Many survive to this day, often only as marginal-MoT runabouts.

Ford Escort Mk III 1.6 Ghia, 1980.

SPECIFICATION

BODY STYLES: hatchback, estate, drophead, commercials

PRODUCTION: 1,857,000

ENGINE & TRANSMISSION: 1117cc, S4 ohv/1296cc/1596cc, S4 ohc/1608cc, S4 ohv diesel, 4sp man, 5sp man, or auto, f/r

POWER: 55bhp @ 5700rpm/69bhp @ 6000rpm/79bhp @ 5800rpm/54bhp @ 4000rpm

MAX SPEED (MPH): 92-103

0-60MPH (SEC): 15.5-10.7

SUSPENSION & BRAKES: coil ifs, coil irs, disc f/drum r

LENGTH (IN)/WEIGHT (LB): 160/1830 - 2024

LAUNCH PRICE: £3374

Escort XR3 1980-82

When Ford dropped the Mk II Escorts, for the time being the RS sub-brand died with them. Top-of-the-range Mk IIIs, on the other hand, were badged as XR3s, and proved to be big sellers. From September 1980 until late 1982, when they were replaced by the fuel-injected XR3i, the three-door XR3s were the fastest of these mainstream Escorts.

Based very closely on the new-generation Escort 1600 Ghia, the XR3 had a tuned overhead-camshaft CVH

Escort XR3, 1980.

SPECIFICATION

BODY STYLES: hatchback

PRODUCTION: see Escort Mk III above

ENGINE & TRANSMISSION: 1596cc, S4 ohv, 4sp man, 5sp man, f/f

POWER: 96bhp @ 6000rpm

MAX SPEED (MPH): 113

0-60MPH (SEC): 9.2

SUSPENSION & BRAKES: coil ifs, coil irs, disc f/drum r

LENGTH (IN)/WEIGHT (LB): 160/2040

LAUNCH PRICE: £5123

engine with 96bhp, this being enough to deliver a top speed of almost 115mph. Early cars had a four-speed transmission shared with the 1600, but the XR3 was easily distinguished by its special alloy wheels, rear spoiler, sports front seats and its extrovert trim and interior features.

From April 1982 the XR3 gained a five-speed manual transmission, which suited it even better. This car, whose front wheels and suspension seemed to be set up with slight positive camber, making it look slightly bow-legged, only had a two-year career before it was replaced by the more sophisticated, and better developed, fuel-injected XR3i model.

Even so, the XR3 sold very well, and the five-speeders in particular became budget-price collectors' cars in the decades which followed.

FRAZER NASH

Although Frazer Nash cars had been on sale since 1924, AFN Ltd (which controlled the brand from 1926) always had to do other things to pay the rent. Before the war the company had imported BMWs, and after the war they would make money by importing Porsches. All pre-war Fraser Nashes were sports cars known as "chain gangs", because of their unique type of chain-drive transmission, and all used proprietary engines.

From 1945 a fresh start was made, and for a brief period AFN joined forces with Bristol to develop new cars, all based on late-1930s BMW engines. This arrangement did not gel, so from 1947 Frazer Nash was once again independent, designing its own sports cars around robust but simple tubular chassis, and with privileged access to the latest Bristol engines and transmissions. All the cars were produced in simply-equipped premises in Isleworth, West London, and many went on to achieve great things in motor racing.

The engineering of the cars was at once simple, robust and advanced but the cars were extremely expensive and thus likely to sell only in tiny numbers. Although Frazer Nash dabbled with the thought of making a cheaper model (a prototype which might have rivalled the Austin-Healey 100 was built in 1952), nothing came of this. With more and more time being spent on the Porsche importing business, the Frazer Nash brand was allowed to fade away.

The last Bristol-engined car was built in 1956, the last Frazer Nash in 1957. The premises survive, much modified and modernised, as a Porsche retail outlet.

High Speed/Le Mans Replica 1948-53

Frazer Nash Le Mans Replica on the 1953 Alpine Rally.

The first post-war Frazer Nash two-seater introduced the combination of a tubular chassis, transverse leaf spring independent front suspension and torsion bar suspension of the rear axle to the rich clientele who wanted a bespoke, hand-built sports car. Bristol supplied the engine (a much-updated BMW 328 design) and the transmission, while Frazer Nash supplied their own body shells.

The "High Speed" had a simple and very basically trimmed two-seater body with cutaway sides, exposed headlamps and cycle-type wings. After one of these cars had taken third place at Le Mans in 1949, new examples were titled "Le Mans Replica", and went on to become the best-selling post-war Frazer Nash.

Specifications varied significantly from car to car (the customer often had his own special requirements), and there were subtle improvements over time. From 1952 this model became Le Mans Replica Mk II, complete with a parallel-tube chassis frame (the design of which was easily adaptable to fit other Frazer Nash models). De Dion rear suspension was adopted for the final run of Mk IIs.

Although this was one of the fastest of Frazer Nashes, it eventually fell from favour because of its very stark and comfortless body shell. Like all such machines from the post-war AFN concern, this sports car handled very well, with precise steering, and had an abundance of character. In the early 1950s it was the sort of car one could drive to a race meeting, plaster up with competition numbers, race, then put back to normal for the drive home. 110mph from a 2-litre engine, of course, was a considerable gait for the period.

In later years, all such Frazer Nash cars became revered and took on a high value. Unhappily, it was possible for replicas (for which, read "fake") to be produced, this being done several times.

Prix de Monte Carlo, 1952. Tony Crook's Le Mans replica leads Manzon's Gordini.

Fast Roadster/Mille Miglia 1950-55

Frazer Nash Mille Miglia.

An attempt to make a more civilised version of the Le Mans Replica was only a partial success, even by Frazer Nash standards.

Originally called the Fast Roadster then (from 1950) the Mille Miglia, this model had a neatly styled full-width two-seater body, with headlamps recessed in the nose of curvaceous front wings – the shape, they say, was originally influenced by the 1940 BMW 328 race car. In some eyes the shape of the Mille Miglia was also likened to that of the MGA, but the Frazer Nash definitely came first, by several years.

To make this the entry-level model, Frazer Nash reduced the power output of the Bristol engine to no more than 100-105bhp, and (as with Bristol 400s of the day) there was a freewheel feature on first gear.

Individual specifications varied from car to car (Frazer Nash was like that) since some customers wanted more power than was officially listed. Most were two-seater sports cars, with simple soft-tops, though Frazer Nash also built two drophead coupés.

Targa Florio 1952-54

Announced in 1952, and therefore using the new parallel-tube chassis frame, the Targa Florio was really a replacement for the Mille Miglia model. In another shuffle of engines and styles, this one was available officially with 100bhp or 125bhp versions of the Bristol engine. The body styling was less curvaceous and less flamboyant than

Frazer Nash Targa Florio.

SPECIFICATION

BODY STYLES: sports car

PRODUCTION: 14

ENGINE & TRANSMISSION: 1971cc, S6 ohv, 4sp man, f/r

POWER: 100bhp @ 5000rpm/125bhp @ 5500rpm

MAX SPEED (MPH): (100bhp) 114

0-60MPH (SEC): (100bhp)10.4

SUSPENSION & BRAKES: leaf ifs, tor rear, drums f&r

LENGTH (IN)/WEIGHT (LB): 150/1848

LAUNCH PRICE: £3035

that of the Mille Miglia had been.

The problem for Frazer Nash, as ever, was that this car cost a lot, prompting many potential clients to settle instead for a Jaguar XK120 at half the price and with even higher performance. The last

of fourteen cars was produced in 1954.

No one ever complained about the performance, however, especially with the 125bhp engine fitted, and like all the related post-war Frazer Nashes this one had bags of character.

Le Mans Fixed Head Coupé 1953-56

Yet another cocktail of chassis, engines and body styles, the Le Mans Fixed Head came along in 1953. In some ways a hard-top version of the Targa Florio sports car, this was the only permanent-roof Frazer Nash put on sale.

Not that it appealed to many people, for in three years only nine such cars were produced, the first having been

The Nottorp/Anderson Frazer Nash Le Mans coupé at Le Mans in 1954.

SPECIFICATION

BODY STYLES: sports coupé

PRODUCTION: 9

ENGINE & TRANSMISSION: 1971cc, S6 ohv, 4sp man, f/r

POWER: 125bhp @ 5500rpm

MAX SPEED (MPH): (E) 125

0-60MPH (SEC): not measured

SUSPENSION & BRAKES: leaf ifs, tor rear (optional DD tor rear), drums f&r

LENGTH (IN)/WEIGHT (LB): 161/1876

LAUNCH PRICE: £3188

raced at Le Mans in 1953 (hence the name chosen). This was the last of the true "production" Frazer Nashes, with more power than most and more toys.

Even the basic specification included the 125bhp version of the Bristol engine (more was available if money changed

hands). This was fitted in the parallel-tube chassis frame, and the De Dion suspension which had recently been developed was available to special order. It was a Le Mans model which was the last of all Bristol-engined Fraser Nashes to be built, in 1956.

Sebring 1954-56

Only three Sebrings were produced, but because of Frazer Nash's narrow horizons this counts as a production car, though a limited one.

Built up around the parallel-tube chassis frame, and with one car constructed from new with coil spring independent front suspension, the Sebring was catalogued as having 140bhp. With such a neat open two-seater sports car body, it looked capable of 125mph.

SPECIFICATION

BODY STYLES: sports car

PRODUCTION: 3

ENGINE & TRANSMISSION: 1971cc, S6 ohv, 4sp man, f/r

POWER: 140bhp @ 5750rpm

MAX SPEED (MPH): (E) 125

0-60MPH (SEC): not measured

SUSPENSION & BRAKES: coil ifs or leaf ifs, DD tor rear, drums f&r

LENGTH (IN)/WEIGHT (LB): 161/1736

LAUNCH PRICE: £3543

Frazer Nash Sebring.

The style itself was unique, but in many ways the car had the proportions of the earlier Mille Miglia. The front end, though, was lifted straight from the Le Mans coupé.

The Sebring was so rare, so powerful, and so rapid that it became one of the most desirable post-war Frazer Nashes. Because only three cars were produced (the £3543 price tag put off almost everyone), survivors are worth a fair fortune.

Continental GT Coupé 1957-58

Once demand for Bristol-engined cars collapsed, Frazer Nash dabbled with the idea of producing a replacement, to be powered by BMW's modern 2.6-litre V8 engine. Only two cars were built, and after the second of these smart coupés had been shown at the Earls Court Motor Show in 1958 the project folded without

SPECIFICATION

BODY STYLES: sports coupé

PRODUCTION: 2

ENGINE & TRANSMISSION: 2580cc, V8 ohv, 4sp man, f/r

POWER: 140bhp @ 5000rpm

MAX SPEED (MPH): 130 (E)

0-60MPH (SEC): not measured

SUSPENSION & BRAKES: coil ifs, leaf rear, drums f&r

LENGTH (IN)/WEIGHT (LB): 153/1875

LAUNCH PRICE: not quoted

The Continental GT Coupé.

a price even being listed.

Technically, the mixture was as expected – the Mk II tubular chassis, transverse leaf or coil spring independent front suspension (the specification was apparently not finalised) and De Dion rear suspension. The new addition to the recipe was the BMW engine and gearbox.

The two-seater coupé body was smart, and looked as if could certainly support the claimed 130mph top speed, but a demand did not develop, and no customer deliveries were ever made.

FRISKY

Captain Raymond Flower, earlier an entrepeneur based in Egypt, returned to the UK in 1956 and collaborated with Henry Meadows Ltd (proprietary engine builders, of Wolverhampton) in developing a new micro-car. After hiring Michelotti to style the bodywork, he previewed the Frisky in 1957, at which stage it had gull-wing doors. However, this layout was thought impractical, and the body was reshaped to a more normal, but still very smart, open roadster. If the Frisky had one Unique Selling Proposition, it was that it was a very attractive-looking machine – and that it was at least a four-wheeler, though with a narrow rear track.

As with all such projects, Frisky relied on the rest of the motor industry for its supplies. GRP bodies were produced by the Guy truck business (which was located very close to Meadows), and the motorcycle-type engine came from Villiers.

The original Frisky Sport sold steadily, which encouraged Flower to try again, first with the startlingly-styled Friskysprint of 1958, and later with a more basic model called the Family Three, which was only a three-wheeler. The Friskysprint project sank without trace, but after a factory move to Sandwich in Kent, Family Threes sold slowly into the early 1960s.

Like many other micro-cars of the period, Frisky eventually died of neglect, both by its makers and by the public, so after the last car had been produced in 1964 the marque perished.

Sport 1957-61

Conceived in 1956, shown as a prototype with gull-wing doors in 1957, then put on sale as conventional drophead or (from late 1958) a fixed-head coupé, the Frisky Sport looked rakish though it was quite tiny. With its Michelotti styling, there seemed to be as much overhang, front and rear, as there was wheelbase.

Like many such micro-car projects, the Frisky was b uilt on a tubular frame, had a motorcycle engine in the mid/rear position, and had a GRP body shell. It was no more than a two- seater but it had quite a brisk performance, which rather confirmed the model name.

Front suspension was by rubber and the Dubonnet type of geometry (think of 1930s Vauxhalls…) though a more conventional coil spring and damper suspension was later adopted, while the rear wheels were set so close together that no differential was thought necessary. Power was by a Villiers twin-cylinder air-cooled two-stroke, while final drive from the motorcycle-type gearbox was by chain. There was no reverse gear – to go backwards it was necessary to set the engine spinning in the other direction – a process that was quite familiar to two-stroke motorcycle owners!

Frisky thought it could do better, and sell more, if it converted this style to a three wheeler, so the closely-similar Family Three took over for the 1960s.

SPECIFICATION

BODY STYLES: drophead coupé, coupé

PRODUCTION: not known

ENGINE & TRANSMISSION: 249cc/324cc, S2 ts, 4sp man, m/r

POWER: 16bhp @ 5500rpm/18bhp @ 5500rpm

MAX SPEED (MPH): 56

0-60MPH (SEC): not possible

SUSPENSION & BRAKES: rubber ifs, coil rear, drums f&r

LENGTH (IN)/WEIGHT (LB): 110/784

LAUNCH PRICE: £450

Frisky Sport.

Family Three 1960-64

Frisky Family Three.

Think of the Frisky Sport, but with a single rear wheel and trailing arm suspension in place of the narrow-tracked back axle. Then use a less powerful choice of engines and somehow squash in almost four-seater accommodation. This was the Frisky Family Three, which sold slowly in the early 1960s. The Prince, with a modified and longer, tail, took over from 1961.

Does anybody remember these strange little vehicles?

SPECIFICATION

BODY STYLES: saloon

PRODUCTION: not known

ENGINE & TRANSMISSION: 197cc/244cc/ 324cc/328cc, 1cyl/S2 ts, 4sp man, m/r

POWER: (244cc engine)11bhp @ 5000rpm

MAX SPEED (MPH): 50 (E)

0-60MPH (SEC): not possible

SUSPENSION & BRAKES: rubber ifs, coil rear, drums f&r

LENGTH (IN)/WEIGHT (LB): 110/672

LAUNCH PRICE: £378 (Prince £397)

GILBERN

Giles Smith and Bernard Frieze (hence the name, Gil-Bern) had both built their own specials, and Frieze had worked for a GRP special bodybuilder in the 1950s, before the pair decided in the late '50s to build complete cars. By doing so they became the last car making company ever to have been born and established in Wales.

Based in very modest premises at Llantwit Fardre, near Pontypridd (a few miles north-west of Cardiff), Gilbern went down the classic route of basing its kit cars on steel multi-tube chassis frames, with glass-fibre (GRP) body shells and proprietary engines, transmissions and suspension parts.

The very first Gilberns were GTs, kit-built creations which relied heavily on BMC running gear (Austin-Healey Sprite or MG MGA), though Coventry Climax engines could also be supplied. Some complete cars were supplied, but

kits did not incur British Purchase Tax, and were therefore more popular.

Moving up-market, Gilbern then introduced its second-generation machine, the Genie, in 1966. This followed the same design, engineering and build philosophy, but used Ford Zephyr/Zodiac V6 engines and running gear. These cars were larger, heavier and more expensive, but they sold steadily, especially after Mecca took control of the company and backed an upgrade which turned the Genie into the Invader in 1969.

An estate car derivative followed in the early 1970s, but Gilbern did not survive the arrival of Value Added Tax in 1973 (there were no exemptions for kit-car manufacturers) and collapsed. It was all over by 1974, and neither of the founders was ever again involved in the motor industry.

GT 1959-67

Although Gilbern was both brave and resourceful, it only ever had the capability to produce its own chassis frames and its own body shells. Everything else had to be bought in, almost all of it as built-up engines, transmissions and suspension components. In the case of the original Gilbern, the GT, BMC was the main supplier.

The GT had a multi-tube chassis built up from small-section rectangular and round tubing. It was by no means scientifically laid out in the Colin Chapman/Lotus manner, but it was sturdy, and simple to repair if necessary. Front suspension and steering were Austin-Healey Sprite derived, and the BMC rear axle was located on coil springs and radius arms; centre-lock wire wheels were a normal fitment.

On the first cars a 42bhp/948cc Sprite engine and gearbox were used, but over time the choice of engines grew, eventually (from 1963) encompassing the 95bhp/1798cc MGB power train. The sophisticated Coventry-Climax FWA overhead-camshaft unit was an early and pricey option and was soon abandoned for lack of demand, as was a supercharged derivative of the 948cc Sprite engine. Overdrive was available from 1963 (as fitted to the rear of the MGB transmission) and all later cars had front-wheel disc brakes..

Gilbern GT, 1959.

The GRP body was a neat and stylish 2+2 fastback coupé, with a rather squared up nose. Fixtures, fittings and extra equipment were often enhanced by the customers who bought the kits, so there was/is really no such thing as a "standard" Gilbern GT.

The GT proved popular, not only because it offered good value as a kit, but also because the completed cars handled well and delivered at least everything that the manufacturer claimed. It was still selling well – up to 150 cars a year in the mid-1960s – when it was displaced by the larger Genie.

SPECIFICATION

BODY STYLES: sports coupé

PRODUCTION: approx 280

ENGINE & TRANSMISSION: 948cc/1588cc/ 1622cc/1798cc, 4cyl ohv, 4sp man, o/d with 1.8-litre, f/r (Coventry Climax 1216cc to special order)

POWER: 68bhp @ 5700rpm/80bhp @ 5600rpm/86bhp @ 5500rpm/95bhp @ 5500rpm

MAX SPEED (MPH): 96-111

0-60MPH (SEC): 17.4-12.0

SUSPENSION & BRAKES: coil ifs, coil rear, early cars drums f/r (disc f/drum r from early 1960s)

LENGTH (IN)/WEIGHT (LB): 152/1582-1915

LAUNCH PRICE: £748

Genie/Invader 1966-74

The Genie followed the same lines as the GT which it replaced, though it was different, from end to end. The same kit-build philosophy was followed – a multi-tube frame, a GRP coupé body, and proprietary running gear – in an appealing package.

Larger than the GT – it was nine inches longer and five inches wider – the Genie was a crisp but rather angular 2+2 seater coupé. It had a much larger cabin than the GT and was powered by the Ford Essex V6 engine from the Zodiac and later the Capri 3000. The rack-and-pinion steering and back axle came from BMC, and there were disc brakes at the front. Like the GT before it, the Genie's

The 3-litre Gilbern Invader, 1969.

SPECIFICATION

BODY STYLES: sports coupé, estate (Invader only)

PRODUCTION: approx 80

ENGINE & TRANSMISSION: 2994cc, V6cyl ohv, 4sp man, o/d, f/r

POWER: 141bhp @ 4750rpm

MAX SPEED (MPH): 115

0-60MPH (SEC): 10.7

SUSPENSION & BRAKES: coil ifs, coil rear, disc f/drum r

LENGTH (IN)/WEIGHT (LB): 159/1990

LAUNCH PRICE: £1752/(Invader) £1790 both as kits.

main attraction was that it was supplied as a well-engineered and very complete kit, at a sensible price.

Poor roadholding and dodgy build quality were failings on earlier versions, but these were addressed when the Genie became the Invader, which had bigger brakes and different suspension settings, together with electric windows and modified front-end styling. Even so, some limitations still persisted, which made it difficult for Gilbern to justify the high selling price.

Not even the introduction of an estate car derivative could save the day, and when the application of VAT bumped up prices in 1973 it came as a death-blow to

the company, which stopped making cars in the very same year.

The Invader estate was introduced in 1970. You could buy the car in kit form for £1695.

GILL

The best way to describe the Gill is as an awful little car that could only ever have existed in the mind of someone who thought that petrol supplies would never ease after the Suez crisis of 1956, and that people really wouldn't mind driving round in shoebox-sized machines as long as they were mobile.

Two years earlier British Anzani (who had a lot to answer for) had supported the birth of the Astra (described earlier), and when that project failed they caused the Gill Getabout to be

born as a two-seater reincarnation of the same machine. The "factory" was based at George Street, in London W1, just north of Oxford Street – which probably meant a tiny workshop that could only work on a handful of chassis at a time. The Gill was no more likely to succeed than the Astra. It failed within a year of being launched – and thoroughly deserved that fate.

This, thank goodness, was the end of British Anzani's automotive delusions.

Getabout 1958-59

Based on the chassis of the Astra Utility (described earlier) the Getabout only finds a place in these pages because it existed – not on merit.

As on the Astra, the chassis featured channel-section side members with a steel floor welded to them and a twin-cylinder air-cooled Anzani motorcycle-

type engine mounted in the tail, driving through a motorcycle gearbox and a chain to the rear wheels. The suspension, at least, was independent all round, by coil-over-shocks and swing axles.

The body of the Getabout was a two/three-seater coupé, in aluminium panels over a wooden frame, with side and rear windows in transparent plastic. Windows in the doors slid fore-and-aft rather than wound down. Access to the engine was through a trap-door in the floor behind the two hammock-type seats, and there was no separate external boot access. The gearchange on the Getabout was an improvement on the

Gill Getabout.

SPECIFICATION

BODY STYLES: coupé

PRODUCTION: not known

ENGINE & TRANSMISSION: 322cc, air-cooled 2cyl 2str, 3sp man, r/r

POWER: 15bhp @ 4800rpm

MAX SPEED (MPH): 55 (E)

0-60MPH (SEC): not possible

SUSPENSION & BRAKES: coil ifs, coil irs, drums f&r

LENGTH (IN)/WEIGHT (LB): 114/715

LAUNCH PRICE: £500

Astra's arrangement, for there was positive-stop operation of the floor-mounted quadrant.

At a price of £500 (or £523 for the "de luxe" model which had bumpers, direction indicators and seat covers) this dreadful machine never had a chance of getting established, for at the time a Ford Popular cost £444 and an Austin A35 £570. The Gill had all the failings of the old Astra, its only merit being excellent fuel economy, though no one seemed to care enough about that to want to buy the car.

In theory there was also going to be a four-seater version to be used as a taxi (one would have loved to see the faces of London's licenced cab authorities when viewing this taxi for the very first time…) but nothing came of it.

GINETTA

Founded by the Walklett family in Essex in the 1950s, Ginetta started by delivering multi-tubular chassis frames for customers to build up around Ford components. The first dual-purpose Ginetta sports car – for use on road or track – was the G4 of 1962. It featured the company's own front suspension but many proprietary components. Having set up in Witham, Ginetta then expanded by producing a fascinating variety of road cars, dual-purpose sports cars, and even single-seaters, before announcing the Sunbeam Stiletto-engined G15 in 1968.

Demand for this and other Ginettas was such that the company decided to move again in 1972, to Sudbury in Suffolk, but this proved to be an over-ambitious step and (out of our period) the company retreated to Witham, where further worthy but slow-selling road and racing sports cars were developed.

In later years the Walkletts sold the Ginetta business to an entrepreneur from the north of England, and although the brand still existed in the early 2000s it was a mere shadow of the company which had shone so brightly in the 1960s.

Only four true road cars – the G4, G10/G11, G15 and G21 – truly qualify for inclusion in this volume; many other Ginettas, too specialised to be genuine road cars, added spice to the marque at the time.

G4 1961-69

The small, sweet and appealing G4 sports car was born in 1961 and sold steadily for the next eight years. At this point the Walklett brothers thought its career was over but, as we shall see, they were wrong – for in much-modified form the G4 would be re-introduced in 1981!

Because Ginetta was not large enough, or rich enough, to design its own engines and running gear, the G4 took shape around modern Ford mechanical components – in this case the recently-announced Anglia 105E, whose engine was already known as the basis of a successful Formula Ford power unit.

Built up around a multi-tubular space frame chassis (with some round- and some square-section tubing), the G4 used independent front suspension of Ginetta design, and located its Anglia 105E rear axle by coil springs, radius arms and an A-bracket. The two-seater body shell, very low, very slippery, and with recessed headlamps, was made from GRP. Parts-bin spotters realised that the windscreen came from an Austin-Healey "Frogeye" Sprite, though the rather flimsy hood and side-screens were by Ginetta themselves.

SPECIFICATION

BODY STYLES: sports car, sports coupé

PRODUCTION: c.500

ENGINE & TRANSMISSION:
997cc/1340cc/1498cc, 4cyl ohv, 4sp man, f/r

POWER: 40bhp @ 5000rpm/54bhp @ 4900rpm/78bhp @ 5200rpm

MAX SPEED (MPH): (997cc) 85

0-60MPH (SEC): not measured

SUSPENSION & BRAKES: coil ifs, coil beam rear, drums f/r at first, then disc f/drum r

LENGTH (IN)/WEIGHT (LB): 140/980

LAUNCH PRICE: £697

Ginetta G4, 1961.

Although the original engine gave a mere 40bhp, the car itself only weighed around 1000lb, so acceleration was brisk, and the claimed top speed of 85mph was competitive. To get more performance, customers could specify Ford's 54bhp 1340cc Classic engine instead. Initially the G4 was only available in part-assembled form for £697 (which avoided Purchase Tax) though kits later cost only £499.

From 1963 the rear-end styling was altered and the Ford rear axle was replaced by a BMC unit, which was lighter and offered more alternative ratios, and soon front disc brakes became optional. From 1964 the latest longer-stroke Ford 1498cc became available, as did the option of a neat removable hard-top. In the mid-1960s the chassis frame was revised and strengthened, while the Series III G4 was given higher-mounted, flip-up headlamps to meet the latest legislation, along with more sturdy bumpers. Many G4s, of course, were used as racing sports cars, running in stripped-out condition, so only a few unmodified true road cars have survived.

Many years later, between 1981 and 1984, the G4 was reintroduced, as a Series IV, at first with a 98bhp 1993cc Ford Pinto engine, though other engines could be (and sometimes were) fitted by the customers.

Even later than that, the G27 of 1985 was really a lineal descendant of the G4 theme. This was the way in which Ginetta stayed afloat until it sold out to Martin Pfaff in the late 1980s.

G10/G11 1965-66

This very smart two-seater had a short but unsuccessful career. The original machine was a V8 (Ford Mustang-powered) monster, whose aim was to win sports car races and also serve as a superfast road car. When this project failed, Ginetta then re-designed it completely, installing MGB power, and offering it as a specialised alternative – to the MGB !

The multi-tube chassis frame had a curvaceous GRP body shell bonded to it on assembly, and was built either as a fastback coupé or as a two-seater open sports car. The resemblance to the

SPECIFICATION

BODY STYLES: sports car, sports coupé

PRODUCTION: 6/12

ENGINE & TRANSMISSION: 4727cc, V8cyl/1798cc, 4cyl ohv, 4sp man, f/r

POWER: 271bhp @ 6000rpm/95bhp @ 5400rpm

MAX SPEED (MPH): 161 (E)/110

0-60MPH (SEC): not measured

SUSPENSION & BRAKES: coil ifs, coil irs (coil beam rear with 4cyl), disc f/disc r (V8) or drum r (4-cyl)

LENGTH (IN)/WEIGHT (LB): 162/ (V8) 1808, (4cyl) not quoted

LAUNCH PRICE: £2729/£1325

Ginetta G10.

current MGB was not entirely accidental, as the MGB's doors (and, on the open version) windscreen and soft top were all specified. Even the GRP nose, though unique, nodded to the MGB by having part-recessed headlamps.

On the V8-engined cars there was a Ford-USA four-speed gearbox and a massive Salisbury rear axle (as used in the Jaguar E-Type). All-independent suspension was by coil springs and wishbones, with big disc brakes all round to look after the 271bhp and the

mountainous torque delivery. Well trimmed inside, the fascia sported a speedometer reading up to 220mph, which impressed schoolboys of all ages.

No doubt because of its high price (£2729 in 1965), the G10 was a complete failure, so Ginetta then reworked the entire design for sale in the UK. Instead of Ford-USA running gear, the Walkletts inserted an MGB power train (engine, gearbox and live rear axle) fitted BMC Mini rack-and-pinion steering gear, and added MGB brakes, which included drums at the rear.

The result was really that of an MGB in a party frock – albeit with Ginetta's chassis and mainly GRP shell – and the ensemble was to be sold at £1325 (built-up) or £1098 (component form). As both of these prices were higher than those of the MGB, and as BMC was predictably reluctant to provide so much gear in order to allow Ginetta to compete with its own model, assembly and delivery were sporadic to say the least. It comes as no surprise, therefore, that the G11 died within one short year of its launch.

G15 1968-74

Earlier Ginettas had been either pure race cars or multi-purpose sports cars which could also be raced and usually were. The G15, launched in 1967, was to be Ginetta's first dedicated road car.

Designed around the rear-mounted Sunbeam Stiletto engine and four-speed transmission, the G15 was a neat two-seater sports coupé. The basis of the design was a tubular steel chassis frame, to the back of which was attached the entire Stiletto overhead-cam engine, transmission and semi-trailing arm

suspension units, with individually designed coil spring front suspension for the front wheels.

The light-alloy Stiletto engine, of course, was shared with other sporty derivatives of the Rootes Group's Imp family of cars, and was a direct development of an earlier Coventry-Climax design. It was a smooth, high-revving little jewel, for which parts were easily available. By the time that the G15 was launched, all the earlier doubts about this engine's reliability had been swept away.

The chassis was clad in a shapely two-seater notchback coupé body echoing certain Ginetta styling themes and fashioned from GRP at the Witham factory in Essex.

Although the engine produced a mere 50bhp, this was a slippery little body and the car's top speed was around 95mph, while the handling balance and traction were well up to Ginetta's usual standards. Because the G15 was such a light car – weighing only about 1100lb unladen – fuel consumption was usually well over 40mpg.

Like other Ginettas of the period, the G15 was sold in kit form so as to avoid the customer paying Purchase Tax on a fully-assembled car. This, in fact, led to the downfall of the model, for when PT was replaced by Value Added Tax (VAT) in 1973, that concession was removed. As the price rocketed, sales slumped, and the G15 was withdrawn in 1974.

Ginetta G15.

SPECIFICATION	
BODY STYLES: sports coupé	
PRODUCTION: c.800	
ENGINE & TRANSMISSION: 875cc, 4cyl ohc 4sp man, r/r	
POWER: 50bhp @ 5800rpm	
MAX SPEED (MPH): 94	
0-60MPH (SEC): 12.9	
SUSPENSION & BRAKES: coil ifs, coil irs, disc f/drum r	
LENGTH (IN)/WEIGHT (LB): 144/1105	
LAUNCH PRICE: £1024	

G21 1973-78

As a follow-up to the successful launch of the G15, Ginetta then developed the larger G21, a pretty front-engined coupé which sold steadily for five years. First reviewed in 1970 with a choice of Ford engines and with independent rear suspension, it was then withdrawn for a re-think and more development. Finally it went on the market in 1973 with a choice of Chrysler UK Rapier engines and a beam rear axle instead. Because VAT had been phased in by this time, The G21 could not be sold advantageously as a kit car, so all the carss were delivered in fully built-up condition.

Like other Ginettas, this car was constructed on a simple, rugged tubular chassis frame, which used square-section steel tubes, with sheet steel fabrications for strengthening. Front suspension and steering were lifted from the Triumph Vitesse/GT6, and the rear axle was from the Ford Cortina, so this truly was a "bitsa", though a surprisingly well integrated one.

The body shell was in GRP (glass fibre), with semi-recessed headlamps, MGB-fashion, and a long, sloping fastback. Many of the cockpit fittings – instruments and controls, for instance – were clearly sourced from Chrysler.

SPECIFICATION

BODY STYLES: sports coupé

PRODUCTION: c.180

ENGINE & TRANSMISSION: 1725cc, 4cyl ohv, 4sp man, o/d, f/r

POWER: 85bhp @ 5200rpm/93bhp @ 5200rpm

MAX SPEED (MPH): 112/117

0-60MPH (SEC): 9.7/9.2

SUSPENSION & BRAKES: coil ifs, coil rear, disc f/drum r

LENGTH (IN)/WEIGHT (LB): 156/1740

LAUNCH PRICE: £1875/£2250

Although sold only as a two-seater, the G21 had a big luggage space or extra stowage shelf behind the seats. The choice of engines was 85bhp (Sunbeam Rapier) or 93bhp (Sunbeam Rapier H120), the latter engine having twin double-choke Weber carburettors.

Although the G21 was a pleasing design, fast but quite civilised in behaviour, it needed work to completely sanitise the handling, which was somewhat twitchy, and the hard ride. The car was also expensive. In 1973, when production began, the 85bhp G21 cost £1875, the near-equivalent 95bhp MGB GT a mere £1547.

When the G21 died in 1978, Ginetta effectively pulled out of the road car market for some years.

Ginetta G21.

GITANE

Here was a brave and – some would say – totally misguided attempt to establish a new brand of luxury GT/sports car. George Fowell, a successful Wolverhampton-based dumper truck business which backed the new venture, had a good name of its own – but no one knew of the Gitane before it was announced.

And why this name ? The origins are lost in the mists of time, but there don't appear to be any connections with the French cigarette of the same title. No matter, in 1961, when the car was conceived, the idea was to build race-ready sports coupés, six of them in 1962 when the new brand was to be announced (the launch came in May 1962), and up to 100 cars in 1963 and beyond.

All this was ambitious, especially as the initial price was set at £2000 (at that time a Jaguar E-Type cost £2036, for example), yet much of the running gear was lifted directly

from the more down-market Mini-Cooper, and peak power was quoted at 83bhp. Fowell told the media that he had plans to adopt an Italian Giannini engine (this company built Formula Junior cars), but this did not come to fruition.

Though designer Gordon Fowell and racer Dan Margulies tried to make an impact by racing the prototype in the Nurburgring 1000km, nothing came of it, and soon afterwards the car retreated into the mists of the Black Country once again.

And that, they say, was that, for the Gitane car never went on to be exhibited at any further British motor shows, no independent tests or impressions ever appeared, nor was there any sign of a serious programme being set up. Even so, this was no ugly duckling. Rather, it was an under-prepared project which deserved, at least, to last longer than one calendar year.

GT 1962

All we really know of this project is of the prototype which was shown immediately before it left for its only public appearance, an unsuccessful foray into the Nurburgring 1000km race of 1962. That prototype, proprietor Gordon Fowell, insisted, was not nearly as sophisticated as the series-built cars which would follow. OK, we will award the benefit of the doubt, and quote differences where appropriate.

The GT was built around the typical special-builder's materials of the day – a multi-tube space frame built of one-inch square section tubing. Although

Gitane GT.

the body style looked as if the engine was up front, in fact the long-stroke Arden-tuned Mini-Cooper engine and its integral gearbox were transversely mounted behind the seats. The cooling radiator was also in the tail, alongside the engine.

Suspension was by race-influenced coil spring/damper and wishbone installations, though Fowell promised that customer cars would be fitted with "Spencer-Moulton" rubber-in-shear units – which effectively meant BMC Mini-Cooper assemblies. Steering was by BMC rack-and-pinion, and Girling disc brakes were fitted all round.

Interestingly, all four were mounted inboard of the specially fabricated magnesium alloy hub carriers.

The body, all-aluminium on the first car (but with some steel promised around the cabin for later machines) was a stressed assembly bolted direct to the chassis frame, with some attempt to simulate a monocoque around the cabin.

In many ways this was a technically adventurous machine which deserved a little longer to make its reputation (or to lose it) in the market place. Unhappily, it never seems to have got that chance.

SPECIFICATION

BODY STYLES: sports coupé

PRODUCTION: 6

ENGINE & TRANSMISSION: 997cc, 4cyl ohv, 4sp man, r/r

POWER: 83bhp @ 7800rpm

MAX SPEED (MPH): 130 (E)

0-60MPH (SEC): not measured

SUSPENSION & BRAKES: coil ifs, coil irs (rubber cone springs on later cars), discs f&r

LENGTH (IN)/WEIGHT (LB): 160/not quoted

LAUNCH PRICE: £2000

GORDON

Gordon 1954-58

This rather strange micro-car was sponsored by one of the UK's leading football concerns, Vernon Industries, and built at Bidston in Cheshire. Its design roots lay in an invalid carriage, the Vi-Car of 1952, though it had grown up, put on weight,

The 197cc Gordon.

and become yet more ugly.

The chassis was a tubular backbone, with only one wheel up front, sprung on motorcycle-style forks, while the bodywork was panelled in steel and had a fold-down canvas roof. The two-stroke Villiers engine lived on the offside of the frame, outside the main bodywork in a little pouch of its own, and drove only the rear wheel on that side. One-up, with engine and driver on the same side of the car, stability was adversely affected. Because the awkward engine position got in the way, there was no space for a door on that side of the car, so access to the simple bench was through a single near-side door instead.

Suspension was all-independent via Metalastik (bonded rubber) bushes at

SPECIFICATION

BODY STYLES: drophead

PRODUCTION: c.40

ENGINE & TRANSMISSION: 197cc, 1cyl ts, 3sp man, r/r

POWER: 8bhp @ 4000rpm

MAX SPEED (MPH): 47

0-60MPH (SEC): not possible

SUSPENSION & BRAKES: rubber ifs, coil irs, drums f&r

LENGTH (IN)/WEIGHT (LB): 134/728

LAUNCH PRICE: £270

the front, and by simple coil springs and trailing arms at the rear, while the brakes were all cable-operated – the rears by a foot pedal, the single front brake by a hand lever!

Perhaps we may never know why Vernons thought this could be a success, for with a 47mph top speed and 0-30mph in 12 seconds, the Gordon was embarrassingly slow, though a potential fuel economy figure of 70mpg-plus on a petroil mixture must have leavened that bread.

Although it was Britain's cheapest "car" when launched at the end of 1954, it was only the Gordon's low annual car tax of £5 which made it at all attractive. Otherwise, in looks and behaviour, it was far too crude to appeal to many. *Motor Cycling* very kindly wrote that: "the Gordon, even in its infancy, will surely establish itself as a leader in its class…", which considerably over-egged the pudding.

GORDON-KEEBLE

After John Gordon's valiant attempts to keep the Triumph-engined Peerless sports car project on the road, he tried again, this time with a much larger and more ambitiously engineered machine, which was engineered for him by Jim Keeble. The Bertone-styled Gordon GT prototype was previewed in March 1960, when an all-steel-bodied prototype appeared at the Geneva Show.

It looked gorgeous, with its 4.6-litre Chevrolet V8 engine it appeared to have all the right credentials, and although *Autocar* gave it the road test treatment later in that year, nothing came of it until 1964. By this time the Chevrolet engine had grown to 300bhp/5.3 litres, and the top speed to close on 140mph.

In the meantime, much development took place. Ex-Jowett chief George Wansborough became interested in financing the project, and took the chair of a company based at premises close to Southampton Airport. To honour the fact that Jim Keeble had designed the car, it was re-named Gordon-Keeble, the type number GK1 emphasising that.

When the car launched in March 1964, pictures showed at least a dozen of the GRP body shells being worked on in the same workshop. It was suspiciously under-priced. In marketing and performance terms it was direct competition for the Aston Martin DB5 of the period, which cost £4248, and this meant that possible clients took much convincing about what they were buying, so the GK1 struggled to gain any sort of reputation; worse, the hoped-for big export sales to the USA never appeared.

George Wansborough had apparently deliberately set a low price, but the company soon found that it was not generating enough cash to have many cars in build at the same time. In spite of a considerable price increase (to £3627 by early 1965), there was no relief, and the company's finances collapsed in May 1965.

This was not quite the end, for two GK dealers, Harold Smith and Geoffrey West, tried to re-launch the car as the "International Touring" (IT), from Keeble Cars at Sholing, an eastern suburb of Southampton. That project lasted less than a year and only a handful of cars were produced.

The final splutter came in 1968 when John de Bruyne bought the remnants of the project and tried to re-launch it as a De Bruyne car at the New York Show in April 1968. That project died almost as soon as it had started, and series production never even commenced.

GK1/IT 1964-66

Like the previous cars with which Jim Keeble had been involved – especially the Triumph-engined Peerless/Warwick of 1958/1960 – the Gordon-Keeble took shape around a sturdy multi-tubular chassis frame and was topped by a glass-fibre shell. There were, however, big advances over his previous projects. Not only was this car powered by a lusty 300bhp/5.3-litre Chevrolet V8 engine, which was backed by a Warner manual transmission, but the De Dion rear suspension and elegant four-seater coupé body were engineered to an altogether higher standard.

The chassis was a complex cats-cradle of rectangular section tubing, much of it 1in square. Gordon Keeble claimed that nearly 300ft of tube was used in each

Gordon-Keeble, styled by Bertone.

frame. It supported the big Chevrolet engine and transmission. Coil spring and wishbone independent front suspension and Marles steering (no power assistance) were matched to a Keeble-designed De Dion rear end, the wheels being located by radius arms and a Watts linkage. Disc brakes were fitted on all four wheels.

The GRP body enclosed a well-trimmed four-seater cabin and was made for Gordon-Keeble by Williams & Pritchard. Because the Italian styling house of Bertone had shaped the car, it bore a strong resemblance to the Iso Rivolta, though GK always claimed that their car had been designed first! The headlamp arrangement, for sure, was straight off the Triumph Vitesse of the period.

Observers think that this was a most unlucky project – a machine which was genuinely capable of great things, though its build and specification quality were never as high as, say, those of Aston Martin. Owing to the rot resistance of the body shell, many Gordon-Keebles have survived, and a brave little owners' club makes sure they always will.

SPECIFICATION

BODY STYLES: sports saloon

PRODUCTION: 99

ENGINE & TRANSMISSION: 5355cc, V8cyl ohv, 4sp man, f/r

POWER: 300bhp @ 5000rpm

MAX SPEED (MPH): 136

0-60MPH (SEC): 7.5

SUSPENSION & BRAKES: coil ifs, De Dion coil rear, discs f&r

LENGTH (IN)/WEIGHT (LB): 190/3165

LAUNCH PRICE: £2798

GSM

Verster de Witt and Bob van Niekerk set up a modest little sports car business in South Africa for which most of the running gear came from the Ford Anglia 100E. Then, in 1960, they were attracted to set up a parallel operation at West Malling, in the UK. Briefly, therefore, a car call the GSM Dart in South Africa, or GSM Delta in the UK (trade mark problems – remember the Daimler Dart of the same period?), was built in two locations at the same time.

As has so often happened, this business was founded more on enthusiasm than on secure long-term prospects. John Scott and his associates helped finance setting up UK assembly and found new premises for the work. GSM's main capital outlay was in getting the tubular chassis and the GRP bodyshell jigs completed, for much of the running gear came from Ford on a cash-with-order basis.

Early Deltas were raced in the UK by luminaries such as Jeff Uren and Keith Holland, which provided much favourable publicity. Unhappily, although this was both a pretty and technically capable little two-seater sports car, it had to be sold at a high price – how many British enthusiasts, for example, would rather pay £1189 for a GSM Delta when they could buy an Austin-Healey Sprite for just £632?

GSM sold more "Darts" in South Africa than "Deltas" in the UK, but finance was always a problem and the business folded little more than a year after the Delta had been launched in the UK.

Delta 1960-61

Starting in South Africa in 1957-58, this sports car project (called "Dart" in that country) made a name for itself, and the founders were offered the chance to set up a parallel operation in Kent. For just two years – 1960 and

SPECIFICATION

BODY STYLES: sports car

PRODUCTION: c.60, plus 116 Darts in South Africa

ENGINE & TRANSMISSION: 997cc, 4cyl ohv, 4sp man, f/r

POWER: 39bhp @ 5000rpm

MAX SPEED (MPH): 80 (E)

0-60MPH (SEC): not measured

SUSPENSION & BRAKES: leaf ifs, coil rear, drums f&r

LENGTH (IN)/WEIGHT (LB): 145/1367

LAUNCH PRICE: £1189

GSM Delta.

1961 – the GSM Delta was built in the UK and was much admired, but it sold only slowly.

Because there was little investment capital available, this was a very cleverly but simply engineered car. The basis was a twin parallel-tube chassis, with transverse leaf and much-modified MacPherson strut independent front suspension, and with the Ford rear axle sprung on coil-over-shock units located by radius arms. Ford provided the new ultra-short-stroke 997cc Anglia 105E engine and gearbox. Although this unit was eminently tuneable, it only produced 39bhp in standard form.

The visual attraction was the neatly-styled two-seater sports car shell, which had a wide but slim front air intake, shallow but noticeable rear fins and (we now know) a Ford Zephyr Mk I windscreen.

A hardtop version was also made available – but this was rather tastelessly inflicted with a reverse-slope rear window. It was GSM's claim that they thought of this feature before Ford, and that it was done to retain the existing boot lid aperture!

In standard form the Delta was an appealing, high-revving, hard-sprung little car but – as happened so often with such projects – it was skimpily and very basically trimmed and it cost far too much to make its own market.

There are one or two survivors.

HEALEY

After spending seven traumatic years in the 1930s guiding Triumph's engineering fortunes around the company's chaotic finances, Donald Healey went to work at Humber Ltd, and spent much spare (stolen?) time working up a new design of sports car. Originally meant to be a Triumph, the scheme collapsed when Triumph's owners declined to back it, so Healey then found backers to set up his own company in Warwick, with capital resources of just £50,000, and secured a supply of Riley engines and transmissions.

From 1945 to 1952 the Healey company's existence was occasionally precarious, but always enterprising. Cleverly, Healey developed one separate steel chassis to accept a variety of different body styles, all of them bought in from coachbuilders. Outwardly, therefore, there were saloons, drophead coupés and sports cars, with Riley, Nash (USA) and Alvis engines, but all shared the same basic mechanical platform and suspension.

Donald Healey was the creator, and the inspiration behind this small company, while his son Geoffrey gradually took on the responsibility of engineering chief. The Healey factory was very simply equipped, but the cars were always fast, nimble and distinguished. A creditable racing programme, which included forays to Le Mans and the Mille Miglia, was a great success.

Healey did not make the hoped-for big breakthrough into the USA, but the early-1950s tie-up with Nash of the USA certainly opened up new possibilities. Fate then stepped in. Healey's project to build a simpler, smaller, cheaper car – the Austin A90-engined Healey 100 – was snapped up at birth by BMC's chairman, Sir Leonard Lord, and was then turned into the Austin-Healey 100 of 1953, which was assembled at Longbridge.

From 1953/54, Healey stopped building its own cars to become an important engineering consultant to BMC, producing (among other important products) the design for the original Austin-Healey Sprite.

Westland/Elliott 1946-50

The original Healey twins, both launched in 1946, shared the new 102in-wheelbase chassis frame which formed the basis of all subsequent Healey cars. History (Geoffrey Healey's books, no less) now tells us that the trailing-link independent front suspension was far too expensive, but it was a very effective system made fashionable by race cars like the Auto Union single-seaters of the late 1930s.

The chassis Healey devised was a simple and rugged structure, with box-section side members and a heavy structure supporting coil spring and trailing link front suspension. At the rear, the Riley axle was located by a torque tube, Panhard rod and coil springs.

Healey's coup was to secure supplies of the excellent 104bhp 2.4-litre Riley engine, which had twin high-placed camshafts and was specially modified for Healey requirements, along with the

The Elliott saloon was 1948's fastest production closed car, capable of 100mph.

Riley gearbox and rear axle. At a stroke, this helped produce one of the fastest cars of the immediate post-war period – both Westland and Elliott could beat 100mph. Vast Lockheed drum brakes (11in diameter at the front, 10in at the rear) kept the performance in check.

Healey built up their own chassis at Warwick, but the two bodies came in from suppliers: the nose and front of these bodies looked identical, for both cars had low-mounted headlamps and extra driving lamps on the nose of the front wings.

The Westland, a four-seater sports tourer with a two-piece windscreen and removable side-screens, came from Westland bodies of Hereford, while the Elliott two-door four-seater saloons (which had Perspex side windows) came from a Reading-based concern whose main business was building shop fronts. Both bodies had timber-framed shells with aluminium skin panels.

The cars were expensive (and the price moved steadily upwards in the early post-war years), but these were excellent machines which handled well and were exceptionally fast by the standards of the day. Since power-assisted steering and disc brakes were not yet available on any cars, the Healeys' heavy steering and drum brakes were quite normal for the period.

Four years after they had gone on sale, both these cars were replaced by later Healeys – the Tickford taking over from the Elliott, and the Abbott (more comprehensively equipped, though) from the Westland. Well before such Healeys once again became fashionable, it was no longer possible to source new panels to restore rusting cars.

Front and rear of the Healey Westland roadster in 1948.

Count Lurani drove this Elliott to class victory in the 1948 Mille Miglia.

The 2443cc Riley engine in the Westland engine bay.

SPECIFICATION

BODY STYLES: saloon (Elliott), roadster (Westland).

PRODUCTION: 101/64

ENGINE & TRANSMISSION: 2443cc, 4cyl ohv, 4sp man, f/r

POWER: 104bhp @ 4500rpm

MAX SPEED (MPH): 102

0-60MPH (SEC): 12.3

SUSPENSION & BRAKES: coil ifs, coil rear, drums f&r

LENGTH (IN)/WEIGHT (LB): 168/2520

LAUNCH PRICE: £1598/£1566

Sportsmobile/Duncan 1948-50

Three more different body styles were added to the Healey range in 1948-49, all of them using the latest B-type version of the chassis and the 104bhp 2.4-litre Riley engine.

The Sportsmobile was a rather undistinguished four-seater drophead coupé (the Abbott which replaced it was much better looking), rather slab-sided and with a more upright nose. A total of 23 examples were made.

The first Duncan was a two-door four-seater saloon, very similar indeed to the Elliott in looks, but coming from Duncan Industries of Norfolk.

SPECIFICATION

BODY STYLES: saloon, sports car (Duncan), drophead (Sportsmobile).

PRODUCTION: 23 Sportsmobile, 39 Duncan

ENGINE & TRANSMISSION: 2443cc, 4cyl ohv, 4sp man, f/r

POWER: 104bhp @ 4500rpm

MAX SPEED (MPH): 102

0-60MPH (SEC): 12.3

SUSPENSION & BRAKES: coil ifs, coil rear, drums f&r

LENGTH (IN)/WEIGHT (LB): 168 (Sportsmobile 180)/2520 (Sportsmobile 2912)

LAUNCH PRICE: (Sportsmobile) £2879, (Duncan) £1985

The Healey Duncan sports roadster was stark in the extreme.

Internally it was more spacious and better-equipped than the Elliott, and also had a larger luggage boot.

Later Duncan also offered a four-seater drophead coupé version, better-equipped inside but not nearly as attractive in the nose as the Westland.

We must also mention the rare and slightly odd Duncan two-seater sports roadster, which was less expensive than the Silverstone (see below) and was aimed at the same sort of market. It had cycle wings and a very stark front end style, quite unlike any other Healey of the period, where radiator grille stripes ran back along the sides of the engine bay, under the bonnet panel, and the spare wheel was bolted on top of the tail section.

None of these cars caught on at the time and are only recalled today, fondly, as curiosities.

1949 Healey Sportsmobile.

Silverstone 1949-50

Although by no means the most common Healey, the Silverstone was the one with the most memorable looks – and the one which was most often campaigned in motorsport events at the time. The Healey company was perhaps too honest for its own bank account's good, for the Silverstone was much cheaper than its other models – it was

SPECIFICATION

BODY STYLES: sports car

PRODUCTION: 105

ENGINE & TRANSMISSION: 2443cc, 4cyl ohv, 4sp man, f/r

POWER: 104bhp @ 4500rpm

MAX SPEED (MPH): 105 (E)

0-60MPH (SEC): 11.0

SUSPENSION & BRAKES: coil ifs, coil rear, drums f&r

LENGTH (IN)/WEIGHT (LB): 168/2072

LAUNCH PRICE: £1246

The Healey Silverstone enjoyed considerable success in the hands of club racers.

launched at only £1246, though most of the production was reserved for export.

Running on the latest version of the 102in chassis frame, the Silverstone was a starkly equipped two-seater. At the rear there was no bumper, but the spare wheel was mounted horizontally in the tail, in a "letter box" with the rearmost arc of the wheel/tyre protruding.

The Riley engine was in exactly the same tune as in other Healeys, but the engine and gearbox were moved eight inches further back in the chassis to improve the roadholding. Because the Silverstone was lighter and more wind-cheating than the other models, this was the fastest Riley-engined Healey of all. The stressed-skin bodywork was made entirely of light alloy. The headlamps were concealed behind the grille and were therefore not

A Silverstone E-type on the Stelvio Pass in the 1952 Alpine Rally.

particularly effective at night.

After 51 early-type Silverstones had been built, a further 51 were produced on what is known as the E-type chassis, these having wider bodies, a bench-type seat and a telescopic steering column. All E-type Silverstones had an air scoop in the bonnet top.

The Silverstone was a great car which the factory and private owners raced with honour – but it was really too stark to appeal to a wider audience.

Tickford saloon/Abbott DHC 1950-54

Yet another variation on what had become a very popular theme, the Tickford and Abbott types were really the second generation of the original Riley-engined Healey theme. Styled by the same sure hands at Healey, two different body shells were mated at first to the C-type chassis. Compared with Westland/Elliott types, the front-end styles were much more integrated, the headlamps being higher and out on the extremities of the front wings. Production did not begin immediately after the Westland and Elliott types had been dropped because for at least a full year the Warwick factory produced nothing but Nash-Healeys.

Both models had a timber body frame clothed in aluminium, both were four-seaters and both had two passenger doors, but one was a saloon, the other a drophead coupé. From mid-1951 both adopted the B-type chassis and gained better headlamps, a front-end facelift and a larger-diameter steering wheel. Then, from late 1951, both cars received the F-type chassis, where the

The Tickford was the best-looking of the Healey saloons.

Riley-style torque tube was abandoned in favour of an open propeller shaft. Telescopic shock absorbers replaced the lever-arm types at the same time. Girling brakes (instead of Lockheed) were also fitted to F-type chassis.

The Tickford model had a two-door saloon body shell by Tickford and was very luxuriously equipped. The Abbott had a very similar two-door four-seater package to the Tickford, but this was a nicely-detailed drophead coupé built by

Abbott at Farnham in Surrey.

Look at the considerable weight of these two models, and you soon see that Healey was piling on the luxury at the expense of outright performance, but no one seemed to mind, as these cars were graceful and well liked. They are among the majority of Warwick Healeys to survive, and deserve that record.

SPECIFICATION
BODY STYLES: saloon (Tickford), drophead coupé (Abbott)
PRODUCTION: 224 Tickford, 77 Abbott
ENGINE & TRANSMISSION: 2443cc, 4cyl ohv, 4sp man, f/r
POWER: 104bhp @ 4500rpm
MAX SPEED (MPH): 104
0-60MPH (SEC): 14.6
SUSPENSION & BRAKES: coil ifs, coil rear, drums f&r
LENGTH (IN)/WEIGHT (LB): 177/2968
LAUNCH PRICE: £1854

The Healey Abbott covertible.

Nash-Healey 1951-54

The long story cut short is that Donald Healey met George Mason (who was President of Nash-Kelvinator) on board the liner *Queen Elizabeth*. A few drinks and a "why can't we ….?" discussion led to the birth of the Nash-Healey project.

This was a marriage between the existing Healey chassis and the Nash six-cylinder engine and gearbox, with Borg Warner overdrive, clad in a full-width three-seater roadster body. Initial cars had a 125bhp 3.8-litre engine, though for 1952 -54 (with a new body style) this was enlarged to a 135bhp 4.1-litre unit. These cars were intended purely for sale in North America, the Nash-Healey never officially being listed for sale in the UK.

The first cars left Warwick at the end of summer 1950, but the model was not launched in the USA until February

1951 Nash-Healey

1951. All were three-seaters with left-hand drive and a Nash-styled grille, in an aluminium-panelled body shell by Panelcraft of Birmingham which featured wind-up windows and a folding soft-top.

By 1952, Healey and Nash had re-jigged production arrangements. After Healey had brought new Tickford and Abbott styles of Riley-engined chassis into production at Warwick, it engaged Farina of Italy not only to restyle the Nash-Healey but also to build the body shells (Nash already a wide-ranging consultancy agreement with Farina.) At the same time the enlarged, more powerful Nash engine was specified. A 1952-54 Nash-Healey, therefore, started life in the UK as a rolling-chassis, was completed in Italy, and was then shipped to the USA for sale.

The Farina Nash-Healey had a sleeker

line than the original, with a one-piece windscreen and a different nose with headlamps incorporated into the grille. Farina also made a few fixed-head coupés.

Much more transatlantic than the Riley-engined Healeys, these cars had (and still have) a following in North America, but to Europeans they are not nearly sporting enough.

Farina-bodied Nash-Healey fixed-head.

SPECIFICATION

BODY STYLES: sports roadster, coupé

PRODUCTION: 253 Panelcraft-bodied cars, 151 Farina-bodied cars

ENGINE & TRANSMISSION: 3848cc/4138cc, 6cyl ohv, 3sp man, o/d, f/r

POWER: 125bhp @ 4000rpm/135bhp @ 4000rpm

MAX SPEED (MPH): 110

0-60MPH (SEC): 9.5

SUSPENSION & BRAKES: coil ifs, coil rear, drums f&r

LENGTH (IN)/WEIGHT (LB): 172/2688

LAUNCH PRICE: Not officially sold in UK

Sports Convertible (G-Type 3-litre) 1951-54

One of the last derivatives of the successful and long-running Healey was the Sports Convertible, which made its debut in October 1951. Think standard G-type Healey chassis, Panelcraft roadster body as supplied for the original Nash-Healeys, and a 106bhp version of the Alvis TA21 3-litre straight-six engine driving through the Alvis four-speed all-synchromesh gearbox.

Deliveries began soon after Nash-Healey body assembly was transferred to Farina in Italy, which freed up capacity at

the Warwick factory. Like the Nash, this Alvis-engined car featured three-abreast bench seating, a vee-screen, wind-up windows in the doors and a fold-away soft top.

Although the Alvis engine's power output was almost the same as that of the Riley, it peaked at lower revs and was more torquey. Even so, Healey body weights had crept up so much that the 3-litre actually accelerated slower than the Westland and Abbott models.

The 3-litre was also expensive, which

explains partly why a mere 25 cars were ever produced at Warwick. Don't forget, though, that the factory was increasingly involved in the Austin-Healey 100 project, and of course in ongoing deliveries of Nash-Healey chassis to Italy for completion.

Purists tend not to rave so much about this car because its engine was not so charismatic as the Riley unit of other Healeys. Yet it was well finished and smart. Just a few survive to make that point today.

BODY STYLES: sports roadster, fixed-head coupé

PRODUCTION: 25

ENGINE & TRANSMISSION: 2993cc, 6cyl ohv, 4sp man, f/r

POWER: 106bhp @ 4200rpm

MAX SPEED (MPH): 100

0-60MPH (SEC): 11.4

SUSPENSION & BRAKES: coil ifs, coil rear, drums f&r

LENGTH (IN)/WEIGHT (LB): (original body) 174/2772

LAUNCH PRICE: £2490

The Alvis-engined Healey G-Type at the 1951 motor show.

HERON

Heron of Greenwich, in south-east London, started life as moulders of glass-fibre – the product being as varied as flower pots and replica suits of armour! Their first body shells were for Austin Sevens. Then they produced their own chassis, clothed it in a two-seater coupé body, and put it on sale as the Europa in 1962. Unhappily, like so many such cars, it was not well-built, well-developed or cheap enough (Heron had to buy Triumph chassis components from a dealer, rather than from the factory). The project died due to lack of interest in only two years.

As ever, the problem was attracting a clientele which would put up with build-quality deficiencies, the lack of a track record, and the lack of after-sales service and back-up. Not even the interest shown by Peter Monteverdi of Switzerland (who eventually put a Heron-based GBM on sale in that country) could rescue it.

Europa 1962-64

This was Heron's first and only complete car. It had a backbone-style chassis, made up from hefty square-section steel tubing, and was available only as a kit with a variety of Ford engines.

There were two major mouldings to the GRP body, one comprising the undertray,

SPECIFICATION

BODY STYLES: sports coupé

PRODUCTION: 12

ENGINE & TRANSMISSION: 997/1340/1498cc, 4cyl ohv, 4sp man, f/r

POWER: From 39bhp @ 5000ropm to 78bhp @ 5200rpm

MAX SPEED (MPH): (78bhp) 115 (E)

0-60MPH (SEC): not measured

SUSPENSION & BRAKES: coil ifs, coil irs, disc f/drum r

LENGTH (IN)/WEIGHT (LB): 136/not quoted

LAUNCH PRICE: £730 (kit)

Heron Europa.

gearbox tunnel and flooring, the other being the upper body. The chassis, which was massive rather than weight-saving, was bonded to these major mouldings, the result being a strong, if simple, unitised-construction.

Much of the suspension was lifted straight from the Triumph Herald, though at the rear Heron provided its own coil-over-shock absorber and transverse wishbone location.

The engine fitted as standard was the small, very over-square 997cc Ford power unit from the Anglia 105E, though larger engines were available for an extra £25.

The overall effect was less than the sum of the parts. Neither the chassis nor the handling was up to scratch, so most people bought a Midget or a Spitfire instead. And one can't blame them...

HILLMAN

Hillman had been founded in Coventry in 1907, but much had changed by 1945. First, in 1928, Hillman merged with Humber (the two companies were next door to each other in Coventry), and then it became a part of the wide-ranging Rootes Group in 1932. By 1939 Hillman had become the entry-level brand of an ever-expanding concern which also included the Rootes-invented Sunbeam-Talbot brand, along with Commer trucks.

From 1945 Rootes private car assembly was concentrated into a modern, ex-"shadow factory" at Ryton-on-Dunsmore, close to Coventry. Hillman concentrated on building the small-medium Minx models, with one type succeeding another in a very stately manner: In the first 20 post-war years, for instance, the long-running Hillman Minx used only three basic body shells and two types of engine. It was not until the 1960s that Hillmans grew up a little (Super Minx), and the company also started building the small rear-engined Imp. Throughout this time Hillman was the base from which

Rootes developed the sporting Sunbeam-Talbots (later Sunbeams), and eventually the slightly more up-market Singer Gazelles and Vogues. Those, effectively, were the brands which had the pizzazz, though it was Hillman, and mass sales, which kept the cash registers ringing.

A long strike at a Rootes body plant in 1962 paralysed the Group and hit hard at company finances, while the huge investment of introducing a new rear-engined "super-mini", the Imp, in 1963 was a massive strain on resources. In 1964, Owing to these factors Rootes sold a large (though not controlling) financial stake to Chrysler of the USA. The American concern converted that to full control in 1967, and from 1970 Rootes became Chrysler United Kingdom.

Before that time, Hillman developed two new family car ranges – the Hunter and Minx of 1966/67, and the all-new Avenger of 1970. Hillman as a brand would then carry on as Chrysler UK's entry-level marque until 1977, when the Chrysler name took over.

Minx Phase I/II 1939-48

The third-generation Minx (it only became known as Phase I after its demise) was launched in September 1939 – the month in which World War Two broke out.

Accordingly it was made only in limited numbers for what was known as "essential" use until 1942, there being a number of non-armoured military transport applications.

Post-war production, of a virtually unchanged design, was begun in 1945. This was the very first Rootes Group car to have a chassis-less (unit-construction) body structure, the style actually picking up many skin panels from the

The 1945 Minx had no fewer than 57 detail improvements, the company said.

SPECIFICATION

BODY STYLES: saloon, drophead, estate, Commer light commercials

PRODUCTION: est. 60,000

ENGINE & TRANSMISSION: 1185cc, 4cyl sv, 4sp man

POWER: 35bhp @ 4100rpm

MAX SPEED (MPH): 59

0-60MPH (SEC): not possible

SUSPENSION & BRAKES: beam leaf front, leaf rear, drums f&r

LENGTH (IN)/WEIGHT (LB): 154/1904

LAUNCH PRICE: £397 in 1945

earlier 1935-39 Minx; Pressed Steel of Cowley provided the saloon car shells. Typical of the late-1930s period for Rootes, there was a simple horizontally-striped grille with separate headlamps.

Most cars were six-light four-door saloons, though some drophead coupé versions, and an estate car (which had evolved from the Minx-based Commer van), were also produced. To meet government financial targets, the vast majority of all these cars were exported.

Conventional from end to end, these

Phase I cars used the 1185cc sidevalve engine which had been launched way back in 1931, a four-speed centre-change gearbox (no synchromesh on first), Bendix cable brakes, and beam axle/half-elliptic spring suspension at front and rear.

A full hydraulic braking system was introduced in 1947, and from late that year Phase II Minxes took over. The new models had a smoothed-out nose with headlamps built into bulbous front wings (which was an improvement), and the "Synchromatic" steering-column gear shift (which was not).

Phase IIs, however, only had a one-year life, for the fourth-generation Minx (which had a completely new monocoque) took over before the end of 1948.

How to sum up these Minxes? Really, as classic "grey porridge", with not even a smidgen of character. Performance was sluggish, handling very ordinary indeed and (until the Bendix system was abandoned) braking not very reassuring. They also rusted badly, and even in the 1960s survivors were few.

Minx Phase II arrived in December 1947, with faired-in headlamps and column change.

Minx Phase III/IV/V 1948-53

Announced in late 1948, the Phase III Minx was the first true post-war Hillman. Although it retained the same drive line as the obsolete Phase II– sidevalve engine, steering-column change gearbox, and spiral bevel rear axle – all this was hidden under a completely new structure and body style, for which the Loewy Studio had been consulted.

Although it looked anonymous in many ways, the body displayed certain Studebaker-influenced details for which Loewy clearly took credit.

Technically, the new Minx contained much the same mixture as before, though at least there was now coil spring and wishbone independent front suspension, this being the very first independently-sprung Hillman model. Regrettably the combination of a steering-column gear change with a bench seat was thought

Minx Phase III, 1949: a new body employing unitary construction.

SPECIFICATION

BODY STYLES: saloon, drophead, estate, light commercials

PRODUCTION: 28,619/90,832/59,777

ENGINE & TRANSMISSION: 1185cc/1265cc, 4cyl sv, 4sp man, f/r

POWER: 35bhp @ 4100rpm/38bhp @ 4200rpm

MAX SPEED (MPH): 63/67

0-60MPH (SEC): 46.6/39.7

SUSPENSION & BRAKES: coil ifs, leaf rear, drums f&r

LENGTH (IN)/WEIGHT (LB): 157/2115

LAUNCH PRICE: £505

essential for post-war tastes, and was retained, and this was still a sluggish, undistinguished type of car. On paper, the chassis should have handled much better than the previous model, but there was little evidence of it on the road.

In true Rootes Group fashion, change came swiftly, for from late 1949 the Phase IV type took over (with a larger 1265cc engine and more substantial bumpers), while Phase V cars arrived in October 1951 with more exterior chromework but few technical up-dates.

All in all, nearly 180,000 cars proved the critics wrong about public taste, and provided much profit for future models. Even so, these were no more desirable than earlier Minxes had been.

Hillman Minx Phase V of 1951 was brightened up with a bit more chrome.

1952 Minx Phase V convertible.

Minx Phase VI/VII 1953-54

By the early 1950s, Rootes had embraced Detroit's philosophy of the "Annual Model Change", which effectively meant making styling changes every year, or making technical changes every year – or both.

Accordingly, in 1953, Rootes announced the Minx Phase VI as a direct evolution of the Phase V, with two principal changes. One was to restyle the front end of all types of the now-familiar body shell, the other being to introduce the Californian Coupé.

The Californian was effectively a hard-top version of the existing drop-head coupe, with a three-piece wrap-around rear window and a duotone colour scheme. Although this car was mechanically unchanged, it was really

A Phase VI Minx, perhaps not the obvious choice for rallying, grinds manfully up a winding pass on the 1953 Alpine Rally.

Minx Phase VI of 1952 had a new oval grille.

Minx Phase VII of 1954 had a slightly longer tail.

SPECIFICATION

BODY STYLES: saloon, drophead coupé, estate, light commercials

PRODUCTION: 44,643/60,711

ENGINE & TRANSMISSION: 1265cc, 4cyl sv, 4sp man, f/r

POWER: 38bhp @ 4200rpm

MAX SPEED (MPH): 67

0-60MPH (SEC): 39.7

SUSPENSION & BRAKES: coil ifs, leaf rear, drums f&r

LENGTH (IN)/WEIGHT (LB): 157/2115

LAUNCH PRICE: £667

the direct ancestor of all Sunbeam Rapiers which would follow in the late 1950s/early 1960s.

Phase VII followed less than a year later, for 1954, these cars having rear-end style changes which included a larger rear window, a slightly enlarged boot and different tail lamps. All this, though, was only a holding pattern – for a brand-new engine was to follow in

the next phase of Minx development.

As far as the character of Phases VI and VII was concerned, they were as anonymous as ever, and not at all interesting to drive, merely slightly shinier and better equipped. Until it was overshadowed by the new Sunbeam Rapier, though, the Californian Coupé was quite a bright spot by previous Hillman standards.

Minx Phase VIII/VIIIA 1954-57

Less than two years before this long-running Hillman range reached the end of its career, it was rejuvenated by the arrival of a brand-new overhead-valve four-cylinder engine. In October 1954, 23 years after it had first been seen, the old sidevalve four was finally made redundant (not on all Minx models, though, until the very end).

For Phase VIII, the new engine was a simple iron block/iron head unit of 1390cc with three main bearings, its initial rating being a mere 43bhp. In

more and progressively more powerful and larger guises, it would be an important part of the Rootes line-up until the late 1970s. Except for adding an anti-roll bar to the front suspension (and deleting the rear bar), there were few other changes: in particular, the steering-column gearshift was retained. Minx Specials kept the old sidevalve engine, but only for a year.

The Phase VIIIA types took over in September 1955, with duotone paint-work in what was innocently called the

"Gay Look", and from this point the sidevalve engine was finally abandoned. Most models in this ageing range were discontinued in mid-1956, though the estate car type continued, on its own, until 1957.

The new overhead-valve engine did little for the Minx's character – though top speed was up from 67mph to 73. The Phase VIII did a great job for Hillman's finances, and the dealers were ecstatic, but car enthusiasts were never excited by these Minxes .

SPECIFICATION

BODY STYLES: saloon, drophead, coupé, estate, light commercials

PRODUCTION: 94,123

ENGINE & TRANSMISSION: 1265cc, 4cyl sv/1390cc, 4cyl ohv, 4sp man, f/r

POWER: 38bhp @ 4200rpm/43bhp @ 4400rpm

MAX SPEED (MPH): (43bhp) 73

0-60MPH (SEC): (43bhp) 29.7

SUSPENSION & BRAKES: coil ifs, leaf rear, drums f&r

LENGTH (IN)/WEIGHT (LB): 157/2115

LAUNCH PRICE: £681

The Minx Phase VIII was the first to get overhead valves. This is the 1955 Californian Coupé.

Husky 1954-57

It took Rootes six years to get round to it, but in October 1954 the Husky arrived, a useful short-wheelbase version of the Minx estate car. Although the wheelbase had been trimmed from 93in to 84in, and there were three instead of five doors, much of the structure and all the front end of the Minx could be retained; the rear loading door opened sideways, which made it very practical

SPECIFICATION

BODY STYLES: estate, light commercials

PRODUCTION: 41,898

ENGINE & TRANSMISSION: 1265cc, 4cyl sv, 4sp man, f/r

POWER: 35bhp @ 4100rpm

MAX SPEED (MPH): 63

0-60MPH (SEC): 27.5

SUSPENSION & BRAKES: coil ifs, leaf rear, drums f&r

LENGTH (IN)/WEIGHT (LB): 146/1925

LAUNCH PRICE: £565

Hillman Husky, introduced in 1955, retained side valves.

indeed in its Commer Cob van version.

Carefully product-planned, the Husky used a slightly de-tuned 35bhp version of the old-style sidevalve engine, which it retained throughout its three-year career. This, by the way, was the first Hillman for some years to have a centre-floor gearchange. The message had finally sunk in – and in any case it was also cheaper to manufacture.

With the rear seat occupied, the luggage space was very limited indeed (and rear-seat legroom was limited), but with that seat empty and folded forward this was a useful little load- carrier. Best not to ask about the handling, which was poor – but then, no one ever bought a Husky as a performance car, did they? And 42,000 customers surely couldn't be wrong ?

Minx Series I/II 1956-58

Seven months after the original Sunbeam Rapier (described later in the book) had been previewed, Rootes finally introduced the new-generation Hillman Minx on which the Rapier was based. The same car, incidentally, gave rise to the Singer Gazelle of 1956- 67.

Here was the first all-new Hillman monocoque to be revealed for eight years and, though we did not know it at the time, this one was going to have a life of eleven very profitable years, during which no fewer than eight different Series would be offered.

Starting again, therefore, Rootes had worked up a smart Loewy-inspired four-door saloon style, on a platform with a 96in wheelbase – this being three inches longer than before. At this stage the running gear was entirely predictable, for the new overhead-valve 1390cc engine was rated at 48bhp, the steering-column gear change was still standard, and there was coil spring and wishbone independent front suspension.

Although the four-door saloon accounted for most of the sales, there was also a two-door drophead coupé derivative, and a five-door estate car would be phased in from June 1957. The estate car had upper and lower tailgate doors. Top speed of the saloons had risen to 77mph.

SPECIFICATION

BODY STYLES: saloon, drophead, estate

PRODUCTION: 202,264

ENGINE & TRANSMISSION: 1390cc, 4cyl ohv, 4sp man or semi-auto, f/r

POWER: 48bhp @ 4600rpm

MAX SPEED (MPH): 77

0-60MPH (SEC): 27.7

SUSPENSION & BRAKES: coil ifs, leaf rear, drums f&r

LENGTH (IN)/WEIGHT (LB): 161/2185

LAUNCH PRICE: £748

Hillman Minx Series II.

Little more than one year later, in August 1957, this new-generation Minx became Series II, with a new front grille design (that Annual Model Change again!), optional Lockheed Manumatic two-pedal control, and a centre-floor gearchange on entry-level Specials. Nothing, however, seemed to last long at Rootes/Hillman in the 1950s, so these cars would all be supplanted by Series III models in the autumn of 1958.

As rust-prone as ever (maybe Pressed Steel were to blame in part, but don't forget that Hillmans were always built down to a price…), these cars handled better than the old Phase types had done but they were still not in any way inspiring. The steering-column gear-change (on the way out, thank heavens) was still awful too. Yet they were a huge commercial success, so can one really complain?

Minx Series III/IIIA/IIIB/IIIC 1958-63

From 1958 to 1963 the Minx went through a whole series of evolutions and development changes which saw engines become larger and more powerful, transmissions improve, and equipment augmented to suit. Best, therefore, to summarise changes as they appeared.

Series III Minxes, of autumn 1958, had

SPECIFICATION

BODY STYLES: saloon, drop-head, estate

PRODUCTION: 3,105/78,052/58,260/Series IIIC unknown

ENGINE & TRANSMISSION: 1494cc/1592cc, 4cyl ohv, 4sp man or auto, f/r

POWER: 49bhp @ 4400rpm/53bhp @ 4600rpm/53bhp @ 4100rpm

MAX SPEED (MPH): 78/79

0-60MPH (SEC): 26.6/23.6

SUSPENSION & BRAKES: coil ifs, leaf rear, drums f&r

LENGTH (IN)/WEIGHT (LB): 161/2200

LAUNCH PRICE: £748

Series IIIA Minx de Luxe, with new tail fins.

49bhp/1494cc, with a revised radiator grille and a modified facia.

Series IIIA Minxes (autumn 1959) had 53bhp/1494cc, a floor gearchange was standardised on all home-market versions, and Smiths Easidrive automatic transmission took over from the unsuccessful Manumatic as an optional extra. At the same time, a rear-end "tail-lift" saw the

arrival of what might be called fold-over rear fins.

Series IIIB Minxes appeared in autumn 1960, the most important change being the use of a hypoid bevel rear axle instead of the old-type spiral-bevel unit.

Series IIIC Minxes (August 1961) had a major upgrade, with a 53bhp/1592cc version of the overhead-valve engine, and to stimulate the market there was also a slight, but genuine, reduction of prices. From this time Rootes began to call the car the "Minx 1600", the "1600" badging actually appearing on the front doors.

Estate car and convertible types were both dropped in mid-1962, to make way for the new Super Minx range, which was concurrently being developed.

All this activity sometimes made it difficult to keep up with evolution of the Minx (especially as some changes were not always made at the same time for export territories), but sales were always strong. Sober analysis sees the basic car improving with every up-date, though no one had a good word to say for the Manumatic or Easidrive transmission options.

Husky Series I/II/III 1958-65

Rootes-watchers who understood product planning could forecast that a second-generation Husky would arrive soon after the new Minx had appeared. In fact they had to wait until the first days of 1958.

As expected, the new Husky Series I was effectively a short-wheelbase, two-door derivative of the latest Minx estate car, though with a side-opening tailgate. It shared the same basic style as the Minx, with a modified version of the new underpan (but with an 86in instead of 96in wheel-base), and the same

The Husky got an ohv engine in 1958. This is the Series III model of 1963.

SPECIFICATION

BODY STYLES: estate, light commercials

PRODUCTION: c. 56,000 up to 1963, Series III unkown

ENGINE & TRANSMISSION: 1390cc, 4cyl ohv, 4sp man, f/r

POWER: 40bhp @ 4000rpm/47bhp @ 4400rpm/41bhp @ 4200rpm

MAX SPEED (MPH): 69-73

0-60MPH (SEC): 41.4-30.0

SUSPENSION & BRAKES: coil ifs, leaf rear, drums f&r

LENGTH (IN)/WEIGHT (LB): 150/2080

LAUNCH PRICE: £699

suspension, engine and running gear.

Like the Minx models of the period, the "Series" Husky came in for regular changes in a seven-year career. These can be summarised as follows:

Series I Husky types originally had 40bhp/1390cc, though from mid-1959 this was increased to 47bhp.

The Series II Husky took over in March 1960, this time with a lowered roof panel, a deeper windscreen, new grille and better-quality seating. From August 1960 the new-type hypoid bevel rear axle was standardised.

The Series III Husky appeared in August 1963, this version having only 41bhp. The bonnet line was lowered, all chassis greasing points were deleted, and a new fascia style was adopted. From September 1964 the Husky got the new corporate all-synchromesh gearbox and a front anti-roll bar.

In common with the early-type Husky, this was never a little car to get excited about, but it did a good, unspectacular job. Compared with the sidevalve models, at least twice as many of these later Husky types were built.

Minx Series V/VI 1963-67

There was no Series IV Minx (that number had been reserved for the Super Minx of 1962, then deferred, then abandoned altogether), so it was late 1963 before the Series V Minxes appeared. From that point there was only a four-door saloon, as more up-market versions had been reserved for the Super Minx instead.

The Series V Minx represented a major revision by any standards, for the monocoque was much changed. Although the platform, the driveline and the basic front-end styling were not changed, there was a new squared-up cabin roof, along with a new fascia and a less wrapped-round rear window, while the "fold-over" tail fins were deleted. 13in wheels (instead of 15in) were standardised, along with front-wheel disc brakes.

In addition we must note that Series V cars, announced in October 1963, had 53bhp/1592cc (manual transmission) or 58bhp/1592cc (auto). Borg Warner automatic transmission was optional, in place of the discredited Smiths Easidrive unit. From September 1964 this model gained a new all-synchromesh gearbox which was being fitted to other Rootes cars at the same time.

Series VI cars arrived in October 1965, with a 1725cc engine producing 65bhp, later detuned to 59bhp. The 1725cc engine was the very first version of this engine family to have a five main bearing crankshaft. The last of these cars

was produced at the beginning of 1967. Like the earlier "Series" Minxes, these were good, steady, continously improving family cars, never very exciting, and

always prone to rusting away. Not many have survived, though the one-make club still loves them.

Minx Series V, 1963.

SPECIFICATION

BODY STYLES: saloon

PRODUCTION: unknown

ENGINE & TRANSMISSION: 1592cc/1725cc, 4cyl ohv, 4sp man or auto, f/r

POWER: 58bhp @ 4000rpm./59bhp @ 4200rpm/65bhp @ 4800 rpm

MAX SPEED (MPH): 80-82

0-60MPH (SEC): 18.6

SUSPENSION & BRAKES: coil ifs, leaf rear, disc f/drum r

LENGTH (IN)/WEIGHT (LB): 161/2200

LAUNCH PRICE: £635

Super Minx I/II/III/IV 1961-67

What had started as a straight replacement for the existing (late 1950s) Minx range eventually became a model range of its own and ran parallel to the Minx until 1966. Thus, what should have been a Series IV Minx actually became the Super Minx. The Super Minx also gave rise to the closely-similar Singer Vogue of 1961-66 and the rather different Humber Sceptre of 1963-67.

While the engine and transmission were very similar to those being used in the contemporary Minx, almost every other component was different. The platform/monocoque was entirely new, with a 101in wheelbase and 51.5in front track (existing Minx – 96in and 49in).

SPECIFICATION

BODY STYLES: saloon, drophead, estate

PRODUCTION: not known

ENGINE & TRANSMISSION: 1592cc/1725cc, 4cyl ohv, 4sp man, o/d or auto, f/r

POWER: 62bhp @ 4800rpm/65bhp @ 4800rpm

MAX SPEED (MPH): 83

0-60MPH (SEC): 22.5-17.9

SUSPENSION & BRAKES: coil ifs, leaf rear, drums f&r (later disc f/drum r)

LENGTH (IN)/WEIGHT (LB): 165/2355

LAUNCH PRICE: £854

Hillman Super Minx was launched in 1961.

Super Minx convertible.

Super Minx estate car, 1965.

The four-door body, also new, had been designed with absolutely no input from outside consultants. At a casual glance it looked as if a reverse-slope rear window had been used – but this was not so, for there was a heavily-wrapped rear window with backward-sloping D and E pillars instead. The tiny, flattened rear

tail fins were a recognition point.

The first Super Minxes had 1592cc engines and 13-inch road wheels, with drum brakes. As usual with Hillman, though, there was constant evolution – four Marks in six years ! – so each type needs its own summary.

Mk I, announced in mid-1961, came

with 62bhp/1592cc, a four-speed gearbox but no first-gear synchromesh, optional Smiths Easidrive automatic transmission, drum brakes all round and a hypoid-bevel rear axle. Estate car and convertible types appeared during 1962.

Mk II, from October 1962, had front-wheel disc brakes as standard, and Borg Warner automatic transmission in place of Easidrive.

Mk III was launched in September 1964, but only as saloon and estate car. It had a restyled cabin incorporating a near-flat rear window and three side windows. An all-synchromesh manual gearbox and fully reclining front-seats both became standard.

Mk IV, appearing in September 1965, had 65bhp/1725cc (this was the final stretch for an engine which had first appeared in 1954), and Laycock overdrive was optional. This model carried on until August 1966 (saloon) and April 1967 (estate car).

Super Minx? In summary, a worthy but totally uncharismatic family car. It did nothing superbly but was competent and, at the time, cheap to run. Tens of thousands of family men wanted no more than that.

Imp/Super Imp 1963-76

Looking back, it was the superbly engineered but unreliable family of Imps which hastened Rootes' downfall and its takeover by Chrysler. To make the Imp (and to secure valuable government subsidies) Rootes was obliged to build the car at Linwood, near Paisley in Scotland, where entire cars had never before been assembled. It was a recipe for disaster which was soon delivered.

The lightweight overhead-camshaft engine evolved from an existing Coventry-Climax design, but every other component of the Imp was new. The same basic design would also appear behind Singer, Sunbeam and Commer (commercial vehicle) badges.

The Imp itself was a two-door four-seater saloon with unusual, rather angular styling. The 875cc engine was in the tail, tipped well over to the right to reduce its height, in unit with a four-speed all-synchromesh transmision driving the rear wheels, and the rear window lifted up to give access to luggage space and to the rear seat. The main luggage container was up front.

A 1972 model Hillman Imp.

All-independent suspension featured coil springs and swing axles in the front, with rack-and-pinion steering, and coil springs with semi-trailing arms at the rear. Drum brakes were standard.

Although the Imp looked good, handled brilliantly (the front suspension was de-cambered from 1967, which made things even better), and was a very practical machine, it had two major problems – build quality and reliability. It also had to compete with the very popular BMC Mini. If the car had been reliable, sales would have followed, but problems persisted. Give a dog a bad name, and all that …

From October 1968 there was an interior facelift, including a new and less ergonomic fascia/instrument layout and more comfortable seating, but in thirteen years (up to the end in 1976) the only mechanical changes were made to enhance the Imp's reliability, not its performance or its function.

Even so, in much developed Rallye Imp guise it was quite a successful competition car, and the related coupés were very pretty indeed.

Super Imp had side chrome. The rear view emphasises the Imp's unique looks.

SPECIFICATION

BODY STYLES: saloon

PRODUCTION: 440,032, all Imp family

ENGINE & TRANSMISSION: 875cc, 4cyl ohc, 4sp man, r/r

POWER: 37bhp @ 4800rpm

MAX SPEED (MPH): 78

0-60MPH (SEC): 25.4

SUSPENSION & BRAKES: coil ifs, coil irs, drums f&r

LENGTH (IN)/WEIGHT (LB): 139/1530

LAUNCH PRICE: £508

Imp Californian 1967-70

Based on the Imp saloon, the Californian was a fastback coupé derivative. Below the waistline, and under the skin, there were no important differences, but the Californian had a re-raked screen, a lowered roof line, and a more definitely sloped rear window, which was fixed in position. The front seats could be reclined, and the front suspension was always de-cambered. In late 1968 the Californian also gained the same interior re-design as the Imp.

This was never a fast car (the closely-related Sunbeam Stiletto had more power and more performance) but it was an appealing "suburban" proposition.

The Imp Californian in 1969.

SPECIFICATION

BODY STYLES: coupé

PRODUCTION: see Imp above

ENGINE & TRANSMISSION: 875cc, 4cyl ohc, 4sp man, r/r

POWER: 37bhp @ 4800rpm

MAX SPEED (MPH): 78

0-60MPH (SEC): 22.1

SUSPENSION & BRAKES: coil ifs, coil irs, drums f&r

LENGTH (IN)/WEIGHT (LB): 139/1560

LAUNCH PRICE: £647

Rallye Imp 1965-67

From 1965, the Rootes "works" Competitions Department built a number (not known – but thought to be several hundreds) of Rallye Imps. These were converted Imps (or Singer Chamois, or Sunbeam Imp Sports), which had enlarged engines, lowered and stiffened suspension, a special instrument panel, and extra slatting in the rear engine cover to keep the compartment cool.

The engine itself was enlarged to 60bhp/998cc, and because this was still basically a Coventry-Climax power unit there was plenty more to come. Race-tuned examples could be persuaded to produce up to 110bhp.

Even in "standard" (ie 60bhp) guise this was an exhilarating little sports saloon, which revved high and sweetly, and could reach up to 95mph. Most were used hard in motor sport, so very few road cars remain. If they have been well loved they are still worth a drive.

SPECIFICATION

BODY STYLES: saloon

PRODUCTION: not known

ENGINE & TRANSMISSION: 998cc, 4cyl ohc, 4sp man, r/r

POWER: 60bhp @ 6200rpm

MAX SPEED (MPH): 92

0-60MPH (SEC): 14.9

SUSPENSION & BRAKES: coil ifs, coil irs, drums f&r

LENGTH (IN)/WEIGHT (LB): 139/1530

LAUNCH PRICE: Special order. £250 for the conversion.

For the Rallye Imp the engine was enlarged from 875cc to 998cc, producing 60bhp. Here are Rosemary Smith and Valerie Domleo on the 1966 Monte Carlo Rally in a works car. Rosemary Smith had won the 1965 Tulip Rally outright in one of these.

Husky 1967-70

Bearing no relation to previous Husky models (which were Minx-based), the third-generation Husky was a high-roof three-door estate car version of the rear-engined Imp. Because of the rear engine position, the load floor of the Husky had to be relatively high (which explains the high roof), yet this was a thoroughly practical load-carrying four-seater, which could swallow up to 25 cu ft of cargo. Naturally there was a van

The Imp-based Hillman Husky.

SPECIFICATION

BODY STYLES: estate, light commercial

PRODUCTION: see Imp above

ENGINE & TRANSMISSION: 875cc, 4cyl ohc, 4sp man, f/r

POWER: 37bhp @ 4800rpm

MAX SPEED (MPH): 76

0-60MPH (SEC): 24.2

SUSPENSION & BRAKES: coil ifs, coil irs, drums f&r

LENGTH (IN)/WEIGHT (LB): 143/1`645

LAUNCH PRICE: £622

derivative, called the Commer Cob.

The basic platform and the rear engine/transmission layout were the same as on the Imp saloon, as were the front end, windscreen and passenger doors, but radial ply tyres were standard

(Imps had cross-ply types).

Unhappily, the Imp's status as a loss-making project meant that the owners, Chrysler, soon cut back on peripheral models, of which the Husky was one. It was only in production for three years.

Hunter 1966-77

Inspired, some say, by the success of the original Ford Cortina, the Rootes "Arrow" project was intended to offer variety in engines, bodies and specifications to suit the pockets and tastes of a wide clientele. The first car to appear, towards the bottom of that product planning spectrum, was called Hillman Hunter – the "Hunter" part of the title already having been used by Singer (another Rootes brand) back in the 1950s.

The running gear – 1725cc engine, four-speed all-synchromesh gearbox, optional overdrive or Borg Warner automatic transmission, hypoid-bevel rear axle and front disc/rear drum braking installation – were all slightly revised derivatives from the Super Minx and Minx models, which were to be superseded. It was the neat four-door saloon/five-door estate car monocoque,

Hillman Hunter.

and the MacPherson strut front suspension assemblies, which were new.

Most importantly, the new Arrow (which we must henceforth call Hunter) was lighter than the Super Minx and handled a whole lot better. Encouraged by Chrysler, Rootes had set about "Fordifying" the Minx/Super Minx product line, making the new car better

looking, faster, better-handling and altogether more responsive than before.

Until 1970 all Hunter saloons used aluminium-headed 1725cc engines, but thereafter the product range widened, so that what had been the "New Minx" (see below) was swept up into the Hunter family, and real complication set in! One example was that the original estate car in this line was titled "Hillman Estate car", only had a 1496cc engine, and was not formally known as a Hunter estate at the time.

From October 1966 Hunters had 72bhp engines and were offered with many different trim and equipment options, but there was no Hunter estate car until the end of 1970, when one became available either with the 1725cc engine or with a 61bhp 1496cc version of it.

Hunter de Luxe estate car.

The rather special Hunter driven to victory in the 1968 London-Sydney Marathon by Andrew Cowan with Brian Coyle and Colin Malkin.

Proliferation into different engine sizes, names and trim levels then followed.

A facelift, involving a new front end and a new fascia/instrument panel, made things even more complicated in 1972, when the GLS (see the separate entry) was added to the range.

From late 1977 Hillman Hunters became Chrysler Hunters, the line being dropped entirely in Europe in 1979. An Iranian-built and renamed version (the Peykan) was produced until the 1980s.

SPECIFICATION

BODY STYLES: saloon, estate

PRODUCTION: c.470,000 all Hunter/Minx types

ENGINE & TRANSMISSION: 1496cc/1725cc, 4cyl ohv, 4sp man, o/d or auto, f/r

POWER: 54bhp @ 4600rpm/61bhp @ 4700rpm/72bhp @ 5000rpm

MAX SPEED (MPH): 83-92

0-60MPH (SEC): 17.8-14.3

SUSPENSION & BRAKES: coil ifs, leaf rear, disc f/drum r

LENGTH (IN)/WEIGHT (LB): 168/2035

LAUNCH PRICE: £838

New Minx 1967-70

Intended to take over from the 1956-67 line of Minxes, the "New Minx" was a down-market version of the Hunter (described above). Because of Chrysler's sometimes misguided attempts at rationalisation, this car only had a life of three years (1967-70), at which point the famous old "Minx" title was buried, and the same car was re-named Hunter DL.

The Minx name came back, however, many years later, after Chrysler had merged more operations with Talbot of France, when there was a "Minx" version of a French car too!

The New Minx's basic engineering was the same as that of the Hunter, though initially the engine was an iron-headed, short-stroke 1496cc version of that car's

engine. When the optional automatic transmission was ordered, it came with an iron-head 1725cc power unit to provide sufficient torque; this engine was optional with manual transmission from 1968.

The Minx handled just as well as the Hunter but it was never as fast or as well equipped. It was a sad end for the popular Minx brand.

Hillman New Minx, a base version of the Hunter.

SPECIFICATION

BODY STYLES: saloon, estate

PRODUCTION: see Hunter above

ENGINE & TRANSMISSION: 1496cc/1725cc, 4cyl ohv, 4sp man or auto, f/r

POWER: 54bhp @ 4600rpm/68bhp @ 4800rpm

MAX SPEED (MPH): 83/90 (E)

0-60MPH (SEC): not measured

SUSPENSION & BRAKES: coil ifs, leaf rear, disc f/drum r

LENGTH (IN)/WEIGHT (LB): 168/2035

LAUNCH PRICE: £733

Hillman GT/Hunter GT 1969-75

The Rootes marketing team was not ready in time to capitalise on the success of the works rally team when Andrew Cowan/Brian Coyle/Colin Malkin won the London-Sydney Marathon of 1968 in a much-modified Hunter. It was the end of 1969 before a rather half-hearted attempt was made to cash in, with a car called Hillman GT.

This new model had a stripped-out specification (at £962 it was cheaper than the entry-level Hunter), with fixed-back high-back seats and a rev-counter mounted in a pod above the instrument panel. Rubber floor mats and Rostyle wheels (Sunbeam Rapier H120-style)

The Hillman GT of 1969 was an improvement, with a 79bhp engine.

SPECIFICATION

BODY STYLES: saloon

PRODUCTION: see Hunter above

ENGINE & TRANSMISSION: 1725cc, 4cyl ohv, 4sp man, o/d, f/r

POWER: 79bhp @ 5100rpm

MAX SPEED (MPH): 96

0-60MPH (SEC): 13.9

SUSPENSION & BRAKES: coil ifs, leaf rear, disc f/drum r

LENGTH (IN)/WEIGHT (LB): 168/2105

LAUNCH PRICE: £962

were standard, as was striping along the flanks. For £33 one could order a "Comfort" pack, which restored the reclining front seats and floor carpets.

This was rather a mish-mash of features and didn't hit the mark. Under the skin was the running gear of the current Sunbeam Rapier – a 79bhp (DIN) at 5100rpm version of the alloy-headed engine, with overdrive as an optional extra. With a top speed of 96mph the Hillman GT could match Ford's class-leading Cortina GT, but no more than that.

A year later Rootes/Chrysler had

second thoughts and made the car into the Hunter GT from October 1970. Though there were no mechanical updates, the interior trim was henceforth at Hunter GL level, with a revised fascia style. This carried on to the mid-life facelift stage, which did not arrive until 1972, when all Hunters got a new fascia/instrument panel.

These were good cars with quite a brisk performance but Chrysler/Hillman made little attempt to promote them, and they were largely ignored by the new-car market. Almost all were extinct by the late 1970s.

Hunter GLS 1972-76

The Hunter GLS did yet better, with 95bhp and a 105mph maximum.

SPECIFICATION

BODY STYLES: saloon

PRODUCTION: see Hunter above

ENGINE & TRANSMISSION: 1725cc, 4cyl ohv, 4sp man, o/d , f/r

POWER: 93bhp @ 5200rpm

MAX SPEED (MPH): 108

0-60MPH (SEC): 10.5

SUSPENSION & BRAKES: coil ifs, leaf rear, disc f/drum r

LENGTH (IN)/WEIGHT (LB): 168/2114

LAUNCH PRICE: £1281

Early in the 1970s, Chrysler took the "high-performance" Hunter image a stage further. In 1972, when a general Hunter facelift saw new front grilles, and a new fascia/instrument panel layout across the range, a new model called the Hunter GLS was launched. This would remain on sale until April 1976.

Basically, the Hunter GLS was a better-equipped Hunter GT, with a four-headlamp nose like that of the closely-related Humber Sceptre. It also had the twin double-choke Weber carburetted Sunbeam Rapier H120 engine, which produced 93bhp. Stiffer suspension produced more sporting handling, and Rostyle wheels (once again of Rapier H120 type) were standard. Overdrive was optional but automatic transmission was not available.

Though it never built up the same sort of reputation as certain fast Fords, the GLS was a capable sports saloon which performed well, in its category, in saloon car racing. The carburation needed dedicated attention to keep it in tune, but the engine was otherwise very strong. When new the GLS cost £1281, which put it uncomfortably higher than cars like – for instance – the 2-litre Cortina of the period.

Avenger 1970-76

Rootes/Chrysler decided to fill a marketing gap below their Minx-Hunter range but above the ageing Imp products with an all-new family car, which became the Hillman Avenger, announced in February 1970. Meant to compete in the Morris Marina/Ford Escort/Vauxhall Viva class, this was a big investment project, for there was no component sharing with any other Rootes/Chrysler car. The platform, the body style, the engine and the transmission line-up were all newly developed.

Based around a 98-inch platform and a monocoque structure, there was a simple overhead-valve four-cylinder engine (two sizes: 1248cc and 1498cc at first), backed by a four-speed all-synchromesh gearbox; the larger engine could also be mated to Borg Warner automatic transmission.

The chassis featured MacPherson struts and rack-and-pinion steering at the front, coil springs and splayed radius arms at the rear, and front disc brakes (drums on some later low-spec entry-level models). This was quite conventional stuff, as was the four-door saloon/five-door estate car styling.

Although the Avenger was a capable little package (later versions were surprisingly fast and nimble, and the high-

Hillman Avenger GL, 1972.

performance Talbot Sunbeam-Lotus of 1979 was a distant descendant), the first cars had a very boring character. Yet despite the fact that they were never inspiring they sold well – 78,000 cars a year at peak – and certainly paid back their investment. The bread-and-butter types, though, were underpowered, which explains why 1295cc and 1599cc engines took over in late 1973.

Chrysler/Hillman learned their product planning lessons from Ford, so there were regular up-dates before the Hillman name was dropped in 1976: an estate car from March 1972, two-door saloons in 1973, a new fascia and instrument design in the same period, and several limited-production high-performance versions.

All in all, not memorable – and almost every one has rotted away.

SPECIFICATION

BODY STYLES: saloon, estate

PRODUCTION : 638,631 all Avengers

ENGINE & TRANSMISSION: 1248cc/1295cc/ 1498cc/1598cc, 4cyl ohv, 4sp man or auto, f/r

POWER: 53bhp @ 5000rpm - 69bhp @ 5000rpm

MAX SPEED (MPH): 81-96

0-60MPH (SEC): 19.8-13.2

SUSPENSION & BRAKES: coil ifs, coil rear, disc f/drum r

LENGTH (IN)/WEIGHT (LB): 161/1895

LAUNCH PRICE: £822

Avenger GT/GLS 1970-76

If not quite a silk purse from a sow's ear, the Avenger GT model was a much better car than the ordinary Avenger from which it was developed. Apart from the use of a four-headlamp front end, and a new fascia/instrument panel incorporating a rev-counter, there were no important style changes.

The engine first fitted was a twin-Stromberg version of the 1498cc power unit and produced 75bhp, which almost (but not quite) delivered a top speed of 100mph, with handling and character to match. Later, from March 1973, the

The 1598cc Avenger GLS.

SPECIFICATION

BODY STYLES: saloon

PRODUCTION: see Avenger, above

ENGINE & TRANSMISSION:
1295cc/1498cc/1598cc, 4cyl ohv, 4sp man or auto, f/r

POWER: 69bhp @ 5800rpm/75bhp @ 5400rpm/81bhp @ 5500rpm

MAX SPEED (MPH): 92-100

0-60MPH (SEC): 14.4-12.2

SUSPENSION & BRAKES: coil ifs, leaf rear, drums f&r

LENGTH (IN)/WEIGHT (LB): 161/1882

LAUNCH PRICE: £1073

The 1498cc Avenger GT two-door of 1973.

engine was enlarged to 1599cc, giving 81bhp, and a 69bhp 1295cc derivative appeared alongside it. In the meantime, from September 1972, the top of the line, with improved trim, fixtures and fittings (but only available in four-door saloon guise), was the 100mph GT-engined GLS, which had a vinyl roof as standard, along with Rostyle wheels.

Like the mainstream Avengers these models carried on until 1976, when the range was rationalised, front-end face-lifted and re-badged Chrysler. If any Avengers deserve to be preserved, it is the GT and GLS types.

Avenger Tiger 1972-73

Here was a car about which Chrysler UK was not very serious, though it built a limited number effectively as motorsport specials. Some of these cars, indeed, performed with honour in British rallies.

There were two types of Tigers: Tiger I (March 1972) with two rectangular headlamps, a bonnet bulge and a boot-lid aerofoil; and Tiger II (October 1972) with quad circular headlamps, no bonnet bulge, the same aerofoil (some cars did not have this) and more refined mechanical equipment.

Recognisable by the striping along the

This is the quad-headlamp Avenger Tiger II.

SPECIFICATION

BODY STYLES: saloon

PRODUCTION: not known

ENGINE & TRANSMISSION: 1498cc, 4cyl ohv, 4sp man, f/r

POWER: 100bhp @ 6000rpm

MAX SPEED (MPH): 105

0-60MPH (SEC): 9.0

SUSPENSION & BRAKES: coil ifs, coil rear, disc f/drum r

LENGTH (IN)/WEIGHT (LB): 161/1882

LAUNCH PRICE: £1500

flanks, the cast alloy wheels (Minilites on the first cars), and the aerofoil (which was for show, not for real aerodynamic improvement), these cars were powered by a much-modified 1498cc Avenger GT engine with re-worked cylinder head, higher compression ratio and twin dual-choke Webers. The suspension was lowered and stiffened, and a brake servo was standard.

Rarely seen, the Stage Two version had an even more highly tuned engine and a competition clutch, giving a top speed claimed to be at least 110mph.

Very few of these cars were built (Chrysler needed to establish sporting homologation and were always evasive about the number), though a proportion remain to this day.

In later years the same engine would be used in the Talbot Sunbeam 1600TI, which had a closely related chassis and running gear.

Roger Bell's works Avenger at Brands Hatch.

HRG

E A Halford, Guy Robins and Ron Godfrey combined their resources, experience and initials in 1936 to found the tiny HRG concern. With an ambition only to make simple, easy-to-build two-seater sports cars, they picked up well-loved features from older cars such as the Frazer Nash and GN (Godfrey had been the "G" of GN). Unhappily, and like other car-makers of their ilk, they were always under-capitalised, and had to take on general engineering contract work merely for their company, based in Tolworth, Surrey, to survive.

Like the pre-war Frazer Nash, the HRG had a very simple chassis and a stark light-alloy bodyshell, but instead of chain drive the HRG used a conventional propeller shaft and spiral bevel axle.

Suspension was by leading quarter-elliptic springs at the front, and half-elliptics at the rear, and was very hard indeed – didn't someone once say that if you saw a "Herg" spring deflect, then something had failed?. Steering was direct, proprietary engines (Meadows at first, but Singer on 1939 and all post-war machines) were used, and there was no silly nonsense about heaters or comfortable cockpits.

As this was a hand-built and relatively expensive "speciality" car, sales and production were always tiny. At its peak HRG delivered 68 cars in 1947, but this dropped rapidly to only eight in 1952 and four in 1953, and profits were hard to generate. The trendily modern HRG "Aerodynamic" of 1946-49 hadn't hit the mark either, so HRG was on borrowed time as the 1950s unfolded.

Not even the very advanced engineering shown by the Twin-Cam of 1955 (the Singer-based engine was shown in an HRG before Singer showed it in one of their own cars) could turn things around, especially as Rootes did not want to service HRG's tiny requirement after they had absorbed Singer in 1955-56. The last HRGs were sold just one year later.

As with similar cars like the "chain-gang" Frazer Nashes, there was always great nostalgia for these appealing machines, which were quicker than they looked, always handled well, and had sack-loads of charisma. Many have survived to this day, some looking and going better than ever.

1100/1500 1939-55

Although the original HRGs had had Meadows engines, from 1939 the more modern, lighter and potentially more powerful overhead-camshaft Singer unit was offered. Except for the handful of twin-cam engined prototypes shown in 1955, this engine was the standard unit for all of the company's post-war production.

HRG's chassis was simplicity itself, with twin parallel channel-section side members linking front and rear (the side members dipping under the line of the rear axle), and with the engine and cockpit sat well back between front and rear wheels. As on the Frazer Nash "chain gang" which had provided some of the inspiration, the tubular front axle was sprung on leading quarter-elliptic leaf springs, with friction-type shock absorbers to help keep things under control.

At the rear, conventional half-elliptic springs were fitted, mounted outboard of the chassis side members. Vertical movement at front or rear, though not negligible, was always very limited – there was no such thing as a soft-riding HRG! Cable brakes, along with a fly-off handbrake, were standard for many years, but the last dozen WS types of 1953-56 had hydraulic brakes instead.

Until 1950 there was a choice of 1074cc or 1496cc Singer engines, each of them backed by the Singer transmission of the period: the short-stroke SM1500-type 1497cc engine was fitted to WS types. Even though the 1100

An HRG on Rest and Be Thankful in the 1952 RAC Rally.

SPECIFICATION

BODY STYLES: sports car

PRODUCTION : 49/99/12

ENGINE & TRANSMISSION:
1074cc/1496cc/1497cc, 4cyl ohc, 4sp man, f/r

POWER: 40bhp @ 5100rpm/65 bhp @ 4800rpm

MAX SPEED (MPH): 75/78

0-60MPH (SEC): not measured/18.4

SUSPENSION & BRAKES: leaf front, leaf rear, drums f&r

LENGTH (IN)/WEIGHT (LB): 143/1512-1624

LAUNCH PRICE: £812 - £882

model was significantly cheaper than the 1500 – £812 instead of £882 in 1946 – most sales, in fact, were of the larger-engined car.

The body style, so characteristic of the late 1930s but not changed for twenty years, was a slim and simply-trimmed two-seater, made of wooden framing and aluminium skin panels, with separate but sweeping front wings and separate headlamps.

Side curtains and a build-it-yourself soft top were both provided, but HRG owners seemed to motor with the top down, almost regardless of the weather.

HRGs were beloved of sporting motorists. Here, a Mercury V8 powered HRG special takes a mudbath on a trial in 1953.

1500 Aerodynamic 1946-49

HRG's post-war nod to modernity was to develop a full-width body which was dubbed the "Aerodynamic". Although briefly successful – 31 cars were built in 1947 alone – it made no lasting impact and was abandoned after only three years.

Under the skin the entire rolling chassis was the same as that of the HRG 1500, the only change being to provide a modified cooling radiator. The body shell, considered attractive for its day, featured built-in headlamps, and consisted of an aluminium skin built up on a framework of lightweight square-section steel tubes. Wind-up windows were provided.

Unhappily, no changes were made to the chassis frame itself, which was really too narrow and which required big extension mounts for this new shell. There was an extension subframe at the rear to support the longer and wider rear end of the body.

The car weighed no less than 250lb more than the standard model, and HRG historians admit that this changed the entire character and behaviour of the chassis. It also didn't help that in 1946 an Aerodynamic cost £991, compared with £882 for the traditional-style 1500.

Scuttle shake, they say, was always a problem, and because heavy items like the spare wheel and the fuel tank (which was mounted in the shell immediately behind the left front wheel) had to be supported, there was more chassis flex than before.

As a result many bodies broke up, and over time a number of Aerodynamics were converted to wear standard HRG bodies. Although the Aerodynamic's top speed was perhaps 8-10mph higher than that of the 1500, acceleration was slower. The Aerodynamic simply wasn't what most potential HRG customers wanted, and it faded away in 1948.

Fashion being what it is, the remaining Aerodynamics are now well liked by classic car aficonados.

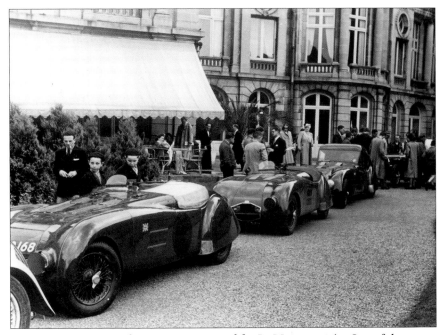

These three HRG Aerodynamics were entered for Le Mans in 1949. One of them, driven by Thompson/Fairman, finished eighth, the other two retiring.

SPECIFICATION

BODY STYLES: sports car

PRODUCTION: 45

ENGINE & TRANSMISSION: 1496cc, 4cyl ohc, 4sp man, f/r

POWER: 65bhp @ 4800rpm

MAX SPEED (MPH): 85 (E)

0-60MPH (SEC): not measured

SUSPENSION & BRAKES: leaf front, leaf rear, drums f&r

LENGTH (IN)/WEIGHT (LB): 162/1708

LAUNCH PRICE: £991

Twin Cam 1955-56

Almost twenty years after the original HRG had been built, the company tried again, this time with an all-new machine which was called, logically enough, the Twin Cam. Launched in February 1955, it caused a real sensation.

Central to the layout of this car was a new twin overhead camshaft derivative of the Singer engine, which HRG's Stuart Proctor had developed, but there was also an entirely new chassis, and running gear. Unhappily, the new project was far too ambitious for a tiny, under-financed concern like HRG to build in numbers, and only four cars were produced before time ran out for the company.

The basis of this front-engine, rear-

The last HRG, the 1955 Twin Cam.

drive car was a twin-tube chassis frame, which had combined coil spring and transverse leaf independent suspension at front and rear.

One astonishing feature was the HRG/Palmer disc brakes (no other British car used discs at this time), for which Lockheed provided the hydraulic circuits. Dunlop rims were five-bolted to magnesium wheel spiders.

The alloy-headed engine produced no less than 108bhp, much more than would ever be seen in modified versions which Singer briefly used for themselves – and that would have a cast iron head. It drove through a more robust version of the usual Singer gearbox.

The full-width light-alloy body was rather curvaceous, and completely unlike

any previous HRG, but in the modern mid-1950s idiom. Lessons had been learned from the problems of the Aerodynamic, and this shell was much more securely mounted to the chassis. From the front the Twin Cam looked rather like a contemporary Ferrari sports car, from the rear rather like an MGA, and there was a large vee-screen.

The Twin Cam was, by definition, too experimental and too expensive to sell well. At £1700, after all, it compared badly with the old-type HRG at £1269 (and especially badly against a Triumph TR2 at £884 or a Jaguar XK140 at £1598). Singer's takeover by Rootes, and the subsequent loss of engine supplies, finally killed off this little-known but promising project.

SPECIFICATION

BODY STYLES: sports car

PRODUCTION: 4

ENGINE & TRANSMISSION: 1497cc, 4cyl 2ohc, 4sp man, f/r

POWER: 95bhp @ 5250rpm/108bhp @ 5750rpm

MAX SPEED (MPH): 100 (E)

0-60MPH (SEC): not measured

SUSPENSION & BRAKES: leaf/coil ifs, leaf/coil irs, discs f&r

LENGTH (IN)/WEIGHT (LB): Not quoted/1624

LAUNCH PRICE: Special order, c. £1700

HUMBER

The dignified Humber concern was one of the pioneers of the British motor industry. Even before the first cars were produced in Beeston and Coventry in 1898, Humber had been building two-wheelers for a generation. From 1908 Humber concentrated its car-making business in Coventry and in 1928 it merged with Hillman: this was a prelude to both marques becoming constituents in the burgeoning Rootes Group, which would then hold control until the end, in 1967.

From 1932 Rootes re-positioned Humber as the up-market brand in the Hillman, Sunbeam-Talbot, Humber collection, and until the arrival of the Sceptre in 1963 Humbers were always the largest and most expensive machines in the stable.

After 1945 Humber's place settled down, with four-cylinder and six-cylinder cars originally called Hawk, Snipe and Super Snipe. Imperial and Pullman models were even larger, as contenders for the private hire and corporate trade. These brands came in for regular rejuvenation, with Hawk and Super

Snipe models invariably sharing the same basic body shells and much hidden engineering.

Though these Humbers were always built in Coventry (from 1947 all were completed at the Ryton factory), their bodies came from a variety of sources, notably from Pressed Steel, and from Rootes' own coachbuilding specialist Thrupp & Maberly.

At the same time as Hillman and (from 1956) Singer sales were rising steadily, those of large Humbers steadily declined, so the Humber badge was then placed on Hillman derivatives and much product identity was lost. Though up-dated persistently, the large Humbers announced in 1957/58 were never replaced, and sales of that breed ended in 1967. The Humber Sceptres based on the Hillman Hunter range carried on until 1976.

In the meantime, the Rootes Group, which had owned Humber since the early 1930s, was itself absorbed by Chrysler of the USA in 1967, the group becoming Chrysler United Kingdom Ltd in 1970.

Hawk Mk I/II 1945-49

The first post-war Hawk was little more than the 1940-model Hillman 14hp which had been shown in December 1939, complete with the still-born facelift of an extended boot "bustle", no running boards and full hydraulic braking. The Hillman 14 had originally been launched in 1937, and shared much of its Pressed Steel body shell with that of the Humber 16hp and Snipe models of the period.

Based on a currently ubiquitous Rootes chassis frame which featured a 114-inch wheelbase and "Evenkeel" independent front suspension (in which a transverse leaf spring also doubled as a wheel locating member), the post-war Hawk had the familiar six-light saloon car style, with exposed headlamps, to

Humber Hawk Mk I, 1945.

which a vertically-striped Humber grille had been added. At the time the standard fitment of a sunshine roof went unremarked.

Under the skin, power came from an obsolescent 1944cc sidevalve engine with an aluminium head. It drove through a four-speed crash-first manual gearbox of Hillman Minx origin which had a centre-floor gearchange. This engine, with a slightly smaller capacity, had been born in the early 1930s for the Humber 12hp, and had not been improved much since then. Rated at a lowly 56bhp, it struggled to provide any sort of performance – a top speed, after much patience, might be up to almost

65mph. Boring – but at least there were very comfortable seats, with loads of leg and hat room, to pass the time in.

In September 1947 Hawk I became Hawk II, the only "improvement" being fitment of the rather unhelpful "Synchromatic" steering-column gearchange, which in the eyes of everyone except salesmen for export markets was a definite backward step.

Even Humber enthusiasts might be hard pressed to find anything kind to say about this car, for performance was almost non-existent, the handling was poor, and these early post-war bodies tried very hard to rust away. Still, there is always period flavour to fall back on.

SPECIFICATION

BODY STYLES: saloon

PRODUCTION: not known

ENGINE & TRANSMISSION: 1944cc, 4cyl sv, 4sp man, f/r

POWER: 56bhp @ 3800rpm

MAX SPEED (MPH): 64

0-60MPH (SEC): 42.1

SUSPENSION & BRAKES: leaf ifs, leaf rear, drums f&r

LENGTH (IN)/WEIGHT (LB): 178/2968

LAUNCH PRICE: £684

Snipe/Super Snipe Mk I 1945-48

SPECIFICATION

BODY STYLES: saloon

PRODUCTION: not known

ENGINE & TRANSMISSION: 2732cc/4086cc, 6cyl sv, 4sp man, f/r

POWER: 65bhp @ 3500rpm/100bhp @ 3400rpm

MAX SPEED (MPH): 69/80

0-60MPH (SEC): 31.2/24.5

SUSPENSION & BRAKES: leaf ifs, leaf rear, drums f&r

LENGTH (IN)/WEIGHT (LB): 178/3332-3360

LAUNCH PRICE: £863/£889

Mk I Super Snipe, 1945, had a 4-litre engine in place of the Hawk's 2-litre unit.

The second of the rationalised range of post-war Humbers was the Snipe. This car was effectively the facelifted-for-1940 model which never saw production before the war.

Based very closely indeed on the Hawk (described above) it had a sidevalve 2731cc six-cylinder engine which had last been seen on the Humber 18hp of 1935-37. The roots of that sidevalve engine went right back back to 1931 and the short-lived Hillman Wizard. By 1945, it may be imagined, it was very close to the end of its useful life.

Technically and structurally, the chassis and body of the Snipe were like the 1945-model Hawk, though with extra cruciform bracing in the chassis frame. At least it kept its centre-floor gearchange until the end in 1948, which was a relief.

The Super Snipe derivative (also a re-born 1940 model), though, was much more enterprising, for it was fitted with the definitive 100bhp sidevalve six-cylinder 4-litre engine. Because this engine could deliver up to 80mph, the car was really quite saleable (police forces bought lots of them). Accordingly, though the Hawk was dropped in 1948, the Super Snipe carried on, as a Mk II (see below).

Very similar in character to the early post-war Hawk, but with even stodgier understeery handling, the Snipes and Super Snipes had more performance to offset their dodgy build and product quality. Just a few of them have survived the dreaded rust bug.

Pullman Mk I 1945-48

Intended for launch in 1939-40 as a weddings/funerals/corporate/mayoral carriage, the Pullman started its working life as a World War Two staff car, and did not become a civilian machine until 1945. Unique among Rootes cars at this time, it used a long-wheelbase version of the Hawk/Snipe/Super Snipe chassis – 127.5in instead of 114in – and a massive coachbuilt limousine body by Thrupp & Maberly.

Although it shared the same basic running gear and suspension (including the "Evenkeel" ifs), along with the same front end styling as the Super Snipe, from the screen backwards it was coachbuilt, spacious, and mighty impressive. Most Pullmans wore seven-seater limousine coachwork but there was also a smart landaulette version in which a soft-top over the rear seats could b e folded back.

This was a Big Beast – it weighed more than 4000lb – and as there was no power-assisted steering it was definitely intended to be driven by a paid (long-suffering?) professional. Not quite as fast as the Super Snipe in a straight line, it devoured fuel at the rate of 16mpg, which made the hard work an expensive business too.

The original post-war Pullman was available for less than three years, when it was replaced by Pullman II, which had an entirely different front-end style.

Since the bodies were all built up on wooden skeletons, most Pullmans had rotted away before the end of the 20th century. Although handling was not their strong point, they were impressive in their staunchly middle-class way.

SPECIFICATION	
BODY STYLES: limousine, landaulette	
PRODUCTION: not known	
ENGINE & TRANSMISSION: 4086cc, 6cyl sv, 4sp man, f/r	
POWER: 100bhp @ 3400rpm	
MAX SPEED (MPH): 80	
0-60MPH (SEC): 24.5	
SUSPENSION & BRAKES: leaf ifs, leaf rear, drums f&r	
LENGTH (IN)/WEIGHT (LB): 198/4005	
LAUNCH PRICE: £1598	

A landaulette version of the Humber Pullman Mk I.

Hawk Mk III/IV/V 1948-54

Announced at the Earls Court Motor Show of October 1948, the Hawk Mk III was the first true post-war Humber. Except for the engine and transmission, which were carry-over items from the ousted Hawk II, every other feature of this car was new. In particular, the "Evenkeel" transverse leaf independent front suspension of previous Humbers had been abandoned.

The Loewy Studio had been consulted regarding the styling of the new body, which was a conventional and rather boxy full-width four-door saloon with headlamps mounted in the nose of the front wings, though there was a conventional upright grille. All in all, it looked rather like an inflated version of the new Minx Phase III, which was launched at the same show.

Under the skin was a new 105.5in-wheelbase chassis frame, complete with box-section side members, cruciform bracing in the centre, and coil spring

1951 Hawk Mk IV had an enlarged engine.

SPECIFICATION

BODY STYLES: saloon, (Mk V only) touring limousine

PRODUCTION YEARS: 10,040/6492/14,300

ENGINE & TRANSMISSION: 1944cc/2267cc, 4cyl sv, 4sp man, f/r

POWER: 56bhp @ 3800rpm/58bhp @ 3400rpm

MAX SPEED (MPH): 71/80

0-60MPH (SEC): 30.7/23.8

SUSPENSION & BRAKES: coil ifs, leaf rear, drums f&r

LENGTH (IN)/WEIGHT (LB): 174/2750

LAUNCH PRICE: £799

independent front suspension. The side-valve engine and four-speed gearbox (with steering column gear change) were exactly as before, though a new type of hypoid bevel rear axle was used.

Inside the car, austerity was still with us and this, combined with a bench front seat and awful fascia/instrument panel styling, didn't make a good showroom impression. This was Rootes product planning at its most cynical, for little attempt had been made to provide good handling or even brisk performance.

Two years after launch the Hawk Mk IV took over, where the principal change was the use of an enlarged 58bhp 2267cc sidevalve engine, and which ran on fatter 15in tyres, though this made

little difference to the overall package.

Then, from Autumn 1952, the Hawk Mk V appeared, this being a face-lifted car with more flamboyant nose styling (which it shared with the then-new Super Snipe Mk IV), and more prominent rear wings. At the same time Rootes made a "touring limousine" version available. It came complete with a removable division, this using all the interior kit from the new Super Snipe. Unsurprisingly, this model was too expensive to appeal to Hawk buyers, and very few were ever sold.

After a two-year life, the Mk V then gave way to yet another derivative – Mk VI – which was the first Hawk to use an overhead-valve engine.

Super Snipe Mk II/III 1949-52

This was the car which motor industry watchers never expected to live for so long, since its junior relative, the Hawk, had just been completely rejuvenated. In spite of this Rootes retained the existing Super Snipe, with improvements, for four more years.

Announced in the autumn of 1949,

the Super Snipe Mk II was effectively a major re-working of the 1945-48 model (and that had its design roots in the 1930s…), all based on the existing body shell and running gear.

Compared with the Snipe Mk I, the Mk II ran on a longer-wheelbase chassis (by 3.5in) which had wider front and rear tracks, though the old-fashioned

"Evenkeel" transverse-leaf front suspension was retained. The lusty 100bhp 4086cc sidevalve engine was also retained, but there was a new gearbox casing allied to a column change.

The body was treated to a new and re-shaped nose with built-in headlamps and recessed driving lamps mounted below them – this virtually bringing it

SPECIFICATION

BODY STYLES: saloon, drophead, limousine

PRODUCTION: 17,064

ENGINE & TRANSMISSION: 4086cc, 6cyl sv, 4sp man, f/r

POWER: 100bhp @ 3400rpm

MAX SPEED (MPH): 81

0-60MPH (SEC): 20.6

SUSPENSION & BRAKES: leaf ifs, leaf rear, drums f&r

LENGTH (IN)/WEIGHT (LB): 188/3696

LAUNCH PRICE: £1144

Maurice Gatsonides (right) took second place in the 1950 Monte Carlo Rally in this Super Snipe.

into line with the latest Thrupp & Maberly Pullman shape. There was an alligator-opening bonnet panel, and running boards, which had been ousted in 1940, now re-appeared. For the first time on the Super Snipe, alternative body styles – saloon, touring limousine and drophead coupé (by Tickford) – were available.

Mk II gave way to Mk III, a relatively minor update introducing Panhard rod location of the rear suspension and detachable rear wheel covers.

This model ran through to the autumn of 1952, selling steadily throughout. It was quite a brisk performer (in a straight line), though it was also a gas guzzler. Few thought it pretty, though the Tickford drophead coupé was very smart. An acquired taste, shared by few – but some examples have survived.

A Super Snipe on the 1952 Monte Carlo Rally, driven by Maurice Gatsonides.

Pullman Mk II/III & Imperial Mk II/III 1948-53

If one understood how Rootes went in for mix-and-match, it was easy enough to work out the lineage of the 1948-53 generation of Pullmans Imperials.

Like the Super Snipe on which it had always been based, the Pullman Mk II used its own version of the latest Super Snipe chassis (the wheelbase had gone up to a magisterial 131in), the latest alligator-

SPECIFICATION

BODY STYLES: saloon, limousine (not on the Imperial)

PRODUCTION: 2200/1526

ENGINE & TRANSMISSION: 4086cc, 6cyl sv, 4sp man, f/r

POWER: 100bhp @ 3400rpm

MAX SPEED (MPH): 78

0-60MPH (SEC): 26.2

SUSPENSION & BRAKES: leaf ifs, leaf rear, drums f&r

LENGTH (IN)/WEIGHT (LB): 211/4648

LAUNCH PRICE: £2171

Humber Pullman Mk III, 1952.

nose bonnet and recessed-headlamp front end, and a slightly revised version of the existing Thrupp & Maberly limousine body. To cover the wider wheel tracks, the rear wings were re-profiled and the doors flared out at the bottom.

In 1948 the Imperial was new – but only in that it was a seven-seater saloon version of the Pullman limousine, sold without the Pullman's division.

Mk IIIs of 1950 had an all-synchromesh transmission but no major visual updates.

To quote one famous historian, these cars were "Definitely for vintage-minded morticians". Unhappily, their wooden-framed bodies were as mortal as the human race, so few have survived. Those which have are looked on with affection, not awe, and are extremely costly to maintain.

Super Snipe Mk IV/IVA/IVB 1952-57

More clever and resourceful product planning from Rootes. Once the new-for-1949 Hawk generation had been launched, it was certain that a Super Snipe derivative would eventually appear. This indeed it did – but not until October 1952, when the Hawk

SPECIFICATION

BODY STYLES: saloon, estate, touring limousine, coachbuilts

PRODUCTION: 9785/676/7532

ENGINE & TRANSMISSION: 4139 cc, 6cyl ohv, 4sp man, o/d or auto, f/r

POWER: 113bhp @ 3400rpm/116bhp @ 3400rpm

MAX SPEED (MPH): 90

0-60MPH (SEC): 16.6

SUSPENSION & BRAKES: coil ifs, leaf rear, drums f&r

LENGTH (IN)/WEIGHT (LB): 197/4025

LAUNCH PRICE: £1482

had already been on sale for four years.

Although it shared the same four-door passenger cabin as the contemporary Hawk, under the skin the Super Snipe was considerably different. The box-section 103.7in-wheelbase chassis frame was treated to coil spring independent front suspension (of Hawk type), and was powered by a broad-shouldered 113bhp 4139cc overhead-valve six-cylinder engine which had already been blooded as a 4750cc unit in Commer commercials. It was mated to the latest four-speed all-synchromesh gearbox.

Compared with the latest Hawk body shell, that of the Super Snipe Mk IV had a much longer nose, though it

The new 1953 Super Snipe Mk IV, now with 4.1-litre ohv engine.

shared the same front-end style. An estate car version eventually became available (from autumn 1955), and there were even a few touring limousines, these being converted at Thrupp & Maberly before being sent to Ryton for complet-ion. In five years there were several updates.

Mk IVA cars came along in autumn 1953, with 116bhp. Mk IVB took over swiftly, in April 1954, with a new fascia style including wood cappings, optional separate front seats and more space in the rear compartment.

From September 1955, the estate car body appeared, along with optional overdrive. This was the point at which peak power was pushed up to 122bhp. Borg Warner automatic transmission be came optional from April 1956.

All this frenetic activity was meant to keep the Super Snipe name alive, but in fact this model was dropped in 1957, there then being a year-long gap before an entirely new type of Super Snipe made its debut.

Though fast and powerful, this was not a car for the connoisseur by any means, especially as it was a heavy old machine without power steering. Fuel economy rarely reached 16mpg, and this factor combined with the model's susceptibility to rust has left few survivors.

Pullman/Imperial Mk IV 1953-54

In 1953-54 the long-running Pullman (limousine) and Imperial (saloon) had one final flourish as Mk IVs, both being re-engined with the 4139cc overhead-valve "Blue Riband" six-cylinder, rated at 113bhp, with an all-synchromesh

Humber Pullman Mk IV.

SPECIFICATION

BODY STYLES: saloon, limousine

PRODUCTION: 414

ENGINE & TRANSMISSION: 4139cc, 6cyl ohv, 4sp man, f/r

POWER: 113 bhp @ 3400rpm

MAX SPEED (MPH): 83 (E)

0-60MPH (SEC): not measured

SUSPENSION & BRAKES: leaf ifs, leaf rear, drums f&r

LENGTH (IN)/WEIGHT (LB): 211/4870

LAUNCH PRICE: £1977

column-change gearbox. There were no styling or equipment updates.

For those tempted to drive such a car, beware, for they weigh upwards of 4870lb and are quite dauntingly long. Splendid comfort in the back, though,

Hawk Mk VI/VIA 1954-57

Rootes planners somehow managed to keep the "class-of-48" Hawks alive until 1957, finally by offering the Mk VI and Mk VIA versions with an overhead-valve engine – the first to appear on Hawks of any sort.

The Mk VI appeared in the autumn of 1954 with an overhead-valve version of the old side-valver (which meant that its original design roots were in the early 1930s). This was a 70bhp 2267cc power unit closely related to the engine then being fitted to Sunbeam Talbots and the Sunbeam Alpine sports car, though with less power. Steering-column gear change was retained, and Laycock overdrive

The 1954 Hawk Mk VI.

became available as an option. The front suspension was stiffened up by the addition of an anti-roll bar as the new Hawk was quite a bit faster.

The only style change was at the rear, where a longer tail and more spacious boot were adopted. One year later, in September 1955, the long-promised five-door estate car finally appeared, a useful and capacious vehicle though it would only have a short life.

The final change came in April 1956, when the Hawk became Mk VIA.

Rootes made much of this by boasting about the de luxe model which became available, but it was no more than a makeover, with new paint and trim options which included wood cappings on the fascia and doors.

By the summer, demand for this car had dropped so far that Rootes had to make price reductions of almost £100, but production then carried on until the spring of 1957, when an entirely new type of Hawk took over.

Estate version of the Hawk Mk VI in 1956.

SPECIFICATION

BODY STYLES: saloon, estate

PRODUCTION: 18,836/9614

ENGINE & TRANSMISSION: 2267 cc, 4cyl ohv, 4sp man, o/d, f/r

POWER: 70bhp @ 4000rpm/75bhp @ 4000rpm

MAX SPEED (MPH): 83 (E)

0-60MPH (SEC): not measured

SUSPENSION & BRAKES: coil ifs, leaf rear, drums f&r

LENGTH (IN)/WEIGHT (LB): 182/3110

LAUNCH PRICE: £986

Hawk Series I/II/III/IV/IVA 1957-67

Humber Hawk Series I, 1957.

Hawk Series IV of 1966 had more angular roof styling.

For a new generation of big Humbers, Rootes commissioned an all-new unit-construction shell – the very first to be used behind a Humber badge – which would double for duty as the basis for a new Hawk and a new Super Snipe. As it happened, the Hawk appeared well over a year before the Super Snipe was ready.

Once placarded as the largest unit-body being built in the UK (but not for long – BMC's C-Series "Farina" cars were on the way !), the Hawk's shell was a sturdy all-steel saloon, with four doors and wrap-around front and rear windows; a five-door estate car would follow in October 1957. The result was a big, spacious and somehow mid-Atlantic looking car, though apparently there had been no influence from previous Rootes styling consultants.

The engine was the 2267cc overhead-valve unit from the previous Hawk, rated at 73bhp, mated to a four-speed column-change gearbox with no synchromesh on first. Laycock overdrive was optional, as was (until 1962) Borg Warner automatic transmission. Drum brakes were standard.

Between 1957, and 1964, when the Hawk received a major re-style, four different series of Hawk were put on sale.

Series I was the original type, first introduced in May 1957.

Series IA took over in October 1959, with different internal gear ratios.

Series II cars followed in October 1960, with front-wheel disc brakes, but with automatic dropped from home-market cars.

Series III came along in September 1962, with a minor rear-window restyle, a larger petrol tank, and automatic transmission no longer available at all.

Series IV Hawks of October 1964 got the same comprehensive cabin re-style as the Super Snipe Series V/Imperial (described below), which is to say that the roof profile was flattened, the rear wrap-around screen was exchanged for near-flat glass, and an extra fixed side-window was fitted behind the rear passenger doors. From this point, too, the Hawk also got an all-synchromesh transmission.

Series IVA Hawks arrived in 1965, the main improvement being the reintroduction of Borg Warner automatic transmission.

Confused? So were many customers, and pundits, which partly explains why sales dropped steadily away, with only 3754 cars built in the last two years. Compared with the Super Snipe (see below) the Hawk, while offering space and comfort, lacked performance, character and exclusivity. This and its stodgy driving characteristics hastened the end of the era of big Humbers, which came in mid-1967.

SPECIFICATION

BODY STYLES: saloon, touring limousine, estate

PRODUCTION: 15,539/6813/7230/6109/ 1746/ 3754

ENGINE & TRANSMISSION: 2267cc, 4cyl ohv, 4sp man, o/d or auto, f/r

POWER: 73bhp @ 4400rpm

MAX SPEED (MPH): 83

0-60MPH (SEC): 20.6

SUSPENSION & BRAKES: coil ifs, leaf rear, drums f&r (later disc f/drum r)

LENGTH (IN)/WEIGHT (LB): 185/3080

LAUNCH PRICE: £1261

Super Snipe Series I/II/III/IV 1958-64

To match the new-generation 1957 Hawk, the Rootes Group eventually announced the new Series of Super Snipe in October 1958. Nothing but the name was carried over from the previous models.

The Super Snipe shared its unit-construction body shell, suspension and general proportions with those of the Series Hawk, but with a glossier front end style. Right from the start, an estate car option was available. All the innovation was under the skin.

Power was by a brand-new six-cylinder 105bhp 2651cc engine which bore startlingly close similarities with the contemporary 3.4-litre Armstrong-Siddeley Sapphire engine. When we remind you that A-S was about to start assembling Sunbeam Alpine sports cars, the co-operative links become more logical. As launched, this engine was linked to a new, all-synchromesh three-speed gearbox (column change, still), with optional Laycock overdrive or Borg Warner automatic transmission. At this stage, servo-assisted four-wheel drum brakes were standard, and power-assisted steering was an optional extra.

The changes and up-dates, then began. Series II cars (October 1959) had a more beefy engine (2965cc/121bhp) and front-wheel disc brakes.

Series III cars (October 1960) had a new and handsome four-headlamp nose (the first ever, we think, on a British car), and a revised interior.

Series IV models (September 1962) got a small power increase, to 124bhp, and a restyled rear window profile. This update then carried the model through to October 1964, when it was replaced by the substantially restyled Series V model.

Compared with the Hawks, these Super Snipes were much faster, though they were still rather elephantine machines and heavy to manoeuvre without power steering. Once the 3-litre engine and front-wheel disc brakes had been standardised, a Super Snipe with power-assisted steering could be quite entertaining to drive. The Series III, after all, was the first-ever 100mph Humber.

Humber Super Snipe Series III estate car, 1960, capacious and luxurious.

SPECIFICATION

BODY STYLES: saloon, touring limousine, estate

PRODUCTION: 6072/7175/7257/6495

ENGINE & TRANSMISSION: 2651cc/2965cc, 6cyl ohv, 3sp man, o/d or auto, f/r

POWER: 105bhp @ 5500rpm/121bhp @ 4800rpm/124bhp @ 5000rpm

MAX SPEED (MPH): 92-100

0-60MPH (SEC): 19.0-14.3

SUSPENSION & BRAKES: coil ifs, leaf rear, drums f&r (disc f/drum r from Series II)

LENGTH (IN)/WEIGHT (LB): 185/3350

LAUNCH PRICE: £1494

A Super Snipe Series I takes a bath on the 1959 Coronation Safari.

Super Snipe Series V/VA and Imperial 1964-67

Rootes treated the big four-door Humber body to a comprehensive facelift in a range of Hawks, Super Snipes and a new derivative, Imperial, in the autumn of 1964. As with the Hawk IV/IVA types, the novelty was in the new cabin, which had a more angular roof profile, with an extra side window behind the rear doors, and no evidence of the previous wrap-around rear window.

On the Super Snipe, the power output crept up from 124bhp to 129bhp, and power-assisted steering finally became

The 1965 Super Snipe Series V.

SPECIFICATION

BODY STYLES: saloon, touring limousine, estate (no estate on the Imperial)

PRODUCTION: 3032

ENGINE & TRANSMISSION: 2965cc, 6cyl ohv, 3sp man, o/d or auto, f/r

POWER: 129bhp @ 5000rpm

MAX SPEED (MPH): 100

0-60MPH (SEC): 16.2

SUSPENSION & BRAKES: coil ifs, leaf rear, disc f/drum r

LENGTH (IN)/WEIGHT (LB): 188/3415

LAUNCH PRICE: £1512

Humber Imperial, 1965.

standard. The Imperial revived a famous old Humber model name, this time applied to what was effectively a super-specified Super Snipe. Although the Imperial was never produced with an estate car body, saloon and touring limousine types were both available. Compared with the Super Snipes, the Imperial cars had automatic transmission as standard, were treated to a pvc leathercloth roof covering, also had power-assisted steering as standard, and were recognised by better trim and interior fittings.

These were the very last of a long line of big Humbers which had first been seen in 1957 (Hawk) and 1958 (Super Snipe). Rootes killed them off in June 1967, and the only Humber to remain on sale was the smaller Hillman-based Sceptre, which was not at all what Hawk and Snipe devotees were used to.

Sceptre I/II 1963-67

During the 1960s Rootes concluded that the Humber badge should be attached to a model smaller than the Super Snipe. The car they chose to do this had originally been scheduled to hit the market as a new Sunbeam Rapier (which explains the front-end style), but a late marketing change followed. The result, introduced in January 1963, was the Sceptre, which was closely based on the new Hillman Super Minx. This

SPECIFICATION

BODY STYLES: saloon

PRODUCTION: 28,996

ENGINE & TRANSMISSION: 1592cc/1725cc, 4cyl ohv, 4sp man, o/d or auto, f/r

POWER: 80bhp @ 5200rpm/85bhp @ 5500rpm

MAX SPEED (MPH): 90/92 (E)

0-60MPH (SEC): 17.1/not measured

SUSPENSION & BRAKES: coil ifs, leaf rear, disc f/ drum r

LENGTH (IN)/WEIGHT (LB): 166/2455

LAUNCH PRICE: £977

The 1592cc Humber Sceptre I, 1963.

Sceptre generation was only ever built as a four-door saloon.

Compared with the Super Minx and Singer Vogue, the Sceptre shared the same platform and basic body shell, suspension and power train, but there was a different four-headlamp nose, and a larger windscreen which actually wrapped over slightly into the roof panel.

All Sceptres had servo-assisted front disc brakes, a manual/overdrive gearbox, and a high standard of trim and equipment including wood on the dash. Original cars were given twin-carburettor 80bhp 1592cc engines linked to a gearbox without first-gear synchromesh. Then the regular up-dates began. A single compound Solex carb-

urettor took over from twin Zeniths in summer 1963, while Rootes's new corporate all-synchromesh gearbox arrived in October 1964.

In the autumn of 1965 the Sceptre became Mk II, the revisions centring around the new 85bhp 1725cc engine, a Borg Warner automatic transmission option, and a revised front end style, still with four headlamps but now built into an unmodified Hillman Super Minx front wing/bonnet structure.

Although the Sceptre of this generation always gave off a whiff of "ugly duckling" (and there was indeed nothing graceful about the handling), it was quite a brisk performer, capable of more than 90mph, and sales figures show that it had been a worthwhile programme. Even so, the next-generation Sceptre, which followed in late 1967, was an altogether better car.

Sceptre II of 1966 had a 1725cc engine and a revised front.

Sceptre 1967-76

The best-selling Humber of all time came towards the end of the story, when Rootes/Chrysler developed the Humber Sceptre as an up-market version of the Hillman Hunter. It was announced one year after the Hunter had gone on sale. Like the earlier-generation Sceptre, the new model was very closely based on the mass-market car, but with some style and mechanical changes to justify the higher price. In some ways this was the "Cortina 1600E" of the range.

Compared with the Hillman Hunter (described above), the Sceptre had a more powerful engine (it was, in fact, the same twin-carburettor tune as the contemporary Sunbeam Rapier). Over-drive was standard and Borg Warner automatic transmission was optional.

Humber Sceptre in 1974.

SPECIFICATION
BODY STYLES: saloon, estate
PRODUCTION: 43,951
ENGINE & TRANSMISSION: 1725cc, 4cyl ohv, 4sp man, o/d or auto, f/r
POWER: 79bhp @ 5100rpm
MAX SPEED (MPH): 98
0-60MPH (SEC): 13.1
SUSPENSION & BRAKES: coil ifs, leaf rear, disc f/drum r
LENGTH (IN)/WEIGHT (LB): 170/2185
LAUNCH PRICE: £1139

The only important styling change was to use a then-unique four-headlamp nose and grille (which would be replicated on the Hunter GLS of the early 1970s). Although the actual body shell was identical to that of the Hunter, a vinyl roof covering was standard, and the interior was more completely equipped, with reclining front seats, a full-length console and a wooden fascia.

Apart from internal revisions and the fitment of a close-ratio gearbox in 1972 (which was when the other Hunters were also modernised), the Sceptre continued, essentially unchanged, until

February 1976.

Amazingly, the smart estate car derivative, complete with built-in roof rack, was not introduced until October 1974 (it was surely justified much earlier than that), so this version had only an 18-month life.

Although it did not have quite as good handling as relatives like the Hillman Hunter GLS, and was not quite a 100mph car, this Sceptre was a nicely-balanced machine, and the sales figures proved that Rootes had a point in putting it on the market. It was the very last Humber.

INVICTA

Noel Macklin and Oliver Lyle got together to build the Invicta sports car in the 1920s. They formed a small company based at Cobham in Surrey and bought in many proprietary components including Meadows engines. However, not even Donald Healey's Monte Carlo rally win in a 4½-litre Invicta in 1931 could stimulate enough sales. By 1935 Macklin had turned to building Railton cars instead, though Invicta struggled on, in London, under new ownership and with less exciting models.

After World War Two, Invicta once again rose from obscurity, this time at Virginia Water in Surrey, with plans to make a technically advanced but monumentally complex new sports saloon. Designer William G Watson (who already had a fine record of his own) was encouraged to finalise a new-generation Meadows-engined car for which development costs were more than £100,000 (in 1947 money, that is), and for which the planned retail price was set at £2940, the original production target being 250 cars a year. Within two years that price had risen stratospherically to no less than £3579.

This project could only have succeeded if enough customers had been found to make each sale extremely profitable, and for cash flow to claw back the debt, but as the new model, called Black Prince, was priced above every British car except the Bentley Mk VI it never looked feasible.

In the end, only seventeen cars were ever sold and the company imploded, still owing mountains to its creditors. After the collapse, the residue of the company and all the existing hardware were absorbed by AFN (the manufacturers of Frazer-Nash sports cars), who tried to interest BMW and then Armstrong-Siddeley in becoming involved, but nothing came of it.

Black Prince 1946-50

Here was one of those very rare birds, a post-war car built with absolutely no pre-war parts, or even any existing hardware, in its design. The Invicta Car Development Co Ltd gave William Watson a free hand to produce what we would now call a "Supercar", which he did, though bankrupting the company in the process.

Built around a sturdy cruciform-braced chassis frame with a 120in wheelbase, the new car, named "Black Prince", featured independent front and rear suspension by longitudinal torsion bars – the front end by Lancia-style sliding pillars, the rear by twin sliding pillars and lower wishbones. To simplify the installation, drum brakes were mounted inboard at the rear, at each side of the differential.

The engine was a magnificent piece of

The Invicta Black Prince had an advanced specification but was too complex.

SPECIFICATION

BODY STYLES: saloon, coupé, coachbuilts

PRODUCTION: 17

ENGINE & TRANSMISSION: 2999cc, 6cyl 2ohc, auto, f/r

POWER: 120bhp @ 5000rpm

MAX SPEED (MPH): 90 (E)

0-60MPH (SEC): not measured

SUSPENSION & BRAKES: tor ifs, tor irs, drums f&r

LENGTH (IN)/WEIGHT (LB): 192/3920

LAUNCH PRICE: £2940

design, which Watson asked Henry Meadows to produce. It was a six-cylinder three litre with twin overhead camshafts and three SU carburettors. It drove through Brockhouse turbo-transmitter transmission, which was an early type of automatic transmission, in fact a multi-stage torque converter. Worryingly, this system had had little development before being chosen to power the Black Prince – and it duly gave trouble.

The original body, a smartly-styled six-light fastback saloon, was made, aircraft-style, of aluminium panels on aluminium alloy box sections, and was originally to have been built by Charlesworth. Nowhere, especially in this body, could any signs of cost-cutting be detected.

Surely no one except a handful of visionaries at Invicta could have expected this monstrously complex machine to succeed, especially as it was heavy, reputedly ponderous, horribly expensive and needed years of development which it never enjoyed.

Amazingly, some of the 17 cars have survived, though non-original parts (especially in the transmission – some now use Jaguar manual gearboxes) have been needed to keep them running.

A rather crude and unshapely drophead coupé body, by Kent, on a Black Prince.

JAGUAR

First there was SS, then SS-Jaguar, with the stand-alone Jaguar marque following in 1945. Although early post-war Jaguars were updated 1930s SS-Jaguar types, the "SS" had dropped out of .the title for all the obvious political reasons. Then, as in later years, this was one of Coventry's most successful marques.

Fiercely independent until 1966, William Lyons's company built its reputation around a philosophy typified by its advertising slogan: Grace, Space and Pace.

With cars usually styled by Sir William himself, and engineering under the tight control of William Heynes, almost every post-war Jaguar was not only a work of art but a fast car with huge character. In the 1950s Jaguar reinforced that impression with a sports car racing programme which saw C-Types and D-Types win the Le Mans 24 Hour race no fewer than five times in seven years.

One vital factor was the magnificent twin-cam XK engine, which powered every new Jaguar – road or race car – in the 1950s and 1960s, but another was the successful attempt to provide remarkable value for money. "How do they do it at the price?" was a constant, despairing bleat from the opposition.

Evolution came in several steps. First there was the new XK engine (1948), then the move to the Browns Lane factory (1951), followed by Jaguar's first unit-construction saloon car (1955), and the takeover of Daimler (1960): all this in spite of a major factory fire in February 1957. The launch of the astonishing new E-Type (1961) was a real milestone, and it was only Sir William's desire for continuity which led him to merge with BMC in 1966.

Unhappily for Jaguar, it became a part of British Leyland in 1968 (and only a small part, at that); it was only sheer luck and, at times, gritted teeth, which allowed the marque to survive. In the 1970s Jaguar's history was complex, sometimes chaotic, and often afflicted by build-quality problems and strikes at the factories.

In 1980, though, John Egan was hired to sort out the mess. The company was floated on the stock market in 1984 and after a period of further independence was taken over by Ford, who expanded the marque mightily as the 2000s opened.

1½-Litre 1938-49

Launched as an SS-Jaguar in 1935, and re-engineered with an overhead-valve Standard engine and an all-steel body shell in 1938, the 1½-Litre went straight back into production after the war and was Jaguar's best-selling car of the period. (Post-war cars became quite unofficially known as Mk IVs.)

Although it had a shorter wheelbase, and was the only four-cylinder car in the line-up, the 1½-Litre shared most of its engineering with the contemporary 2½- and 3½-Litre models.

The basis of the car was a solid box-section chassis frame with beam axles and half-elliptic leaf spring suspension at

Jaguar 1½-Litre saloon.

SPECIFICATION

BODY STYLES: saloon

PRODUCTION: 5861 post-war, 5119 pre-war

ENGINE & TRANSMISSION: 1776cc, 4cyl ohv, 4sp man, f/r

POWER: 65bhp @ 4600rpm

MAX SPEED (MPH): 72

0-60MPH (SEC): 25.1

SUSPENSION & BRAKES: beam leaf front, leaf rear, drums f&r

LENGTH (IN)/WEIGHT (LB): 173/2968

LAUNCH PRICE: £684

front and rear. Although Jaguar sourced body pressings from many suppliers, it assembled the all-steel four-door shell, painting it and trimming it in Foleshill, a northern suburb of Coventry. The style was attractive but already beginning to look too "traditional", for the exposed headlamps and flowing front wings were definitely of 1930s and not post-war origin. At least the cars made after the war got heaters, which pre-war types had not had. Incidentally, the 1938-39 drophead coupé version of the 1½ did not re-appear in 1945.

Since 1937-38, the 1776cc engine (by no means the "1½-litre" that the model title suggested!) had been built for Jaguar by courtesy of the Standard Motor Co, and was backed by a Standard gearbox, though with a special Jaguar remote-control gearchange. The same engine was also used in the 1945-49 period in the Triumph Roadster/1800 saloon models. Amazingly, Jaguar stuck to a Girling mechanical braking installation.

This car was the entry-level Jaguar model of the range, yet it cost no less than £684 when it was reintroduced – although by comparison, say, with the Rileys of the period (which were competitors) it still offered formidable value. It was a very attractive car and, because of the high standard of trim, furnishings and equipment, felt like a true gentleman's sporting carriage, but it was no greyhound, for the top speed was only a little above 70mph.

Jaguar, in any case, was no longer committed to this end of the market, so when the Mk V range took over in 1949 there was no 1½-litre in the line-up.

2½-Litre/3½-Litre 1938-49

These early post-war Jaguars were the archetypal "Mk IVs" that everyone wanted – if, that is, they could raise the money, and gain a place in priority delivery queues. Similar in appearance and in structure to the 1½-Litre, they shared the same cabin dimensions but rode on a longer wheelbase ahead of that cabin – 120in instead of 112.5in – and had slightly wider wheel tracks, all this being done to accommodate the lengthy six-cylinder engines. Before the war these units had been made by Standard (though there was no equivalent Standard engine), but from 1945 they were manufactured by Jaguar them-selves.

Like the smaller-engined car, they rode on a box-section chassis frame with half-elliptic springing on front and rear beam axles. Handsome wire-spoke wheels discreetly veiled the massive mechanically operated drum brakes. The engines had pushrod-operated overhead valves, and were conventional enough, but (with credit going to Harry Weslake for cylinder head work) were deep breathers: the 2½-Litre gave 105bhp and the 3½-Litre produced a torquey and rousing 125bhp. They also gave you hot feet.

If the aerodynamic qualities of this body had been better (with huge free-standing headlamps and separate wings there was no chance, really…) the 3½-

Jaguar 3½-Litre saloon of 1946.

Interior of a six-cylinder Jaguar.

Litre could certainly have been a 100mph car. Even as it was, this was one of the fastest, most covetable of the early post-war crop of British cars. By 1960, however, survivors could be had for £20.

Most were long, sleek, all-steel four-door saloons, though from 1947 there was the alternative of a smart two-door drophead coupé, most of these going off to export markets. Unhappily, both bodies proved to be rust-prone, as Jaguar's anti-corrosion treatment was none too effective at the time.

How would Jaguar improve on this package? With better suspension and a more roomy cabin. The Mk V, which followed, offered all that, and more besides.

Jaguar 3½-Litre drophead.

SPECIFICATION

BODY STYLES: saloon, drophead

PRODUCTION: 1861/4420 post-war, 1856/1306 pre-war

ENGINE & TRANSMISSION: 2663cc/3485cc, 6cyl ohv, 4sp man, f/r

POWER: 105bhp @ 4600rpm/125bhp @ 4500rpm

MAX SPEED (MPH): 91/91

0-60MPH (SEC): 17.0/16.8

SUSPENSION & BRAKES: beam leaf front, leaf rear, drums f&r

LENGTH (IN)/WEIGHT (LB): 186/3584-3668

LAUNCH PRICE: £889/£991

Mk V 2½-Litre/3½-Litre 1949-51

If William Lyons had got his way, what we now know as the Mk VII would have appeared earlier, and there would have been no need for the Mk V. Tooling priorities, though, got in the way, so the large and elegant Mk V counts as one of the nicest "stop-gap" Jaguars of all time.

Hidden away was a brand-new 120in-wheelbase chassis frame, complete with long-travel independent front suspension, the springing medium being longitudinal torsion bars. Chassis side members swept up and over the rear axle, and a hydraulic braking system kept everything in check. There was a choice of engines – the 2½-litre and 3½-litre six-cylinder units, which had been lifted straight out of the now-obsolete "Mk IV" models, but there was no 1½-litre model any more.

Shaped and tooled in a tearing hurry, the body styling was a fascinating halfway house between what had gone before and what Jaguar had in mind for the future. More capacious than the "Mk IV", it had semi-recessed headlamps, wheel spats at the rear, and for the first time on a Jaguar the chassis carried steel disc wheels instead

The Jaguar Mark V was launched in 1949.

of centre-lock wires. The profile surrounding the side windows would be seen, in modified form, on several Jaguar models in the future

Most Mk Vs were four-door saloons but in 1950 and 1951 there was also a two-door drophead coupé, in which a lot of wood was used in the framing of the shell and the doors. Although these cars looked bigger than the "Mk IVs", and the chassis

was certainly more robust, the weight increase was minimised.

The result was a pair of fine, purposeful, sporting cars, of which the larger-engined model easily outsold the smaller. The Mk Vs helped prepare Jaguar fans for the Mk VIIs which followed. The cars were sumptuously furnished inside but, like "Mk IVs", it was a pity that they really weren't very well built.

SPECIFICATION

BODY STYLES: saloon, drophead

PRODUCTION: 1690/8803

ENGINE & TRANSMISSION: 2663cc/3485cc, 6cyl ohv, 4sp man, f/r

POWER: 102bhp @ 4600rpm/125bhp @ 4250rpm

MAX SPEED (MPH): 90 (E)/91

0-60MPH (SEC): not measured/14.7

SUSPENSION & BRAKES: tor ifs, leaf rear, drums f&r

LENGTH (IN)/WEIGHT (LB): 187/3696

LAUNCH PRICE: £1189/£1263

Mark V drophead coupé.

XK120 1948-54

Here was the sensation of the decade – the all-new Jaguar sports car which changed the face of Jaguar, of British sports car motoring, and of performance cars all over the world. Not only did it use the world's first quantity-production twin overhead camshaft

engine, but it was the first-ever sports car to have a regular top speed of more than 120mph. At the launch price of only £1263 it looked like – and indeed was – a bargain.

Conceived in a hurry to "blood" the new engine before it went into the Mk

VII saloon for which it was originally intended, the XK120 used a new 102in-wheelbase chassis which was effectively a shortened version of the Mk V/Mk VII frame, with the same independent front suspension by longitudinal torsion bars, and with huge 12in diameter drum brakes, plus steel disc or centre-lock wire wheels.

The 3442cc engine had seven main bearings, a cast iron block, and a cast aluminium head, with two lines of valves opposed at 70 degrees. At the start of what would be a long career, it was rated at a claimed 160bhp, and drove through a four-speed gearbox of Moss design.

The body style, by William Lyons, was a rakish two-seater, the first 240 cars being constructed of aluminium panels on a wooden skeleton. Then, from mid-1950, to meet the completely unpredicted level of demand for the new Jaguar, Pressed Steel supplied an all-steel body shell which looked identical but was completely different under the skin. Both had removable side curtains.

Much development followed in the

The 1949 Jaguar XK120 looked wonderful from every angle.

next six years. Two uprated versions of the engine were eventually offered, producing 180bhp and 210bhp; some cars were converted retrospectively. The smart fixed-head coupé version went on sale in March 1951, the svelte drophead coupé (with wind-up windows) following in April 1953.

Looking back, the XK120 was by no means perfect, for its brakes could not

always cope with the performance, the steering was heavy, the driving position cramped and awkward, and there was not enough space in the cockpit. No matter – Ian Appleyard proved how good it could be as a rally car, and the customers queued up for years. The steel cars rusted badly (but there are many restored survivors), and the aluminium cars are now highly-prized icons.

SPECIFICATION

BODY STYLES: sports car, sports coupé, drophead

PRODUCTION: 12,055

ENGINE & TRANSMISSION: 3442cc, 6cyl 2ohc, 4sp man, f/r

POWER: 160bhp @ 5000rpm/180bhp @ 5000rpm/210bhp @ 5750rpm

MAX SPEED (MPH): (160bhp) 125

0-60MPH (SEC): (160bhp) 10.0

SUSPENSION & BRAKES: tor ifs, leaf rear, drums f&r

LENGTH (IN)/WEIGHT (LB): 174/2856

LAUNCH PRICE: £1263

The imperturbable Stirling Moss at the wheel of an XK120 at Silverstone.

The drophead coupé version of the XK120 arrived in 1953.

Mk VII/VIIM 1950-56

Although the Mk VII was Jaguar's second new post-war saloon, it was the first to have a Pressed Steel shell and the first to use the twin-camshaft XK engine. Jaguar would have introduced it earlier had the tooling been ready, which explains why the Mk V was a stop-gap.

There were three principal features – the up-dated 120in chassis already found under the Mk V, the twin-cam engine, and the large but carefully-shaped four-door saloon car body, which represented a huge investment for the still-small Jaguar concern. The car was completely up-to-date in style, with recessed headlamps and recessed driving lamps below

Jaguar Mk VIIM.

them, and with a two-piece vee-screen.It had a much roomier interior than any previous Jaguar, finished in the same attractive wood-and-leather style. The 160bhp engine was "as XK120", but on this car there were servo-assisted brakes.

Most early cars went for export, UK deliveries beginning in earnest in 1951. The original specification was quite basic, though Borg Warner automatic transmission became optional from March 1953, and Laycock overdrive could be had from January 1954.

From October 1954 the Mk VII became the Mk VIIM model, using the 190bhp engine of the XK140, and with a modified nose which featured free-standing driving lamps on the front bumper, engine bay air intakes below the headlamps, and a wrap-around rear bumper.

Both types were fast (not many saloon cars, of any nationality, could achieve 100mph in the mid-1950s), but they were also heavy and drank a lot of fuel. Yet they were nimble enough to win saloon car races and rallies at top level. Great value at the time, they were built down to strict cost targets, which explains why the bodies rusted badly.

SPECIFICATION

BODY STYLES: saloon

PRODUCTION: 47,190 all Mk VII family

ENGINE & TRANSMISSION: 3442cc, 6cyl 2ohc, 4sp man, o/d or auto, f/r

POWER: 160bhp @ 5200rpm/190bhp @ 5500rpm

MAX SPEED (MPH): 100/102

0-60MPH (SEC): 14.3/13.6

SUSPENSION & BRAKES: tor ifs, leaf rear, drums f&r

LENGTH (IN)/WEIGHT (LB): 197/3864

LAUNCH PRICE: £1276/£1616

The Mk VII's biggest rallying exploit was an outright win in the 1956 Monte Carlo Rally, driven as here by Ronnie Adams. PWK 700 was a works Mk VIIM which had many outings, including in saloon car racing.

XK140 1954-57

Jaguar's second thoughts on the XK theme involved making the car more comfortable, more versatile, and more powerful, so that it would appeal even more to the North American market, where most sales were achieved.

Basically the XK140 (there was no XK130) was a modified XK120 with an enlarged cabin. To achieve this the

SPECIFICATION

BODY STYLES: sports car, sports coupé, drophead coupé

PRODUCTION: 8884

ENGINE & TRANSMISSION: 3442cc, 6cyl 2ohc, 4sp man, o/d or auto, f/r

POWER: 190 bhp @ 5500rpm/210bhp @ 5750rpm

MAX SPEED (MPH): (190bhp) 121

0-60MPH (SEC): (190bhp) 8.4

SUSPENSION & BRAKES: tor ifs, leaf rear, drums f&r

LENGTH (IN)/WEIGHT (LB): 174/3136

LAUNCH PRICE: £1598

Fixed-head XK140 coupé: more headroom and heavier bumpers than the XK120.

engine was pushed three inches further forward. It was now rated at 190bhp (or 210bhp in optional Special Equipment guise), and Alford & Alder rack-and-pinion steering was standardised, but otherwise the chassis was much the same before.

The body, though recognisably developed from the XK120, had a different

XK140 drophead coupé, 1955.

front grille, much more substantial bumpers, a bulkhead which had been pushed forward, and a rearranged cabin so that "+2" seating could be accommodated in the fixed-head and drophead coupé models. To suit the expanded cabin, there was a significantly larger roof on the fixed-head coupé.

The options list got bigger and bigger, for overdrive was an option on all types, while from October 1956 Borg Warner automatic (of Mk VII type) was made

available on fixed-heads and dropheads though not on the roadster.

Because the XK140 was considerably heavier than the XK120, and because the front/rear weight distribution was biased more towards understeer, the XK140 was not quite the outstanding success that its predecessor had been. It was, however, a very competent and very fast sports car. Purists might prefer the XK120, and there are those who are more drawn by the looks of the XK150.

Cabin of the XK140 drophead, with classic Jaguar dash.

2.4/3.4 (Mk I) 1955-59

Jaguar's 2.4 was not only its first-ever monocoque production car but also the first to use a short-stroke version of the XK engine. Developed with the active assistance of the Pressed Steel Company (who not only built the shells but also engineered the structure), this was the first "small" new Jaguar of the post-war period. At launch it weighed a substantial 900lb less than the contemporary Mk VIIM.

Built around a 107.4in. wheelbase, the four-door saloon was given a 112bhp 2483cc version of the XK engine which was 50lb lighter than the 3.4-litre unit. It was fed by two downdraught Solex carburettors in place of the 3.4's SUs. In retrospect the screen and door pillars look too thick and the front grille aperture too small, but all this was done to ensure ample strength in the all-steel shell. Rear wheel covers were standard. As on larger Jaguars of the day, the Moss gearbox was standard, and the Laycock

The 2.4 was the first unit-construction Jaguar.

overdrive was optional. Because disc brakes were still in their infancy, servo-assisted drum brakes were fitted.

The front suspension, by coil springs and wishbones, with Burman worm-and-nut steering, was a real innovation, as was rear suspension by means of cantilever leaf springs, radius arms and a short Panhard rod. For styling, rather than any other reason, the rear track was 4.5in narrower that that of the front

end; it was even narrower than that of the Morris Minor!

Well though not lavishly equipped, like other Jaguars the 2.4 had a wooden fascia and leather seats. In theory there was an entry-level "Standard" model but this was rarely seen, most being Special Equipment types.

Bargain or not, the 2.4 was underpowered, so the 3.4-litre, offered from March 1957, was more than welcome.

SPECIFICATION

BODY STYLES: saloon

PRODUCTION: 19,992/17,405

ENGINE & TRANSMISSION: 2483cc/3442cc, 6cyl 2ohc, 4sp man, o/d or auto, f/r

POWER: 112bhp @ 5750rpm/210bhp @ 5500rpm

MAX SPEED (MPH): 102/120

0-60MPH (SEC): 14.4/9.1

SUSPENSION & BRAKES: coil ifs, leaf rear, drums f&r (discs f&r from 1957)

LENGTH (IN)/WEIGHT (LB): 181/3024-3192

LAUNCH PRICE: £1344

3.4 with wire wheels and cutaway spats.

Dashboard and controls of the 2.4.

Its 210bhp engine guaranteed more than 120mph, the package including a bigger front grille, cutaway rear spats, a heavy duty rear axle and (for the first time on this car) an automatic transmission option. The extra performance meant that the 3.4 was now under-braked, a failing made good from September 1957 when four-wheel Dunlop discs and/or centre-lock wire wheels both became optional. From this date 2.4s got the wider radiator grille and the automatic option too. Thus made safe, the Mk I (as the cars became known) carried on until the autumn of 1959, when the Mk II took over.

First impressions persisted, and were correct. With too much front end weight and a narrow rear track these cars understeered badly, then kicked their tail out. Their styling was not as sleek as the Mk IIs which followed. Even so, the 3.4 in particular made a real name for itself.

Mark Is and Mk VIIIs in the Browns Lane factory.

XKSS 1957

If ever there was a predecessor to the legendary E-Type, the XKSS was it. As a thinly disguised road-car conversion of the D-Type racing sports car, the XKSS offered staggering performance with cramped two-seater accommodation. Except for the provision of a full-width screen, an extra door on the passenger's side and a very rudimentary soft-top, this was as raw a 1950s-style racing two-seater as Jaguar could devise.,

The original D-Type was revealed as a works racing car in 1954, with a sinuous style whose aerodynamic shape had evolved by Malcolm Sayer via mathematical calculations and a great deal of aerospace experience. In its racing form there was a cover over the "passenger seat", a wrap-around screen, and a fin behind the driver's head.

The structure centred around a magnesium alloy monocoque centre tub, with a complex bolt-on multi-tubular front end which supported the engine,

The rare Jaguar XKSS, a lightly "civilised" D-Type.

torsion bar independent front suspension and steering rack. Rear suspension of the heavy beam axle was by transverse torsion bars and trailing links. Dunlop centre-lock disc wheels and four-wheel disc brakes were standard, the latter enabling the D-Type to outbrake all its rivals.

The engine was a highly-tuned derivative of the XK unit which, with three dual-choke Weber carburettors, produced 250bhp. Coupled with a new all-synchromesh gearbox, this proved to be a bomb-proof combination for long-distance sports car racing. In "single-seater" form the D-Type would achieve 170mph, and with the later factory-only long nose and fin refinements that figure increased to beyond 180mph.

Limited production of the D-Type began in 1955, but by the end of 1956 orders had dried up. With no fewer than 29 near-complete D-Types in stock, Jaguar decided to convert most of them

An XKSS alongside a C-Type, the model which won at Le Mans in 1951 and 1953.

to road cars, developing the XKSS in double-quick time. The new model was launched in January 1957, but with only 16 cars completed, the balance were destroyed in the factory fire of 12 February 1957.

In the 1970s the XKSS was so popular that several D-Types were converted, retrospectively. In later years, several XKSSs were turned into D-Types. Confusing – but logical, as both were quite sensational machines.

SPECIFICATION

BODY STYLES: sports car

PRODUCTION: 16

ENGINE & TRANSMISSION: 3442cc, 6cyl 2ohc, 4sp man, f/r

POWER: 250bhp @ 5500rpm

MAX SPEED (MPH): 144

0-60MPH (SEC): 5.5

SUSPENSION & BRAKES: tor ifs, tor rear, discs f&r

LENGTH (IN)/WEIGHT (LB): 154/2015

LAUNCH PRICE: export only: US$6900 (equivalent to £2464)

Mk VIII 1956-58

Six years after the Mk VII had gone on sale, Jaguar launched the third version of the model, this time calling it Mk VIII, and giving it a more powerful 210bhp engine which would soon be shared with the XK150 sports car.

Although the basic shape of this massive saloon car was not changed, there was now a one-piece curved windscreen, a bolder grille treatment and, because of a strategically placed chrome strip, the chance to build the car in two-tone paint schemes.

Inside the Mk VIII, the trim level was improved still more. As usual, automatic transmission cars (most of them, as it transpired) had a bench front seat, while the seats were squashier and larger than ever before. Reutter reclining front seats were optional from mid-1958. Although there was no power steering at first, this became optional on left hand drive export-market cars from April 1958. The 210bhp engine pushed the top speed up towards 110mph, which soon demonstrated that the drum brakes, with 4000lb to bring to a halt from very high speeds, had truly reached their limits. Discs would replace them on the next model.

Although the Mk VIII was a good, sometimes exhilarating, large car, it was not as well-rounded as the Mk IX which would follow – and that would be the last derivative of a long-running family.

SPECIFICATION

BODY STYLES: saloon

PRODUCTION: 6212

ENGINE & TRANSMISSION: 3442cc, 6cyl 2ohc, 4sp man, o/d or auto, f/r

POWER: 210bhp @ 5500rpm

MAX SPEED (MPH): 107

0-60MPH (SEC): 11.6

SUSPENSION & BRAKES: tor ifs, leaf rear, drums f&r

LENGTH (IN)/WEIGHT (LB): 197/4032

LAUNCH PRICE: £1830

A curved windscreen and optional two-tone paint came with the Jaguar Mk VIII of 1957.

XK150/XK150S 1957-61

To replace the XK140, but without investing in a new chassis, Jaguar evolved the XK150, which had a more rounded and somehow less lithe body style than previous XKs. The crown line of the wings, along the flanks, dipped far less sharply than before; at the styling stage this was done by rotating and re-cropping the existing front wings.

Mechanically, Jaguar took the XK chassis just about as far as it would go. First of all, servo-assisted four-wheel disc brakes were standardised, while the power output of the engine was pushed up even further – to 210bhp as standard (though 190bhp was still theoretically still available). Both overdrive and Borg Warner automatic transmission were extras. Steel wheels were standard but

Rear view of the XK150 roadster.

rarely seen, the majority of cars having the optional centre-lock wires.

Although the body style was essentially fresh and featured a wrap-around screen and a much larger radiator grille, the car was still a recognisable descendant of the

XK140, with a number of XK140 pressings, sometimes modified. Fixed-head and drophead coupé types were announced first, while the open roadster variety (with wind-up windows) arrived in March 1958.

There was a big reshuffle in 1958 when the 3781cc engine option was offered, along with the XK150S model. Power outputs now ranged from 220bhp (two SUs, 3.8-litre), through 250bhp (three SUs, 3.4-litre) to 265bhp (three SUs, 3.8-litre), an intriguing choice for all

Jaguar enthusiasts. A Powr-Lok limited-slip differential was standard on the XK150S.

Although this was an even heavier car than the XK140 had been, the 265bhp XK150S could reach 136mph, making it real competition at the time for all but Ferrari. Complete with its disc brakes, it was a thoroughly safe superfast machine, but because of its style (the phrase "middle-age-spread" was often quoted) it was not generally considered as desirable as the earlier XK types.

In 1961 the XK150 and XK150S were replaced by the E-Type, bringing the 13-year XK pedigree to a close.

Jaguar XK150 drophead coupé, 1957.

SPECIFICATION

BODY STYLES: sports car, sports coupé, drophead coupé

PRODUCTION: 9395, of which 1466 XK150S

ENGINE & TRANSMISSION: 3442cc/3781cc, 6cyl 2ohc, 4sp man, o/d or auto, f/r

POWER: 190bhp @ 5500rpm/210bhp @ 5500rpm/220bhp @ 5500rpm/250bhp @ 5500rpm/265bhp @ 5500rpm

MAX SPEED (MPH): (210bhp/265bhp) 123/136

0-60MPH (SEC): (210bhp/265bhp) 8.5/7.6

SUSPENSION & BRAKES: tor ifs, leaf rear, discs f&r

LENGTH (IN)/WEIGHT (LB): 177/3190

LAUNCH PRICE: £1764

XK150S fixed-head coupé, 1958.

Mk IX 1958-61

The Mk IX was the last derivation of the Mk VII, which had appeared in 1950. Launched in October 1958, it was a revised Mk VIII, now with a 220bhp 3781cc XK engine and four-wheel disc brakes. This combination guaranteed

Jaguar Mk IX, 1958, a further update of the big saloon and now with 220bhp.

SPECIFICATION

BODY STYLES: saloon, limousine

PRODUCTION: 10,009

ENGINE & TRANSMISSION: 3781cc, 6cyl 2ohc, 4sp man, o/d or auto, f/r

POWER: 220 bhp @ 5500rpm

MAX SPEED (MPH): 114

0-60MPH (SEC): 11.0

SUSPENSION & BRAKES: tor ifs, leaf rear, discs f&r

LENGTH (IN)/WEIGHT (LB): 197/3980

LAUNCH PRICE: £1995

not only a top speed of 114mph but also a safe chassis to go with it.

The Mk IX was the first 3.8-litre engined Jaguar saloon and it also had Burman power-assisted steering as standard. By this time the vast majority of cars built had automatic transmission, which meant that they also had a bench front seat. Using this bench seat layout, a few limousine conversions were also

produced. The last cars were produced in September 1961.

In this case the last was definitely the best. Although the Mk IX was outdated, in that its styling was a decade old and it was very heavy, it handled as well as ever and was the fastest and safest of all types. A manual/overdrive example (rare by any standards these days) is a remarkably satisfying classic car.

2.4/3.4/3.8 Mk II 1959-67

Roy Salvadori, Jack Sears and Sir Gawaine Baillie in Mk IIs in the Molyslip Trophy race at Brands Hatch in 1962.

Better in every way than the Mk Is which they replaced, the Mk IIs were faster, more capable, better equipped and better looking. The 3.8, in particular, was one of the fastest high-speed bargains on the market, and could reach 125mph. This explains why they had a long career (if you include 240/340 types, almost ten years), and spawned off several sub-types.

First there was the restyle, which included half-doors instead of full-frame doors, more glass at the side, an enlarged rear window, extra driving lamps built into the nose, and a three-inch wider rear track. The 2.4-litre engine was boosted to 120bhp, and there was lusty 220bhp3.8-litre derivative too.

Four-wheel disc brakes were now standard and wire-spoke wheels (fitted to many cars) were optional. A new fascia finally placed the speedomete and rev-counter dials ahead of the driver's eyes. Reclining front seats were still an option. Power-assisted steering started out as an export-only option, but UK customers could have it from late 1960. From late 1965 Jaguar's new corporate all-

SPECIFICATION

BODY STYLES: saloon

PRODUCTION: 25,173/28,666/30,141

ENGINE & TRANSMISSION:
2483cc/3442cc/3781cc, 6cyl 2ohc, 4sp man, o/d or auto, f/r

POWER: 120bhp @ 5750rpm/210bhp @ 5500rpm/220bhp @ 5500rpm

MAX SPEED (MPH): 96/120/125

0-60MPH (SEC): 17.3/11.9/8.5

SUSPENSION & BRAKES: coil ifs, leaf rear, discs f&r

LENGTH (IN)/WEIGHT (LB): 181/3192-3304

LAUNCH PRICE: £1534

Jaguar Mk II, 1960, a spectacular success.

synchromesh gearbox was fitted instead of the slightly ponderous old Moss unit. Following a realignment of the range, the Mk IIs gave way to the 240/340 types in September 1967.

Police and escaping robbers both loved the 3.8 Mk IIs in equal measure, not only for their high performance but also for their remarkably competent handling. The only disappointed Mk II customers were those who bought 2.4s, only to find that they would not reach 100mph.

In later years these cars unfortunately descended into the furry-dice/crude customising bracket, and the great majority simply rusted away. Even so, a good, well-restored 3.4 or 3.8 is a gem.

The 3.8 loved to go racing. Jack Sears is driving this one at Brands Hatch in 1960.

240/340 1967-69

With the S-Types and 420 on the market, Jaguar really had too many models. Accordingly, in autumn 1967 the Mk IIs were dropped and replaced (as a short-term measure) by the 240/340 models. Mechanically these were like the equivalent Mk IIs, though the 240 got a 133bhp 2483cc engine.

The most significant changes involved making the cars entry-level models once again by reducing the level of equipment. Bumpers were slimmed down, front driving lamps had already disappeared, and there was Ambla (plastic) rather than leather upholstery.

This was a short-term strategy, which resulted in only 7246 cars being sold, but it filled the gap until the new-generation XJ6 (complete with its 2.8-litre engine) was up and running.

Slimline bumpers distinguish the Jaguar 240 (above) and 340 (below) from the Mk II.

SPECIFICATION

BODY STYLES: saloon

PRODUCTION: 4446/2800

ENGINE & TRANSMISSION: 2483cc/3442cc, 6cyl 2ohc, 4sp man, o/d or auto, f/r

POWER: 133bhp @ 5500/210bhp @ 5500rpm

MAX SPEED (MPH): 106/115

0-60MPH (SEC): 12.5/8.8

SUSPENSION & BRAKES: coil ifs, leaf rear, discs f&r

LENGTH (IN)/WEIGHT (LB): 179/3192-3360

LAUNCH PRICE: £1365

E-Type 3.8 1961-64

This was the most sensational of all Jaguar's new models, for it was lighter, smaller, faster and altogether more beautiful than the XK150s which it replaced. The original 1961 production car had evolved from a racing sports project of 1957, but was different in many ways. An obvious evolution of the D-Type race car, the E-Type combined a central steel monocoque tub with a tubular front section to support the engine and gearbox, front suspension, steering and cooling radiator.

Like the D-Type, the E-Type was shaped after much mathematical analysis (Malcolm Sayer once again), ending up as a long-nosed two-seater, with a choice of roadster or fixed-head coupé styles; for the roadster there was a removable hardtop option too. The headlamps were hidden behind shaped glass shields, and the bumpers were fixed direct to the body panels, which made them decorative rather than useful. Another quirk was that the driver could not see the nose, or how far it stretched, so nose-to-tail nibbles could be frequent.

Torsion bar independent front suspension and rack-and-pinion steering were an evolution of 1950s layouts, but the twin coil-over-damper independent rear suspension was an innovation; the same basic geometry would be adopted for many future Jaguars. Centre-lock wire spoke wheels were standard.

The 265bhp 3781cc engine was almost the same as the XK150S unit, and the Moss gearbox was as archaic as ever, with a slow change and poor synchromesh. A limited-slip differential was standard.

Jaguar E-Type 3.8 roadster.

Unlike earlier XKs, there were no overdrive or automatic options.

The brakes (with Kelsey-Hayes servo) and the cross-ply tyres were not really a match for the 150mph top speed, and over the years good-quality radials and later-type servos have often been fitted to preserved cars.

The early E-Type was charismatic, very fast and very desirable, so road-holding,

E-Type on road test in 1961

braking and cabin shortcomings (it was extremely cramped in there, with basic seating) were easily forgiven. Even so, the 4.2-litre engined car which followed in 1964 was a much better all-round package.

Dashboard of the roadster.

SPECIFICATION

BODY STYLES: sports car, sports coupé

PRODUCTION: 15,490

ENGINE & TRANSMISSION: 3781cc, 6cyl 2ohc, 4sp man, f/r

POWER: 265bhp @ 5500rpm

MAX SPEED (MPH): 149

0-60MPH (SEC): 7.1

SUSPENSION & BRAKES: tor ifs, coil irs, discs f&r

LENGTH (IN)/WEIGHT (LB): 176/2688

LAUNCH PRICE: £2098

E-Type fixed-head coupé..

E-Type 4.2 SI 1964-68

Jaguar's second thoughts on the E-Type theme were much more satisfactory: except on the grounds of early-design purity, this is the most desirable of all six-cylinder E-Types. With a better engine, a much better gearbox, better seating and more devel-opment, this is the E-Type the original car should have been.

Compared with the original, the structure and styling had not changed, but there was much improvement hidden away. The engine was enlarged to the definitive 4235cc, giving 265bhp – no more power than before but significantly more torque – and this was the very first Jaguar to use a new, all-synchromesh, four-speed gearbox, allied to a diaphragm clutch. The electrical system went to negative earth, and an alternator was standard.

A Lockheed vacuum brake servo replaced the unsuccessful Kelsey-Hayes unit of the 3.8s, and the seats were now much larger and more squashy. The

fascia was revised, and a centre console was also fitted. Radial-ply tyres were already optional, and became standard from October 1965.

These cars sold strongly until 1968, and for the last year were really "Series 1½" types as some of the modifications due for S2 models were introduced: for example the headlamps lost their glass

covers, and there were changes to the fascia/instrument/switchgear layout.

Though no faster than the 3.8 model (extra engine torque was balanced by extra weight) these were fine cars, which sold well and still have huge charm. It was to preserve cars such as this that the E-Type re-manufacturing industry developed.

SPECIFICATION

BODY STYLES: sports car, sports coupé

PRODUCTION: 9550/7770

ENGINE & TRANSMISSION: 4235cc, 6cyl 2ohc, 4sp man, f/r

POWER: 265bhp @ 5400rpm

MAX SPEED (MPH): 149

0-60MPH (SEC): 7.4

SUSPENSION & BRAKES: tor ifs, coil irs, disc f&r

LENGTH (IN)/WEIGHT (LB): 176/2856

LAUNCH PRICE: £1896

4.2-litre E-Type fixed-head was externally the same as the 3.8.

E-Type 2+2 1966-71

A lot of clever re-engineering went into producing the 2+2, which is one reason for it not appearing until mid-1966. Although it was based on the fixed-head coupé 4.2, the 2+2 had a nine-inch longer wheelbase, with a completely re-profiled rear floor and fixed-head roof which allowed a pair of occasional seats to be fitted in. The immediate result was that the deeper windscreen looked a little too upright,

though this would be amended, with a different glass sweep, from late 1968. Because of the cabin re-shaping the 2+2 never looked as good as the two-seaters

All 2+2s shared the same engine, manual transmission and suspension layout as the two-seaters, but this was the first and only six-cylinder E-Type to have a Borg Warner automatic trans-mission option. Once the two-seater E-

Types became S2, the 2+2 took on all their changes, including the exposed headlamps, optional power-assisted steering, and optional steel disc wheels. Air conditioning was available on export LHD examples.

Although not the best-seller in the range – Jaguar sold less than 2000 2+2s each year, this model was such a success that its platform was used as the basis of the Series III (V12-engined) cars which followed in 1971. Although 2+2s were not as fast (139mph) as the two-seaters, and didn't handle quite as well, they were versatile and have survived, restored, in big numbers.

SPECIFICATION

BODY STYLES: sports coupé

PRODUCTION: 10,930

ENGINE & TRANSMISSION: 4235cc, 6cyl 2ohc, 4sp man or auto, f/r

POWER: 265bhp @ 5400rpm

MAX SPEED (MPH): 139

0-60MPH (SEC): 7.4

SUSPENSION & BRAKES: tor ifs, coil irs, discs f&r

LENGTH (IN)/WEIGHT (LB): 184/3108

LAUNCH PRICE: £2245

The 2+2 version of the E-Type. This is a Series II with open headlamps.

E-Type SII 1968-71

The SII arrived at the end of 1968, inspired by a raft of new USA exhaust emission and safety legislation. Directly developed from the S1 (and the unofficial "S1½" of 1967-68), this further refined the six-cylinder line, though not everyone liked the visible changes

As on later 2+2s, the headlamps were exposed and moved forward, and rocker switches featured on the fascia. Disc wheels and power-assisted steering both became optional. At the front of the car, the cooling air/radiator intake was made considerably larger. Air conditioning was now optional on left hand drive cars.

Cars sent to the USA suffered badly from new exhaust emission rules, their

E-Type Series II roadster.

strangled engines, fitted with Zenith-Stromberg carburettors, producing less than 200bhp – though this evil was not forced on home-market customers.

The SII was only on sale for two and a half years, for in 1971 it was replaced by the Series III car, which had the brand new V12 engine.

SPECIFICATION

BODY STYLES: sports car, sports coupé

PRODUCTION: 13,490

ENGINE & TRANSMISSION: 4235cc, 6cyl 2ohc, 4sp man, f/r

POWER: 265bhp @ 5400rpm

MAX SPEED (MPH): 143

0-60MPH (SEC): 7.2

SUSPENSION & BRAKES: tor ifs, coil irs, discs f&r

LENGTH (IN)/WEIGHT (LB): 176/2856

LAUNCH PRICE: £2163

Series II fixed-head coupé.

E-Type SIII V12 1971-75

The third-generation E-Type, introduced in March 1971, was a classic
case of "new wine in old bottle", for it
was effectively a revised SII type, on the
longer wheelbase of the 2+2, but with
the new 5.3-litre V12 engine squeezed in
under the bonnet.

Although the style was much as before,
the big new engine had forced many
changes on the engineers. Visually, the
nose featured a decorative front grille,
the wheel arches were flared to cover
wider-section tyres and wheels as well as
wider wheel tracks, and most cars were
delivered with steel disc wheels, though
centre-lock wires were optional. All cars
now had the same 105in-wheelbase
platform, which meant that the open
two-seater was more spacious than
before. The closed car used a modified
version of the 2+2 coupé shell. Inside,
there were few changes to the established
fascia and instrument panel, though
more cars were fitted with the optional
air conditioning.

The massive V12 engine, a superb
unit, was lightly tuned and very torquey,
so many customers went for the optional

Series III E-Type V12.

Borg Warner Type 12 automatic transmission in place of of the four-speed
manual gearbox. Power-assisted steering
was standard equipment, and a lift-off
GRP hardtop was optional on the open
two-seater model.

This, the last of the E-Types, was
somewhat "softer" than its predecesors,
and the ageing lineage of the chassis and
the cockpit packaging was more

apparent. In the UK, the last of the
fixed-head coupés was produced in
February 1974, and the last SIII cars of
all were produced in the winter of
1974/75.

Theoretically, the XJ-S (introduced
later in 1975) would replace the E-Type,
but as the two cars had completely
different characters the public was never
likely to accept that.

*These wheels were the standard fitment
on V12 E-Types.*

SPECIFICATION

BODY STYLES: sports car, coupé

PRODUCTION: 15,290

ENGINE & TRANSMISSION: 5343cc, V12cyl
ohc, 4sp man, auto, f/r

POWER: 272bhp @ 5850rpm

MAX SPEED (MPH): 146

0-60MPH (SEC): 6.4

SUSPENSION & BRAKES: tor ifs, coil irs,
discs f&r

LENGTH (IN)/WEIGHT (LB): 185/3304

LAUNCH PRICE: £3123

Series III with optional hard top and wire wheels.

Mk X/420G 1962-1970

Jaguar was proud of the Mk X at the time, but now, maybe, they would agree that it was too big and too heavy. As a replacement for the Mk IX, it was the biggest car Jaguar had ever made. Apart from the XK engine and the choice of manual or automatic transmissions, the rest of the car – the monocoque structure, steering, suspension and braking – was new.

Built on a 120in-wheelbase platform, this was a very wide and heavy car, with a vast bonnet and four headlamps. Power was supplied by the triple-SU 265bhp 3781cc engine, almost identical to that of the then-new E-Type. Most customers chose Borg Warner automatic transmission and a few opted for manual with overdrive, but there were very few who chose the (Moss-type) manual 'box alone.

There were no suspension similarities with older Jaguars. The coil spring independent front end was new, while the

The Jaguar Mark X, Britain's widest car, as introduced in 1962.

double coil-over-shock independent rear suspension was technically like that of the E-Type. Power-assisted steering (very light indeed, rather disconcerting) was standard, as were four-wheel disc brakes complete with the troublesome Kelsey-Hayes servo.

The ultra-wide interior featured the usual Jaguar combo of wooden fascia, leather seats and good-looking trim. The front seat was a vast divided bench

From October 1964, the Mk X got the E-Type's 4235cc engine, and (rarely, as it happened) Jaguar's new all-synchromesh gearbox to go with it. In addition, Marles Varamatic power-steering took over from Burman, while Borg Warner Model 8 automatic took over from the old-type DG 'box. The Kelsey-Hayes servo was dropped and replaced by a Lockheed vacuum servo, and air

conditioning became optional.

A year later Jaguar introduced a limousine derivative. There were no exterior changes but there was no front-seat adjustment; only 18 were made. Finally, from October 1966, the Mk X became the 420G, which was little more than a name change and a few extra bits of brightwork and interior padding; 24 of the cars were limousines. This car carried on for four years, incidentally donating its platform and all the running gear to the Daimler DS420 Limousine.

Then, as now, the Mk X/420G was seen as too large, too heavy, too profligate, and too softly sprung to be an enjoyable open-road machine. Unlike the Mk II (one of its contemporaries) it never became an enthusiast's car, nor was it much loved in later years.

Interior of the Mark X, as sumptuous as ever.

Most of the changes made for the 420G were under the skin, but for external recognition there was a full-length chromed waist strip and a prominent central grille bar.

SPECIFICATION

BODY STYLES: saloon, limousine

PRODUCTION: 24,282

ENGINE & TRANSMISSION: 3781cc/4235cc, 6cyl 2ohc, 4sp man, o/d or auto, f/r

POWER: 265bhp @ 5500rpm/265 bhp @ 5400rpm

MAX SPEED (MPH): 120/122

0-60MPH (SEC): 12.1/9.9

SUSPENSION & BRAKES: coil ifs, coil irs, discs f&r

LENGTH (IN)/WEIGHT (LB): 202/3990

LAUNCH PRICE: £2393

S-Type 1963-1968

Sir William Lyons's third thoughts on a "compact" Jaguar came along in late 1963. The Mk I had been supplanted by the Mk II in 1959, and for 1963 the entire rear end of the car was reworked, complete with the E-Type/Mk X-style independent rear suspension and an extended tail.

It wasn't quite a straightforward as that. Though the front half of the platform, the front end, suspension and doors were all carried over, the roof line was different, the rear of the platform was totally different, and now there were twin fuel tanks, one tucked into each wing. Not only that, but the headlamps were slightly hooded, the side lights had migrated from the top to the bottom of the front wings, and there was a different grille.

The engines fitted were 210bhp 3442cc or 220bhp 3781cc (no 2.4 option, not even in export markets, please note), and

S-Type Jaguar: familiar nose and an elongated tail.

Substructure of an S-Type at Browns Lane, with a jury-rigged seat for the driver.

SPECIFICATION

BODY STYLES: saloon

PRODUCTION: 24,900

ENGINE & TRANSMISSION: 3442cc/3781cc, 6cyl 2ohc, 4sp man, o/d or auto, f/r

POWER: 210bhp @ 5500rpm/220bhp @ 5500rpm

MAX SPEED (MPH): 120 (E)/121

0-60MPH (SEC): not measured/10.2

SUSPENSION & BRAKES: coil ifs, coil irs, discs f&r

LENGTH (IN)/WEIGHT (LB): 187/3584-3696

LAUNCH PRICE: £1669

were like those of the Mk II, as were all three transmission options. For the first 18 months, the S-Type was inflicted with the old Moss gearbox, but from March 1965 the new all-synchromesh gearbox took its place.

Changes included removing the front driving lamps and downgrading interior equipment from September 1967 to give

the 420 (see below) a better chance in the showrooms, but the end came when the XJ6 appeared in autumn 1968.

Compared with the Mark II the S-Type was a heavier car but it offered much better handling balance. There's not a lot in it, really, though in later years the S-Type almost became the "forgotten Jaguar".

420 1966-1968

Jaguar's fourth iteration of the Mk I/Mk II/S-Type theme was called the 420, and it looked very much like the much larger Mk X. The resemblance, though, was purely visual, there being no common parts.

How was it done? The S-Type shell and all-independent platform were retained, except that the body was given a more bluff four-headlamp nose. Only one

engine was available, this being a 245bhp 4235cc version of the XK power unit, clearly different from and more powerful than the unit fitted to S-Types. Varamatic power-assisted steering, Girling four-wheel disc brakes and Borg Warner Model 8 automatic transmission all helped to update what was now an ageing design.

With a top speed of nearly 125mph this

was the fastest of all the cars in this long-maturing family, the "go" being matched by excellent handling, the equal of the S-Type's. Yet it didn't get the same raffish reputation as the Mk II.

There was a badge-engineered Daimler Sovereign version of the 420 too – utterly identical except in grille and tiny trim details. The 420 gave way to the XJ6 in the autumn of 1968.

SPECIFICATION

BODY STYLES: saloon

PRODUCTION: 9600

ENGINE & TRANSMISSION: 4235cc, 6cyl 2ohc, 4sp man, o/d or auto, f/r

POWER: 245bhp @ 5500rpm

MAX SPEED (MPH): 123

0-60MPH (SEC): 9.9

SUSPENSION & BRAKES: coil ifs, coil irs, discs f&r

LENGTH (IN)/WEIGHT (LB): 188/34696

LAUNCH PRICE: £1930

Jaguar 420, 1967, with Mark X-style front and S-Type tail.

XJ6 SI 1968-1973

Years in the making, and subject to several technical upheavals along the way, the XJ6 took over from all existing Jaguar saloons except the 420G in the autumn of 1968. It was Jaguar's first all-new platform/body shell (Pressed Steel did the honours) in seven years. In a life which stretched through 18 years, and three distinct iterations, until the 2000s it was the best-selling Jaguar of all time.

The XJ6 was built on an a 108.75in-wheelbase platform and wore a magnificently styled four-door saloon body. It came with the latest XK engines and the usual choice of manual, overdrive or automatic transmission. If the power outputs look puny by comparison with older Jaguars, this is because strict DIN measuring standards had been applied (originally they were quoted at 180bhp for the 2.8 and 245bhp for the 4.2, which was much more reassuring !). The

Jaguar XJ6, photographed in 1968 before launch.

short-stroke, shallow-block 2792cc XK engine was new for this car, and would be used in no other.

The new platform rode on familiar, but new-in-detail coil spring independent suspension; this time, though, steering was by Adwest power-assisted rack-and-pinion, very accurate and a major innovation. Wheel rims were six inches (the widest yet on a Jaguar) , and Dunlop radial-ply tyres were standard (previously, radials were optional, except on 420Gs).

Interior trim and equipment were an update of what we already knew from S-Types and 420s, with a new and effective heater system, and (for export only) optional Delanair air conditioning. From October 1972, and very rare for a time, a 4.2-litre model with a four-inch longer wheelbase was offered alongside the standard-wheelbase saloon. The Daimler Sovereign version of the XJ6 appeared in October 1969.

There is no question that this was the most refined Jaguar ever developed: though the ride was plush-smooth, the handling was superb. Not many customers bothered to explore the limits, which were very high indeed. The SI gave way to a revised SII in 1973, and a face-lifted SIII in 1979. By any measure this was a very long-running success story.

At the time of writing the SI XJ6 is an undervalued classic. Will its day come?

SPECIFICATION

BODY STYLES: saloon

PRODUCTION: 19,426/58,972

ENGINE & TRANSMISSION: 2792cc/4235cc, 6cyl 2ohc, 4sp man, o/d or auto, f/r

POWER: 140bhp @ 5150rpm/173bhp @ 4750rpm

MAX SPEED (MPH): 117/124

0-60MPH (SEC): 11.0 (E)/8.8

SUSPENSION & BRAKES: coil ifs, coil irs, discs f&r

LENGTH (IN)/WEIGHT (LB): 190/3388-2703

LAUNCH PRICE: £1797

The same car getting some exercise on road test.

XJ12 SI 1972-1973

The new V12 engine had already appeared in the latest E-Type, but it was not fitted in Jaguar's big saloon until July 1972, in a car badged XJ12. Because the XJ6/XJ12 range was up-dated to Series II in October 1973, this meant that the original XJ12 had a very short life.

The XJ6 structure had just enough space in the engine bay for the massive V12 engine (which had four Zenith-Stromberg carburettors) to be inserted. There was so much under-bonnet heat in this model that the battery now had to have its own cooling fan!

The 5.3-litre Jaguar XJ12 arrived in 1972.

SPECIFICATION

BODY STYLES: saloon

PRODUCTION: 3,238

ENGINE & TRANSMISSION: 5343cc, V12cyl ohc, auto, f/r

POWER: 265bhp @ 5850rpm

MAX SPEED (MPH): 146

0-60MPH (SEC): 7.4

SUSPENSION & BRAKES: coil ifs, coil irs, discs f&r

LENGTH (IN)/WEIGHT (LB): 190/3881

LAUNCH PRICE: £3726

Automatic transmission was standard equipment (there was no manual gearbox option), but the chassis, suspension, power-assisted steering, fascia/ instrument panel and all the cabin equipment were virtually the same as on the XJ6.

From October 1972, a longer-wheelbase version was also available, the two types going forward together until the Series II

models took over in October 1973.

Compared with the XJ6, the XJ12 was faster, even smoother and more silent than the six-cylinder car, though its fuel consumption could be appallingly high, sometimes no better than 11-12mpg. For all that, these cars – particularly the original short-wheelbase types – became real collectors' pieces.

XJ6 SII 1973-1979

In October 1973, after five years of the original model being on sale, the XJ6 became Series II. The basic design was not changed but the front-end styling was altered, with a facelift including a

SPECIFICATION

BODY STYLES: saloon

PRODUCTION: 69,772

ENGINE & TRANSMISSION: 3442cc/4235cc, 6cyl 2ohc, 4sp man, 5sp man, o/d or auto, f/r

POWER: 160bhp @ 5000rpm/173bhp @ 4750rpm

MAX SPEED (MPH): 117/124

0-60MPH (SEC): 10.9/8.8

SUSPENSION & BRAKES: coil ifs, coil irs, discs f&r

LENGTH (IN)/WEIGHT (LB): 195/3708

LAUNCH PRICE: £4795/£3674

Jaguar XJ6 Series II, with shallower grille and raised bumper.

raised bumper and different grille. Inside, there was a new and much-simplified instrument panel.

At first this car was only available with the 4235cc engine, for the earlier 2.8-litre had died with the end of the Series I (except, briefly, for some export markets). There was a choice of standard or long-wheelbase saloons.

Overdrive became standardised on manual-transmission cars from February 1974, and the shorter-wheelbase saloon was discontinued from September 1974. A 3442cc-engined version was introduced in April 1975 (the capacity was the same as that of the 1950s unit but the engine was rather different internally). This 3.4-litre car had the longer-wheelbase shell, and the overdrive gearbox as standard. Finally, from the summer of 1978, the Rover SD1-type five-speed gearbox took over from four-speed-plus-overdrive – though very few such cars were ever delivered as almost all XJ6s were now bought with automatic transmission.

After a turbulent five-year career, during which British Leyland's finances sometimes threatened its very existence and build quality sometimes fell away, the Series II gave way in March 1979 to the extensively changed Series III models.

Officers from Avon and Somerset police on patrol in a Series II XJ6.

XJ12 SII 1973-1979

Series II XJ12L. L versions had slightly longer rear doors and more legroom.

SPECIFICATION

BODY STYLES: saloon

PRODUCTION: 14,226

ENGINE & TRANSMISSION: 5343cc, V12cyl ohc, auto, f/r

POWER: 265bhp @ 5850rpm/285bhp @ 5750rpm

MAX SPEED (MPH): 146/147

0-60MPH (SEC): 7.4/7.8

SUSPENSION & BRAKES: coil ifs, coil irs, discs f&r

LENGTH (IN)/WEIGHT (LB): 195/4116

LAUNCH PRICE: £4702

Because it was so closely "twinned" with the six-cylinder XJ6, when that car progressed to Series II, so did the XJ12. Like the original type, the massive V12 engine was mated to automatic transmission (a manual gearbox was not available), and in this case the car was only ever available in longer-wheelbase form. Visually it was almost impossible to pick the differences between six-cylinder and V12-engined cars, as both had the same facelifted nose, raised bumper and intake details. For the first series of cars, too, the engine was still rated at 265bhp and was fed by four Zenith-Stromberg carburettors.

In May 1975 the engine was given Bosch-Lucas fuel injection and up-rated to 285bhp, and at the same time the interior trim was revised. Officially, at this point, the car was named XJ 5.3 though the old name of XJ12 stuck. In spite of its heavy fuel consumption, and the fact that world-wide oil prices were rocketing, this car sold strongly for the next four years, until displaced by the Series III Model.

XJC (Coupé) 6cyl and V12 1975-1977

There were times when Jaguar enthusiasts thought that these cars would never go on sale. Previewed in October 1973 (when the SII saloons were launched), they were promised for sale in mid-1974, but deliveries did not start until early 1975. Within three years, though, they would be extinct.

Mechanically these coupés were based on the original (not longer) wheelbase version of the XJ6/XJ12 SII platform. They shared the same front end, front wings, screen, fascia/instrument panel and back end as the saloons, but had a unique two-door body. The vinyl roof covering was not only a styling feature but hid the welded joints of the pressed-steel roof panel. Most people called the cars coupés, but they were really roomy enough to qualify as two-door saloons.

There were two versions, the XJ6C having the 4.2-litre six-cylinder engine, the XJ5.3C having the latest fuel-injected 285bhp V12. All, except a few of the six-cylinder cars, had automatic transmission. Performance, handling,

Only Series II XJs were offered with the coupé body. This is an XJ12C.

ride and general ambience were the same as were offered by the four-door saloons, although prices were inevitably higher.

Because the doors were large and heavy (more so than on the saloons), in-service problems with sealing from water and wind persisted, and the doors were also known to sag as the bodies got older. Yet it was pricing rather than engineering which held sales back – in June 1975, why pay £6850 for an XJ 5.3C when you could pay £5960 for a V12-engined saloon, which had two extra doors and more cabin space? Needing to rationalise their assembly lines, Jaguar dropped these graceful but short-lived coupés in October 1977.

SPECIFICATION

BODY STYLES: two-door saloon/coupé

PRODUCTION: 6505/1873

ENGINE & TRANSMISSION: 4235cc, 6cyl 2ohc/5343cc, V12cyl ohc, 4sp man, o/d (6-cyl only) or auto, f/r

POWER: 173bhp @ 4750rpm/285bhp @ 5750 rpm

MAX SPEED (MPH): 124/148

0-60MPH (SEC): 8.8/7.6

SUSPENSION & BRAKES: coil ifs, coil irs, discs f&r

LENGTH (IN)/WEIGHT (LB): 190/3724-3885

LAUNCH PRICE: £5480/£6850

The XJ6C on standard road wheels, as against the Kent alloys on the V12 model.

XJ-S (1975-81 spec)

Jaguar could not expect the pundits to welcome a saloon-based car that tried to take over from the much-loved E-Type, so in September 1975 the new XJ-S had a difficult reception. However, the new car already had a proven basis as it was based on the platform of the fuel-injected XJ12.

Although larger and heavier than the E-Type, the XJ-S actually had the better aerodynamic shape (Jaguar was proud of this, but wouldn't really explain why…) and could top 150mph in its initial form.

Based on a short-wheelbase version of the XJ6/XJ12 platform, it had cabin sides extended by a pair of odd-looking "flying buttresses" which linked them to the tail lamps. There was "almost four-seater" accommodation. The nose featured large rectangular headlamps (or four circular ones on North American cars). The fascia and instrument layout, not at all Jaguar in flavour, was unique to the XJ-S, and there was a two-spoke padded steering wheel.

Almost all cars would have automatic

1977 Jaguar XJ-S.

transmission, but until March 1979 a four-speed manual gearbox was also available (just 352 such cars were produced). Peak XJ-S sales would be reached in the 1980s, and early sales were at a best rate of nearly 4000 cars a year.

Because the XJ-S's looks were always controversial, the fuel consumption high, and the initial reliability record not good enough, sales lagged in the late 1970s, and for a time in 1980 no XJ-Ss were produced at all. Even so, the car had such

high performance, and excellent ride and handling qualities, that a change of fortune would follow in the 1980s when the original model was transformed by a new "HE" (High Efficiency) V12 engine. In the end there would also be cabriolet and convertible versions, along with new-generation six-cylinder models.

By 1996, when the last XJ-S was produced, no fewer than 115,413 cars had been made, during more than 20 years of production.

SPECIFICATION

BODY STYLES: sports coupé

PRODUCTION: c15000 pre-HE model of 1981

ENGINE & TRANSMISSION: 5343cc, V12cyl ohc, 4sp man, or auto, f/r

POWER: 285bhp @ 5500rpm

MAX SPEED (MPH): 153

0-60MPH (SEC): 6.9

SUSPENSION & BRAKES: coil ifs, coil irs, discs f&r

LENGTH (IN)/WEIGHT (LB): 182/3902

LAUNCH PRICE: £8900

The rear end of the XJ-S, with characteristsic "flying buttresses".

Not everyone liked the dashboard of the early cars.

XJ6 SIII 1979-1986

In March 1979, more than ten years after the XJ6 had originally gone on sale, Jaguar turned it into the SIII, with few mechanical changes but with a revised superstructure. The style, which had been re-touched by Pininfarina, featured a more angular roof, more glass area, and a cleaned-up nose. Different tail lamp shapes, too, told their own story. Inside the car, there was further

change to the fascia, yet more comfortable seating, and the same style of two-spoke steering wheel as on the contemporary XJ-S.

As before, there were 3442cc and 4235cc versions of the now-venerable twin-cam XK engine, though the larger type was finally given Bosch-Lucas fuel injection for all markets. This boosted the home-market car's peak power to

205bhp, which delivered a top speed of 131mph – the fastest so far on a six-cylinder engined Jaguar. Some manual transmission cars were built (not many, in truth), and they now had the five-speed gearbox introduced very late on SII types.

Early in the career of this model Jaguar's corporate fortunes took a turn for the better, the company's image gradually improved, and the SIII would go on to be a very successful and well-liked model. Few significant technical changes were to be made in the seven-year life of the car, and by the time the last car was produced in October 1986, no fewer than 122,452 of all types had been built.

In all respects these cars were the equal of, sometimes better than, the SIIs they replaced, as during the 1980s Jaguars' build quality and reliability seemed to improve steadily. Along with the XJ 5.3 SIII (XJ12 SIII), they would eventually be displaced by a new-generation Jaguar saloon known to all as the "XJ40" type.

SPECIFICATION

BODY STYLES: saloon

PRODUCTION: 122,452

ENGINE & TRANSMISSION: 3442cc/4235cc, 6cyl 2ohc, 5sp man, or auto, f/r

POWER: 160bhp @ 5000rpm/205bhp @ 5000rpm

MAX SPEED (MPH): 117/131

0-60MPH (SEC): 10.9/8.6

SUSPENSION & BRAKES: coil ifs, coil irs, discs f&r

LENGTH (IN)/WEIGHT (LB): 195/4033

LAUNCH PRICE: £11,189/£12,326

Jaguar XJ6 Series III, introduced in 1979.

XJ12 SIII 1979-1992

Early in 1979, when the XJ6 became SIII, the XJ12 (XJ 5.3, as British Leyland wanted it called) was up-dated at the same time. The third-generation V12-engined model, therefore, got the restyled cabin, with more angular roof, more glass area and different front and rear treatments, along with all the changes to the interior.

Mechanically there were virtually no changes at first (though from 1981, just out of our period) the engine would be upgraded to XJ-S HE levels, with 299bhp. Because the V12 version of the

SPECIFICATION

BODY STYLES: saloon

PRODUCTION YEARS: 14,229

ENGINE & TRANSMISSION: 5343cc, V12cyl ohc, auto, f/r

POWER: 285bhp @ 5750rpm/299bhp @ 5500rpm

MAX SPEED (MPH): 150

0-60MPH (SEC): 8.1

SUSPENSION & BRAKES: coil ifs, coil irs, discs f&r

LENGTH (IN)/WEIGHT (LB): 195/4234

LAUNCH PRICE: £15,015

Series III XJ12, with "pepperpot" alloy wheels.

next-generation Jaguar was to be delayed for some time, this SIII would remain in production for many more years than the six-cylinder version.

Accordingly, the car's name would eventually be changed to Sovereign (from late 1983), at which point GM400 automatic transmission was adopted, and sales continued slowly but

steadily until December 1992, when the last example was produced at Browns Lane. In that time, Jaguar claimed, no fewer than 177,243 SIII types (Jaguar and Daimler-badged varieties), and 402,848 XJ6-family models of all types had been produced – an all-time record for the Jaguar concern.

JENSEN

Starting as a specialist coachbuilder of buses, trucks and cars, Jensen of West Bromwich revealed its very first "own-brand" car in 1936. Brothers Richard and Alan Jensen kept the company afloat throughout the Second World War, and then from 1946 began to expand their activities.

Early post-war experiments with a Meadows-engined car were abandoned, after which Jensen forged strong links with Austin, from whom they bought engines and other components. Alongside the production of their own PW and Interceptor models they undertook contracts to build bodies for the Austin A40 Sports, Austin-Healey 100/3000 and Sunbeam Tiger. Jensen even assembled the first P1800s for Volvo, from bodies supplied by Pressed Steel.

It wasn't easy to stay afloat financially, so from 1959 the Norcros Group took control, then William Brandt succeeded Norcros in 1968, and USA motor trader Kjell Qvale completed the revolution in 1970.

In the 1960s Jensen not only embraced Chrysler V8 engine power, but (from 1966) FF four wheel drive technology, and Italian styling. The new-generation Interceptor became their best-selling car, and from 1972 there was also the Lotus-engined Jensen-Healey sports car, which transmuted itself into the Jensen GT in 1975.

Hit by the after-effects of the energy crisis of 1973/74, Jensen went into receivership in September 1975, and all series production ended early in 1976.

Attempts to revive the brand in the 1980s and 1990s were unsuccessful.

PW 1946-51

Previewed in 1946, the PW (for "Post War") model was based on the pre-1939 H-Type Jensen, though with a smart new body style and a straight-eight twin-cam Meadows 4-litre power unit producing 130bhp. All manner of development troubles saw this engine abandoned. A few cars got pre-war type Hudson eight-cylinder engines, but most were fitted with a 130bhp six-cylinder Austin Princess engine instead. That was the start of Jensen's long-term links with Austin (later BMC), and a great deal of contract body assembly of Austins and Austin-Healeys.

The separate box-section chassis of the PW incorporated coil spring independent front suspension featuring a broad-based tubular bottom wishbone at each side. There were coil

The rather stylish Jensen PW echoed the lines of pre-war models.

springs for the rear axle, which had an archaic worm drive. This was changed to an Austin hypoid-bevel unit from 1949. Brakes, by Girling, were all hydraulic. The original Meadows engine was closely related to the twin-cam straight six used in the Invicta Black Prince, but in the end only three were fitted (and reportedly never sold). The Hudson "eights" were, literally, old stock from the 1939 H-Type.

Austin's triple-SU Princess engine took over in 1949, but only as a last-minute interim rescue job – its main use would be in the forthcoming Interceptor.

The bodies were built by Jensen. There was a four-door saloon and a cabriolet, both with handsome semi-razor edge styling, built on an ash frame with steel or aluminium panels. This was a heavy, unresponsive, pre-war flavoured car which was seen as both expensive and unproven. The fact that a mere 17 (13 of them with Austin engines) were sold tells its own story.

SPECIFICATION

BODY STYLES: saloon, drophead

PRODUCTION: 17

ENGINE & TRANSMISSION: 3860cc, 8cyl, 2ohc/4205cc, 8-cyl, sv/3993cc, 6cyl, ohv, 4sp man, f/r

POWER: (3993cc) 130bhp @ 4300rpm

MAX SPEED (MPH): 90 (E)

0-60MPH (SEC): not measured

SUSPENSION & BRAKES: coil ifs, coil rear, drums f&r

LENGTH (IN)/WEIGHT (LB): 197/3248 - 3556

LAUNCH PRICE: £1998/£2842

Interceptor 1950-57

Jensen's second post-war model, called the Interceptor, avoided all the pitfalls of the PW. Apart from the Austin Sheerline engine and transmission, this was a completely different car from the PW, cheaper and definitely more modern, though still a machine which did not find a large market.

Smaller, six inches lower, and lighter than the PW, which soon gave way to this new car, the Interceptor looked astonishingly like the Austin A40 Sports which followed – the reason, simply, was that Jensen's Eric Neale had styled both. Based on the cruciform-braced Austin A70 Hampshire/Hereford chassis frame, but with a longer (114in) wheelbase and much stiffening, it used modified Austin independent front suspension, along

Jensen Interceptor convertible, a large and effortless touring car.

with conventional half-elliptic leaf rear suspension for the hypoid-bevel rear axle. Front and rear track dimensions were like those of the Austin too, and a Girling hydro-mechanical braking system was standard. An all-hydraulic system followed in the early 1950s.

The two-door body was of composite construction – some wood, some steel, some aluminium – the entire front assembly being hinged at the nose to give excellent access to the engine bay. At first the only body on offer was an occasional four-seater cabriolet on which the entire rear screen panel was made from Perspex and swung down into a recess when the hood was lowered. A permanent hardtop (Jensen called it a saloon) followed in 1952; this is also

when overdrive was made available.

Although never a major seller (technically and visually it was soon overtaken by the 541 model), the Interceptor re-established Jensen as a car-maker. Like the PW it was too big and somehow too elephantine to be a truly fast car, though high gearing gave easy cruising. A few of the 88 cars built have survived, as well-regarded rarities.

The Interceptor saloon had a fabric roof covering.

SPECIFICATION

BODY STYLES: saloon, drophead

PRODUCTION: 88

ENGINE & TRANSMISSION: 3993cc, 6cyl ohv, 4sp man, o/d, f/r

POWER: 130bhp @ 3700rpm

MAX SPEED (MPH): 95

0-60MPH (SEC): 13.1

SUSPENSION & BRAKES: coil ifs, leaf rear, drums f&r

LENGTH (IN)/WEIGHT (LB): 183/2800

LAUNCH PRICE: £1999

541 1954-59

In the mid-50s, when it was launched, the 541 was a wickedly attractive car – a genuinely sporting two-door four-seater, big enough to be called a saloon and sleek enough to be a sports coupé.

Only the engine, transmission and basic front suspension (all from Austin) were carried forward from the Interceptor, for the chassis was now a 105in-wheelbase steel platform which included large-diameter longitudinal tubes, small pressings, foldings and reinforcements. Drum brakes were fitted at first, but four-wheel Dunlop discs followed in late 1956.

The glassfibre-bodied Jensen 541 was futuristic looking in 1954, and was capable of 115mph.

The chassis was topped by a glass-fibre body (the first prototype shown had a metal shell) in which the whole of the front-end could be lifted up for engine bay access. In addition, a flap in the front air intake could be closed to cut off air flow into the engine bay. There were only three major mouldings, and the doors were actually in light alloy.

As usual with Jensens of this period, power came from the Austin D-Series six-cylinder engine of 3993cc, and Laycock overdrive was optional. Interior equipment was simple but well-laid-out, this being a much more modern car than the Interceptor had ever been. Without going anywhere near a wind tunnel Jensen had produced a very

efficient body shape, for this car could beat 110mph with ease and cruise at 90-100mph.

Still costly, of course, this was a Jensen which appealed to more people because of its good looks and its outstanding abilities. Its handling was never light (power-assisted steering on Jensens was a decade away), but the 541 was a very fast and capable open-road car. Because of the GRP shell's long-life capability, many have survived.

The 541 looked happier on wire wheels.

SPECIFICATION

BODY STYLES: sports saloon

PRODUCTION: 226

ENGINE & TRANSMISSION: 3993cc, 6cyl ohv, 4sp man , o/d, f/r

POWER: 125bhp @ 3700rpm

MAX SPEED (MPH): 116

0-60MPH (SEC): 10.8

SUSPENSION & BRAKES: coil ifs, leaf rear, drums f&r (disc f&r from late 1956)

LENGTH (IN)/WEIGHT (LB): 176/3135

LAUNCH PRICE: £2147

541R 1957-60

In late 1957 the 541 was joined by the 541R (the "R", they say, stood for rack-and-pinion steering). It was a more powerful, more specialised car than the original 541.

The first 43 R-Types used BMC engines producing 140bhp, but from 1958 the car was de-tuned to 130bhp, with a different cylinder head and two instead of three SU carbs. A Jaguar-

SPECIFICATION

BODY STYLES: sports saloon

PRODUCTION: 193

ENGINE & TRANSMISSION: 3993cc, 6cyl ohv, 4sp man, o/d, f/r

POWER: 140bhp/130bhp @ 3700rpm

MAX SPEED (MPH): 124

0-60MPH (SEC): 10.6

SUSPENSION & BRAKES: coil ifs, leaf rear, discs f&r

LENGTH (IN)/WEIGHT (LB): 176/3260

LAUNCH PRICE: £2866

The 541R of 1957: disc brakes and more power.

type Moss gearbox was now used, and Laycock overdrive was standard. Four-wheel disc brakes and the already-mentioned rack-and-pinion steering were all standard. Many examples had centre-lock wire wheels and looked very handsome.

With the original triple-SU engine, the 541R was a genuine near-125mph machine, putting it close to the Aston Martin class. It was expensive but it was an appealing package – and there was still more to come from this very well-balanced chassis.

541S 1960-63

What was the easiest way for Jensen to give the 541R a larger cabin, and better roadholding? Easy really: cut the chassis and bodyshell tooling in half down the middle, widen them both by exactly four inches, and then start again. Since the tooling was quite simple in each case, this could be done with minimal disruption.

The 541S, therefore, was 67in wide instead of 63in, with a 1.5in higher roof line, yet this was done so carefully that the style didn't seem to have changed much. If Jensen had not adopted a conventional nose, with an orthodox egg-crate grille aperture, casual observers

The 541S was four inches wider than the 541R, and slower.

would probably not have noticed.

Compared with the 541R, the running gear was very similar, though on this car GM Hydramatic automatic transmission (as manufactured by Rolls-Royce and also supplied to BMC for the D-Series engined Princesss) became standard. The Moss gearbox with Laycock overdrive was still available to special order until March 1962, then dropped altogether.

Elsewhere the specification was very familiar, for the engine was a direct carryover from the 541R, as were the front and rear suspension, rack-and-

pinion steering, and servo-assisted four-wheel Dunlop disc brakes. Inside the cabin, though, the fascia layout was new, while a radio and safety belts were both standard.

The 541S was a bigger, heavier and (especially in automatic transmission form) less wieldy machine than the 541R it replaced. Not only that, but it was 10-15mph slower than before (transmission losses had much to answer for), and it was expensive. The miracle, therefore, was that Jensen managed to sell 127 of them before the much-changed C-V8 arrived in 1963.

SPECIFICATION

BODY STYLES: sports saloon

PRODUCTION: 127

ENGINE & TRANSMISSION: 3993cc, 6cyl ohv, 4sp man, o/d or auto, f/r

POWER: not quoted

MAX SPEED (MPH): 109

0-60MPH (SEC): 12.4

SUSPENSION & BRAKES: coil ifs, leaf rear, discs f&r

LENGTH (IN)/WEIGHT (LB): 178/3415

LAUNCH PRICE: £3097

C-V8 1961-66

For the C-V8, in 1962, Jensen swung into line with competitors such as Bristol by adopting a Chrysler V8 engine and transmission to replace the older Austin/Hydramatic combination. Although the chassis and GRP body shell had both evolved from the 541S, the performance was quite transformed. Especially in later form, a C-V8 was one of the fastest-accelerating of all contemporary British cars.

Chrysler claimed 305bhp for the original 5.9-litre engine, which may have been optimistic, but there was much more torque than before. Almost all cars had the Chrysler Torqueflite automatic transmission; a few used a Chrysler manual three-speeder with

The Jensen C-V8, introduced in 1962 with a 5.9-litre Chrysler V8 engine.

Laycock overdrive behind it. One quirk was that brake and clutch operation was servo assisted, the vacuum reservoirs actually being in the chassis tubes, which were sealed off for that purpose.

Compared with the 541S there were significant style changes, though the

same basic body shell was retained. Not only was a rather ungainly slanted four-headlamp nose (two larger, two smaller) chosen, but the rear quarters were altered and the tail became more of a notchback. As before, the doors had aluminium skins. The C-V8 was a nicely equipped two-door almost-four-seater, but it still lacked power steering.

In the autumn of 1963 the Mk II arrived, with Armstrong adjustable Selectaride dampers (first use on a British car) and improvements to the ventilation. A brawnier 330bhp 6276cc Chrysler engine was fitted from April 1964.

The Mk III version was introduced in July 1965. Most changes were cosmetic, including the fitment of equal-sized headlamps, a larger screen, and a gloss rather than matt finished wood fascia panel, but there were no significant mechanical improvements.

Before the C-V8 was dropped at the end of 1966 in favour of the new Interceptor, it gained a reputation as a very fast car with good handling. If only

it could have looked nicer (opinion was always divided about the styling) it would have sold even better. At least its GRP body shell meant that corrosion was minimised. A force to be reckoned with on the road, even today.

The CV-8 had distinctive four-headlamp front-end styling.

Interceptor 1966-76

Here was the most handsome Jensen ever built. Engineers, artists and Jensen buffs all agree about this. Whereas the GRP-bodied C-V8 had simply been big and impressive, its successor with Italian styling was big, beautiful and practical too. For classic fans though, there would be one major problem – rust, for these cars were bodied in sheet steel.

Original cars were styled by Touring of Milan, with bodies produced at Vignale of Turin, but series production always took place in the UK. The body was large and brawny but very attractive, with an almost-four-seater cabin and a vast lift-up hatchback rear window.

These Interceptors used developments of the C-V8 chassis platform, which

Interceptor II in 1969.

came complete with massively torquey Chrysler power. Only 23 early cars had manual gearboxes, and Chrysler Torqueflite transmission was always more popular; by 1969 all cars were built with automatic transmission.

Here was an immensely capable machine with supercar performance and four-wheel discs to keep everything in check. Only the lack of power-assisted steering (optional from late 1967 and standard from October 1968) made an Interceptor hard to drive.

In a ten-year life the cars were steadily improved. The Mk II (October 1969) had style changes, particularly on the fascia, while the Mk III (October 1971) had yet more styling updates and alloy road wheels. At that point, the 7.2-litre 385bhp SP version appeared, and a 330bhp version of this engine was fitted in Mk III Interceptors from January 1973.

Later, in 1974, a convertible version of the Interceptor was launched. No fewer than 467 of these would be sold in less than two years before the company went into liquidation. Even later there was a fixed-head coupé (no hatchback) derivative of that drophead. The four wheel drive FF model of 1966-71 deserves its own analysis and is described below.

If you could live with the possibilities (and later with the horrible realities) of corrosion, if you could afford the considerable fuel consumption, and if you could come to terms with the usual specialist-car build-quality problems, this was truly a great car. Expensive to restore, but much too good to be consigned to the scrapheap.

Interceptor as launched in 1966, with its distinctive Touring of Milan styling.

FF 1966-71

Jensen's bravest ever move was to co-operate with FF (Ferguson Formula) of Coventry to evolve a four wheel drive version of the new Interceptor. This was the world's first ever series-production four wheel drive private car, and it was let down only by the expense of manufacture and the need to set up each car individually before it went to a customer.

After a rather undistinguished C-V8-based prototype had been built in 1965, the production car was launched alongside the Interceptor. Apart from the fact that it had a four-inch longer wheelbase to accept the front-end transmission fixtures, the FF looked almost the same as the Interceptor. To identify, look for two cooling vents in the front wings rather than one on the Interceptor.

For the drive to the front wheels, FF's installation consisted of a transfer gearbox

The four wheel drive Jensen FF, recognised by its dual side vents.

behind the automatic transmission, a front propeller shaft running alongside the engine, a differential ahead of the engine, and driveshafts thence to the front wheels. Compared with the Interceptor, the front end of the chassis was much changed, there was an extra front sub-frame to support the differential, and twin coil-over-shocks were needed on each side of the front suspension. Not only that, but aircraft-style Dunlop Maxaret anti-lock braking was also standard – this pulsed much slower than a modern ABS system would do.

Functionally and technically the FF was a great car. It handled well, it was very fast,

and its four wheel drive system was very effective, but it was also very expensive – £5340 instead of the Interceptor's £3743 – and there were recurring problems in service.

Jensen wisely built only right hand drive cars (an LHD installation was physically nearly impossible to arrange) but pulled the plug at the end of 1971 when demand was falling and profits were still some distance away. In five years, only saloons were produced.

Even so, forget the complication and face up to the in-service problems. If you can afford one, this is a pioneering classic car that must be preserved.

SPECIFICATION

BODY STYLES: saloon

PRODUCTION: 320

ENGINE & TRANSMISSION: 6276cc, V8 cyl ohv, auto, f/4

POWER: 325bhp @ 4600rpm

MAX SPEED (MPH): 130

0-60MPH (SEC): 8.4

SUSPENSION & BRAKES: coil ifs, leaf rear, discs f&r

LENGTH (IN)/WEIGHT (LB): 191/4030

LAUNCH PRICE: £5340

JENSEN-HEALEY

Kjell Qvale's main reason for taking control of Jensen in 1970 was to promote the birth of a new sports car brand which would link Jensen with Donald Healey (whose association with BMC/British Leyland was about to be dissolved).

In March 1972, the result was the arrival of the Jensen-Healey sports car. This had a body shell manufactured by Jensen at West Bromwich, but the company could not afford to design and build its own chassis and running gear.

Accordingly, the new car was something of a "bitsa" (bits of this and bits of that). The engine came from Lotus in Norfolk – this was the first use of the 16-valve unit which would power all mid/late-1970s Lotus cars too. The transmission was

bought in from Chrysler UK, and the suspension came from Vauxhall.

Although the Jensen-Healey sold quite well, its prospects (particularly in North America, where Qvale's other businesses were centred) were hit by the energy crisis of 1973, and by quality problems with the brand-new engine. Later cars were better than early ones, and a "sporting-estate" version (badged purely as the Jensen GT) was added to the range, but when the parent company ran into financial trouble the Jensen-Healey brand was dragged down with it.

Jensen ceased trading in the spring of 1976, at which point the Jensen-Healey also perished.

Sports 1972-76

In 1972, Jensen was well placed to build a new volume-production sports car. In previous years it had built all the bodies for the Austin-Healey 3000, and had also built complete Volvo P1800s and Sunbeam Tigers. The Jensen-Healey, though, would have no "Healey" components of any sort.

It was engineered around a conventional unit-construction steel body with rather bland styling. Under the skin there was an amalgam of bought-in components. The car was powered by the original 1973cc 16-valve twin-cam Lotus engine. Chrysler UK supplied the gearbox as found in the Sunbeam Rapier H120. The coil spring independent front suspension, rack-and-pinion steering and coil spring rear suspension were all Vauxhall (Viva GT/Victor FD) units.

The Jensen-Healey was faster than the obvious competition – the 95bhp

The 1972 Jensen-Healey Sports used a Lotus engine, Chrysler UK transmission and Vauxhall suspension.

SPECIFICATION

BODY STYLES: sports car

PRODUCTION: 10,504

ENGINE & TRANSMISSION: 1973cc, 4cyl 2ohc, 4sp man/5sp man, f/r

POWER: 144bhp @ 6500rpm

MAX SPEED (MPH): 119

0-60MPH (SEC): 7.8

SUSPENSION & BRAKES: coil ifs, coil beam rear, disc f/drum r

LENGTH (IN)/WEIGHT (LB): 166/2340

LAUNCH PRICE: £1810

MGB, for instance – and offered the same sort of no-nonsense ride and handling. It also had the same sort of character. Inside, the cabin was neatly trimmed, there being no attempt to provide occasional rear seats, though when the Jensen GT appeared (see below) that omission was rectified. In the early stages there was no plan to offer alternative transmissions.

Early cars suffered from so-so build quality, and were soon seen to need better anti-corrosion protection, but Jensen set about making improvements. From August 1973 there were trim and equipment improvements, including an artificial wood-grain finish on the dashboard. Then, from November 1974, a Getrag five-speed gearbox took over from the Chrysler

four-speeder. Self-adjusting brakes were also standardised, and a real wood finish appeared on the dashboard.

Deliveries were often limited by a shortage of engines, but the principal reason why the Jensen-Healey project was not a success was that the cars did not sell as well as had been hoped in North America. The last cars were made before the end of 1975, though the Jensen GT carried on for a few weeks longer.

If the project had been backed by a larger concern (as Austin-Healey had been by BMC) there would have been a definite future for this car, but it lacked the brand image and dealer network to achieve that. Because the engines were none too reliable at first, "classic" values never built up, so survivors are still quite cheap.

GT 1975-76

In an effort to expand its market, Jensen added a "sporting estate" derivative of the Jensen-Healey sports car in July 1975, aiming to attract the same customers as might otherwise buy a Reliant Scimitar GTE or a Ford Capri II. Because of the parent company's financial problems this was a short-lived project which lasted less than a year, assembly ceasing in April 1976.

Based very closely on the Jensen-Healey two-seater, the Jensen GT (no "Healey" name, please note) featured a square-back estate car rear with a large lift-up glass tail gate. The petrol tank had been re-poistioned, and occasional rear seats had

Jensen GT, 1975.

somehow been squeezed on to the modified platform.

Electric window lifts were standard, as was a burr-walnut fascia/instrument panel, but mechanically the GT model was nearly identical to the definitive five-speed Jensen-Healey two-seater. There was now a front anti-roll bar. Rear springs were stiffer than before, to take account of the extra 120lb over the rear wheels.

Although the performance was almost the same as that of the two-seater, the price was substantially higher. In July 1975 the GT cost all of £4198 against the Jensen-Healey at £3130 (or a Ford Capri 3000 Ghia at just £3099). The Jensen

GT, therefore, faced an uphill battle to generate sales, but had little chance to prove that it could.

16-valve Lotus twin cam gave 144bhp.

SPECIFICATION

BODY STYLES: sports hatchback

PRODUCTION: 507

ENGINE & TRANSMISSION: 1973cc, 4cyl 2ohc, 5sp man, f/r

POWER: 144bhp @ 6500rpm

MAX SPEED (MPH): 119

0-60MPH (SEC): 8.7

SUSPENSION & BRAKES: coil ifs, coil beam rear, disc f/drum r

LENGTH (IN)/WEIGHT (LB): 166/2417

LAUNCH PRICE: £4198

JOWETT

Jowett, of Bradford in Yorkshire, started out by manufacturing engines for other people (including the Scott motorcycle), and then moved into the manufacture of motor cars in 1910. In the 1920s and 1930s, still independent, Jowett was making simple and inexpensive machines, almost all with flat-twin engines. The company's slogan was "The little engine with the big pull". A flat-four-engined model was introduced in 1936. Then, as later, the company tried to make as many components in-house as possible.

During the busiest period of World War Two, Jowett hired Gerald Palmer to design an all-new family car, the result being the launch of the Javelin saloon, which went on sale in 1947. Along with the pre-war style Bradford estate/commercial vehicle, this car kept the factory at Idle, Bradford, very busy until the early 1950s, by which time the smart Jupiter two-seater sports car had also joined the range. Gerald Palmer had moved on and Ray Lunn had arrived, but he found few resources to encourage enterprise and there were no signs of Jowett being absorbed by a larger car-maker.

In the 1940s and 1950s Jowett's problem was that it was under-capitalised, with an old-fashioned and basically-equipped factory. Although Javelin bodies were provided by Briggs Motor Bodies (from Doncaster), Jowett found that it had to sell cars at quite a high price, and demand fell away.

By 1953, sales were slow, stocks of unsold cars were high, and Jowett owed much to its suppliers. At the same time, works Jupiters had been raced at Le Mans. They gave a creditable performance, but racing was expensive. This, and a lot of quality problems with later Jowett-built transmissions, led to huge financial losses. Briggs was taken over by Ford, but body supplies would have been assured if only Jowett could have paid for them – and used them.

Sadly, it could not. Development of a Javelin successor was well advanced, but there were no signs of it being tooled up for production. In 1953/54 the fragile business collapsed and the old firm of Jowett finally went out of business. There was no last-minute rescue, and the pretty little Jupiter R4 project died at birth.

Bradford 1946-53

Introduced in 1938 on an 8hp van, the chassis which inspired the post-war Bradford was immediately available when peacetime activities recommenced. The Bradford, more than any other British car of the mid-to-late 1940s, was a pre-war model which ought really to have been rendered obsolete as soon as possible, but because of post-war shortages (and a low price helped too), the Bradford was still on sale in 1953.

The chassis was very simple indeed – half-elliptic leaf springs front and rear, with mechanical braking, powered by the final version of Jowett's pre-war flat-twin sidevalve engine. With no more than 19bhp at first, and a three-speed gearbox, this antiquated vehicle truly represented

The trusty Jowett Bradford went out of production in 1953. Its flat-twin engine could trace its roots back to before the First World War.

motoring at at the most basic level.

Yet it sold and sold. Most early post-war types were van-bodied, but the Bradford estate car (actually it was more of a van with windows) finally went on sale in 1947. It was only the general shortage of post-war cars which made the Bradford at all saleable, though many people liked the idea of a low-speed slogger which was mechanically very simple. On the flat, even a modest 50mph was unattainable.

From the end of 1949 the engine advanced to what Jowett called the CC type, which meant that much had been re-designed. A heady 25bhp was finally

available, along with synchromesh on top and second gears. This helped to produce a death-defying top speed of 53mph, but the ride was still hard and bouncy, the body crudely equipped, the brakes poor, and the styling a full decade out of date.

By January 1953 a large number of unsold Bradfords were in stock at Idle, so assembly finally came to an end, and the last cars dribbled out of the plant later in the year.

All in all, what the Bradford had going for it was its "Jowett-ness" and its dogged devotion to duty. At any other time in history it would have sunk without trace.

SPECIFICATION

BODY STYLES: estate, commercials

PRODUCTION: 38,241

ENGINE & TRANSMISSION: 1005cc, flat-2cyl sv, 3sp man, f/r

POWER: 19bhp @ 3500rpm/25bhp @ 3500rpm

MAX SPEED (MPH): (25bhp) 53

0-60MPH (SEC): not possible

SUSPENSION & BRAKES: beam leaf front, leaf rear, drums f&r

LENGTH (IN)/WEIGHT (LB): 144/1904

LAUNCH PRICE: £320

Javelin 1947-53

Although the Javelin was powered by a front-mounted flat-four engine, there were no direct technical links with Jowett's past and no parts were shared with older, pre-war Jowett private cars.

Like almost all British cars of this period it seemed to be underpowered, but the Javelin was a very capable saloon car which sold well in spite of rather high pricing (and, later, a known history of mechanical problems). The handling was extremely highly regarded, which explains why and how it would become a useful rally car.

The 50bhp 1486cc overhead-valve engine was mated to a newly-designed

The Jowett Javelin was an advanced design for 1947, its launch year.

four-speed synchromesh gearbox, which suffered – though not as badly as many rivals – from a steering-column change. Because the body had been so carefully profiled (quite miraculously so by the standards of the day), a near-80mph top speed was available.

This was a surefooted car, with torsion bar independent front suspension and rack-and-pinion steering, allied to torsion bar springing of the beam rear axle. It wore a smart four-door fastback saloon body, in steel, built by Briggs Motor Bodies at Doncaster. The first cars, delivered in mid-1947, had a metal dashboard with rectangular

instruments, but series production and deliveries did not really start until 1948.

Jowett tried hard to update and modernise the Javelin as time went by, though there was a losing battle against engine failures (not solved until a revised crankshaft was introduced in 1952), and a constant struggle to make reliable gearboxes. In 1950 a De Luxe model was offered, having Connolly leather upholstery and full instrumentation, and from 1951 Jowett began manufacturing its own gearboxes. An engine oil

cooler was standard by 1952, as was all-hydraulic braking. Sales fell away in 1952-53, and well before Jowett admitted that it was in major difficulties the Javelin's career was effectively over.

For the enthusiastic driver who wanted his saloon to look good, yet keep him interested in hard driving, the Javelin was a fine machine, with a better chassis than many of its competitors. Unhappily, its mechanical problems, and the almost inevitable tinworm, mean that few have survived into the new century.

SPECIFICATION

BODY STYLES: saloon

PRODUCTION: 23,307

ENGINE & TRANSMISSION: 1486cc, flat-4cyl ohv, 4sp man, f/r

POWER: 50bhp @ 4100rpm/53bhp @ 4500rpm

MAX SPEED (MPH): 78/83

0-60MPH (SEC): 22.2/20.9

SUSPENSION & BRAKES: tor ifs, tor rear, drums f&r

LENGTH (IN)/WEIGHT (LB): 168/2156

LAUNCH PRICE: £819

Side view shows the Javelin's distinctive fastback styling.

Jupiter 1950-53

In forty years of trading, only one Jowett sports car – the Jupiter – was ever put on sale. Only available between 1950 and 1953, this relied heavily on the Javelin saloon for its running gear, and on the engineering company ERA for its tubular chassis. Although the car looked good, it needed more power – and to go on a weight loss diet – and eventually it could not compete with cars like the Triumph TR2, so sales were disappointing.

Unable to design its own sports car, Jowett asked ERA of Dunstable to come up with a suitable chassis. This company provided an archetypal large-tube layout which had been designed by ex-Auto Union GP engineer Professor Eberan von Eberhorst. First shown in 1949 as an "ERA-Javelin", the car went on sale as the Jupiter in March 1950.

The engine, transmission, steering-

A Jowett Jupiter outside the factory in 1950.

column gear change and suspension units were all Javelin-derived (with significantly more power from the engine), but the body on this 93in chassis was totally new, A two/three-seater drophead coupé, made of steel internal panels with aluminium skins, enclosed a bench seat, but there was

no exterior access to the luggage compartment in the long, sloping tail. The whole of the front end, hinged at the bulkhead, could be swung up for engine bay access.

As expected from a Javelin-derived car, the handling was good, but performance was no more than brisk. Special factory-backed (and much lighter) R1 race cars performed with honour in the Le Mans 24-hour sports car race, but a lot more performance was needed to satisfy the demands of the North American market.

Development changes included a fully hydraulic braking system from early 1951 and a more powerful 63bhp engine from January 1953. After a re-design of the body, the Mk 1a, complete with opening boot lid, appeared in October 1952, though original Mk Is (old body stock, really) were still available at home in 1953.

A much smaller and lighter successor to the Jupiter, the R4, with a smooth glass-fibre body, appeared in October 1953. It showed the signs of becoming a 100mph sports car but was killed when Jowett collapsed, and only three prototypes were made.

The Jupiter is ideally summarised as "if

A Jupiter braking hard on the 1953 MCC Rally.

The Wisdom/Wise Jupiter which took 16th place at Le Mans in 1950.

only" – if only it had been lighter, if only it had had a floor gearchange, and if only it could have sold at a lower price, it might have succeeded. The most favourable

epitaph is that this was the last Jowett to remain in (limited) production at Idle, after the last Javelins had been produced. It is quite a collector's car today.

SPECIFICATION

BODY STYLES: sports car

PRODUCTION: 825

ENGINE & TRANSMISSION: 1486cc, Flat-4cyl ohv, 4sp man, f/r

POWER: 60bhp @ 4750rpm/63bhp @ 4500rpm

MAX SPEED (MPH): (60bhp) 84

0-60MPH (SEC): (60bhp) 16.8

SUSPENSION & BRAKES: tor ifs, tor rear, drums f&r

LENGTH (IN)/WEIGHT (LB): 168/2100

LAUNCH PRICE: £1017

At Le Mans the Jupiter led the 1.5-litre class, breaking by 14 miles a record set by Aston Martin in 1935.

LAGONDA

Founded at Staines in 1906 by Wilbur Gunn, Lagonda rose rapidly to be a noted vintage and then thoroughbred car manufacturer. After a refinancing trauma in 1935, W O Bentley became chief designer, and it was his team which laid down the first post-war model, though Bentley then moved out following an unsavoury trademark dispute with his old employers at Rolls-Royce.

Industrialist David Brown came to the rescue of the financially stretched company in 1947, and soon merged the brand with another car maker, Aston Martin, which he had also purchased. From that juncture, Aston Martin Lagonda assembled all its products at Feltham in Middlesex (not far from what became Heathrow Airport), until David Brown once again moved the operation, this time to the old Tickford factory at Newport Pagnell, Bucks, in 1957.

After World War Two the pre-war Lagondas did not go

back into production. The first post-war product was the 2.6-litre model, with the excellent new twin-cam six-cylinder engine which was soon adopted for use in the Aston Martin DB2 and subsequent models. The 2.6-litre was succeeded by the 3.0-litre type in 1953, but Lagonda was always the less glamorous side of David Brown's personal plaything, so a subsequent Lagonda, called the Rapide, was no longer individual but based on a longer-wheelbase version of the Aston Martin DB4 chassis, and was the first Lagonda to be assembled at Newport Pagnell.

From 1964 the Lagonda name disappeared for years, only returning in 1974 on a badged version of an Aston Martin. This was followed by a four-door Aston Martin Lagonda in 1976, startlingly styled by William Towns. The last of these was produced in 1990. The Lagonda badge then disappeared into the "heritage" cupboard, and never re-appeared.

2.6-Litre 1948-53

Engineered during and immediately after World War Two by W O Bentley's design team, the 2.6-litre model was previewed before it was ready for sale. Lagonda could not afford to put the car on the market, but after David Brown's rescue of the failing company it was finalised, and went on sale in 1948.

Every component, nut and bolt was new (which explains the original inability to put it on sale). The design centred around a massively strong cruciform-shaped chassis, with all-independent suspension, inboard rear brakes and the excellent new twin overhead camshaft 105bhp 2580cc six-cylinder engine. The still-born prototype used an electrically-controlled Cotal epicyclic gearbox, but production cars had a conventional four-speed part-synchromesh unit from David Brown Industries; at launch the Cotal box was "available as an extra", but no such cars were delivered. Unhappily, the synchromesh-gearbox cars were inflicted with a steering-column gearchange.

The Lagonda 2.6-Litre saloon arrived in 1948.

The first bodies were four-door coachbuilt saloons, lovingly assembled at Feltham, though from 1949 there was also a smart two-door four-seater drophead coupé from Tickford, which at the time was still independent of David Brown. The fascia was quite simple, with all instruments grouped centrally on the dashboard, which meant that it was simple enough to provide right- or left-hand drive.

From autumn 1952 the 2.6 progressed to Mk II, though only as the four-door saloon. Engine power went up to 125bhp (this mirrored power increases applied to Aston Martin DB2s of the period), the seating and interior were improved, and (as one pundit later wrote) "a proper heating and demisting system" was included. Rear seat access was improved by the fitment of longer doors, and Smiths Jackall jacking was fitted. There were no Mk II dropheads.

Before this car gave way to the much-changed 3-Litre of 1953, the media learned all about the over-steery handling, but that was easily forgiven because this was such a well-made, rapid and impressive machine. Not too many survive, but they stack up well against any other so-called GT car of the period.

Lagonda 2.6-Litre drophead.

SPECIFICATION	
BODY STYLES: saloon, drophead	
PRODUCTION: 484 Mk I, 26 Mk II	
ENGINE & TRANSMISSION: 2580cc, 6cyl 2ohc, 4sp man, f/r	
POWER: 105bhp @ 5000rpm/125bhp @ 5000rpm	
MAX SPEED (MPH): (105bhp) 90	
0-60MPH (SEC): (105bhp) 17.6	
SUSPENSION & BRAKES: coil ifs, tor irs, drums f&r	
LENGTH (IN)/WEIGHT (LB): 188/3400	
LAUNCH PRICE: £3110/£2996	

3-Litre 1953-57

The second generation of post-war Lagonda, introduced during 1953, used the same basic chassis and running gear as the 2.6-Litre, but with a larger engine, more power, and a completely new body style.

Launched at the 1953 Paris Salon, the 3-Litre featured a smooth new body styled and made by Tickford. It was a traditional coachbuilt affair, with steel panels on a timber frame, available from the start as a two-door saloon or as a very elegant two-door drophead coupé. The styling of the 2.6-Litre had its roots in the past, but the 3-Litre displayed a totally contemporary shape, much admired by the industry. HRH The Duke of Edinburgh gave it the Royal seal of approval by buying two different examples.

The twin-cam six-cylinder engine had been enlarged to 2922cc, giving 140bhp, and because of the more bulky body the car's weight had risen by 215lb. Even so, its top speed, at 104mph, easily surpassed the 2.6-Litre's. The column gearchange was still standard at first.

In 1954 Lagonda introduced a four-door saloon version which was available alongside the two-door at first but displaced it completely in 1955. From 1956, the 3-Litre evolved into the Series II, with a centre-floor gearchange at last. Only five of the Series IIs built had convertible coachwork.

More desirable than the 2.6-Litre, the 3-Litre's principal problem was its high price - £3203 for the saloon in 1953, and £3901 for the Series II version in 1956. In the autumn of that year David Brown had to impose a price cut, to £2994, but this was no lasting solution, for only 81 Series II types were ever sold.

Like the 2.6-Litre, this very elegant 3-Litre was enjoyed by the wealthy buyer who might otherwise have purchased a Bristol, or something exotic and foreign. Still an oversteering chassis when pressed, it was nevertheless a fine car. It was the last individually-engineered Lagonda.

The Lagonda 3-Litre, launched in 1953.

SPECIFICATION	
BODY STYLES: saloon, drophead	
PRODUCTION: 270	
ENGINE & TRANSMISSION: 2922cc, 6cyl 2ohc, 4sp man, f/r	
POWER: 140bhp @ 5000rpm	
MAX SPEED (MPH): 104	
0-60MPH (SEC): 12.9	
SUSPENSION & BRAKES: coil ifs, tor irs, drums f&r	
LENGTH (IN)/WEIGHT (LB): 196/3615	
LAUNCH PRICE: £3203	

Rapide 1961-64

The Rapide of 1961 was a rather awkward cuckoo, seen as such by all traditional Lagonda customers, who shunned it almost completely. Effectively a longer-wheelbase, rebodied version of the Aston Martin DB4, but with De Dion rear suspension, it was not special enough, fast enough or beautiful enough to make a mark.

Called the Rapide (reviving a famous Lagonda name of the 1930s), this new model was based on the steel platform of the DB4, stretched by 16in, and incorporated a De Dion rear end sprung on transverse torsion bars. Like the DB4, it had

Lagonda Rapide of 1961, now with 4 litres.

SPECIFICATION	
BODY STYLES: saloon	
PRODUCTION: 54	
ENGINE & TRANSMISSION: 3995cc, 6cyl 2ohc, 4sp man or auto, f/r	
POWER: 236bhp @ 5000rpm	
MAX SPEED (MPH): 130 (E)	
0-60MPH (SEC): not measured	
SUSPENSION & BRAKES: coil ifs, tor DD rear, discs f&r	
LENGTH (IN)/WEIGHT (LB): 196/3780	
LAUNCH PRICE: £5251	

servo-assisted (by Kelsey Hayes) four-wheel Dunlop disc brakes and split hydraulic circuits. It also had the DB4's new-generation twin-cam six-cylinder 3995cc engine, giving 236bhp. The Rapide's two twin-choke Solex carburettors made a very odd induction system.

To match this, Borg Warner automatic transmission was standard equipment. The DB4's four-speed all-synchromesh manual gearbox was theoretically a no-cost option, though very rarely ordered.

The four-door body featured a rather awkwardly-styled nose incorporating four headlamps and a so-called "Lagonda" grille. The body was built at Newport Pagnell but styled by Touring of Milan,

and featured that company's Superleggera construction system of small-diameter tubes to shape the shell, with steel inner and aluminium outer panels to clothe them. Wood, leather and deep carpets all featured strongly in the interior, along with an extremely complex heating and ventilation system.

The Rapide never really took off – the astronomical price didn't help, nor did the rather undistinguished and slightly confused styling. As it turned out, sales and assembly rarely exceeded one car a month. The car was too big, maybe, and was somehow unloved by the factory and by the AML enthusiasts. It died away, little missed, in 1964.

LANCHESTER

Once a proud British motoring pioneer, Lanchester had hit hard financial times in 1931 and been absorbed by BSA, which already controlled Daimler. Within months it was clear that BSA intended Lanchester to become the "entry-level" marque to introduce aspiring motorists to the Daimler brand. From 1932 until the outbreak of war, a series of Daimler-engineered Lanchesters were designed, some of them being very close indeed to their Daimler relatives. By this time Lanchester cars had embraced Girling independent front suspension, along with the fluid-flywheel pre-selector transmission which Daimler had pioneered.

After 1945, though still centred at the Daimler factory in Coventry, Lanchester took something of a back seat. Its first post-war car was the small LD10, which had almost been

ready for launch in 1939-40, but there were no other Lanchesters until 1950, when the original 14 (later called the Leda) previewed the Daimler Conquest which would share much of the engineering.

The third and last post-war Lanchester was stillborn, for although the new Sprite (previewed in 1954) was technically interesting, and had little in common with contemporary Daimlers, it was all set to swallow too much of Daimler's manufacturing resources and was killed off at the pre-production stage.

At the time, Daimler hoped to revive the Lanchester brand in due course, but their takeover by Jaguar put a stop to that, and the Lanchester marque disappeared into the spare-names cupboard, where it has remained for the last fifty years.

LD10 1946-51

If the Second World War had not broken out Daimler would certainly have launched the LD10 in 1940 as a replacement for the Eleven model and to go alongside the larger Roadrider de Luxe. In the event, the LD10's development had to be frozen, and in 1945/46 all the tooling was dug out of store so that the car could go ahead, complete with a late-1930s style all-steel four-door six-light body which was to be supplied by Briggs Motor Bodies.

Technically, the LD10 was typical of what Lanchester had evolved in the late 1930s, which means that the separate channel-section chassis frame had main side members which swept under the line of the spiral-bevel back axle, and that there was Girling-type coil spring independent front suspension. Girling

Lanchester LD10, a pleasant and well-made car. This is an early six-light model.

SPECIFICATION

BODY STYLES: saloon

PRODUCTION : 3050, of which 575 with Barker coachwork

ENGINE & TRANSMISSION: 1287cc, 4cyl ohv, 4sp pre-S, f/r

POWER: 40bhp @ 4200rpm

MAX SPEED (MPH): 68

0-60MPH (SEC): 36.8

SUSPENSION & BRAKES: coil ifs, leaf rear, drums f&r

LENGTH (IN)/WEIGHT (LB): 158/2576

LAUNCH PRICE: £672

mechanical brakes – quite archaic by modern (mid-1940s, that is) standards – were fitted.

The overhead-valve engine was a four-cylinder version of the straight-six that had been used in the pre-war Roadrider de Luxe, reasonably powerful but hampered by having to drag along a rather heavy (nearly 2600lb) car whose aerodynamic characteristics were only average. The fact that there were inevitably efficiency losses through the fluid-flywheel transmission didn't help either.

The Autocar described the LD10's interior as "plain but tastefully finished …unusually roomy for a Ten", noting that the front seats were adjustable for height, and that the upholstery was

leather; on the other hand, a heater was still an extra-cost option.

The all-steel Briggs body was replaced by a rather different four-light coach-built (aluminium on wood framing) Barker body in 1949, but neither car sold in big numbers. Both types, it seems, were alarmingly ready to rot away, which the vast majority duly did. When the new Fourteen/Leda model was ready in 1950, the LD10 was dropped to make way for it.

In looks, in performance and in character the LD10 was exactly what Lanchesters aspired to be in those days – gentle, dignified and reassuringly middle class. No one ever got excited driving such a car, but they were never alarmed either.

14/Leda 1950-54

In the post-war era, Daimler had great ambitions for Lanchester. In the 1950s, not only did the company develop its own medium-sized Daimler, the Conquest, but preceded it with a Lanchester 14 which used the same rolling chassis and basic body style. For confirmation of this, it is only necessary to compare the body of the Lanchester, launched in October 1950, with the Daimler Conquest of 1953.

The Lanchester, which carried type number LJ200, used the same 104in-wheelbase chassis frame as the later Daimler, the same laminated torsion bar independent front suspension, the same fluid-flywheel pre-selector transmission, the same Girling hydro-mechanical braking, and the same style of four-door six-light coachwork, but there were two important differences. Not only did the original Lanchester have a coachbuilt body shell, based on a wooden skeleton with steel panels, but it also had a four-cylinder 60bhp 1968cc engine.

The engine itself was really two thirds of the new Daimler Regency power unit (same bore, stroke, valve gear and accessory drives, and using much of the same machining) which would follow in a matter of months.

Other than in the front view, the body looked the same as the more popular Conquest would look. Interestingly, in 1952 the "home-market" coachbuilt body was joined by an identical-looking all-steel (Pressed Steel Co.) shell for export. Thus the 14 became the Leda,

Lanchester 14, photographed in September 1950 prior to launch.

the steel body soon becoming the normal fitment; at the time, Lanchester claimed that it was lighter than the coachbuilt body. A drophead coupé would eventually join this range from late 1951, complete with a hydraulic-powered soft top. Both cars had high-

quality wood, carpet and leather in the cabins. Neither fast nor exciting, these cars somehow encouraged one to drive gently and simply enjoy the quality. Who was it who once called a Lanchester the ideal "retired Colonel's car"? They were right.

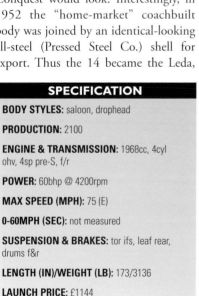

SPECIFICATION

BODY STYLES: saloon, drophead

PRODUCTION: 2100

ENGINE & TRANSMISSION: 1968cc, 4cyl ohv, 4sp pre-S, f/r

POWER: 60bhp @ 4200rpm

MAX SPEED (MPH): 75 (E)

0-60MPH (SEC): not measured

SUSPENSION & BRAKES: tor ifs, leaf rear, drums f&r

LENGTH (IN)/WEIGHT (LB): 173/3136

LAUNCH PRICE: £1144

Lanchester 14 drophead at Earls Court in 1951. This may have been the only example.

Sprite 1955-56

By any standards, this was the oddest Lanchester ever conceived – the only one to have a unit-construction body/chassis unit, the only one to have (Hobbs) automatic transmission, and the only one to have this unique 1622cc engine. Prototypes were exhibited at the motor show in October 1954, with a slab-sided body, but the production car of late 1955 looked more like a Leda that had shrunk in the wash. Not that this much mattered, for Daimler pulled the plug after only 13 pre-production cars had been assembled.

This was a big investment programme. Not only was the steel monocoque shell new (aluminium would be used for closing panels), but so was the coil spring independent front suspension, though that was changed to a longitudinal torsion bar layout in late 1955.

The engine was a simple overhead-valve design, a four-cylinder derivative of the Daimler Conquest unit (same bore, stroke, valve gear, camshaft drive details, for instance), but the Hobbs transmission, a four-speed device with planetary gears and a twin-plate friction clutch, was a complicated affair. This was to be the only production contract awarded to Hobbs.

Like most Lanchesters, this one was too heavy, and it was underpowered. Built down to a price (it was strange to see a Daimler-Lanchester model with Vynide upholstery and a washable pvc head-

Lanchester Sprite prototype at the 1954 motor show.

lining), it was offered at £1078 in 1954, and in late 1955 with restyled body at £1227. That price put it way out ahead of obvious competition such as the MG Magnette ZA (£915), and would have made it difficult to establish a sales base.

Revealed prematurely, and developed while the controversy over Sir Bernard Docker's management methods was raging, the Sprite was cancelled in the winter of 1955/56, after the tooling for the unique 172in-long saloon body had been completed. It can be no coincidence that Sir Bernard was sacked immediately after this turbulent period.

This was the very last Lanchester of all to be produced, for the Leda/LJ200 had already died. The "Sprite" model name, presumably, was then returned to BMC to

use on its new small Austin-Healey sports car. At least one Lanchester Sprite still survives, the miracle being that the complex transmission is still in one piece.

SPECIFICATION

BODY STYLES: saloon

PRODUCTION: 13

ENGINE & TRANSMISSION: 1622cc, 4cyl ohv, 4sp auto, f/r

POWER: 60bhp @ 4200rpm

MAX SPEED (MPH): 65 (E)

0-60MPH (SEC): not measured

SUSPENSION & BRAKES: tor ifs, leaf rear, drums f&r

LENGTH (IN)/WEIGHT (LB): 172/2688

LAUNCH PRICE: £1228

LAND-ROVER

Immediately after the end of World War Two, Rover found itself with a large but empty factory at Solihull (near Birmingham), and needed work to fill it. Because of the shortage of sheet steel supplies, Rover cars could not fill that gap. Casting around for a new product, as a stop-gap, Rover decided to introduce a light four wheel drive machine for agricultural use. Branded Land-Rover in 1948, that stop-gap soon became a major part of Rover's business, eventually out-selling the private car business by a considerable margin.

The first Land-Rovers were closely based on the famous US Jeep layout, but they soon took on a character of their own. Although they used Rover private-car engines at first, all other pieces were unique and, over the years, an astonishing number of wheelbase lengths and body derivatives were put on sale. By the late 1950s, too, engines specially designed for Land-

Rover use were also developed.

Because fashion was less important than function, model changes were never frequent. Series I types did not give way to Series II until 1958, and Series III would not follow until 1971. The most important advance of all came in 1970, when the new Rover V8-engined Range Rover was put on sale. This product became a world leader.

Land-Rovers and Range Rovers were built alongside Rover private cars at Solihull until the early 1980s, after which Solihull became a dedicated 4x4 plant, and was expanded mightily in later years, with new model ranges, and constant revisions to the "classic" model, which was eventually re-named Defender.

Land-Rover was a Rover brand until 1966, a Leyland brand until it was absorbed within British Leyland (and all its successors), but was finally sold off to Ford in 2000.

SI 1948-58

The original Land-Rover, which went on sale in 1948, set an engineering style which has been retained for more than half a century. The formula of solid steel chassis frame, aluminium body shell, front-mounted engine, four-wheel drive and beam axles may have changed in every detail over time, but the layout of the 2000s-type Defender was still recognisably developed from the original of 1948.

The first Land-Rovers had an 80in-wheelbase chassis, rock-hard leaf springs, sturdy beam axles front and rear, hydraulic brakes, a high ground clearance, and a whole raft of options which included winches and power take-offs. The first types were simple pick-ups, with 50bhp 1595cc Rover 12hp private car engines. Side curtains, not windows, could be attached to the doors, the windscreen could be removed, and the

An early Series I Land-Rover.

fascia/instrument panel was basic beyond belief. Headlamps were hidden behind mesh in the front grille. In fairness, though, this was more of an all-can-do agricultural machine which could be driven on the road, rather than a dedicated private car. One important pecuniary advantage was that these machines attracted no Purchase Tax (which was the precursor of VAT).

Changes were frequent. A station wagon body version was offered from 1948-51 (killed off because Purchase Tax was applied). The engine was enlarged to 1997cc (52bhp) in 1952. A choice of wheelbases – 86in and 107in – took over in 1954, these both going up again to 88in and 109in in 1956. By this time

vans and other station wagons had been added, and the headlamps had come out into the open.

The very first dedicated diesel engine option, with a 2052cc power unit giving 51bhp, was introduced in June 1957. Thus equipped, the Series I then gave way to the rather different Series II in April 1958.

Though the chassis and the few steel body parts could all rust away, the rest of an early Land-Rover was virtually indestructible, so that many survived for decades. Because of the cheerful, unburstable, go-anywhere, do-anything character of the machine, it soon spawned one-make preservation clubs, and thousands are still in use today.

SPECIFICATION

BODY STYLES: utility/estate/van/specials

PRODUCTION: 1.4 million plus, all SI to SIII models

ENGINE & TRANSMISSION: 1595cc/1997cc, 4cyl ioe, or 2052cc, 4cyl ohv diesel, 4sp man, f/4

POWER: 50bhp @ 4000rpm/52bhp @ 4000rpm/51bhp @ 3500rpm

MAX SPEED (MPH): 55/58/55 (E)

0-60MPH (SEC): not available

SUSPENSION & BRAKES: leaf beam front, leaf rear, drums f&r

LENGTH (IN)/WEIGHT (LB): 132 – 174/ 2594 - 3275

LAUNCH PRICE: £450

SII and SIIA 1958-61/1961-71

Land-Rover reworked the original design into the Series II, though the character was not degraded. Visual changes included more rounded outer wings, but in all other basic ways the chassis, engine, transmission, accommodation, and the add-on optional features list were preserved, even augmented.

From April 1958 SIIs got the barrel-side style changes, wider wheel tracks and a brand-new 77bhp 2286cc petrol engine (which shared some machine tooling facilities with the diesel).

Only three years later, in September 1961, the SIIA replaced the SII, with no visual changes, but with a larger 62bhp 2286cc diesel engine. From

April 1967, but only on 109in-wheelbase types, there was an additional six-cylinder 83bhp 2625cc engine option, this being ex-Rover P4 passenger car, though de-tuned.

In 1968-69, headlamps were moved outboard from the grille to the fronts of the wings, and a new heavy-duty 1-ton payload version followed. This broad-

Land-Rover Series II.

based range carried on until October 1971, by which time a total of more than 750,000 of all types had been produced, before being replaced by the yet further modified Series III models.

The SIIs were more powerful, more versatile and better developed than the SIs, though the rock-hard ride and rugged durability remained, and they too built up a big following. Many were still in use, at work even, at the end of the twentieth century.

SIII 1971-85

Time moved slowly as far as Land-Rover evolution was concerned, so when SIIA became SIII in 1971 there were few visual changes to make the point. Compared with the SIIA, which the SIII replaced, the same basic four wheel drive chassis, choice of petrol and diesel engines, and the myriad body styles and accessory packages, were all continued.

On the outside the only update was at the front, where the wing-mounted headlamps flanked a new-type radiator grille in injection-moulded plastic. Owners camping out in the bush could no longer remove the grille to use it as a barbecue grid!

Internally, changes were more sweeping, for there was a totally new fascia and instrument display, which looked much more car-like, while for the first time there was a smart three-abreast seating package too, as an option.

Under the skin there was a brand-new all-synchromesh main gearbox dedicated to Land-Rover models (the old transmission had been Rover car-derived), the engines were slightly upgraded, and brakes were enlarged to

Land-Rover Series III in 1972.

suit. From August 1974, a Fairey-designed overdrive was made optional. The millionth Land-Rover, by the way, was built in June 1976.

From March 1979 there was a new engine option, the light-alloy V8 (see Rover cars of the period) taking over from the obsolete 2.6-litre "six". Compared with its use in cars, the 3.5-litre V8 was much detuned, but it was amazingly torquey in consequence. To make space for this bulkier (but not heavier) engine, the front-end style was modified, with a new grille, further forward than before and flush with the fronts of the wings.

The original "leaf-spring" Land-Rover therefore reached maturity, and would be built until the mid-1980s, when it was finally replaced by the

Ninety and One-Ten types. It was typical of Land-Rover that these models had a completely new chassis but much the same exterior styling.

SPECIFICATION

BODY STYLES: utility/van/estate/specials

PRODUCTION: see SI above

ENGINE & TRANSMISSION: 2286cc, 2286cc diesel, 4cyl ohv/2625cc, 6cyl ioe/3528cc, V8 ohv, 4sp man, f/4

POWER: 70bhp @ 4000rpm/62bhp @ 4000rpm/86bhp @ 4500rpm/91bhp @ 3500rpm

MAX SPEED (MPH): 68/ (E) 60/69/81

0-60MPH (SEC): 29.1/not measured/31.7/26.1

SUSPENSION & BRAKES: beam leaf front, leaf rear, drums f&r

LENGTH (IN)/WEIGHT (LB): 143 – 175/2953 - 3459

LAUNCH PRICE: £1002

Series III Land-Rover V8 with truck cab, 1979.

LEA-FRANCIS

To quote that eminent historian Michael Sedgwick: "Cars appeared in fits and starts from the Lea-Francis concern, which originally made bicycles".

This Coventry based car maker started series production in 1920, fell out of the market in the early 1930s, then re-appeared in 1938 with new capital and a pair of excellent Riley-clone twin high camshaft four-cylinder engines.

Updated versions of the 1939-40 models appeared immediately after the war, and in spite of their obsolescence the company seemed to thrive until the early 1950s. By that time a pair of chunky but only partially-successful sports cars had appeared, time had been found to engineer independent front suspension, and the engines had been used with honour in motor racing.

Time, and modern fashions, finally caught up with the company in 1954, for the old-fashioned models had stopped selling, and the marque disappeared for some time. In 1960 there was an extraordinarily misguided attempt to revive the brand with a hideously-shaped sports car, the Lynx (which used a Ford Zephyr engine), but this was a total failure, and Lea-Francis finally withdrew from the market.

Years after the Coventry company closed down, trademark rights were bought up. In the 1980s and 1990s several attempts were made to re-launch the brand, but without success.

12hp/14hp 1946-54

Originally introduced in 1938, when the Lea-Francis brand was revived, this chassis was significantly up-dated for a re-launch in 1946, though the pre-war drophead coupés and tourers were not seen again.

In March 1946 the re-introduced cars looked just like the 1939 models, complete with exposed headlamps and a central driving lamp mounted ahead of the characteristic grille. The bodies, produced by Lea-Francis themselves, had the sloping tail which was a recognition point. They had steel floorpans but were built on an ash wood frame panelled mainly in aluminium

Lea-Francis 14, 1951.

sheet. There was a four-door saloon at first, and a five-door "woody" type of estate car (1767cc only), but a hardtop coupé would follow.

The chassis was strictly traditional, with beam axles and half-elliptic leaf springs at front and rear. There were Girling mechanical brakes, and Burman steering with a long drag link to the front axle. The engines, new in 1938, but cloned from the Riley 12/4 (Riley's chief designer, Hugh Rose, had jumped ship to take on the job) were of 1496cc (55bhp) and 1767cc (65bhp). The latter was larger than the pre-war version and would go on to make a fine name for itself in sports car and even single-seater motor racing. Very few 1496cc-engined

12s were built, the model being dropped within three years.

Realising that their cars would have to be up-dated, Lea-Francis introduced many revisions. From 1948 there was a six-light body style, as an alternative to the original, while from September 1949 independent front suspension by longitudinal torsion bars was grafted on to a modified chassis frame (but not until 1950-51 on the woody). The front-end style was changed in September 1950, with restyled front wings and recessed

headlamps, while the entire body line was lowered by two inches and the rear end was reshaped. Full hydraulic brakes appeared in 1951 to replace the hydro-mechanical system (hydraulic front, rod rear), but there were few other changes before 1953 when sales petered out.

Well liked despite their old-fashioned ambience, and with good rather than sensational performance, these cars were lifted by their fine engine, but there was not much long-term appeal and very few now remain.

SPECIFICATION

BODY STYLES: saloon, coupé, estate

PRODUCTION: 3137

ENGINE & TRANSMISSION: 1496cc/1767cc, 4cyl ohv, 4sp man, f/r

POWER: 55bhp @ 4700rpm/65bhp @ 4700rpm

MAX SPEED (MPH): 70 (E)/77 (E)

0-60MPH (SEC): not measured

SUSPENSION & BRAKES: beam leaf front (tor ifs from 1949), leaf rear, drums f&r

LENGTH (IN)/WEIGHT (LB): 179/2800-2912

LAUNCH PRICE: £951

Lea-Francis woody estate, a not uncommon sight in the 1950s.

12hp/14hp Sports 1947-49

Only a year after the post-war saloons became available, Lea-Francis showed the first of its new sports cars, which would have a short and relatively successful career in the late 1940s and early 1950s.

Developed quickly and, no doubt, on the cheap, the 14hp Sports used a short-wheelbase version of the 12/14hp saloon's leaf-sprung chassis (99in instead of 111in), clothed by a rather "interim" two-seater body style. This had a recessed-headlamp nose (modern) but cutaway doors with removable side curtains (traditional), and the spare wheel stowed, in view, on the tail under a pressed cover. Body construction was traditional, with a wood frame and mostly aluminium skin panels.

Lea-Francis 14 Sports had twin carburettors and over 70bhp.

Early cars were listed with the 12hp 1496cc engine, but very few seem to have been delivered before the lustier 1767cc power unit was standardised instead. In late 1948, and just like the saloons, this car gained the new torsion bar independent front suspension, but

production ended in 1949 ahead of the launch of the much more powerful 2½-litre sports model.

Lea-Francis's problem, as ever, was that to make a profit it had to set high prices, and the 12/14hp sports had to battle against Jaguar's XK120 at the

same price level, so it was no contest. A good and solid car, with a top speed of around 87mph, it was not outstanding enough to make a reputation. Not even the substitution of the 2½-litre engine could make up for that.

SPECIFICATION

BODY STYLES: sports car

PRODUCTION: 129

ENGINE & TRANSMISSION: 1496cc/1767cc, 4cyl ohv, 4sp man, f/r

POWER: 64bhp @ 5300rpm/77bhp @ 5100rpm

MAX SPEED (MPH): 80 (E)/87

0-60MPH (SEC): not measured/19.2

SUSPENSION & BRAKES: beam leaf front (to ifs for 1949), leaf rear, drums f&r

LENGTH (IN)/WEIGHT (LB): 156/2128-2457

LAUNCH PRICE: £1266/£1276

The Lea-Francis 18hp Sports Special of 1947 was the basis for the Connaughts.

14/70 and 18hp 1949-53

Lea-Francis's second post-war model was a useful mechanical up-date of the earlier 12/14hp models, but the car was still demonstrably old-fashioned in many ways. When previewed in October 1948 it was only available with the 65bhp 1767cc engine, which could deliver a 75mph top speed. Most of the first batch of these cars were sent to export markets.

With a chassis based on that of the often-changing 12/14hp, this was the first-ever Lea-Francis to be given the new torsion bar independent front suspension, although the Girling hydro-mechanical brakes were retained. As had

been the case on the earlier cars, this chassis delivered rather a hard ride, for the frame swept under the rear axle, which rather limited the available movement of the rear suspension.

The body was a brand new and rather slab-sided six-light style, with a wing crown line sweeping across both doors to a point at rear wheel hub level. This was the first Lea-Francis to be given recessed headlamps and a rounded nose, and to distinguish it from its close relation Lea-Francis liked it to be called the 14/70. From late 1950 the

car's potential was greatly improved by the use of the 95bhp 2496cc engine, which gave an estimated 90mph top speed, and by 1952 full hydraulic brakes were available – but this 18hp was an expensive car, costing £1700, which compared badly with the price of the rather more desirable Jaguar Mk VII, for instance.

It wasn't an elegant saloon, or a high performer, so it only had the Lea-Francis name on which to trade. Not fashionable then, and certainly not fashionable later, it was soon forgotten.

SPECIFICATION

BODY STYLES: saloon

PRODUCTION: 252

ENGINE & TRANSMISSION: 1767cc/2496cc, 4cyl ohv, 4sp man

POWER: 65bhp @ 4700rpm/95bhp @ 4000rpm

MAX SPEED (MPH): 75 (E)/90 (E)

0-60MPH (SEC): not measured

SUSPENSION & BRAKES: tor ifs, leaf rear, drums f&r

LENGTH (IN)/WEIGHT (LB): 181/2912-3020

LAUNCH PRICE: £1276

Lea-Francis 18hp, an attempt at modern styling.

2¹/₂-Litre Sports 1950-53

Announced in September 1950, as a direct replacement for the earlier 14hp sports, this car combined the 14hp model's structure and body with the latest torsion bar independent front suspension and the larger and altogether beefier four-cylinder 2496cc engine.

In all its chassis and body details, this was a reprise of 14hp Sports theme, with Girling hydromechanical brakes, and

Lea-Francis 2¹/₂-litre Sports could touch 100mph.

SPECIFICATION

BODY STYLES: sports car

PRODUCTION: 77

ENGINE & TRANSMISSION: 2496cc, 4cyl ohv, 4sp man, f/r

POWER: 95bhp @ 4000rpm

MAX SPEED (MPH): 95 (E)

0-60MPH (SEC): not measured

SUSPENSION & BRAKES: tor ifs, leaf rear, drums f&r

LENGTH (IN)/WEIGHT (LB): 168/2570

LAUNCH PRICE: £1394

this time it delivered a 95-100mph top speed. If (a big "if") Jaguar's XK120 had not been available, the car might have been more successful. Though it was not agile, it was certainly solidly built and purposeful.

It remained on sale for three years but did little for Lea-Francis as in that time only 77 cars found customers, the major problem being that the car was priced at £1394 – more than the XK120 and 25mph slower. Even with the full hydraulic brake installation of later cars, this was an impossible handicap.

Lynx 1960

The ill-starred Lynx project of 1960 might just claim to be the worst-ever attempt to kick-start the career of a moribund concern. Having been out of the market for years, though still trading and getting by with sub-contract engineering work, the company gained a new chairman in 1960, and he commissioned the design of the Lynx.

This was a real lemon, visually if not technically. The Lynx had no technical connection with any previous Lea-Francis, nor its engineers with reality, it seemed. It was little more than an up-market type of "special" which used

pieces from all round the industry. Because its chief engineer was an ex-Jaguar personality, it was no surprise to find many XK items in the specification.

The 99in-wheelbase chassis was based on twin 3.5in-diameter steel tubes

SPECIFICATION

BODY STYLES: sports car

PRODUCTION: 3

ENGINE & TRANSMISSION: 2553cc, 6cyl ohv, 4sp man, o/d, f/r

POWER: 107bhp @ 4700rpm

MAX SPEED (MPH): 110 (E)

0-60MPH (SEC): not measured

SUSPENSION & BRAKES: tor ifs, leaf rear, discs f&r

LENGTH (IN)/WEIGHT (LB): 180/2575

LAUNCH PRICE: £2096

Lea-Francis Lynx's bizarre looks attracted no takers.

which passed under the rear axle. Torsion bar independent front suspension was matched to a half-elliptic rear end. Power was by a tuned-up 2553cc Ford Zephyr engine producing 107bhp compared with the 85bhp of the standard Ford. It drove through a Moss four-speed gearbox with Laycock overdrive which had been lifted straight out of the Jaguars of the day. Rack-and-pinion steering, four-wheel Dunlop disc brakes and optional centre-lock disc wheels made up an interesting, though not distinguished, set of running gear.

The body style, by Bristol Designs Ltd, was frankly awful, a mess of conflicting curves with an over-large wrap-around screen, a rather droopy nose and a circular-type grille. Abbey Panels had built the steel-bodied prototypes. Amazingly, there was even a proposal to offer a Perspex hardtop as an optional extra.

Whitewall tyres were fitted to the prototype. 2+2 seating was provided inside the cockpit, the fascia/instrument layout (complete with TR3A/Austin-Healey type of steering wheel) looking like other British sports cars of the day. Wind-up windows were provided, the handbrake being on the outside of the driver's seat, Rootes-style.

The car exhibited on the Lea-Francis stand at Earls Court was painted in mauve with gold brightwork, which told us all we needed to know about the new chairman's tastes and his marketing skills. At £2096 (when a 100bhp Triumph TR3A cost just £991) the Lynx had no chance, and the public ignored it. Within weeks, it seems, the project died the death – yet the prototypes were sold off to a private owner, and survived into the "classic" era.

LLOYD

The brainchild of Roland Lloyd of Grimsby, this marque started life in 1935 as maker of a motorcycle-engined delivery van, a project which did not survive the war. The post-war product, the 650, was surprisingly advanced, and almost entirely designed and manufactured by Lloyd itself. Launched in 1946, it struggled on for just four years, but with many in-house instead of proprietary components the price was always too high.

After the last car was produced in 1951, spare parts were available for a good number of years, but Lloyd never again tried to build a new model.

650 1946-51

Amazing, really, that a car designed out of the motor industry mainstream – it was conceived and manufactured in Grimsby – should be so technically and visually appealing. Years before Alec Issigonis made it famous, Roland Lloyd produced a radical new front wheel drive layout with a backbone chassis, all-coil independent suspension and a water-cooled vertical twin two-stroke engine.

Because the engine had full-pressure oiling, messy petroil fuel was not needed. The transmission was all-synchromesh, even on reverse gear – to this day few

The Lloyd 650, made in Grimsby.

other makes, even big multi-nationals, offer such a feature.

All 650s were two/four-seater roadsters, smoothly-styled for the period, though cost limitations saw the headlamps still exposed to the wind, being mounted on the front wings. Then, as later, the problem lay in the price, not the engineering. A 650 cost £480 at a time when Ford's four-seater Prefect saloon cost only £352, which was a very considerable disadvantage.

Front suspension was by what Lloyd called "oil-damped coil springs", with double wishbones at the front and a similar though simpified arrangement at the rear. The body, simply styled and constructed, was of the usual composite type, mounted on long, flimsy-looking outriggers from the central backbone frame.

This was a technically brave, if unorthodox, layout but the car never truly caught on, and Lloyd made no money from the project. Although the last 650 model of all was built in 1951, Lloyd offered spares and service support until 1983, a truly honourable existence.

SPECIFICATION

BODY STYLES: open roadster

PRODUCTION: approx 600

ENGINE & TRANSMISSION: 654cc, 2cyl ts, 3sp man, f/f

POWER: 18bhp @ 2450rpm

MAX SPEED (MPH): 55 (E)

0-60MPH (SEC): not possible

SUSPENSION & BRAKES: coil ifs, coil irs, drums f&r

LENGTH (IN)/WEIGHT (LB): 147/1344

LAUNCH PRICE: £480

LOTUS

Engineering genius Colin Chapman built the first Lotus cars as Austin Seven specials, then in 1952 founded the Lotus Engineering Co, in Hornsey, North London, to build two-seater sports cars with multi-tube chassis frames. By the end of the 1950s, Lotus Cars Ltd had been formed, and the more advanced Seven and the monocoque-shelled Elite were on sale, but Lotus had also developed an F1 team.

The 1960s were an exciting time for Lotus, not only because they produced successful and technically advanced F1 and Indy 500 single-seater race cars, but also because they developed their own twin overhead camshaft road-car engine, the Elan, Plus 2 and Europa road car families, and assembled the Lotus-Cortina saloon for Ford. First of all the company moved to Cheshunt in Hertfordshire then, from 1966/67, based themselves on Hethel Airfield, near Norwich.

Subsequently, all manufacturing rights to the Seven were sold off to Caterham Cars in 1973.

Later, there were completely new 16-valve engines, Esprit and Elite road cars and a series of great single-seater racers. Always surrounded by controversy, and ready to interpret motorsport regulations to suit his own opinions, Chapman clashed with the FIA, supplied 16-valve engines to Jensen (Jensen-Healey) and Talbot (Sunbeam-Lotus), set up an engineering consultancy division, engineered the De Lorean for production, then died suddenly in 1982. After this, Lotus company ownership changed hands repeatedly in the 1980s and 1990s. New models, and owners, came and went, and cars like the Talbot Sunbeam-Lotus and the Vauxhall Lotus-Carlton were built under licence, until the Far Eastern Proton concern took control and introduced an element of stability.

Mk VI 1953-56

Although the Mk VI was strictly a kit-car, which Lotus never assembled at its cramped Hornsey premises, it was the company's first production machine, for at least 100 examples were produced in three years.

The basis of the design was a light (only 63lb) but sturdy multi-tube chassis frame, the tubing being well triangulated. Extra chassis strength was ensured by riveting all the aluminium body skin panels to this frame. The body shape set up a basic styling theme for the Mk VII (Seven) which followed, for it combined separate front wings and cowled rear wings, with a squarish grille. On the Mk

Lotus Mark VI in 1953, with its creator Colin Chapman at the wheel.

VI, the headlamps were hidden away behind the grille.

There were few creature comforts and very little trim. This car was so low, and so basically simple, that there was no provision for doors, and the soft top and weather protection could best be described as sketchy.

Independent front suspension was by a divided-axle (swing-axle) layout with coil-over-shock absorbers, the Ford-based rear beam axle being sprung on coil springs and located by a torque tube and Panhard rod. Strange steering geometry was needed to match up to the movements of the divided front axle (but it seemed to work!), and many minor chassis and running gear components were lifted straight off the Ford Prefect/10hp/Popular 103E of the time,

including those models' cable-operated drum brakes.

The base car was marketed with a Ford sidevalve engine and a close-ratio conversion of the Ford three-speed gearbox, but several other engine and transmission combinations were available – notably the 1508cc Ford Consul and the 1250cc MG XPAG unit found in TCs and TDs. Power outputs thus spanned 36bhp to 54bhp.

The Mk VI is best described as a motorcycle on four wheels, for it offered as much immediate involvement with the road, similarly direct handling, and about as much weather protection. It was a very successful start to Lotus's road-car operations, and was the obvious ancestor of the long-running Seven which followed.

SPECIFICATION

BODY STYLES: sports car

PRODUCTION: approx 100

ENGINE & TRANSMISSION: 1172cc, 4cyl sv, 3sp man, 4sp man, f/r

POWER: 36bhp @ 4500rpm

NOTE: Other Ford or BMC engines/power outputs also available

MAX SPEED (MPH): 80 (E)

0-60MPH (SEC): not measured

SUSPENSION & BRAKES: coil ifs, coil rear, drums f&r

LENGTH (IN)/WEIGHT (LB): 121/c.1000

LAUNCH PRICE: Dependent on engine chosen, and whether supplied by customer. £110 for the basic frame, £75 for the body shell

Seven S1 1957-60

When Lotus introduced the Seven in 1957, it could not have known that further-evolved versions of the car would still be in production nearly fifty years later! Yet the fact is that the lineage of the modern Caterham Super Seven can be traced back easily, and directly, to that Seven.

Although it looked similar to the Mk VI, the Seven was different in almost every detail, not least in the use of an even lighter multi-tube chassis frame, coil spring and wishbone independent front suspension, Morris Minor 1000 rack-and-pinion steering, and a BMC beam rear axle. Wire spoke wheels (15in diameter) were optional, and Girling hydraulic brakes were standard. The suspension was firm, but not shatteringly so, and the steering response was instant – this was even more of a "motorcycle on four wheels" than the Mk VI had been.

Cycle-type front wings and separately-positioned headlamps mounted on front wing support tubes were all part of the new car's theme. The body was ultra-low and ultra-lightweight, with no doors and only very basic wet-weather protection.

The search for ultimate lightness and simplicity, and the ability to supply this machine with various engines and transmissions, was retained. Early Sevens had 40bhp 1172cc sidevalve Ford engines, but a 75bhp 1098cc Coventry-Climax followed in 1958, and a 37bhp 948cc BMC engine followed in 1959. By this time some Sevens had swept front wings (the USA was supplied first) to meet local regulations – and cars were being produced at a more modern and more spacious factory at Cheshunt.

Because Seven owners built up their cars from kits, no two original Sevens were the same, or contained the same equipment. That is all part of the charm they hold today.

An early Lotus Seven.

No doors, no sidescreens, but there is a hood.

SPECIFICATION

BODY STYLES: sports car

PRODUCTION: 251

ENGINE & TRANSMISSION: 1172cc, 4cyl sv, 3sp man/948cc, 4 cyl ohv, 4sp man/1098cc, 4 cyl ohc, 4sp man, f/r

POWER: 40bhp @ 4500rpm/40bhp @ 5000rpm/75bhp @ 6250rpm

MAX SPEED (MPH): 76/83/104

0-60MPH (SEC): 17.8/12.1/9.2

SUSPENSION & BRAKES: coil ifs, coil rear, drums f&r

LENGTH (IN)/WEIGHT (LB): 129/960 - 1008

LAUNCH PRICE: £511 (as a kit)

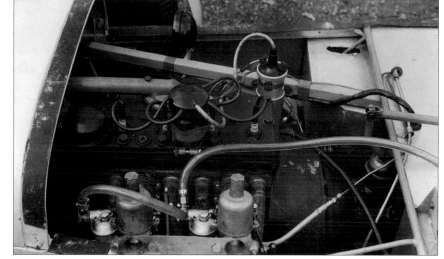

Under the bonnet, this Seven has a Ford 1172cc sidevalve engine fed by twin SUs, enough for nearly 80mph.

Seven S2 1960-68

The second series Seven appeared in mid-1960, looking almost exactly like the original S1 but with a raft of changes and improvements. The S1 had lasted for three seasons, but this type was on sale for no less than eight years.

The chassis of the S2 was a slightly simplified version of the S1's, with a different "A-frame" type of rear axle location. A relocated (Triumph Herald) rack-and-pinion steering took over, along with a Standard back axle, and 13in disc wheels were now fitted, with no wire wheel option. Visually, the S2 now used GRP mouldings for the nose cone and front and rear wings, and almost all cars were now being supplied with flared and swept front wings.

Lotus Seven S2 had flared front wings. This is the 95bhp Super Seven 1500.

The big change was in the choice of engines. The costly Coventry-Climax engine was no longer available, for before long the "base" S2 came with Ford's latest 105E overhead-valve 997cc power unit. This, and larger derivatives (up to 1498cc), could be Cosworth-tuned, and a further alternative was BMC A-Series engines, as lifted from the Austin-Healey Sprite.

With the largest engine and up to 95bhp, the Seven was now a seriously quick car, so front-wheel disc brakes were soon standardised. Production moved from Cheshunt to Hethel in 1966-67, before the S2 gave way to the S3 in 1968.

SPECIFICATION

BODY STYLES: sports car

PRODUCTION: 1362

ENGINE & TRANSMISSION: 1172cc, 4cyl sv, 3sp man/948cc/997cc/1340cc/1498cc, 4cyl ohv, 4sp man, f/r

POWER: 40bhp @ 4500rpm-95bhp @ 6000rpm

MAX SPEED (MPH): 80-103

0-60MPH (SEC): 14.3-7.7

SUSPENSION & BRAKES: coil ifs, coil rear, drums f&r (disc f/drum r on high-powered versions)

LENGTH (IN)/WEIGHT (LB): 132/960 - 1064

LAUNCH PRICE: £587 (as a kit)

Plenty of work awaits these young men in April 1964.

The Super Seven Cosworth as seen from above.

Seven S3 1968-70

Theoretically, the third series of Seven – the S3 – was only going to be on sale for two years, after which the very different Series 4 would take over. The customers did not see it like that. After Lotus cut adrift and sold off all Seven-manufacturing rights to Caterham Cars, the S3 would be reborn in 1974 as the Caterham Seven. Production then continued – and still continues – into the new century.

The S3 looked just like the S2 (though cycle-type wings were no longer available), but the line-up of engines had changed once again. The new car's "base"

The Series 3 Lotus Seven.

engines were unmodified cross-flow Ford "Kent" Escort GT (1297cc) or Cortina GT (1598cc). A high-output 120bhp 1598cc engine by Holbay was soon added, and (from late 1969) the Super Seven Twin Cam SS model had a 115bhp 1558cc Lotus Twin-Cam engine (only 13 were made).

The S3 used a Ford Mexico-type rear axle, with wider rear wings (in GRP) to cover the wider track, Ford road wheels were now standard, as were front-wheel disc brakes. All in all, this type was up to

200lb heavier than the S2, but the clientele loved the higher performance they were offered, the S3 becoming the best-selling Seven so far.

Although production of new Lotus-built cars actually ended late in 1969, the final deliveries did not take place until mid-1970. It would start up again, this time as the Caterham Super Seven, in Kent, in 1974.

The S3, as agreed by all Lotus fanatics, was the ultimate in Sevens, for it had lost none of the sporting appeal of the original and was now faster and more stable than ever before. Thousands of

Only 13 Super Seven Twin Cam SS models were made.

enthusiastic customers who bought these, and the Caterham versions, would never have anything else.

SPECIFICATION

BODY STYLES: sports car

PRODUCTION: 385

ENGINE & TRANSMISSION: 1297cc or 1598cc, 4cyl ohv/1558cc, 4cyl 2ohc, 4sp man, f/r

POWER: 72bhp @ 6000rpm-125bhp @ 6200rpm

MAX SPEED (MPH): 99-110

0-60MPH (SEC): 7.7-6.5 (E)

SUSPENSION & BRAKES: coil ifs, coil rear, disc f/drum r

LENGTH (IN)/WEIGHT (LB): 133/1210 - 1260

LAUNCH PRICE: £775 (as kit)

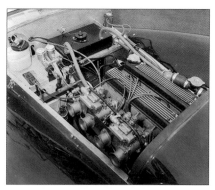

Engine of the Twin Cam SS.

Business-like cockpit of the Twin Cam SS.

Seven S4 1970-72

Though called Series 4, this derivative of the Seven was different from the S3 in many ways. The same basic layout – multi-tube frame, two-seater sports body, familiar-looking style – was retained, but almost every component except bought-in engines and running gear was different.

The chassis frame now had a 90-inch

SPECIFICATION

BODY STYLES: sports car

PRODUCTION: 887

ENGINE & TRANSMISSION: 1297cc/1598cc, 4cyl ohv/1558cc, 4cyl 2ohc, 4sp man, f/r

POWER: 72bhp @ 6000rpm/115 bhp @ 5500rpm

MAX SPEED (MPH): 100/116

0-60MPH (SEC): 8.8/8/7

SUSPENSION & BRAKES: coil ifs, coil rear, disc f/drum r

LENGTH (IN)/WEIGHT (LB): 145/1276

LAUNCH PRICE: £895 (kit)

Seven S4 , last of the Lotus-built Sevens.

wheelbase, with a more spacious cockpit area, and was stiffened by flat steel cockpit sides and engine bay panels. The new car's bodywork, made entirely of GRP, was altogether more angular, with a squarer nose profile, and had its flared front wings sweeping all the way past the cutaway cockpit sides to meet up with the rear wheelarches. The tail was

squared up, with the spare wheel mounted upright at the rear. The bonnet was hinged at the front and lifted up completely for engine bay access, while for the first time the weather equipment included sliding side-screens.

Front suspension was by Europa-style double wishbones and coil springs, Burman provided a new rack-and-pinion steering, and the rear axle location was now by a pair of fore-and-aft Watts linkages, with a triangulated arm for lateral location.

The engines offered were basically the same ones as had been available for the S3, though very few 1297cc power units were ever supplied, most cars being ordered with 84bhp 1598cc Ford power, and only a few with 115bhp 1558cc Lotus-Ford twin-cams.

The S4 was much more successful at home than Colin Chapman had forecast (he apparently hated the looks), though it may be significant that after Graham Nearn's Caterham concern took over manufacture, they soon dropped it in favour of reviving the S3.

Although the S4 was never as fashionable as the S3, it sold just as well and performed in the same way. Its looks were distinctive, but after nearly 50 years of production of "normal" Sevens, it is a rare, almost forgotten beast today.

Elite 1958-63

Colin Chapman's new front-engined Elite, previewed in 1957, but not in series production until the winter of 1958-59, was not only a beautiful sports coupé but was also technically advanced: it was the first car in the world to be built around a reinforced glass-fibre monocoque structure. From late 1959, all Elites were assembled at the new Cheshunt factory.

In that exquisitely sleek two-seater coupé, which was shaped with so much "tumblehome" in the doors that the windows could not be retracted (they had to be removed instead!) there was only a little steel reinforcement (mainly tubular), around the front suspension and engine/transmission mountings, plus the door hinges and windscreen. The shell itself comprised only three major mouldings – floor, structural centre section, and the one-piece outer skin – after which moveable panels such as doors and bonnet panel could be bolted into place.

Power came from the celebrated and very lightweight Coventry-Climax overhead-camshaft engine – the 1216cc FWE type was specially developed for

Lotus Elite, 1958, the world's first unit-construction glassfibre car.

An Elite outside the Lotus factory, among noticeably loftier Ford Classics.

SPECIFICATION

BODY STYLES: sports coupé

PRODUCTION: 988

ENGINE & TRANSMISSION: 1216cc, 4cyl ohc, 4sp man, f/r

POWER: 71bhp @ 6100rpm/83bhp @ 6250rpm

MAX SPEED (MPH): 112/118

0-60MPH (SEC): 11.4/11.0

SUSPENSION & BRAKES: coil ifs, coil irs, discs f&r

LENGTH (IN)/WEIGHT (LB): 148/1455

LAUNCH PRICE: £1951

this car. It was mated to a BMC B-Series gearbox at first, or a ZF transmission on SE derivatives of the SII type. Early cars were available with 71bhp (single carburettor) or 83bhp, though very few low-power types were sold.

Four-wheel independent suspension featured coil springs and wishbones at the front, and Chapman struts with fixed-length half-shafts at the rear. Four-wheel disc brakes, rack-and-pinion steering and centre-lock wire-spoke wheels were all standard.

Series II types, available from October 1960, had a different rear suspension location. More power was available from the FWE engine, the rating eventually going up to 105bhp; such cars were sold as Super 95, Super 100 and Super 105 types.

Beautifully styled, excellent to drive, and with wonderful performance and handling, the Elite was let down by build quality problems, the lack of decent in-cabin ventilation, and serious noise transmission problems from the hull-mounted transmission. As a racing sports car it was always a class leader, and few more attractive shapes have ever been conceived. Because the body shell was essentially rot-proof, many Elites have survived, and are highly prized.

Elan 1962-71

The Elan signalled a new beginning for Lotus – the end of space-frame chassis or GRP monocoques, the arrival of a family of road cars with pressed-steel backbone chassis, soft-sprung all-independent coil-spring suspension (Chapman struts at the rear), smooth GRP body styles (with pop-up headlamps), and an in-house designed twincam engine. Many, incidentally, were sold as tax-free kits for completion at home, and after 1966/67 all were manufactured at the Hethel factory in Norfolk.

The engine, based on the bottom end of the Ford Cortina design, but with a special light-alloy eight-valve twin-cam cylinder head, was central to all 1960s Lotus road cars. In the Elan it was mated to a close-ratio Ford-derived gearbox. Soft, all-independent suspension, four-wheel Girling disc brakes, and lightweight construction added up to an astonishingly fast and nimble two-seater which was only let down by Lotus's sometimes casual attitude to build quality. The first 22 cars had 1498cc engines but a 1558cc unit was adopted before series production began; all early engines, it is thought, were subsequently converted to the larger capacity.

The Elan remained in production for more than a decade (latterly as the higher-powered Sprint), becoming better built, of a higher quality and somewhat heavier as time passed. Original Elans (retrospectively known as Series Is) were all two-

Lotus Elan S1, 1963, with optional hardtop.

The backbone chassis of the Elan.

seater roadsters, with a removable hardtop option from 1963.

Series 2 Elans arrived in November 1964, with a polished (instead of matt) fascia panel, lockable glove box, re-styled rear lamp clusters, and optional centre-lock disc wheels. One year later, the permanent fixed-head coupé derivative (S3) joined the range. From early 1966 a 115bhp "Special Equipment" engine became optional too.

From mid-1966 the open-top version became S3, with fixed window frames around the drop glasses. In March 1968 the S4 took over. It had flared wheelarch lips, a revised fascia, and a bonnet bulge to clear alternative carburettors. From late 1968, for almost a year, single-choke Stromberg carburettors replaced twin-choke Webers.

This range was then replaced by the more powerful Elan Sprints (which looked the same) from early 1971.

Each and every Elan was a joy to drive – very fast for its size, with remarkable roadholding – though with rather a cramped two-seater cabin. Build quality and longevity were always a problem, and the backbone frames could rust badly, but many have survived. They are as desirable today as they were in their youth.

Elans at Goodwood in 1966.

The 1966 Elan S4. Centre-lock wheels had arrived with the S2.

The cockpit of the Elan sported a wooden dashboard.

SPECIFICATION

BODY STYLES: sports car, sports coupé

PRODUCTION: approx 12,200, all types

ENGINE & TRANSMISSION: 1498cc/1558cc, 4cyl 2ohc, 4sp man, f/r

POWER: 100bhp @ 5700rpm/105bhp @ 5500rpm/115bhp @ 6000rpm

MAX SPEED (MPH): 110-122

0-60MPH (SEC): 9.0 (E) -7.6

SUSPENSION & BRAKES: coil ifs, coil irs, discs f&r

LENGTH (IN)/WEIGHT (LB): 145/1516

LAUNCH PRICE: (1498cc) £1499, (1558cc) £1312

Elan Sprint 1971-73

The final derivative of the popular little original-type Elan was the Sprint. Introduced in February 1971, the Sprint featured a "Big Valve" version of the 1558cc twin-cam engine. In later years, analysts suggested that the 126bhp output claimed was optimistic. Most cars were sold in "sponsors' livery" – red over white, as featured on the contemporary Lotus F1 single-seaters. As before, open sports car or closed (bubble-top) coupé types were both on offer.

Compared with the previous Elan S4, there were no significant style changes,

SPECIFICATION

BODY STYLES: sports car, sports coupé

PRODUCTION: See Elan

ENGINE & TRANSMISSION: 1558cc, 4cyl 2ohc, 4sp man, f/r

POWER: 126bhp @ 6500rpm

MAX SPEED (MPH): 121

0-60MPH (SEC): 6.7

SUSPENSION & BRAKES: coil ifs, coil irs, discs f&r

LENGTH (IN)/WEIGHT (LB): 145/1590

LAUNCH PRICE: £1686 (as kit) – not available as completely built-up car.

Elan Sprint.

and the four-speed gearbox was not changed either. This was the fastest of all such Elans – 0-60mph in 6.7 seconds was a stirring performance for a little 1.6-litre car – and it was still ostensibly sold as a Build-It-Yourself machine to eliminate the payment of British Purchase Tax. When VAT replaced Purchase Tax in 1973, it was inevitable that the Elan would speedily die, which it did, early in that year.

Elan Plus 2/Plus 2S 1967-69/1969-71

To follow up the success of the Elan, Lotus then introduced the Elan Plus 2, which used the self-same engine, transmission and general chassis layout, but with a longer-wheelbase frame (96in instead of 84in), wider wheel tracks and a totally different GRP body. All these cars were manufactured at Hethel.

SPECIFICATION

BODY STYLES: sports coupé

PRODUCTION: 5200, all Plus 2 types

ENGINE & TRANSMISSION: 1558cc, 4cyl 2ohc, 4sp man, f/r

POWER: 118bhp @ 6250rpm

MAX SPEED (MPH): 118

0-60MPH (SEC): 8.9

SUSPENSION & BRAKES: coil ifs, coil irs, discs f&r

LENGTH (IN)/WEIGHT (LB): 168/1882

LAUNCH PRICE: £1923

Lotus Elan Plus 2, 1969.

Although the Plus 2 model bore obvious family resemblances to the Elan, this was an altogether bulkier, heavier machine. All cars had servo-assisted brakes, and development changes mirrored those of the smaller two-seater Elan.

As reflected in its model name, the Plus 2 had a larger cabin, with two occasional seats tucked in behind the

The Elan Plus 2 had a full complement of instruments.

individual front seats, all covered by a shapely bubble-top roof, and weighed at least 350lb more than the two-seater. Because of this, Lotus made the "Special Equipment" twin-cam engine standard – the result being that with 118bhp the Plus 2 delivered a 118mph top speed.

Only one year after launch, the Plus 2 progressed to Plus 2S, at which point the kit-car build option was no longer available. Mechanically there were no updates but the interior trim was enhanced. As with the two-seater, the Plus 2S model would be replaced by a more powerful 126bhp version, called

the Plus 2S 130, in 1971.

Although not quite as crisp-handling a car as the two-seater Elan, and still just as subject to quality-control vagaries, the Plus 2 family was very well liked and has survived in fair numbers, although many have suffered chassis rot at some time.

Elan Plus 2S 130 and 130/5 1971-74

In parallel with the Elan, when the "Big Valve" 126bhp engine became available, it was fitted to the larger car as well, the model name then becoming Plus 2S 130. There were no changes to the style, the exterior decoration, or the interior – all the up-grading went into the engine.

Performance was enhanced – *Autocar*

recorded a top speed of 121mph and 0-60mph acceleration in 7.4 seconds – but the soft ride and inch-accurate steering were just as good as before.

In October 1972 a newly-developed five-speed gearbox became available, this being intended for the still-secret Elite for 1974, and actually having Austin Maxi gear wheels inside a new

casing. This five-speed model carried the ungainly title of Plus 2S 130/5, and would be built alongside the four-speed car.

Sold as a "built-up" car, the Plus 2S 130 and Plus 2S 130/5 did not suffer when VAT was introduced in 1973, but carried on steadily until 1974, when finally displaced by the new Elite.

Elan 130 +2S, 1971, had the same 126bhp "Big Valve" engine as the Elan Sprint.

SPECIFICATION

BODY STYLES: sports coupé

PRODUCTION: see Plus 2S

ENGINE & TRANSMISSION: 1558cc, 4cyl 2ohc, 4sp man, 5sp man, f/r

POWER: 126bhp @ 6500rpm

MAX SPEED (MPH): 121/120

0-60MPH (SEC): 7.4/7.5

SUSPENSION & BRAKES: coil ifs, coil irs, discs f&r

LENGTH (IN)/WEIGHT (LB): 168/1954

LAUNCH PRICE: £2676/£2716

Europa S1/S2 1966-71

The mid-engined Lotus Europa S1, 1966.

At the end of 1966, when previewed, the Europa caused a real sensation for it was Britain's first mid-engined sports car. Although similar to the Elan in its engineering philosophy – a folded-steel backbone chassis covered by a two-seater GRP body shell – it was Renault-powered, and different in every detail.

To keep its price right down, Lotus made the Europa as simple as possible, so the engine/transmission assembly was a tuned version of that normally found in the front-engined Renault 16 family hatchback, effectively turned back-to-front. The engine was ahead of the line of the rear wheels, the transaxle driving those rear wheels. Soft coil spring inde-pendent suspension was fitted all round, but braking was by front discs and rear drums.

On the first cars, which were all built at Hethel, and initially for export only, the body shell was bonded to the chassis frame on assembly, which later rendered major maintenance and restoration very difficult, but this feature was abandoned when the S2 Europa arrived in 1968.

This, in some ways, was the "people's Lotus", for it was priced at only £1667 (fully built-up) in 1968. Although it was a small and neatly-engineered machine, its engine was none too powerful. Even so, an efficient aerodynamic shape

helped deliver a top speed of 109mph, and the handling was as good as every Lotus enthusiast expected.

Inevitably, more power was demanded than the Renault engine could supply,

Europa S1 and S2 models had engines and transmissions from the front wheel drive Renault 16..

so from late 1971 the Europa got the Lotus twin-cam engine and became the Europa Twin-Cam.

SPECIFICATION	
BODY STYLES: sports coupé	
PRODUCTION: 9230, all Europa types	
ENGINE & TRANSMISSION: 1470cc, 4cyl ohv, 4sp man, m/r	
POWER: 78bhp @ 6500rpm	
MAX SPEED (MPH): 109	
0-60MPH (SEC): 10.7	
SUSPENSION & BRAKES: coil ifs, coil irs, disc f/drum r	
LENGTH (IN)/WEIGHT (LB): 157/1375	
LAUNCH PRICE: £1667	

Europa Twin-Cam/Special 1971-75

In 1971 Lotus up-rated the mid-engined Europa design by dumping the underpowered Renault engine in favour of the 105bhp 1558cc Lotus twin-cam unit. At the same time the style was altered by the reduction of the "sail" panels at the rear quarters of the GRP body shell.

This was an advance on the original car (the top speed was 117mph), but only one year later the Twin-Cam gave way to the Special, which looked exactly the same, but was fitted with the "Big Valve" 126bhp engine. There was also the option of a Renault 12 Gordini-based five-speed gearbox, which would be standardised in March 1974.

The Special could reach 121mph and was a very fast and nimble car, afflicted

only by the rather small cabin of the Europa model range.

Even after the arrival of VAT in 1973 (which meant that all subsequent

Europas had to be sold in fully built-up condition), sales continued at a steady pace. The last cars of all were produced in September 1975.

Lotus Europa Special, 1972, had the "Big Valve" engine and a five-speed gearbox.

SPECIFICATION
BODY STYLES: sports coupé
PRODUCTION: see Europa S1/S2
ENGINE & TRANSMISSION: 1558cc, 4cyl 2ohc, 4sp man, 5sp man, m/r
POWER: 105bhp @ 6000rpm/126bhp @ 6500rpm
MAX SPEED (MPH): 117/121
0-60MPH (SEC): 7.7/7.0
SUSPENSION & BRAKES: coil ifs, coil irs, disc f/drum r
LENGTH (IN)/WEIGHT (LB): 157/1557-1588
LAUNCH PRICE: £1996/£2370

Europa Special in the familiar John Player livery, showing chopped-down butresses.

Elite and Elite 2.2 1974-83

Lotus planned a new generation of road cars in the 1970s, all of them to be powered by a new 16-valve twin overhead camshaft engine which had an aluminium cylinder block and would be laid over in the engine bays at 45 degrees (though Lotus did not admit it for years, this was actually because a 90-degree V8 derivative was already envisaged).

The first of these cars was the front-engined Elite of May 1974, which had a sporting estate/hatchback body and rode on a new 98in-wheelbase steel backbone chassis.

The new engine was matched to a newly-developed five-speed gearbox (which used BL Austin Maxi internals), and as usual with such a Lotus there was soft, long-travel independent suspension by coil springs all round.

The Elite was a much larger car than the Elan Plus 2S 130/5 which it replaced – longer, wider, heavier and with a larger cabin. It had a rather sharp-edged GRP body with flip-up headlamps in the nose and 2+2 seating. Surprisingly, the rear seats were sculptured and could not be folded forward to increase load space; in this respect, rivals such as the Reliant Scimitar GTE had a great advantage.

The cabin was plushily comfortable, with an all-new fascia/instrument panel layout, and because the chassis was a backbone the central tunnel was very substantial indeed. On the early cars the steering wheel was a very starkly styled twin-spoke design.

Development changes included the option of power-assisted steering and air

Lotus Elite S1, launched in 1974.

conditioning from late 1974, and optional automatic transmission from January 1976 (few people took this up – only 60-70 a year, Lotus admitted). At the end of 1975 the Eclat coupé appeared (this is described separately). It was based on the Elite chassis and the front part of the body shell.

From May 1980, the Elite was up-rated to Elite 2.2, this car having the enlarged and more torquey engine, matched to a Getrag five-speed gearbox. Starting from that period the chassis frame was treated to a hot-dip zinc-plate galvanising process (which was intended to deal with earlier corrosion problems), while 7in Speedline alloy road wheels became the standard fitment. Style changes included a tidied-up fascia with higher-quality wood facings, while externally there were Rover SD1 rear lamp clusters, and headlamp operation was henceforth to be by electricity rather than by engine vacuum.

Though the Eclat was the cheaper, more down-market car, it seemed to

appeal more than the Elite, so in 1983 the hatchback car was quietly phased out of production.

Not always well-built and, like many such Lotuses of the period, widely thought – with some justification – to be less than completely reliable, an Elite in first-class order and on top form was nevertheless a fast, capable and stylish car. Even so, Lotus's sporting hatchback experiment was never to be repeated.

SPECIFICATION

BODY STYLES: sports hatchback

PRODUCTION: 2535

ENGINE & TRANSMISSION: 1973cc/2174cc, 4cyl 2ohc, 5sp man, or auto, f/r

POWER: 160bhp @ 6200rpm/160bhp @ 6500rpm

MAX SPEED (MPH): 124/127

0-60MPH (SEC): 7.8/7.5

SUSPENSION & BRAKES: coil ifs, coil irs, discs f&r

LENGTH (IN)/WEIGHT (LB): 176/2440

LAUNCH PRICE: £5445/£16,142

Eclat and Eclat 2.2 1975-82

Launched in October 1975, the Eclat was effectively a conventional fastback coupé version of the new-style Elite. The rolling chassis was effectively the same, the front half, the doors, and the bottom rear half of the GRP body shells were shared, and it was only the roof and sloping tail (with its small separate boot lid) which were unique to the Eclat.

Lotus deliberately set the specification and prices a little further downmarket than the Elite of the period. The original "base" Eclat (Type 520), for instance, had a four-speed (Ford Capri-type) gearbox and steel road wheels, though other models had the BL-based five-speeder. Air conditioning, alloy wheels, power steering and automatic transmission were also optional. Many

of the Eclats supplied to customers were, as it transpired, well-loaded with such options.

The Sprint 520 and 521 versions of 1977 were anything but, being the same car mechanically as others (except for a lowered final drive ratio, to give smarter acceleration), but with a different trim and badging specification.

As with the closely-related Elite, from

May 1980 the Eclat was uprated to Eclat 2.2, with the galvanised chassis frame, the 2174cc engine and the Getrag five-speed gearbox; all the previous options except for the four-

SPECIFICATION

BODY STYLES: sports coupé

PRODUCTION: 1519

ENGINE & TRANSMISSION: 1973cc/2174cc, 4cyl 2ohc, 4sp man, 5sp man, or auto, f/r

POWER: 160bhp @ 6200rpm/160bhp @ 6500rpm

MAX SPEED (MPH): 129/127

0-60MPH (SEC): 7.9/7.5

SUSPENSION & BRAKES: coil ifs, coil irs, discs f&r

LENGTH (IN)/WEIGHT (LB): 176/2440

LAUNCH PRICE: £5729/£15,842

Lotus Eclat, 1975, had a fastback tail.

speed Ford gearbox and the pressed-steel road wheels were still on offer.

The Eclat then carried on until July 1982 (there was a Riviera special edition in late 1981), after which it was replaced by the Eclat-based Excel (which had several important Toyota components fitted).

Esprit S1/S2/S2.2 1976-78/1978-80/1980-81

Introduced in 1975, modified and yet again modified over the years, the basic design of the mid-engined Esprit would survive until 2004/5, when the last of the type (then powered by a Lotus V8 engine) was produced. Lotus sold the Esprit for just as long as it was commercial, there being no doubt that the the original Ital Design/Giugiaro body style and the Peter Stevens facelift (from 1987) had much to do with this.

Although the Esprit was a direct replacement for the Europa, there were no mechanical links between the two cars. The Esprit had a new steel backbone chassis with a 96in wheelbase, all-round coil spring suspension, and disc brakes for all four wheels, the rears being inboard. The Lotus 16-valve engine, rated at 160bhp, was poitioned immediately behind the cramped two-seater cabin. The five-speed gearbox was a modified Citroen SM/Maserati Merak-type unit.

The low, wide, squat body was fashioned in GRP, the cabin being best described as snug, with surprisingly constricted footwell space. Even though the Esprit was a very fast and compact car (130mph was easily possible in original cars), the ride was soft and pliant, while the handling was

Lotus Esprit.

remarkable, if tending towards oversteer. It took time for Lotus to make the car as refined as they had originally planned.

Although the car was launched in October 1975, the first deliveries did not take place until June 1976, and after only two years (in August 1978) the Esprit became S2, complete with style and equipment changes in the cabin, and with wider-rim alloy road wheels (Speedline instead of Wolfrace). The front spoiler was integrated more smoothly than at first, and Rover SD1 rear lamp clusters were fitted.

Then came an interim car, the Esprit 2.2 of May 1980, which had a galvanised chassis frame and the 2174cc version of the engine. This car carried on for only 11 months, to April 1981, when it was replaced by the much changed Esprit S3.

Interior of the Esprit.

Esprit on the test track with headlamps raised.

SPECIFICATION

BODY STYLES: sports coupé

PRODUCTION: 2092, all types

ENGINE & TRANSMISSION: 1973cc/2174cc, 4cyl 2ohc, 5sp man, m/r

POWER: 160bhp @ 6200rpm/160bhp @ 6500rpm

MAX SPEED (MPH): 135/134

0-60MPH (SEC): 8.0/6.7

SUSPENSION & BRAKES: coil ifs, coil irs, discs f&r

LENGTH (IN)/WEIGHT (LB): 165/2218

LAUNCH PRICE: £7883/£11,124/£14,951

Esprit Turbo 1980-87

Always planned, but years in the making, the turbocharged Esprit was not announced until February 1980 (deliveries began in August), all the original cars being liveried in the colours of Essex Petroleum, the F1 team's contemporary sponsors. Cars based on the new design, with progressively more and more power, would remain on sale until the end of the century.

Although it was based on the layout of the mid-engined Esprit (and looked very similar), the Turbo had many important differences. Not only was this the first use of the turbocharged dry-sump version of the 2174cc twin-cam engine, but the engine was installed in a completely re-engineered backbone chassis frame which also had a different layout of independent rear suspension. The engine itself did not have an intercooler (that would not be incorporated for some years), and the same Citroen/Maserati five-speed transmission was retained.

Style differences include a larger wrap-around front bumper and deep new spoiler. There were also skirts along the

The 210bhp Esprit Turbo of 1980.

body sides, incorporating ducts to channel fresh air into the engine bay, a more prominent rear spoiler, and special 15in alloy road wheels.

After the first 100 Essex-liveried cars had been produced, from April 1981 the Turbo became available in conventional colours, and with air conditioning as an extra, rather than as standard. On all these cars, trim and instrumentation were similar to those of normally-aspirated Esprits. "Essex" cars had an extra "communications panel" in the roof.

Development changes included the fitment of a normal wet-sump lubrication system from March 1983, an enlarged and fully carpeted boot compartment from January 1984, and a glass sun-roof option from the same time. From October 1986 the Turbo was uprated to Turbo HC (High Compression), with 215bhp (instead of 210bhp), and fatter-section tyres. This car was finally displaced

by the revised-style "X180" Esprit in October 1987.

All Esprit Turbos were phenomenally fast and nimble two-seaters, let down only by Lotus's then-legendary reputation for the poor reliability of its cars. Nevertheless, many examples have been preserved by classic car owners.

SPECIFICATION

BODY STYLES: sports coupé

PRODUCTION: see Esprit

ENGINE & TRANSMISSION: 2174cc, 4cyl 2ohc, 5sp man, m/r

POWER: 210bhp @ 6000 rpm

MAX SPEED (MPH): 148

0-60MPH (SEC): 6.1

SUSPENSION & BRAKES: coil ifs, coil irs, discs f&r

LENGTH (IN)/WEIGHT (LB): 165/2653

LAUNCH PRICE: £16,982

Interior of the Esprit Turbo.

MARAUDER

Before the Marauder there was the Rover Special, an overweight and underpowered single-seater race car which had been designed by Peter Wilks, Spencer King and George Mackie, all engineers at the Rover company in Solihull.

Branching out on their own, this trio then evolved a two/three-seater sports tourer, basing it on a lightly-modified version of the then-new Rover P4 75 passenger car chassis and all its running gear, and called it the Marauder. Wilks and Mackie ran the business, while Spen King stayed behind at Rover (where he would later design the various turbine-engined prototypes and the Range Rover 4x4).

The first cars were assembled at Dorridge, near Birmingham (and very close to Rover at Solihull), actually in premises owned by Richard Mead, who built the bodywork. Assembly was later moved to premises at Kenilworth, near Coventry, with bodies provided by Abbey Panels.

Due to the high prices set, sales were always slow, and by 1952 the business had to close down, its funds exhausted. Peter Wilks and George Mackie both returned to work at Rover – Wilks eventually becoming technical director of that concern, being responsible for the highly successful P6 family car of the 1960s.

There was no attempt to revive the Marauder, but most of the cars have survived.

A/100 1950-52

To Rover watchers who had already seen the new P4 four-door saloon, the origins of this new sports tourer, the Marauder, were obvious. Not only was the rolling chassis a direct development of that of the P4, but a number of P4 body panels were employed in the construction.

Compared with the Rover P4 chassis, the Marauder had its wheelbase shortened from 111in to 102in, though the coil spring independent front suspension and steering gear, along with the conventional leaf-sprung rear end and Girling hydro-mechanical brakes, were left alone. Few changes were made to the six-cylinder 75bhp Rover engine with its overhead inlet and side exhaust valve arrangement, or to the internals of its gearbox, which incorporated a freewheel device; overdrive was optional, years before such a fitting was ever offered on a Rover.

Only 15 Rover 75-based Marauders were built.

The engine and gearbox assembly was moved back in the frame to improve the weight distribution, and instead of the P4's steering-column gearchange there was a neat remote-control centre-floor change.

With its long bonnet and short tail, the steel-panelled Marauder was very different from the P4, but a number of styling cues gave the game away.

The first four bodies were built by Richard Mead at Dorridge, the balance (of only 15 cars built) coming from Abbey Panels of Coventry (the same company would provide bodywork for specialist competiton cars like the Jaguar C-Type and D-Type).

Although the initial 1950 price of £1236 rocketed to more than £2000 in 1952, this operation could not turn a profit – and the higher the price, the less interest there seemed to be. Marauders, like the P4s from which they were developed, were heavy and rather lumbering cars, not likely to endear themselves to enthusiastic drivers. Their bodies rusted out badly, although the running gear, being by Rover, was very long-lived.

Most of the 15 cars built survive.

SPECIFICATION

BODY STYLES: sports roadster

PRODUCTION: 15

ENGINE & TRANSMISSION: 2103cc, 6cyl ioe, 4sp man, o/d, f/r

POWER: 80bhp @ 4200rpm

MAX SPEED (MPH): 89

0-60MPH (SEC): 18.4

SUSPENSION & BRAKES: coil ifs, leaf rear, drums f&r

LENGTH (IN)/WEIGHT (LB): 166/2576

LAUNCH PRICE: £1236

MARCOS

Jem Marsh had already been involved in the kit-car/tuning/accessory end of the market for some years (first of all he had run Speedex, of Luton, then worked for Leslie Ballamy's LMB concern for a time), before he got together with Frank Costin to set up Marcos in 1963.

Originally based in Luton then, from 1963, in Bradford-on-Avon in Wiltshire, Marcos developed Costin's plans for a sports car built from carefully shaped and stressed sheets of marine plywood, with a GRP body shell, which stood up remarkably well to open-road use. In the next decade, many such machines were produced (almost all of them in partly-complete kit form to avoid the customer paying Purchase Tax). A whole variety of engines was used, and it was only the practical necessity of meeting new North Amrican crash test standards which inspired a change to a steel tube chassis in 1969. This coincided with the move to a new factory, at Westbury.

The first Marcos was the rather ungainly GT, really intended for sports car racing though some road cars were built, but the Marcos which struck gold was the smart Dennis Adams-styled coupé which followed in 1964. Originally offered with a 1.8-litre Volvo P1800-type engine, but latterly with smaller, larger, and different Ford and Volvo power units, it proved very successful.

To keep the pot boiling, Marcos also developed the Mini-Marcos, which was a rather nasty little coupé using Mini parts, while the larger Mantis was a complete styling and marketing disaster. As the sale of cars to the USA became more and more problematical, Marcos's finances wobbled, and sales came to an abrupt end in 1971.

This led to liquidation, but in the late 1970s Jem Marsh somehow revived the business, carrying on building a whole series of re-engineered and restyled Adams-type cars until the early 2000s.

GT 1960-63

This was the first collaboration between Jem Marsh and Frank Costin. Costin, a De Havilland aircraft engineer, had already shaped the successful Vanwall F1 cars and Lotus Eleven racing sports cars, but this was his first essay into structures. Knowing much about the De Havilland Mosquito fighter-bomber, he chose a complex structure of spruce and marine plywood, to which special-builder Marsh fitted a variety of proprietary hardware.

Although the very first GT looked ungainly, with a narrow nose and cycle-type wings, cars which were sold from late 1960 had a more normal full-width nose and headlamps, though they also had a rather odd-looking coupé canopy which featured a wrap-around screen.

Ford provided engines (Anglia 105E or Classic 109E, both of which could be tuned to choice), these being well canted over towards the right to reduce the bonnet height. Marcos was also ready to supply a BMC-engined version if the customer wanted that. Front

suspension and rack-and-pinion steering were from the Triumph Herald, the rear axle came from the Austin/Nash Metropolitan or the Standard Ten, and Girling front-wheel disc brakes were also fitted.

The build quality was poor and the cabin equipment was sparse, but this car handled extremely well. Because it was light, and because the engines were so tuneable, the Marcos endeared itself to motorsport drivers, and to those who wanted a fast car. In spite of its World War Two heritage, though, most prospective customers distrusted the wooden construction, and sales were limited. Quite a rarity today.

A Marcos GT competing in a Historic Sports Car Championship event.

SPECIFICATION

BODY STYLES: sports coupé

PRODUCTION: 29

ENGINE & TRANSMISSION: 997cc/1340cc, 4cyl ohv, 4sp man, f/r

POWER: 39bhp @ 5000rpm/54bhp @ 4900rpm (tuned-up version available to special order)

MAX SPEED (MPH): (1340cc) 95 (E)

0-60MPH (SEC): not measured

SUSPENSION & BRAKES: coil ifs, leaf rear, disc f/drum r

LENGTH (IN)/WEIGHT (LB): 145/1000

LAUNCH PRICE: £830 (kit form)

1800/1500/1600/1650 1964-68

This astonishingly attractive coupé, with long shark-like nose, sharply-raked screen, two-seater cabin and cut-off tail, first appeared in 1964. Like the earlier ugly duckling GT it had a chassis constructed of spruce and marine ply with a GRP body shell, the running gear and all the chassis and transmission being proprietary, or modified production car parts. Local steel reinforcement around suspension and engine mounting points helped the integrity of the assembly. All cars had front-wheel disc brakes and the same basic style, with the front air intake hidden under the overhanging nose.

The original car was powered by a 114bhp Volvo P1800 engine with

Marcos 1600.

SPECIFICATION

BODY STYLES: sports coupé

PRODUCTION: not known

ENGINE & TRANSMISSION:
1778cc/1499cc/1599cc/1650cc, 4cyl ohv, 4sp man, (o/d with 1778cc), f/r

POWER: 114bhp @ 5800rpm/85bhp @ 5300rpm/88bhp @ 5400rpm/95bhp @ 5500rpm/120bhp @ 5400rpm

MAX SPEED (MPH): 106-117

0-60MPH (SEC): 12.5 (E) -8.7

SUSPENSION & BRAKES: coil ifs, DD coil rear, (from 1965) coil rear, disc f/drum r

LENGTH (IN)/WEIGHT (LB): 161/1658

LAUNCH PRICE: £1606-£1860

overdrive gearbox and was equipped with a complex De Dion-type rear suspension.

From 1965-66, though, the Volvo engine/transmission gave way to Ford Cortina-based engines with Ford gearboxes, no overdrive, and a Ford beam rear axle. This was suspended on coil springs and located by radius arms and a Panhard rod.

Several different tunes of Ford engine were available, ranging from an 85bhp unit with twin Stromberg carburettors to the very special Lawrencetune 120bhp 1650cc engine.

In all cases, these were fast road cars which under certain circumstances

could be used in club motorsport. At peak they were being built at 10 cars per week (Morgan levels), and because all were produced before the cut-off date of September 1969, all had the unique wood chassis.

Like Lotus cars of the period, these Marcos machines often looked better than they could deliver in quality terms, and partly because of Marcos's sometimes cavalier attitude to customers' complaints, demand for them was always limited.

Even so, when a Marcos was working well it was a joy to drive – and a surprising number still provide that pleasure today.

2-Litre/2.5-Litre/3-Litre 1968-71

The second-generation of long-nose, short-tail Marcos sports coupés bowed in during 1968, when the first of the V4 and V6 Ford-engined types came along, and it wasn't long before the Volvo straight-six-cylinder unit was also made available. These engines were more powerful and heavier than the straight fours they eventually replaced, though the basic style and chassis specification of the coupés did not change.

One major change came in September

1969, when the pressure of meeting new USA crash test regulations led Marcos to abandon the wooden chassis, and to replace it with a more conventional square-tube steel chassis frame instead. This weighed 175lb, and was mounted to the body shell at 47 points. This frame then formed the basis of all Marcos cars based on this body style, including those produced after the company was revived at the end of the 1970s.

Although a few Triumph 2.5-litre six-cylinder engines were fitted, the vast majority of cars had Ford engines for the British market, and big Volvos for export, particularly to the USA where that engine was already being marketed in de-toxed form.

Volvo-engined types were particularly popular, and an automatic version was made available, but it was those cars, and difficulties in financing them, which led to Marcos's collapse in 1971.

Marcos 3-litre.

Mini-Marcos 1965-74

Marcos never supplied these machines as complete cars, only as DIY kits. They had a character all of their own. Launched in late 1965, the Mini-Marcos was effectively a simply-trimmed GRP monocoque, shaped as a two-seater coupé, which customers could fit in place of the crashed or rusted-out remains of a Mini body. All Mini-Marcos, therefore, had transversely-mounted engines with front-wheel drive, and all of them used sturdy (but rust-prone) Mini sub-frames at front and rear. Firm all-independent suspension, accurate rack-and-pinion steering and instant handling response were typical Mini features.

Although Marcos listed two basic specifications – one based on the humble 850 Mini, the other on the 1275cc-engined Mini-Cooper S 1275 – customers could, of course, use whatever Mini base suited them, and the number of permutations was large. A Mini-Marcos, therefore, might have "dry" (rubber) or "wet" (Hydrolastic) suspension, all-drum brakes or disc front/drum rear, and many were treated to non-standard road wheels.

What they all had was a rather dumpy body, and build quality which depended entirely on the skills and energy of the customer who completed the car. Even though the structure was rot-resistant, the sub-frames were not, so many cars were simply dumped as being worthless after a number of years.

The Mini Jem of the late 1960s and early 1970s was a lineal descendant of this machine, using the same GRP shell and Mini mechanicals, and the Midas had connections too.

Being supplied as DIY kits, build quality was variable.

Mini-Marcos, 1965.

Mantis 1970-71

Other authorities have described the Mantis as being bizarre, and we would not argue with that. The tragedy is that although the chassis and running gear were quite competently engineered, assembled, and put on sale, the body shape was very strange indeed. Accordingly, because the Mantis was marketed at such a high price – at £3185 it cost nearly £500 more than the svelte and attractive Jaguar E-Type 2+2 – it struggled to build up a clientele.

With an eye on the potentially lucrative US market, Marcos contrived a longer-wheelbase car with 2+2 seating in a closed coupé style and the Triumph 2498cc six-cylinder engine. Initially this engine was launched in European TR6 tune, complete with Lucas fuel injection, but fitting the "federalized" version of this power unit for North American sale would have made sense. An overdrive gearbox was standard, with Borg Warner automatic transmission promised for the future.

The car's basis was a square-section steel tube chassis frame, clothed in the GRP coupé body, and though the details were different the front and rear suspension designs were like those of the smaller two-seater Marcos models, the front end being from the Triumph Vitesse, the rear axle from the Ford Capri 3-litre.

Mechanically the car seemed promising but the styling repelled many. Maybe the original design featured hidden headlamps, but as announced a pair of fixed, semi-recessed, rectangular lamps were fitted instead. The lower feature line of side windows, too, was controversial, and this was a car with big overhangs at front and rear.

All in all, not a visual success, and Marcos's financial problems in the winter of 1970-71 only helped to kill it off abruptly. Only 32 examples of the Mantis were sold – and not many people seem to care how many have survived.

Marcos Mantis, 1970, not much loved.

SPECIFICATION

BODY STYLES: sports coupé

PRODUCTION: 32

ENGINE & TRANSMISSION: 2498cc, 6cyl ohv, 4sp man, o/d, f/r

POWER: 150bhp @ 5700rpm

MAX SPEED (MPH): 125 (E)

0-60MPH (SEC): not measured

SUSPENSION & BRAKES: coil ifs, coil beam rear, disc f/drum r

LENGTH (IN)/WEIGHT (LB): 187/2300

LAUNCH PRICE: £3185

METROPOLITAN

Who originally called this car a "motoring cuckoo"? It certainly had every qualification. First built by Austin on behalf of the American Motors company of the USA, it later took on a life of its own, gained a badge of its own, and would eventually be sold, in smallish numbers, in the UK for the last four years of its career.

Early in the 1950s Austin secured a contract to assemble a new small car for American Motors, the deal being that AMC would provide the styling, while Austin would engineer the car, use their own running gear to power it, and assemble every car at Longbridge. Suitably badged as Nash or Hudson products – both were "Metropolitans" – they would be marketed solely in the USA, for although the British public were shown the cars, they could not buy them.

Hidden away was an amalgam of A40 and some A30 components. The new car was launched in 1954 with an A40 engine but from 1956 the larger A50 engine was fitted instead. Finally, from the spring of 1957, AMC allowed Austin to start selling the car outside the USA, which they chose to do, purely as a "Metropolitan". UK sales, in fact, were limited (only about 9400 were sold at home), and the last Metropolitan of all was built in 1961.

Even so, with more than 100,000 produced for all markets, and with all the financial risks underpinned from the USA, this had been a very profitable project.

1200 1954-56

For sale only in the USA, the original Nash/Hudson Metropolitan was a short, stubby two-door machine where four-seats were somehow crammed into a small cabin. In order to maximise the available luggage boot space, the spare wheel was externally mounted, on the tail, under a cover; there was no external access to the boot in any case. Like other Nashes of the period, both front and rear wheels were partly cowled by fixed wing panels.

These cars were fitted with a 1.2-litre A40 engine driving through a three-speed column-change gearbox. The suspension was based on the A30's, and this was a distinctly built-down-to-a-price machine whose only assets in the US market were a low price and small size.

Let's be quite clear about this – the road-holding was poor, the equipment stark, and the general character bargain-basement, but Austin didn't mind this as they had struck a very profitable deal to build the cars. The British, in any case, were not allowed to buy this model.

The original type, in fact, lasted for only two years, for AMC decided that they did after all require more power, so the 1500 took over from April 1956.

Metropolitan 1200.

SPECIFICATION

BODY STYLES: saloon, drophead

PRODUCTION: 20,007

ENGINE & TRANSMISSION: 1200cc, 4cyl ohv, 3sp man, f/r

POWER: 42bhp @ 4500rpm

MAX SPEED (MPH): 72

0-60MPH (SEC): 27

SUSPENSION & BRAKES: coil ifs, leaf rear, drums f&r

LENGTH (IN)/WEIGHT (LB): 149/1850

LAUNCH PRICE: not sold in UK. All cars exported to USA, with Nash or Hudson badges

1500 1956-61

At facelift time, Nash specified the larger and more powerful 1489cc Austin/BMC B-Series engine, which produced 47bhp instead of 42bhp, so although this odd-looking machine still looked far too transatlantic for British tastes, it was somewhat more lively than

SPECIFICATION

BODY STYLES: saloon, drophead

PRODUCTION: 84,361 of all badged types produced, of which 9400 "Metropolitan" for UK delivery

ENGINE & TRANSMISSION: 1489cc, 4cyl ohv, 3sp man, f/r

POWER: 47bhp @ 4100rpm

MAX SPEED (MPH): 75

0-60MPH (SEC): 24.8

SUSPENSION & BRAKES: coil ifs, leaf rear, drums f&r

LENGTH (IN)/WEIGHT (LB): 149/1850

LAUNCH PRICE: £714

Metropolitan 1500. No Metropolitan was much good at corners.

before. Compared with the original, there was a more tasteful mesh front grille, and a kinked chrome strip along the flanks to allow two-tone paintwork to be specified.

The first UK-version right hand drive Metropolitans – badged just that – were shown in April 1957, although deliveries to Nash and Hudson in the USA continued.

It was difficult to categorise the Metropolitan, except that it could be colourful, briefly fashionable and showy – for if ever there was a start to the

"hairdresser's car" pedigree this was it. No red-blooded male ever bought one, though a surprising number of smart ladies of a certain age most certainly did.

There was only one important update, in 1959 (on UK cars from summer 1960), when an opening boot lid was provided, and the spare wheel was finally mounted inside.

The end came in April 1961, and no attempt was ever made to replace this model. Its unusual looks and style have earned it a certain following today

MG

Invented by Cecil Kimber of Morris Garages in the 1920s, MG was encouraged to grow independently by proprietor Lord Nuffield, then swept into his Nuffield Organisation in 1935. By 1939, most MGs had become up-market relatives of other Nuffield marques – Morris, and particularly Wolseley – but had kept their sports car pedigree (the TA/TB types) alive. MG's biggest advantage was that it assembled its cars at Abingdon, south of Oxford, in a dedicated plant.

Post-war expansion concentrated on a succession of sports cars – TC, TD, TF and the all-new MGA, but saloons like the YA and Magnette ZA types became commercially important too. From the mid-1950s, BMC (which had absorbed Nuffield) imposed its will on MG, and all future models except the Twin-Cam used corporate engines and transmission assemblies.

With Austin-Healey assembly concentrated at Abingdon from 1957-58, this became a dedicated BMC sports car factory, so 1960s MG saloons like the Magnette Mk III and the 1100 were always assembled elsewhere. Although vast numbers of Midgets and MGBs were produced at Abingdon until the end of the 1970s, there was precious little new-model development in that time. With these ancient sports cars dying by inches, British Leyland management then closed down (and razed) the factory at the end of 1980.

The MG brand was then resurrected in the 1980s, first of all on a series of Austin-based family cars, before the MG R-V8 and mid-engined MGF revived the sports car fortunes. In the 2000s British Leyland's descendant, Rover Group, later MG Rover, continued to build MG-badged saloons and hatchbacks in satisfying, commercially successful quantities, until MG Rover's demise in 2005

TC 1945-49

When the war ended, MG was quite unprepared for peacetime car production, and had laid no plans during the war years. Accordingly, the team looked around, decided that the late-1930s TA/TB sports cars were still saleable, and came up with the TC. With only minor changes from the TB (a wider cockpit was the most important marketing change), the two-seater TC became a best-seller and set MG on its path to post-war fame and fortune. The Tickford-bodied drophead coupé (seen on the TA and TB) never re-appeared.

Based on a slim chassis frame with channel side members, the TC had very hard half-elliptic leaf spring suspension at front and rear, lever-type dampers and very direct steering. Centre-lock wire-spoke wheels were standard, the spare

1946 MG TC, not much changed externally from the 1936 TA.

being exposed behind a large slab tank. The chassis itself was quite flexible, so wheel hop was a known habit, and hard braking on uneven surfaces could be a chancy business,

Power was by Nuffield's modern XPAG engine (less powerful versions were used in Morris 10 and Wolseley 10 saloons), and although it was rated at only 54bhp it was already known to be very tuneable.

Built by Morris Bodies in Coventry, the two-seater body was a simple coachbuilt structure with a wooden (ash) frame and steel skin panels. Exposed headlamps and long sweeping front wings were all in the

1930s-style MG tradition. Doors were hinged at the rear, and the seat was a full-width bench. The windscreen could be folded flat if required.

Because its aerodynamic characteristics were awful the TC could only reach 75mph, though acceleration was brisk – and no-one ever complained about the car's character or its sporting credentials. Even though the suspension was technically obsolete (the contemporary YA saloon had independent front suspension which was much better), this was still a very successful car. Today, it seems, TCs are more popular than ever – and deservedly so.

SPECIFICATION

BODY STYLES: sports car

PRODUCTION: 10,000

ENGINE & TRANSMISSION: 1250cc, 4cyl ohv, 4sp man, f/r

POWER: 54bhp @ 5200rpm

MAX SPEED (MPH): 75

0-60MPH (SEC): 22.7

SUSPENSION & BRAKES: beam leaf front, leaf rear, drums f&r

LENGTH (IN)/WEIGHT (LB): 140/1735

LAUNCH PRICE: £480

YA/YB 1947-53

Much delayed by the war (prototypes had been seen running around Oxford in 1939), the YA was MG's first post-war saloon, the first-ever MG to have independent front suspension, and the first to be made available with left-hand drive. As ever at this time, it was a carefully product-planned Nuffield corporate design; although it used its own chassis, the engine was a de-tuned TC unit and the body shell was a modified version of the four-door Morris Eight Series 8.

Although Y-Types only had 46bhp and a top speed of a mere 71mph, they were appealing machines, with sturdy box-section chassis (underslung at the rear), and soft coil spring independent front suspension allied to rack-and-pinion

MG Y-Type saloon on the Weston Rally.

steering. There was no servo brake assistance (it was not really needed because of the car's restricted performance), yet this felt like a real little sports saloon.

The all-steel body was quite narrow and cramped, but it had the sort of traditional MG front end with exposed headlamps which appealed to many potential customers. Inside the cabin there were plenty of MG details and badges, along with a wooden fascia, leather seats, a sprung-spoke steering wheel and a slick direct-action centre gearchange.

Although not cheap – at £672, it cost more than twice the £301 of the related

Morris Eight Series E – it was well-integrated, and sold steadily.

From January 1952, the YA turned into the YB, with few mechanical or style changes but with two-leading-shoe brakes, a front anti-roll bar, 15in wheels and a new hypoid-bevel rear axle. Production ended, without a flourish, in August 1953, the Y-type's replacement being the all-new and very different Magnette ZA.

YAs and YBs are still well regarded in the MG movement, many of the survivors now featuring T-type tuning mods to give considerably more powerful 1250cc engines.

SPECIFICATION

BODY STYLES: saloon

PRODUCTION: 6158/1301

ENGINE & TRANSMISSION: 1250cc, 4cyl ohv, 4sp man, f/r

POWER: 46bhp @ 4800rpm

MAX SPEED (MPH): 71

0-60MPH (SEC): 28.2

SUSPENSION & BRAKES: coil ifs, leaf rear, drums f&r

LENGTH (IN)/WEIGHT (LB): 161/2184

LAUNCH PRICE: £672

YT 1948-50

MG YT tourer, 1948

SPECIFICATION

BODY STYLES: tourer

PRODUCTION: 877

ENGINE & TRANSMISSION: 1250cc, 4cyl ohv, 4sp man, f/r

POWER: 54bhp @ 5200rpm

MAX SPEED (MPH): 75 (E)

0-60MPH (SEC): 16.0 (E)

SUSPENSION & BRAKES: coil ifs, leaf rear, drums f&r

LENGTH (IN)/WEIGHT (LB): 164/2110

LAUNCH PRICE: not officially available in UK

MG's late-1940s four-seater tourer, the YT, was aimed squarely at export markets, for it never officially went on sale in the UK. Under the skin was a YA-type rolling chassis, complete with independent front suspension, though the engine was always in higher (TC) tune.

The novelty was in the body style, which shared themes with the TC and, later, the TD, but had nothing in common with either. In fact the YT shared front-end Y-Type panels back to the passenger bulkhead, but was unique beyond that point. Made by Morris Bodies in Coventry, the shell was based on a traditional wooden frame, with steel panelling which later was sadly prone to corrosion and deterioration.

The YT had two doors with cutaway sides, and four seats, though space in the rear was constrained by the fold-back soft-top mechanism.

In spite of the export-only title, left and right hand drive types were produced, and a few were delivered to customers in the UK. The YT did not sell as well as hoped, and was therefore dropped after only two seasons. Just a few remain in these islands, and are worth more than Y-Type saloons, if only for their rarity.

TD Midget 1949-53

Who would think that the TD sports car, which in the early 1950s became MG's runaway best-seller so far, was lashed up in a tearing hurry during 1949, with only a single proto-type ever being produced. Reading the runes, MG had seen the TC's appeal rapidly dying, so they produced a shorter, much-changed version of the YA saloon's chassis frame (it swept up and over the axle at the rear), and hastily evolved a wider but still traditional-looking two-seater body to cover it.

Although it had the TC's engine and gearbox, much of the rest of the TD's running gear was drawn from the Y-

MG TD succeeded the TC in 1950.

Type, including the coil spring independent front suspension and the new-type hypoid-bevel rear axle. As far as the enthusiasts were concerned, the only backward step was to make steel disc wheels standard, for centre-lock wires were never made available, even as an option. Early cars had plain wheels, but perforated wheels were adopted from late 1950.

The style was similar to the TC's, though squatter, and there was still a wood-framed body, a bench seat, and removable side curtains. On the TD, though, speedometer and rev-counter were ahead of the driver's eyes.

The TD did everything better than the

TC had ever done. It handled better, rode better, had more precise (rack-and-pinion) steering, was slightly faster, was rather more roomy in the cabin, and was available with left-hand drive, which the TC had never been. The vast majority of TDs were exported (particularly to the USA), but sales were so high that latter-day survivors were guaranteed.

TD IIs, slightly changed, followed in summer 1951, and later there was a TD Mk II, which was very different and had a tuned-up 60bhp engine. Even so, by 1953 competition in the shape of the Triumph TR2 was looming, and MG needed to do more – the TF being the result.

SPECIFICATION

BODY STYLES: sports car

PRODUCTION: 29,664

ENGINE & TRANSMISSION: 1250cc, 4cyl ohv, 4sp man, f/r

POWER: 54bhp @ 5200rpm/60bhp @ 5500rpm

MAX SPEED (MPH): 80/81

0-60MPH (SEC): 19.4/16.5

SUSPENSION & BRAKES: coil ifs, leaf rear, drums f&r

LENGTH (IN)/WEIGHT (LB): 145/1930

LAUNCH PRICE: £569

TF1250 Midget/TF1500 Midget 1953-55

Although the MG management wanted to produce an all-new car in 1953 (it would come in the form of the MGA in 1955) the powers at BMC refused permission, so a speedy facelift of the TD, called the TF, had to make do. Unhappily, every MG enthusiast realised that it was bound to be an interim model and it never sold very well.

Peak power was pushed up slightly to 57bhp, and wire-spoke wheels once again became available as an option, but the TF used the same rolling chassis as the TD had done. The centre section of the body, too, was unchanged. Ahead of the screen the nose was lowered and the radiator grille raked back, with more flowing wings and semi-recessed headlamps, while the rear end was slightly elongated to suit. Inside the car there were separate seats (at last!), and a new fascia in which the instruments were located in a central panel.

At any other time (or in 1950, for instance, when the TD was new) this would have been received with acclaim – but not in 1953. With a top speed of just 80mph the TF could not really compete, so from mid-1954 (and without a flourish – it was never officially launched in the UK) the engine was enlarged to

63bhp/1466cc. This version was called the TF1500 (badges to that effect were usually found on bonnet sides), and was an 85mph machine which was better, if still not competitive with the opposition.

Agile, elegant in its own semi-traditional way, and definitely endowed with all the right Abingdon sports car genes, the TF held the line for less than two years.

If nothing else, for enthusiasts it is noted as the last MG to use a traditional body style and to use a Nuffield as opposed to a BMC engine. Even so, what goes around, comes around – once the classic car movement had matured, TFs became more desirable than the TD, and have remained that way. The TF is perhaps the prettier car.

TF followed TD in 1953. This is the TF 1500 model of 1954.

SPECIFICATION	
BODY STYLES: sports car	
PRODUCTION: 6200/3400	
ENGINE & TRANSMISSION: 1250cc/1466cc, 4cyl ohv, 4sp man, f/r	
POWER: 57bhp @ 5500rpm/63bhp @ 5000rpm	
MAX SPEED (MPH): 80/85	
0-60MPH (SEC): 18.9/16.3	
SUSPENSION & BRAKES: coil ifs, leaf rear, drums f&r	
LENGTH (IN)/WEIGHT (LB): 147/1930	
LAUNCH PRICE: £780	

Magnette ZA/ZB 1953-58

MG revived a famous name of the 1930s, Magnette, in 1953, though on a four-door saloon car rather than a sports car. As a direct replacement for the old YA/YB type, it was different in every way, and qualified as the very first of the "BMC-MGs", as opposed to the "Nuffield-MGs" which had dominated the scene at the Abingdon factory since the mid-1930s.

Engineered in parallel with the Wolseley 4/44 (which had appeared a year earlier), the Magnette had a smart semi-fastback four-door monocoque structure, to which a curved version of the MG grille had been neatly blended. Sufficient wood and leather inside, along with a remote control centre gearchange, made it very acceptable, though the original fascia panel, in metal but painted to resemble wood, was a cheapening touch.

This was the very first BMC car to use the all-fresh B-Series engine, four-speed gearbox and hypoid back axle – all of which would eventually go into the MGA. Purists were horrified at first but soon realised that the ZA's performance

MG Magnette ZA, 1954.

was quite acceptable: they also found out how much the engine could be tuned for motorsport use. In any case, the ZA had rack-and-pinion steering and good open-road handling, which made up for a lot.

Things improved further over time. A proper wooden fascia arrived at the end of 1954, and at the end of 1956 the ZB took over, this car having a touch more power, the (unsuccessful) option of Manumatic two-pedal control, and the

Varitone alternative, where the rear window was much enlarged and a two-tone colour scheme was available.

Monotone Varitones (and, yes, there were such things!) with manual transmissions were the best of a good bunch. Most people enjoyed the best-handling and briskest-performing MG saloon so far produced. Years later they still would, as the very different Austin-based Magnette Mk III which followed was a great disappointment.

A Magnette leading a Jaguar Mk I and a Wolseley 4/44 on the circuit.

MGA 1500 1955-59

Although it took MG 20 years to shake off its 1930s technical traditions, the result, first seen in 1955, was worth it. Conceived in 1952, when MG wanted to use TD/TF running gear under its shapely skin, the MGA eventually went on sale with BMC B-Series engine, transmission and rear axle instead, these being close relations of those in use in the contemporary Magnette ZA.

Significantly larger than the TF1500 which it replaced, the MGA used a rock-solid separate chassis frame, with box-section side and cross-bracing members, to which TF-type independent front suspension, along with rack-and-pinion steering, was attached. The sleek full-width two-seater body shell was all steel (the first-ever for an MG sports car), with detachable side-curtains and an enclosed boot compartment (another MG sports car innovation). A heater was still an optional extra, as were centre-lock wire-spoke wheels and, eventually, a lift-off hardtop.

For the MGA, the B-Series engine produced 72bhp (68bhp at launch, raised

The MGA was launched with a 1500cc engine in 1955.

very shortly afterwards), which was enough to guarantee a top speed of nearly 100mph, a huge advance on the TF1500. Overdrive was not available – nor would it be until the MGB arrived seven years later. From October 1956 there was an alternative bubble-top coupé derivative, which had wind-up windows. Warm and civilised, this apparently suffered from interior noise problems.

By comparison with any previous MG sports car, the MGA, though perhaps too

heavy, was a huge advance, with more performance, more comfort, and handling as good as that of any TD or TF. Once again, it raised MG sales to new heights, before being superseded by the MGA 1600 in 1959.

The coupé version of the MGA.

An MGA on the 1956 Alpine Rally.

MGA 1600/1600 MKII 1959-62

In mid-1959 MG replaced the original MGA with the MGA 1600, which looked exactly the same as before but came with a number of useful improvements.

The engine was enlarged to a more meaty 1588cc, giving 78bhp, and at the same time Lockheed front disc brakes were added – these being totally different from the brakes on the Twin-Cam model.

As before, Roadster and bubble-top coupé versions were marketed, and sales continued to be particularly strong in North America.

The third phase of MGA production came in June 1961 (so this last type would be in production for little more than a year), when the 1600 Mk II appeared. Compared with the 1600, the Mk II had an 86bhp 1622cc version of the B-Series engine. Although there were no sheet metal style changes, there was a new and slightly recessed front grille, and horizontal-pattern instead of vertical pattern tail lamps. This was the fastest of the pushrod-engined MGAs.

But not the rarest. Following the demise of the Twin-Cam, MG found itself with several hundred spare sets of chassis components. This led to the rather crafty marketing of the 1600 and 1600 Mk II "De Luxe" models, which effectively had Twin-Cam chassis, centre-lock disc wheels and four-wheel disc brake installations, but were fitted with the ordinary pushrod engines of the day. Though they were no faster in a straight line than the mainstream cars, they were undoubtedly the best-equipped, and best-balanced, of the family.

In total, more than 100,000 MGAs of all types were produced before the new monocoque MGB took over, which proves just what a successful and well-liked car this was. With great looks and good handling, the only complaints were that this car was either over-heavy or under-engined for its task.

MGA 1600. Recessed grille and horizontal tail lamps show that this car is a Mk II.

Dashboard of the 1600 Mk II.

SPECIFICATION

BODY STYLES: sports car, sports coupé

PRODUCTION: 31,501/8719

ENGINE & TRANSMISSION: 1588cc/1622cc, 4cyl ohv, 4sp man, f/r

POWER: 79bhp @ 5600rpm/86bhp @ 5500rpm

MAX SPEED (MPH): 101/101

0-60MPH (SEC): 14.2/13.7

SUSPENSION & BRAKES: coil ifs, leaf rear, disc f/drum r (disc f/disc r on De Luxe)

LENGTH (IN)/WEIGHT (LB): 156/2015

LAUNCH PRICE: £940

MGA Twin Cam 1958-60

Although the Twin Cam set out with a great purpose – to provide an all-conquering "class" car for motorsport, it ended up as an unreliable indulgence which BMC had to kill off because of high warranty claims and falling sales.

Based on the mainstream MGA, but visually different because of its Dunlop centre-lock disc (not wire) wheels, the Twin Cam had a unique twin overhead camshaft engine of 108bhp/1588cc, which drew its inspiration from Jaguar's XK power unit and the Coventry-Climax race units. Only the block came from the pushrod B-Series, the rest being special.

The rack-and-pinion steering gear had to be relocated to clear the bulky engine, and four-wheel Dunlop disc brakes kept the performance in check. There was plenty of that – the top speed was at least 113mph, and bubble-top coupés may have been even faster – but the selling price was always high (£1266 in 1958),

MGA Twin Cam had Dunlop centre-lock wheels.

and unreliability problems were legion.

Sales started well, but by late 1959 they had nearly dried up. Engine trouble, and oil consumption problems, led to the car's withdrawal in March 1960 though by that time solutions had been discovered. Bolstered by this knowledge, many Twin Cams have survived, and they are much coveted.

Inlet side of the MGA Twin Cam's unique engine.

SPECIFICATION

BODY STYLES: sports car, sports coupé

PRODUCTION: 2111

ENGINE & TRANSMISSION: 1588cc, 4cyl 2ohc, 4sp man, f/r

POWER: 108bhp @ 6700rpm

MAX SPEED (MPH): 113

0-60MPH (SEC): 9.1

SUSPENSION & BRAKES: coil ifs, leaf rear, discs f&r

LENGTH (IN)/WEIGHT (LB): 156/2185

LAUNCH PRICE: £1266

An MGA Twin Cam waits for its crew to sign on for the 1962 Morecambe Rally. Alongside is an Austin-Healey 3000 and ahead a TR4.

Magnette Mk III/IV 1959-68

It's difficult to be kind to this car, which took over from the much-admired Magnette ZB and all too soon reduced that badge to ridicule once again. The new Magnette Mk III had nothing to with MG except for its badging, as it was merely one of the five derivatives of the Austin-Morris B-Series Farina-styled machines which were rolling out across the network. It was not built at Abing-don but at Cowley, and true-blue MG enthusiasts would have nothing to do with it.

Based on the mundame Austin A55 saloon which had just been launched, the Magnette Mk III had the same all-steel four-door saloon monocoque, the same lumbering chassis with too-narrow tracks, and an MG grille. The B-Series engine produced 64bhp – exactly the same as the outgoing Magnette ZB – and there was a walnut veneer fascia, with the speedometer ahead of the driver's eyes; there was no rev-counter, though. Except in detail, all this was identical with the new Riley 4/68 too.

Like the other B-Series Farinas, the Magnette was quite spacious inside, but it didn't handle at all well and certainly was not a "driver's car". BMC clearly realised this so, from late 1961, the Mk IV took over, which was certainly an improvement but still far from brilliant.

For the Mk IV the engine capacity was increased to 1622cc, giving 68bhp, and automatic transmission was offered as an option. Equally important, under the same basic body shell the Mk IV had a longer wheelbase and wider tracks, plus anti-roll bars at front and rear, so it handled much better than before. So too did the Riley 4/72.

All in all, the Mk IV was better than the Mk III, but not a patch on the Magnette ZB. It tells us a lot about BMC's mark-eting skills that it carried on selling until 1968 with virtually no improvement over the 1961 specification.

MG Magnette Mk IV, 1961, another of BMC's multi-badged "Farina" range.

SPECIFICATION

BODY STYLES: saloon

PRODUCTION: 16,6748/14,356

ENGINE & TRANSMISSION: 1489cc/1622cc, 4cyl ohv, 4sp man or auto, f/r

POWER: 64bhp @ 4800rpm/68bhp @ 5000rpm

MAX SPEED (MPH): 84/86

0-60MPH (SEC): 20.6/19.5

SUSPENSION & BRAKES: coil ifs, leaf rear, drums f&r

LENGTH (IN)/WEIGHT (LB): 178/2507

LAUNCH PRICE: £1013

Midget MK I/II/III/IV 1961-74

Although "Midget" was MG's most famous model title of the 1930s and 1940s, it was shelved in 1955 when the TF1500 was dropped. Six years later, when MG developed a new badge-engineered version of the Austin-Healey Sprite, the name was revived. This, in fact, was the first monocoque-hulled MG sports car.

Except in tiny details of trim and badging, the Sprite and Midget of the day were always identical, though Midgets tended to sell better in certain export

The MG Midget, 1961.

SPECIFICATION

BODY STYLES: sports car

PRODUCTION: 25,681/26,601/ 13,722/100,246

ENGINE & TRANSMISSION: 948cc/1098cc/1275cc, 4cyl ohv, 4sp man, f/r

POWER: 46bhp @ 5500-65bhp @ 6000rpm

MAX SPEED (MPH): 86-94

0-60MPH (SEC): 20.0-14.1

SUSPENSION & BRAKES: coil ifs, leaf rear, drums f&r (disc f/drum r for 1963 onwards)

LENGTH (IN)/WEIGHT (LB): 138/1525

LAUNCH PRICE: £670

territories where sports car tradition counted for a lot. The Mk I Midget was launched one week after the arrival of the Mk II Sprite, but thereafter the two cars tracked each other until the Sprite/Austin Sprite breathed its last in 1971.

Midget Mk Is had 46bhp/948cc and quarter-elliptic leaf rear suspension, then in October 1962 they got 56bhp/1098cc

Simple dash of the 1961 Midget.

Mk I Midget with optional hard top and with its sliding side windows in position.

Mk II Midget of 1964 gained winding windows.

The dashboard of the MK II Midget, now more refined.

and front-wheel disc brakes. Mk IIs arrived in spring 1964, with 59bhp, half-elliptic leaf-spring rear suspension and wind-up windows, Mk IIIs followed in late 1966 with 65bhp/1275cc, then Mk IVs appeared in late 1969 with Rostyle wheels and different equipment.

All such Midgets had chrome bumpers, rather cramped two-seater cockpits, and

optional removable hardtops. Except for slight decorative changes, the only obvious visual differences were from 1964 (wind-up windows/larger screen), and from early 1972 (round-profile rear wheel arches instead of flat-top profile).

From late 1974 this Midget would be replaced by the similar-looking Midget 1500, which came with the Triumph

Spitfire engine and black impact-resistant bumpers.

The A-Series-engined Midgets sold well, all of them being appealing, effective and very tuneable little sports cars with nimble handling. It is generally agreed that the 1275cc-engined cars were the best of the bunch, and thousands have been preserved.

The MG Midget Mk III, 1966, with engine enlarged to 1275cc.

Midget Mk IV arrived in 1969. It had a black grille and sills.

From 1972 the Mk IV Midget had these rounded rear wheel arches.

1100/1300 1962-73

Announced at the same time as the new front wheel drive Morris 1100, the MG 1100 a tuned-up and better-trimmed derivative of that car, and was always built alongside it at Cowley. Apart from having the archetypal MG front grille, and a higher standard of trim and furnishing inside the cabin, the MG looked almost exactly like the Morris (and, of course, the Austin 1100 which would follow); the speedometer display, in fact, was Austin 1100- type.

All this family shared the same Farina-styled monocoque hull – in two-door saloon or four-door saloon forms but with no other versions – and all used the revolutionary new all-independent "riding on liquid" Hydrolastic suspension. Front-wheel disc brakes, with rear

MG 1100 four-door, 1962.

drums, were fitted to all types. The A-Series engine was transversely mounted, and in the MG's case was usually fitted with twin SU carburettors.

Unlike the larger Magnette with which it shared badging and showrooms, the MG1100 was an appealing little car – with 85mph initially it was brisk rather than fast, with soft suspension and a strange, rather floaty ride.

Two-door types were "export only" until 1968, after which there was an about-face in product planning: they became standard after that! Early developments included fitting a proper tree-wood fascia from early 1963, and reclining front seats became optional early in 1966. In mid-1967, for the last few months of the Mk I's life, there was a 58bhp single-SU 1275cc engine option, of which 564 were produced.

From October 1967, Mk IIs took over from the Mk I, complete with chopped-back tail fins, and optional AP automatic transmission from 1967 to 1969. 1100 Mk IIs were rare, and the model was dropped in March 1968, but the 1300s were progressively improved from 1967. The 58bhp engine was upgraded to a

MG 1100 demonstrates its Hydrolastic suspension.

twin-carburettor 65bhp version from April 1968, and an all-synchromesh manual gearbox was phased in by mid-summer of that year.

Then, from late 1968, the 1300 became Mk II, with a twin-SU 70bhp engine, closer-ratio gears, radial ply tyres and a brand-new instrument display featuring circular instruments (and a rev counter, at last!). This was not a unique specification, as the Austin/Morris 1300GTs shared it for a time.

Naturally, and as expected, the 1300 Mk II was not only the best, but also the best-liked, of all this family of front wheel drive ADO 16 types. It had the attractive combination of performance (97mph, flat out), ride, roadholding and character which was lost when future, different, MG saloons came along.

MG 1300 two-door, 1967.

Under the bonnet of the MG 1300.

SPECIFICATION

BODY STYLES: saloon

PRODUCTION: 124,474/32,935

ENGINE & TRANSMISSION: 1098cc/1275cc, 4cyl ohv, 4sp man or auto, f/f

POWER: 55bhp @ 5500rpm-70bhp @ 6000rpm

MAX SPEED (MPH): 85-97

0-60MPH (SEC): 18.4-14.1

SUSPENSION & BRAKES: Hydro ifs, Hydro irs, disc fr/drum r

LENGTH (IN)/WEIGHT (LB): 147/1820

LAUNCH PRICE: £799

MGB and MGB GT 1962-80

Everyone, surely, knows that the legendary MGB was MG's best-selling and longest-lived sports car of all time. It was the world's best-selling sports car for many years, even after it was discontinued, and it was not until the 2000s that the Mazda MX-5/Miata took away that crown.

The MGB was based on a sturdy new steel monocoque body/chassis unit, but much of its running gear was developed directly from that of the long-running MGA. The engine was a 95bhp/1798cc stretch, the gearbox and rear axle were the same, and the front suspension was also very similar. As before, disc or wire-

MGB in left hand drive form.

spoke wheels were to choice, while front-wheel disc brakes were standard.

The new car was attractive and immensely strong. There were wind-up windows in all types (the MGA Roadster had used removable side curtains), and the car handled just as well as the MGA had done. Only the open-top roadster was available at first.

Evolution was steady. Laycock overdrive became optional almost at once, the engine gained a five-bearing crankshaft from late 1964, and a very smart and practical fastback/hatchback coupé, the MGB GT, appeared in the autumn of 1965. After a stronger rear axle was standardised in 1965, the specification then settled down until the Mk II appeared in late 1967.

Mk IIs featured an all-synchromesh gearbox as standard (it was shared with the contemporary MGC), Laycock overdrive was still optional, and a Borg Warner automatic gearbox became a new transmission alternative; there were no significant changes to the engine or to the cars' performance.

British Leyland took control in 1968. From that point, and for the next twelve years, the MGB was subject to many cosmetic makeovers, though none to the

MGB GT arrived in 1965.

performance, and because of exhaust emission regulations engine power in the USA cars gradually eroded away. From late 1974 the massive "black bumper" specification was phased in, and the cars' weight went up. By 1980, when it was finally dropped, the MGB was not nearly as good a car as the early Mk IIs had been, and it did not handle as well either.

Everyone has their own opinion of the MGB, but most agreed that it was right for its time, in terms of handling,

performance and image. The tragedy was that British Leyland never lavished attention on it in the way they did with the rival Triumph concern.

Useful hatchback of the MGB GT.

This is the MGB Berlinetta offered by Jacques Coune of Brussels, an attractive variation on the standard car.

SPECIFICATION

BODY STYLES: sports car, sports coupé

PRODUCTION: 513,272, all MGB types

ENGINE & TRANSMISSION: 1798cc, 4cyl ohv, 4sp man, o/d or auto, f/r

POWER: 95bhp @ 5400rpm

MAX SPEED (MPH): 103

0-60MPH (SEC): 12.2

SUSPENSION & BRAKES: coil ifs, leaf rear, disc f/drum r

LENGTH (IN)/WEIGHT (LB): 153/2030 (GT 2260)

LAUNCH PRICE: £834

MGB cockpit was spacious and could accommodate tall drivers.

Plenty of room in front of and around the MGB's simple engine.

MGB Mk II, 1970, with revised grille and syncrhomesh on first gear.

In 1974 the MGB received these black bumpers and a raised ride height.

MGC 1967-69

BMC (not British Leyland, who killed it off in short order) clearly saw the MGC as a spiritual successor to the old Austin-Healey 3000, for as one model disappeared, the other came on the scene. Based on the modern MGB monocoque, but with many front-end changes, the MGC had a re-designed Healey 3000-style six-cylinder engine.

Although it looked very like the MGB – only bonnet bulges and larger wheels/tyres gave the game away – the MGC was very different under the skin. The lengthy and heavy 2912cc engine ruined the weight distribution, though the new all-synchromesh gearbox was an advance. As with the latest MGB, overdrive and Borg Warner automatic transmission were options, and there was of course a choice of open roadster or fixed-head GT bodywork. Due to lack of space up front, the independent front suspension was by longitudinal torsion bars in place of coil springs.

Pundits didn't like the early cars,

MGC, 1967, with characteristic bonnet bulge to accommodate the six-cylinder engine.

MGC GT.

SPECIFICATION

BODY STYLES: sports car, sports coupé

PRODUCTION: 8976

ENGINE & TRANSMISSION: 2912cc, 6cyl ohv, 4sp man, o/d or auto, f/r

POWER: 145bhp @ 5250rpm

MAX SPEED (MPH): 120

0-60MPH (SEC): 10.0

SUSPENSION & BRAKES: coil ifs, leaf rear, drums f&r

LENGTH (IN)/WEIGHT (LB): 153/2460

LAUNCH PRICE: £1102

dubbing them nose-heavy and unresponsive, so MG worked hard to make improvements.

From autumn 1968 there were wholesale reshuffles of gearbox ratios and overall gearing, but this wasn't enough to forge a new image. British Leyland cut its losses by killing the MGC after two years on sale, even

though almost 9,000 had been sold.

There's no hiding the fact that the MGC didn't handle as well as the MGB or the Austin-Healey 3000, yet if you wanted sports-car motoring at limited engine speeds, without effort, then it was a good contender. Perversely, MGCs are better liked today than they were in the late 1960s.

MGB GT V8 1973-76

It was only after Ken Costello's private enterprise V8 conversions had proved their point that British Leyland authorised the development of a V8-engined version of the MGB. Although the light-alloy Rover V8 (which was virtually in Range Rover tune at this time) could easily be fitted to roadster or GT types, for marketing reasons the only car to go

on sale was the MGB GT V8. Except for a handful of development cars which were sent to North America, every production car was built with right hand drive, for sale in the UK.

The conversion was simple enough – once a suitable twin-SU carburation set-up had been evolved (to fit snugly under the bonnet), the 90-degree V8 engine

fitted easily into the existing engine bay; as it actually weighed no more than the normal 1798cc engine, no significant changes were needed to spring or damper settings. Overdrive transmission was standard, and unlike the MGC there was no automatic transmission option. Radial ply tyres were standard as were cast alloy road wheels.

Because this was a hurried, low-budget project there were no style changes, either to the exterior or to the cabin, and it was only the badging which gave the game away. Like other MGBs of the period, this car was given the "black bumper" and raised ride height treatment from the autumn of 1974, which did little for the looks and nothing at all for the handling.

Although this was the fastest MGB-based car of all, it was always handicapped by a high price. When announced, the MGB GT V8 cost £2294, which compared badly with, for instance, the Ford Capri 3000GXL's £1824. British Leyland put out stories that low sales were due to a lack of engine supplies, but this was nonsense.

Here, unhappily, was another British Leyland car which was better than its initial reputation suggested, for it rode and handled as well as any other MGB but was much faster and delivered its performance effortlessly. In later years it was to become a collectors' piece, and deservedly so.

SPECIFICATION

BODY STYLES: sports coupé

PRODUCTION: 2591

ENGINE & TRANSMISSION: 3528cc, V8cyl ohv, 4sp man, o/d, f/r

POWER: 137bhp @ 5000rpm

MAX SPEED (MPH): 124

0-60MPH (SEC): 8.6

SUSPENSION & BRAKES: coil ifs, leaf rear, disc f/drum r

LENGTH (IN)/WEIGHT (LB): 153/2387

LAUNCH PRICE: £2294

MGB GT V8, 1973.

Midget 1500 1974-79

The final iteration of the Midget was introduced in October 1974, and was not the car which its original development team would have wished. Faced, however, with ever-tightening exhaust emission and safety/crash-test regulations in the North American market, this was the only way that its popular sports car's career could be extended.

The old Midget Mk IV and its BMC A-Series engine could not meet new emissions requirements, so, using as a basis the pre-1972 "square-wheelarch" Midget (the "round-wheel-arch" car could not meet the new crash-test targets), the revised car was given a lightly-modified Triumph Spitfire 1500 engine and its all-synchromesh gearbox (which was also used in the Morris Marina). Vast but carefully shaped black polyurethane bumpers were fitted at front and rear, and the

Last of the Midgets, the 1500 of 1974.

SPECIFICATION

BODY STYLES: sports car

PRODUCTION: 73,899

ENGINE & TRANSMISSION: 1493cc, 4cyl ohv, 4sp man, f/r

POWER: 66bhp @ 5500rpm

MAX SPEED (MPH): 101

0-60MPH (SEC): 12.3

SUSPENSION & BRAKES: coil ifs, leaf rear, disc f/drum r

LENGTH (IN)/WEIGHT (LB): 141/1700

LAUNCH PRICE: £1351

ride height was raised to an appropriate level. A front anti-roll bar was standard, as were Rostyle wheels; centre-lock wires were available as an optional extra.

The result was the fastest Midget of all (it was the only derivative which could beat 100mph), but one which did not handle very well or even look as good as its ancestors had once done.

Nevertheless, this was a car which kept the pot boiling for several more years (an average of about 15,000 cars was built annually in 1975 to 1978 inclusive), most of the production as ever being sold to North America.

Sales fell away steadily in 1979, so British Leyland announced not only that Abingdon would close in 1980, but that the Midget would be killed

off at the end of 1979. Thus it was, but so many cars remained unsold in the USA that deliveries continued over there for nearly another year.

Because this version used a Triumph engine, MG fanatics do not remember it fondly; yet it was significantly faster than any "real" Midget and had an all-synchromesh gearbox too. It takes a lot to satisfy some people...

MIDAS

Harold Dermott's D & H Fibreglass Techniques Ltd took over the defunct Mini-Marcos project in 1975, set about re-engineering it, and turned it from a rather scruffy minimal-motoring kit car into something more like a properly sorted small coupé, which happened to lean heavily on Mini/Mini-Cooper expertise for its running gear. Richard Oakes re-styled the car, placing the headlamps further inboard, and altering the side and window profile.

Cars called Midas Bronze were sold as fairly basic body shells, fully trimmed and furnished shells, or as complete cars, so it was often difficult to put a typical price on an ensemble. The business originally operated from a mill at Greenfield, near Oldham, but then moved to Corby, Northants in 1982. The even better Midas Gold was introduced in 1985, but after a fire devastated the premises in 1989 the company went into liquidation. GTM then took over the remants of the project in 1991.

Bronze 1978-88

Quoting a settled specification for this car is rather like trying to pin jelly to a wall, for different varieties of BMC Mini running gear and suspensions were used, the style changed subtly over the years, and the inventive Dermott made continual changes.

The basic structure was a two-seater GRP monocoque coupé, with two passenger doors and a lift-up hatchback. Transversely-mounted Mini engine and gearbox, and "dry" front suspension units, were fitted at the front, though Midas provided a specially-engineered

SPECIFICATION

BODY STYLES: sports coupé

PRODUCTION: c.350

ENGINE & TRANSMISSION: 848cc/998cc, 4cyl ohv, 4sp man, o/d or auto, f/r

POWER: 34bhp @ 5500rpm/41bhp @ 5400rpm/55bhp @ 5800rpm

MAX SPEED (MPH): 75 (E) -90 (E)

0-60MPH (SEC): not measured

SUSPENSION & BRAKES: rubber ifs, coil irs, disc f/drum r

LENGTH (IN)/WEIGHT (LB): 137/1120

LAUNCH PRICE: £650 (fully-trimmed shell), c.£1200 (complete car)

The Mini-based Midas Bronze.

galvanised steel sub-frame to mount it all. At the rear, early cars had standard Mini suspension at first, but a special coil spring and trailing arm set-up (with adjustable dampers) followed.

By the early 1980s Midas was confident enough to exhibit its cars at the British motor shows. They now used the standard Mini Metro power-pack, which was of course a direct develop-

ment of the classic Mini layout.

By the time the style had changed to incorporate flared wheelarches, and cars were being built with cast alloy wheels, the Midas was a very purposeful-looking car, light years ahead of the old Mini-Marcos from which it had stemmed. From 1985 it was supplanted by the Midas Gold, of which a cabriolet derivative was also available.

MINI

Although the Mini did not officially become a brand on its own until 1969, I have treated all Minis that way. In fact BMC introduced two tiny and identical transverse-engined front wheel drive saloon cars, badging them as Austin Se7en and Morris Mini-Minor, in August 1959, and it was only in the face of determined preferences by the public that these were eventually known as Austin Mini and Morris Mini from early 1962. Except in badging, and in the location of dealer showrooms, the two types were always identical.

The first higher-performance Mini, the 997cc engined Mini-Cooper, followed in the autumn of 1961, the very first 1071cc Mini-Cooper S followed in early 1963, and in 1964 not only the 970cc and 1275cc Mini-Cooper S models but also the 998cc Mini-Cooper all came along.

Other derivatives were badged as Rileys and Wolseleys (these are described separately), vans appeared, and there was the cute Mini Moke as well.

Soon after British Leyland was set up, management decided to expand the brand and to give it a separate identity. From late 1969, therefore, the Minis lost their separate Austin and Morris badges and received significant trim and equipment updates. At the same time British Leyland introduced the Clubman types with the elongated square nose..

Although the range gradually contracted, and sales declined, Minis continued on sale through the 1970s, 1980s and 1990s, until the last "classic" Mini of all was produced in October 2000. In the meantime BMW of Germany had taken control of the Rover Group, and therefore of the Mini brand. When the acrimonious split from Rover came in 2000, BMW rid itself of Rover but retained the Mini brand and introduced a brand-new generation in 2001 which went on selling strongly as the 2000s progressed.

All in all, when assembly of hat became known as "classic" Minis ended, an impressive grand total of 5,387,862 Minis of all shapes, sizes, badges, and trim levels had been produced through four decades.

Mk I 1959-67

Everyone knows everything about the Mini, right? That it was Issigonis's masterpiece. That it was the first to combine the front-engine, front wheel drive formula into a tiny package. That it went on to sell more than five million. But all that took time. It was two years before any engine except the 848cc power unit was used.

The first cars were two-door saloons, built at Longbridge as Austin Se7ens, and at Cowley as Morris Mini-Minors. The standard specification included 34bhp 848cc engines, rubber suspension, tiny 10in wheels, sliding windows in the doors, and drop-down boot lids. The interior trim and equipment were

Mk I Mini, the Austin Se7en version with crinkly grille.

SPECIFICATION

BODY STYLES: saloon, estate, light commercials

PRODUCTION TOTAL: 5,387,862 Minis, all types

ENGINE & TRANSMISSION: 848cc, 4cyl ohv, 4sp man or auto, f/f

POWER: 34bhp @ 5500rpm

MAX SPEED (MPH): 72

0-60MPH (SEC): 27.1

SUSPENSION & BRAKES: rubber ifs, rubber irs, drums f&r (Hydro F and R from 1964)

LENGTH (IN)/WEIGHT (LB): 120/1380

LAUNCH PRICE: £497

cheap-and-cheerful, with only one central instrument, and with a very sharply raked steering wheel.

The longer-wheelbase (by four inches) "woody" estate car versions (Austin Countryman/Morris Traveller) arrived in September 1960, complete with twin sideways-opening rear doors, with vans and even a tiny pick-up all in the growing range; all-metal estates appeared in October 1962. This was a time when basics, de Luxes, Supers and Super De Luxes appeared with frequency.

From September 1964, Hydrolastic

suspension (inter connected front-to-rear) replaced rubber on saloons, but not on estate types, and AP automatic

The Morris Mini-Minor: note the different grille pattern.

Instrument and controls of an early Mini, with the straight gear lever.

Mini Traveller.

The Mini van suited many purposes.

An Austin Seven being used to demonstrate the abilities of Dunlop tyres on an ice rink in 1962.

transmission was optional from October 1965. By that time a quarter of a million Minis of all types were built every year, and they had built up a following in all walks of life.

The Mini's winning combination of tiny but ingenious packaging, marvellous handling, responsive steering and an enormously appealing character was irresistible. It was only the continuing dodgy build quality problems which let the side down.

Original-type Minis were replaced by Mk IIs in October 1967.

Mk II/III 1967-92

In October 1967, the Mini progressed to MkII, with a choice of 848cc or 998cc engines, an enlarged rear window, different front grille, larger tail lamps, and enhanced trim. As before, a four-speed manual gearbox was standard and

SPECIFICATION

BODY STYLES: saloon, light commercials

PRODUCTION: see Mk I

ENGINE & TRANSMISSION: 848cc/998cc, 4cyl ohv, 4sp man or auto, f/f

POWER: 34bhp @ 5500rpm/38bhp @ 5250rpm

MAX SPEED (MPH): 72/75

0-60MPH (SEC): 27.1/26.2

SUSPENSION & BRAKES: Hydro ifs, Hydro irs, drums f&r (rubber F and R from late 1969)

LENGTH (IN)/WEIGHT (LB): 120/1395

LAUNCH PRICE: £509

Mark II Mini with restyled grille but retaining external door hinges and sliding windows.

the AP automatic 'box was optional. Hydrolastic suspension was standard, as were sliding windows in the doors. There was still no Hydrolastic on estate cars (and no sign, now, of pick-ups).

By summer 1968 an all-synchromesh manual gearbox was fitted to all models, but the major change came in November 1969. At this point what was known as the "ADO20" body shell was adopted, complete with wind-up windows, concealed door hinges, and larger door apertures. More significantly, there was a reversion to rubber ("dry") suspension. At this point, individual "Austin" and "Morris" badges disappeared. Henceforth, all such cars were simply "Minis". The new basic models were known as Mini 850 and Mini 1000 and were only sold as saloons; estate cars were now a version of the Mini Clubman.

This was the basis of the two-door Mini saloons which then carried on in production for another thirty years – long after the period covered in this book – though in that time there would many trim changes and specification improvements, many special editions, a 1098cc engine from 1975, front disc brakes, and 12in wheels.

Names and detail spec changes came and went. For 1979-80, for instance,

The Mark III Mini 850. This is the base model, with no frills whatsoever.

there was an 850 City, an entry-level model, plus an 850 Super De Luxe, but all 850s were killed off when the Mini Metro appeared. This was when the Mini City gained a 998cc engine, and it

would live on for twelve more years. The Mayfair would arrive in 1982, the Sprite would follow that, and a profusion of Special Editions kept interest alive until the end.

Cooper Mk I 1961-69

Inspired by an F1 constructor, but produced at Longbridge by BMC, the Mini-Cooper was the first of the higher-performance Minis. Available only as a two-door saloon, but badged as an Austin or a Morris, this was an endearing little basic competition car, soon to be trumped by the even more excitingly specified Cooper S.

Compared with ordinary Minis, the Mini-Cooper had a long-stroke twin-SU 55bhp 997cc version of the engine, closer gear ratios, a remote-control gear change, and tiny front-wheel disc brakes.

SPECIFICATION

BODY STYLES: saloon

PRODUCTION: 24,860/39,364

ENGINE & TRANSMISSION: 997cc/998cc, 4cyl ohv, 4sp man, f/f

POWER: 55bhp@ 6000rpm/55bhp @ 5800rpm

MAX SPEED (MPH): 85/90

0-60MPH (SEC): 17.2/14.8

SUSPENSION & BRAKES: rubber ifs, rubber irs, disc f/drum r (Hydro f and r from 1964)

LENGTH (IN)/WEIGHT (LB): 120/1440

LAUNCH PRICE: £679

A Mini-Cooper holding off opposition in the form of a Ford Anglia, an MG 1100 and a Jaguar Mk 2 in **The Motor** *Six Hours race in 1962.*

Though better than the drums, these discs were still liable to fade and would soon be improved.

This specification did not last long: from January 1964, a shorter-stroke and higher-revving 55bhp 998cc engine was adopted, and from the autumn of 1964 Hydrolastic suspension (inter-connected, front to rear) replaced the original rubber suspension. For motorsport purposes many optional extras were available, and were often fitted on assembly. Reclining front seats (popular) were optional from 1965. On the other hand, AP automatic transmission was never available.

Mini-Coopers had a duotone colour scheme (the roof panel usually being white, or black, depending on the main body colour), along with different grilles and extra quarter bumpers for identification.Inside the cars, there was a new three-instrument fascia.

Fashionable at first, but overshadowed by the Mini-Cooper S from the mid-1960s, the Mini-Cooper carried on until late 1967 when it became Mk II.

The Mini-Cooper Mk I was introduced in 1961.

Cooper S (970, 1071, 1275) 1963-67

This most specialised Mini came along to boost the motorsport potential of the car, and was turned into a formidable pocket rocket. Using technology first blooded in Formula Junior racing, the engines were higher-revving, deeper-breathing, and more robust.

Compared with the Mini-Cooper, the Cooper S had larger front disc brakes, radial ply tyres as standard and, from late 1965, wider 4.5in wheel rims. More and more optional extras were available as time passed. As with the Mini-Cooper, there were Austin and Morris versions which seemed to sell equally well.

Mini Cooper S, with perforated wheels and an S over the bonnet badge.

SPECIFICATION

BODY STYLES: saloon

PRODUCTION: 963/4031/14,313

ENGINE & TRANSMISSION:
970cc/1071cc/1275cc, 4cyl ohv, 4sp man, f/f

POWER: 65bhp @ 6500rpm/70bhp @ 6000rpm/76bhp @ 5800rpm

MAX SPEED (MPH): 92 (E)/95/97

0-60MPH (SEC): not measured/12.9/10.9

SUSPENSION & BRAKES: rubber ifs, rubber irs, disc f/drum r (Hydro f and r from 1964)

LENGTH (IN)/WEIGHT (LB): 120/1440

LAUNCH PRICE: £671

Paddy Hopkirk at the wheel of a 1071cc Mini Cooper S in 1963.

All models were fitted with twin SU carburettors The first version was the 70bhp 1071cc (1963-64), which was soon displaced in 1964 by twins, the 65bhp 970cc and 76bhp 1275cc types. The 1071cc car was good enough to win the 1964 Monte Carlo rally (with Paddy Hopkirk driving it), the short-stroke, high-revving 970S (1964-65) was a specialist "class car" for 1-litre motor-sport, while the 1275S (1964 onwards) was the all-can-do road car, rally car, and successful race car.

All 1071Ss had rubber suspension, all but a few 970Ss had rubber suspension, but from late 1964 the 1275S was fitted with Hydrolastic suspension. Among the development changes for the 1275S model were optional reclining front seats from 1965, with twin fuel tanks (11 gallons capacity) and an engine oil cooler standard from January 1966.

By general acclaim, this was the best of all Mini derivatives, and its legend lived on, such that many more Cooper S cars seem to have been "created" in more recent years than were originally produced. The 1275S sold better as time passed, and was displaced by the Mk II in 1967. Forty years on, it still provides spirited motoring.

A Cooper S holding off a Chevrolet Camaro at the Spa circuit in 1967.

Cooper Mk II 1967-69

Austin Mini-Cooper Mk II, 1967.

SPECIFICATION

BODY STYLES: saloon

PRODUCTION: 16,396

ENGINE & TRANSMISSION: 998cc, 4cyl ohv, 4sp man, f/f

POWER: 55bhp @ 5800rpm

MAX SPEED (MPH): 90

0-60MPH (SEC): 14.8

SUSPENSION & BRAKES: Hydro ifs, Hydro irs, disc f/drum r

LENGTH (IN)/WEIGHT (LB): 120/1440

LAUNCH PRICE: £631

From late 1967, the Cooper became Mk II, picking up the body changes already described under Mini Mk II. All Mk IIs had Hydrolastic suspension. An all-synchromesh gearbox was standardised in summer 1968.

This was the last of the Mini-Coopers, there being no equivalent in the "de-badged" Mini range in 1969/70.

Cooper S Mk II/III 1967-71

When the mainstream Mini range became Mk II, so did the 1275S (though the 970S and 1071S types had been dropped years earlier). As with the other cars, Austin and Morris badges were retained. By this time Hydrolastic suspension, twin fuel tanks, an engine oil cooler and 4.5in wide wheels had become established as standard equipment. An all-synchromesh gearbox was standardised from summer 1968.

The Mk II was shortlived, and was replaced by the de-badged Mk III in March 1970. Like others of its ilk, it

Austin Mini-Cooper S Mk II.

SPECIFICATION

BODY STYLES: saloon

PRODUCTION: 6329/19,511

ENGINE & TRANSMISSION: 1275cc, 4cyl ohv, 4sp man, f/f

POWER: 76bhp @ 5800rpm

MAX SPEED (MPH): 97

0-60MPH (SEC): 10.9

SUSPENSION & BRAKES: Hydro ifs, Hydro irs, drums f&r

LENGTH (IN)/WEIGHT (LB): 120/1440

LAUNCH PRICE: £849

used the latest body shell (but there were no duotone colour schemes), which included wind-up windows, but it retained Hydro-lastic suspension. Of the 19,511 cars produced before June 1971, the vast majority were shipped overseas as CKD kits.

Records do not make this clear, but it is possible that in 1971 some late models were produced with "dry" rubber suspension, yet this reversion was never officially announced.

Mini-Cooper S Mk III, 1970, was no longer badged as an Austin or Morris.

Clubman 1969-82

With future crash-test regulations in mind, BMC developed the longer, square-nosed Clubman, although it was British Leyland who put it on sale at the end of 1969. This was a commercially successful attempt to broaden the Mini's appeal without altering the basics of the front wheel drive chassis.

Apart from the longer nose, the Clubman had wind-up windows in the doors, a new-style instrument display, and a three-spoke steering wheel, plus face-level ventilation and more up-market trim and seating. It was available as a two-door saloon or as an estate car, the estate now being all-steel (for the facsimile woody had been abandoned).

Technically, the Mini-Clubman used the latest 38bhp 998cc engine, with all-synchromesh trasnmission and a remote-

Clubman estate had fake wood side trims.

control gearchange, plus optional AP automatic transmission. The first saloons had Hydrolastic suspension, but "dry" rubber suspension was re-introduced in

mid-1971; estate cars always used dry suspension.

Development changes included radial ply tyres from 1973, and adoption of a

The Mini Clubman, introduced in 1969.

SPECIFICATION

BODY STYLES: saloon, estate

PRODUCTION: 473,189

ENGINE & TRANSMISSION: 998cc/1098cc, 4cyl ohv, 4sp man or auto, f/f

POWER: 38bhp @ 5250rpm/41bhp @ 4850rpm/45bhp @ 5250rpm

MAX SPEED (MPH): 75-82

0-60MPH (SEC): 21.0-17.9

SUSPENSION & BRAKES: Hydro ifs, Hydro irs, drums f&r (rubber f and r on estates, all cars from 1971)

LENGTH (IN)/WEIGHT (LB): 125/1406

LAUNCH PRICE: £720

45bhp 1098cc engine for manual cars from late 1975 (automatics always had a 41bhp 998cc unit). A cosmetic update in May 1976 included redesigned switchgear on the steering column, enhanced interior trim and a revised grille.

The Clubman saloon was dropped in August 1980 to make way for the Mini Metro, the estate car derivative staying on until 1982. These cars, though derided by Mini purists because of their looks, sold extremely well, and had all the dynamic qualities of the original Minis. Today, though, the mockers hold sway, so few Clubmen have been preserved and loved.

1275GT 1969-80

Determined to rid themselves of the "Cooper" badge – one reason was to cheapen the cars' specification, the other to eliminate royalty payments to John Cooper himself – British Leyland set out to replace the Mini-Cooper and Cooper S with a new, high-performance version of the long-nose Mini-Clubman. The resulting 1275GT was commercially and dynamically capable, but it never had the same charisma or appeal.

Based on the Mini-Clubman shell, the 1275GT had a single-SU 59bhp 1275cc engine, and all-synchromesh

SPECIFICATION

BODY STYLES: saloon

PRODUCTION: 110,673

ENGINE & TRANSMISSION: 1275cc, 4cyl ohv, 4sp man, f/f

POWER: 59bhp @ 5300rpm/54bhp @ 5300rpm

MAX SPEED (MPH): (59bhp) 90

0-60MPH (SEC): (59bhp) 13.3

SUSPENSION & BRAKES: Hydro ifs, Hydro irs, disc f/drum r (rubber f and r from1971)

LENGTH (IN)/WEIGHT (LB): 125/1555

LAUNCH PRICE: £834

The 1969 Mini 1275GT did not win the hearts of Mini-Cooper fans.

manual transmission. Automatic transmission was not available. Rostyle wheels and Cooper S disc front brakes were standard. Inside the car, there was a variation of the Clubman instrument display, this time with three circular dials.

Hydrolastic suspension was standard at first, but a change to "dry" rubber springing came in 1971. From June 1974, 12-inch front wheels, larger disc brakes and a 7.5-gallon fuel tank were fitted. Peak power was reduced at this time, but the change was never publicly acknowledged.

The same basic cosmetic updates as the Clubman followed in May 1976, and Dunlop Denovo run-flat tyres were standardised from August 1977. The last 1275GT was produced in August 1980, immediately ahead of the launch of the Mini-Metro.

Moke 1964-68

BMC first tried to sell this car to the British military as a lightweight personnel carrier, but after it was turned down by the military the model was redeveloped for civilian fun-car use.

Except as a fine-weather machine the Mini Moke had no practical uses, for it was starkly trimmed, with poor wet-weather protection, and it lacked four-wheel drive, but no one seemed to care. It was rugged, it was simple, and in the "swinging" days of the 1960s it was fun.

Structurally, the Moke had a brand-new steel structural tub, based on that of the Mini saloon, to which all the running gear of the original 850 Mini was bolted – transverse engine, front-wheel drive, and all-independent rubber suspension. The

Mini- Moke, 1964.

SPECIFICATION

BODY STYLES: open-top utility

PRODUCTION: 14,518, UK-assembly

ENGINE & TRANSMISSION: 848cc, 4cyl ohv, 4sp man, f/f

POWER: 34bhp @ 5500rpm

MAX SPEED (MPH): 65

0-60MPH (SEC): 21.8

SUSPENSION & BRAKES: rubber ifs, rubber irs, drums f&r

LENGTH (IN)/WEIGHT (LB): 120/1176

LAUNCH PRICE: £405

only exception was the fuel tank, which was located on one of the longitudinal sponsons.

The vast windscreen could be folded flat, and for wet-weather protection there was a canvas roof supported by removable poles. Big, flappy and altogether inadequate side curtains were optional equipment. On the first examples, all seats except that for the driver were optional too! Storage space was, quite literally, non-existent.

Although there were Austin and Morris versions, both types looked identical, all were painted Spruce Green, and all were

assembled at Longbridge. Production in the UK lasted for less than four years, and there was never any proposal to fit Hydrolastic suspension or larger engines.

In the 1970s and 1980s, Moke assembly was transferred successively to Australia and later to Portugal.

Driving and enjoying the Mini-Moke was an acquired taste, for here was a machine which was no faster than an ordinary Mini saloon, merely more open to the elements, just as hard-sprung, and more extrovert. Even so, in the 1960s, and to a certain class of customer, it was the coolest car on the planet.

MORGAN

Family-owned when set up in 1910, and still family-owned at the start of the 21st century, Morgan always treated motor car manufacture as a steady and traditional business. Then, as later, manufacture was at Malvern Link in Worcestershire, using separate chassis frames, wooden-framed open-top bodies, and Morgan's own unique type of sliding-pillar independent front suspension.

For many years the company only built three-wheeler machines – always with two front wheels and with rear-wheel drive – the move to producing four-wheelers being delayed until 1936

After World War Two, closely related three-wheeler and four-wheeler types were produced in parallel. The last three-wheeler was produced in 1952. The Standard-Triumph engined Plus 4 of 1950 was joined by the re-born 4/4 in 1955, but although there was a minor front-end re-style in the mid-1950s Morgans of 1980 still looked much

the same as they had in 1945. One aberration – the Plus 4 Plus coupé of 1963 – was just that, an aberration. Morgan wrote it off to experience, and never again diverted from their traditional product and traditional styling as the 20th century came to a close.

Although time never actually stood still at Morgan (and one model looked much like another), sweeping or revolutionary changes rarely took place. Accordingly, the move to a 2.1-litre Standard engine in 1950 (and to Triumph TR power from 1954), the revival of the 4/4 with Ford power for smaller models in 1955, and a change to Rover V8 power in 1968 were the big talking points of our period.

Even as the new century opened, Morgan was still in business at Malvern Link, still making between 12 and 15 cars a week, and still building recognisable descendants of the products described below. Only one radically new model, the Aero 8 of 2000, had so far broken with tradition.

F4/F-Super 3-wheeler 1936-51

The F-Type 3-wheelers were really a left-over from the 1930s (the new 4/4 had all but swamped them by the end of the 1930s, after all), but the old model plodded on steadily until the early 1950s, when orders for the Plus 4 finally filled up the Malvern Link works and forced them out.

All F-Types had a simple ladder-type chassis frame with Z-section side members and Morgan's own super-stiff sliding-pillar independent front sus-pension, in which the coil springs surrounded the telescopic dampers. The simple and rugged Ford-UK side-valve engine – Anglia or Prefect type – sat up front, driving a rear-mounted three-speed gearbox through a central torque tube, with final drive to the single rear wheel being by chain. Rear suspension was by a simple cantilever leaf spring.

F-Types – two-seaters or four-seaters – all used the traditional coachbuilt type of body, framed in (untreated) wood, with steel panelling. Flared front wings flanked a proud near-vertical radiator, and the style looked remarkably Morgan car-like, yet the narrowing tail ended by surrounding the exposed spare wheel.

Here was no-frills motoring at its best, for such Morgans were always noted not only for their rock-hard ride and direct steering, but also for their ultra-sporting character. The engines, of course, were simple, sturdy but distinctly mundane Ford units, yet they were quite powerful enough for the capabilities of the chassis.

SPECIFICATION

BODY STYLES: sports tourer

PRODUCTION: 632 post-war

ENGINE & TRANSMISSION: 933cc/1172cc, 4cyl sv, 3sp man, f/r

POWER: 23bhp @ 4000rpm/30bhp @ 4000rpm

MAX SPEED (MPH): 65 (E)/70 (E)

0-60MPH (SEC): not measured

SUSPENSION & BRAKES: coil ifs, leaf irs, drums f&r

LENGTH (IN)/WEIGHT (LB): 132/896

LAUNCH PRICE: £263 in 1945

The Ford sidevalve-engined Morgan F4 3-wheeler began life in the 1930s.

4/4 1936-50

Morgan 4/4, 1947.

Introduced in 1936, and the very first Morgan four-wheeler sports car, the original 4/4 (which was only retro-spectively known as the Series I), had started life with Coventry-Climax

SPECIFICATION

BODY STYLES: sports car, drophead coupé

PRODUCTION: 1720, of which 1084 post-war

ENGINE & TRANSMISSION: 1267cc, 4cyl ohv, 4sp man, f/r

POWER: 40bhp @ 4300rpm

MAX SPEED (MPH): 77

0-60MPH (SEC): 26.0

SUSPENSION & BRAKES: coil ifs, leaf rear, drums f&r

LENGTH (IN)/WEIGHT (LB): 136/1624

LAUNCH PRICE: £455

engines, but a special overhead-valve Standard 1267cc engine became available (never used in any Standard, incidentally)..

Starting again in 1946, Morgan reintroduced a slightly up-dated 4/4, this time only building it with the 40bhp 1267cc Standard engine and a separate Moss gearbox. By any measure this was a spritely little car, just as effective as the MG TC of the period.

In many ways an evolution of the F-Type 3-wheeler, the 4/4 had a more sturdy chassis frame, still with Z-section side members and with sliding pillar front suspension, but now, of course, with a beam rear axle above the line of the full-length chassis side members. Mechanical brakes were still standard, as were pressed-steel disc wheels.

At the front, the body style of the 4/4 was really an development of the F-Type 3-wheeler's proportions, with more sweeping front wings. As in 1939, no fewer than three different body types were available, all on the same 92in-wheelbase chassis frame – a two-seater sports (this was the most popular), a four-seater sports, and a rather elegant two-seater drop-head coupé which had a nicely tailored fold-away soft-top.

All such Morgans were built down to a price (£455 in 1946 for the two-seater), so they were certainly not meant to last for ever. The chassis and running gear lasted well, but the timber framing of the bodies eventually rotted away, and all surviving original-type 4/4s will have been rebuilt at least once during their lifetime.

Plus 4 1950-68

The change from 4/4 to Plus 4 was forced on Morgan by Standard, who could no longer supply the 1267cc engine, but it turned out to be the making of the company. Even at first, with the relatively agricultural Standard Vanguard engine, the Plus 4 was a formidably effective sports car. Once the more highly tuned TR units were added, it could be a winner on the race track, in rallies, in trials and on the road.

Starting in 1950, Morgan lengthened the wheelbase of the 4/4 chassis to 96 inches and added two inches to the track. Stiffening up the frame all round, and changing suspension settings from rock hard to merely very hard, they prepared the car to accept the large and heavy 68bhp 2088cc Standard Vanguard engine, and provided hydraulic brakes for the first time. A Moss gearbox was mounted

Morgan Plus 4 two-seater, 1950, powered by the Standard Vanguard engine.

Plus 4 trialling in the early 1950s.

separately from the engine, several inches back in the frame. There were no styling changes at first, and the usual three body styles were listed.

Thereafter changes and improvements came regularly. In 1953 the style changed to incorporate a sloping radiator; one year later this change was completed, to include a curved cowl

SPECIFICATION

BODY STYLES: sports car, drophead coupé

PRODUCTION: 3737, all types

ENGINE & TRANSMISSION:
1991cc/2088cc/2138cc, 4cyl ohv, 4sp man, f/r

POWER: 68bhp @ 4000rpm/90-100bhp @ 4800rpm/100bhp @ 4600rpm/104bhp @ 4700rpm.

MAX SPEED (MPH): 85-105

0-60MPH (SEC): 14.1-9.7

SUSPENSION & BRAKES: coil ifs, leaf rear, drums f&r at first; disc f/drum r from 1959

LENGTH (IN)/WEIGHT (LB): 140/1876

LAUNCH PRICE: £652

The Plus 4 four-seater in 1959. By now the Triumph TR engine was fitted.

concealing the radiator. The 90bhp 1991cc Triumph TR2 engine was fitted from 1954, the 100bhp TR3 engine from 1956, front disc brakes were optional from 1959 and standard from 1960. Wire wheels were available from 1959 and wider bodies were phased in during that year. The enlarged 2138cc 100bhp TR4 engine came on stream in 1962 and was upgraded to 104bhp from 1965.

With Morgan, though, it is best not to be too specific about the facts, as special provision was sometimes made for special customers. The Plus 4 kept on selling well (there was always a waiting list) until it was displaced by the Plus 8 in 1968.

4/4 Series II to Series V 1955-68

Morgan re-introduced the 4/4 name in 1955, maintaining a strong visual connection to the earlier type, though with virtually no common or carry-over components or panels. The new 4/4, in fact, was based on the chassis frame of the much more powerful Plus 4 (see above), with that car's wheelbase and (from 1960) the same wheel tracks.

Like the Plus 4, the latest 4/4 had the Z-section chassis frame, the sliding-pillar front suspension, and the steel-panelled wood-framed body with the latest curved and laid back radiator grille. In this case, though, only the two-seater sports body was available, and disc wheels (not wires) were standard. Amazingly, Hartford-type

4/4 Series II two-seater, 1955, fitted with the 1172cc Ford sidevalve engine.

friction dampers were still fitted.

From 1955 to 1960 SIIs used the Ford sidevalve 1172cc engine with its allied three-speed gearbox and a crude push-pull gearchange protruding from the fascia. This ensemble gave a 71mph top speed. Aquaplane tuning kits were available which helped boost this. Then the changes came.

Series III (1960-61) had Ford's new Anglia 105E 39bhp 997cc engine, a four-speed gearbox, two-inch wider tracks and Armstrong piston-type dampers. The body shell was widened to be the same as that of the Plus 4, so there was more cockpit space.

Series IV (1961-63) had 54bhp 1340cc engines and front-wheel disc brakes.

Series V (1963-68) had 60bhp 1498cc engines. A Competition version with 78bhp was also available.

All had the same hard-riding, direct-steering pre-war character, which attracted a steady stream of customers. The later the model, with power increasing but still very simple mechan-

SPECIFICATION

BODY STYLES: sports car

PRODUCTION: 386/58/114/639

ENGINE & TRANSMISSION: : 1172cc, 4cyl sv, 997cc/1340cc/1498 cc, 4cyl ohv, 4sp man, f/r

POWER: 36bhp @ 4400rpm/39-78bhp @ 5000rpm

MAX SPEED (MPH): 71/78/80/94

0-60MPH (SEC): 29.4/25.8/18.6/11.9

SUSPENSION & BRAKES: coil ifs, leaf rear, drums f&r (later disc f/drum r)

LENGTH (IN)/WEIGHT (LB): 144/1428 - 1516

LAUNCH PRICE: £639

4/4 Series V four-seater

4/4 1600 1968-81

In late 1968 Morgan re-worked the 4/4 once again, turning it into the 4/4 1600, a genuine 100mph car which almost made up for the loss of the Plus 4, that model having just been replaced by the new Plus 8.

Based on the 4/4 Series V, but now with a choice of two-seater or four-seater bodies, it had a choice of 74bhp or 88bhp 1599cc cross-flow Ford Kent engines. No larger and no more roomy than before, it now had the choice of disc or centre-lock wire-spoke wheels.

This was the perfect entry-level Morgan and it sold well and steadily until the early 1980s, when supplies of the Kent engine finally ran out. Then (well out of our period) new-fangled Ford CVH and even Fiat twin-cam four-cylinder engines were fitted instead.

SPECIFICATION

BODY STYLES: sports car

PRODUCTION: 3708

ENGINE & TRANSMISSION: 1599cc, 4cyl ohv, 4sp man, f/r

POWER: 74bhp @ 4750/88bhp @ 5400rpm

MAX SPEED (MPH): 100 (E)/102

0-60MPH (SEC): not measured/9.8

SUSPENSION & BRAKES: coil ifs, leaf rear, disc f/drum r

LENGTH (IN)/WEIGHT (LB): 144/1516

LAUNCH PRICE: £858

Morgan 4/4 1600 four-seater, 1968.

Plus 4 Super Sport 1961-68

Morgan was so impressed by Chris Lawrence's club racing performance in Morgans that it commissioned him to produce a limited number of specially tuned TR3/TR4-type engines for their own use. Chassis specification was not

SPECIFICATION

BODY STYLES: sports car

PRODUCTION: 102

ENGINE & TRANSMISSION: 1991cc/2138cc, 4cyl ohv, 4sp man, f/r

POWER: 115bhp@ 5500rpm/120bhp @ 5500rpm

MAX SPEED (MPH): 115 (E)

0-60MPH (SEC): 7.6 (E)

SUSPENSION & BRAKES: coil ifs, leaf rear, disc f/drum r

LENGTH (IN)/WEIGHT (LB): 140/1680

LAUNCH PRICE: £1314

The Plus 4 Super Sports, introduced in 1961, with Lawrencetune TR engine and part light-alloy body.

changed, but wherever possible light-alloy body panels were used instead of steel.

The result was the Plus Four Super Sport of which, reputedly, only 102 examples were made. Not really intended as a road car, it was bought for use as a "starter racing car", and performed its task very successfully.

Plus 4 Plus 1963-66

Almost as soon as this car had been launched, Morgan wished they had not done it. For once in his long and carefully thought through business life, Peter Morgan was persuaded to produce a "modern Morgan". The Plus 4 Plus, of which only 26 examples would be sold, looked like no other Morgan ever produced, before or afterwards.

Under the skin, this car was pure mid-1960s Plus 4, which is to say that it had the 104bhp 2138cc Triumph TR4-type

engine and its related four-speed gearbox, plus the same rock-hard suspension as ever. In order to keep the body shell in one piece, they say, the chassis was beefed up here and there to stop it flexing.

The body was a full-width two-seater bubble-top fixed-head in GRP and was produced by EB Plastics. It had an elongated, quite shapely tail. There were elements of the just-obsolete Lotus Elite in the style, but somehow this didn't

quite work on the Morgan chassis. Unusually for a Morgan, not only did the windows wind up and down, but the windscreen was curved, and there were exterior door handles and a separate boot compartment.

To the existing Plus 4's virtues and vices the Plus 4 Plus added a cramped, noisy cabin. The combination of svelte coupé and Vintage springing did not work. It was a failure. Morgan will forget it if you promise to do the same.

SPECIFICATION

BODY STYLES: sports coupé

PRODUCTION: 26

ENGINE & TRANSMISSION: 2138cc, 4cyl ohv, 4sp man, f/r

POWER: 104bhp @ 4700rpm

MAX SPEED (MPH): 105 (E)

0-60MPH (SEC): not measured

SUSPENSION & BRAKES: coil ifs, leaf rear, disc f/drum r

LENGTH (IN)/WEIGHT (LB): 152/1820

LAUNCH PRICE: £1275

The glassfibre-bodied Plus 4 Plus found very few buyers.

Plus 8 1968-2004

For Morgan, the launch of the Rover V8-engined Plus 8 was a major step – it was the first important engine change to be made to the traditional body/chassis layout since 1960 (and even that had been a Ford like-for-like swap). Not only that, but the new car had a significantly longer wheelbase and wider track than the Plus 4 which it replaced.

Launched in September 1968, this model went on to become an all-time Morgan best-seller (6233 were produced before assembly ended in 2004), and it changed steadily and consistently in a 36-year career. In the context of this book we can only describe the original specification.

Though wider and longer than the Plus 4 – two inches in the wheelbase, two inches in the track – the Plus 8's original chassis design was precisely the same as

SPECIFICATION

BODY STYLES: sports car

PRODUCTION: 482 to the first spec, 6233 of all versions

ENGINE & TRANSMISSION: 3528cc, V8cyl ohv, 4sp man, f/r

POWER: 161bhp @ 5200rpm

MAX SPEED (MPH): 124

0-60MPH (SEC): 6.7

SUSPENSION & BRAKES: coil ifs, leaf rear, disc f/drum r

LENGTH (IN)/WEIGHT (LB): 147/1979

LAUNCH PRICE: £1478

Morgan Plus 8.

before, this including the use of a separately-mounted Moss four-speed gearbox. All cars had new-design 15in cast alloy road wheels, and all were made with the familiar two-seater sports car style, and a steel-panelled body. No other derivative was ever officially available.

The engine was the light-alloy 90-degree V8 used by Rover since late 1967, this being a re-engineered version of the Buick V8 of 1960-63. The engine would go on to have a legendary life in a number of Rovers and other cars; it was finally dropped in 2004.

Compared with any earlier Morgan the Plus 8 had startling acceleration, but its top speed was limited to about 125mph by its awful aerodynamics.

In April 1972 a Rover 3500S gearbox replaced the ancient Moss, and due to Rover's own policy the engine was actually downrated to 143bhp DIN in 1973. Rack-and-pinion steering became

optional in 1983, power went back up to 155bhp in 1976, a five-speed Rover SD1 gearbox arrived at the same time, and at that period new 14in alloy wheels were fitted. By 1976, a 3-inch track increase, in two stages, had pushed out the overall width to 62in, and annual production had settled to between 150 and 200 cars.

Later still, and outside our period, there would be still wider tracks, lighter bodies, larger and more powerful versions of the engine (including fuel-injected types), and several generations of fascia/instrumentation styles.

Once launched, the Plus 8 was an instant best-seller by any Morgan standards, and enormous waiting lists eventually built up. Although the company did not consider it obsolete even at the end of the 1990s (and the order book proved that), the launch of a brand-new Morgan, the Aero 8, finally saw it die off.

MORRIS

In the 1930s the Nuffield Organisation, of which Morris was by far the largest marque, had been Britain's market leader. In the late 1940s, however, a humdrum series of new models, and ageing management, made it an obvious takeover target. After Lord Nuffield, who had founded the business in 1912, finally sold out to Len Lord at Austin, it was soon subsumed into the BMC monolith which arose.

Before the mid-1950s, Morris's fortunes were buoyed up by the Morris Minor (and by MG sports cars), but from that point new Morris-labelled cars were usually no more than re-badged Austins. Although BMC retained different Austin and Morris dealer chains, which competed with each other head on, in almost every British high street, the only real difference was that Morris cars were usually (not invariably!) assembled at Cowley, near Oxford, while Austins were built at Longbridge.

Alec Issigonis had inspired the post-war Morris Minor – great chassis and suspension, disappointing engine – but he despaired of any further corporate enterprise and left in 1952. When you study the Oxford MO, and the Series II which followed in 1954, you can see why! The last Nuffield-Morris (as opposed to BMC-Morris) to reach the public was the Isis of 1955, and even by then there were new-generation BMC engines under the skin.

In the 1960s Morris Minis, Coopers, 1100s and Oxfords were produced in huge quantities, but all were no more than re-badged clones of Austins. The marque entered the 1970s as a component of British Leyland, though only one major new model, the Marina was launched, in 1971. The Marina then sold steadily throughout the decade, transmuted into the Ital in the early 1980s, before the last Morris of all was built in 1984.

8 Series E 1938-48

To get the assembly lines full after the war, Morris dug some of its existing tooling out of store and re-introduced the 8 Series E, which had originally been launched at the end of 1938. Although it had recessed headlamps which made it look relatively modern, it still ran on a separate chassis frame, with beam front and rear axles and a 918cc sidevalve engine, so this was definitely *vieux jeu* in a rapidly changing world.

Even by Morris standards, the only thing to be boasted about was the low selling price – £301 if you could fight your way up the priority waiting list – for this was a sluggish old machine at which 50mph cruising seemed to be quite enough, with no heater, radio or any other diversions to keep one interested.

At the time, and certainly not in the more recent "classic" era, there was nothing to excite any client's heart, for the ride was hard, the acceleration ponderous, and the style positively anonymous. Amazingly, with a different chassis, a revised front end, and a better engine, the Series E became an MG Y-Type, which was an entirely different proposition.

The Series E sold like 5-cent hamburgers in the car-starved 1945-48 period, but Issigonis's Minor, which succeeded it, represented a complete revolution for the Morris image.

Morris 8 Series E had been introduced in 1938.

SPECIFICATION

BODY STYLES: saloon

PRODUCTION: 120,434, of which 52,919 post-war

ENGINE & TRANSMISSION: 918cc, 4cyl sv, 4sp man, f/r

POWER: 30bhp @ 4400rpm

MAX SPEED (MPH): 58

0-60MPH (SEC): not possible

SUSPENSION & BRAKES: beam leaf front, leaf rear, drums f&r

LENGTH (IN)/WEIGHT (LB): 144/1704

LAUNCH PRICE: £301

10 Series M 1938-48

Compared with its contemporary, the 8 Series E, the 10 Series M was at once more advanced yet visually less pleasing. The monocoque structure and the overhead-valve 1140cc engine were forward looking, yet the beam axle front suspension, and the separate headlamp front end were both traditional.

Introduced in 1938, and one of the stars of the last pre-war Earls Court Show, the Series M was aimed at Morris's most profitable and largest market. As an obvious competitor to cars like the Austin Ten and the Hillman Minx, Nuffield judged that it needed to be to be a

The Morris 10 Series M had an ohv engine and unitary construction.

conventional machine – and it was.

Post-war types, which looked exactly like the 1938-39 models at first, got off to a flying start, as tens of thousands had been built during the war for military purposes, many of them with utility bodywork. Even so, after the first 8,000 cars had been produced with the old-style flat radiator, a new and more rounded radiator shell was standardised. This shape was originally evolved for use in the Hindustan Ten,

which was assembled in India.

An anti-roll bar was fitted to the front suspension, but this was not a car that handled well (even though Alec Issigonis had been involved in its design). Yet it sold well, especially as the initial launch price in 1945/46 was a mere £378.

A few have survived, mainly because some Morris enthusiasts believe that this was the last of the real Morris cars which deserved their attention.

SPECIFICATION

BODY STYLES: saloon

PRODUCTION: 53,566 post-war

ENGINE & TRANSMISSION: 1140cc, 4cyl ohv, 4sp man, f/r

POWER: 37bhp @ 4600rpm

MAX SPEED (MPH): 62

0-60MPH (SEC): not measured

SUSPENSION & BRAKES: beam leaf front, leaf rear, drums f&r

LENGTH (IN)/WEIGHT (LB): 158/2044

LAUNCH PRICE: £378

Minor MM 1948-53

Designed by Alec Issigonis, Nuffield's new Minor would have been an all-new post-war product if the company had allowed a brand-new engine to be chosen: in the end, this very modern machine was lumbered with the ancient and under-powered sidevalve four of the Morris 8 Series E, which had its roots in the early 1930s.

The original Minor had a sturdy unit-construction body with rounded styling. The body was widened at a late stage in the development phase, and featured small low-mounted headlamps at each side of the grille and had a split wind-screen. Gear changing was by a long and rather willowy centre lever, and the trim was both simple and cheap, but these trifling issues were overshadowed by the

car's magnificent roadholding and balance. The novelties (which rivals would not match for some years) were independent front suspension by torsion bars and wishbones, and inch-accurate rack-and-pinion steering.

Because it was new, looked new, and handled like no other British small car had ever done, we forgave the performance, which was dismal. Although the top speed was 62mph, one rarely saw a Minor MM going faster than 45mph on the road.

Original types were sold only as two-door saloons and convertibles, for the four-door saloon did not appear until 1950. From 1949 (on cars for export to North America), and from early 1951 (all models) the front-end style was altered so that larger 7-inch headlamps sat higher on

the front wings. After the BMC merger, the Minor was speedily modified to use the new A-Series engine, so this MM type disappeared in 1952/53.

SPECIFICATION

BODY STYLES: saloon, drophead

PRODUCTION TOTAL: 176,002

ENGINE & TRANSMISSION: 918cc, 4cyl sv, 4sp man, f/r

POWER: 27bhp @ 4400rpm

MAX SPEED (MPH): 62

0-60MPH (SEC): 36.5

SUSPENSION & BRAKES: tor ifs, leaf rear, drums f&r

LENGTH (IN)/WEIGHT (LB): 148/1652

LAUNCH PRICE: £359

The sidevalve Morris Minor MM, 1948, distinguished by its low-set headlamps.

Interior of the Minor MM. This one has both heater and radio.

Oxford MO 1948-54

Although the new Oxford MO looked much like an inflated Minor MM, there were no shared panels, no shared running gear – and Alec Issigonis was not involved in the design. Introduced in October 1948, the MO was one of four cars (the Morris Six, the Wolseley 4/50 and Wolseley 6/80 were the others) which shared the same basic hull/four-door passenger cabin.

The MO, however, was the only one to use a brand-new sidevalve 1476cc engine, and had the shortest wheelbase of all these types. Like the Minor MM (though the details were different) the new Oxford had torsion bar suspension and a steering rack, but don't get too excited, as the handling was strictly "Nuffield family car", and there was an awful steering-column gearchange.

Early cars were only available as four-

SPECIFICATION

BODY STYLES: saloon, estate, commercials

PRODUCTION TOTAL: 159,960

ENGINE & TRANSMISSION: 1476cc, 4cyl sv, 4sp man, f/r

POWER: 41bhp @ 4200rpm

MAX SPEED (MPH): 71

0-60MPH (SEC): 31.0

SUSPENSION & BRAKES: tor ifs, leaf rear, drums f&r

LENGTH (IN)/WEIGHT (LB): 166/2212

LAUNCH PRICE: £505

Morris Oxford MO, 1952 and still with side valves.

door saloons; a two-door "woody" estate car followed in 1952, and for the commercial sector there were also vans and pickups. Except to point out that it must have been a commercial success, this was a singularly characterless Morris. Compared with other power units in the Nuffield Organisation, the side-valve engine was an old-fashioned disgrace, the performance was negligible, and the unit-construction bodyshell tended to rust away. But it was a comfy car.

Six 1948-53

Here was Morris's first post-war six-cylinder engined model, and it was a commercial failure which disappeared from view after a life of only five years. Although it was one of the four new cars (Oxford MO, and the two Wolseleys) which shared the same four-door hull, in many ways it was a waste of Nuffield's resources.

SPECIFICATION

BODY STYLES: saloon

PRODUCTION TOTAL: 12,400

ENGINE & TRANSMISSION: 2215cc, 6cyl ohc, 4sp man, f/r

POWER: 70bhp @ 4800rpm

MAX SPEED (MPH): 83

0-60MPH (SEC): 22.4

SUSPENSION & BRAKES: tor ifs, leaf rear, drums f&r

LENGTH (IN)/WEIGHT (LB): 177/2688

LAUNCH PRICE: £608

Morris Six, 1949, cousin of the MO and very closely related to the Wolseley 6/80.

How to sum up the Six? Think of the much more appealing Wolseley 6/80, but with a less powerful, single-SU version of the 2213cc overhead-cam engine (70bhp instead of 72bhp – but the difference felt much larger), a less distinctive nose, and a less distinctive interior. Cam-gear steering was not a patch on the rack-and-pinion of smaller Morris models of this period, and the steering column gearchange became obstructive as the linkage wore.

Not many Brits bought the Six (at least 7000 were exported), and Nuffield did little to promote it. Soon after the BMC merger was finalised, the Six came under sentence of death. The last was produced in March 1953, and its notional replacement, the Isis, did not appear until 1955.

Minor SII 1952-56

Immediately after the merger of Nuffield with Austin (the foundation of BMC), the planners set about developing the second series – SII – of the Morris Minor line. Simply, this involved ditching the old-fashioned sidevalve 918cc engine of the MM and replacing it with the brand-new Austin-designed A-series overhead-valve 803cc unit and its related gearbox.

The SII was available in four-door saloon form from late 1952, and in all forms from February 1953. The engine was smaller, lighter and slightly more powerful than before, yet the Minor could still only reach 60/62mph. Better acceleration was only achieved by giving the car low gearing, so to many it was an engine-screaming, gutless wonder which deserved more power

Morris Minor Series II gained overhead valves, using the Austin A30's 803cc engine.

and higher gearing. To complete the range, BMC announced a new "woody"-bodied Traveller (estate), a related van and a pick-up from 1953, this providing a stable family which would continue for many years into the future.

Minor changes such as an Austin A30-based back axle (early 1954) and a new horizontally-slatted grille and re-styled fascia (October 1954) were made, but the last SII of 1956 was much like the first and the car remained underpowered to the end. It was replaced by the more successful Minor 1000.

First of the Minor Travellers was the Series II.

SPECIFICATION

BODY STYLES: saloon, drophead, estate, light commercials

PRODUCTION: 269,838

ENGINE & TRANSMISSION: 803cc, 4cyl ohv, 4sp man, f/r

POWER: 30bhp @ 4800rpm

MAX SPEED (MPH): 62

0-60MPH (SEC): not measured

SUSPENSION & BRAKES: tor ifs, leaf rear, drums f&r

LENGTH (IN)/WEIGHT (LB): 148/1652

LAUNCH PRICE: £582

Minor Series II van, much favoured by the Post Office.

Oxford II/III/IV 1954-60

Conceived before the BMC merger, but one of the very first models to use the brand-new corporate B-Series engine, the bulbous Oxford Series II took over from the sidevalve-engined Oxford MO in 1954 .

Apart from the model name there was no carryover from the old Oxford MO. The new car had a completely new

monocoque hull (in longer-wheelbase form this would be shared with the forthcoming Morris Isis), though the

SPECIFICATION

BODY STYLES: saloon, estate, commercials

PRODUCTION: 145,458

ENGINE & TRANSMISSION: 1489cc, 4cyl ohv, 4sp man or semi-auto, f/r

POWER: 50bhp @ 4800rpm

MAX SPEED (MPH): 73

0-60MPH (SEC): 29.0

SUSPENSION & BRAKES: tor ifs, leaf rear, drums f&r

LENGTH (IN)/WEIGHT (LB): 170/2464

LAUNCH PRICE: £745

Morris Oxford Series II, 1954, was surprisingly roomy.

design of the torsion bar front suspension and rack-and-pinion steering looked familiar.

The running gear – 50bhp 1489cc engine, four-speed gearbox and hypoid-bevel rear axle – was all from the new B-Series parts bin. This, at least, was a technical advance, but the retention of a steering-column gearchange was not. The interior style was such that the fascia was a long way ahead of the bench front seat, and the steering column and steering wheel were considerably offset. An Olde English "woody" estate car Traveller sold alongside the four-door saloon.

Not a great car by any means, but a sturdy and reliable one. A facelift in 1956 (to Series III saloon) and in 1957 (to Series IV steel-bodied Traveller estate car) didn't advance things much. The new Traveller, incidentally, had four doors, so was more versatile than the woody's two-door body.

Engine power had been increased to 55bhp, and two-pedal semi-automatic

Oxford Series III, 1956, with scalloped bonnet and two-tone paint.

Manumatic transmission became an option, and the facelift included longer rear wings and a rather contrived duotone paint job along the flanks. The fascia and control layout was much improved. At least a centre-floor gearchange was optional from the spring of 1958.

Oxford Travller, 1955, had only two doors but a huge load area.

Isis 1955-58

It's easy to see how product planners arrived at the Isis. Seeking to replace the unsuccessful Morris Six of 1948-53, Nuffield/BMC engineers were told to take the new-generation Morris Oxford Series II cabin and centre structure, lengthen the wheelbase by 10.5 inches, and install the brand-new BMC C-Series six-cylinder 2639cc engine.

As with the Oxford, four-door saloon and two-door woody station wagon versions were to be available. Isis was chosen not only because that was the name given to the Thames as it flowed through Oxford but also because there had already been a Morris Isis in the pre-war period.

Built only for three years – 1955 to 1958 – the Isis was no more successful

The Isis replaced the Morris Six in 1955.

SPECIFICATION

BODY STYLES: saloon, estate

PRODUCTION TOTAL: 8,541 SI, 3,614 SII

ENGINE & TRANSMISSION: 2639cc, 6cyl ohv, 4sp man, o/d or auto, f/r

POWER: 86bhp @ 4250rpm/90bhp @ 4500rpm

MAX SPEED (MPH): 86

0-60MPH (SEC): 17.8

SUSPENSION & BRAKES: tor ifs, leaf rear, drums f&r

LENGTH (IN)/WEIGHT (LB): 178/2960

LAUNCH PRICE: £802

than the Six had been, though it was a somewhat more distinguished car, and had nothing visually in common with the competing Wolseley 6/90 of the period. This, the only 'Morris' model to use the C-Series engine, had 86bhp and a top speed of 86mph (symmetrical figures, at least…) but was unfortunately lumbered with a steering-column gear change.

The Isis soon gained a Borg-Warner overdrive option, and from late 1956 the Isis became SII (at the same time as the Oxford became SIII. Confused? So were many other people…). It received the same facelift of the wings and tail, and a

welcome upgrade to the fascia/control layout. Not only that, but the engine now had 90bhp, the manual gearchange lever was now installed between front seat and door (on the right of the RHD driver's seat, for example) as on the latest Wolseley 6/90 and Riley Pathfinder models, and there was the new option of Borg-Warner automatic transmission.

Not that all this made a mediocre car much better, for it was always found to be floppy, under-damped, under-steery and very ungainly when hurried along.

This, in fact, was the last six-cylinder engined Morris. A slightly ignominious exit, some might say…

Cowley/Cowley 1500 1954-59

Perhaps the original Cowley – the "bullnose" of the 1920s – was the most famous Morris of all time, but the 1950s version was probably the most obscure. Does anyone even remember that there was a Cowley at this time?

The story is easily told. Set on selling every possible permutation of every new model, BMC decided to produce an entry-level version of the Oxford SII of 1954. Stripping out some equipment, using the smaller 1200cc 40bhp version of the new B-Series engine and getting rid of some brightwork produced the

SPECIFICATION

BODY STYLES: saloon

PRODUCTION: 17,413/4623

ENGINE & TRANSMISSION: 1200cc/1489cc, 4cyl ohv, 4sp man or semi-auto, f/r

POWER: 42bhp @ 4500rpm/55bhp @ 4400rpm

MAX SPEED (MPH): 65/73

0-60MPH (SEC): 37.5/27.1

SUSPENSION & BRAKES: tor ifs, leaf rear, drums f&r

LENGTH (IN)/WEIGHT (LB): 170/2464

LAUNCH PRICE: £702/£799

A Morris Cowley mingles with Veterans on the London-Brighton Run.

new Cowley. In the mid-1950s the only real reason to buy one of these instead of an Oxford was its selling price – £702 against £745 – but this difference was not enough to cause a huge rush to buy. Morris/BMC nevertheless sold a respectable 17,413 Cowleys in the first two years, so when the Oxford SII-to-SIII

facelift came at the end of 1956, the Cowley became Cowley 1500. As both Cowley and Oxford models henceforth shared exactly the same running gear (even to the Manumatic transmission option), there was even less daylight between the two, so the Cowley died away, unsung, early in 1959.

Minor 1000 1956-71

The Minor 1000 took over from the SII in the autumn of 1956, not only with a larger and more powerful engine, but with revised gearing and a remote-control gearchange. All these improvements, incidentally, would be shared with the Austin A35 and (from 1958) with the first of the Austin-Healey Sprites.

The 948cc engine had a higher output (37bhp instead of 30bhp) and was more torquey too, while the gear-box ratios and overall gearing were both revised and made more suitable. At a stroke, the top speed was pushed up from 62mph to 73mph, the Minor 1000 having a much more sporty and robust character. Visually, the only important change was that all types were given a one-piece windscreen,

The 948cc Morris Minor 1000 arrived in 1956.

while the rear window of the saloons was enlarged considerably.

The Minor 1000 then stayed in production until 1971, with improvements along the way, principally in October 1962 when the latest and quite lively 48bhp 1098cc engine took over from the 948cc unit. Glovebox lids came and went, and some trim items were uprated, but not much else

changed. To commemorate the building of the millionth Minor, a series of lilac-hued "Minor Million" saloons were built in 1960.

After British Leyland was founded, the Minor range was gradually trimmed. The convertible was dropped in June 1969, the saloon was discontinued in November 1970, and the last Traveller was built in April 1971, 23

years after the launch of the original Minor. For obscure British Leyland product planning reasons, some of the last vans were badged as Austins.

Tourer ceased production in 1969.

Minor 1000 Traveller.

SPECIFICATION

BODY STYLES: saloon, drophead, estate, light commercials

PRODUCTION: 554,048 948cc and 303,443 1098cc

ENGINE & TRANSMISSION: 948cc/1098cc, 4cyl ohv, 4sp man, f/r

POWER: 37bhp @ 4750rpm/48bhp @ 5100rpm

MAX SPEED (MPH): 73/74

0-60MPH (SEC): 25.9/24.8

SUSPENSION & BRAKES: tor ifs, leaf rear, drums f&r

LENGTH (IN)/WEIGHT (LB): 148/1652

LAUNCH PRICE: £603

Oxford V/VI 1959-71

Except in its badging details, and in the detail of its launch and demise, this Farina-styled Oxford was effectively the same car as the contemporary Austin A55/A60 models from which it was cloned. The running gear, the performance and the cost of ownership of the two cars was effectively identical, though of course they were always sold through different dealer networks and, for some reason, the Morris was usually priced a few pounds higher than the Austin.

Announced in March 1959, all Oxford Series Vs or (from late 1961) Series VI types, were produced at Cowley. The estate car (Traveller) appeared at the end of 1960, and was dropped in February 1969. The valiant old saloon, little changed at all during the 1960s, was finally discontinued in April 1971. It was immediately replaced by the Morris Marina. See Austin A55/60 for a full description.

The Oxford VI Traveller.

Morris Oxford V, 1959.

SPECIFICATION

BODY STYLES: saloon, estate

PRODUCTION: 296,255

ENGINE & TRANSMISSION: 1489cc/1622cc, 4cyl ohv, or 1489cc diesel, 4sp man or auto, f/r

POWER: 52bhp @ 4350rpm/61bhp @ 4500rpm/40bhp @ 4000rpm

MAX SPEED (MPH): 78/81/66

0-60MPH (SEC): 23.6/21.4/39.4

SUSPENSION & BRAKES: coil ifs, leaf rear, drums f&r

LENGTH (IN)/WEIGHT (LB): 178/2473-2520

LAUNCH PRICE: £816

Oxford VI of 1961.

The Morris Oxford was not an inspiring drive but it was tough. This one is competing in the South African Safari.

1100/1300 1962-73

Although we have already described the Austin 1100/1300 models in detail, it was the Morris-badged version which first met its public, actually in August 1962. The Morris 1100, therefore, had a year's clear run in the market place before the Austin went on sale.

Apart from the badging, the only real difference from the Austin was in the fascia/instrument panel design. Options (including automatic transmission), extra features and facelifts all arrived at

The Morris 1100 was available from 1962.

SPECIFICATION

BODY STYLES: saloon, estate

PRODUCTION TOTAL: approx 743,000

ENGINE & TRANSMISSION: 1098cc/1275cc, 4cyl ohv, 4sp man or auto, f/f

POWER: 48bhp @ 5100rpm/58bhp @ 5250rpm/70bhp @ 6000rpm

MAX SPEED (MPH): 78/88/93

0-60MPH (SEC): 22.2/17.3/15.6

SUSPENSION & BRAKES: Hydro ifs, Hydro irs, disc f/drum r

LENGTH (IN)/WEIGHT (LB): 147/1780 - 1900

LAUNCH PRICE: £661

1969 Morris 1300GT

Morris 1300 Traveller.

the same time on both models.

Because the Morris Marina arrived in 1971, the 1100 and 1300 were dropped at that time, except in some export markets, though Travellers (ie estate cars)

continued, cosmetically upgraded as "Mk IIIs", until 1973.

As with the Austin equivalents, a few diehards have kept these cars on the road, but most have now rusted away.

1800 1966-73

Once again, we can save ourselves some space here. Except for its grille, badging, and tiny details of its equipment, the Morris 1800 was always exactly the same car as the Austin 1800. The only real difference, in this case, was that the Austin had been launched in October 1964, while the Morris first appeared in March 1966.

Like the Austin, the Morris 1800 became Mk II in May 1968, but at least the higher performance (96bhp) 1800S appeared first, in October 1968. The

Morris Mk II 1800, 1969. This is the 95bhp S model.

SPECIFICATION

BODY STYLES: saloon

PRODUCTION TOTAL: 95,271

ENGINE & TRANSMISSION: 1798cc, 4cyl ohv, 4sp man or auto, f/f

POWER: 80bhp @ 5000rpm/86bhp @ 5300rpm/96bhp @ 5700rpm

MAX SPEED (MPH): 90/93/99

0-60MPH (SEC): 17.1/16.3/13.7

SUSPENSION & BRAKES: Hydro ifs, Hydro irs, disc f/drum r

LENGTH (IN)/WEIGHT (LB): 164/2645

LAUNCH PRICE: £873

1800S was dropped in 1972 to make way for the six-cylinder 2200 model, but the 86bhp version soldiered on until 1975.

Like the Austin, too, the Mk III version of March 1972 had a floor-mounted handbrake, and a rod-operated gearchange, but apart from small revisions to the front grille and the equipment there was little to make it worth giving the car a new model name.

Have any survived? Because the hull, though rust-prone, was solid, there are a few. While they're not everybody's idea of a classic, they're not expensive, simple to work on and make a change from a Cortina.

2200 1972-75

Apart from its badging, and the fact that it was sold through a different dealer chain, the 2200 was the same six-cylinder front wheel drive car as the Austin 2200. See that entry for details.

SPECIFICATION

BODY STYLES: saloon

PRODUCTION: 20,865 Morris and Austin 2200s

ENGINE & TRANSMISSION: 2227cc, 6cyl ohc, 4sp man, or auto, f/f

POWER: 110bhp @ 5250rpm

MAX SPEED (MPH): 104

0-60MPH (SEC): 13.1

SUSPENSION & BRAKES: Hydro ifs, Hydro irs, diasc f/drum r

LENGTH (IN)/WEIGHT (LB): 167/2620

LAUNCH PRICE: £1325

The six-cylinder overhead-camshaft Morris 2200.

Marina 1971-80

In 1968, newly-founded British Leyland needed a rival for Ford's all-conquering Cortina, and engineered the ADO28 (called Morris Marina) accordingly. Conventional in every way, it used a new 96in-wheelbase platform, and offered a choice of four-door saloon, two-door "coupé" (actually a fastback saloon) and five-door estate car to face up to Ford.

The engine choice was conventional – A-Series and B-Series (the latter in single- or twin-carburettor tune) – with all-synchromesh manual, or automatic, transmissions. For "image" reasons, the MGB-tune TC engine never got an automatic option though.

The big mistake, hindsight now tells us, was to use modified Morris Minor/ Wolseley 1500-style torsion bar independent front suspension, for this guaranteed awful understeer at first (a hasty recall for modifications never entirely cured the problem). This, and the fact that cars were not always properly built, and strikes were hitting hard at British Leyland, damaged the Marina's reputation considerably. The first 1.3-litre types had drum brakes all round, but disc front/drum rear is normal wear on all other Marinas.

At the outset the price was right and careful product planning had lined up a big choice of derivatives, so businesses bought the cars in large numbers for their fleets. Early performance types were TCs, though these became HLs for 1976, when the Marina became Marina 2. From 1977 there was a rare diesel-engined Marina,

Morris Marina 1300 saloon, 1971, dull and not very worthy either.

The TC Coupé was a bit more exciting, its engine being more or less to MGB tune.

sold only as a four-door saloon in export markets; only 3870 such cars were built.

From mid-1978 there was a big engine carve up when the venerable 1798cc unit was dropped and replaced by the 78bhp 1695cc overhead-camshaft O-Series. From this point there was a much improved fascia design, but this engine only came with the four-door saloon body. It was a 98mph car, and originally cost £3029, which tells how bad inflation

had been during the 1970s.

All Marinas were dropped to make way for the Ital in mid-1980, but as this was only a much facelifted Marina some people didn't really notice the difference. Although the Marina family sold well and certainly made money for British Leyland, it is chiefly remembered for its poor handling, a complete lack of character and doubtful build quality. It's hard to these cars as candidates for restoration.

SPECIFICATION

BODY STYLES: saloon, two-door coupé, estate

PRODUCTION: 659,852

ENGINE & TRANSMISSION: 1275cc/1798cc, 4cyl ohv/1695cc 4cyl ohc/1489cc diesel, 4sp man, or auto, f/r

POWER: 60bhp @ 5250rpm-95bhp @ 5500rpm

MAX SPEED (MPH): 86-100

0-60MPH (SEC): 16.8-12.1

SUSPENSION & BRAKES: tor ifs, leaf rear, (ear;y 1275cc) drums f&r (all others) disc f/drum r

LENGTH (IN)/WEIGHT (LB): 167/1949 - 2117

LAUNCH PRICE: £923

A 1979 Morris Marina Mk II 1700L estate.

Ital 1980-84

Here was the Morris badge's final fling. With help from a noted Italian styling house (hence the name of the new model), the Ital was effectively a seriously modified Marina, complete with a new face and a longer tail. This time around, though, there was no two-door coupé – all cars being either four-door saloons or five-door estates.

Original cars had the choice of 61bhp 1275cc A-Series or 78bhp 1695cc O-Series engines, then from late 1980 there was also a 1993cc 90bhp version of the O-Series unit, but this was available only with automatic transmission, which was of course optional on other Itals too. In fact the 1993cc engine was dropped from the range in May 1982.

Under the platform, which kept the Marina's 96in wheelbase, nothing much had changed, for the age-old torsion bar front end was retained, with leaf-spring rear suspension which tended to tramp when provoked.

Inside the car, the fascia was totally different from that of the Marina, and in the showrooms the customer could choose between a bewildering number of trim packs – L, HL and HLS, which became SL and SLX from late 1982.

This model was dropped in February 1984, though the last cars did not leave the showrooms until much later that year. With the end of the Ital, the Morris marque died away too. Like its parent, the Marina, it is not a car to cherish.

The Ital replaced the Marina in 1980 but no one got very excited.

SPECIFICATION

BODY STYLES: saloon, estate

PRODUCTION: 175,276

ENGINE & TRANSMISSION: 1275cc, 4cyl ohv/1695cc/1993cc, 4cyl ohc, 4sp man, or auto, f/r

POWER: 61bhp @ 5300rpm/78bhp @ 5150rpm/90bhp @ 4750rpm

MAX SPEED (MPH): 91/98/101

0-60MPH (SEC): 15.2/12.5/11.7

SUSPENSION & BRAKES: tor ifs, leaf rear, disc f/drum r

LENGTH (IN)/WEIGHT (LB): 171/2070 - 2163

LAUNCH PRICE: £3736

18-22 Series (AD071 series) 1975

This car was the Morris equivalent of the Austin 18-22, and was virtually identical to the Austin in every detail, except for the actual

SPECIFICATION

BODY STYLES: saloon

PRODUCTION: 19,000, including Austin and Wolseley types

ENGINE & TRANSMISSION: 1798cc, 4cyl ohv/2227cc, 6cyl ohc, 4sp man, or auto, f/f

POWER: 82bhp @ 5200rpm/110bhp @ 5250rpm

MAX SPEED (MPH): 96/104

0-60MPH (SEC): 14.9/13.5

SUSPENSION & BRAKES: HydraG ifs, HydraG irs, disc f/drum r

LENGTH (IN)/WEIGHT (LB): 175/2557-2600

LAUNCH PRICE: £2117/£2424

Morris 18-22, on sale for only eight months.

badging, and the showrooms where it was sold. Like the Austin and Wolseley models, this car had only an eight-month life, and would be submerged into the "Princess" marque after that. See the Austin 18-22 entry.

O G L E

David Ogle was a successful industrial designer, working at Murphy, who built radios and TVs, before starting his own business, Ogle Design at Letchworth in Hertfordshire. Before the end of the 1950s he, armed with only 18 employees, had an urge to design and build his own cars – the first result being the Riley-based Ogle 1.5.

That toe-in-the-water exercise was not successful, but the second contract – the Ogle Mini SX1000 – was much more fruitful. Sales, marketing and production were developing well until Ogle himself was killed in a road crash in May 1962; he

was only 40 years old. Even though his partner, John Ogier, was an accomplished businessman and race driver, and Tom Karen soon arrived as managing director and chief designer, the Ogle brand never really developed any further.

After that Ogle Design became even more famous as consultants to other companies – most notably, in this period, to Reliant on the various Scimitars, GTEs, and the Bond Bug. Even in the 1990s the Ogle name was still around, although no new car shapes had recently been credited to the company.

1.5 1961-62

This short-lived project was David Ogle's first take on the way his car-making ambitions should develop. Strangely, Ogle chose the Riley 1.5 saloon as its basis, though the majority of that car's unit-construction body was cut out and abandoned.

Only the Riley floor pan (cut off ahead of the rear axle line), some front-end inner panels and the bulkhead were retained, along with the front suspension, steering, engine/transmission unit and rear axle. Extra stiffening panels were added along the under-door sills. At the rear there was a complex multi-tube chassis extension (with square-section

The Ogle 1.5, 1960.

tubing) which had been engineered by race-car designer John Tojeiro, the Riley rear axle being suspended on coil-over-shocks and located by no fewer than three radius arms.

The body style, in glass-fibre, was a 2+2 seater fastback coupé (from some angles you could confuse it with a Gilbern GT). There were soft leather seat covers, rear seats which were very definitely hammocked to increase the headroom, and a fascia incorporating

an instrument pod ahead of the driver's eyes.

Although it was a smart car, there were two major problems. One was that the chassis was reputedly not torsionally stiff enough, the other more important one being that at £1574 it was too expensive (the Riley 1.5 saloon cost £816 and an MGA coupé, for instance, £1027). With no order book building up, Ogle speedily abandoned this one and turned to the more promising SX1000 project instead.

SPECIFICATION

BODY STYLES: sports coupé

PRODUCTION: 8

ENGINE & TRANSMISSION: 1489cc, 4cyl ohv, 4sp man, f/r

POWER: 60bhp @ 4800rpm

MAX SPEED (MPH): 88

0-60MPH (SEC): 20.1

SUSPENSION & BRAKES: coil ifs, coil rear, drums f&r

LENGTH (IN)/WEIGHT (LB): 165/1975

LAUNCH PRICE : £1574

SX1000 1962-64

This egg-like Mini-based coupé, launched just a year after the unsuccessful Ogle 1.5, looked a lot more promising – once again, that is, until one looked at the price tag. This

time round David Ogle had taken the bare bones of a BMC car – the then-new Mini-Cooper – and added his own interpretation of what a sports coupé should look like.

It was costly because manufacture involved taking a complete Mini-Cooper, cutting and stripping it down to the front end/platform/sub-frames state, and building up from there. To stiffen up the platform (the GRP body could not possibly help) there was extra metal stiffening in the sills, bulkhead and rear end.

The two-seater body shell was made from glass-fibre, and looked rather like an Ogle 1.5 which had shrunk in the wash, although on this occasion there was a more pleasing nose, with four headlamps in the corners of the grille. Because the SX1000 was only 46.5in high, the Microcell seats had to be dropped on to the floor pan, and headroom over the rear "shelf" was distinctly marginal. The very first prototype had an 848cc Mini engine, but production cars were sold with Mini-Cooper engines or (from 1964, just before the end came) with 1275S power units instead.

Although the Ogle Mini sold at a silly, inflated price – in 1962 one paid £640 for the Mini-Cooper before it was vandalised, then another £550 for the conversion – there was a clientele who wanted style, and a bit more performance, and were willing to pay for it. But, let us be honest about this, it fell into the "indulgence" category, a market sector which was small.

SPECIFICATION

BODY STYLES: sports coupé

PRODUCTION: 66

ENGINE & TRANSMISSION: 997cc/1275cc, 4cyl ohv, 4sp man, f/f

POWER: 55bhp @ 6000/76bhp @ 5800rpm

MAX SPEED (MPH): (76bhp) 102 (E)

0-60MPH (SEC): (76bhp) 15.0 (E)

SUSPENSION & BRAKES: rubber ifs, rubber irs, disc f/drum r

LENGTH (IN)/WEIGHT (LB): 134/1507

LAUNCH PRICE: £1190

Ogle SX1000, 1962, had Mini mechanicals.

OPPERMAN

Before it turned to automotive manufacture, Opperman was a well-regarded precision and general engineering company, with three factories in Hertfordshire, the largest being at Stirling's Corner, on the A1 (Great North Road) just out of London.

Just before the Suez Crisis struck, Opperman decided that there was money to be made from cheap-and-cheerful small cars, commissioning the ubiquitous Lawrie Bond to engineer a new rear-engined four-wheeler for them to sell. The result was the Unicar saloon, which would have short-lived and ephemeral success. Its problem was that it looked crude, sounded crude and was unrefined to drive, so not even a reasonable price could make up for its lack of attractions.

Even so, in 1958 the Unicar was joined by the more sporty-looking Stirling (named after the factory location, not the racing driver…) but production of that car never even got started. Conspiracy theorists suggest that BMC had a hand in killing off the Oppermans, by threatening sanctions against their mutual suppliers – but it's more likely that the public simply didn't like what it was being offered.

Whatever the reasons, Opperman pulled out of the car-making business early in 1959, and never attempted to make a comeback.

Unicar 1956-59

Opperman had none of the expertise needed to engineer their own mini-car, so the Unicar was commissioned from the amazingly inventive Lawrie Bond, who at the time was no longer connected with Bond cars and was working on the then-new Berkeley sports car. Like several other Bond-designed vehicles of the day, the Unicar was an advanced yet at the same time crudely engineered machine.

This very basic four-wheeler had two doors and 2+2 accommodation (willing children could be slotted into the rear). Its GRP body shell was moulded around tubular aluminium sub-frames and reinforcements. There were two basic hammock-style front seats, and a padded rear shelf which also doubled as a cover for the battery – and for access to the air-cooled twin-cylinder motorcycle engine.

The Unicar was a mixture of modern, archaic, and plain bizarre. Coil spring independent front suspension was good, but the noisy and smelly two-stroke engine, with final drive by chain, was an anachronism and doomed the car to mediocrity. The rear axle, with no differential and with one coil-over-shock suspending it, was crude.

The asking price of £400 was superficially attractive (yet Britain's cheapest "real" car, the Ford Popular

100E, for instance, cost very little more at £414). Some Unicars were sold, tax-free, as kits. Mind you, to make up for the very down-market image and equipment provided, the Unicar had to be cheap. Amazingly, a handful of these machines have survived.

The motorcycle-engined Opperman Unicar, 1956-59.

Stirling 1958-59

In a fit of enthusiasm, Opperman then decided to take the Unicar theme one stage further by styling its own fastback coupé shape (think of an NSU Sport Prinz, which did it better, and you'll get the picture) around the existing Unicar layout. The "Stirling", as it was christened, was named after the location of the factory where it was to be built.

This time around they chose a larger 424cc Excelsior engine and offered hydraulic brakes, but not even calling it the "Family Speed Saloon" could do the trick.

Opperman Stirling coupé.

In theory, deliveries would begin in 1959, but they never did. Maybe it was the much higher price than the Unicar (all of £541 – you could buy a year-old Austin-Healey Sprite for less) and maybe it was the manifest crudities which put people off. Who knows?

If you discount the "killed-by-BMC-influence" conspiracy theory, we think it failed because it was a thoroughly unsaleable car. Apparently one example survives.

OPUS-HRF

Special-builder/converter Neville Trickett somehow convinced the patrician Rob Walker that it might be amusing, even profitable, to put a "fun-car" kit of parts on sale in the 1960s. By engineering the body and chassis so that standard Ford pieces could be bolted into place, it would be possible for almost anyone with a garage to complete the job.

Amazingly Walker, who owned a thriving garage business at Warminster in Wiltshire, agreed with him. Walker, whose interests really lay in F1 (where he ran a successful private team) and in real sports cars, let others do the marketing which, considering the Opus-HRF's looks, was surprisingly successful.

As happened so often with projects of this sort, sales were much slower than expected, so Rob Walker hived off the operation to one Roy Dickenson of Bristol in 1970, but it all died the death in 1972.

Opus-HRF 1966-72

It was one of those very silly open-top two-seaters, the sort which appealed to Neville Trickett and his pals, and which he thought might appeal to others. Opus-HRF provided the basics of an open-top two-seater machine which looked as if it might find a home in midget or banger racing, on a fairground, in a specialised driving test, or on a dry warm day at the seaside. Although Opus-HRF specified what ought to be purchased to complete the car, the customer was expected to source these bits himself.

The simple and rugged tubular chassis supported a glass-fibre bathtub-like two-seater body with an enormous windscreen. The radiator was vertical, the headlamps were bolted to the side of the radiator surround, and cycle-type wings were the standard wear.

The rest of the running gear was pure Ford. Early cars used a 997cc Anglia 105E powertrain, but later cars used larger-capacity Ford engines, all from the same Anglia/Escort/Cortina family; some cars, for sure, did not line up with the typical specification printed here.

The front end, crude and obviously so, was the transverse leaf sprung beam axle of the obsolete Ford Popular 100E but the rest, according to Opus-HRF would "accept all Ford parts without modification". Some cars had 10-inch Mini wheels, some used 13-inch Ford wheels. Not that this made any difference to the steering geometry.

To bowdlerise Cosworth's legendary founder, Keith Duckworth on other subjects, such a car was "daft, plain daft" – but it appealed to a couple of hundred extroverts.

SPECIFICATION

BODY STYLES: sports car

PRODUCTION: c.250

ENGINE & TRANSMISSION:
997cc/1298cc/1599cc, 4cyl ohv, 4sp man, f/r

POWER: 39bhp @ 5000rpm/71bhp @ 6000rpm/88bhp @ 5400rpm

MAX SPEED (MPH): not measured

0-60MPH (SEC): (1298cc) 7.0 (E)

SUSPENSION & BRAKES: beam leaf front, leaf rear, drums f&r

LENGTH (IN)/WEIGHT (LB): 122/900

LAUNCH PRICE: With 1298cc engine, £670 fully-built. Kits, various packages, from £112

Opus-HRF.

PANTHER

Panther-Westwinds was set up by car enthusiast and industrial designer Robert Jankel in 1972, using premises at Byfleet, near Weybridge, which had previously been occupied by the Cooper F1 motor racing team. Jankel, who was the son-in-law of the famous bandleader Joe Loss, set out unashamedly to develop a series of "pastiche" cars reminiscent of early motor cars. He always insisted that these were not, and were never intended to be, replicas.

The original, best-selling, model was the J72, a Jaguar-powered two-seater reminiscent of the 1930s-type SS100, after which there were the Ferrari FF (1974) and the De Ville (monstrous, and trying to ape the Bugatti Royale). The Rio of 1975 was no more than a re-skinned Triumph Dolomite Sprint, and has no place here, but the Vauxhall-engined Lima, which was Morgan-sized, was a more serious proposition.

Panther hit financial problems in 1979, and was bought up by Young C. Kim of South Korea; Robert Jankel left the company shortly afterwards. Without its charismatic founder, Panther then lurched from crisis to crisis. The Kallista was a Ford-engined derivative of the Lima, which was good, but the four wheel drive Sierra Cosworth-engined Solo was a total marketing disaster.

Ssang Yong of Korea took control in 1987 and the business was moved to Korea in 1992, but nothing came of this, and the enterprise (and the marque) died completely in 1996.

J72 (Later known as Brooklands) 1972-81

This, the original Panther, was built on strictly traditional lines, with a tubular chassis frame and, at first, a coil-sprung beam front axle (independent suspension followed). There was also a coil-sprung rigid rear axle (at first), with wire-spoke wheels and four-wheel disc brakes, all topped by a coachbuilt (aluminium panels on a wooden frame) two-seater sports car body with separate front wings and massive separate headlamps.

Power, transmission and almost all the chassis components came from current Jaguars – using either the six-cylinder XK or the still-new 5.3-litre V12 engines. In fact there were very few V12-engined versions, as Panther could not gain regular supplies from the Jaguar factory. Some cars even had automatic transmission – no wonder that Jaguar purists shuddered whenever they encountered a J72. Specifications often followed customers' particular requirements, and some development changes were made this way too, so beware pedants arguing about the mechanical specification.

More practical than the SS100, from which its styling was inspired, it had a much more roomy cockpit. Endowed with colossal acceleration (though not top speed as the aerodynamics were awful), this was not a car for the self-effacing. Call it a retro-car, call it a poseur's car if you will, but there is no doubt that it made an impact. Amazingly, as many were sold as the original SS100 had sold in the 1930s, but those were different times.

Panther J72 V12.

SPECIFICATION

BODY STYLES: sports car

PRODUCTION: c.300

ENGINE & TRANSMISSION: 3781cc/4235cc, 6cyl 2ohc/5343cc, V12cyl ohc, 4sp man, o/d or auto, f/r

POWER: 190bhp @ 5000rpm/266bhp @ 5750rpm

MAX SPEED (MPH): 114/136 (E)

0-60MPH (SEC): 6.4/not measured

SUSPENSION & BRAKES: coil beam front (coil ifs from 1977), coil rear (later cars with coil irs), discs f&r

LENGTH (IN)/WEIGHT (LB): 160/2504

LAUNCH PRICE: £4380/£5285/£9500

The Panther J72 with sidescreens erected.

FF 1974-75

Panther's second pastiche came in 1974, when an attempt was made to replicate the late-1940s Ferrari 125S body style, complete with separate front wings, atop a contemporary Ferrari chassis and running gear. Amazingly, Ferrari agreed to supply 330GTC rolling chassis (though that car was no longer available from Maranello), and Panther's craftsmen did the rest in Surrey.

Originally produced at the request of Willy Felber of Switzerland (already a Panther dealer), the FF made its debut at the Geneva Show in March 1974. The style was somewhat up-dated from the

Panther FF had a Ferrari 330GTC engine.

SPECIFICATION

BODY STYLES: sports car

PRODUCTION: 12

ENGINE & TRANSMISSION: 3967cc, V12cyl ohc, 5sp man, f/r

POWER: 300bhp @ 7000rpm

MAX SPEED (MPH): 160 (E)

0-60MPH (SEC): 4.5 (E)

SUSPENSION & BRAKES: coil ifs, coil rear, discs f&r

LENGTH (IN)/WEIGHT (LB): 154/2100 - 2204

LAUNCH PRICE: c. £13,000

late 1940s style, with the headlamps semi-recessed into the sides of the nose, the sidelamps at the front of the flowing wings, and a bonnet air intake for the 300bhp 3967cc V12 engine. The spare wheel sat out in the open, clamped to the tail.

It's worth remembering that the Ferrari 330GTC "donor" car had a 275GTB/4-style multi-tube frame, with four-wheel independent suspension and the V12

engine driving the rear-mounted five-speed transaxle by means of a stout torque tube.

Though the pedigree was appealing, and the style quite cute, at an estimated UK price of £13,000 this car was always going to be too expensive; for comparison, a contemporary Jaguar E-Type V12 cost less than a third of this, at £3812, which maybe explains that so few FFs were actually sold.

De Ville 1974-85

Looked at from the point of view of aesthetics, the Panther De Ville was simply awful. Though large, impressive

The Panther de Ville. What a mess.

SPECIFICATION

BODY STYLES: saloon, drophead

PRODUCTION: c.60

ENGINE & TRANSMISSION: 4235cc, 6cyl 2ohc/5343cc, V12 ohc, 4sp man, o/d or auto, f/r

POWER: 190bhp @ 5000rpm/ 266bhp @ 5750rpm

MAX SPEED (MPH): 127 (E)/137 (E)

0-60MPH (SEC): not measured/not measured

SUSPENSION & BRAKES: coil ifs, coil irs, discs f&r

LENGTH (IN)/WEIGHT (LB): 204/4264 - 4368

LAUNCH PRICE: £21,965/£17,650

and admittedly beautifully built, it represented everything that was wrong with the "replicar" movement of the 1970s. Some say that it was inspired by the Bugatti Royale – but we remind you

that that was a commercial failure too!

The De Ville was huge. Based on an all-tubular chassis frame, and no less than 204in long, like the J72 sister (sports) model it was powered by well-proven Jaguar hardware. Most cars had the massive 5.3-litre V12, but some had the traditional (and definitely ageing by that time) 4.2-litre XK power unit, and most were also matched to Borg Warner automatic gearbox. Independent coil spring suspension was fitted at front and rear, many components being lifted directly from the Jaguar parts bin of the day, and of course power-assisted steering was standard.

The body style spoke (or rather shrieked) for itself. It was traditional in that it had separate headlamps, flowing front wings, running boards and a vertical radiator which aped that of Bugatti. All this enclosed a big and rather angular four-door saloon body (though a few two-door convertibles, and even the occasional six-door stretch type were both made). The boot, by the way, was a separate trunk, in traditional coach-built style, and the spare wheel sat behind that.

Separate reclineable front seats, wall-to-wall walnut-veneer fascia, and every possible fixture or fitting were standard, the standard instruments and controls once again being Jaguar-derived. All in all, this was a totally over-the-top machine which appealed to very few people. Many years later, perhaps it was inevitable to find "the baddies" in Walt Disney's 102 Dalmations rushing round in a brightly liveried De Ville..

Lima 1976-82

Compared with earlier Panthers, the Lima was a much more serious proposition. Smaller, lighter, cheaper and altogether more practical than cars like the J72, the Lima aimed directly at the Morgan market, with some success.

The original Lima, a two-seater sports car, took shape around the pressed-steel underpan/platform of the contemporary Vauxhall Magnum, and had that car's overhead-camshaft 2279cc engine. Panther beefed up the platform and used all the Vauxhall's chassis and suspension components.

As one expected of Panther at this time, the body styling was really a modernised 1930s "retro" (perhaps as successful as anything Morgan was building at the time), with a mainly glass-fibre body shell, though it used MG Midget door assemblies. Headlamps were set out in the open, front wings swept back, and there were running boards below the doors. All but

Panther Lima, 1976.

the first cars had a big "cow-catcher" front spoiler under the bumper.

The two seats were set well back, just ahead of the line of the Vauxhall rear axle, and the tail was rounded off but carried an exposed spare wheel. Many Vauxhall instruments and controls were used in the fascia display.

From late 1978 the Lima became Mk II, with a new, all-Panther, tubular steel chassis which replaced the beefed-up Vauxhall platform and made the car altogether more rigid. By this time the smaller 1759cc Vauxhall overhead-cam

engine, and even automatic transmission, had become available. To special order, a few cars also got turbo-charged engines.

If only Panther's name had not been tainted by the diehards, the Lima might have sold better than it did, for in performance, roadholding, comfort and equipment it beat the existing Morgan 4/4 1600. Even so, it provided valuable cash flow to Panther for years, and was eventually replaced by the Kallista of 1982, which had Ford mechanicals in place of the Vauxhall components.

SPECIFICATION	
BODY STYLES: sports car	
PRODUCTION: 897	
ENGINE & TRANSMISSION: 1759cc/2279cc, 4cyl ohc, 4sp man, auto, f/r	
POWER: 96bhp @ 5200rpm/108bhp @ 5000rpm	
MAX SPEED (MPH): 107 (E)/115	
0-60MPH (SEC): not measured/6.7	
SUSPENSION & BRAKES: coil ifs, coil rear, disc f/drum r	
LENGTH (IN)/WEIGHT (LB): 142/1800 - 1950	
LAUNCH PRICE: £8997/£4998	

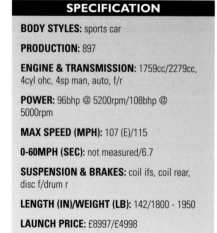

The 178bhp Panther Turbo Lima.

PARAMOUNT

Garage employees Bill Hudson and Sam Underwood of Stanton, in Derbyshire, often dreamed of building "their" car, and finally made one, in a tiny workshop at Swadlincote. Based on a new chassis frame, and a coachbuilt four-seater body, this machine picked up readily available Ford Prefect pieces, and was named Paramount.

This amateurish operation creaked slowly into operation in 1950 at Woodville nearby but, under-capitalised, lacking marketing skills, and with no image already behind the badge, it struggled to settle down. Only seven cars were built before a capital injection allowed assembly to move once again, this time to Melbourne, where the company was known as Meynell Motors.

Predictably, after only six cars had been produced, this all ended in tears, the result being that Camden Motors, a large and flourishing concern of motor traders, bought up the business, and re-established it near their company HQ at Leighton Buzzard. By previous standards, production then leapt, and from 1954 the engine was changed for the larger, heavier and more powerful overhead-valve Ford Consul unit.

It was a false dawn, however, for customers were still hard to find. The end came in 1956 when Welbeck Motors bought up the old stock – 26 cars, no less – and sold them off cheaply. No more was ever heard, in the motor industry, of Bill Hudson or Sam Underwood.

Ten/1½-litre 1950-56

The Paramount definitely falls into the "high hopes" category of post-war motoring, for the company's founders knew little about engineering, but just loved cars and wanted to have their own to sell. After producing a prototype based on the post-war Alvis chassis, they sensibly moved down-market to offer a tubular-framed machine with old-style sidevalve Ford Prefect components.

The original Paramount was an odd mixture – rigid modern chassis with independent front suspension, but 1930s-style running gear. It had a smart coachbuilt body (wooden frame, steel and aluminium panelling) in the form of a four-seater tourer with a vee-windscreen. The looks suggested an 80mph-plus performance, but with only an anaemic Ford engine and its three-speed transmission the car

struggled to reach even a lowly 65.

The transverse leaf spring front end was independent (though Leslie Ballamy might not have recognised it as wishbones were also involved), but this was the only enterprising part of the running gear.

Not even Camden Motors could persuade people that this sluggish tourer was worth £995 (which it cost in 1952), so a change to the Ford Consul 1508cc engine was made in 1954. That, at least, delivered 80mph, but there was still a

distinct lack of charisma, and by 1956 not even a hardtop derivative could help the cause. Later cars had twin fuel tanks – one each hidden in the front wings behind the wheel arches.

After Welbeck Motors bought up the bankrupt stock they discovered one new but two-year-old Ford Prefect-powered version among them. They managed to move them on but were not interested in continuity or development. Where have they all gone? Gone to scrap yards, we guess, almost every one.

SPECIFICATION

BODY STYLES: saloon, drophead

PRODUCTION: c.150

ENGINE & TRANSMISSION: 1172cc, 4cl sv/1508cc, 4cyl ohv, 3sp man, f/r

POWER: 30bhp @ 4000rpm/47bhp @ 4400rpm

MAX SPEED (MPH): 65 (E)/72

0-60MPH (SEC): not measured/31.2

SUSPENSION & BRAKE: leaf ifs, leaf rear, drums f&r

LENGTH (IN)/WEIGHT (LB): 166/2072 - 2436

LAUNCH PRICE: £632/£1014

The Paramount was made 1950-56. Early cars made do with Ford's 1172cc sidevalve unit, but an overhead-valve 1508cc Consul engine became available later.

PEEL

Before 1962, Peel Engineering Co. had led a blameless existence in the Isle of Man, specialising in GRP (glass-fibre) mouldings for industry, including bathtubs. They then astonished the motoring business by producing what they rightly claimed to be the smallest car in the world.

This was a truly minuscule single seater which certainly had no rivals in its packaging or its marketing approach. Like all other tiny cars of the period, it relied extensively on motorcycle technology of the period – in this case the use of a DKW motorcycle engine and transmission – while the structure was developed by its own GRP specialists.

The original P50 was so bizarre, and so obviously vulnerable to assault by any other motor vehicle (including, even, other and larger tri-cars) that it failed to make its mark. To get themselves out of a fix, therefore, Peel developed a larger, tubbier, and more bizarre-looking two-seater, calling it the Trident, but this was even less of a success.

Hurt by what they thought was the British motoring public's failure to appreciate real enterprise, Peel then took the Mini-Marcos route, with a similar-looking GRP coupé which relied totally on BMC Mini running gear. That failed too, so it was all over by 1967.

P50 1962-66

An air of incredulity surrounded the entire Peel P50 project, for it was an almost ludicrously tiny three-wheeler, with tiny ambitions (except to be a new type of "peoples" car), only one seat, and absolutely no attempt at providing refinement.

The very first Peel, shown in November 1962, had one front wheel and twin rears, though a few test drives soon convinced the engineers that two fronts and one rear would be more stable.

With a monocoque glass-fibre body structure, and the tiny DKW moped engine tucked away behind/under the seat, the P50 provided only one door (on the near side, for safety purposes), and one headlamp. Naturally there was no reverse gear – if you wanted to go backwards you dismounted and tugged the P50 by means of a handle provided at the rear!

At a mere 53 inches long, the P50 was the smallest "car" in the world – ever –

SPECIFICATION	
BODY STYLES: saloon	
PRODUCTION: 75	
ENGINE & TRANSMISSION: 49cc, 1cyl ts, 3sp man, m/r	
POWER: 4.2bhp @ 6500rpm	
MAX SPEED (MPH): 38 (E)	
0-60MPH (SEC): not possible	
SUSPENSION & BRAKES: coil ifs, coil irs, drums f&r	
LENGTH (IN)/WEIGHT (LB): 53/132	
LAUNCH PRICE: £200	

Peel P50, 1962. The most basic transport.

and was extremely cheap at £199.50. It was delivered from the factory in a wooden box – which some buyers continued to use as a rudimentary garage!

Crude in the extreme, with a very noisy interior, it was difficult for the P50 to be taken seriously.

Just a few people did take it seriously,

however – and their cars have survived, though you are unlikely ever to see one. The Trident which followed was an enlarged derivative of the P50.

Trident 1965-66

Based on the same minimalist layout as the (even smaller) Peel P50, the Trident was claimed to be a two-seater, for two could just about squeeze into the bubble, side by side.

The Trident's body consisted almost entirely of a forward-hinged section, which had a weirdly profiled but flat windscreen and a clear bubble-top dome roof.

Slightly larger (at 72in long), it could still turn in no more than 96 inches, so there was really no need for a reverse gear, which was not provided. Boldly, Peel priced the Trident at even less than

the P50 – it sold for a mere £190 – but this really could not generate much enthusiasm, even if the larger Vespa 100cc engine was fitted. The project died off in just over a year.

SPECIFICATION

BODY STYLES: saloon

PRODUCTION: 45

ENGINE & TRANSMISSION: 49cc, 1cyl ts, 3sp man, m/r

POWER: 4.2bhp @ 6500rpm

MAX SPEED (MPH): 40 (E)

0-60MPH (SEC): not possible

SUSPENSION & BRAKES: coil ifs, coil irs, drums f&r

LENGTH (IN)/WEIGHT (LB): 72/not quoted

LAUNCH PRICE: £190

Peel Trident.

Viking 1965-67

This was a glass-fibre 2+2 coupé, with in-built steel linking front and rear sub-frame mountings to which the customer added Mini running gear.

SPECIFICATION

BODY STYLES: coupé

PRODUCTION: c.50

ENGINE & TRANSMISSION: 848cc, 4cyl ohv, 4sp man, f/f

POWER: 34bhp @ 5500rpm

MAX SPEED (MPH): 75 (E)

0-60MPH (SEC): not measured

SUSPENSION & BRAKES: rubber or Hydro ifs, rubber or Hydro irs, drums f&r

LAUNCH PRICE: £230 for body kit + cost of donor car

Peel Viking, 1965.

PEERLESS

Although the name was connected with a company which had sold reconditioned US Peerless trucks in the 1920s, there was no US or commercial vehicle connection in the 1950s. Instead Bernie Rodger used the old premises at Slough, became involved with John Gordon to engineer a new chassis, and launched the Triumph TR3-based Peerless GT in 1957; deliveries began in 1958.

As with so many other projects of this period, the idea was good, but it was was let down by crudities in the quality of finish (GRP bodies still had a long way to go before they were acceptable) and the inescapably high price.

Initial publicity was good – a works car performed with honour in the Le Mans 24 Hour Race – but that still didn't bring in the punters. Cash flow was certainly present at Peerless, but mostly in the wrong direction, and although the company once forecast that it would be making 25 cars a week there were never enough sales to make this a reality.

By February 1960 – and less than two years after deliveries had begun – Peerless filed for bankruptcy, owing £13,700 in unpaid Purchase Tax, and about £50,000 to its other creditors. Revival, though, came almost at once, in the shape of the near-identical Warwick GT.

GT 1958-60

How to summarise this car? Probably as a good idea, with smart looks and a credible mechanical and performance package, but built badly, and sadly lacking almost every type of refinement and the reliability needed to bolster a lasting reputation.

Based on a multi-tube chassis frame with square-section tubes (how would the specialist car industry have managed without this?), the original Peerless prototype had a mainly aluminium-panelled body with some GRP mouldings. However, by the time deliveries began in mid-1958, bodies were all-glass-fibre, made by James Whitson and Co. of West Drayton, in Middlesex.

From front to rear the running gear was pure Triumph TR3, complete with the unburstable 1991cc wet-liner engine, the overdrive transmission, centre-lock wire-spoke wheels, and the coil spring independent front suspension. The De Dion rear suspension, though, was a real novelty. The body style was long and low, with 2+2 accommodation and slight hoods (fashionable at the time) over the headlamps.

If it had been built properly (without squeaks, rattles, leaks or breakdowns – they all happened on a Peerless) the GT might have sold better, even though it was expensive. It had the usual special-builders' problems though, and demand

SPECIFICATION

BODY STYLES: sports coupé

PRODUCTION: c.325

ENGINE & TRANSMISSION: 1991cc, 4cyl ohv, 4sp man, o/d, f/r

POWER: 100bhp @ 5000rpm

MAX SPEED (MPH): 103

0-60MPH (SEC : 12.8

SUSPENSION & BRAKES: coil ifs, DD leaf rear, disc f/drum r

LENGTH (IN)/WEIGHT (LB): 162/2240

LAUNCH PRICE: £1498

soon fell away when word got around.

The Warwick GT, which leapt Phoenix-like from the flames, was a better proposition.

The TR-powered Peerless GT.

PIPER

Motorsport engineer George Henrotte, Campbells Garage of Hayes in Kent, and stylist Tony Hilder all had a hand in setting up the Piper project. The result, first previewed in 1967, was the startlingly beautiful GT (later the GTT would become the "production car"), which started life as a kit-car project to which one was invited to fit Ford Cortina-type engines and components.

Series production of a sort began in 1968 when one Brian Sherwood took up the project, founded Piper Cars, and began building cars at Wokingham, near Reading. All cars concentrated on using Ford four-cylinder engines. Bill Atkinson joined the company at this time, and carried on after Sherwood was killed in a road accident while driving his Piper.

By 1971 the GTT had progressed to P2, which involved a longer-wheelbase chassis and the original rectangular headlamps being replaced by twin circular ones, after which (from 1972) larger single lamps popped up when needed.

After Piper Cars failed financially, Atkinson and Tony Waller tried again, this time with Emmbrook Engineering of South Willingham, in Lincolnshire, but by 1974 the imposition of VAT on kit-car sales was hurting Piper just as hard as all other such firms, and the automotive project was abandoned. Amazingly, in later years the company turned to making luxury bathroom equipment, and prospered mightily at that, but there was no further attempt to re-enter the motor industry.

GTT/P2 1968-74

First there was the GTA, then the GTT production kit car – which is to say that it was partly assembled by Piper before being collected by the customer for completion at home, to save himself paying purchase tax on a fully built-up car.

It was built around a multi-tube chassis frame in which many members were made from the ubiquitous square-section tubing. This frame was designed to accept proprietary components such as Triumph Herald front suspension, steering and disc brakes, but a Ford beam rear axle. It was to be powered by one of several different Ford four-cylinder engine and gearbox combinations. Rear axle location was by triangulated radius arms.

The body shell, moulded from glass-fibre, was an extremely attractive two-seater coupé, with a long nose, a vast and heavily wrapped-around screen, deep side windows, and a big rear window glass covering a very short tail. It was, literally, as low as it looked – at 41 inches.

Changes included re-designing the GTT to become the P2 in 1971, at which point the chassis was lengthened by six inches, sturdy outriggers were added to the chassis, the pedal box became adjustable, and the original rectangular headlamps gave way to paired circular headlamps behind Perspex shields. One

SPECIFICATION

BODY STYLES: sports coupé

PRODUCTION: c.50/100

ENGINE & TRANSMISSION: 997cc/1298cc/1599cc, 4cyl ohv, 4sp man, f/r

POWER: 39bhp @ 5000rpm/71bhp @ 6000rpm/88bhp @ 5400rpm

MAX SPEED (MPH): (88bhp) 120 (E)

0-60MPH (SEC): not measured

SUSPENSION & BRAKES: coil ifs, coil beam rear, disc f/drum r

LENGTH (IN)/WEIGHT (LB): not quoted

LAUNCH PRICE: £1435

year later, in 1972, yet another headlamp change saw single circular headlamps hidden behind covers which could be flipped up by a hydraulic mechanism.

Various one-off engined types were sold, but the majority of cars had cross-flow Ford Kent power units. By this time the price had rocketed to £2500, which put it into E-Type territory. For that reason, and the usual resistance to kit cars, sales were always slow, and after VAT had been imposed they dried up altogether.

In many ways a race-influenced design which had been re-developed for the road, the Piper would no doubt have accepted higher-power engines if customers had asked for them. Quite a number of these striking-looking machines survived the 20th century.

Piper GTT.

POWERDRIVE

Although Powerdrive did not last long as a car-making enterprise – set up in 1955, it was all over by 1958 when the company collapsed – it was later revived as the Coronet, which has already been described.

The Powerdrive project was set up to build a super-economy car at Wood Green in North London. Like many such cars, it relied on very simple engineering – a tubular chassis, a coachbuilt light-alloy body and a motorcycle-type engine – but this, by definition, embraced crudeness to keep down the price.

Almost every entrepreneur who thought he could insult the British motorist's intelligence by aiming so low came a cropper, and Powerdrive was no exception. Not even the onset of petrol rationing in the winter of 1956-57 could give this square little three-wheeler machine a good grounding, and it failed in 1958.

Roadster 1955-58

Announced in 1955, the Powerdrive was aimed at the "graduate-from-motorcycles" market, for it was more of a three-wheeler with bodywork than a motor car with three wheels. Two front wheels and one rear wheel at least provided the most stable platform possible. Designer David Gottlieb devised a tubular chassis with a rear-mounted British Anzani two-stroke motorcycle engine. The three-speed motorcycle gearbox was in unit with engine, and final drive was by chain. Gear-changing was by a dash-mounted

The Powerdrive.

SPECIFICATION

BODY STYLES: roadster

PRODUCTION: not known

ENGINE & TRANSMISSION: 322cc, 2cyl ts, 3sp man, r/r

POWER: 15bhp @ 4800rpm

MAX SPEED (MPH): (E) 60

0-60MPH (SEC): not measured

SUSPENSION & BRAKES: coil ifs, coil irs, drums f&r

LENGTH (IN)/WEIGHT (LB): 148/840

LAUNCH PRICE: £382

lever in a visible gate. Coil spring and swinging arm independent front suspension and hydraulic braking were enterprising, as were the swing-axle rear end and the electric starter, but the rest of the running gear was of two-stroke motorcycle standards, the result being noisy, smelly and slow transport. The body, of aluminium with steel reinforcements, was shaped to make it look as if there were two rear wheels. Vents in the rear flanks told you where the engine was. Plastic sidescreens and a fold-back soft top completed a very basic specification.

PRINCESS

If only British Leyland had been as adept at making money as it was at changing its mind, all would have been well, but…

Way back in the 1950s, Princess had been a model name for up-market Austins, and from 1959 that allegiance was transferred to Vanden Plas models instead. From 1975, however, Princess became a marque of its own – at least as far as the 18-22 (ADO 71) family was concerned, for "Princess" stayed on as a model name for a particular Allegro until 1980 as well!

From late 1975 what we may now call "Princess Princess" types were all re-badged versions of the large 18-22 front wheel drive Austin, Morris and Wolseley models cars which had only been launched earlier in that year.

First-generation Princesses, therefore, were produced with 1.8-litre B-Series and 2.2-litre E6 engines, and from 1978 these were replaced by the Series II models which used 1.7- and 2.0-litre O-Series and 2.2-litre E6 engines. There was no further development, and in 1982 the entire range was dropped, in favour of the Austin Ambassador, which was a hatchback derivative of the Princess II – the version which it should always have been.

1800/2200 1975-78

The newly-created Princess 1800 and 2200 took over smoothly from the similarly-engined Austin, Morris and Wolseley models in September 1975, with no technical changes and the very minimum of trim and equipment alterations. The 1798cc versions had four-headlamp noses, and six-cylinder

Princess 1800 had quad headlamps.

SPECIFICATION

BODY STYLES: saloon

PRODUCTION: 84,867 (1800)/63,443 (all 2200 to 1982)

ENGINE & TRANSMISSION: 1798cc, 4cyl ohv/2227cc, 6cyl ohc, 4sp man, or auto, f/f

POWER: 82bhp @ 5200rpm/110bhp @ 5250rpm

MAX SPEED (MPH): 96/104

0-60MPH (SEC): 14.9/13.5

SUSPENSION & BRAKES: HydraG ifs, HydraG irs, disc f/drum r

LENGTH (IN)/WEIGHT (LB): 175/2557-2638

LAUNCH PRICE: £2237/£2562

2227cc-engined versions had near-rectangular headlamps as a recognition point. There were 1800 and 1800HL, 2200HL and 2200HLS types, the top-most model being equivalent to the very short-lived 1975-model Wolseley Six.

Very few changes were made to these cars in three years, and from July 1978 they were replaced by the Series II, where the principal innovation was a new range of overhead-camshaft four-cylinder engines.

Like the dumpy old-type British Leyland models they replaced, all these Princesses were handsome, soft-riding, and remarkably good handling machines, with vast five/six-seater cabins, though they never captured the sales that they seemed to deserve and never came as hatchbacks. For too long, there were well-justified complaints about build quality, and British Leyland's reputation for awful labour relations did not help either.

1700/2000/2200 Series II 1978-81

From mid-1978 this Princess range became Series II. Though there were no external style changes, the range was re-aligned. The old 1798cc engine had been dropped, and in its place came two versions of the new overhead-camshaft O-Series engine – in 87bhp 1695cc and 93bhp 1993cc form. The existing six-cylinder 2227cc engine carried on as

Princess II.

SPECIFICATION

BODY STYLES: saloon

PRODUCTION: 41,134/35,498/see above

ENGINE & TRANSMISSION: 1695cc/1993cc, 4cl ohc/2227cc, 6cyl ohc, 4sp man, or auto, f/f

POWER: 87bhp @ 5200rpm/93bhp @ 4900rpm/110bhp @ 5250rpm

MAX SPEED (MPH): 99 (E)/98/104

0-60MPH (SEC): not measured/14.6/13.5

SUSPENSION & BRAKES: HydraG ifs, HydraG irs, disc f/drum r

LENGTH (IN)/WEIGHT (LB): 175/2510 - 2638

LAUNCH PRICE: £3725/£4390

before. Automatic transmission was optional for all three engines.

As before there were three trim levels – 1700L/1700HL/2000HL, along with the usual 2200HL/2200HLS. HL and HLS interiors had been smartened up considerably, there being circular instrument dials and a genuine wood fascia surrounding them. 1700HLS and

2000HLS types were added from spring 1979, and from that time the only six-cylinder type on sale was the 2200HLS.

Production of these cars carried on steadily until the end of 1981, when the entire Princess range was replaced by a much-changed hatchback model known as the Austin Ambassador. Princesses are now so rare as to be almost invisible.

RANGE ROVER

By the 1960s there was a yawning market gap at Rover between the utilitarian Land Rover and the well-crafted middle-class Rover cars. The company spent time trying to deal with that gap, and projects originally known as "Road Rovers" eventually evolved into a new type of 4x4.

Acting independently of product planners, ace engineer Spen King developed a massive new 4x4, to use the company's newly-acquired V8 engine, and conceived a smart four/five-seater body style totally different (and much more up-market) from the Land Rover. This went into production at Solihull in 1970, and became an important part of that operation for the next generation.

Starting gently – it sold only 5510 copies in the first full year – the Range Rover soon became the icon of the countryside, and the middle and upper-middle classes in general. While specifications gradually improved, and interior appointments became more and more luxurious, the go-anywhere four wheel drive capabilities were never degraded. Once the Discovery (which used a Range Rover chassis) had joined the range, these modern 4x4s outsold the traditional type of Land Rover "Defender".

The Range Rover was always a very profitable long-term project, and successive generations have emphasised that position. When Rover private car assembly moved from Solihull to Longbridge, the Range Rover became the most prestigious brand to stay behind.

BMW approved the development of a third-generation type for the 2000s, and after Ford bought up Land Rover it once again took the limelight at Solihull.

Range Rover 1970-96

Although decades of Land Rover experience went into the original Range Rover, there was absolutely no carryover of components. Apart from using a de-tuned version of the Rover's alloy V8 engine, here was a motor industry rarity – an all-new machine.

Built up on a sturdy box-section 100in-wheelbase chassis frame, the Range Rover used the traditional four wheel drive layout – engine up front, main gearbox behind it, with the high/low ratio arrangements and transfer box behind that, and separate propeller shafts to front and rear axles. Beam axles, front and rear, were suspended on coil springs, and four-wheel disc brakes were standard.

The original body style was a three-door estate car (the rear door was a two-piece, upper-and-lower, arrangement), built up of an inner steel structure with aluminium skin panels. Although original types had plastic seat coverings and washable mats on the floor, this machine was trimmed and equipped to an altogether higher standard than the Land Rover had ever been.

Although 100mph was not quite available at first, and fuel economy could be as low as 12-14mpg, there was always a queue to buy, and the Range Rover became an absolute fixture among the countryside set. After 1970, a whole raft of changes and improvements would follow – diesel engines, automatic transmissions, five-door bodies, and special editions – such that the original Range Rover would actually remain in production for a quarter of a century. In the first decade, however, innovations arrived only slowly – optional power-assisted steering from January 1973 and Fairey overdrive from early 1978 being the highlights. Even so, there would be no five-door derivative until 1981, nor an automatic transmission option until 1982. The first fascia re-style would come in 1984, and the first fuel-injected engine in 1985.

Early examples had very soft suspension, so it was a brave driver who pushed on hard on the roads to the limit of its abilities, but that wasn't the point. Any hill, swamp or ice field that could be beaten by a Land Rover could also be beaten by a Range Rover, in style and without breaking sweat...

Range Rover in its element.

SPECIFICATION
BODY STYLES: estate
PRODUCTION: 317,615, all types
ENGINE & TRANSMISSION: 3528cc, V8cyl ohv, 4sp man, f/4
POWER: 135bhp @ 4750rpm
MAX SPEED (MPH): 99
0-60MPH (SEC): 12.9
SUSPENSION & BRAKES: coil beam front, coil rear, discs f&r
LENGTH (IN)/WEIGHT (LB): 176/3880
LAUNCH PRICE: £1998

RELIANT

First there was Raleigh, then there was Reliant. The connection was Tom Williams, who had designed a three-wheeler for the cycle-building Raleigh company, bought the rights in it, and set up his own Reliant company in Tamworth to produce the same three-wheeler. After the Second World War, Reliant first prospered with Austin Seven-engined three-wheelers, but eventually turned to machines with an own-brand four-cylinder engine. From the early 1960s the company began to build sports cars (at first in conjunction with Sabra of Israel). Early Sabres were crudely engineered, but Ogle-styled Scimitars were much better, and the sporting-hatchback Scimitar GTE went on to be a great success.

Expansion at Tamworth led to Reliant also making the three-wheeler Robin, whose handling quirks made it infamous, and there was a four-wheeler Rebel to keep marginal motorists happy. Reliant even went so far as to buy up Bond in 1969 – some say to eliminate their major three-wheeler competitors from the market place.

After the Scimitar GTE faded away in the 1980s, Reliant's fortunes gradually slumped, for the smaller Michelotti-styled Scimitar SS1 was no beauty, and Robin/Rialto three-wheeler sales gradually declined. Several changes of ownership and several financial crises later, Reliant finally closed its doors in the early 2000s.

Regal MkI-VI 1952-62

Designed entirely at Tamworth, the Regal became Britain's archetypal three-wheeler, a car which thousands of ex-motorcyclists used to make their first transition from two wheels towards full car ownership. Based around a sturdy box-section chassis, with a single front wheel, but with a front-mounted four-cylinder engine driving the rear axle, it was simple, reliable – and cheap to run.

Like all this generation of Regals, the first car used Reliant's own version of the old sidevalve Austin Seven engine, the front wheel being suspended on a leading arm with torsion bar springing.

Early cars had coachbuilt body shells – aluminium panels on a traditional wood skeleton – but from 1956 glass-fibre was used instead, though the ash frame was retained. Early cars were soft-top tourers, but once GRP was adopted a two-door saloon took over and the style became significantly more rounded.

Evolution was slow but sure, so Mk Vs (1959) had a much sharper nose style, some versions had sliding sidescreens in the doors, and before the end came in 1962 the ancient Austin engine had been persuaded to produce 18bhp.

Although these machines built their own ever-expanding market – in the last two years, nearly 8500 Mk VIs were produced, or 40 per cent of the ten-year total – their reputation was founded on lightness, operating economy, and the fact that three-wheelers were always cheaper to licence with British authorities. They were certainly not very stable when pushed hard on corners, nor were they luxuriously trimmed, but the clientele didn't seem to mind that.

The Reliant concern made money, thrived, expanded, and made ever better three-wheelers as the years passed by, which is more than can be said for almost all their rivals.

A 1962 Regal van.

The Austin Seven-engined Reliant Regal Mk I, 1952.

SPECIFICATION

BODY STYLES: saloon, tourer, commercials

PRODUCTION: 20,359, all derivatives

ENGINE & TRANSMISSION: 747cc, 4cyl sv, 3sp man/4sp man, f/r

POWER: 16bhp @ 4000rpm/18bhp @ 4000rpm

MAX SPEED (MPH): 60/63

0-60MPH (SEC): not measured

SUSPENSION & BRAKES: tor ifs, leaf rear, drums f&r

LENGTH (IN)/WEIGHT (LB): 1234/890

LAUNCH PRICE: £300

Regal 3/25, 3/30 1962-73

To replace the old Austin Seven-engined Regal, Reliant produced an entirely new three-wheeler in 1962. Not only did it feature a brand-new chassis frame (still with only one front wheel), and an all-glass-fibre body, but it had its own in-house overhead-valve four-cylinder engine with alloy block and head castings. Launched as the 3/25 (where 25 represented the claimed power output) this Regal would be around for more than ten years and more than 105,000 examples.

The new car had coil spring inde-

1968 model Regal de Luxe used a 29bhp version of Reliant's own engine.

SPECIFICATION

BODY STYLES: saloon, estate, commercials

PRODUCTION: 105,824, all types

ENGINE & TRANSMISSION: 598cc/701cc, 4cyl ohv, 4sp man, f/r

POWER: 24bhp @ 5250rpm/29bhp @ 5000rpm

MAX SPEED (MPH): 64/73

0-60MPH (SEC): not measured/29.6

SUSPENSION & BRAKES: coil ifs, leaf rear, drums f&r

LENGTH (IN)/WEIGHT (LB): 135/896

LAUNCH PRICE: £450

pendent front suspension and a more sturdy chassis which provided greater stiffness and crash protection at the front, but otherwise the layout was as before. The 598cc engine was more powerful and more torquey than the previous unit.

The new glass-fibre body featured sharp-edged styling with headlamp hoods and a reverse-slope rear window (Ford Anglia 105E-style).

An estate car derivative joined the range from the mid-1960s, and from 1967 the

family was up-dated to 3/30, with a 29bhp 701cc derivative of the little engine. From late 1964, too, there was a four-wheeler evolution of this car, called the Rebel (separately described), and until the early 1970s the Regal was very much the mainstay of Reliant's business.

Like the early Regals, this generation of three-wheelers sold strongly on their virtues of lightness, operating economy, and reduced annual licencing fees. In 1973, the Regal's replacement was the well-known Robin.

Rebel 1964-73

When Reliant introduced the Rebel in September 1964, it caused quite a surprise, as it was a lineal

SPECIFICATION

BODY STYLES: saloon, estate

PRODUCTION: 3500

ENGINE &TRANSMISSION: 598cc/701cc/748cc, 4cyl ohv, 4sp man, f/r

POWER: 27bhp @ 5250rpm/31bhp @ 5000rpm/35bhp @ 5500rpm

MAX SPEED (MPH): 63/68/72

0-60MPH (SEC): not measured/35.9/not measured

SUSPENSION & BRAKES: coil ifs, leaf rear, drums f&r

LENGTH (IN)/WEIGHT (LB): 138/1178

LAUNCH PRICE: £525/£592/£845

descendant of the recently rejuvenated Regal three-wheeler type. This was one of the first cross-over models (four wheels instead of three wheels) that the British motor industry had achieved.

Although the Rebel used the same

The Reliant Rebel 700 Estate: four wheels and no frills.

598cc engine, four-speed gearbox and spiral-bevel back axle as the Regal, it was much more than a mere conversion. Much heavier, in any case, it had a new box-section chassis frame in which the engine was mounted much further forward than it could ever go in the three-wheeler, with Triumph Herald coil spring front suspension but with worm-and-peg steering. Full hydraulic brakes were fitted, and the spare wheel was mounted up front, under the bonnet, atop and to one side of the engine.

The two-door four-seater saloon body was Ogle-styled, but essentially rather plain, very simply trimmed and equipped. Even though it was capable of 63mph, and handled in a neat but unobtrusive way, the Rebel was too costly to attractive a huge order book. Initially priced at £525, it had to compete with the basic Mini (£470) and basic Ford Anglia 105E (£479) – which it could not do.

Reliant persisted with this car, though, phasing in the 701cc engine in October 1967, launching an estate car at the end of 1967, then pushing up the engine to 748cc in September 1972, but the last car was produced in December 1973. It would be two more years before the even larger-engined Kitten appeared to fill the gap.

Sabre and Sabre Six 1961-63/1962-64

It was only after Reliant co-operated with Sabra of Israel in building a sports car that they considered launching a similar car for British and export markets. The result, at first, was a real "Ugly Duckling" which improved persistently but never won the hearts of the public. At least the Sabre taught Reliant how to do a lot better – with the Scimitar which followed.

To save time, Reliant chose an LMB chassis frame, complete with Leslie Ballamy's patented swing axle/coil spring front suspension. The rear axle was located by Watts linkages and sat under coil springs, and Reliant clothed the chassis in a GRP body shell of their own manufacture. For the original car, the Sabre (later known as the Sabre 4), they fitted a 72bhp Ford Consul 1703cc engine and a Ford four-speed gearbox.

Not only was the nose far too long, and the performance below par, but the "split-axle" front suspension suffered from awful bump steer. The revised version of late 1962 was given a shorter and much more attractive nose, while a new and optional fastback hardtop (with a sharply cut-off tail) looked much better too. The Sabre 4, however, did not last beyond the end of 1963.

Reliant Sabre, 1961.

The Sabre 6 of late 1962, complete with a six-cylinder 2553cc 109bhp Ford engine, was a more promising machine, especially after mid-1963 when the chassis was altered to accept Triumph TR4-type coil spring and wishbone front suspension.

Nothing, however, could shake off the original "special builder" image, and because by 1963 the Sabre 6 cost £1016 when a TR4 cost £907 and an Austin-Healey 3000 just £1046, Reliant had to fight an uphill battle on cost, image and build-quality grounds. In a straight line the Sabre 6 was fast (109mph), but the handling was none too special, and refinement was lacking. Only a few cars have survived.

Sabre Six coupé of 1962.

A Sabre Six SE2S on the Spa-Sofia-Liège rally in 1963.

SPECIFICATION
BODY STYLES: sports car, sports coupé
PRODUCTION: 208/77
ENGINE & TRANSMISSION: 1703cc, 4cyl ohv/2553cc, 6cyl ohv, 4sp man, or o/d, f/r
POWER: 72bhp @ 4400rpm/90bhp @ 5000rpm/109bhp @ 4800rpm
MAX SPEED (MPH): 93/109
0-60MPH (SEC): 14.4/9.9
SUSPENSION & BRAKES: coil ifs, coil rear, disc f/drum r
LENGTH (IN)/WEIGHT (LB): 165 (later 160)/1756-2212
LAUNCH PRICE: £1165/£1156

Scimitar SE4A 1964-66

Compared with the lumpy Sabre series, the Scimitar of 1964 was a vastly better car in all respects. It had a much-improved chassis (there was little connection with that of the Sabre Six), an excellent 2+2-seater coupé body styled by Ogle Design, and a well-equipped interior. This was the first of a family of Scimitars which would run, successfully, until the mid-1980s.

The sturdy 92in-wheelbase chassis featured box-section side members and reinforcements, used Triumph TR4-type coil spring front suspension and rack-and-pinion steering, and the Ford rear axle was sprung on coil-over-shock absorbers, with a fore-and-aft Watts linkage on each side. That rear end, in fact, was always controversial (because of linkage details, in effect the axle itself became a massive anti-roll bar), and was changed in favour of twinned trailing arms from September 1965. Front disc brakes and centre-lock wire-spoke wheels were standard.

The body, in glass-fibre, was a smooth and nicely-profiled fixed-head coupé, the fascia had a wood veneer finish, and there were small (not quite useless, but it was close) "+2" seats in the rear.

Power was by a triple-SU converted Ford Zephyr power unit, backed either by the Ford gearbox and optional overdrive,

Reliant Scimitar SE4A used the Ford straight-six engine.

or even (though these were rare) by the ZF 4S12 four-speeder (without overdrive, which could not be fitted).

All in all, this the SE4 was a remarkable turn-round by Reliant – not only in performance, but also in handling, looks, and build quality. However, this model would be dropped in October 1966, when Ford could no longer supply the straight-six engines (as that particular engine had gone out of series production). Instead, the same car was re-worked (see below) to accommodate Ford's new V6 power unit.

SPECIFICATION	
BODY STYLES: sports coupé	
PRODUCTION: 297	
ENGINE & TRANSMISSION: 2553cc, 6cyl ohv, 4sp man, and o/d, f/r	
POWER: 120bhp @ 5000rpm	
MAX SPEED (MPH): 117	
0-60MPH (SEC): 11.4	
SUSPENSION & BRAKES: coil ifs, coil rear, disc f/drum r	
LENGTH (IN)/WEIGHT (LB): 167/2200	
LAUNCH PRICE: £1292	

Scimitar SE4B/C 1966-70

SPECIFICATION	
BODY STYLES: sports coupé	
PRODUCTION: 590 3-Litre, 117 2.5-litre	
ENGINE & TRANSMISSION: 2495cc/2994cc, V6cyl ohv, 4sp man, o/d or auto, f/r	
POWER: 112bhp @ 4750rpm/136bhp @ 4750rpm	
MAX SPEED (MPH): 111/121	
0-60MPH (SEC): 12.3/10.0	
SUSPENSION & BRAKES: coil ifs, coil rear, disc f/drum r	
LENGTH (IN)/WEIGHT (LB): 167/2305	
LAUNCH PRICE: £1395/£1516	

Scimitar SE4B, now Ford V6-powered.

From late 1966, Reliant's Scimitar was re-engined with the brand new Ford V6 power units. Originally with the 136bhp 2994cc engine but from August 1967 with the 112bhp 2495cc unit as optional equipment, the Scimitar specification settled until November 1970, when the line was discontinued.

Except for listening out for the exhaust beats, it was difficult to pick these Scimitars out from the original straight-six types, though steel disc wheels had replaced the wire-spoke variety. Under the skin, though, the ZF gearbox had been withdrawn, and there were minor changes to trim and equipment.

Even though it was a heavier car, the 3-litre V6 version was significantly faster than the straight-six had been. It had also received further attention to ride, handling and refinement, and was a very saleable proposition – the production figures confirm this.

In 1970, though, the larger and even more versatile Scimitar GTE, with its entirely different body style, had taken all the limelight at Tamworth.

Scimitar GTE SE5/SE5a 1968-75

In October 1968, Reliant unveiled the Scimitar GTE and established a new type of body style – what many pundits called the "sporting estate". Effectively, this was a sports coupé, but with a square-back body style and a vast rear window which also doubled as a loading door. Because the GTE was longer and wider than the existing conventional coupé, it was an "almost four-seater", which appealed to many people.

Although the old Scimitar's Triumph-based front suspension/steering and the same coil-sprung rear axle were retained, the chassis was different, for the wheelbase was up by seven inches, the wheel tracks by seven inches, and the detailing of the pressings was totally new, especially at the rear end where they supported the big load platform.

The cabin style was much like that of the two-seater Scimitars, though far more spacious, and Reliant had arranged for the rear seat backrests to fold forward to maximise the load platform area For packaging reasons the spare wheel was up front, ahead of the radiator, and accessible by lifting up the bonnet panel.

First of the GT estates, the Scimitar GTE SE5 of 1968.

The latest type of 3-litre Ford V6 engine was specified (the 2.5-litre version was also mentioned at launch time but never reached the showrooms). Overdrive was an optional extra, Borg Warner automatic transmission was available from October 1969, and overdrive actually became standard from April 1971.

By any previous Reliant standards this car was a best-seller, well liked by the pundits, the media, and the customers too. Improvements over time to the interior, to the precise engine tune and to the gearbox ratios kept the car up to scratch. Even so, after a seven-year run, Reliant decided it was time for a complete re-design, the even larger SE6 type being the result.

SPECIFICATION

BODY STYLES: sports hatchback coupé

PRODUCTION: 4311 SE5, 5105 SE5a

ENGINE & TRANSMISSION: 2994cc, V6cyl ohv, 4sp man, o/d or auto, f/r

POWER: 138bhp @ 5000rpm

MAX SPEED (MPH): 121

0-60MPH (SEC): 8.9

SUSPENSION & BRAKES: coil ifs, coil rear, disc f/drum r

LENGTH (IN)/WEIGHT (LB): 170/2500

LAUNCH PRICE: £1759

Rear of the GTE had plenty of glass area.

GTE interior, with leather seats and full instrumentation.

Scimitar GTE SE6/SE6a 1976-80

In late 1975 (sales began in February 1976), Reliant performed deep-seated surgery on the Scimitar GTE. Though superficially it looked the same as ever, there was a new chassis frame with a four-inch longer wheelbase and three-inch wider wheel tracks. The glass-fibre body moulds had been cut up, hot-cross-bun style, re-fashioned, and modified to suit.

It was a masterstroke, not only in keeping continuity and a proven image, but in reducing tooling change costs to a minimum. Mechanically, the new frame supported almost the same kit as before, though power-assisted steering was to be optional, and the suspension was softer than before. A 20-gallon fuel tank was

The longer and wider Scimitar GTE SE6 replaced the SE5.

SPECIFICATION

BODY STYLES: sports hatchback

PRODUCTION TOTAL: 4420

ENGINE & TRANSMISSION: 2994cc, V6cyl ohv, 4sp man, o/d or auto, f/r

POWER: 135bhp @ 5000rpm

MAX SPEED (MPH): 119

0-60MPH (SEC): 10.0

SUSPENSION & BRAKES: coil ifs, coil rear, disc f/drum r

LENGTH (IN)/WEIGHT (LB): 175/2770

LAUNCH PRICE: £4367

now standard, and there were dual-circuit brakes.

Unless one looked carefully, the body style appeared to be unchanged, yet the whole shell was larger and there was more glass. One front-end recognition point was the use of larger 7-inch outer headlamps. The fascia layout was much changed too.

This was a good effort, as *Autocar*'s testers agreed: "…almost every item for which we had any criticism has been rectified. The result has been a much more refined product…"

The GTE was now at the height of its reputation, and sold well for four years before supplies of the old-type Ford V6 engine ran out. The result was that it was once again updated in 1980.

Scimitar GTE (SE6b)/GTC (SE8b) 1980-86

The final variation on the Scimitar GTE theme appeared in March 1980, when the chassis was re-engined with a Ford-Germany V6 and a convertible version of the car, to be known as the GTC, was launched. These two models would carry on the Scimitar brand until 1986.

This was the only Scimitar to be available as a hatchback and a drophead coupé. The GTC was announced at once, and in many of its body features it was like the Triumph Stag. The running gear was entirely shared with the latest GTE, but the drophead coupé body (still in GRP) had a fold-away soft-top and a

Scimitar GTE SE6B.

permanently fixed T-bar which not only acted as a roll cage if needed, but also provided valuable stiffening to the shell itself. Compared with the GTE there were style and layout changes in the tail, for this car had a separate lift-up boot lid, and a rather squared-off tail.

Both revised cars – GTC and GTE – had 135bhp 2792cc engines, as fitted to the contemporary Ford Granada and Scorpio models, and as with previous models they were available with a four-speed manual gearbox (with overdrive as standard), or with Borg Warner three-speed automatic transmission. No fewer than 300 cars were produced in 1980 alone – too many as subsequent events showed – and from December 1980 there was a further possibility, an optional bolt-on hardtop for the GTC, in which case the folding soft-top was deleted. The hardtop cost £437 and weighed a hefty 66lb. It was standardised in later years. After this, both types

continued, essentially unchanged, until mid-1986, though sales dried up almost completely after 1982 and only three cars a week were being produced. This pedigree of Reliant Scimitar finally died out in November 1986.

Scimitar GTC, 1980

GTC with hardtop in place.

SPECIFICATION

BODY STYLES: sports hatchback coupé, drophead

PRODUCTION TOTAL: 437 GTE, 442 GTC

ENGINE & TRANSMISSION: 2792cc, V6cyl ohv, 4sp man, o/d or auto, f/r

POWER: 135bhp @ 5200rpm

MAX SPEED (MPH): 119

0-60MPH (SEC): 10.0

SUSPENSION & BRAKES: coil ifs, coil rear, disc f/drum r

LENGTH (IN)/WEIGHT (LB): 175/2421

LAUNCH PRICE: £10,324

Robin 1973-81

The Robin was a direct successor to the Regal, and although it had the same basic chassis its styling, by Ogle Design, was quite different. This was a three-wheeler often mocked by snobbish pundits, especially after being used as the butt of jokes by TV series like Mr Bean. Other three-wheeler Reliants were some-times dubbed (wrongly) as Robins (like the Regals used in *Only Fools and Horses*), the media sometimes referring to them Robin Reliants!

Though the Robin's chassis frame was more robust than before, the basic layout was the same as that of the Regal

1975 Reliant Robin.

SPECIFICATION

BODY STYLES: saloon, commercials

PRODUCTION: not known

ENGINE & TRANSMISSION: 748cc/848cc, 4cyl ohv, 4sp man, o/d or auto, f/r

POWER: 32bhp @ 5500rpm/40bhp @ 5500rpm

MAX SPEED (MPH): (32bhp) 72

0-60MPH (SEC): (32bhp) 22.5

SUSPENSION & BRAKES: coil ifs, leaf rear, drums f&r

LENGTH (IN)/WEIGHT (LB): 131/946

LAUNCH PRICE: £801

3/30, with many components carried over. At first the engine was eased out to 748cc, giving 32bhp, but a 40bhp 848cc derivative took over in 1975.

The two-door body exhibited a more rounded silhouette than the Regal's – not craggy, with no sign of hooded headlamps, and it featured a very practical lift-up hatchback. From the screen backwards, the whole of the cabin would be shared by the Kitten which was to follow. Trim and equipment were kept simple, because Reliant had to keep down the overall weight to maintain fuel economy.

Robins sold steadily, at up to 10,000 a

year, until the early 1980s, when the same basic chassis was once again re-bodied, this time by a wedge-style machine known as the Rialto. That car was not liked by everyone, so some years later the Robin would be re-introduced.

Like the Regal, the Robin was a brisk performer in a straight line, but the single front wheel chassis could provide perilous handling if pushed too far. No serious motorist – only those types who wanted truly marginal accommodation, equipment and costs – ever took a three-wheeler Reliant seriously. But we must ask the question, can a quarter of a million buyers all be wrong?

Kitten 1975-82

Reliant Kitten had a certain charm.

The concept was simple enough. If the Rebel had been a four-wheeler relative of the 1960s Regal, then the Kitten was the four-wheeler derivative of the Robin. Although having a four-wheeler rear-drive chassis, a different box-section frame and naturally a unique four-seater saloon style, the technical link between the two cars was obvious. The choice of the name – "Kitten" – was carefully made to stress what a non-competitive, non-macho machine this was.

Sitting on an 84in-wheelbase chassis frame, with simple coil spring and wishbone front suspension with rack-and-pinion steering, the Kitten was powered by the latest 40bhp 848cc version of Reliant's own light-alloy engine (for the first time, this engine had

an SU carburettor), and the same basic gearbox as was used in the Robin three-wheeler. Being both light and low-powered, it needed no more than drum brakes all round, and Mini-type 10in wheels were standard. The Kitten was seven inches shorter than the Rebel.

The Ogle-styled GRP body shell, though conventional at the nose, from the screen back was based closely on that of the Robin three-wheeler. It was available as a saloon (really a hatchback, as the rear window opened, with a very high rear sill) or as an estate car. The trim, fascia and instruments were all much as found in the Robin.

Because the three-door estate version

had already appeared, there were virtually no other developments over time. However, from January 1981, reclining front seats and a heated rear window were standardised. Selling much slower than Reliant had hoped – even in the inflationary 1970s the high initial price cannot have helped – the Kitten died of neglect in December 1982, and no attempt was made to replace it.

The Kitten was a brisk little mover (faster than the Mini, and more economical too), but it gave a hard and nervous ride and, of course, it did not handle as well as the much cheaper (£1299) Mini. Perhaps this was one reason why it sold so slowly.

SPECIFICATION

BODY STYLES: saloon, estate

PRODUCTION: 4551

ENGINE & TRANSMISSION: 848cc, 4cyl ohv, 4sp man, f/r

POWER: 40bhp @ 5500rpm

MAX SPEED (MPH): 78

0-60MPH (SEC): 19.6

SUSPENSION & BRAKES: coil ifs, leaf rear, drums f&r

LENGTH (IN)/WEIGHT (LB): 133/1159

LAUNCH PRICE: £1499

RILEY

Proudly based in Coventry since Victorian days, Riley had been building cars since 1903. Having hit hard times in 1938, it was then swept into the Nuffield Organisation but retained much of its autonomy at first.

Integration into Nuffield (and, from 1952, BMC) took a long time. Early post-war RM series Rileys were designed in Coventry and still used all-Riley components – engines, chassis and bodies. Yet this practice was sure to come to an end.

In 1949 Riley assembly was moved down to the MG factory at Abingdon, and the first Nuffield-designed model was the Pathfinder of 1953. In fact this was the last Riley to use a Riley-designed engine, for the 2.6 which followed was no more and no less than a re-badged Wolseley 6/90.

With Nuffield subsumed into BMC, there was further rationalisation. BMC clearly decided that new Rileys would be

better-equipped, sometimes faster, derivatives of Austin-Morris cars, and although a Riley dealer chain would be maintained, the cars would never again be individually shaped or engineered. The 1.5 was an upmarket Wolseley 1500 (both cars used a Morris Minor platform), the 4/68 was a derivative of the Austin A55, and the appealing little Elf was a booted and bustled front wheel drive Mini. Once started, that process was never likely to be reversed, as every Riley of the 1960s was based on corporate engineering and assembled either at Longbridge (the old Austin plant) or at Cowley (Morris).

According to BMC accountants, Riley's strategy was profitable, but from 1968 – after British Leyland was formed – the new management decided to dump a once-famous brand. The last Riley was produced in 1969, and the badge then disappeared into the parts bin.

1½-Litre RMA/RME 1946-55

The first of the post-war Rileys, previewed in 1945 and on sale from 1946, used the 1930s-type Riley engine and transmission, but every other component was new. By finding time during the war years Riley had engineered a brand-new chassis frame, and designed a rakish body shell for it.

Although this car was always too heavy, it must have been aerodynamically efficient – 78mph from only 55bhp was a real achievement – and the style, complete with semi-recessed headlamps, was distinctive. Built by traditional methods – a wooden frame with pressed steel structural and skin panels – it had a divided screen, a slim four-door cabin and individual front seats. The interior was somehow "clubby" in ambience, and there was a fabric covering for the roof. The

The 1952 1½-litre RME had rear wheel spats and no running boards.

original fascia layout, with scattered dials and instruments, was replaced by a more integrated layout from late 1949.

The "12/4" engine with its twin high camshafts was very familiar to Riley owners but the chassis, with torsion bar independent front suspension, rack-and-pinion steering, drive via a torque tube to the rear axle, and hydro-mechanical brakes, was all new.

Assembly moved from Coventry to Abingdon in 1949, and type RME cars took over from Type RMA in late 1952. RMEs had helmet-type front wings, and the running boards were removed. Out of sight there was a simpler rear suspension – with half-elliptic leaf springs but no torque tube – and the brakes were now

hydraulically operated all round.

The 1½-litre RM-Series was a car of great charm, with formidable roadholding and steering response for its day, though its acceleration was sorely affected by its weight. For that reason, and in spite of its higher price, the 2½-litre version was better regarded.

Riley 1½-litre RMA.

SPECIFICATION

BODY STYLES: saloon

PRODUCTION: 10,504 RMA, 3446 RME

ENGINE & TRANSMISSION: 1496cc, 4cyl ohv, 4sp man, f/r

POWER: 55bhp @ 4500rpm

MAX SPEED (MPH): 78

0-60MPH (SEC): 25.1

SUSPENSION & BRAKES: tor ifs, leaf rear, drums f&r

LENGTH (IN)/WEIGHT (LB): 179/2688

LAUNCH PRICE: £710

2½-Litre RMB/RMD/RMF 1946-53

Big brother to the 1½-litre type, by late 1940s standards the "16hp" 2½-litre Riley was reckoned to be a performance car. It shared the same chassis and low-slung four-door body as the 1½-litre, but the 2½-litre had a longer wheelbase (119in instead of 112.5in) to accommodate the bulkier and heavier 2443cc engine.

Though the engine was of 1937 vintage (it was launched just before Nuffield absorbed Riley) it was very powerful and torquey – and was in fact adopted by Healey for their own post-

The 2½-litre RMD drophead coupe of 1948-51.

war sports cars. It suited the character of this car perfectly. The combination of the longer wheelbase, which improved the look, and 100bhp ("only" 90bhp until 1948), made this a real sports saloon.

The smart two-door drophead coupé derivative joined it from 1948 to 1951 (502 were produced), and a very special three-seater Roadster was also built (described next), but it was the saloons which sold so well; some performed with great honour in races and rallies.

Assembly was at Coventry until 1949, and at Abingdon thereafter. Like the 1½-litre type, the 2½-litre gained a more stylish fascia in 1949, and the more conventional rear suspension in 1952, but (unlike the 1½-litre) there were no styling updates at that time.

2½-litres were well-loved and were often driven very hard when they were new. Because of their performance, and their purer pedigree compared with later "BMC-Rileys", in later years they became much prized by the Riley enthusiasts' movement.

In 1953 the 2½-litre was dropped in favour of the very different Pathfinder.

1948 Riley 2½-litre RMB in Police service. The bonnet is longer than on the smaller-engined cars.

SPECIFICATION

BODY STYLES: saloon, drophead

PRODUCTION: 8959, including Roadster

ENGINE & TRANSMISSION: 2443cc, 4cyl ohv, 4sp man, f/r

POWER: 90bhp @ 4000rpm/100bhp @ 4500rpm

MAX SPEED (MPH): 95

0-60MPH (SEC): 15.2

SUSPENSION & BRAKES: tor ifs, leaf rear, drums f&r

LENGTH (IN)/WEIGHT (LB): 186/3136

LAUNCH PRICE: £1125

2½-Litre RMC Roadster 1948-50

In theory we Brits never knew much about the Riley 2½-litre Roadster (RMC) model, as it did not officially go on sale in the UK until late in its life. Aimed principally at the export market, particularly North America, it was built for only two years, during which 507 examples were sold. By 1949 it was listed for UK sale at £1225.

The chassis was pure Riley 2½-litre RMB, as basically was the front end of the body back to the bulkhead, though the radiator and bonnet line were 1.5in lower. Aft of the bulkhead, however, this was a very different car – a two- or three-seat Roadster with a bench seat.

The specially-styled coachbuilt body had a long and sweeping tail, cutaway

Riley RMC three-seater roadster.

SPECIFICATION

BODY STYLES: sports roadster

PRODUCTION: 507

ENGINE & TRANSMISSION: 2443cc, 4cyl ohv, 4sp man, f/r

POWER: 100bhp @ 4500rpm

MAX SPEED (MPH): 98

0-60MPH (SEC): 19.0

SUSPENSION & BRAKES: tor ifs, leaf rear, drums f&r

LENGTH (IN)/WEIGHT (LB): 186/3080

LAUNCH PRICE: (1949) £1225

doors, removable side curtains and an exposed spare wheel at the rear. In its description, *The Autocar* noted that the "long tail of the body provides a luggage boot of prodigious capacity.. The lid of this conceals the twin fillers of the fuel tank, which contains 20 gallons".

There were very large and solid chrome-plated bumpers, four over-riders at front and rear, and a steering-column gearchange on the left hand drive cars which made up the majority of deliveries. The windscreen was arranged to fold flat if the weather was encouraging – which abroad rather than in Britain it often is.

Road tests showed that this was almost a 100mph car, which handled equally as well as the RMB saloons, but the best that could be said of the gearchange is that it freed up space in the front seat. A few right hand drive cars were produced, and they happily got a centre-floor gearchange.

In the UK this Roadster was a distinct rarity, and a rather gangly one at that. Like the saloons, though, it was quicker than most rivals. Rot in the timber frame has been its greatest enemy.

Pathfinder 1953-57

Although the vision behind the new BMC/Nuffield-inspired Pathfinder, was clear, the execution was always flawed. To replace the 2½-litre RM Series models, BMC allowed Nuffield to develop a big new saloon which would have much in common with a new large Wolseley (the 6/90 launched in 1954), but which would retain the legendary twin high camshaft Riley engine and would have torsion bar independent front suspension. The Pathfinder was always assembled at the MG factory at Abingdon.

Apart from the 2.4-litre engine, everything else about the Pathfinder (which, inevitably, became nicknamed "Ditchfinder") was new, for this was a bigger, bulkier and heavier car than the old 2½-litre model. It was built around a new separate chassis frame with the torsion bar front end, but there was at first a complex type of rear axle location, with coil-over-shock springing, semi-trailing torque arms and a Panhard rod. The gearbox was a new corporate BMC design with side-mounted selector rods and a right-hand floor gearchange on the outside of the driver's seat, Bentley fashion.

The all-steel four-door body, thought handsome by many, looked smooth and modern but had to be adapted to use a traditional Riley front grille. Pity about the bench front seat, but such things were still fashionable.

Deliveries did not begin until mid-1954, after which changes were frequent.

Riley Pathfinder driven by John Bremner in the 1956 Monte Carlo Rally, where it was placed 69th. An Austin A90 lies upside down behind.

Borg-Warner overdrive became optional from late 1955, and extra Panhard rod location was added to counter a tendency for the rod to tear out of its mounting, with "Ditchfinding" results.

The third chassis development arrived in late 1956, when the rear coil springs were dumped in favour of conventional half-elliptic leaf springs, Borg Warner automatic transmission became optional, and there was a new fascia design. Even so, production was discontinued in

January 1957, after which there was an interval of some months before its replacement (the 2.6) arrived.

Although the Pathfinder was faster and much more roomy than the old RM-Series had been, few Riley traditionalists warmed to it. The handling, especially of early types, wasn't up to much, nor was the build quality, and many objected to the obvious visual and technical links with the Wolseley 6/90. Could have been a great car, but missed several targets.

SPECIFICATION

BODY STYLES: saloon

PRODUCTION: 5536

ENGINE & TRANSMISSION: 2443cc, 4cyl ohv, 4sp man, o/d or auto, f/r

POWER: 110bhp @ 4400rpm

MAX SPEED (MPH): 98

0-60MPH (SEC): 16.7

SUSPENSION & BRAKES: tor ifs, coil rear (leaf rear from 1956), drums f&r

LENGTH (IN)/WEIGHT (LB): 183/3450

LAUNCH PRICE: £1382

The Pathfinder shared its styling, but not its engine, with the Wolseley 6/90.

2.6 1957-58

Hold on to your hats, for here was a classic BMC case of scissors and paste. To replace the slow-selling Pathfinder (and also to get rid of the old twin high cam Riley engine, which was no longer used in any other private car), BMC introduced the 2.6.

Looking rather like the Pathfinder, but very different under the skin, the 2.6 was really a badge-engineered Wolseley 6/90 Mk III; apart from the traditional Riley

Riley 2.6, 1958. This one did have the Wolseley's BMC C-type engine.

SPECIFICATION

BODY STYLES: saloon

PRODUCTION: 2000

ENGINE & TRANSMISSION: 2639cc, 6cyl ohv, 4sp man, o/d or auto, f/r

POWER: 97bhp @ 4750rpm

MAX SPEED (MPH): 93

0-60MPH (SEC): 17.4

SUSPENSION & BRAKES: tor ifs, leaf rear, drums f&r

LENGTH (IN)/WEIGHT (LB): 186/3610

LAUNCH PRICE: £1411

grille there were absolutely no unique Riley parts in the specification.

Like the latest 6/90 and the final Pathfinder, the box-section chassis featured torsion bar front suspension and half-elliptic rear springs, but the engine/transmission line-up was pure BMC 2639cc C-Series, with 97bhp – it had more torque but less peak power than the Pathfinder. The right-hand gear change was retained, and there was a full range of transmission

options. Smaller road wheels but a higher stance meant that the 2.6 didn't look as sleek as the Pathfinder, and a very con-trived duotone colour scheme didn't help either.

No one apart from BMC's cost accountants liked this one, for only 2000 cars were sold from 1957 to 1959, and virtually no one mourned its passing. It was the very last of the large Rileys, for all future models would have much smaller four-cylinder engines.

1.5 1957-65

In 1957, first there was the Wolseley 1500 (described below) and then, from November, there was the Riley 1.5, both of them sharing the same body structure, basic body style, and running gear. As was the way of things at BMC, the Wolseley was really an up-market Austin, and the Riley was meant to have a more sporty character.

The development process had been tortured, but the parentage of this car was clear. Although the 1.5 had a stubby unit-construction four-door saloon body, the platform was that of the Morris Minor 1000, from which also came – though modified – the front and rear suspension and the rack-and-pinion steering gear.

The B-Series engine/transmission installation, however, was really a de-tuned MGA outfit, for the twin-SU engine produced 62bhp and the gear-box featured a neat remote-control

The Riley 1.5, 1961 model.

floor change. Trim and furnishing were rather bitty and multi-coloured, though separate front seats were standard and there was a wood fascia featuring a rev-counter.

Although the 1.5 did not handle with the same crispness as the Minor 1000, it was a brisk little machine, but its top speed of 84mph was a little disappointing. Independent specialists soon proved that the 1.5 could be turned into an effective racing saloon car, though rallying success eluded it.

Although it stayed in production for eight years, there was little evolution in that period. The Mk II model of 1960 featured hidden bonnet and boot hinges, but few other changes, while the Mk III of 1961 had a slightly revised front-end style but no other innovation. At no time did overdrive become available.

By the early 1960s the 1.5 (and the Wolseley 1500) were really forgotten cars, though down-market Austin Lancer and Morris Major versions had been introduced for domestic assembly in Australia. Many people respected the 1.5, but no one really seemed to love it enough to preserve and improve later examples. Today, we reckon, this is an anonymous machine.

Pat Moss and Ann Wisdom in this 1.5 won the Coupe des Dames in the 1961 Sestrières rally.

SPECIFICATION	
BODY STYLES: saloon	
PRODUCTION: 39,568	
ENGINE & TRANSMISSION: 1489cc, 4cyl ohv, f/r	
POWER: 62bhp @ 4500rpm	
MAX SPEED (MPH): 84	
0-60MPH (SEC): 17.4	
SUSPENSION & BRAKES: tor ifs, leaf rear, drums f&r	
LENGTH (IN)/WEIGHT (LB): 153/2060	
LAUNCH PRICE: £864	

Riley 1.5s were useful on the circuits. Here the driver is E Lewis, in the Molyslip Trophy at Brands Hatch in August 1962.

4/68 and 4/72 1959-69

By 1959 BMC was at the height of its badge-engineering expertise and strategy. To summarise the Riley 4/68, imagine a Farina-styled Austin A55 or Morris Oxford Series V, but with more power (64bhp instead of 52bhp), a unique front-end style, cropped rear wings, and a pseudo "gentleman's club" interior with a glossy wooden fascia, a rev-counter, separate front seats and a remote-control floor gearchange. As the last of the five B-Series "Farina" cars to be launched, the 4/68 was really a clone of the MG Magnette Mk III, with which it shared the same engine, transmission

Riley 4/68, 1959, another variation on the BMC-Farina theme with leather, walnut and twin carburettors.

and much the same performance.

Though the 4/68 was by no means outstanding, BMC's marketing machine did a good job on it, so that it sold faster than any of the recent "real" Rileys had ever done. Yet its tracks were too narrow, its suspension was too soft, and there was a distinct lack of character.

BMC realised this, so from late 1961 the 4/68 became the 4/72, with a 68bhp 1622cc engine, wider tracks, a longer wheelbase, front and rear anti-roll bars and much improved handling. Borg Warner automatic transmission became optional but never made much impact on sales.

Nothing much did, really – for BMC never sold more than 3000 a year after 1961, and by the late 1960s sales were down to around 1000 a year. Not that anyone seemed to mind, for the 4/72 soon went off into its own twilight world as BMC's front wheel drive cars

Riley 4/72, 1961, with 1622cc engine and widened track.

took all the headlines and the sales.

Riley enthusiasts will be happy for you to forget all about the 4/72, which was killed off in the autumn of 1969, at which point the Riley brand also died. It was certainly not a car by which to remember one of Britain's oldest and most illustrious marques.

SPECIFICATION

BODY STYLES: saloon

PRODUCTION: 10,940/14,151

ENGINE & TRANSMISSION: 1489cc/1622cc, 4cyl ohv, 4sp man, or auto, f/r

POWER: 64bhp @ 4800rpm/68bhp @ 5000rpm

MAX SPEED (MPH): 84/86

0-60MPH (SEC): 20.6/19.5

SUSPENSION & BRAKES: coil ifs, leaf rear, drums f&r

LENGTH (IN)/WEIGHT (LB): 178/2507

LAUNCH PRICE: £1028/£1088

Elf 1961-69

Clever marketing, or cynical product planning? Make up your own mind about the Elf, for it was really no more or less than a dolled-up Mini. The advantages were the increase in stowage space and a more up-market specification, the disadvantage being the higher price.

Launched in the autumn of 1961, the Elf (with its sister car the Wolseley Hornet) was based on the layout and two-door body shell of the contemporary 848cc-engined Mini, complete with a transversely-mounted engine and front-wheel drive, but it was fitted with a longer tail (the boot, therefore, being larger, though in this case the boot lid opened upwards, and could not extend the platform), and had a different nose which incorporated the traditional Riley grille.

Inside the car, there was a full-width wooden fascia, with gloveboxes on each side of the central instrument display and – wait for it – a chrome-plated gear-lever, along with better-than-expected trim and furnishings and a lot more sound-deadening material.

Over the years the specification advanced. From autumn 1963 the Elf became Mk II, with 38bhp/998cc, which gave a little more oomph, and from late 1964 the suspension was

Riley Elf I, 1961.

changed from rubber cone springs to interconnected Hydrolastic.

The Mk III Elf of October 1966 used the same mechanical package as the Mk II, but was given wind-up windows in the doors, "eyeball" ventilation in the fascia, and a remote-control gearchange of Mini-Cooper type. AP automatic transmission became optional from late 1967, and an all-synchromesh manual

gearbox was standard from mid-1968.

The Elf's driving character was like that of the Mini, but the customers (most of whom appeared to be in a higher age bracket) really fell for the Riley badging and the quieter, more salubrious in-cabin environment. Since most 21st-century Mini fanatics like to talk about maximum performance, cars like the Elf (and Hornet) tend to be disdained these days.

SPECIFICATION

BODY STYLES: saloon

PRODUCTION: 3522/17,816/9574

ENGINE & TRANSMISSION: 848cc/998cc, 4cyl ohv, 4sp man, (from late 1967) auto, f/f

POWER: 34bhp @ 5500rpm/38bhp @ 5250rpm

MAX SPEED (MPH): 71/77

0-60MPH (SEC): 32.3/24.1

SUSPENSION & BRAKES: rubber ifs, rubber irs (Hydrolastic springs from late 1964), drums f&r

LENGTH (IN)/WEIGHT (LB): 129/1435

LAUNCH PRICE: £694

The Elf sported a walnut veneer dash.

Kestrel 1100/Kestrel 1300 1965-69

Along with the Wolseley 1100, with which it was always twinned, the Riley Kestrel of 1965 was the last of the BMC ADO 16 (Austin/Morris 1100) types to be launched, bringing the total of derivatives to six. "Kestrel" of course, revived a famous old Riley model name of the 1930s.

All had transversely-mounted A-Series engines, front-wheel drive, Hydrolastic independent suspension at front and rear, front-wheel disc brakes, and crisp styling by Farina. Unlike other types, the Kestrel was only ever built as a four-door saloon.

Mechanically, it shared its running gear – particularly its engine size and state of tune – with the MG 1100 of the period,

the two cars being built on the same assembly line at the old Morris factory at Cowley. Visually, however, Riley traditionalists were kept happy by the Riley-style front grille and by the walnut veneer dashboard, which incorporated a circular speedometer and rev-counter, making the Kestrel different from MG and Wolseley models.

As with the MG and Wolseley, changes and up-dates came regularly, and were mainly mechanical. Original types had 55bhp 1098cc engines, but only manual transmission; in summer 1967 a 58bhp 1275cc engine became optional.

From late 1967, the cars became 1300s and Mk II 1100s along with other ADO

16s, receiving cropped tail fins. A few 1100s were produced, some listed with AP automatic transmission, but most were 58bhp 1275cc cars, which also came with an automatic transmission option. The 1100 Mk II was dropped in February 1968. After this the 1300s got 65bhp, and all-synchromesh transmission was standardised during the year. Along with some trim improvements, the engine was further up-rated, to 70bhp, from September 1968, at which point the Kestrel 1300 officially became the Riley 1300 Mk II.

Production finally came to an end the summer/autumn of 1969.

Like the MGs and Wolseleys (and the Vanden Plas Princesses too) these Kestrels were brisk, well-appointed and relatively sporting cars. New car buyers realised they were purchasing a badge, not uniqueness, and so too do today's preservers.

Kestrel 1300n.

SPECIFICATION

BODY STYLES: saloon

PRODUCTION: 21,529, all types

ENGINE & TRANSMISSION: 1098cc/1275cc, 4cyl ohv, 4sp man, or auto, f/f

POWER: 55bhp @ 5500rpm/58bhp @ 5250rpm/65bhp @ 5750rpm, 70bhp @ 6000rpm

MAX SPEED (MPH): 85 - 97

0-60MPH (SEC): 18.4 - 14.1

SUSPENSION & BRAKES: Hydro ifs, Hydro irs, disc f/drum r

LENGTH (IN)/WEIGHT (LB): 147/1820 - 1850

LAUNCH PRICE: £781/£852

ROCHDALE

Here was another special-building concern which got better, and more professional, as the 1950s turned into the 1960s, eventually producing a series of remarkably competent sports coupés. Because the company was established in Rochdale, the choice of the marque name was unsurprising.

Way back, it had built aluminium bodies for racing cars, but turned to glass-fibre from 1952. A combined tubular/glass-fibre body/chassis structure was then developed, and the company's first kit-supplied vehicle was the Olympic of 1960. Owners Harry Smith and Frank Butterfield (originally they were panel beaters) shaped an attractive coupé style, into which they first of all fitted BMC running gear and, then, from 1962, Ford Cortina components. Unhappily, a fire at the factory in the early stages hampered deliveries just when they were needed.

Although these cars sold in respectable numbers (and there are still Rochdale fanatics today who swear by them), there was not enough business to underpin the company's future, so the last example was produced in 1968.

Olympic I 1960-62

Having announced an attractive looking glass-fibre coupé body, Rochdale then advanced by mating it with tubular strengthening sections and provided it with all the appropriate suspension and steering pick-up points. With a choice of BMC or Ford running gear, the customer was then encouraged to complete his own car. At this early stage he could choose a frame with Morris Minor/Riley 1.5-style wishbone front suspension, or swing axles. Rochdale claimed that, after delivery as a kit, the car could be completed in no more than 50 man-hours.

The majority of cars sold in the next two years had the BMC B-series 1489cc engine and transmission, a car thus equipped being the subject of a full road test in *The Motor* in 1961. Even with only 60bhp it could beat 100mph, which made it faster than the MGA of the period (which cost £724, very little more than the Rochdale), and almost as fast as the TR3A, but the brakes were drums all round.

The structure was rigid and virtually rot-proof, though (as ever with such small manufacturers) the cockpit specification was no more than mediocre, and build quality was distinctly average, especially as the body shell was provided as a self-coloured moulding. Even so, there were real carpets on the floor, and wind-up windows were provided in the doors. BMC instruments filled the fascia display.

SPECIFICATION

BODY STYLES: sports coupé

PRODUCTION: c.150

ENGINE & TRANSMISSION: 1489cc, 4cyl ohv, 4sp man, f/r

POWER: 60bhp @ 4800rpm

MAX SPEED (MPH): 102

0-60MPH (SEC): 11.9

SUSPENSION & BRAKES: tor ifs, coil rear, drums f&r

LENGTH (IN)/WEIGHT (LB): 147/1540

LAUNCH PRICE: £670 (as kit)

Olympic II 1960-62

From 1962, Rochdale changed tack by specifying Ford Cortina-type engine and transmission components

SPECIFICATION

BODY STYLES: saloon

PRODUCTION: 21,529, all types

ENGINE & TRANSMISSION: 1098cc/1275cc, 4cyl ohv, 4sp man, or auto, f/f

POWER: 55bhp @ 5500rpm/58bhp @ 5250rpm/65bhp @ 5750rpm, 70bhp @ 6000rpm

MAX SPEED (MPH): 85-97

0-60MPH (SEC): 18.4-14.1

SUSPENSION & BRAKES: Hydro ifs, Hydro irs, disc f/drum r

LENGTH (IN)/WEIGHT (LB): 147/1820 - 1850

LAUNCH PRICE: £781/£852

Rochdale Olympic.

for their Olympic, staying faithful to that source of supply for the next six years. At the same time, the mono-coque was revised, with a lifting tail-gate and a bigger bonnet.

Front suspension and steering now came from the Triumph Herald (which therefore provided a remarkably tight steering lock), twin fuel tanks were fitted, and Rochdale also claimed a better, higher-quality, interior, though this was still not up to, for instance, MGB standards.

Although this was a quick car – at 111mph it was certainly quicker than the equivalent MGB or TVR Grantura – and economical (which meant that the aerodynamic performance was clearly good too) – the build quality was never good enough. By the late 1960s the demand for Rochdales had fallen away, so the Olympic was dis-continued, and there was no successor. A pity, as it was a good car of its type.

RODLEY

This strange concern went public in 1954 and disappeared within a year. Few seemed to know where the inspiration had come from, and none seemed to care where it went. With a capital of a mere £20,000, the Rodley Automobile Company (of Rodley, near Leeds) was set up to make an ultra-economical car, one shaped in such an angular fashion that no complex press tooling was required. Up to 50 or 60 a week were proposed (Britain's Co-operative Society was supposedly a big backer), but since this looked like, and apparently was, a truly awful car, such an ambition was never realised.

Designed by a Mr Henry Brown (of whom the motor industry knew nothing, for he apparently had no track record), the Rodley 750 did not follow any accepted trends, so the use of an ultra-rough motorcycle-type engine was apparently not considered a handicap. The public thought otherwise, and customers never apparently materialised.

Were any such cars ever delivered? Experts of that period cannot remember ever seeing one on the road. At least Brown did better with his next car project – which was the Scootacar, produced nearby.

750 1954-55

Whoever thought up the Rodley 750 cannot have had much of a marketing nose, for this seems to have been the crudest, ugliest and least refined motoring machine known to man. Sitting on a separate frame was a boxy two-seater "coupé" body in pressed steel, with a fold-back roof panel. In fact it was advertised as a four-seater, but space in the rear was extremely cramped and impractical.

The car sat on a stubby box-section chassis (this machine was only 112in long – eight inches shorter than the Mini would be). Power came from a noisy,

The Rodley.

SPECIFICATION

BODY STYLES: saloon

PRODUCTION: not known

ENGINE & TRANSMISSION: 747cc, V2cyl sv, 3sp man, r/r

POWER: 20bhp @ 3800rpm

MAX SPEED (MPH): 55 (E)

0-60MPH (SEC): not possible

SUSPENSION & BRAKES: coil ifs, leaf rear, drums f&r

LENGTH (IN)/WEIGHT (LB): 112/1000

LAUNCH PRICE: n/a

rough and no doubt smelly vee-twin JAP motorcycle-type engine behind the seats. Drive to the rear wheels was through a motorcycle trans-mission, and final drive to the axle was by exposed chain. With cable brakes, a hard ride and virtually no creature comforts, it brought a new meaning to the phrase "marginal motoring". No one, anywhere, ever seemed to know much about this car, for it was never road tested and, as far as is known, no survivors remain.

ROLLS-ROYCE

Founded in 1904, "The Best Car in the World" thereafter, and pre-eminent until the 1930s, Rolls-Royce built its reputation by taking infinite pains. No engineering problem, no solution, was too much trouble for founder Henry Royce, and his successors carried this forward. The Ghosts, and the Phantoms which followed, were superbly built machines. From 1931, incidentally, Rolls-Royce came to control Bentley, whose 1930s products became more Rolls-Royce-like with every passing season.

Up to 1939, Rolls-Royce built rolling chassis at Derby, allowing approved coachbuilders to complete their cars. From 1945, though, chassis assembly moved to the ex-aero-engine factory at Crewe. Early post-war Silver Wraiths carried on the 1930s "chassis-only" tradition, but the Silver Dawn, and the Silver Clouds which followed, were wholly built at Crewe.

The Silver Shadow of 1965 ushered in mountains of innovation, which was good enough to make this car, its Bentley relatives, and the coachbuilt types which also appeared, into best-sellers by any previous standard. Hit by aero-engine finance problems, Rolls-Royce called in the Receiver in 1971, though the cars side barely faltered, and sales continued to boom: the first Corniche was launched within weeks of the collapse.

Floated off in 1973, Rolls-Royce was not independent for long. It was taken over by Vickers from 1980, and survived happily until 1998 when a bitter takeover dispute saw VW capture Bentley and BMW take control of Rolls-Royce. By the early 2000s, BMW had built a brand-new factory at Goodwood, the latest product being almost entirely BMW-ised under the skin.

Silver Wraith 1946-59

The original post-war Rolls-Royce, the Silver Wraith, used a long-wheelbase version of the "rationalised" chassis which had been adopted for the Bentley Mk VI, but retained one old tradition – that all the bodies were specially constructed by coachbuilders.

Compared with the Bentley, the Silver Wraith used a 127in wheelbase (instead of 120in), and its engine was de-tuned; though never revealed, unofficially its peak power was 120-125bhp. As with the Bentley, there was coil spring independent front suspension and a four-speed gearbox with the gearchange located on the right of the driver's seat (or on the steering column with left-hand drive). Drum brakes, hydraulically operated and a gearbox-driven servo,

Rolls-Royce did not offer standard bodywork on the Silver Wraith. Hooper were the coachbuilders of this Touring Limousine.

were part of the layout.

Rolling chassis were assembled at Crewe and were then delivered to approved coachbuilders for the body to be attached. Many of these were

A 1953 Silver Wraith with Hooper "Empress" coachwork.

Typically splendid rear compartment of a Hooper Touring Limousine.

SPECIFICATION

BODY STYLES: various coachbuilts, mainly limousines

PRODUCTION: 1783

ENGINE & TRANSMISSION: 4257cc/4566cc/4887cc, 6cyl ioe, 4sp man, or auto, f/r

POWER: never quoted

MAX SPEED (MPH): 85 (E), 90 (E), 95 (E)

0-60MPH (SEC): not measured

SUSPENSION & BRAKES: coil ifs, leaf rear, drums f&r

LENGTH (IN)/WEIGHT (LB): 206/4700-5200

LAUNCH PRICE: £3802

limousines in the grand tradition – almost all of them featuring the vertical RR radiator, with massive headlamps to each side, though a few were stylish drophead coupés, and there were also occasional horrors which somehow slipped through the net. Most such bodies had traditional ash skeletons with steel or aluminium skin panels, though more and more light alloy internal castings also appeared in later years.

Development changes, over time, included the 4556cc engine from mid-1951, the 4887cc engine from mid/late 1954, and more power from late 1956. Rolls-Royce-GM Hydramatic transmission was available from late 1952 (this soon took over almost all orders). The wheelbase was increased to 133in from mid-1951 (first deliveries, January 1952).

Although sales dropped away in the mid-1950s, there was a continuing demand. This model, in fact, would be replaced by the even larger Phantom V in 1959.

Always heavy, always exclusive, and always expensive, the Silver Wraith was not a driver's car, but it had unbeatable dignity and a "top drawer" image. Naturally, many of these splendid cars have survived.

Silver Wraith chassi, ready for the coachbuilder.

Silver Dawn 1949-55

Introduced in 1949, originally for export only, and available in the UK from 1953, the Silver Dawn was the very first Rolls-Royce to have standard, factory-fitted, saloon coachwork. The rolling chassis had the same 120in. wheelbase (shorter than that of the Silver Wraith) as the Bentley Mk VI, and all suspension and steering installations were the same. Left hand drive versions had a steering-column gear change, right-handers the right-side floor change of the Mk VI.

Traditionalists do not like to admit

The Silver Dawn was the first Rolls-Royce to be supplied with standard bodywork. This is an early small-boot model.

this, for though it naturally had the Rolls-Royce radiator, and less powerful versions of the 4257cc/4556cc engines, the Silver Dawn was almost a clone of the contemporary Bentley Mk VI/R-Type. The instrument panel was different, as was the marking of the instruments, but otherwise as many components as possible were shared.

The 4556cc engine was adopted in 1951, and the long-tail body style was

SPECIFICATION	
BODY STYLES: saloon, coachbuilts	
PRODUCTION: 761	
ENGINE & TRANSMISSION: 4257cc/4556cc, 6cyl ioe, 4sp man, auto, f/r	
POWER: not quoted	
MAX SPEED (MPH): 85/87 (E)	
0-60MPH (SEC): 17.5/16.2 (E)	
SUSPENSION & BRAKES: coil ifs, leaf rear, drums f&r	
LENGTH (IN)/WEIGHT (LB): 200/4060	
LAUNCH PRICE: £3250	

A small number of Silver Dawns received special bodies. This 1954 example is by James Young.

phased in towards the end of 1952. Rolls-Royce-GM Hydramatic transmission was fitted towards the end of 1952: though optional in theory, it immediately spelt the end of the manual transmission on this car.

Although not a fast car – 75mph was the best easy cruising speed to use – this at least was the first post-war Rolls-Royce which the owner, as opposed to the chauffeur, was intended to drive. Big, solid, reassuring, but above all well built, the Silver Dawn was a perfect ancestor to the larger Silver Cloud which was to follow.

The 4.6-litre long-boot Silver Dawn.

This same car is actually one of Harold Radford's ingenious Countryman conversions, featuring, among other things, this complete picnic equipment.

Phantom IV 1950-56

Way back in the early 1950s, unless you were royalty, a head of state or a dictator, you could neither order nor take delivery of a Phantom IV. Here was a colossal Rolls-Royce by any standards – not many pre-war cars were as huge as these machines, surely – which was not only very rare, but had a straight-eight version of the now ubiquitous six-cylinder engine found in other contemporary Rolls-Royce and Bentley types.

The chassis, with its 145in wheelbase, was the final stretch of the Bentley Mk

The straight-eight Phantom IV was supplied to very special customers. This is the Duchess of Kent's Mulliner-bodied limousine.

SPECIFICATION

BODY STYLES: coachbuilts

PRODUCTION: 18

ENGINE & TRANSMISSION: 5675cc, 8cyl ioe, 4sp man, auto, f/r

POWER: not quoted

MAX SPEED (MPH): 95 (E)

0-60MPH (SEC): not measured

SUSPENSION & BRAKES: coil ifs, leaf rear, drums f&r

LENGTH (IN)/WEIGHT (LB): 227/5000

LAUNCH PRICE: never quoted (special orders)

VI/Silver Dawn/Silver Wraith frame, retaining the same front and rear suspension, steering, brakes and transmission. Each car was hand built. The bodies were massive, larger than those built on the Silver Wraith but in some cases similarly styled.

With only 18 cars built in six years, all specifications were individual. Only two cars were fitted with automatic transmission and none had power-assisted steering (pity the poor chauffeur). Twelve cars were exported, and five went to members of the British royal family. Until recent years one, at least, was still an important member of the Buckingham Palace fleet.

Phantom IVs were hard work to drive, incredibly thirsty, and too big to park almost anywhere, but their rarity made them infinitely desirable. As you might expect, most of them still exist.

Silver Cloud I 1955-59

The Silver Cloud took over from the Silver Dawn in April 1955. Apart from the automatic transmission and the 4887cc six-cylinder i.o.e engine, every component of the car was new. It was a considerable success.

It does not diminish the reputation of the car at all to point out that it was identical to the Bentley S1 of the same period (1955-1959). Except for the radiator grille, the badging and identification of the product, there was not an ounce of difference between the two cars.

For all details of modifications and updates, see the Bentley S1 entry.

SPECIFICATION

BODY STYLES: saloon, coachbuilts

PRODUCTION: 2359

ENGINE & TRANSMISSION: 4887cc, 6cyl ioe, auto, f/r

POWER: not quoted

MAX SPEED (MPH): 106

0-60MPH (SEC): 13.0

SUSPENSION & BRAKES: coil ifs, leaf rear, drums f&r

LENGTH (IN)/WEIGHT (LB): 212/4480

LAUNCH PRICE: £3385

Rolls-Royce Silver Cloud I, 1955.

A Silver Cloud estate car conversion by H J Mulliner and Harold Radford.

Long-wheelbase Silver Cloud with division.

Phantom V/VI 1959-92

The Phantom V was related to the Silver Cloud II as the Silver Wraith had been to the Silver Dawn. In other words, it used the same package of mechanical running gear, but in a much longer-wheelbase version of the chassis, and was fitted with hand-crafted special coachwork, almost all of it of the formal limousine variety.

The original Phantom Vs were built on a 145in-wheelbase version of the Silver Cloud II chassis, with the same brand-new design of 6¼-litre V8 engine, mated to the familiar RR-GM Hydramatic four-speed automatic gearbox. There was power-assisted steering, but drum brakes, with that famous friction servo.

The majority of Phantom Vs were fitted with either H J Mulliner or Park

Phantom V seven-passenger Park Ward limousine, just short of 20 feet long.

Ward seven-seater limousine coachwork (ash frame, steel and alloy panelling, much hand-crafting involved), though a number were bodied by the James Young concern, and there were even some sports saloons in which the owner got to do his own driving.

From 1963, the Phantom V got the more powerful Silver Cloud III type of V8 engine, and by this time the merged Mulliner-Park-Ward business was supplying almost every body in the same style; from 1967, in any case, there was no alternative to this supply, though a few (very few) examples would have drop-top landaulette coachwork).

Phantom V became Phantom VI during 1968, these cars having separate air-conditioning systems in the front and rear compartments, and a four-headlamp nose as used on the last of the Silver Clouds. Ten years later, from 1978, the chassis was up-dated with the 6¾-litre engine and GM400 three-speed automatic transmission. The Phantom VI then carried on, quietly, and built in tiny numbers, until 1992, when this long-running line of separate-chassis coachbuilt cars finally became obsolete.

Like the earlier Silver Wraith and Phantom IV, these last Phantoms were meant to glide along gently, smoothly, and with immense dignity, which they always did. In later years, for those few who could afford the colossal upkeep and restoration bills, they became very desirable indeed; many of the 1241 built survived.

SPECIFICATION

BODY STYLES: coachbuilts

PRODUCTION: 1241

ENGINE & TRANSMISSION: 6230cc/6750cc, V8cyl ohv, auto, f/r

POWER: not quoted

MAX SPEED (MPH): 101/105 (E)

0-60MPH (SEC): 13.8/not measured

SUSPENSION & BRAKES: coil ifs, leaf rear, drums f&r

LENGTH (IN)/WEIGHT (LB): 238/5600 - 6000

LAUNCH PRICE: £8905

Even more splendid is this Phantom VI landaulette.

Silver Cloud II/III 1959-65

As with the original Silver Cloud, it is enough to state that the V8-engined Silver Cloud II, and the later four-headlamp Silver Cloud III, were identical to the Bentley S2 and Bentley S3 models of the same period – 1959-62, and 1962-65.

For all details, see the appropriate Bentley entry.

SPECIFICATION

BODY STYLES: saloon, coachbuilts

PRODUCTION: 5013

ENGINE & TRANSMISSION: 6230cc/6750cc, V8cyl ohv, auto, f/r

POWER: not quoted

MAX SPEED (MPH): 113/116

0-60MPH (SEC): 11.5/10.8

SUSPENSION & BRAKES: coil ifs, leaf rear, drums f&r

LENGTH (IN)/WEIGHT (LB): 212/4650

LAUNCH PRICE: £5802/£5517

The 1959 Silver Cloud II was unchanged in appearance but a V8 engine replaced the previous model's straight six.

Silver Cloud III is identified by its twin headlamps.

Special bodies could still be had, like this 1963 Park Ward Silver Cloud III coupé.

Silver Shadow I 1965-77

Except in details like the radiator grille and the badging, the Silver Shadow was the same car as the Bentley T-Series, and received the same improvements, up-dates and development changes at exactly the same time.

The only significant difference, in marketing terms, was that customer demand for the Silver Shadow soared while sales of the T-Series Bentley faded away. It was indeed not long before the Silver Shadow was well on its way to becoming Rolls-Royce's best-selling motor car of all time.

For all technical and development details, please refer to the Bentley T-Series entry.

In 1977 the Silver Shadow was replaced by the Silver Shadow II.

The Rolls-Royce Silver Shadow as launched in 1965.

SPECIFICATION

BODY STYLES: saloon, limousine, coachbuilts

PRODUCTION: 19,497/10,560

ENGINE & TRANSMISSION: 6230cc/6750cc, V8cyl ohv, auto, f/r

POWER: not quoted

MAX SPEED (MPH): 115/117

0-60MPH (SEC): 10.9/10.2

SUSPENSION & BRAKES: coil ifs, coil irs, discs f&r

LENGTH (IN)/WEIGHT (LB): 204/4660

LAUNCH PRICE: £6670/9272

Long-wheelbase Silver Shadow saloon.

Silver Shadow 2-door H J Mulliner Coupé/Convertible 1966-71

This is getting monotonous. These smart two-door four-seater Rolls-Royces, saloons from 1966 and drop-head coupés from 1967, were the same cars as the Bentley T-Series types also built at the Mulliner Park Ward factory in north-west London. Supremely elegant, both would be transformed into Corniche models at the same moment, in early 1971.

For all details, see the Bentley T-Series 2-door entry.

Silver Shadow Mulliner Park Ward Coupé.

SPECIFICATION

BODY STYLES: saloon, drophead

PRODUCTION: 1073

ENGINE & TRANSMISSION: 6230cc/6750cc, V8cyl ohv, auto, f/r

POWER: not quoted

MAX SPEED (MPH): 115/120 (E)

0-60MPH (SEC): not quoted/9.6

SUSPENSION & BRAKES: coil ifs, coil irs, discs f&r

LENGTH (IN)/WEIGHT (LB): 204/4978

LAUNCH PRICE: £9849

Silver Shadow Mulliner Park Ward Convertible.

Silver ShadowII/Silver Wraith II 1977-80

By the late 1970s, the Silver Shadow had almost extinguished its stablemate, the T-Series Bentley, and in 1977 both were updated at the same time. Although the principal layout, monocoque, engineering and style were not changed, the second-series cars benefited from the latest split-level air conditioning system (as pioneered in the Rolls-Royce Camargue of 1975), which was accompanied by a magnificently detailed new fascia. A major innovation

was rack-and-pinion steering, which with suspension revisions gave much improved handling, and there were minor styling changes including black-faced bumpers and an under-bumper front spoiler.

At the same time the longer-wheelbase version of the car, available with a built-in limousine division, was named Silver Wraith II. Although these cars cost a lot more they sold well – for one in five of the second-generation cars were Silver Wraiths, usually doing sterling service as cars for high-powered businessmen.

Sales, and the reputation of the model, held up well for more than three years before the Silver Shadow was finally displaced by the totally re-shaped Silver Spirit of 1980.

The 1977 Silver Shadow II was distinguished by its black-faced bumpers.

SPECIFICATION

BODY STYLES: saloon, limousine

PRODUCTION: 8425/2135

ENGINE & TRANSMISSION: 6750cc, V8cyl ohv, auto, f/r

POWER: not quoted

MAX SPEED (MPH): 119

0-60MPH (SEC): 9.4

SUSPENSION & BRAKES: coil ifs, coil irs, discs f&r

LENGTH (IN)/WEIGHT (LB): 205/4930 [Wraith 209/(with division) 5260]

LAUNCH PRICE: £22,809/£26,887

Rear view of the Silver Shadow II.

Silver Wraith II, 1977.

Camargue 1975-86

Rolls-Royce's "Delta" project, a full-sized four-door hardtop coupé, was the very first post-war car from Crewe to feature styling by an overseas consultant

– Pininfarina of Italy. Having been instructed that they were obliged to keep the traditional RR radiator shape, and to use the existing Silver Shadow platform

and running gear, the Italian company did a great job.

The new car, badged Camargue, was introduced in March 1975. As ever,

Rolls-Royce was secretive about the power output, though it admitted that the four-choke Solex carburettor added 10 per cent to previous peak figures.

The body shell was produced at Rolls-Royce's Mulliner Park Ward subsidiary in north-west London, mainly from steel, though all the opening panels were in aluminium. The two-door four-seater body and its fittings were up to usual Rolls-Royce standards, but this was the car on which automatic split-level air conditioning was introduced, as standard equipment, and this required a

The Camargue's looks were controversial. It was a Pininfarina design.

SPECIFICATION

BODY STYLES: coupé

PRODUCTION: 530

ENGINE & TRANSMISSION: 6750cc, V8cyl ohv, auto, f/r

POWER: not quoted

MAX SPEED (MPH): 118 (E)

0-60MPH (SEC): not measured

SUSPENSION & BRAKES: coil ifs, coil irs, discs f&r

LENGTH (IN)/WEIGHT (LB): 204/5175

LAUNCH PRICE: £29,250

completely new fascia and instrument panel layout.

Because the Camargue was so costly, and had less accommodation than Silver Shadow saloons offered, its sales were always limited. From 1977, the Silver Shadow II type of suspension, with rack-and-pinion steering, was adopted for the Camargue, and body assembly moved to Motor Panels of Coventry in 1978. Silver Spirit-type rear suspension arrived in 1979, and fuel-injected engines for

the US market from 1981. There were no styling changes in eleven years, and the last car of all (by then priced at £83,122) was built in 1986.

Like all Silver Shadow-based models, the Camargue was not really much of a driver's car, but rather a vehicle in which to live and to be seen. Beautifully and carefully built, it was never totally taken into the inner hearts of the Rolls-Royce movement, and no replacement for it ever came forward.

Corniche 1971-94

The original Corniches were no more than lightly modified and up-dated versions of the Mulliner Park Ward two-door models already described, but they would enjoy an astonishing 23-year career. Though based on the original Silver Shadow platform of 1965, the Corniche outlived that car by a very long time, and would take on more and more features from the later Silver Spirit.

Introduced in March 1971, the Corniche was originally available as a two-door saloon and a drophead coupé. The saloon (1108 built) would be discontinued at the end of 1980, while the drophead version carried on until 1994. At all times, this Rolls-Royce was mirrored by a near-identical Bentley, though that was renamed "Continental" from 1984.

Generally speaking, up-dates to this car followed what was taking place on Silver Shadow (until 1980) and Silver Spirit

Rolls-Royce Corniche convertible.

(1980 onwards)saloons, but occasionally the Corniche got preferential treatment. Split-level air-conditioning came in 1975/76 while the revised Silver Spirit-type independent rear end was adopted in March 1979, before the Silver Spirit was announced.

Bosch fuel injection was standardised for the USA market from 1981, but not for all markets until 1985-86. From 1988 cars for all markets became Corniche II (the USA was first in 1986), and for 1990 the car became Corniche III when the Silver Spirit adaptive suspension damping system was fitted. Corniche IV came along in 1992, with the latest four-speed GM automatic transmission, and the last cars were built at the end of 1994.

These Corniches were magnificently well built, excellently detailed, and

Corniche saloon.

SPECIFICATION

BODY STYLES: saloon, drophead

PRODUCTION TOTAL: 6277, all types

ENGINE & TRANSMISSION: 6750cc, V8cyl ohv, auto, f/r

POWER: not quoted

MAX SPEED (MPH): (original type) 120

0-60MPH (SEC): (original type) 9.6

SUSPENSION & BRAKES: coil ifs, coil rear, discs f&r

LENGTH (IN)/WEIGHT (LB): 205/4930

LAUNCH PRICE: £12,829

provided their driver and passengers with every indulgence. Later cars could reach 130mph, and although the suspension was always too soft for this level of performance, the Corniche provided an extremely restful means of

driving long distances at speed.

Complex, by no means corrosion-free, and expensive to maintain, these cars have almost all survived and, still commanding high prices, were very much part of the scene in the early 2000s.

Silver Spirit/Silver Spur 1980-92

The problem here is knowing not where to start, but where to stop. Although it used an updated Silver Shadow-style platform, suspension, and running gear, the Silver Spirit was new in October 1980. That basic four-door saloon body shell would then carry on, through a mass of different derivatives and model names, until the end of the century. In this case, though, the sensible cut-off is in 1991-92, when the first-generation Silver Spirit and Silver Spur models were finally supplanted. Silver Spirit referred to the standard-length (120.5in) wheelbase, while Silver Spur referred to the longer-wheelbase (124.5in) types.

Based on the latest evolution of the Silver Shadow platform, complete with a much-modified independent rear suspension, the latest cars used the same V8 engine, automatic transmission, complex self-levelling suspension, and high-pressure hydraulic braking system. Body shells had a similar envelope to the Silver Shadow, but were less angular and even slightly bulkier than before.

Right away, the Rolls-Royce versions outsold their Bentley equivalents by a factor of at least ten to one. All, of

Rolls-Royce Silver Spirit.

course, had the sumptuous equipment expected of a Rolls-Royce, with acres of leather, thick carpets, real tree wood, and one of the most effective and complex split-level air-conditioning systems ever developed. All USA-market cars had Bosch fuel injection, though this would not feature on other cars until 1987. This, Rolls-Royce stated, gave more than 20 per cent extra peak power.

Changes and improvements followed regularly (especially on the Bentley side, where the renaissance included a turbocharged model from 1982). Anti-lock braking was standardized for 1987 (when prices ranged between £68,944 and £81,702), but the first-generation range was phased out at the end of the 1980s to make way for the Series II types, which were equipped with adaptive suspension damping.

Over the years, not only were there Bentley equivalents, but also stretched limousines (some with six doors), along with extensively modified 1990s types known as Silver Dawn and Flying Spur. Accordingly, it is easy (though not cheap) to find parts and restoration expertise for all these cars, though no one should imagine that running one can be done on a small budget. All cars, without exception, had soft suspension, which limited their cornering abilities, but all had excellent and comprehensive

equipment. Many later owners treated them as objects of affection rather than driving machines.

The Silver Spur had a longer wheelbase, and an Everflex roof covering.

ROVER

Here was yet another Coventry-based company which started by building pedal cycles and which later began selling cars, in Rover's case in 1904. Independent and prosperous by 1939, its Coventry factory was blitzed, so post-war operations began in Solihull, south-east of Birmingham.

Like other car makers, Rover took time to introduce new post-war models, so the 1939-40 cars (generically coded P2) were revived at first. As an interim step the Land Rover was launched in 1948 (this is a separate marque, already described). Two long-running passenger cars, the P4 (1949) and the P5 (1958), emphasised a staid, dignified market image, but the technically advanced P6 (1963) changed all that and made Rover seem altogether more sporty.

Rover then bought up Alvis in 1965, and was itself absorbed by Leyland in 1967. As a component of British Leyland from 1968, it prospered by using the newly-acquired V8 engine, and then introduced yet another marque, Range Rover, in 1970. From 1972 there was a close co-operation with Triumph, at British Leyland's behest, and, a new big hatchback (the SD1) was launched in 1976, but by the 1980s Rover was fast becoming just another much-abused badge within British Leyland/BL.

After a complicated series of corporate changes, name changes, ownership by BMW, and partial sales, what had been BMC in the 1960s and British Leyland in the 1970s became MG-Rover, but no trace of genuine Rover pedigree remained. and MG-Rover itself expired in 2005.

10 P2 1946-47

Rover had completed its wide range of P2 models in 1938, with the smallest car in its range, the 1389cc 10. This was re-introduced in 1946 and available only as a four-door saloon, with bodywork by Pressed Steel.

Rover 10 P2 saloon, 1946.

Like all P2s it was based on a simple 105.5in-wheelbase chassis frame with channel-section side members. There were half-elliptic springs front and rear, Burman steering, and Girling rod-operated brakes. The four-cylinder engine shared the same tooling as the

12hp, 14hp and 16hp and the same 100mm stroke. There was synchro-mesh on top and third gears, and Rover also supplied a freewheel as standard. Automatic chassis lubrication was a feature.

Post-war, only a six-light saloon body

was offered (in 1939 there had been a coupé, which was not revived), this having a typically Rover "middle-class" ambience to the cabin, including a neat and nicely laid out wooden fascia, a spring-spoke steering wheel and separate front seats, along with a very precise remote-control centre-floor gearchange. Heaters were standard for 1947 models.

As an entry-level model, this Rover had no performance pretensions – 50mph was a good, though not exciting, cruising speed – but it was well built, well equipped, and extremely durable. It is almost extraordinary that, in the car-starved post-war period, it sold relatively slowly. Very very few have survived – because the larger six-cylinder cars were more appealing to collectors.

12 P2 1946-47

Based on the same technical layout as the 10hp model, though with a longer wheelbase (112in instead of 105.5in), and a 2.5in wider track (giving more space in the rear compartment) the 12 was even more typical of the pre-war Rover pedigree. It had originally been

Rover 12 P2, 1946

SPECIFICATION

BODY STYLES: saloon, sports tourer

PRODUCTION: 4840

ENGINE & TRANSMISSION: 1496cc, 4cyl ohv, 4sp man, f/r

POWER: 53bhp @ 4200rpm

MAX SPEED (MPH): 67

0-60MPH (SEC): not measured

SUSPENSION & BRAKES: coil ifs, leaf rear, drums f&r

LENGTH (IN)/WEIGHT (LB): 170/2912

LAUNCH PRICE: £646

launched at the end of 1936.

The bodies of this model were coachbuilt in-house at Solihull, using wooden (ash) frames clad in pressed-steel panels, and Rover offered no fewer than three different styles, a six-light saloon, a four-light "sports saloon" and – in 1947 only – a rather awkwardly-styled two-door sports tourer. All carried their headlamps high, and separate, on each side of the vertical radiator.

The engine was a 1496cc four-cylinder unit giving 53bhp. It was a larger version of the 10hp engine, and one which had been seen in Rovers since 1933. It used the same gearbox, freewheel and mechanical brakes. Little faster than the 10hp (it was more powerful, but heavier), the 12hp's extra length gave it better looks. The six-light took the most sales, only 760 four-light sports saloons and 200 sports tourers being sold.

14/16 P2 1946-47

The 14 and 16 models, which were really only separated by the size of their six-cylinder engines, were the

The six-cylinder Rover 14 had a longer bonnet than the 10 and 12.

SPECIFICATION

BODY STYLES: saloon

PRODUCTION: 1705/4150

ENGINE & TRANSMISSION: 1901/2147cc, 6cyl ohv, 4sp man, f/r

POWER: not quoted/66bhp @ 4600rpm

MAX SPEED (MPH): 72/78

0-60MPH (SEC): 41.3/not measured

SUSPENSION & BRAKES: leaf front, leaf rear, drums f&r

LENGTH (IN)/WEIGHT (LB): 173/3136

LAUNCH PRICE: £704/£742

largest of the revived pre-war models. These cars had first been seen at the end of 1936, and retained their elegant but distinctly traditional styling.

One step up from the 12, the 14 and 16 models had an even longer wheelbase – 115in instead of 112in – but the same rear axle width and basic body contours. Both shared the same technical layout – half-elliptic leaf springs, mechanical braking, four-speed part-synchromesh gearbox, and a freewheel – and were available with coachbuilt six-light saloon or four-light sports saloon bodies, all with four passenger doors.

The engines were six-cylinder versions of the fours used in the smaller models – sharing the same 100mm stroke, though with unique bore and piston sizes.

By any standards, these were nicely-equipped, well-behaved and very dignified middle-class machines. The 16, in particular (it sold better than the 14) was a good long-distance car, though because of its great weight it never showed much acceleration.

It was the style of these cars though, not the engineering, which inspired the P3 models which were to follow.

P3 60/75 1948-49

Although the short-lived P3 models – they were only built in 1948 and until August 1949 – looked very like the P2 cars which they replaced, they were entirely different under the skin. In particular, there was a box-section chassis with coil spring independent front suspension, and a brace of new engines, four-cylinder and six-cylinder, which shared the same overhead inlet/side exhaust valve layout.

Both cars had a 110.5in wheelbase, with the chassis frame ending ahead of the rear axle, so that the rear springs

The P3 60 and 75 at the 1948 motor show.

SPECIFICATION

BODY STYLES: saloon

PRODUCTION: 1274/7835

ENGINE & TRANSMISSION: 1595cc, 4cyl ioe/2103cc, 6cyl ioe, 4sp man, f/r

POWER: 50bhp @ 4000rpm/72bhp @ 4000rpm

MAX SPEED (MPH): 72/75

0-60MPH (SEC): not measured/29.4

SUSPENSION & BRAKES: coil ifs, leaf rear, drums f&r

LENGTH (IN)/WEIGHT (LB): 169/2950-3070

LAUNCH PRICE: £1080-/£1106

were hooked up under the body shell at the rear. This was ingenious but caused all kinds of trouble when the steel body shell eventually began to rust away. There was coil spring independent front suspension of the Girling variety, and hydro-mechanical brakes.

The engines would be a feature of Rover cars and Land Rovers for the next twenty years. Their overhead inlet and side exhaust valve arrangement was similar to but not the same as that used by Rolls-Royce/Bentley at the same time. As before, there were four-speed gearboxes with freewheels.

Though the style looked like that of the P2, these were all-steel (instead of coachbuilt, with a wooden skeleton), and almost every panel was different. As before there were six-light (saloon) and four-light (sports saloon) types. As delivered from Solihull, they had free standing headlamps and one, centrally-mounted, extra driving lamp.

Compared with the P2s, the P3s were faster though no more agile. The "60" model (with a 1.6-litre engine) was rather underpowered – the public realising this, and buying far more of the more expensive "75" types.

P4 75/90 1949-59

The car which affectionately became known as the "Auntie" Rover was previewed in September 1949. In many different guises – there would be several engine changes over the years – it would remain in production until 1964.

Compared with the P3, the chassis frame and the body were entirely new, though the same six-cylinder engine (complete with overhead inlet and side exhaust valves), four-speed transmission and freewheel were retained. The box-section chassis was full-length this time,

The 1949 P4 Rover 75, known today as the "Cyclops".

sweeping up and over the rear axle line, with a new type of long-travel coil spring independent front suspension, and hydro-mechanical Girling brakes.

The body, provided by Pressed Steel, was a sober-looking four-door, initially with an extra "Cyclops" type of driving lamp in the centre of the grille, and a rather truncated tail. It was only sold as a saloon, though elements would be used in the Marauder sports tourer (described separately). Inside, there were leather seats, good carpets, lots of wood cappings and facings, and a steering-column gear change. The car's character, ambience, and manner of motoring were "gentlemen's club", with a soft ride, a hushed interior, and no question of haste.

Gradually, but insistently, major changes took place over the years. In

In 1952 the P4 appeared with a revised front end. This is the 90 model, introduced in 1954.

At this time Rover were busy with the development of their gas turbine car. Here it is in 1952.

A few P4s received special bodies. This is a 1953 75 drophead coupé by Pinin Farina.

Hazel Dunham's Rover on the 1954 Monte Carlo Rally.

SPECIFICATION

BODY STYLES: saloon

PRODUCTION: 43,241/35,903

ENGINE & TRANSMISSION: 2103cc/2230cc/ 2638cc, 6cyl ioe, 4sp man, or o/d, f/r

POWER: 75bhp @ 4200rpm/80bhp @ 4500rpm/90bhp @ 4500rpm/93bhp @ 4500rpm

MAX SPEED (MPH): 82-90

0-60MPH (SEC): 23.1-18.4

SUSPENSION & BRAKES: coil ifs, leaf rear, drums f&r

LENGTH (IN)/WEIGHT (LB): 178/3265-3310

LAUNCH PRICE: £1106/£1297

1951 a full hydraulic braking system was adopted. In March 1952 the original "Cyclops" style of front end was abandoned in favour of a conventional grille.

In the autumn of 1953 the twin-carb 90bhp 2638cc-engined 90 model joined the 75, and the gearbox at last gained synchromesh on second gear. (There was also a new four-cylinder 60 model, described separately). From this point the cars got a centre-floor gearchange, with adjustable lever alignment.

In autumn 1954 the 75 model received an 80bhp 2230cc engine in place of the

2103cc unit, along with a slightly enlarged tail/boot and a wrap around rear window. In autumn 1955 Laycock overdrive became optional; with overdrive fitted, the freewheel had to be abandoned. Finally, in autumn 1956, a front-end facelift included "sharper" front wings.

Still selling strongly, these cars were effectively replaced by the larger-engined, more powerful 100 and 110 models which followed in late 1959. Not that the 90 had been that slow: with overdrive it was a relaxed 80mph cruiser.

P4 60/80 1953-59/1959-62

SPECIFICATION

BODY STYLES: saloon

PRODUCTION: 9666/5900

ENGINE & TRANSMISSION: 1997cc, 4cyl ioe/2286cc, 4cyl ohv, 4sp man, or o/d, f/r

POWER: 60bhp @ 4000rpm/77bhp @ 4250rpm

MAX SPEED (MPH): 77/86

0-60MPH (SEC): 23.2/22.8

SUSPENSION & BRAKES: coil ifs, leaf rear, drums f&r(disc f/drum r on 80 model)

LENGTH (IN)/WEIGHT (LB): 178/3106 - 3246

LAUNCH PRICE: £1163/£1269

The four-cylinder Rover 60 of 1953.

Though it was the smooth six-cylinder P4s which made most of the headlines and garnered most sales, Rover also had four-cylinder types on sale for almost a decade. To keep the permutations down to a minimum, these cars took up the style changes as and when offered on the sixes, but had their own running gear.

From late 1953, the 60 used a 60bhp 1997cc engine which was a four-cylinder version of the 90's unit and similar to that being used in the Land Rover (described separately). Overdrive was optional from 1956/57 (no freewheel in that case).

From late 1959 the earlier engine was dumped in favour of the 77bhp 2286cc four-cylinder of the contemporary Land Rover. This engine was certainly more powerful but it was also rather agricultural. On the 80 model over-drive was standard, as were front wheel disc brakes.

Because on the P4 there was really no substitute for six-cylinder smoothness, these four-cylinder cars never sold well – less than 16,000 in nine years – so the sub-family was abandoned from mid-1962.

P4 105R/105S/95/100/110 1956-64

Commencing in late 1956, Rover introduced yet another wave of new six-cylinder engined P4 derivatives – some more powerful than before, one with automatic transmission, and all intended to squeeze every sale out of a long-established design. Like the earlier models, all these cars shared the same four-door saloon style and furnishings, with leather seating and wood cappings. The only way to pick one type from another was really by the badging.

Changes came thick and fast. In October 1956 two new derivatives were launched, the105R and 105S, both with 2625cc 108bhp engines.

105R (R for Roverdrive) featured a unique automatic transmission which included a torque converter, a manual clutch, two-speed-and-reverse gearbox, and Laycock overdrive. This transmission was heavy and resulted in sluggish performance. The launch price of the 105R was £1650. It was not popular, and was phased out in the summer of 1958.

105S (S for Sporting) had a four-

Rover 105S, 1956.

speed manual gearbox, with Laycock overdrive as standard. The launch price was £1596, and in summer 1958 the model became the 105 (without the S). It would be dropped in the summer of 1959.

In September 1959 the P4 100 appeared, as a direct replacement for the 90 and 105 models. Looking the same as its predecessors, the new car had a single-carb 104bhp 2625cc engine, and overdrive and front-wheel disc brakes. The initial price was £1538, and the 100 carried on until mid-1962.

Another rationalisation, in September 1962, saw the 80 and 100 models dropped and two new ones – the 95 and 110 – introduced.

The 95 had 102bhp/2625cc, still with front-wheel disc brakes, but without overdrive. It was priced at £1373. The 110 had 123bhp/2625cc, with overdrive as standard, and front-wheel disc brakes. The price was £1534

These were the last of a long-running, refined and very civilised family. Production finally ended in July 1964.

Rover 100, 1959, had a new seven-bearing engine.

SPECIFICATION

BODY STYLES: saloon

PRODUCTION: 3540/5215/3680/ 16,521/4620

ENGINE & TRANSMISSION: 2625cc, 6cyl ioe, 4sp man, o/d or auto (105R only), f/r

POWER: 102bhp @ 4750 to 123bhp @ 5000rpm

MAX SPEED (MPH): 94 - 100

0-60MPH (SEC): 18.0 – 15.9

SUSPENSION & BRAKES: coil ifs, leaf rear, disc f/drum r

LENGTH (IN)/WEIGHT (LB): 179/3287 - 3416

LAUNCH PRICE: £1596

P5 3-Litre 1958-67

The first new-style Rover for nine years was the P5, which came on the scene in September 1958. Though it used a development of the six-cylinder engine which had become familiar in P4s, along with the same family of manual gearbox and overdrive transmission, the structure and body style were all new.

This was a much larger car than the P4, running on a 110.5in wheelbase, powered by a 115bhp 2995cc engine, and with a more capacious four-door passenger cabin. The normal saloon would be joined by a lower-roof coupé model in autumn 1962. This derivative had half-frame doors, which lightened the interior. All P5s had a monocoque structure, with a massive sub-frame supporting engine, transmission and front suspension. As you

Rover P5 3-Litre saloon and coupé. These are Mk III models of 1965.

SPECIFICATION

BODY STYLES: saloon, four-door coupé

PRODUCTION: 56,524

ENGINE & TRANSMISSION: *2995cc, 6cyl ioe, 4sp man, o/d or auto, f/r

POWER: 115bhp @ 4500rpm/129bhp @ 4750rpm/134bhp @ 5000rpm

MAX SPEED (MPH): 96/102/107

0-60MPH (SEC): 16.2/17.7/15.0

SUSPENSION & BRAKES: tor ifs, leaf rear, drums f&r (disc f/drum r from late 1959)

LENGTH (IN)/WEIGHT (LB): 187/3556 - 3640

LAUNCH PRICE: £1764

*****NOTE :** 25 cars with 2445cc engines, and 131 cars with 2625cc were produced for export markets from 1962 to 1965.

would expect, the cabin was luxuriously equipped, but without ostentation

In 1958 four-wheel drum brakes were fitted, but front-wheel discs followed in the summer of 1959. A manual gearbox was standard (no synchromesh on first gear), with optional overdrive, or there was the option of Borg Warner automatic transmission.

Further developments were frequent. From May 1960 overdrive was standard (though it could be deleted by special order), while power-assisted steering was optional from October 1960.

Mk II models followed in autumn 1962, with 134bhp (manual/overdrive) or 129bhp (automatic), there now being a

remote-control centre-floor change for manual cars. Power-assisted steering was standard on the new Coupé, and later on saloons from August 1964.

Mk IIIs appeared in September 1965, with detail style changes, and the 134bhp engine for all transmissions. Seating was revised, with individual seating in the rear.

Through their lives these cars were always built carefully, ran beautifully smoothly, and were the very epitome of dignity on wheels. Government ministers naturally favoured them. In later years the bodies rusted and were expensive to restore, but the mechanics lasted well. The last cars were built in August 1967, when the V8-engined P5B took over.

P5B 3½-Litre 1967-73

Officially titled 3½-Litre, but always popularly known as the P5B, this was the very first of Rover's new V8-engined cars (there would be several more). Once built by the Buick Division of General Motors (which explains the "B" of the code name), the engine was a mainly light-alloy unit which had been re-engineered by Rover. Bulkier but no heavier than the old straight-six, Rover's V8 would have a life

extending over nearly forty years.

All P5Bs were produced with this 151bhp 3528cc unit and had Borg Warner automatic transmission as standard. The P5 body, still available in saloon and coupé form, had real (not sham) Rostyle road wheels, but was otherwise visually little changed, needing boot lid badges to signal the difference from the old car. Power steering and front-wheel disc brakes

Rover P5B V8 3.5-litre saloon, 1967.

SPECIFICATION

BODY STYLES : saloon, four-door coupé

PRODUCTION: 20,600

ENGINE & TRANSMISSION : 3528cc, V8cyl ohv, Auto, f/r

POWER : 151bhp @ 5200rpm

MAX SPEED (MPH) : 108

0-60MPH (SEC) : 12.4

SUSPENSION & BRAKES : tor ifs, leaf rear, disc f/drum r

LENGTH (IN)/WEIGHT (LB) : 187/3498

LAUNCH PRICE : £2009

The P5B coupé.

were standard equipment.

Much quicker than the 3-Litre, and with a top speed of nearly 110mph, this smooth and impressive car sold steadily for six years and was changed very little in that time. Saloons and coupés continued side by side until May 1973, when the last car was assembled.

The P5Bs – the coupé in particular – were the most desirable of all the P5 family, and built up quite a following as the classic car movement got under way.

P6 2000 and P6 2000TC 1963-73

Here was a very rare thing, a car new from end to end and top to bottom. New structure, new engine, new transmission and new engineering philosophy – the Rover P6 was a very different type of car from the P4 which it would replace and the larger P5.

The P6's structure was known as "base unit", a monocoque to which every one of the skin panels was bolted into place. It was only ever put on sale by Rover as a four-door saloon, though some private-enterprise estate car conversions were later produced. The 89bhp1978cc engine was

Rover P6 2000, a completely fresh and unexpected design.

SPECIFICATION

BODY STYLES: saloon

PRODUCTION: 246,260, all four-cylinder P6 types

ENGINE & TRANSMISSION: 1978cc, 4cyl ohc, 4sp man, or auto, f/r

POWER: 89bhp @ 5500rpm/110bhp @ 5500rpm

MAX SPEED (MPH): 104/108

0-60MPH (SEC): 14.6/11.9

SUSPENSION & BRAKES: coil ifs, coil DD rear, discs f&r

LENGTH (IN)/WEIGHT (LB): 179/2760/2822

LAUNCH PRICE: £1264

2000TC on rare optional wire wheels.

a brand new overhead-camshaft four, and there was also a new all-synchromesh gearbox. The coil spring independent front suspension had a complex linkage, and at the rear there was a sophisticated De Dion suspension. Four-wheel disc brakes and radial ply tyres were all in the standard specification.

The result was an agile handling package which lacked only two things at first: higher performance and more equipment options. However, these were to come, as in October 1966 the higher-powered 110bhp 2000TC (already launched in export markets) was put on sale in the UK. Centre-lock wire wheels (rare) became an option. At the same time the original 2000 became known as 2000SC, and the 2000 Automatic, with 89bhp, was introduced. In October 1969 Delanair air conditioning became optional.

In September 1970 came a mid-life facelift including the use of a honeycomb grille, re-styled skin panels, and a bonnet with "power bulges". The TC got a revised fascia and instrument display.

Finally, in September 1973, the 2000 range was dropped, to be replaced by the 2200 models – the same basic car with larger and more powerful, engines. Some prefer the purity of the original concept

The Morrison/Syer Rover 2000 on the 1965 Acropolis Rally.

P6 2200SC/2200TC 1973-77

In October 1973, Rover gave the long-running P6 saloon a final facelift, which would see it through the last few years of its career.

The P6's familiar overhead-camshaft engine was given a larger bore – 90.5mm instead of 85.7mm - which increased the swept volume to 2205cc. As before there were single-carburettor (SC) types, now with 98bhp, and twin-carburettor (TC) types with 115bhp, and as before automatic transmission was available, but only with the more flexible single-carburettor engine.

Apart from some minor trim and equipment changes in the cabin, and the use of different badges, there were no visual differences from the last of the 2000 models. These changes, though, appear to have come too late, for the 2200 sold rather slowly compared with the 2000 – on average only 10,000 a year.

The last of this long-running line was made in February 1977.

Rover 2200TC.

SPECIFICATION	
BODY STYLES: saloon	
PRODUCTION: 32,370	
ENGINE & TRANSMISSION: 2205cc, 4cyl ohc, 4sp man, or auto, f/r	
POWER: 98bhp @ 5000rpm/115bhp @ 5000rpm	
MAX SPEED (MPH): 101/108	
0-60MPH (SEC): 13.4/11.5	
SUSPENSION & BRAKES: coil ifs, coil DD rear, discs f&r	
LENGTH (IN)/WEIGHT (LB): 179/2822	
LAUNCH PRICE: £20-19/£2139	

P6B 3500 and 3500S 1968-76

As they had done with the P5, Rover somehow managed to squeeze the new alloy V8 under the bonnet of the P6 (2000) structure. The company tried to impose the name "Three Thousand Five" on the public but they ignored that, and the car universally came to be known as the 3500, or sometimes as the P6B (B for "Buick", of course).

Originally launched in April 1968, the P6B had 144bhp at 5000rpm and Borg Warner automatic transmission, with no manual transmission option. Power-assisted steering was an optional extra, but the rest of the advanced chassis was little changed (nor, indeed, needed much up-dating to cope with the extra power and torque).

The original car carried on until late 1970, when it received the same mid-life facelift already described for 2000 models. Even so, there was great demand

Rover P6 3500, 1968.

SPECIFICATION

BODY STYLES: saloon

PRODUCTION : 79,057, all V8 P6Bs

ENGINE & TRANSMISSION: 3528cc, V8cyl ohv, 4sp man, or auto, f/r

POWER: 144bhp @ 5000/150bhp @ 5000rpm

MAX SPEED (MPH): 117/122

0-60MPH (SEC): 9.5/9.1

SUSPENSION & BRAKES: coil ifs, coil DD rear, discs f&r

LENGTH (IN)/WEIGHT (LB): 180/2862

LAUNCH PRICE: £1801

The 122mph Rover 3500S, fitted with a manual gearbox as standard.

H R Owen Ltd offered estate car conversions on the 3500.

for a manual transmission car, this finally being satisfied in October 1971 when the 3500S appeared. This car originally had a 150bhp version of the engine, which was slightly re-rated in 1973 to 143bhp.

These V8s were very popular, especially with those who wanted performance but not bulk, and good handling to go with it. 3500s proved very popular with the British police force, who shrugged off the lack of stowage and took advantage of the performance. Except that the hull eventually proved to be quite rust-prone, this was a very complete car in every way.

3500 (SD1) 1976-86

If Rover's P8 project had not been cancelled by British Leyland, there might never have been a new 3500 – or, as it is always known, the SD1 (the project code). SD1 was started in the early 1970s, but did not appear until June 1976. Apart from the light-alloy V8 engine (as carried over from the P5B,

P6B and Range Rover), it was new from end to end. Until 1982, assembly was at Solihull.

Compared with the innovative P6 this was an utterly conventional car. The structure (originally made at Castle Bromwich, which later became a Jaguar facility) was an all-steel monocoque, the

front suspension classic MacPherson, and there was a coil-sprung beam axle (with self-levelling) at the rear. The engine was an up-dated version of the P6B unit, while the five-speed gearbox and the axle were newly engineered by Triumph. Rack-and-pinion power steering was standard, and automatic transmission was optional.

Other derivatives were planned (see 2300/2600, below), but this was the top-of-the-range model from the beginning. Though the cabin package was quite

Rover SD1 3500S, 1979.

SPECIFICATION

BODY STYLES: hatchback

PRODUCTION: 303,345, all SD1 types

ENGINE & TRANSMISSION: 3528cc, V8cyl ohv, 5sp man, or auto, f/r

POWER: 155bhp @ 5250rpm

MAX SPEED (MPH): 123

0-60MPH (SEC): 8.4

SUSPENSION & BRAKES: coil ifs, coil rear, disc f/drum r

LENGTH (IN)/WEIGHT (LB): 185/2989

LAUNCH PRICE : £4750

restricting (it was no match for the new-generation Ford Granada of the period, for instance), the driving position and the road manners were much more sports-saloon than executive-magic-carpet. Few people seemed to notice that the steering wheel was not truly circular, for the seats were fully reclineable, the instrument panel lavishly equipped, and the trim (if properly built and assembled) definitely up-market in feel.

Electric window lifts arrived in late 1977, and leather seats as an option from mid-1978.

In July 1979 a V8S version arrived, mechanically the same but with gold-painted wheels and even more interior equipment including leather seating; air conditioning was optional from late 1979.

From late 1980 the 3500 became the 3500SE, and the V8S gave way to the Vanden Plas, the improvements being cosmetic and in equipment level. Early in 1982 SD1 assembly was moved to Cowley – Cowley cars also having extra engine options. Automatic transmission would become standard in May 1984.

If only these cars had been properly built, and the build quality maintained, they ought to have been best-sellers, for they were fast, nimble and attractive. Unhappily, British Leyland's problems were all but terminal at this time, corrosion was soon seen to afflict the cars, and sales dragged.

2300/2600 (SD1) 1977-86

Announced in October 1977, and then built in parallel with other SD1s, the 2300 and 2600 types were powered by a new overhead-camshaft in-line six-cylinder engine which was actually designed and developed by Triumph. In almost every other respect, including the overall style, and the equipment options, it was easy to see the connection with the 3500.

The 123bhp 2300 was the entry-level model, with only a four-speed gearbox as standard, though the 3500's five-speeder, and automatic transmission,

The 1977 Rover SD1 2300 (right) and 2600 (left).

SPECIFICATION

BODY STYLES: hatchback

PRODUCTION: see SD1 totals above

ENGINE & TRANSMISSION: 2350cc/2597cc, 6cyl ohc, 4sp man/5spd man, or auto, f/r

POWER: 123bhp @ 5000rpm/136bhp @ 5000rpm

MAX SPEED (MPH): 111/117

0-60MPH (SEC): 11.9/10.7

SUSPENSION & BRAKES: coil ifs, coil rear, disc f/drum r

LENGTH (IN)/WEIGHT (LB): 185/2787

LAUNCH PRICE: £5645/£5800

were both options. The 136bhp 2600 was the classic "gap filler" between 2300 and 3500, this car not only having more power, but also the five-speed gearbox as standard, the automatic transmission as an option, and picking up most of the 3500's trim and decorative equipment as standard too. Power steering was optional at first, but standard (2600 only) from 1979.

Once launched, and on sale, these versions rarely got the publicity, or the marketing attention, of the V8-engined parent model, but both sold well, and would stay in production until 1986. As with the 3500, assembly was moved to Cowley in 1981/82. Automatic transmission became standard on 2600s from May 1984.

Like the 3500, these cars would have had a better reputation if the build quality had been of a higher standard. Compared with the 3500, it seems, few have survived.

RUSSON

After the War, when almost any type of car would apparently find customers, some strange concoctions appeared. The Russon, conceived and developed in Stanbridge, Bedfordshire, with production at Eaton Bray, was one of these, and had been designed by D A Russell. Although it looked gawky (even by 1951 standards), it did at least have four wheels, and gave the impression of a conventional car which had shrunk in the wash – or perhaps an overgrown fairground machine.

Like most such projects, though, it had very simple engineering, and was manufactured with very rudimentary tooling. Russon advertised it as "Britain's Lowest Priced Four-wheeler Car", but at a price of £424 for the so-called "production" car, it really was no sort of a bargain and demand was virtually non-existent. The entire project imploded within a year or so, and no more was heard of it.

Minicar 1951-52

Someone, somewhere, must have been looking at fairground dodgem cars, for the Russon looked unmistakeably like a grown-up version of that breed. Although the awkwardly-styled two/three-seater tourer body hid quite enterprising chassis engineering, it was never likely to appeal to a mass market.

The basis of the machine was a twin-tube chassis frame with tubular cross-

The Russon Minicar.

SPECIFICATION

BODY STYLES: tourer

PRODUCTION: 15

ENGINE & TRANSMISSION: 197cc, 1cyl ts/250cc, 2cyl ts, 3sp man, m/r

POWER: 8bhp/10bhp

MAX SPEED (MPH): 45 (E)/ 45 (E)

0-60MPH (SEC): not possible

SUSPENSION & BRAKES: coil ifs, coil irs, drums f&r

LENGTH (IN)/WEIGHT (LB): 128/560-616

LAUNCH PRICE: £424

bracings, there being coil-over-shock-absorber springs all round and rack-and-pinion steering. The engine, as you might expect, was a motorcycle-type air-cooled two-stroke unit, with motorcycle gearbox and chain drive, all behind the seats.

The first car used a 197cc JAP engine, but "production" cars were powered by a twin-cylinder Excelsior Talisman.

The body was built by traditional coachbuilt methods, with a wood, steel and aluminium skeleton, all clad in aluminium skin panels.

Crude? Certainly. Worth preserving? Depends on your point of view.

SCOOTACAR

You have to start by taking projects like the Scootacar seriously, even if they look weird, are tiny, and seem to have very little to offer. One might ask why an established company like Hunslet Holdings of Leeds, who knew all about building railway locomotives and other large pieces of railway machinery, should decide to go into the mini-car market ?

The legend is that a Hunslet director's wife wanted something smaller than her Jaguar, so that she could go shopping in Leeds – and it had to be British! Henry Brown, who had been connected with the failed Rodley project (described earlier), moved in to do the design job, and though no one at Hunslet admitted to knowing anything about cars, in its own way it was a success, for with minimal capital outlay it sold more than 1000 examples.

Hunslet made sure that conventional automotive engineering did not get in the way by developing and building the car in Leeds. This, maybe, was not a good precedent, as Henry Brown's earlier project, the awful Rodley, had already been produced in that part of the world.

Although the Scootacar was completley ignored by most of the motoring press, *The Motor* devoted no fewer than three pages to a root-and-branch assessment of this quirky design, suggesting that it might be an "easy to park second string".

On the basis that few people expected too much of it, the Scootacar pottered along until 1965, having had an engine up-date and a slight styling up-date along the way, when Hunslet retired from the automotive business and reverted to railway engineering.

Coupé 1958-61/1961-65

Think of a conventional bubble car such as an Isetta or a Heinkel, squeeze it to narrow it to 52in wide, and let the roof rise up to 60in. Then, with a bit of suitable smoothing of panels, you

have the two-seater Scootacar. Unique in so many ways, it was a three-wheeler (two front wheels) which featured tandem seating for two – the "pillion" passenger sat atop the rear-mounted

motorcycle engine – with the driver controlling not a wheel, but handlebars.

The basis of the design was a simple steel platform chassis, with coil spring independent suspension all round (the rear end doubled as the chain drive for the transmission), hydraulic front brakes (Morris Minor type), and cable brake operation of the single rear wheel. The engine – a single-cylinder Villiers at first, but with a twin-cylinder transplant towards the end (only 10-20 of those were made) – was mated to a motorcycle gearbox, and final drive was by chain.

The body shell was of glass-fibre, with a fixed roof and only one door (to the left side of the car), this slim coupé being equipped with winding windows. The package was so small that, even with only 8in wheels, the spare had to live outside, on the tail, where it doubled as a bumper.

After an initial burst of enthusiasm, sales of the Scootacar fell away, and not even a facelift (with a more bulbous nose and a slightly longer tail) could

Scootacar Coupé.

SPECIFICATION

BODY STYLES: saloon

PRODUCTION: c.1000, all types

ENGINE & TRANSMISSION: 197cc, 1cyl ts/324cc, 2cyl ts, 4sp man, m/r

POWER: 8bhp @ 4000rpm/16bhp @ 5000rpm

MAX SPEED (MPH): 50/68 (E)

0-60MPH (SEC): not possible/not measured

SUSPENSION & BRAKES: coil ifs, coil irs, drums f&r

LENGTH (IN)/WEIGHT (LB): 84/500

LAUNCH PRICE: £298

rescue it. As with so many such cars, it was the BMC Mini which killed it off for good.

For conventional motorists, there was much to get used to in the Scootacar, including direct steering, rough-and-ready gear-changing – the lever was to the right of the seat – and the hard ride. Even though it had no heating, and only a single windscreen wiper, it had its own appeal, and a surprising number have survived.

SINGER

Way back in the 19th century, Singer of Coventry had started by building pedal cycles, then motor cycles, before finally producing cars from 1905. By the late 1920s Singer was one of Britain's most important car makers, the fourth largest in output terms, but retreated after the depression of the early 1930s. Even so, by 1939 the company had rather old-fashioned factories in Coventry and Birmingham.

After 1945, the company started its post-war programme with the SM1500/Hunter saloon, which sold well but not well enough to make a lot of money. By the mid-1950s, therefore, Singer was still solvent, but not making enough money to invest in new models. As an example, the twin overhead camshaft engine developed both for the Hunter and for HRG was expensive, and not properly prepared for sale until it was too late.

The Rootes Group therefore made an agreed takeover in 1955-56, and set about re-shaping Singer as one of its own

Hillman-based brands: Lord Rootes himself had been a Singer apprentice, so there was a personal connection to be indulged.

For the next fifteen years there always seemed to be a Singer equivalent to any new Hillman – slightly more upmarket, and slightly more decorated. The Gazelle was close to the Minx, the Vogue to the Super Minx, and the cute little Chamois to the rear-engined Imp. By this time, separate Singer assembly facilities had long gone, for the cars were being produced alongside Hillmans (and Sunbeams) at Ryton near Coventry, or at Linwood in Scotland.

Singer sales were brisk, and profitable for the Rootes Group, but after Chrysler took control of Rootes it began dismantling the pyramid of brands. Accordingly, in 1970 the last Singers of all were re-badged as Sunbeams, and the historical links were finally lost.

Nine Roadster/4A 1939-51

Anxious to get back into civilian car production as soon as possible, Singer re-introduced the 1939-vintage Nine Roadster. Like MG's TC, it was a thoroughly backward-looking machine which would surely have died an early death if there had not been such a shortage of new cars of any type. For the first four years, almost all production went to export markets.

Although Singer built the Roadster alongside the Super Ten saloon of the period, there were many differences to negate any economies of scale – the Roadster's different chassis frame, smaller

SPECIFICATION

BODY STYLES: sports car, coupé

PRODUCTION: c. 6900, all post-war Roadster/4A/4AB types

ENGINE & TRANSMISSION: 1074cc, 4cyl ohc, 3sp man, 4sp man (on 4A), f/r

POWER: 36bhp @ 5000rpm

MAX SPEED (MPH): 65

0-60MPH (SEC): 37.6

SUSPENSION & BRAKE : leaf front (coil ifs on 4A), leaf rear, drums f&r

LENGTH (IN)/WEIGHT (LB): 150/1708

LAUNCH PRICE: £493/£576

Singer Nine Roadster.

engine and three-speed gearbox among them. The body style was traditional-British of the 1930s, with sweeping front wings, separate headlamps, a vertically-slatted grille, and a body of aluminium panelling on a wooden skeleton.

The frame itself had leaf springs and solid axles at front and rear, brakes were mechanical, and the overhead-camshaft engine's promise was masked by the car's bulk, for this was a four-seater open tourer. From September 1949, Singer upgraded the Roadster to become the

Roadster 4A, this having the Hunter's four-speed gearbox, complete with a remote-control change. But it wasn't long before an even better Roadster, the 4AB (separately described) killed it off.

The Roadster's problem was always that it was never as good as the earlier Singer sports cars of the mid-1930s, nor as fast and charismatic as the competing MGs of the period. Except for curiosity and "quaintness" value, there was really little reason for preserving Roadsters for posterity – and few have been.

Nine Roadster 4AB 1950-52

The Roadster Type 4AB, available on the UK market from the autumn of 1950 was a logical (and ultimately short-lived) update of the existing Roadster 4A, in that it was given a new chassis, with independent front suspension, without alteration to the styling, method of body construction or engine performance.

SPECIFICATION

BODY STYLES: sports car

PRODUCTION: see above

ENGINE & TRANSMISSION: 1074cc, 4cyl ohc, 4sp man, f/r

POWER: 36bhp @ 5000rpm

MAX SPEED (MPH): 65

0-60MPH (SEC): 37.5

SUSPENSION & BRAKES: coil ifs, leaf rear, drums f&r

LENGTH (IN)/WEIGHT (LB): 152/1736

LAUNCH PRICE: £576

Singer Nine Roadster 4AB, 1950.

The suspension was lifted from the Singer SM1500 saloon, and quite transformed the roadholding, and the hydro-mechanical brakes were an advance, but nothing else could transform the four-seater tourer's appeal, so in 1951 it was supplanted by yet another derivative, that one being the SM Roadster.

Super Ten/Super Twelve 1938-49

The Super Ten, of pre-war vintage, was re-launched in January 1946, a car of traditional looks and behaviour with one major selling point – that it had the single-overhead camshaft engine for which Singer was famous. The rest of the car was pure 1930s. Although no one admitted to anything at the time, much of the steel body shell was the same as that used in the Hillman Minx of the day.

The chassis was ladder-style with cruciform bracing and half-elliptic leaf springs at front and rear, but at least the brakes were hydraulic. The 1194cc

Singer Super Ten, an update of the pre-war model.

engine (slightly enlarged compared with 1939) produced 37bhp, and was backed by a newly-developed four-speed gearbox which had a remote-control centre-floor shift. For post-war cars there was a new fascia.

The Super Twelve was the sister car, with a longer wheelbase and 11 inches longer overall, all this being arranged to accommodate the larger 1525cc engine at the front. There was an extended boot compartment at the rear, though the rest of the cabin was little changed.

Neither car was ever going to break any records, or astonish the market place, but as cars up-market of the similar Hillmans and Morris, they kept Singer dealers happy until the post-war SM1500 could come on stream.

The 1.5-litre Singer Super Twelve.

SPECIFICATION

BODY STYLES: saloon

PRODUCTION: 11,595 post-war

ENGINE & TRANSMISSION: 1194cc/1525cc, 4cyl ohc, 4sp man, f/r

POWER: 37bhp @ 5000rpm/43bhp @ 4000rpm

MAX SPEED (MPH): 62/68

0-60MPH (SEC): not measured/37.1

SUSPENSION & BRAKES: leaf front, leaf rear, drums f&r

LENGTH (IN)/WEIGHT (LB): 155/2240, 166/2576

LAUNCH PRICE: £509/£768

SM1500/Hunter 1948-54/1954-56

Singer's first new post-war saloon car, initially called the SM1500, seemed to take ages to come to the market. Originally previewed in 1947, it was not built in numbers until the end of 1948, and home deliveries (to priority customers) began in 1949.

Singer had tried hard. The smart, modern-looking four-door body, albeit with a rather anonymous nose, was all-steel (from Pressed Steel), and rode on a new box-section chassis frame which had coil spring independent front suspension; for Singer, the use of all-hydraulic braking was a novelty.

Naturally the engine was a four-cylinder overhead-camshaft unit, different from that of the old Super Twelve (larger bore, shorter stroke, and 1506cc instead of 1525cc) and producing a very satisfactory 48bhp, but it only delivered a 71mph top speed. As everyone had suspected, this meant that the rather slab-fronted and slab-sided body was not aerodynamically efficient. As usual on post-war British cars there was a bench front seat and the gear change was on the steering column.

By 1951 Singer had seen the obvious (to historians) marketing error, so a slightly smaller, shorter-stroke 1497cc engine was adopted to set the car in a lower class. In 1952, a twin-carb 58bhp derivative became optional, this being the time when a new fascia style and a larger rear window were adopted.

From September 1954, the SM1500 turned into the Hunter (that name would be handed down to Hillman in the 1960s), with a new front end incorporating a traditional Singer grille, and with a GRP bonnet/bonnet valance panel, though the 48bhp and 58bhp engines continued as before and the gear shift lever was still on the steering column. Even so, the GRP panelling was not a success, and a reversion to pressed steel came in 1955.

At the very end of the run, a stripped out Hunter S appeared and a centre-floor (Roadster-type) gear change became available, but the Rootes takeover condemned the Hunter to death; it duly died in 1956. It had been a good car – a great improvement over the Super Ten and Super Twelve types – but was never sufficiently outstanding in performance, looks or behaviour to match cars like the Hillman Minx, for prices were always too high.

Singer SM1500, a good car but not a good looker.

SPECIFICATION

BODY STYLES: saloon

PRODUCTION: 17,382/4772

ENGINE & TRANSMISSION: 1506/1497cc, 4cyl ohc, 4sp man, f/r

POWER: 48bhp @ 4200rpm/58bhp @ 4600rpm

MAX SPEED (MPH): 71/76

0-60MPH (SEC): 33.7/23.5

SUSPENSION & BRAKES: coil ifs, leaf rear, drums f&r

LENGTH (IN)/WEIGHT (LB): 174/2520 - 2688

LAUNCH PRICE: £799/£975

SM Roadster 1951-55

Announced during 1951, the SM Roadster was the final development of the ageing Roadster which had been fresh in 1939, acceptable in 1945, but frankly out of date by the 1950s.

To the 4AB chassis (complete with coil spring independent front suspension and hydro-mechanical brakes), Singer added the larger and more powerful 48bhp 1497cc SM1500 engine but made few other changes, and sent all the early supplies to export markets.

Here was an old-fashioned car with a 73mph top speed (the aerodynamic

SPECIFICATION

BODY STYLES: sports car

PRODUCTION: 3440

ENGINE & TRANSMISSION: 1497cc, 4cyl ohc, 4sp man, f/r

POWER: 48bhp @ 4600rpm/58bhp @ 4600rpm

MAX SPEED (MPH): 73/77

0-60MPH (SEC): 23.6/20.2

SUSPENSION & BRAKES: coil ifs, leaf rear, drums f&r

LENGTH (IN)/WEIGHT (LB): 151/1820

LAUNCH PRICE: £724/£829

Singer SM Roadster.

performance was still awful).

Before domestic deliveries began in 1953 a more powerful engine producing 58bhp from 1497cc became optional. Although this pushed up to the top speed to 77mph, the SM Roadster was no longer competitive, especially against the likes of the TR2, and it struggled even to survive until 1955, when it quietly faded away. When is the last time you saw one?

The 1953 glassfibre-bodied SMX Roadster, a project abandoned after only a handful had been made.

Hunter 75 1955-56

This is a fascinating footnote to the SM1500/Hunter story. In October 1955, just before the Rootes Group took over Singer, the company announced the Hunter 75, in which the great novelty was a twin-cam version of the existing 1497cc engine.

This, an iron-head derivative of the much more powerful engine already seen in the HRG Twin-Cam (previously

SPECIFICATION

BODY STYLES: saloon

PRODUCTION: 20

ENGINE & TRANSMISSION: 1497cc, 4cyl 2ohc, 4sp man, f/r

POWER: 75bhp @ 5250rpm

MAX SPEED (MPH): 85 (E)

0-60MPH (SEC): not measured

SUSPENSION & BRAKES: coil ifs, leaf rear, drums f&r

LENGTH (IN)/WEIGHT (LB): 174/2688

LAUNCH PRICE: £1150

Singer Hunter 75.

described), had lines of valves opposed at 90 degrees, and retained a three-bearing crankshaft. It was fuelled by two downdraught Solex carburettors. Amazingly, Singer kept the usual steering-column gearchange though they did at least make the brakes larger, and turn over to Girling for supplies.

At a launch price of £1150, this car was

much more costly than the existing Hunter (£975), which might have made on-going sales difficult. Not that this mattered, for after about 20 engines had been built Rootes abruptly cancelled the programme. We doubt whether any cars have survived.

No independent road appraisals were ever published.

Gazelle I and II 1956-57/1957-58

The first "Rootes" Singer appeared in September 1956, effectively a new-generation Hillman Minx, re-engined with the Singer Hunter-type overhead-camshaft engine, but using a Minx gearbox and its steering-column change. This was merely an interim model, for the Gazelle which followed in 1958 had the Hillman Minx engine instead.

SPECIFICATION

BODY STYLES: saloon, drophead, estate

PRODUCTION: 4344/1582

ENGINE & TRANSMISSION: 1497cc, 4cyl ohc, 4sp man, o/d, f/r

POWER: 49bhp @ 4500rpm

MAX SPEED (MPH): 78

0-60MPH (SEC): 23.6

SUSPENSION & BRAKES: coil ifs, leaf rear, drums f&r

LENGTH (IN)/WEIGHT (LB): 164/2255

LAUNCH PRICE: £898

Singer Gazelle I convertible, 1956.

Based on the new-type Hillman Minx monocoque, in four-door saloon guise with a wrap-around rear window, and

(soon) a two-door drophead coupé, the new Gazelle used the same front and rear suspensions, and the styling differed only by having a so-called Singer front grille and badging, with a walnut-grained fascia panel. The Hunter engine produced 49bhp at a time when the equivalent Minx engine produced 48bhp, so there was really no difference in performance between the brands.

It was typical of Rootes that derivatives built up rapidly. From autumn 1957 the Gazelle became Mk II, with an estate car body added to the range, and with optional Laycock overdrive. The Mk II, though, was only produced for a few months. Rootes wanted to position Singer up-market of the Hillman brand, but with less performance than the Sunbeams which were priced even higher. This gave the Singer brand a slowly-developing middle-class image. There is no argument, though, that the Gazelle was never more than a "Minx in a party frock", mirroring all the changes which were made to the equivalent Hillman of the day.

Gazelle IIA to IIIC 1958-63

As with the Minx of the period, Rootes went in for rapid-fire changes with the Gazelle which gradually updated its appearance and enhanced its specification. The IIA of February 1958 lost the overhead-camshaft Singer engine in favour of an overhead-valve 56bhp 1494cc Hillman Minx unit, so there was now little to choose, mechanically, between the two brands.

Best to summarise what happened, and when, as follows :

The Mk IIA had the 56bhp 1494cc Minx engine, but was otherwise like the Mk II

The Mk III of September 1958 was mechanically identical, but now with duo-tone paintwork and a number of trim changes.

The Mk IIIA of September 1959 had style changes like the Minx, including "rolled-over" tail fins and a deeper front screen, plus a 60bhp engine with twin downdraught Zenith carburettors, closer ratio gears and a centre floor gear-change (the column change was retained for export models). Smiths Easidrive automatic transmission became an option.

The Mk IIIB of August 1960 reverted to a single-carburettor engine and inherited the new Rootes corporate hypoid-bevel rear axle.

The Mk IIIC of July 1961 (the seventh sub-division of Gazelles in five years!) had a 53bhp 1592cc engine. This was also the model which saw the convertible option dropped in February 1962, and the estate car in March 1962.

Through all this marketing turmoil the same basic style, in exterior and interior terms, continued, and the sober, no-hurry, middle-class character remained, along with the spongy, heavy steering As a policy, though, it obviously worked, which was confirmed by the steadily rising sales figures.

SPECIFICATION

BODY STYLES: saloon, drophead, estate

PRODUCTION: 3824/10,929/12,491/13,272/15,115

ENGINE & TRANSMISSION: 1494cc/1592cc, 4cyl ohv, 4sp man, or auto (from Mk IIIA), f/r

POWER: 56bhp @ 4600rpm/60bhp @ 4600rpm/53bhp @ 4100rpm

MAX SPEED (MPH): 82

0-60MPH (SEC): 21.4

SUSPENSION & BRAKES: coil ifs, leaf rear, drums f&r

LENGTH (IN)/WEIGHT (LB): 164/2255

LAUNCH PRICE: £898

Gazelle IIIC.

Gazelle V 1963-65

There was no Gazelle Mk IV (that numeral had been reserved for the car which became the Singer Vogue), so in autumn 1963 the Gazelle sequence leapt from Mk IIIC to Mk V. This was an important juncture, for it brought significant styling and mechanical changes.

There was only one shape of Mk V, the four-door saloon, this sharing the same new squared-up cabin (which no longer had a wrap-around rear window) as the equivalent Hillman Minx, the Series V. It had reclining front seats as standard, and a new-style fascia layout, though the familiar Rootes-Singer front end was retained. Mechanically, there were now two 1592cc engines, which were rated at 53bhp for manual transmission cars, or 58bhp for automatic transmission. At the same time, the chassis got front disc brakes, and 13in wheels, plus a "nogrease-point" chassis. From October 1964 this model gained a new all-synchromesh manual gearbox. The optional automatic transmission got a centre-floor quadrant selector lever.

SPECIFICATION

BODY STYLES: saloon

PRODUCTION: 20,022

ENGINE & TRANSMISSION: 1592cc, 4cyl ohv, 4sp man, or auto, f/r

POWER: 53bhp @ 4100rpm/58bhp @ 4000rpm

MAX SPEED (MPH): 79

0-60MPH (SEC): 24.9

SUSPENSION & BRAKES: coil ifs, leaf rear, disc f/drum r

LENGTH (IN)/WEIGHT (LB): 164/2255

LAUNCH PRICE: £723

Gazelle V, 1963.

Gazelle VI 1965-67

The last variation on the long-running Minx-type Gazelle appeared in October 1965, this time with the final stretch of the Rootes engine, a 1725cc five-bearing power unit, and with negative earth electrics.

There were very slight front-end style changes (the grille was now fixed to the

SPECIFICATION

BODY STYLES: saloon

PRODUCTION: 1482

ENGINE & TRANSMISSION: 1725cc, 4cyl ohv, 4sp man, or auto, f/r

POWER: 65bhp @ 4800rpm/59bhp @ 4200rpm

MAX SPEED (MPH): 82

0-60MPH (SEC): 20.5

SUSPENSION & BRAKES: coil ifs, leaf rear, disc f/drum r

LENGTH (IN)/WEIGHT (LB): 164/2225

LAUNCH PRICE: £757

Gazelle VI, 1965.

front panel instead of swinging up with the bonnet when it was opened) but little else of significance.

Early cars had significantly more power – 65bhp instead of 59bhp – than the

majority of those built. For once, though, this was a Gazelle which sold very slowly; the last was built in March 1967. Its successor was based on the latest-generation Hillman Minx/Hunter.

Vogue I/II 1961-64

Singer's Vogue, announced in July 1961, was actually based on the new Hillman Super Minx, though its launch preceded it by three months. It was originally planned as a new Gazelle (to

be named Gazelle Mk IV) but the policy changed at a later stage. Old Gazelle and new Vogue continued alongside for five years. The Humber Sceptre of 1963 was another close relation.

The new Vogue shared the same basic unit-construction four-door saloon as the Hillman Super Minx, as well as the chassis and most of the running gear. It had the same 62bhp 1592cc engine, and four-wheel drum brakes. Overdrive and Smiths Easidrive automatic transmission were both optional equipment. For the Singer application there was a different, four-headlamp front-end (with Singer-type grille), and the interior included a walnut veneer fascia panel.

An estate car derivative appeared in May 1962 but unlike the Super Minx

The 1.6-litre Singer Vogue, an upmarket Hillman Super Minx.

SPECIFICATION

BODY STYLES: saloon, estate

PRODUCTION: 7423/20,021

ENGINE & TRANSMISSION: 1592cc, 4cyl ohv, 4sp man, o/d or auto, f/r

POWER: 62bhp @ 4800rpm

MAX SPEED (MPH): 83

0-60MPH (SEC): 20.9

SUSPENSION & BRAKES: coil ifs, leaf rear, drums f&r (disc f/drum r on Vogue II)

LENGTH (IN)/WEIGHT (LB): 165/2410

LAUNCH PRICE: £929

the Vogue was never offered as a convertible. Saloon and estate both progressed to Vogue II level in October 1962, with disc front brakes, Borg Warner instead of Easidrive automatic transmission, and a "no-greasing" chassis, but no styling changes.

As with other Singers of the period, this Vogue was no more and no less than a better-dressed Hillman: sturdy, conventional and nicely trimmed in the manner of Rootes cars of the period. No-one ever got excited about them, but Rootes sold them in shed-loads.

Vogue III/IV 1964-65/1965-66

Introduced in the autumn of 1964, this was a thorough up-date of the original Vogue package, with different styling and a much more powerful engine. In some ways the Vogue III moved a long way away from the Hillman Super Minx, and towards the Humber Sceptre.

Not only was the saloon car cabin completely re-shaped, with a six-light style and flattened rear window, but the 78bhp 1592cc Sceptre-tune engine (which had an aluminium cylinder

The 1964 Vogue IV, now with 1725cc engine.

SPECIFICATION

BODY STYLES: saloon, estate

PRODUCTION: 10,000/10,325

ENGINE & TRANSMISSION: 1592cc/1725cc, 4cyl ohv, 4sp man, o/d or auto, f/r

POWER: 78bhp @ 5000rpm/85bhp @ 5500rpm

MAX SPEED (MPH): 90/92 (E)

0-60MPH (SEC): 14.1/13.5 (E)

SUSPENSION & BRAKES: coil ifs, leaf rear, disc f/drum r

LENGTH (IN)/WEIGHT (LB): 165/2410

LAUNCH PRICE: £845/£896

head) was installed, along with the new corporate all-synchromesh gearbox. The automatic gearbox selector quadrant was now on the centre floor, and reclining front seats had become standard. This was the first 90mph Vogue, and it was a more attractive package.

The Vogue III was only available for a year, for in October 1965 it became Series IV and received the long-stroke five-bearing 85bhp 1725cc engine. No fewer than 10,325 such cars were produced before yet another type of

Vogue, the Hillman Hunter-based car, took its place.

Vogue IV estate car, 1965.

Chamois 1964-70

The only real novelty in this rear-engined saloon was its name. Unlike other Rootes models of the period, it was not a recycled model from the past, but a new one picked up out of the "trade mark" bin.

Apart from having a slightly higher level of trim and equipment and – strange, this – wider-rim road wheels, the Singer Chamois was a complete clone of the Hillman Imp/Super Imp models already described.

SPECIFICATION

BODY STYLES: saloon, coupé

PRODUCTION: saloon 40,678, coupé 4971

ENGINE & TRANSMISSION: 875cc, 4cyl ohc, 4sp man, r/r

POWER: 37bhp @ 4800rpm

MAX SPEED (MPH): 78

0-60MPH (SEC): 25.4/22.1

SUSPENSION & BRAKES: coil ifs, coil irs, drums f&r

LENGTH (IN)/WEIGHT (LB): 139/1530, 141/1530

LAUNCH PRICE: £582 saloon, £665 coupé

Singer's version of the Hillman Imp, the Chamois. In 1968 it gained twin headlamps.

Mk I became Mk II in autumn 1965, the front suspension was de-cambered in the spring of 1967, and a different fascia style and a four-headlamp nose were adopted from October 1968.

The Chamois Coupé, launched in 1967, was mechanically identical to the Hillman Imp Californian of the 1967-70 period, and shared the same smart coupé body, though like the Chamois saloon it had slightly more up-market trim and fittings.

Like all other Singers, the Chamois was abandoned in April 1970.

Chamois Sport 1966-70

Always contemporary with the Sunbeam Imp Sport, the Chamois Sport was a very close copy of that car, sharing all its chassis, its monocoque and its chunky saloon style, with the cooling louvres in the rear engine cover.

SPECIFICATION

BODY STYLES: saloon

PRODUCTION: 4149

ENGINE & TRANSMISSION: 875cc, 4cyl ohc, 4sp man, r/r

POWER: 51bhp @ 6100rpm

MAX SPEED (MPH): 90

0-60MPH (SEC): 16.3

SUSPENSION & BRAKES: coil ifs, coil irs, drums f&r

LENGTH (IN)/WEIGHT (LB): 141/1640

LAUNCH PRICE: £665

The 51bhp Chamois Sport.

Compared with the Imp Sport, though, it had one minor but obvious advantage in terms of equipment and attraction – which was that from October 1968 it had the same smart four-headlamp nose which had already been seen on the Sunbeam Stiletto.

Like other Singers, it was dropped in April 1970, after which the Sunbeam Imp Sport soldiered on alone.

New Gazelle 1967-70

Like all other Singers of the 1960s, the latest-generation Gazelle was mechanically almost identical to the equivalent Hillman – in this case the new "Arrow"-type Minx.

Manual transmission versions had the 1496cc engine, while automatics had the more powerful (iron cylinder head) 1725cc power unit. There was no overdrive option. Compared with the Minx, though, this Gazelle had a

Singer New Gazelle, 1967-70.

SPECIFICATION

BODY STYLES: saloon

PRODUCTION: 31,482

ENGINE & TRANSMISSION: 1496cc/1725cc, 4cyl ohv, 4sp man, or auto, f/r

POWER: 54bhp @ 4600rpm/61bhp @ 4700rpm

MAX SPEED (MPH): 84/90

0-60MPH (SEC): 17.8/14.6

SUSPENSION & BRAKES: coil ifs, leaf rear, disc f/drum r

LENGTH (IN)/WEIGHT (LB): 168/2035

LAUNCH PRICE: £798

different fascia with circular dials, a wood veneer dashboard, Ambla seats and carpets on the floor – plus of course, the Singer-like shape to the front grille. It was also distinguished by its rectangular headlamps.

As with previous Gazelles, customers were buying the badge, but no more performance and no better roadholding. Even so, Rootes/Chrysler sold more than 31,000 before the Singer name was swept away.

New Vogue 1966-70

For "Hillman Hunter" read "Singer Vogue", for this new Vogue V was really no more than a Hunter in formal clothing. It came as four-door saloon and (from April 1967) five-door estate car and had a goodly expanse of wood veneer on the fascia, with circular instead of strip instrumentation, but the chassis and running gear were almost the same as those found in the Hunter.

All Vogues used the same body style as the Gazelle, and all used the 1725cc version of the engine. A manual gearbox was standard, with overdrive as an option, or automatic transmission could be specified at extra cost. There was a power-boost from October 1967. These were sound cars which did their job well.

Singer New Vogue estate car.

SPECIFICATION

BODY STYLES: saloon, estate

PRODUCTION: 47,655

ENGINE & TRANSMISSION: 1725cc, 4cyl ohv, 4sp man, o/d or auto, f/r

POWER: 61bhp @ 4700rpm/72bhp @ 5000rpm

MAX SPEED (MPH): 90

0-60MPH (SEC): 14.6

SUSPENSION & BRAKES: coil ifs, leaf rear, disc f/drum r

LENGTH (IN)/WEIGHT (LB): 168/2035

LAUNCH PRICE: £911

STANDARD

Founded in 1903, Standard of Coventry expanded gradually until the 1930s, when the dynamic John Black (later Sir John) turned it into one of Britain's "Big Six" car makers. After a busy war spent producing military machinery of many sorts, Standard faced 1945 with two new strands to its business. One was that Sir John had bought up the bankrupt remains of Triumph, the other was that he secured a vast contract to produce Ferguson tractors in the ex-aero-engine factory at Banner Lane.

After the revival of the 1930s-style Standards, then the introduction of the first "Standard-Triumphs", the first true post-war Standard was the Vanguard of 1948. Five years later the new Standard Eight and Ten saloons founded a family of cars (their engine would be used until 1980), after which successive models of Vanguards and the Ten-based Pennant

kept the pot boiling.

By this time, though, the Standard business was in turmoil. Management now favoured Triumph instead of Standard, and dissolved the link with Ferguson in 1958 (which severely hit their cashflow and profits). They then made huge investments in the new Triumph Herald project, buying up suppliers and building a new assembly hall. When a Vanguard replacement (the "Zebu") stalled at the development stages, and the Vanguard quietly expired, the game was up for the marque.

Even though Leyland rescued the business (and would make much of Triumph in the years which followed), it allowed the Standard brand to fade away: the last of all was produced in 1963, though the Triumph side of the business would then carry on until 1984.

8hp 1938-48

Launched in 1938, the smallest Standard car was reintroduced in 1945, just ten days after VE Day, as an interim model which would kick-start the company's post-war programme.

When new, the 8hp had been an ambitiously-specified car, aimed at the heart of Austin and Morris territory, for it had transverse leaf spring independent front suspension when its rivals stuck to a beam axle. That was still a good selling point in 1945, but the 28bhp 1009cc sidevalve engine really let the side down, for the 8 could not reach 60mph under any circumstances. There was one big advance – pre-war cars had been lumbered with a three-speed gearbox, but from 1945 the 8 was given the same four-speeder as was used in the larger 12/14 models.

Standard 8hp, revived in 1945 and a best-seller.

SPECIFICATION

BODY STYLES: saloon, drophead, tourer, estate

PRODUCTION: 53,099, post-war

ENGINE & TRANSMISSION: 1009cc, 4cyl ohv, 4sp man, f/r

POWER: 28bhp @ 4000 rpm

MAX SPEED (MPH): 58

0-60MPH (SEC): not possible

SUSPENSION & BRAKES: leaf ifs, leaf rear, drums f&r

LENGTH (IN)/WEIGHT (LB): 139/1680

LAUNCH PRICE: £314

There was a sturdy box-section chassis with an 83in wheelbase, which meant that four-seater accommodation was marginal, while the Bendix mechanical brakes were a throwback to the past. Several steel bodies were provided, all of them with two passenger doors. The saloon bodies were made by Fisher & Ludlow, and tourer, drophead and estate variants were offfered.

These cars were built down to a price, starting at £314, for Sir John Black was determined to fight Austin and Morris head-on, just as he had set out to do in 1939. He succeeded too, for the 8 outsold the Austin 8, and matched the Morris 8 Series E for three whole years.

Sturdy? Yes. Memorable? Not really, but still remembered fondly as starter-motoring for many war-weary motorists.

The Standard 8hp drophead coupé.

Tourer version of the 8hp.

12/14hp 1937-48

The fastback Flying Standards dated right back to 1936, and were revised as up-dated notchbacks in 1938. All the tooling for these survived the war and they were re-introduced in May 1945, selling well until displaced by the all-new Vanguard in 1948. The body was three inches wider than on the pre-war cars, to give extra passenger space, and the rear axle was lenghtened to suit. Much of the chassis engineering of the 14 was also used in the tubular-framed Triumph 1800 Roadster and 1800 saloon of the period.

Backward-looking in almost every way apart from having transverse leaf independent front suspension, they used simple sidevalve engines, and retained very traditional styling. The 14hp model was "export only" at first, but eventually filtered on to the domestic scene too.

The chassis, with channel-section side members and little cross-bracing, was underslung at the rear, which limited rear axle movement. Gearboxes had four forward speeds, and there was a spiral bevel rear axle; stubborn to the last, Standard also clung on to Bendix mechanical brakes.

The 12 was launched at once, with a 44bhp 1609cc engine, the 14 following in 1946 with a 1776cc unit giving 51bhp. Although a 65bhp overhead-valve version of the larger unit already existed and was used in the Triumph 1800 models and in the Jaguar 1½-litre, the Standard did not specify it for the 14, preferring to use the original and

The Standard 14hp was another postwar revival. It could do almost 70mph.

simple sidevalve version instead.

Most of the 12s and 14s produced were saloons, though there were some drophead coupés and a few estate cars. Trim was advertised as "de Luxe", and there was leather seating and a forward-opening windscreen

Stodgy but worthy, and with no great performance, these cars did a good job for the company, selling strongly in a car-starved market, and gave reliable service, but they are not much remembered today. Most of them, in any case, had rusted away by the mid-1950s.

SPECIFICATION

BODY STYLES: saloon, drophead, estate

PRODUCTION: 32,188 post-war

ENGINE & TRANSMISSION: 1609cc/1776cc, 4cyl ohv, 4sp man, f/r

POWER: 44bhp @ 4000rpm/49bhp @ 3800rpm

MAX SPEED (MPH): 65/68

0-60MPH (SEC): 36.0/32.8

SUSPENSION & BRAKES: leaf ifs, leaf rear, drums f&r

LENGTH (IN)/WEIGHT (LB): 165/2492-2520

LAUNCH PRICE: £480/£576

Standard 12 drophead coupé, 1946.

Vanguard I 1948-53

Immediately after capturing the contract to manufacture Ferguson tractors, Sir John Black took another "Brave Pill", and committed Standard to an all-new medium-sized range of cars. The Vanguard, previewed in 1947, and on sale from mid-1948, was not only the car which Standard wanted to sell abroad, but was also to inspire new Triumph models (Triumph was owned by Standard), and to provide engines to Ferguson for the tractor.

Styled, they say, with careful reference to the 1942 Plymouth, the Vanguard was technically conventional, having a cruciform-based channel-section chassis, floppy coil spring independent front suspension, an all-steel four-door saloon

The six-seater Standard Vanguard as first launched in 1948.

SPECIFICATION

BODY STYLES: saloon, estate, commercials

PRODUCTION: 184,799

ENGINE & TRANSMISSION: 2088cc, 4cyl ohv, 3sp man, or o/d, f/r

POWER: 68bhp @ 4200rpm

MAX SPEED (MPH): 77

0-60MPH (SEC): 22.0

SUSPENSION & BRAKES: coil ifs, leaf rear, drums f&r

LENGTH (IN)/WEIGHT (LB): 164/2654

LAUNCH PRICE: £544

body with a fastback shape, and what became feted as an unbreakable wet-liner four-cylinder engine.

The bad news for keen drivers was the the bench front seat, the three-speed gearbox with a steering-column change – and the car's considerable weight. Its awful handling and poor fuel economy would not have mattered if the body had been rust-resistant. No such luck, there, though. Saloons were soon joined by estate cars and by vans, while the Belgian assemblers (Imperia) built some convertibles, and the Australians many pick-ups.

Overdrive became available from 1950 (the Vanguard was a trail-blazer for the British industry in this respect), and there was a minor front-end restyle in 1952, but the much-changed Vanguard II then took over in early 1953.

The Phase I Vanguard got a new grille in 1952.

Vanguard II 1953-55

Although the new-style Vanguard II took over from the original type in March 1953, this was only a short-term change, as it would be phased out in the autumn of 1955 – in other words it had a production life of two and a half years. Mechanically there were few changes, but the body shell was mainly new.

Although the wheelbase and chassis layout had not altered, there was now much more rear seat passenger space. This had been found by completely re-shaping the body aft of the front doors from the original swept style to a notchback shape. At the same time there were longer rear doors, the shell was four

The notchback Vanguard Phase II, 1953.

inches longer, and there was a more capacious boot. From this point there were also two-door and four-door estate cars, derived from the vans which were selling so well in some territories.

Inside the cabin, however, it was situation normal, with the bench seat and steering-column gearchange discouraging spirited driving but enabl-ing three of you to get matey in the front. Leather upholstery was an option. Technically, the big advance was to provide a hydraulically-operated (instead of cable-operated) clutch release. Laycock overdrive was optional, as it had been since 1950 on earlier Vanguards.

From February 1954, Standard added a diesel engine alternative. This was the very first time there had been a diesel-engined British private car, but the results were disappointing. Totally different from the petrol power unit, the engine was the one being used in the Ferguson tractor, but it was 97lb heavier, and produced a miserable 40bhp. Rough, noisy and not even very economical, the diesel struggled to beat 65mph. It was not a success, and was not carried forward to the next-generation Vanguard.

Vanguard III/Vignale 1955-61

The Phase III Vanguard kept the familiar 2088cc engine and its allied three-speed steering-column gearchange but was new in many other respects. Not only was it a unit-construction car (previous Vanguards had used a separate chassis), but Pressed Steel provided the structure, and the car was considerably lower than its predecessor.

Styled by an American consultant, Carl Otto, the Phase III looked transatlantic in some ways, there being the suggestion of a "dollar grin" up front, with soup-plate tail lamps at the rear. The four-door body hid a robust and conventional frame with an 8-inch longer wheelbase than before. There was coil spring independent suspension at the front, ordinary leaf springs at the rear, and steering which was by no means as precise as many would like.

The engine and gearbox were much as before, and there was an overdrive option. As usual, too, there was a bench front seat. An estate car was added from October 1956, and automatic transmission became

Vanguard III, 1955, just as tough as the Vanguards that came before it.

optional from late 1957, while from early 1958 a four-speed manual gearbox (with floor gearchange) became available at extra cost.

From October 1958, the Vanguard became "Vignale Vanguard" (the styling changes had been inspired by Michelotti, who had links with the Italian concern). Within the same basic monocoque, Vignales had larger front and rear windows, new grille and tail lamps, two-tone colour schemes and upgrades inside the cabin. The Vignale carried on after the announcement of the Vanguard Six in late 1960, now with the four-speed floor-change transmission as standard. The last car was produced in August 1961.

None of these cars was exciting to drive or prestigious to own, but they were rugged and simple, and were well-liked in export markets. Unhappily they were as rust-prone as most Pressed Steel cars of this period.

Maurice Gatsonides drove this works Vanguard III into eighth place in the 1956 Monte Carlo Rally.

Vanguard Sportsman 1956-58

Oh dear ! We must be thankful that the Sportsman was not launched as a "new Triumph Renown", for that is how it had been conceived – the radiator grille and badging make that clear. Even as a Vanguard Sportsman, and available only as a four-door saloon, it was a commercial catastrophe, for only 901 were sold in an eighteen-month career.

Based on the Vanguard III, but with the

Vanguard Sportsman, 1956: 90bhp and 90mph.

SPECIFICATION
BODY STYLES: saloon
PRODUCTION: 901
ENGINE & TRANSMISSION: 2088cc, 4cyl ohv, 3sp man, o/d, f/r
POWER: 90bhp @ 4500rpm
MAX SPEED (MPH): 91
0-60MPH (SEC): 19.2
SUSPENSION & BRAKES: coil ifs, leaf rear, drums f&r
LENGTH (IN)/WEIGHT (LB): 174/2772
LAUNCH PRICE: £1231

different front grille, a 90bhp 2088cc engine which was a hybrid of Triumph TR3 and Vanguard, overdrive as standard and larger brakes, the Sportsman offered a lot more performance without parallel improvements in handling or image.

Inside the car there were two-tone seats, but the bench front seat and steering-column change were certainly not the

mark of a sports saloon. The Sportsman came too early to benefit from a four-on-the-floor gearbox, and fortunately there was no automatic option either.

It was expensive – £1231 at launch compared with £939 for the existing Vanguard III – so when it was discontinued, in March 1958, no one seemed to mind very much.

Eight 1953-59

The new-generation Eight, introduced in 1953, five years after the previous model, shared nothing with it except the name. It was a brand-new four-door saloon model, with an engine and transmission which (in evolved forms) would power other Standards and Triumphs until 1980.

As direct competition for cars like the Austin A30, Morris Minor and Ford Anglia, the new Eight used a stumpy unit-construction body which had been ruthlessly stripped out to save costs. Original cars had no separate access to the boot area (that was found by folding down the rear seats), and had sliding windows front and rear. Yet the engine had overhead valves and was very tuneable, and the handling was safe and predictable.

Soon after the Eight was joined by its big brother, the Ten (see opposite), a long period of improvement began, with peak power gradually rising and better

The 803cc Standard Eight, 1953, a rival to the Austin A30 and Morris Minor.

equipment gradually being standardised. During 1954 De Luxe models got wind-up windows, these being adopted by all Eights from May 1955.

From late 1955 there was a Super Eight, with more equipment, and from March 1957 Laycock overdrive (operating on top, third and second) became optional at £63.75. Weeks later an opening boot lid was adopted for all models, these becoming the "Gold Star" models, with a

mesh front grille added; by that time peak power had risen to 33bhp. There were no major changes after that until the Triumph Herald took over, and the last Eight was built in July 1959.

Although the stripped-out early models sold well, it was the better-equipped late models which were best. Always overshadowed by the Tens, then swamped by the Heralds, these were good, profitable, but ultimately not memorable cars.

SPECIFICATION

BODY STYLES : saloon

PRODUCTION TOTAL: 136,317

ENGINE & TRANSMISSION : 803cc, 4cyl ohv, 4sp man, or o/d, f/r

POWER : 26bhp @ 4500rpm/30bhp @ 4500rpm/33bhp @ 5000rpm

MAX SPEED (MPH) : 61-66

0-60MPH (SEC) : (33bhp) 39.8

SUSPENSION & BRAKES : coil ifs, leaf rear, drums f&r

LENGTH (IN)/WEIGHT (LB) : 143/1484

LAUNCH PRICE : £481

Five Standard Eights and an Austin A30 on the Tulip Rally in 1956. The A30 eventually led the Standards home.

Ten 1954-61

In March 1958, five months after the launch of the new Eight, the larger, faster and more up-market Ten was introduced. Based on the same four-door monocoque, it had a larger 948cc engine and was always better equipped.

Apart from the new 33bhp engine (that figure would be nudged up to 37bhp by 1957-58) the most important improvements were the opening boot lid and the wind-up windows, both of which the Eight originally lacked. Though the Ten had a fully trimmed interior it was still a simple car, with no pretensions to high performance or sporty handling. Exterior identification was by a Vanguard-like front grille.

Although not at the same frenetic pace as with the Eight (which had a lot more ground to make up!), changes followed regularly. The estate car version (called

The 948cc Standard Ten had an opening boot as well as a grille and hubcaps.

the Companion) arrived in October 1954, with four passenger doors and twin outward-opening loading doors. The trim was a bit basic, this becoming clear when the van equivalent joined in.

The Family Ten of March 1956 combined Ten running gear with simpler Super Eight trim and equipment (and therefore no external boot lid). At £615 instead of £646 it was an intriguing offering, though it would not be sold after 1957.

From late 1956 Standard fell for the hype surrounding two-pedal control and offered "Standrive" as an option, but this was not a success. Optional overdrive, however, from March 1957 onwards, was a useful fitting.

Once the Ten was joined by the much re-styled Pennant in October 1957, it

took a back seat. The last saloon was built in July 1959. In the meantime, from April the estate had been given Pennant-style front body pressings and an interior upgrade. The last of those was not built until January 1961.

SPECIFICATION

BODY STYLES: saloon, estate, commercials

PRODUCTION: 172,500

ENGINE & TRANSMISSION: 948cc, 4cyl ohv, 4sp man, or o/d, or semi-auto, f/r

POWER: 33bhp @ 4500rpm/35bhp @ 4500rpm/37bhp @ 5000rpm

MAX SPEED (MPH): 69

0-60MPH (SEC): 38.3

SUSPENSION & BRAKES: coil ifs, leaf rear, drums f&r

LENGTH (IN)/WEIGHT (LB): 143/1652

LAUNCH PRICE: £581

Standard Ten Companion at the 1954 motor show.

Pennant 1957-59

In the 1950s, Standard knew almost as much as the Rootes Group about badge engineering and facelifts. In October 1957, just four years after the Eight/Ten family had been launched, the Pennant was introduced, this being, effectively, a better-equipped and more garishly styled version of the Ten.

Standard's own stylists added a new hooded-headlamp, full-width-grille nose

The 1957 Standard Pennant, a sharpened-up version of the 10.

SPECIFICATION

BODY STYLES: saloon

PRODUCTION: 42,910

ENGINE & TRANSMISSION: 948cc, 4cyl ohv, 4sp man, o/d or semi-auto, f/r

POWER: 37bhp @ 5000rpm

MAX SPEED (MPH): 66

0-60MPH (SEC): 34.9

SUSPENSION & BRAKES : coil ifs, leaf rear, drums f&r

LENGTH (IN)/WEIGHT (LB): 142/1745

LAUNCH PRICE: £729

and rear tail fins to the basic Ten four-door shell. Inside the car was a new fascia style, along with a remote control centre-floor gear change.

Power was pushed up to 37bhp, and overdrive was an optional extra (popular) as was the two-pedal control "Standrive" (a commercial flop). Two-tone upholstery and duotone paintwork were both standard.

At £729 (£75 more than the Ten) the Pennant was no bargain, but it sold quite briskly for two years before being displaced by the Triumph Herald. Like the Eights and Tens, these cars were no great performers, although twin-carburettor tuning kits could turn them into brisk machines – second and third places on the 1958 RAC rally was a worthy performance.

Ensign 1957-61

Ensign! There was a good old Standard name which had not been seen for decades. Any competent product planner could have written the spec for this car: a stripped-out Vanguard III with a smaller version of the wet-liner engine, less equipment, more modest decoration, a different, less flashy front style, and a lower price. All

The Ensign was the same size as the Vanguard but had only 1670cc to propel it.

SPECIFICATION

BODY STYLES: saloon, estate

PRODUCTION: 18,852

ENGINE & TRANSMISSION: 1670cc, 4cyl ohv, 4sp man, or o/d, f/r

POWER: 60bhp @ 4000rpm

MAX SPEED (MPH): 78

0-60MPH (SEC): 24.4

SUSPENSION & BRAKES : coil ifs, leaf rear, drums f&r

LENGTH (IN)/WEIGHT (LB): 172/2531

LAUNCH PRICE: £900

present and correct – a car which sold steadily to fleets, and also to British military organisations.

New in October 1957, the Ensign was the first of this Vanguard-based family to get a four-speed gearbox with centre-floor gearchange (still a bench front seat, though) – a great advance which, we are sure, made Vanguard customers jealous until it became optional on their cars in 1958 ! On the Ensign, as on the Vanguard, overdrive was an extra – but

automatic would never be an option on this type.

It received the basic body style changes of the new "Vignale" Vanguard in October 1958 – essentially, larger screen, larger rear window and different rear lamp treatment – but the Ensign was not otherwise changed much until August 1961, when it was finally discontinued. The Ensign De Luxe, which was different in several ways, did not then appear until May 1962.

Ensign De Luxe 1962-63

Soon after they took control of Standard, Leyland began juggling available assets in a bid to generate sales (and cash) as an interim measure before new Triumphs could come on stream. The Ensign De Luxe, therefore, was the very last new-model Standard but it had no new engineering.

Introduced in May 1962, and only in production for a year, the De Luxe took over where the original Ensign had left

Ensign de Luxe of 1962 had a 2.1-litre engine. This is the estate version.

SPECIFICATION

BODY STYLES: saloon, estate

PRODUCTION: 2318

ENGINE & TRANSMISSION: 2138cc, 4cyl ohv, 4sp man, or o/d, f/r

POWER: 75bhp @ 4100rpm

MAX SPEED (MPH): 88

0-60MPH (SEC): 18.2

SUSPENSION & BRAKES: coil ifs, leaf rear, drums f&r (optional disc f/drum r)

LENGTH (IN)/WEIGHT (LB): 172/2660

LAUNCH PRICE: £848

off in August 1961. The same structure, body style and choice of four-door saloon or five-door estate car remained, as did the rugged, straightforward suspension and relatively simple trim and furnishings. This time around, though, the old wet-liner engine was of 2138cc (like that of the contemporary TR4), but had a single Solex carburettor and produced 75bhp.

The latest Vanguard four-speed all-synchromesh gearbox (with central change) was standard, and once again overdrive was optional. Disc brakes became optional. Inside the cabin, there was a bench front seat, with a simple new instrument binnacle and circular dials.

This was a hard-working slogger of a car, sometimes found in military use or in far-flung territories, but never sought out by enthusiastic motorists.

Vanguard Luxury Six 1960-63

Here was the last throw of the dice for the Vanguard brand. The structure, style and running gear were basically those of the existing "Vignale" Vanguard (which continued alongside the new model), but the engine was the brand-new six-cylinder unit which had evolved from the existing Herald four-cylinder. This engine, by the

SPECIFICATION

BODY STYLES: saloon, estate

PRODUCTION: 9953

ENGINE & TRANSMISSION: 1998cc, 6cyl ohv, 3sp man, 4sp man, o/d or auto, f/r

POWER: 80bhp @ 4400rpm

MAX SPEED (MPH): 87

0-60MPH (SEC): 17.0

SUSPENSION & BRAKES: coil ifs, leaf rear, drums f&r (disc f/drum r optional)

LENGTH (IN)/WEIGHT (LB): 172/2660

LAUNCH PRICE : £1021

way, would go on to power many Triumphs – TRs, GT6s, Vitesses and 2000s – in the next two decades.

With its 80bhp output, the new 1998cc six gave a worthy performance boost to the old Vanguard chassis. It was backed by the same choice of three-speed, four-speed or overdrive gearboxes (though few three-speeders were actually sold). Automatic transmission was available from early 1961. Trim and furnishings were better than on the Vignale types, with a new instrument display.

Recirculating-ball steering took over, and a front anti-roll bar was standard. Front-wheel disc brakes became optional from mid-1961, after which point most Vanguard Sixes seemed to have them.

This was always meant to be an interim model, bridging the gap between the old Vanguard and the Triumph 2000 which would follow but which was not yet ready. Though much quieter, smoother and

more refined than the old wet-liner four-cylinder engine, the new six could not transform the Vanguard's reputation or its character completely. The car was still too big, too lumpy, and too ordinary in the handling department. Yet it was the last Standard of all and should be remembered on that account.

The Vanguard Luxury Six, 1960, had the body of the Vignale Vanguard with a 2-litre six-cylinder engine that was later to go into the Triumph 2000.

SUNBEAM

The Rootes Group bought up Sunbeam in 1935, when the company was struggling; three years later it was folded into the "Sunbeam-Talbot" marque, which thrived from 1938 until the mid-1950s.

Rootes revived Sunbeam, on its own, for the Alpine sports car of 1953, then abandoned the "Talbot" side of the business a year later. Thereafter Sunbeam prospered, as the "sporty" marque in the collection of different Rootes brands. Long-running models which not only succeeded commercially but also made much money for the company included the Rapier sports saloons and the Alpine sports cars.

1960s diversions included the Ford V8-powered Tigers, and sportier versions of the Hillman Imp (Sunbeam Imp Sport/Stiletto), but once Chrysler took control in 1967 there was no more innovation on that score, and the last Sunbeam was produced in 1976. The marque then became a model name – thus, late in the 1970s, a Chrysler Sunbeam hatchback appeared, and from 1979 there was also the Talbot Sunbeam-Lotus (a successful competition car by any standards). After Chrysler sold out to Peugeot in 1978, Sunbeam was put under sentence of death – the last car to wear the badge being built in 1981.

Alpine 1953-55

Rootes dealer George Hartwell had the inspiration for this project and built the first one-off. Rootes then put the Alpine production car on sale in March 1953. Originally for export only, it went on UK sale in autumn of that year.

Very closely based on the existing chassis and running gear of the Sunbeam-Talbot Mk IIA saloon car of the day, the two-seater Alpine also used the same front-end pressings but had entirely different centre and rear bodywork, laid out in two-seater form with a long, sweeping tail.

The chassis was stiffened up, with more

The Sunbeam Alpine was first shown in 1953. This one has aeroscreens in place of the standard one-piece windscreen.

SPECIFICATION

BODY STYLES: sports car

PRODUCTION: 3000

ENGINE & TRANSMISSION: 2267cc, 4cyl ohv, 4sp man, or o/d (from late 1954), f/r

POWER: 80bhp @ 4200rpm

MAX SPEED (MPH): 95

0-60MPH (SEC): 18.9

SUSPENSION & BRAKES: coil ifs, leaf rear, drums f&r

LENGTH (IN)/WEIGHT (LB): 168/2900

LAUNCH PRICE: £1269

robust main side members and with an extra tubular cross member behind and under the engine/gearbox assembly. Front suspension and anti-roll bar settings were stiffened too, and the steering was made more direct. The engine was more highly tuned than the saloon's, and the gear ratios were altered. Unhappily, the saloon's steering-column gear change was retained.

Compared with the new competition from Austin-Healey, the Alpine was too heavy and not agile enough, but it could cruise at high speeds, acquitted itself well in tough rallies and sold steadily. Although made more desirable with the fitment of

overdrive, it was killed off in mid-1955 ahead of the launch of the entirely different Sunbeam Rapier.

Stirling Moss and John Cutts in a works Alpine on the '53 Alpine Rally. Moss won a Coupe des Alpes and came 14th overall.

MK III 1954-57

Earlier versions of this car had been badged as Sunbeam-Talbots, but from this point Rootes ditched the "Talbot". This aligned the latest saloons with the newly-launched Sunbeam Alpine two-seater, which was in any case

closely related. Compared with the Sunbeam-Talbot 90 which it replaced at the end of 1954, the Mk III had a minor front-end facelift and three "portholes" on each side of the bonnet. Many examples had a duotone colour scheme. The fascia

was revised to incorporate provision for fitting the new optional rev-counter, and there were larger, more luxurious front seats. Engine power went up to 80bhp (this was the same tune as in the Alpine two-seater), and Laycock overdrive on top gear only, became a desirable option.

Castles of Leicester (the main Rootes dealer in that city) converted cars to have a centre floor gearchange and a different boot opening arrangement, but this was a private-enterprise product, unconnected with the factory.

Assembly of the saloon carried on until early 1957, when this graceful line of sporting cars died out. The drophead had disappeared after 1955. Like its predecessors, the Mk III was heavy to handle and the column change was no fun, but it went well enough, and was robust enough, to gain an outright win in the 1955 Monte Carlo Rally and good placings in many other demanding events.

SPECIFICATION

BODY STYLES: saloon, drophead

PRODUCTION: c 2250

ENGINE & TRANSMISSION: 2267cc, 4cyl ohv, 4sp man, or o/d, f/r

POWER: 80bhp @ 4200rpm

MAX SPEED (MPH): 91

0-60MPH (SEC): 18.4

SUSPENSION & BRAKES: coil ifs, leaf rear, drums f&r

LENGTH (IN)/WEIGHT (LB): 168/2950

LAUNCH PRICE: £1127

The Rootes team of Mk IIIs at the Stockholm start of the 1956 Monte Carlo Rally. Sheila van Damm and Ann Hall are beside the car. Rootes won the team prize.

Rapier I and IA 1955-58

The original Rapier of 1955 founded a long-line of Sunbeam sports saloons and convertibles which, in the Rootes hierarchy, were always faster that the Hillmans on which they were based, and rather more sporty than the Humbers with which they sometimes shared components.

In many ways a direct descendant of the Hillman Minx Californian coupé (but endowed with more panache), the Rapier was a two-door pillarless sports saloon derivative of the Hillman Minx "Series" cars (though it preceded them by seven months), sharing the same platform, basic

The 1.4-litre Sunbeam Rapier I, 1955, was based on the Hillman Minx.

SPECIFICATION

BODY STYLES : saloon

PRODUCTION TOTAL: 7477

ENGINE & TRANSMISSION : 1390cc, 4cyl ohv, 4sp man, o/d, f/r

POWER : 63bhp @ 5000rpm/67bhp @ 5400rpm

MAX SPEED (MPH): 85/85

0-60MPH (SEC) : 21.7/19.4

SUSPENSION & BRAKES : coil ifs, leaf rear, drums f&r

LENGTH (IN)/WEIGHT (LB) : 161/2280

LAUNCH PRICE : £1044

running gear, general proportions, and almost identical front-end style, though with duotone colour schemes, and with drop-down rear quarter window glasses.

In this case the engine was a 63bhp 1390cc development of the modern small Rootes unit (the new Minx would have only 48bhp), still with steering-column gearchange, and Laycock overdrive was standard. Immediate experience showed that it needed more performance, so from October 1956 the Rapier became Series IA, with a twin-Zenith 67bhp version of the 1390cc engine

Thus equipped the car could reach 85mph, although it really needed crisper

handling and better brakes to make it competitive with, say, the MG Magnette ZA of the period. By comparison with what was to come, this was rather a milk-and-water Rapier, but Rootes had to learn somewhere – and would certainly do so in the next few years!

Even so, the company started a serious motorsport programme with this model, which included sending cars on the Mille Miglia, and providing wheels for Peter Harper to take a respectable fifth place in the 1958 Monte Carlo rally.

Most of these cars, however, rusted away within a decade, which maybe explains why they never became fashionable.

Rapier II 1958-59

Launched just one week after Peter Harper's fine Monte performance in a Mk IA, the Rapier Series II signalled the next step towards making the Rapier into a successful sports saloon.

Compared with the Series I/IA cars, which it replaced, the Series II kept the same basic platform/structure/style, but had a more traditional "Sunbeam" grille up front, along with a pair of sharply-detailed tail fins. Not only that, but a drophead coupé derivative (like that of the contemporary Minx) was added to the range.

This was the first Rootes car to gain the

Rapier II, now 1.5 litres, 1958.

Paddy Hopkirk and Jack Scott in a Rapier II on the 1959 Alpine Rally.

1494cc engine, tuned to produce 68bhp, and with significantly more torque than before. Twin down-draught Zenith carburettors were retained, and (thank goodness!) a remote-control floor gearchange was standardised, though overdrive was now optional instead of standard as it had been on the early cars.

Clearly there could be more to come, but because this car could reach 90mph, and handled better than its predecessors, the Series II was already a considerable improvement.

SPECIFICATION

BODY STYLES: saloon, drophead

PRODUCTION: 15,151

ENGINE & TRANSMISSION: 1494cc, 4cyl ohv, 4sp man, or o/d, f/r

POWER: 68bhp @ 5200rpm

MAX SPEED (MPH): 90

0-60MPH (SEC): 20.2

SUSPENSION & BRAKES: coil ifs, leaf rear, drums f&r

LENGTH (IN)/WEIGHT (LB): 161/2280

LAUNCH PRICE: £1044

Rapier III/IIIA 1959-61/1961-63

Rootes rarely left a model alone for long in the 1950s. The Rapier Series III took over from the SII in October 1959, only 20 months after that model had first appeared.

There were few style changes this time (apart from slightly changed duotone

SPECIFICATION

BODY STYLES: saloon, drophead

PRODUCTION: 15,368/17,354

ENGINE & TRANSMISSION: 1494cc/1592cc, 4cyl ohv, 4sp man, or o/d, f/r

POWER: 73bhp @ 5400rpm/75bhp @ 5100rpm

MAX SPEED (MPH): 92/90

0-60MPH (SEC): 16.5/19.3

SUSPENSION & BRAKES: coil ifs, leaf rear, disc f/drum r

LENGTH (IN)/WEIGHT (LB): 163/2300

LAUNCH PRICE: £986/£1000

A Rapier IIIA on the 1962 RAC Rally. The engine was now of 1.6-litres.

paint treatment), but there were important technical improvements. Picking up the work which had gone into the new Alpine two-seater, the new Series III got a 73bhp1494cc engine,

with an aluminium cylinder head, closer-ratio gears and – most important, this – front-wheel disc brakes.

At the same time, there was now a wood veneer finish to the fascia, and from October 1960 Rootes also phased in a new-type hypoid bevel (instead of spiral bevel) rear axle.

The Series III was only in production for a year and a half. From April 1961 the Series IIIA took over, this up-grade having the latest 1592cc version of the Rootes engine giving 75bhp. But there were no style changes or badging changes to point out the difference.

Many think this was the time when Rapiers were more competitive than anything else in their class. The III and IIIA certainly excelled in rallying. In the 1962 Monte, for example, Rapiers finished third and fourth overall, won their class, and took the team prize. The sales figures were very healthy too.

On the Rapier IIIA the contrasting side stripe went straight through to the tail and did not extend up to the peak of the fin.

Rapier IV 1963-65

With the arrival of yet another new type, the Rapier "Series" now reached SIV, all of eight years after the original, less complete, Rapier package had been launched.

Introduced in October 1963, the SIV had the latest 79bhp version of the engine, with a Solex compound-choke carburettor, 13-inch instead of 15-inch wheels, gear ratio changes to match, a

Sunbeam Rapier IV, 1963: smaller wheels and flatter bonnet.

SPECIFICATION

BODY STYLES: saloon

PRODUCTION: 9700

ENGINE & TRANSMISSION: 1592cc, 4cyl ohv, 4sp man, o/d, f/r

POWER: 79bhp @ 5000rpm

MAX SPEED (MPH): 92

0-60MPH (SEC): 17.0

SUSPENSION & BRAKES: coil ifs, leaf rear, disc f/drum r

LENGTH (IN)/WEIGHT (LB): 163/2300

LAUNCH PRICE: £877

diaphragm spring clutch, a brake servo and – from October 1964 – a new all-synchromesh gearbox.

Style changes included a lowered bonnet line, a different front grille, "SIV" badging, and different side flashing. Inside the car there were reclining front seats, a revised fascia,

and a steering column adjustable for reach. There was no convertible version, however, this having been dropped when the SIIIA was phased out.

Probably the best Rapier yet, it was unfortunately dropping behind the times, as lighter, faster Ford Cortina GTs were beginning to make inroads.

Rapier V 1965-67

The last of this generation of Rapiers – SV – appeared in October 1965, ten years after the original type had first appeared. This car was given an 85bhp 1725cc five-main-bearing engine (very

closely related to the Sunbeam Alpine of the period), and a negative-earth electrical system, but virtually no other significant changes.

The Rapier's heyday had passed,

however, and sales of only 3759 cars in two years proved that the public had finally tired of it. The next-generation Rapier would be a very different type of car.

SPECIFICATION

BODY STYLES: saloon

PRODUCTION: 3759

ENGINE & TRANSMISSION: 1725cc, 4cyl ohv, 4sp man, o/d, f/r

POWER: 85bhp @ 5500rpm

MAX SPEED (MPH): 95

0-60MPH (SEC): 14.1

SUSPENSION & BRAKES: coil ifs, leaf rear, disc f/drum r

LENGTH (IN)/WEIGHT (LB): 163/2300

LAUNCH PRICE: £908

The last of this family was the Rapier V, launched in 1965 with a 1.7-litre engine.

Alpine I 1959-60

If Rootes's new Alpine had not had to compete with two established rivals – the MGA and the TR3A – it might have built up more sales. Yet it was a stylish, well-equipped and effective two-seater, which Rootes would continue to sell, in five versions, for nine years.

The Alpine was typical of Rootes's resourceful product planning. It was built on a short-wheelbase version of the Minx/Rapier platform (actually it came from the Husky estate car!), and the running gear was up-rated from the Rapier of the day. It was given a smart two-door sports body with prominent fins; a lift-off aluminium hardtop was

The 78bhp Sunbeam Alpine I, 1959, a pleasingly unfussy design.

SPECIFICATION

BODY STYLES: sports car

PRODUCTION: 11,904

ENGINE & TRANSMISSION: 1494cc, 4cyl ohv, 4sp man, or o/d, f/r

POWER: 78bhp @ 5300rpm

MAX SPEED (MPH): 98

0-60MPH (SEC): 14.0

SUSPENSION & BRAKES : coil ifs, leaf rear, disc f/drum r

LENGTH (IN)/WEIGHT (LB): 155/2135

LAUNCH PRICE: £972

optional. The soft-top, when furled, hid under fold-back steel cover panels behind the seats.

The roadholding was adequate, an improved version of the Rapier's, but the running gear was a real advance. There was not only an output of 78bhp from the twin-carburettor1494cc engine, but also optional overdrive, and front-wheel disc brakes as standard, hidden behind 13-inch disc wheels. Centre-lock wire-spoke wheels were a desirable option.

Because this car could approach 100mph (making it Rootes's fastest medium-sized car), it was a good start to a long career, especially as North America seemed to like the styling and bought large numbers. Yet (and this was typical of Rootes) there was a long way to go, for the Alpine SI was on sale for only about 15 months !

Anoraks will need to know that Armstrong-Siddeley assembled all these cars – as they would until 1962.

Alpine II 1960-63

Alpine IIs appeared in October 1960, and would carry on until early 1963. Compared with the first

type, they featured 80bhp1592cc versions of the engine, though there were few other important changes.

Assembly moved back to Rootes's own factory at Ryton-on-Dunsmore from the spring of 1962.

Engine capacity of the Alpine II was increased to 1.6 litres.

Alpine III 1963-64

The third phase of Alpine development saw the Alpine III appear early in 1963. This time around, the pedigree was split into two sub-lines. The Roadster continued as before, with 82bhp/1592cc, while the "GT" version came with a smart angular-shaped hardtop and a walnut dash but with a less powerful 77bhp version of the engine. Although the hardtop could be removed, no soft-

The Alpine III of 1963.

top was supplied with the GT.

Both cars got stiffened-up suspension, telescopic rear dampers, an adjustable steering column, and twin fuel tanks (one each inside the rear wing pressings). There were quarter-lights for the windows, more comfortable fully reclining seats and a more plush interior.

Surprisingly, the new GT, which cost £900 compared with £840 for the Roadster, was not at all popular, so the split-line experiment would not be carried forward to the next model. Within a year the SIII had been ousted by the SIV. The Rootes planners were embarrassed.

Alpine IV 1964-65

Early in 1964, the Alpine IV took over from the Alpine III, which had been on sale for less than a year. Once again there were changes in marketing emphasis – and this time also in visual details.

Only one type of engine was provided for 1964, this being the 82bhp/1592cc unit, though now with a single Solex

compound-choke carburettor. However, for the first and only time in this sports car family, there was an automatic transmission which, predictably to those outside the company, proved to be a marketing failure. From autumn 1964, the new corporate all-synchromesh manual gearbox was fitted, as it was to all other medium-sized Rootes cars of

the period. Overdrive was an option.

The big styling change was that the prominent rear fins had been cropped back, and new-type tail lamps had been specified. There was also a walnut veneer fascia. Along with the angular hardtop as introduced in 1963, this made the fully-facelifted Alpine look even smarter than before.

SPECIFICATION

BODY STYLES: sports car

PRODUCTION: 12,406

ENGINE & TRANSMISSION: 1592cc, 4cyl ohv, 4sp man, or o/d or auto, f/r

POWE : 82bhp @ 5200rpm

MAX SPEED (MPH): 98

0-60MPH (SEC): 14.9

SUSPENSION & BRAKES: coil ifs, leaf rear, disc f/drum r

LENGTH (IN)/WEIGHT (LB): 156/2220

LAUNCH PRICE: £852

The tail fins were cut back for the Alpine IV, and the grille had a single bar.

Alpine V 1965-68

The fifth and final derivative of the Alpine – Alpine V – appeared in October 1965, less than two years after the facelifted SIV had first appeared. To bring it into line with other cars in the same family, it was given the five-main-bearing 1725cc engine, this time with no less than 93bhp and with twin semi-

SPECIFICATION

BODY STYLES: sports car

PRODUCTION: 19,122

ENGINE & TRANSMISSION: 1725cc, 4cyl ohv, 4sp man, or o/d, f/r

POWER: 93bhp @ 5500rpm

MAX SPEED (MPH): 98-100

0-60MPH (SEC): 13.6

SUSPENSION & BRAKES: coil ifs, leaf rear, disc f/drum r

LENGTH (IN)/WEIGHT (LB): 156/2220

LAUNCH PRICE: £878

The 1965-68 Alpine V, with 1725cc engine, was the last of the line.

downdraught Zenith-Stromberg carburettors. An alternator and an oil cooler were both standard. The automatic transmission option seen briefly on SIV types was abandoned.

This, no question, was the best of all the Alpines, and could just reach 100mph. Handling was now good, if not super-

sporting, and the trim and equipment were definitely superior to the major domestic rival. But because Chrysler (which had just taken over Rootes in 1967) found the Alpine unprofitable, it was killed off early in 1968. The market thus lost a pleasant, comfortable open car ideal for fast touring.

Harrington Alpine Series A/B/C 1961-63

With a great deal of behind-the-scenes support from Rootes, a conversion by Thomas Harrington of Hove was built between 1961 and 1963. Official, or unofficial? Let's just say that George Hartwell was a great friend of the Rootes family, and that he was also chairman of Harrington…

There were three different types of Harrington, all based on the SII Alpine (though one or two stragglers seem to

have been built on an SIII base, these being dubbed Series D).

The Series A cars, announced in March 1961, had the original boot lid/rear deck carved away, to be replaced by a smooth fastback in GRP, with a small boot lid on the tail. The seating became 2+2, with reclining Microcell seats in the front, while trim and equipment levels were enhanced. The engines were normally not super-tuned, but three different

tuning stages were available, the most extreme costing £215.

Series B cars, on sale from October 1961 and better known as "Harrington Le Mans", had a modified version of the hardtop, with the tail fins cropped off so that the waistline fell, rather than rose, towards the rear, and with a cropped-off rear panel. The usual engine tune, by Hartwell, offered an output of 104bhp at 6000rpm.

The Series C models, announced in October 1962, moved back a little more towards standard. Although based on the completely reshaped "Le Mans" (Series B) cars, they kept the original Rootes shape of rear fins, though there was yet another version of the rear-end cut-off. In an attempt to promote sales (there was a helpful Purchase Tax reduction at about the same time), the price was reduced to £1197.

Although these were very effective sports coupés – one such car competed with honour as a "works" car at Le Mans in 1961 – they never sold as well as the Robins & Day dealership had hoped, mostly because they were much more expensive than the ordinary Alpines on which they were based. In later years, though, rarity made them most desirable within the Sunbeam enthusiasts' movement. Many consider the Series B to be the best looking.

The Harrington Alpine Series B Le Mans, usually supplied with a 104bhp engine.

SPECIFICATION

BODY STYLES: sport coupé

PRODUCTION: c.400-450, all Harringtons

ENGINE & TRANSMISSION: 1592cc, 4cyl ohv, 4sp man, o/d, f/r

POWER: up to 104bhp @ 6000rpm

MAX SPEED (MPH): (93bhp Stage II) 99 (96bhp) 101

0-60MPH (SEC): (93bhp Stage II) 12.7 (96bhp) 13.0

SUSPENSION & BRAKES: coil ifs, leaf rear, disc f/drum r

LENGTH (IN)/WEIGHT (LB): 155/2168 - 2275

LAUNCH PRICE : From £1225 (£1300 in Stage II tune); Le Mans model £1495

Tiger I 1964-67

Because the concept came via Carroll Shelby in California, and the same Ford-USA V8 engine was used, the Tiger was sometimes known as the "poor man's Cobra". Actually it was at the same time much more and rather less that that. Although it was launched in April 1964, initial sales were USA-only, with UK sales not starting until mid-1965.

Production cars were made by sending

V8 4.2-litre Sunbeam Tiger.

SPECIFICATION

BODY STYLES: sports car

PRODUCTION: 6495

ENGINE & TRANSMISSION: 4261cc, V8 ohv, 4sp man, f/r

POWER: 136bhp @ 4200rpm

MAX SPEED (MPH): 117

0-60MPH (SEC): 9.5

SUSPENSION & BRAKES: coil ifs, leaf rear, disc f/drum r

LENGTH (IN)/WEIGHT (LB): 156/2200

LAUNCH PRICE: £1446

Alpine IV (later Alpine V) body shells to Jensen at West Bromwich, where changes needed to install different running gear were made, and the entire car was then assembled there. Externally, the only change was to add chrome striping along the flanks, along with different badges, while the tyres were fatter. The running gear, however, was very different.

Motive power was by a torquey 136bhp 4261cc Ford V8 engine, which drove through a non-Rootes four-speed gearbox and a more robust rear axle. At the front there was rack-and-pinion steering (of which the geometry was suspect), with a Panhard rod for extra rear axle location.

The result was a rumbly, fast and extrovert machine, with pleasingly effortless performance, whose only predictable problems were a tendency to overheat in hot conditions, and to devour its brakes and tyres.

Tiger II 1967

If only Chrysler had not taken control of Rootes by 1967, the Tiger II might have had a longer life, but as that company was not about to commit any of its cars to using a rival's V8 for a long period, it was produced only in the first half of 1967.

Behind its egg-crate grille, it was a better car in all respects. The Ford V8 had been

Tiger II, 4.7 litres, a cross-hatch grille and side stripes.

SPECIFICATION

BODY STYLES: sports car

PRODUCTION: 633

ENGINE & TRANSMISSION: 4727cc, V8cyl ohv, f/r

POWER: 174bhp @ 4400rpm

MAX SPEED (MPH): 122

0-60MPH (SEC): 7.5

SUSPENSION & BRAKES: coil ifs, leaf rear, disc f/drum r

LENGTH (IN)/WEIGHT (LB): 156/2574

LAUNCH PRICE: Not officially available in UK

up-gunned to 174bhp/4727cc, the gear ratios were made wider, and twin radius arms were added to the rear suspension to provide even better location.

With a top speed of at least 122mph, this was a formidable machine, with more potential still lurking away, and hidden, but company politics and the impending end to Alpine assembly made it into a very short-lived lost cause. Naturally the surviving cars (many seem to be still around) are much loved, and some Tiger Is have been rebuilt to Tiger II standard in more recent years.

Imp Sport/Sport 1966-76

It was always part of Rootes's long-term plan that the radically-engineered Imp should evolve into a complete family. In advance, therefore, any enthusiast could write his own specification for the Sunbeam version – ie more power and better equipment than the Hillman Imp which founded the family.

Announced in October 1966, the Imp Sport looked almost exactly like the Hillman version, though with different wheel trims and a louvred engine bay cover at the rear. Wider wheels helped improve the already great handling, and the interior was enhanced with extra instuments.

The engine was given twin Zenith-Stromberg carburettors and produced no less than 51bhp at a rousing 6100rpm; it could easily be revved to 7000rpm. Technically and in its chassis the Sunbeam was twinned with the Singer Chamois

Sport, receiving de-cambered front suspension early in 1967 and a revised fascia style in October 1968. When the Singer sister car was dropped in 1970, the Sunbeam was given a four-headlamp nose and re-christened "Sport". It then carried on, little modified, until 1976, when all Imp assembly closed down.

Although history has not been kind to the Imp, early engine problems had been solved when the Imp Sport appeared.

Sunbeam Imp Sport had a twin-carburettor 51bhp engine.

SPECIFICATION

BODY STYLES: saloon

PRODUCTION: c.10,000

ENGINE & TRANSMISSION: 875cc, 4cyl ohc, 4sp man, r/r

POWER: 51bhp @ 6100rpm

MAX SPEED (MPH): 90

0-60MPH (SEC): 16.3

SUSPENSION & BRAKES: coil ifs, coil irs, drums f&r

LENGTH (IN)/WEIGHT (LB): 141/1640

LAUNCH PRICE: £665

Stiletto 1967-73

Another mix-and-match car from Rootes was the Sunbeam Stiletto, which combined the low-roof fastback style of the Hillman Imp Californian with the 51bhp engine of the Sunbeam Imp Sport, the latest de-cambered front suspension, and the four-headlamp nose

SPECIFICATION

BODY STYLES: coupé

PRODUCTION: c.10,000

ENGINE & TRANSMISSION : 875cc, 4cyl ohc, 4sp man, r/r

POWER: 51bhp @ 6100rpm

MAX SPEED (MPH): 87

0-60MPH (SEC): 17.6

SUSPENSION & BRAKES: coil ifs, coil irs, drums f&r

LENGTH (IN)/WEIGHT (LB): 141/1625

LAUNCH PRICE: £726

The Sunbeam Stiletto was introduced in 1967.

of the Singer Chamois Sport.

But there was more. Announced in October 1967, the Stiletto also had a smart and unique fascia, with circular dials instead of a strip speedometer, along with reclining front seats. That fascia, incidentally, was never used on any other Imp-family derivative. Stilettos also had a black vinyl roof covering.

All in all, this was a good little sports saloon, and a handsome one too, but it did not sell as well as its specification promised. It was lost in a spate of cost-cutting in 1973.

Rapier 1967-76

The second-generation Rapier, based on the new-type Hillman Hunter but with an entirely different body style, was introduced in October 1967 and soldiered on for nine years under Chrysler tutelage. Although a better car in every way than the earlier Rapiers, the Rapier's time had gone, especially as this new version was not a car which could claim a motorsport heritage or record.

The Rapier shared its entire platform,

SPECIFICATION

BODY STYLES: coupé

PRODUCTION: 46,204, incl. H120 and "Arrow" Alpine types

ENGINE & TRANSMISSION: 1725cc, 4cyl ohv, 4sp man, o/d or auto, f/r

POWER: 79bhp @ 5100rpm

MAX SPEED (MPH): 103

0-60MPH (SEC): 12.8

SUSPENSION & BRAKES: coil ifs, leaf rear, disc f/drums r

LENGTH (IN)/WEIGHT (LB): 175/2275

LAUNCH PRICE: £1200

The new Rapier, introduced in 1967 and based on the Hillman Hunter.

MacPherson front and leaf-spring rear suspension with the Hillman Hunter and the new-type Humber Sceptre, while its aluminium-headed engine was the same 79bhp 1725cc unit as that of the Sceptre, as was the four-speed plus overdrive gearbox. Amazingly in view of Rootes's negative experience with this installation, Borg Warner automatic transmission was optional, though rarely taken up.

The body featured two doors and a full four-seater cabin, with a long, sweeping fastback roof, plus four headlamps. The body shape must have been

aerodynamically efficient because this was the fastest car to use that engine !

Although the Rapier also bequeathed its engine/transmission to the Hunter GT model in the early 1970s, it received very few styling or technical up-dates in the 1970s, and sold steadily until April 1976. It was, of course, the car from which two other Rootesmobiles – the "Arrow"-type Alpine, and the Rapier H120 – were evolved.

This Rapier was perhaps too heavy, and did not handle as crisply as some of its rivals, but in most respects it was a very effective package.

Rapier H120 1968-76

Some people thought this was a case of "too little, too late". Why, they asked, did it take 14 years for Rootes/Chrysler to apply proper tuning to this engine? Yet when it arrived the Rapier H120 proved a very effective way of up-rating the performance of the new Rapier.

Announced in October 1968, the H120 used Holbay expertise to produce more power from the five-bearing 1725cc engine, but it needed a pair of expensive Weber dual-choke carburettors to do that. Holbay could produce more power from the engine than

Rapier H120.

SPECIFICATION

BODY STYLES : coupé

PRODUCTION: see Rapier, above

ENGINE & TRANSMISSION: 1725cc, 4cyl ohv, 4sp man, o/d, f/r

POWER: 105bhp @ 5200rpm

MAX SPEED (MPH): 105

0-60MPH (SEC): 11.1

SUSPENSION & BRAKES: coil ifs, leaf rear, disc f/drum r

LENGTH (IN)/WEIGHT (LB): 175/2300

LAUNCH PRICE: £1599

Rootes/Chrysler was ready to authorise, which may explain the otherwise meaningless H120 title. The full 120bhp would have been nice, though…

As fitted to the Sunbeam Rapier, the 105bhp Holbay engine helped boost top speed nearer to 110mph, and with its prominent rear spoiler, exuberant styling stripes along the flanks and Rostyle wheels, this was really a very noticeable car too.

Tyres were wider-section than those of the ordinary Rapier, and naturally there

was no automatic transmission option. This mechanical package, incidentally, was later fitted to the Hillman Hunter GLS which followed in 1972; such a car had already won the London-Sydney Marathon of 1968, and would be a race-car contender in the 1970s.

Like the Rapier, the H120 was a satisfactorily fast car, but perhaps too heavy and too ponderous to suit the fast-developing marketplace, Even so, Chrysler kept it in production, little changed, until 1976.

Alpine 1969-75

The third Rootes/Chrysler car to carry the "Alpine" badge was totally different from earlier Alpines, so was immediately accused of being a nasty case of badge-engineering.

SPECIFICATION

BODY STYLES: coupé

PRODUCTION: see Rapier, above

ENGINE & TRANSMISSION: 1725cc, 4cyl ohv, 4sp man, or o/d or auto, f/r

POWER: 72bhp @ 5500rpm

MAX SPEED (MPH): 91

0-60MPH (SEC): 14.6

SUSPENSION & BRAKES: coil ifs, leaf rear, disc f/drum r

LENGTH (IN)/WEIGHT (LB): 175/2220

LAUNCH PRICE: £1086

The 1969 Sunbeam Alpine was a budget version of the Rapier.

Announced in October 1969, the "Arrow"-type Alpine was closely based on the new-generation Rapier (launched 1967), with the same two-door fastback body style and a four-headlamp nose, but with a less powerful engine and simplified equipment.

This particular Alpine shared the same

1725cc engine, but in single-carburettor Hillman Hunter tune, which meant only 72bhp. Overdrive and automatic transmission were optional, and cross-ply tyres were standard until 1972. Minor updates were made in March 1972, but the Alpine always sold slowly, and was dropped in 1975.

Vogue 1970

When the ancient Singer brand was abandoned in April 1970, the

SPECIFICATION

BODY STYLES: saloon, estate

PRODUCTION: not known

ENGINE & TRANSMISSION: 1725cc, 4cyl ohv, 4sp man, o/d or auto, f/r

POWER: 72bhp @ 5000rpm

MAX SPEED (MPH): 90

0-60MPH (SEC): 14.6

SUSPENSION & BRAKES: coil ifs, leaf rear, disc f/drum r

LENGTH (IN)/WEIGHT (LB): 168/2035

LAUNCH PRICE: £1070

Sunbeam Vogue Estate.

Vogue was re-named Sunbeam, with no changes except for badges. This model was short-lived, and was dropped after only six months, in October 1970.

SUNBEAM-TALBOT

Although Sunbeam sold its first car in 1901, and the British arm of Talbot followed in 1903, the two did not join forces until 1938. Stricken by the financial collapse of the Sunbeam Talbot Darracq combine, both had been snapped up by the Rootes Group in 1935, who invented a new joint marque, Sunbeam-Talbot, in 1938. Before War broke out, no fewer than four new "Rootes Sunbeam-Talbot" models – Ten, 2-Litre, 3-Litre and 4-Litre – were launched. Only two of them would be revived in 1945.

Originally there were two post-war Sunbeam-Talbots, the Ten and the 2-Litre, both of them being Hillman-based. Built in London at first, these were strictly interim models, but assembly soon moved to the main Rootes factory at Ryton-on-Dunsmore, near Coventry, and the first true post-war types, the 80 and the closely-related 90, followed in 1948.

For the next few years the Sunbeam-Talbot 90 pedigree was progressively developed (the 80 had been short-lived), but in some markets the "Talbot" name was not used, and when the 90-based Sunbeam Alpine was introduced in 1954, for this 'made-up marque the writing was on the wall.

It all ended late in 1954, when an improved version of the 90 Mk IIA became the Sunbeam (no "Talbot") Mk III. The "Talbot" name would be revived many years later, from mid-1979, years after Rootes had sold out to Chrysler, who had themselves sold out to Peugeot. In such ways are famous names degraded.

Ten 1938-48

SPECIFICATION

BODY STYLES: saloon, drophead

PRODUCTION: 1415, post-war

ENGINE & TRANSMISSION: 1185cc, 4cyl sv, 4sp man, f/r

POWER: 41bhp @ 4500rpm

MAX SPEED (MPH): 67

0-60MPH (SEC): 38.7

SUSPENSION & BRAKES: beam leaf front, leaf rear, drums f&r

LENGTH (IN)/WEIGHT (LB): 156/2184

LAUNCH PRICE: £620

The Hillman Minx-based Sunbeam-Talbot Ten had begun life before the War.

Originally launched in August 1938, the Ten's very basic leaf-spring chassis had evolved from the mid-1930s Hillman Aero Minx, which had become a Talbot Ten in 1935, and then advanced to "Sunbeam-Talbot" status in

1938. The engine and transmission were almost pure sidevalve Minx (though with an aluminium cylinder head), the chassis frame swooped under the rear axle (restricting rear spring travel), and Bendix mechanical brakes were still fitted. Steel wheels were tricked up with fancy covers.

Two body styles were available – a four-door saloon and a two-door drophead coupé – other pre-war styles not being continued. Assembly began in August 1945, and would continue until mid-1948. This was a classic Rootes case of pretty bodywork covering humdrum running gear, but maybe the customers were not unhappy with a 67mph top speed and snail-like acceleration. For sure they were disappointed by the hard ride, and by the dodgy brakes – but this was post-war when almost any car, of any type, could be sold at a profit.

While the mechanicals of the Ten were nothing to write home about, it was nicely trimmed, attractively styled, and has plenty of period flavour.

2-Litre 1939-48

Think of the Ten, but with a 3.5-inch longer wheelbase. All the stretch was ahead of the screen, being needed to cover the larger, Humber-derived, sidevalve 1944cc engine,

SPECIFICATION

BODY STYLES: saloon, drophead

PRODUCTION: 1124, post-war

ENGINE & TRANSMISSION: 1944cc, 4cyl sv, 4sp man, f/r

POWER: 56bhp @ 3800rpm

MAX SPEED (MPH): 70

0-60MPH (SEC): 29.1

SUSPENSION & BRAKES: beam leaf front, leaf rear, drums f&r

LENGTH (IN)/WEIGHT (LB): 159/2492

LAUNCH PRICE: £799

The 2-Litre, powered by the 56bhp sidevalve engine from the Humber Hawk.

which produced 56bhp, 15bhp more than the Ten. The choice of bodies – saloon and drophead – was the same as for the Ten and the basic chassis design was the same, but with hydraulic brakes. With the 2-Litre it was only the performance (better), and the fuel consumption (worse), which made a talking point.

Only 1124 examples were sold. The same basic chassis was found under the 80 and 90 replacement models.

80 1948-50

Here was the first genuine post-war Sunbeam-Talbot. Launched in July 1948, the style of the new twins – 80 and 90 - was sleek, and not shared with any other Rootes Group model, but what it hid was disappointing. Under the skin, except for the wider rear axle and the hydraulic brakes, the 80 was still mainly Sunbeam-Talbot Ten, and that was a pre-war design, with beam axles at both ends.

The novelties, therefore, were in the body style and in the engine. The four-seater bodies – a four-door saloon and a two-door drophead coupé – had attractive and curvaceous styles, the saloon carrying on that famous feature of a pillarless joint (glass on glass) between the rear passenger doors and the rear quarter windows. The headlamps were built into the nose, as were two extra driving lamps.

The engine was an overhead-valve conversion of the 1185cc Hillman Minx power unit which, with 47bhp, was an advance on the old Ten, but this was partly offset by the use of a steering-column gearchange.

There's no way of hiding this – the 80 was underpowered, and too heavy, to do

SPECIFICATION

BODY STYLES: saloon, drophead

PRODUCTION: 3500

ENGINE & TRANSMISSION: 1185cc, 4cyl ohv, 4sp man, f/r

POWER: 47bhp @ 4800rpm

MAX SPEED (MPH): 73

0-60MPH (SEC): 36.4

SUSPENSION & BRAKES: beam leaf front, leaf rear, drums f&r

LENGTH (IN)/WEIGHT (LB): 168/2605

LAUNCH PRICE: £889

anything other than back up the 90. The handling was distinctly pre-war, the gearchange awful, and the performance abysmal. It lasted for only two years – the miracle being that 3500 such cars were sold.

The 1948 Sunbeam-Talbot 80, with only 1185cc, was underpowered.

90 Mk I/Mk II/Mk IIA 1948-54

Here was the second of the 80/90 twins of July 1948, which shared the same style and choice of bodies until 1950. Only the engines were different.

Though the original 90 was lumbered with the ancient pre-war type of chassis, at least it had 64bhp from its 1944cc sidevalve engine to do battle with the steering-column gearchange, and could reach 80mph, a respectable sports saloon performance for that period. Unlike the 80, though, this was a car only at the beginning of its development.

In October 1950 the 90 became the Mk II, complete with a brand new chassis frame which included coil spring independent front suspension, Panhard rod rear axle location, an overhead-valve 70bhp 2267cc version of the engine, and a modified front end without the extra driving lamps and with headlamps raised to give a more attractive line. There were also air intakes either side of the radiator grille. Changes to the transmission included closer gearbox ratios, and this was the first Sunbeam-Talbot to use a

The new Sunbeam-Talbots developed an illustrious rallying career. Stirling Moss drove this 90 into second place in the 1952 Monte Carlo Rally.

hypoid-bevel rear axle. Overdrive did not become an option until the introduction of the Mk III version.

The Mk II 90 was an 86mph car – tough, and chuckable if hard on the biceps – which made its mark in rallying (Stirling Moss took second in the 1952 Monte Carlo rally). It did much to boost the marque's image.

In October 1952, after two years, Mk II evolved into Mk IIA, now having 77bhp instead of 70bhp and no rear wheel covers. It also had pierced road

wheels and enlarged brakes to improve the other half of performance. By this time the top speed could approach 90mph – but how much better this car would have been if it had had a floor gearchange.

In October 1954 the Sunbeam-Talbot badge was abandoned, though it was not the end for this chassis, or motor car. The two-seater Sunbeam Alpine sports car had already appeared, and from this point the saloon was modified and renamed Sunbeam Mk III.

The three-position 90 drophead coupé was very good looking.

SPECIFICATION

BODY STYLES: saloon, drophead

PRODUCTION: 4000/5493/10,888

ENGINE & TRANSMISSION: 1944cc/2267cc, 4cyl ohv, 4sp man, f/r

POWER: 64bhp @ 4100rpm/70bhp @ 4000rpm/77bhp @ 4100rpm

MAX SPEED (MPH): 80/86/81

0-60MPH (SEC): 22.5/24.3/20.8

SUSPENSION & BRAKES: (Mk I) beam leaf front, (Mk II and IIA) coil ifs, leaf rear, drums f&r

LENGTH (IN)/WEIGHT (LB): 168/2830 - 2905

LAUNCH PRICE: £991/£991/£1170

Sheila van Damm, Francoise Clarke and Anne Hall crewed this works Mk IIA on the 1953 Monte, but only managed 90th place.

SWALLOW

Once upon a a time the "'Swallow" trade mark belonged to William Lyons, but he had sold off Swallow Coachbuilding long before the definitive Jaguar concern became an established marque. By the 1950s Swallow had passed through several hands, and was controlled by Tube Investments, which was a large British steel and components supplier.

The Doretti project was inspired by the prospect of sales in the USA, the name being chosen as a salute to the formidable Dorothy Deen, whose Cal Sales concern was already selling many sports cars in that continent. Economically the project revolved around Standard-Triumph's willingness to sell TR2 running gear, while Tube Investments and Swallow would look after chassis supplies

and body shell production respectively, with assembly concentrated at Walsall, north of Birmingham. Even before sales began, the project achieved notoriety when a prototype crashed outside the gates of Standard's HQ, injuring Standard's managing director, Sir John Black.

Aesthetically the Doretti was a very pretty two-seater car, but because it borrowed so much from the TR2, including some of that car's rorty character, Swallow never found it easy to justify a higher price for slightly less performance.

In the end, the project died away of its own accord, with only about 250 cars sold. A Mark 2 Doretti was already being proposed, including a hard-top coupé derivative, but nothing came of it.

Doretti 1954-55

Launched in 1954, the Doretti relied almost completely on Triumph's new TR2 sports car for its running gear, though Swallow had evolved its own chassis and body designs. The idea was not to compete head-on with the TR2, but to selling a much smarter two-seater sports car of similar performance at a higher price – £1102 compared with £887 for the TR2 of the day.

Although all the running gear – engine, gearbox, overdrive, rear axle, front suspension and steering, instruments and many other cockpit fittings – were those of the then-new Triumph TR2, the chassis and body were completely new. The engine and gearbox, in fact, were set significantly further back than the TR2, while the wheelbase, at 95in, was seven inches longer than that of the TR2, and the front track was wider.

The ladder-type chassis was mainly

The 1954 Swallow Doretti had Triumph TR mechanics.

tubular (since the sponsoring parent company was Tube Investments, this was reasonable), while the smart Barchetta-type two-seater body shell had steel inner structural panels, but alloy skins. To many people, one definite advance over the TR2 was that the doors were not cut away at the side and wind-up windows were standard, so bad-weather motoring was not such a raw experience.

The Doretti was a very competent machine. It was not as fast as the TR2 but it handled well. However, it suffered by being an unknown quantity in the marketplace at first, and the higher price always militated against it. Sales of the car had already begun to stagnate before Tube Investments decided to call it a day. Had Standard-Triumph threatened to withhold supplies? We don't think so.

SPECIFICATION

BODY STYLES: sports car

PRODUCTION: 250

ENGINE & TRANSMISSION: 1991cc, 4cyl ohv, 4sp man, or o/d, f/r

POWER: 90bhp @ 4800rpm

MAX SPEED (MPH): 100

0-60MPH (SEC): 12.3

SUSPENSION & BRAKES: coil ifs, leaf rear, drums f&r

LENGTH (IN)/WEIGHT (LB): 156/2156

LAUNCH PRICE: £1102

The stillborn Mk II Swallow Doretti coupé, also known as the Sabre.

TALBOT

As already mentioned under Chrysler UK, Peugeot bought out Chrysler's European interests in 1978, and from late summer 1979 re-badged all Chrysler-UK cars as Talbots.

Although Peugeot seemed to be serious about this enterprise, it soon lost heart. The ex-Rootes/ex-Chrysler-UK factory at Linwood, in Scotland, was abandoned in the early 1980s. Though several new European Talbots (but no all-British types) appeared in the early 1980s, the Talbot badge was dropped again in 1985-86, and the old Rootes/Chrysler factories in Britain were turned over to manufacturing French Peugeots.

Sunbeam 1979-81

Starting in the late summer of 1979, the Chrysler Sunbeam hatchback was rebadged as the Talbot Sunbeam. In a late, and minor, facelift, dated January 1981, larger, flush-mounted headlamps were fitted, though this was not a very noticeable change. Because its platform/chassis/running gear were based on those of the Avenger, when that larger car was dropped in May 1981, the Sunbeam hatchback died along with it.

For all technical details, see the Chrysler-UK entry.

Talbot Sunbeam 1.3GL, 1979.

Sunbeam 1600Ti 1979-81

On sale from mid-1979 as a Chrysler, but re-badged as a Talbot from late summer 1979, the Sunbeam 1600Ti was effectively a highly-tuned derivative of the Sunbeam 1600.

Based on the standard three-door hatch, the 1600Ti had a 100bhp version of the 1598cc engine, with two twin-choke Weber carburettors, a different camshaft profile, and a freeflow exhaust system. The gearbox, final drive and braking system was the same as before, though there were

The 1600Ti was launched as a Chrysler. All but the very first were badged as Talbots.

SPECIFICATION

BODY STYLES : hatchback

PRODUCTION: 10,113

ENGINE & TRANSMISSION : 1598cc, 4cyl ohv, 4sp man, f/r

POWER : 100bhp @ 6000rpm

MAX SPEED (MPH) : 107

0-60MPH (SEC) : 10.7

SUSPENSION & BRAKES : coil ifs, coil rear, disc f/drum r

LENGTH (IN)/WEIGHT (LB) : 151/2037

LAUNCH PRICE : £3779

wider wheels and tyres, front and rear spoilers, a sporty steering wheel and a full array of instruments.

In marketing terms, this car was always overshadowed by the Sunbeam-Lotus (see below), which had an illustrious competition record. While its carburation needed regular attention to keep the engine in tune, this was otherwise a rather simply engineered car.

In character, the 1600Ti was extrovert, there being a lot of under-bonnet engine noise from the Webers, more exhaust noise than on other Sunbeams, and a harder ride. The handling was good and sporting, though a little twitchy, and it was possible to get fuel consumption down to no more than 20mpg, which was a legacy of using Webers.

By no means as famous as contemporary fast Fords, the 1600Ti was nevertheless a fast and nimble hatchback. It was only on sale for two years and the last cars were produced in May 1981.

Sunbeam Lotus 1979-83

Like all the best homologation specials the Sunbeam-Lotus was engineered as a car for use in motorsport, with de-tuned cars sold in small numbers for road use. Works cars shone in the World Rally Championship, winning the Manu-facturers' title in 1981.

Originally set up as a joint project between Chrysler and Lotus, the co-operative agreement carried on when re-badging took place in summer 1979. In fact, almost all these road cars were badged as Talbots, for very few cars had been made before then.

Though it looked much like any other Talbot Sunbeam (the special wheels and the unique horizontal-motif colour schemes gave the game away, of course), it was totally different under the skin. Up front was a Lotus 2174cc 16-valve twin-cam engine (closely related to that fitted to Lotus Elite/Eclat/Esprit road cars), fitted with Dell'Orto carburettors and installed with the cylinder block leaning over at 45 degrees towards the

Talbot Sunbeam Lotus, with a 2.2-litre 150bhp twin-cam engine and five-speed gearbox.

near side of the car. It was backed by a five-speed ZF gearbox and a stronger Chrysler/Talbot rear axle. The brakes, amazingly, were the same size as those of other Sunbeams, though the wheels were special six-inch rim alloys.

Talbot built these cars at Linwood, to "rolling chassis" stage, and transported them to Lotus in East Anglia, where engines, transmissions and other details were slotted into place at a factory at Ludham airfield.

These road cars were developed in a great hurry but they were surprisingly reliable, and even refined (though the ZF gearbox was never as quiet as quality controllers would like). The ride was hard, and the character always robustly sporting. Talbot dealers hated having to work on them because they did not understand the Lotus engines.

As with the 1600Ti, the style inherited

flush headlamps from January 1981, but Linwood built no more rolling chassis after May 1981. Lotus carried on assembling unsold cars until 1982, and the car was not officially discontinued until January 1983.

Of the 2308 cars produced, only 1184 were initially sold in the UK. Because of this car's character, and its sporting record, a high proportion have survived into the new century.

Henri Toivenen slings a Talbot Sunbeam Lotus sideways on his way to winning the 1980 RAC Rally.

SPECIFICATION

BODY STYLES: hatchback

PRODUCTION: 2308

ENGINE & TRANSMISSION: 2174cc, 4cyl 2ohc, 5sp man, f/r

POWER: 150bhp @ 5750rpm

MAX SPEED (MPH): 121

0-60MPH (SEC): 7.4

SUSPENSION & BRAKES: coil ifs, coil rear, disc f/drum r

LENGTH (IN)/WEIGHT (LB): 151/2166

LAUNCH PRICE: £6995

Alpine 1979-85

Soon after the Chrysler Alpine was rebadged as a Talbot Alpine in late 1979, a series of changes and up-dates followed.

From January 1980, the front-end style was changed to incorporate a sloping-back nose rather than a sloping-forward nose. At the same time there was a new 1600SX model which featured an 87bhp

1592cc engine, with automatic trans-mission and power-assisted steering as standard. A five-speed manual gearbox was optional from March 1981, then standard from September 1981. At this time, all Alpines inherited a new four-dial fascia.

As the 1980s progressed, the 1442cc-engined cars disappeared in September

1982, and the 1294cc-engined cars in December 1983. The 1592cc version carried on, becoming the Alpine Minx/Alpine Rapier (special trim up-grade) editions from October 1984, until the entire range was dropped in September 1985. The Solara (see below) was a conventional four-door saloon derivative of this hatchback.

SPECIFICATION

BODY STYLES: hatchback

PRODUCTION: 185,827, plus 27,250 Minx/Rapier

ENGINE & TRANSMISSION: 1294cc/1442cc/1592cc, 4cyl ohv, 4sp man, 5 sp manual, or auto, f/5

POWE : 68bhp @ 5600rpm/85bhp @ 5600rpm/87bhp @ 5400rpm

MAX SPEED (MPH) : 90-100

0-60MPH (SEC) : 16.9-12.9

SUSPENSION & BRAKES : tor ifs, coil irs, disc f/drum r

LENGTH (IN)/WEIGHT (LB) : 167/2314

LAUNCH PRICE : £3872

The five-door Talbot Alpine GLS.

Solara 1980-85

Starting in May 1980, Talbot (i.e. Peugeot) added a conventional three-box four-door saloon version of the Alpine to its range, naming it Solara. Mechanically, and in almost every detail, the model range was similar.

SPECIFICATION

BODY STYLES: saloon

PRODUCTION: 98,150

ENGINE & TRANSMISSION: 1294cc/1592cc, 4cyl ohv, 4sp man, 5sp man, or auto, f/r

POWER : 67bhp @ 5600rpm/72bhp @ 5200rpm/87bhp @ 5400rpm

MAX SPEED (MPH): (E) 90/93/100

0-60MPH (SEC): not measured/13.9/11.6

SUSPENSION & BRAKES: tor ifs, coil irs, disc f/drum r

LENGTH (IN)/WEIGHT (LB): 173/2231-2416

LAUNCH PRICE: £4069

1.6-litre Talbot Solara SX, 1980.

The Solara ran on the same 102.5in. wheelbase platform as the Alpine. The overall length went up by six inches from 167in to 173in. The 1442cc engine was never offered, there being a 67bhp 1294cc 1300LS along with 72bhp or 87bhp 1600 types. 1300s had a four-speed gearbox, while 1600s had five-speed manual or automatic transmission options.

As with the Alpine, there were development changes over the years. Special editions – Sceptre, Vogue, Minx and Rapier – would all appear, while five-speed gearboxes eventually became standard on less pricy models. From October 1984 until the end, Minx and Rapier models were only available with 1592cc engines.

In character, in style, and in performance, the Solaras were almost the same as the Alpines, and they sold well, but for only five years. When the Solara disappeared, so did the Talbot brand.

Avenger 1979-1981

The Chrysler Avenger range was rebadged as the Talbot Avenger range from late 1979, and carried on until April/May 1981, when it was finally dropped.

For all technical details, see the Chrysler-UK (or even the late Hillman) entries.

Talbot Avenger GLS estate, 1980.

TORNADO

Like several other makers of glass-fibre components and mouldings, Tornado, of Rickmansworth, north-west of London, run by Bill Woodhouse, progressed to building sports car body shells in the mid-1950s. From there it was only a short step to designing a new tubular chassis frame, picking up an appropriate set of production-car running gear, and offering full-blown sports car kits for Build-It-Yourself, tax-free, assembly.

The first of a short-lived breed was the Typhoon, which looked flashy but hid humble Ford sidevalve running gear. Once customers made it clear that they could handle more power, Tornado expanded to launch the Tempest, which used modern small-Ford engines and transmissions.

So far, so good, but an attempt to launch the Thunderbolt,

complete with a Triumph TR3A engine, was a total failure, not because it was a poor car but because it was vastly more expensive than the TR itself.

Tornado took that on board, and started again from scratch with the neat Talisman coupe, which not only looked contemporary, and had a very sleek fastback body style, but also had a new and neatly engineered chassis with modern Ford running gear. This car sold steadily, if not spectacularly, but after Tornado's attempts to link up with a mass-market manufacturer failed, the automotive side of the business quietly folded.

In the 1980s, an owners' consortium tried to revive the Talisman, but failed.

Typhoon 1958-62

The original Tornado road car was a kit car which could be supplied in many forms – chassis only, body only, bits added, or bits deleted. Although it was really no way to found a credible kit-car business, its low prices helped it to catch on, and Typhoons were sold for four years.

The tubular chassis frame, with cross-bracings, had an 86in wheelbase, but for

special purposes Tornado would also supply it in 90, 96 and 100in form too; the last was for the very rare four-seater version. The front end was yet another derivative of the LMB split-axle independent system, but with coil-over-shock absorbers. The Ford rear axles were sprung on coil-overs, with a torque tube (standard Ford type) and a Panhard rod for location.

The glass-fibre body was smoothly styled, with a wrap-around windscreen that looked suspiciously like the rear window of a British family car. Years before Reliant thought of it, there was even a "Sportsbrake" derivative too, an ungainly concoction, with a square "estate" roof and a large lift up tailgate.

The running gear was from the old-fashioned Ford Anglia/Prefect, with side-valve engines and a three-speed gearbox, though at least there was a remote-control gearchange. Girling mechanical brakes were thought to be enough to keep the ensemble in check.

Like all such kit cars, the Typhoon was rough-and-ready in some ways, but at those prices no one was really complaining. It was too slow, though, and rather bizarrely styled.

A Tornado Typhoon being driven with enthusiasm.

Tempest 1960-62

The next Tornado to hit the kit-car market was more ambitious and more costly. In 1960 Tornado launched the Tempest, which looked similar to the Typhoon and shared much of the original's chassis but had an ultra-modern, high-revving, overhead-valve Ford Anglia 105E engine and its related gearbox. Anxious to cover all

The Tempest followed the Typhoon in 1960 and was built to accept the Ford Anglia 105E ohv engine.

SPECIFICATION

BODY STYLES: sports car, coupé

PRODUCTION: c.15

ENGINE & TRANSMISSION: 997cc/1340cc, 4cyl ohv, 4sp man, f/r

POWER: 39bhp @ 5000rpm/54bhp @ 4900rpm

MAX SPEED (MPH): not measured/87

0-60MPH (SEC): not measured/19.2

SUSPENSION & BRAKES: coil ifs, coil rear, drums f&r

LENGTH (IN)/WEIGHT (LB): 148/1092

LAUNCH PRICE: £630 as kit/£919 as complete car

bases, Tornado stated that Triumph Herald and BMC A-Series running gear could also be fitted instead.

This time around, the old LMB-type front suspension had been abandoned in favour of Triumph Herald coil spring suspension and its related rack-and-pinion steering. The brakes were now, thankfully, hydraulic. The body

style was much as before, though some cars had front bumpers and all had faired-in headlamps.

Unhappily the prices quoted by the company deterred almost everyone, for in spite of the Tempest representing a step-change advance in chassis engineering this machine was a failure and only about 15 examples were sold.

Thunderbolt 1960

Every entrepreneur has his blind spot, and in Tornado boss Bill Wood-house's case it was in thinking that he could match the big boys with a far more expensive and, frankly, rather badly detailed and built "special".

In this case, Tornado widened the Tempest chassis, fitted larger drum

brakes and a huge 15-gallon fuel tank, retained much of the Triumph and Ford componentry from the Tempest, but installed the 100bhp Triumph TR3A engine and gearbox instead.

Although the installation of this power plant suggested a top speed of nearly 110mph, that velocity was never going

to be achieved in much style, or safety. We simply cannot see how Tornado expected to sell many two-seater Thunderbolts at £1550 when the TR3A of the day cost only £991. Neither could the public, it seems, and this project died immediately, reputedly only with a single prototype built.

Tornado Thunderbolt: only one built.

SPECIFICATION

BODY STYLES: sports car

PRODUCTION: 1

ENGINE & TRANSMISSION: 1991cc, 4cyl ohv, 4sp man, f/r

POWER: 100bhp @ 5000rpm

MAX SPEED (MPH): 108 (E)

0-60MPH (SEC): not measured

SUSPENSION & BRAKES: coil ifs, coil rear, drums f&r

LENGTH (IN)/WEIGHT (LB): 148/1540 - 1624

LAUNCH PRICE: £795 as a kit, £1500/£1665 as a complete car

Talisman 1961-64

By comparison with earlier Tornados, the Talisman was a vastly more attractive machine, with a neatly styled 2+2-seater fastback coupé body. This time around, the chassis, engine weight and power, and fittings were nicely balanced and integrated. Tornado deserved to sell more cars than they did – 186 is the official production figure – but the high price, and the lack of an established reputation, were always big problems.

The 96in-wheelbase chassis featured a twin-tube tubular backbone (half-way towards the layout of the later TVRs, some say), with Tornado-designed coil spring independent suspension at front and rear, rack-and-pinion steering (with a crash-collapsible Triumph Herald column), and a braking system which featured front-wheel discs. Although the ride was quite hard (the car had originally been evolved on the race track), this was a much more capable layout than that of any earlier Tornado.

Having learned their lesson with the awful Thunderbolt, Tornado powered the Talisman with modern, light, Ford engines and their related gearboxes. Standard or Cosworth-tuned engines could be supplied to a customer's requirements. All this was matched by a well trimmed and instrumented interior with Microcell front seats and a '+2' shelf in the rear. Surprisingly, there were Mini-like Perspex sliding windows in the passenger doors.

High hopes, high hopes – but when sales gradually faded away in 1964, the Talisman project was quietly closed down. Few survived to the end of the century, even though an owners' consortium once proposed to get the car (or at least the major chassis and body shell components) back into production.

SPECIFICATION

BODY STYLES: sports coupé

PRODUCTION: 186

ENGINE & TRANSMISSION: 1340cc/1498cc, 4cyl ohv, 4sp man, f/r

POWER: 54bhp @ 4900rpm/60bhp @ 4600rpm/78bhp @ 5200rpm

MAX SPEED (MPH): (75bhp) 102

0-60MPH (SEC): (75bhp) 10.1

SUSPENSION & BRAKES: coil ifs, coil irs, disc f/drum f&r

LENGTH (IN)/WEIGHT (LB): 150/1250

LAUNCH PRICE: £875 in kit form/£1299 as complete car

The 2+2-seater Talisman, 1961-64.

TOURETTE

First seen as the Progress Supreme in 1956 before going on sale as the Tourette in 1957, this tiny egg-like three-wheeler was another of those super-economy machines which sank without trace as soon as the Suez Crisis disappeared.

Originally conceived by Carr Bros of Purley, Surrey, it was eventually put on sale by another company, but still based in the same town. Like all such machines, it had the simplest possible engineering, the lightest possible bodywork, and was powered by a two-stroke motorcycle engine, the attractions being a very low price, or the remarkable (claimed) fuel economy.

Only a Supreme (sorry about that) optimist would have expected to sell many of these machines, and there were no tenough of them in the world. Although *The Autocar* once described the Tourette as a "pretty little beetle" (they were not referring to the VW…), there were few who wanted to pay good money for one, and it sank without trace within a year.

As far as is known, the sponsors of this product never again tried to break into the automotive market.

Supreme 3-wheeler 1957

The best way to describe this machine is as a minimum-size three-wheeler intended to support up to three passengers (one preferably very small) on a bench seat, surrounded by egg-shaped styling in plastic.

Based on a simple-to-make tubular steel chassis frame, with ubiquitous coil-over-shock suspension, it had a two-stroke single-cylinder motorcycle engine just behind the seat, driving via a motorcycle gearbox by chain to the single rear wheel. It rode on 8-inch tyres. The makers of the Scootacar, which we have already described, may have looked at this device before proceeding.

The Tourette had very little going for it except a low price and encouraging fuel economy. If you wanted to drive with a

Tourette Supreme three-wheeler, with 197cc two-stroke power.

SPECIFICATION

BODY STYLES : sports tourer, optional hardtop

PRODUCTION : c.30

ENGINE & TRANSMISSION : 197cc, 1cyl ts, 4sp man, f/r

POWER : 8bhp @ 4000rpm

MAX SPEED (MPH) : 50 (E)

0-60MPH (SEC) : not possible

SUSPENSION & BRAKES : coil ifs, coil irs, drums f&r

LENGTH (IN)/WEIGHT (LB) : 104/430-450

LAUNCH PRICE : Junior £288/ Senior £312

motorcycle licence you could buy a "Junior" model with three speeds and no reverse, but other mortals ordered a "Senior" with four speeds and a reverse gear, and paid an extra £24 for the privilege.

Egon Brutsch, who designed such cars in Germany, was responsible for the layout, and his German connections allowed the Tourette to use Messerschmitt wheels, brakes, hubs and stub axles.

Because it had to accommodate twin front wheels and a width of 54in, but was only 104in long, the rounded GRP body looked bulbous from any angle. All cars were self-coloured in Ivory, twin headlamps were semi-recessed, and there were no doors (the body sides were cut away), but at least one could order a bolt-on glazed hardtop, which actually looked quite neat.

Would you have liked it? Apparently almost no-one did, so, with no more than 30 cars sold, it counts as a total failure.

TRIDENT

If horses were involved, and if bloodstock lines were important, we would point out that the Trident was originally a new TVR project with Italian (Fiore/Fissore) styling input, but with much influence from a TVR dealer, Bill Last of Suffolk.

The TVR Trident prototype was shown at Geneva in 1965, but faded when the company collapsed into liquidation. In the fog of what followed, Bill Last somehow acquired the prototype, insisted that he had bought the rights (the next TVR management always disputed this), re-engineered it, and put the new Trident Clipper into production in Suffolk in 1967; a move, from Woodbridge to Ipswich, soon followed. Though the TVR version had used a typically TVR multi-tube chassis, Last changed everything so that a modified Austin-Healey 3000 platform could be used as the main structural member instead.

In spite of the bad blood between Last and TVR, Trident carried on making cars, which were originally powered by American V8 engines. These cars were expensive, and not very well-built, but sold slowly until the early 1970s. Even so, not even a front-end restyle (with rectangular headlamps for some models), and a change to the use of a modified Triumph TR6 chassis frame, could secure the company's future.

Juggling with model names – Clipper, Venturer, Tycoon – and with engines (Ford V6, Triumph straight six, Ford-USA V8, Chrysler-USA V8) all added to the confusion, the company eventually going into liquidation in 1975.

A reformed company started up again in 1976, using a beam-axle conversion of the chassis and intending to produce Venturers and Clippers, but it was short-lived. The last Trident of all, it seems, was built in 1978.

Clipper 1967-78

This was the first Trident production car and was originally based around a much-modified Austin-Healey 3000 chassis, internal structure and front suspension, though power came from a Ford-USA V8 (later Chrysler-USA) engine and its related transmissions.

The Clipper was a sharp-edged fastback two-door 2+2-seater coupé with semi-recessed headlamps and a distinct ridge along the waistline linking front to rear. The body was styled by Trevor Fiore (in conjunction with the Italian styling house, Fissore) but built by Trident in glass-fibre.

Engine specifications changed (Chrysler V8s were adopted from 1972), and most British cars were sold with automatic transmission, but a truly major revision came for 1971, when Trident re-engineered the car yet again, this time to use a Triumph TR6 chassis frame, which featured semi-trailing-link coil spring independent rear suspension.

These were smart-looking cars, restyled in 1972 to incorporate a shorter nose and four circular headlamps), but were always too expensive and none too well built. Demand was always very limited, and fell away completely by the mid-1970s. Very few now remain.

The V8-powered 1967 Trident Clipper.

SPECIFICATION

BODY STYLES : sports coupé, drophead

PRODUCTION TOTAL: c.130 produced, all Trident types

ENGINE & TRANSMISSION : 4727cc/4942cc/5562cc, V8cyl ohv, 4sp man, or auto, f/r

POWER : 275bhp @ 6000rpm/223bhp @ 4000rpm/243bhp @ 4800rpm

MAX SPEED (MPH) : 137 (E)

0-60MPH (SEC) : 5.0 (E)

SUSPENSION & BRAKES : coil ifs, leaf beam rear (AH) or coil irs (from 1971, TR6), disc f/drum r

LENGTH (IN)/WEIGHT (LB) : 165/not quoted

LAUNCH PRICE : £3456

Venturer V6/Tycoon 1969-78

Both these types, being lineal derivatives of the Clipper, used smaller-capacity British engines in an attempt to stimulate a demand.

The Venturer V6 was a Ford-UK V6-powered car, introduced in late 1969. Manual, overdrive or automatic transmission were all available. The independent-suspension TR6 chassis frame was adopted for 1971, the Ford V6 power was uprated at the end of the year (like that used in contemporary Ford Capris), and a new and shorter nose, with rectangular headlamps came along in 1972.

Trident Venturer V6.

SPECIFICATION

BODY STYLES: sports coupé, drophead

PRODUCTION: 1969-78 (c.130, all Tridents)

ENGINE & TRANSMISSION: 2498cc, 6cyl ohv/2994cc, V6cyl ohv, 4sp man, o/d or auto (auto only with 2498cc), f/r

POWER: 152bhp @ 5500rpm (Tycoon)/128bhp @ 4750rpm/138bhp @ 5000rpm (Venturer V6)

MAX SPEED (MPH): 120-125

0-60MPH (SEC): 7.5 (E)/not measured

SUSPENSION & BRAKES: coil ifs, leaf rear (AH) coil irs (from 1971, TR6), disc f/drum r

LENGTH (IN)/WEIGHT (LB): 165/not quoted

LAUNCH PRICE: £1840 as kit, £2400 built-up

From late 1971, the Venturer was joined by the Tycoon, which was also offered as a drophead coupé and was powered by a 152bhp fuel-injected Triumph TR6 engine of 2498cc. Only available with Borg Warner automatic transmission (which the TR6 never had, since it did not really suit the torque characteristics of the engine), the Tycoon was a marketing failure, and apparently only seven such cars were ever built.

TRIKING

This enterprising little business was set up in 1979 by technical artist Tony Divey, who was a long-time Morgan fanatic. After engineering and building his first personal prototype, later nicknamed the "Old Lady", in 1978, he decided to put the Triking car on sale. Working from Marlingford, near Norwich in East Anglia, Divey set out to re-create a three-wheeler with the shape and (modernised) character of the legendary Morgan Super Sports of the 1930s. It is no coincidence that he received out-of-hours help from friends he had made at the Lotus factory, which was situated not too far away.

With a car which looked for all the world like that Morgan, though with modern, purpose-built or purpose-modified running gear, he achieved a ferociously fast little machine. Although this was never a project meant to sell in big numbers (and at a 1979 starting price of £4500 for a part-completed kit it was certainly not cheap), Divey's tiny business found that there was there was a slow but steady demand for the Triking. By the time there was a major design change, in 1990, just 100 examples of this frisky little machine had been built.

In the years which followed, there would be a new chassis, a new front-end style, lightweight racing versions, and even supercharged derivatives.

Triking 1979-90

Looking for all the world like a Morgan three-wheeler of the 1930s (which is exactly what designer Tony Divey was trying to replicate), the Triking was different from end to end, and was powered by a lusty air-cooled 90-degree V-twin Moto Guzzi motorcycle engine. This was linked to a Guzzi five-speed motorcycle gearbox (which did not have a reverse ratio), and there was shaft drive to the single rear wheel.

Up front there was coil spring and wishbone front suspension (only the Triumph upright was a proprietary item), with Triumph rack-and-pinion steering, though the wheels were centre-lock wires of motorcycle type. To accommodate the shaft drive to the single rear wheel, this sat

The Triking used a Moto Guzzi V-twin motorcycle engine

under a simple coil-over-shock suspension assembly, with trailing-arm location.

The combined chassis frame/body structure was fabricated from simple pressings and foldings – some square section steel tubing, some sheet steel and some aluminium.

The engine was up front and out in the breeze, and the body featured a narrow nose, a two-seater open-to-the-weather cockpit, and a tail which swept closely around the rear wheel. There was virtually no overhang at front or rear.

The body skin itself was fabricated from aluminium sheet, there were no doors because the cockpit had cutaway sides, and the windscreen was a low vee-shape, enough (but only just enough) to keep the

rain out. The exhaust pipes – two of them, chrome-plated throughout – swept along the body sides, well below the level of the cockpit cutaways.

Like the Morgan after which it was so clearly styled, the Triking had very firm suspension but handled extremely well and readily, there being the usual tendency for the (driven) rear wheel to skip sideways on bumpy corners. It was not, in other words, a completely practical or indeed sensible car – but engineer Divey never intended it to be so.

A select number of customers got a great deal of fun from their Trikings, all without having to worry about wet rot or dry rot in the body framing, for there was no wood there at all.

SPECIFICATION

BODY STYLES: sports car

PRODUCTION: 100

ENGINE & TRANSMISSION: 844cc/949cc, V2cyl ohv, 5sp man (no reverse), f/r

POWER: 56bhp @ 6750rpm/71bhp @ 6500rpm

MAX SPEED (MPH): 105 (E)

0-60MPH (SEC): not measured

SUSPENSION & BRAKES: coil ifs, coil irs, discs f&r

LENGTH (IN)/WEIGHT (LB): not quoted/780

LAUNCH PRICE: £4,500 + for a kit, depending on degree of completion

TRIUMPH

Like other Coventry-based car-makers, Triumph began in the 19th century by producing pedal cycles, then moved on to motor cycles, and only entered the four-wheeler business in 1923. In the next 16 years, several changes of management (including Donald Healey at the technical helm from 1934 to 1939), and two financial crises, led to Receivership in 1939. During the War, in 1944, the Triumph brand was bought up by Standard.

Starting in 1946 with the 1800 Roadster and Saloon models, Triumph was reborn. The razor-edged Mayflower was another step, but it was the new TR2 sports car of 1953 which made all the difference. From 1959, a range of Triumph Heralds signalled the incipient end of small Standards, and after the arrival of the Spitfire sports car and 2000 saloon the revolution was complete. The last Standard was built in 1963, and thereafter all cars were badged as Triumphs.

Leyland rescued Standard-Triumph from bankruptcy in 1961 and rebuilt the marque in the 1960s, not only with new saloons such as the Vitesse but also with new-generation TRs (TR4-TR6). The assembly line in Coventry was joined by a new facility at Speke, in Liverpool.

After British Leyland was formed, Triumph moved closer to Rover in the early 1970s, and co-operated closely on future products. Though Dolomites were pure Triumph, there was some Triumph engineering in the new Rover 3500 of 1976, and much Rover input into the TR7. As British Leyland's fortunes went from bad to worse, the last real Triumph (the TR7) was killed off in 1981, and the Cowley-built Acclaim that followed was no more than a re-badged Honda.

After a complex series of takeovers, mergers, rescues and corporate divorces, the dormant Triumph brand came to be held by BMW.

1800 Roadster/2000 Roadster 1946-48/1948-49

As Triumph's new owners, Standard decided to re-launch the old marque by developing two new models around the same basic tubular chassis (different wheelbases, though), using running gear based on the Standard Flying Fourteen, and the 1776cc engine currently being built for the Jaguar 1½-litre saloon. Thus the new 1800 Roadster and Saloon came to market at the same time.

The Roadster ran on a 100in wheelbase, the 63bhp 1776cc engine being linked to a Flying Fourteen gearbox, with a steering-column gearchange mounted on the right of the column. The rear axle was positioned above the main tubular side members. Also lifted

The Triumph 1800 Roadster, powered by the same engine as the 1½-litre Jaguar.

SPECIFICATION

BODY STYLES: drophead coupé

PRODUCTION: 2501/2000

ENGINE & TRANSMISSION: 1776cc/2088cc, 4cyl ohv, 4sp man/3-spd man, f/r

POWER : 63bhp @ 4500rpm/68bhp @ 4200rpm

MAX SPEED (MPH): 77

0-60MPH (SEC): 25.2/24.8

SUSPENSION & BRAKES: (1800) leaf ifs (2000) coil ifs, leaf rear, drums f&r

LENGTH (IN)/WEIGHT (LB): 169/2541 - 2828

LAUNCH PRICE: £889/£991

from the Standard Flying Fourteen was the independent front suspension by transverse leaf spring.

The body was a three-abreast Roadster with wind-up windows and a divided bench seat, built around a wooden skeleton and with mainly aluminium panels. This was the last production car in the world to be fitted with a dickey (or rumble) seat, which was only exposed when the boot lid was opened up and swung backwards to reveal a padded backrest.

From the autumn of 1948 there were no more supplies of old-type engines

and suspension units, so the Roadster was re-arranged as the 2000 Roadster, this time with a 68bhp 2088cc Standard Vanguard engine with its associated three-speed gearbox and rear axle. The gearchange lever moved to the left side of the steering column. Production finally ran out in October 1949.

Though smart and well-equipped in their own way, neither of these Roadsters went or handled like a sports car, so their appeal was limited. In later years, and because of their dickey-seat feature, they were treated as loveable curiosities, and a number have survived.

1800 saloon 1946-49

Mechanically, the original razor-edge style 1800 saloon was the sister car to the 1800 Roadster, though it had a longer 108in-wheelbase version of the tubular chassis. All the rest of the running gear – the overhead-valve 1776cc engine, the Standard Flying Fourteen gearbox, rear axle and transverse-leaf front suspension – was like that of the Roadster.

The body was built by Mulliners of Birmingham and was the usual coach-built amalgam of a seasoned ash frame

Triumph 1800 saloon, 1946.

SPECIFICATION

BODY STYLES: saloon

PRODUCTION: 4000

ENGINE & TRANSMISSION: 1776cc, 4cyl ohv, 4sp man, f/r

POWER: 63bhp @ 4500rpm

MAX SPEED (MPH): 75

0-60MPH (SEC): 29.1

SUSPENSION & BRAKES: leaf ifs, leaf rear, drums f&r

LENGTH (IN)/WEIGHT (LB): 175/2828

LAUNCH PRICE: £889

with panelling mainly in aluminium. As on the Roadster there was a divided bench front seat and the column-change gear lever was on the right of the column. Gear changing was not a pleasure. Leather seating, a wooden dashboard and nice detailing all added to the appeal. Although the style looked archaic to some, Standard's managing director, Sir John Black, was a great fan and insisted it should look like that.

As noted in the 1800 Roadster entry, the supply of Standard Flying Fourteen components ran down at the end of 1948, so a change to the Vanguard engine and gearbox was inevitable; this would happen in early 1949.

Like the Roadster, the 1800 saloon was a worthy but by no means agile car – certainly not a sports saloon, but with its own type of dignity. As long as you didn't rush it, everything was OK…

2000/Renown saloon/Limousine 1949-54

From 1949 to 1954, this razor-edged Triumph went through three iterations, the final product being very different from the original of 1946

In February 1949 the 1800 (see above) became the 2000 (Type TDA), equipped with the 68bhp 2088cc Standard

SPECIFICATION

BODY STYLES: saloon, limousine

PRODUCTION: 2000/9301/190

ENGINE & TRANSMISSION: 2088cc, 4cyl ohv, 3sp man, or o/d, f/r

POWER: 68bhp @ 4200rpm

MAX SPEED (MPH): 75

0-60MPH (SEC): 25.1

SUSPENSION & BRAKES: (2000) leaf irs (Renown) coil ifs, leaf rear, drums f&r

LENGTH (IN)/WEIGHT (LB): 175- 181/2828-3024

LAUNCH PRICE: £991/£1440

The Vanguard engine was also used in the Renown. This is a rare Renown Limousine with sliding division and a 111-inch wheelbase.

Vanguard engine and its related three-speed gearbox and rear axle. The column change moved to the left of the column. The original tubular chassis and

transverse leaf spring front suspension was retained. This, though, was only an interim model because from October 1949 the interim 2000 became the

Renown. This had an entirely different chassis, a 108in-wheelbase version of the Standard Vanguard frame, with pressed box-section structural members, side members which swept up and over the rear axle, and Vanguard-type coil spring independent front suspension.

In June 1950 Laycock overdrive became optional (priced at £64 at the time) – it was introduced to the closely-related Standard Vanguard at the same time. Renowns had Vanguard-type instrumentation in a revised centre fascia.

In autumn 1951 Triumph introduced a smart limousine version of this body, with its wheelbase lengthened by three inches to provide more rear-seat leg room. This change was so subtly applied that it was difficult to spot the difference in body lines. Only 190 limousiness were sold, but the same longer wheelbase and substantially altered body structure were applied to the saloons as well. This was the TDC range.

Thus finalised, the Renown soldiered on until October 1954, by which time it had virtually disappeared off Britain's new-car radar: not even a substantial price reduction in June 1953 could stimulate new demand. Yet the 1800/200 saloon had managed an eight-year life. There was no direct replacement – though the Standard Vanguard Sportsman (see entry) might have been one if the corporate daydreamers had got their way.

Mayflower | 1949-53

Standard's Sir John Black was so fixated on razor-edge styling that when the time came to produce a new small Standard-Triumph, he insisted on the theme being used again. Accordingly, although the new Mayflower of 1949 (sales began in mid-1950) had unit-construction body engineering (the first ever for Standard-Triumph), it still looked like a Renown which had shrunk in the wash, and ungainly with it. To quote a sage of the period, "It's got a Queen Anne front and Mary Ann sides".

Riding on an 84in wheelbase, this strange bodywork hid a slightly smaller version of the old 1930s-type sidevalve Standard Flying Ten engine (1247cc instead of 1267cc), which was backed by the ubiquitous Vanguard three-speed gearbox and its related rear axle. The Mayflower was nothing if not over-engineered. Naturally (this was the export-conscious 1940s), there was a steering-column gearchange. Independent front suspension, by coil springs

Triumph Mayflower in 1949, with older Standards behind.

and wishbones, was all new – and would eventually be used in modified form in the TR2 sports car family.

Although this was a small two-door saloon, it was relatively well-equipped (up to Standard's perceived "Triumph" standards), with leather seat coverings and pile carpets, and a fascia clearly related to the 1800/2000 saloon's layout. This emphasis on the quality of the furnishings was a good thing, because the performance, with only a 38bhp engine, was no great shakes, and neither was the handling. A proposal to use an overhead-valve version of the engine (as supplied to Morgan) was still-born.

Although Fisher & Ludlow built the saloon bodies, Triumph previewed a two-door convertible with a body conversion by Mulliners, but after only ten such cars had been built this was cancelled.

Amazingly, considering that its image and engine were both obsolete, the Mayflower's popularity increased over time, but as the same factory space was needed to build mass-market Standard Eights and Tens, it was dropped in mid-1953. In character, the Mayflower could be described as quaint, or endearing, but not technically exciting. Those that have not rusted away have gathered together into a thriving little club to look after their survival.

SPECIFICATION

BODY STYLES: saloon, drophead

PRODUCTION: 34,000

ENGINE & TRANSMISSION: 1247cc, 4cyl sv, 3sp man, f/r

POWER: 38bhp @ 4200rpm

MAX SPEED (MPH): 63

0-60MPH (SEC): not measured

SUSPENSION & BRAKES: coil ifs, leaf rear, drums f&r

LENGTH (IN)/WEIGHT (LB): 154/2016

LAUNCH PRICE: £480

TR2/TR3 1953-55/1955-57

After a false start in 1952 (the "20TS" prototype had to be completely re-engineered), the TR2 went on sale in the autumn of 1953. Cars in this "side-screen" family would then be built for the next nine years, and sold very well in export markets. All such cars shared the same box-section separate chassis frame and two-seater body.

Built on an 88in-wheelbase frame, the TR2 was powered by a twin-SU version of the Standard Vanguard's 1991cc wet-liner engine, producing 90bhp. The four-speed gearbox was a development of the Vanguard's unit, but with a neat, stubby remote-control gearchange. Laycock overdrive was a very popular optional extra. The result was a fast and (at first) astonishingly economical combination; later cars seemed to trade off fuel economy for more weight and more power.

The bucket seats had little space behind for extra passengers (but later cars could have an optional "occasional" rear seat. Removable side-screens were provided, with a simple fold-away soft top, or a removable hardtop (very popular) to keep the rain out. Centre-lock wire wheels were optional and many TR2s had them.

The two-seater body started life with full depth passenger doors, but no sills: what became known as the "short-door" style took over from October 1954. Build quality and rot-proofing were so-so, which explains why many cars rusted

Front and rear views of the production TR2 in 1953.

The Wadsworth/Brown TR2 took 15th place at Le Mans in 1954, recording a staggering 34.6mpg in the process.

away, but classic car enthusiasts were later able to buy replacement panels to keep them on the road.

In autumn 1955 the TR2 gave way to the TR3, looking the same except for an egg-crate front grille, and from late 1956 this became Britain's first series-production car to have front-wheel disc brakes as standard. Power crept up from

90bhp through 95bhp to 100bhp meantime. The TR3 then gave way to the face-lifted TR3A for 1958.

Early cars had dodgy handling (limited rear wheel movement didn't help), but radial ply tyres seem to have cured much of that. As with cars like the MGA, the TR2/TR3's charm was in its two-seater Britishness – an appeal that never faded.

SPECIFICATION

BODY STYLES: sports car

PRODUCTION: 8628/13,377

ENGINE & TRANSMISSION: 1991cc, 4cyl ohv, 4sp man, or o/d, f/r

POWER: 90bhp @ 4800rpm/95bhp @ 4800rpm/100bhp @ 5000rpm

MAX SPEED (MPH): 103

0-60MPH (SEC): 11.9

SUSPENSION & BRAKES : coil ifs, leaf rear, drums f&r (disc f/drum r from late 1956)

LENGTH (IN)/WEIGHT (LB): 151/1848

LAUNCH PRICE: £787/£976

The 1955 TR3 had a grille at the front of the intake.

TR3A/TR3B 1957-62

From 1958 the TR3A took over, still with a TR2/TR3-type body, but with a full-width "dollar-grin" front end, in which the headlamps were slightly recessed. There were exterior door handles for the first time. These cars sold even better than before, especially in North America.

Technically, little was changed at first, though an option (rarely taken up, it seems) of a larger 2138cc engine added to the variety. Assembly of TR3As ended in the autumn of 1961, to let the new-style TR4 (see below) take over.

Six months later, early in 1962, a North America-only TR3B model went back on sale, assembled at a satellite factory in Birmingham. Looking like the TR3A, there were two series – the first 530 cars being TR3A clones, the other 2801 having 2138cc as standard, with the new all-synchromesh TR4 gearbox. This batch was completed before the end of the year.

A 1960 TR3A with factory hardtop.

The TR3A/TR3B models were better than the earlier types in every way, though no faster. They seemed to handle better, and with their exterior door handles and locking boot lids were also more owner-friendly. Thousands have survived.

TR3As have arrived in the Standard-Triumph competitions workshop to be prepared for the 1958 Monte Carlo Rally. Competitions manager Ken Richardson has a look.

David Seigle-Morris and Vic Elford in a works TR3A won their class in the 1960 Alpine Rally.

SPECIFICATION

BODY STYLES: sports car

PRODUCTION: 58,236/3331

ENGINE & TRANSMISSION: 1991cc/2138cc, 4cyl ohv, 4sp man, or o/d ,f/r

POWER: 100bhp @ 5000rpm/100bhp @ 4600rpm

MAX SPEED (MPH): 105 (E)

0-60MPH (SEC): not measured

SUSPENSION & BRAKES: coil ifs, leaf rear, disc f/drum r

LENGTH (IN)/WEIGHT (LB): 151/2050

LAUNCH PRICE: £1050

Herald/Herald S 1959-64

Because Fisher & Ludlow (taken over by BMC) refused to supply any more body shells to Standard-Triumph, Alick Dick (who replaced Sir John Black in 1954) took a big gamble when what became the new Triumph Herald was commissioned. To make the new model possible, he had to agree to a separate-chassis design, with the body made up of large bolt-together sections. This explains why so many different types of Herald and Vitesse could be built.

The new Herald had a chassis frame with strong backbone members, independent front and rear suspension, and rack-and-pinion steering. The car's tight steering lock (25 feet, equal to that of a London taxi cab) was remarkable, though the swing-axle rear end was criticised for its on-the-limit tuck-under tendencies: all Heralds and (until late 1968) Vitesses had the same characteristics. Two different tunes of the 948cc engine were chosen, that used in the Coupé and Convertible having 45bhp (by 1960 it was optional on the saloon too). were chosen, The Standard Pennant gearbox was fitted, along with a chassis-mounted differential.

Three two-door body shells, all inter-

The 948cc Triumph Herald, 1959.

SPECIFICATION

BODY STYLES: saloon, drophead, coupé

PRODUCTION: 116,121

ENGINE & TRANSMISSION: 948cc, 4cyl ohv, 4sp man, f/r

POWER: 35bhp @ 4500rpm/45bhp @ 6000rpm

MAX SPEED (MPH): 71/79

0-60MPH (SEC): 31.1/23..2

SUSPENSION & BRAKES: coil ifs, leaf irs, drums f&r

LENGTH (IN)/WEIGHT (LB): 153/1764

LAUNCH PRICE: £702

related, and all with the same front end, windscreen and doors, were made available inside two years. The entire front end was hinged at the nose, and swung up to give unparalleled access to the mechanicals

The interior was a mix of enterprise and crudity – a collapsible steering column and remote-control gearchange balanced by poor-quality fascia coverings and downmarket trim.

A four-door saloon model was developed, but never built in the UK. Eventually it was built in numbers in India, becoming the Standard Gazel.

The Herald's launch came in April 1959. Saloons and 2+2-seater coupés were available at once, and the drophead version arrived in March 1960. Sales would have been stronger if build quality had been better, and there's no doubt that the dodgy reputation acquired by the rear suspension took its toll. The original 948cc models gave way to the much better Herald 1200 in 1961, though one entry-level survivor, the stripped-out Herald S (strangely, with optional front discs from October 1961) carried on until early 1964.

Rolling chassis of the Herald.

Herald 1200 1961-70

Triumph was ready to launch the 1200 in 1961, but Leyland, having taken over by then, trumpeted it as their

SPECIFICATION

BODY STYLES : saloon, drophead, coupé, estate, commercials

PRODUCTION: 294,711

ENGINE & TRANSMISSION: 1147cc, 4cyl ohv, 4sp man, f/r

POWER: 39bhp @ 4500rpm/48bhp @ 5200rpm

MAX SPEED (MPH): 74/77

0-60MPH (SEC): 28.6/25.8

SUSPENSION & BRAKES: coil ifs, leaf irs, drums f&r (optional disc f/drum r)

LENGTH (IN)/WEIGHT (LB): 153/1771

LAUNCH PRICE: £708

The Herald 1200 came along in 1961.

own idea. Of such economies with the truth are legends born…

The basic design of the original Herald was not changed, but there was more power and torque, an extra body option, and much higher standards of trim and build quality. The new saloon, coupé and convertible were introduced at once, with a smart (and fast-selling) estate car version revealed just one month later.

The 1200 was better built than its predecessor, with tidier and more complete trim and a wooden fascia, although there was still only a single instrument on it. A 39bhp 1147cc engine was fitted to all models in the range. Thus revised, the new Herald appealed to more people, and sold well – except for the coupé, whose appeal vanished when it no longer had more performance than the saloon, so it was finally dropped in October 1964.

Front-wheel disc brakes were optional from October 1961, and a short-lived Courier van version arrived early in 1962 (it would die out in 1966). The standard engine tune was uprated to 48bhp from November, and the 1200 then led a steady existence for some years. Indeed, even after the 13/60 models arrived (see below), the Herald 1200 continued, but only as a saloon car, until mid-1970.

Perseverance pays off, for although the Herald 1200 was basically no more than an improved version of the original, it sold dramatically better, for nearly ten years. Triumph also improved the rear suspension so that the cars handled more surely in later years. Undoubtedly these Heralds were a considerable commercial success.

Herald 12/50 1963-67

The Herald 12/50 was a different enough variant to qualify for a separate entry.

Only sold as a saloon, it was marketed with a fold-back fabric sun-roof as standard (such things were rare

Herald 12/50 came with a sunroof as standard.

SPECIFICATION

BODY STYLES: saloon

PRODUCTION: 54,807

ENGINE & TRANSMISSION: 1147cc, 4cyl ohv, 4sp man, f/r

POWER: 51bhp @ 5200rpm

MAX SPEED (MPH): 78

0-60MPH (SEC): 25.2

SUSPENSION & BRAKES: coil ifs, leaf irs, disc f/drum r

LENGTH (IN)/WEIGHT (LB): 153/1855

LAUNCH PRICE: £635

in the UK at that time), and with a 51bhp 1147cc engine as standard and front disc brakes. Announced in March 1963, it was then produced until replaced by the up-rated 13/60 models in August 1967.

TR4 1961-65

The second-generation TR, launched nine years after the original, used the same chassis layout, but was updated in every other aspect. This, the first of the "Michelotti" TRs, would go on to father the TR4A, the TR5/TR250, and the TR6.

The TR4's chassis frame was basically that of the outgoing TR3A, but with a four-inch wider track front and rear, and rack-and-pinion steering. The engines, 1991cc and 2138cc, were basically as before, though this time the 1991cc unit was optional (and very rarely chosen). Behind it, an all-synchromesh four-speed gearbox was new, with Laycock overdrive optional as usual. Also optional were centre-lock wire-spoke wheels.

The new all-steel body style featured fully recessed headlamps and a full-width bonnet which hinged at the nose. The bonnet panel needed a long power bulge to clear the dashpots of the SU carburettors. The windscreen was larger, wind-up windows were a feature, and the cockpit was roomier than before. A new

Works TR4 on the 1962 Alpine Rally.

SPECIFICATION

BODY STYLES: sports car

PRODUCTION: 40,253

ENGINE & TRANSMISSION: 1991cc/2138cc, 4cyl ohv, 4sp man, or o/d, f/r

POWER: 100bhp @ 5000rpm/100bhp @ 4600rpm

MAX SPEED (MPH): 105/109

0-60MPH (SEC): not measured/10.9

SUSPENSION & BRAKES: coil ifs, leaf rear, disc f/drum r

LENGTH (IN)/WEIGHT (LB): 154/2184

LAUNCH PRICE: £1095

The 1961 Triumph TR4 was a longer and wider car than the TR3A.

type hardtop was in two pieces, with a large wrap-around rear window and a removable roof panel; customers could order a vinyl fabric top (a "Surrey Top") instead of that panel.

Changes over time included the use of Zenith-Stromberg carburettors in place of SUs (with no changes to advertised power outputs), new front suspension members, and revised seats. There were no changes to the chassis layout, though – restricted rear wheel movement was still a problem – which led to complaints about the hard ride and bump steer.

Not that Triumph was too worried. for the TR4 sold very well indeed, and independent rear suspension was already planned.

TR4 with the new two-piece hardtop.

Dove GTR4 1962-65

Like the Sunbeam Harrington Alpine, here was another sports coupé in the "High Hopes" category, where the sponsors of a converted sports car thought it should sell much more than it did. As coachbuilders, Harringtons of Hove had a hand in both products, but in this case it was a Triumph dealer from Wimbledon, Doves, which defied the odds.

Built as a private-enterprise project, though with the tacit approval of the factory, the Dove GTR4 was a conversion of the standard TR4. To build it, the

SPECIFICATION

BODY STYLES: sports coupé

PRODUCTION: c.55

ENGINE & TRANSMISSION: 2138cc, 4cyl ohv, 4sp man, or o/d, f/r

POWER: 100bhp @ 4600rpm

MAX SPEED (MPH): 106

0-60MPH (SEC): 12.0

SUSPENSION & BRAKES: coil ifs, leaf rear, disc f/drum r

LENGTH (IN)/WEIGHT (LB): 156/2660

LAUNCH PRICE: £1250

Dove GTR4.

entire rear deck and boot lid were removed, the fuel tank was relocated under the rear floor, and a full-length GRP roof panel was grafted into place, with a large lift-up rear window. An occasional rear seat was installed.

The result was a pleasing car, though it inevitably weighed more than the Roadster, or even the TR4 hardtop model. It was also a very useful machine, the major problem being that at £1250 (plus optional extras) it was significantly more costly than the £907 (Roadster) or £949 (Hardtop) TR4s supplied by the factory. And maybe, just maybe, other Triumphs dealers would have sold Doves if they were not having to advertise the skills of a rival.

Statistics are difficult to come by, but it is possible that a handful of TR4A based Doves were also produced. Officially, at least, Dove GTR4 assembly came to an end when the live-axle TR4 died in 1965.

A nice rarity if you can find one.

TR4A 1965-67

The second-generation Michelotti-style TR was the TR4A, visually almost identical to the TR4, but now with a new, stiffer chassis frame, and coil spring independent rear suspension which was closely related to that of the modern Triumph 2000 saloon (in the USA, by the way, a beam rear axle alternative remained, but this was never

The TR4A, with independent rear suspension, arrived in 1965.

SPECIFICATION

BODY STYLES: sports car

PRODUCTION: 28,465

ENGINE & TRANSMISSION: 2138cc, 4cyl ohv, 4sp man, or o/d, f/r

POWER: 104bhp @ 4700rpm

MAX SPEED (MPH): 109

0-60MPH (SEC): 11.4

SUSPENSION & BRAKES: coil ifs, coil irs (some leaf rear in USA), disc f/drum r

LENGTH (IN)/WEIGHT (LB): 154/2240

LAUNCH PRICE: £968

offered in the rest of the world).

The car was a little heavier than the TR4, but this was balanced by a slight power increase from the old wet-liner engine. As before, there was the choice of a two-piece hardtop, or a half-and-half "Surrey top", and – as ever on a TR – Laycock overdrive was optional.

The handling was better than on the

TR4 because the wheels spent more time in touch with the ground (there was much more rear-wheel travel), but by this time some customers were actually beginning to question the engine's gruff character. The TR4A, therefore, stayed on the market for less than three years – and this was the last-ever Triumph car to use this engine.

TR5 1967-68

Although it still looked almost the same as the TR4 of 1961 (you had to look carefully at badges to spot the difference), the TR5 was very different under the skin. It was not only the first TR to use a six-cylinder engine, but also the very first to use fuel-injection; for the USA market injection was not used, which explains why the TR250 is a different car, separately described.

The six-cylinder TR5, 1967.

SPECIFICATION

BODY STYLES: sports car

PRODUCTION: 2947

ENGINE & TRANSMISSION: 2498cc, 6cyl ohv, 4sp man, or o/d, f/r

POWER: 150bhp @ 5500rpm

MAX SPEED (MPH): 120

0-60MPH (SEC): 8.8

SUSPENSION & BRAKES: coil ifs, coil irs, disc f/drum r

LENGTH (IN)/WEIGHT (LB): 154/2268

LAUNCH PRICE: £1212

The chassis, all-independent suspension, gearbox options and rear axle (no live axle option at the rear, this time) were like those of the TR4A. The engine was effectively a long-stroke version of the Vanguard Six/Triumph 2000 unit, with a new cylinder head. With a more ambitious camshaft grind, and Lucas fuel injection, peak power went up to a

The 2498cc fuel-injected TR5 engine.

very healthy 150bhp (compared with 104bhp for the outgoing TR4A), which completely transformed the performance. This, in fact, was the first 120mph TR, which could compete on level terms with cars like the old Austin-Healey 3000 or the brand new MGC.

Servo-assisted brakes, radial ply tyres

and Rostyle wheels were all standard, Centre-lock wire wheels, overdrive and the two-piece lift-off hardtop were still optional, as on the TR4s. The handling was softer than that of the old-type traditional TRs, and was something of an acquired taste, but unreconstructed TR2 owners would have loved it.

Because the restyled TR6 (described below) was already under development, the TR5 was to be a very short-lived model. Announced in October 1967, it was officially rendered obsolete in January 1969; this explains the low production figure, and thus the scarcity of survivors.

TR250 1967-68

Because of the arrival of new exhaust emission regulations in North America, the TR5 could not go to the USA or Canada. The new 2498cc six-cylinder engine was still used, but it came with twin Zenith-Stromberg carburettors and a mere 104bhp.

Much smoother running than the

TR250, produced for North America only.

SPECIFICATION

BODY STYLES: sports car

PRODUCTION: 8484

ENGINE & TRANSMISSION: 2498cc, 6cyl ohv, 4sp man, or o/d, f/r

POWER: 104bhp @ 4500rpm

MAX SPEED (MPH): 110 (E)

0-60MPH (SEC): 10.6

SUSPENSION & BRAKES: coil ifs, coil irs, disc f/drum r

LENGTH (IN)/WEIGHT (LB): 154/2268

LAUNCH PRICE: not officially sold in UK

TR4s, the new car, as far as the Americans were concerned, was no more and no less than a TR4A with compulsory independent rear suspension (diehards over there didn't like that) and with none of the old masochistic joys of a rough four-cylinder engine.

Even so, in just one selling year – 1968

– Triumph sold 8484 of them. A recognition point applied to all TR250s was a multi-stripe decal across the nose of the bonnet and down the front wings.

After only a year the TR250 would be replaced in North America by the TR6 , again with carbutettors instead of injection. It was never sold in the UK.

TR6 1969-76

A restyled (by Karmann) derivative of the TR5/TR250 models, the TR6 was the last and the best-selling of all separate-chassis TRs. On sale from the first days of 1969, the TR6 used the same basic chassis as before, but with a much-changed bodyshell featuring new front-end sheet metal, re-positioned headlamps (furtheroutboard), and a squared-off tail which gave a slightly larger boot. The doors and windscreen were unchanged from the Michelotti TRs. This was the time, too, when a more angular one-piece lift-off hardtop was introduced as an option.

Although North American and "Rest of the World" cars were very different

Triumph TR6, 1973 model.

SPECIFICATION

BODY STYLES: sports car

PRODUCTION: 94,619

ENGINE & TRANSMISSION: 2498cc, 6cyl ohv, 4sp man, or o/d, f/r

POWER: 104bhp @ 4500rpm/106bhp @ 4900rpm/124bhp @ 5000rpm/150bhp @ 5500rpm

MAX SPEED (MPH): (104bhp) 110-120

0-60MPH (SEC): 10.5-8.2

SUSPENSION & BRAKES: coil ifs, coil irs, disc f/drum r

LENGTH (IN)/WEIGHT (LB): 159/2473

LAUNCH PRICE: £1334

from each other, both carried "TR6" badges. In North America the 2498cc engine had twin Zenith-Stromberg carburettors, and about 105bhp at first (this varied slightly, year on year, as regulations changed), while Rest of the World cars retained Lucas fuel injection. Until late 1972 fuel-injected cars had 150bhp, thereafter being re-rated as 124bhp (DIN) though this was not as serious a drop as it seems.

Development changes included a cosmetic facelift, a revised fascia in 1972, a Stag-type gearbox in mid-1971, a different (J-Type) overdrive to coincide with the re-rated injection engine for 1973, no wire-spoke wheel option after mid-1973, and vast crash-resistant black bumper over-riders for 1975 model year North American cars. Even though the all-new TR7 appeared in January 1975, the TR6 carried on for another eighteen months, the last being produced in mid-1976. With nearly 100,000 built, the TR6 outsold all of its TR predecessors.

Softer in some ways than the TR5 had been, and better-equipped, the TR6 was really the last of Britain's hairy-chested sports cars. It remains a very popular choice today.

Herald 13/60 1967-71

The last major re-alignment in the Herald range came in October 1967 when the 13/60 (available as saloon, convertible or estate car) supplanted the 1200 and 12/50 type; as an entry-level model, however, the old 1200 would carry on for three more years.

The basic design – separate chassis, tight-turning steering, swing-axle rear suspension, lift-up front bodywork, and

The 1296cc Herald 13/60 convertible.

SPECIFICATION

BODY STYLES: saloon, drophead, estate

PRODUCTION: 82,652

ENGINE & TRANSMISSION: 1296cc, 4cyl ohv, 4sp man, f/r

POWER: 61bhp @ 5000rpm

MAX SPEED (MPH): 84

0-60MPH (SEC): 17.7

SUSPENSION & BRAKES: coil ifs, leaf irs, disc f/drum r

LENGTH (IN)/WEIGHT (LB): 153/1876

LAUNCH PRICE: £700

bolt-together body sections – was carried forward, the only important style change being a new nose with larger headlamps and a bonnet profile borrowed from the Vitesse.

The engine was enlarged to 1296cc, with a single Zenith-Stromberg carburettor and an eight-port cylinder head, giving 61bhp, so performance increased, and front-wheel disc brakes were made standard instead of optional. 13/60s all shared a better-equipped fascia, but the 12/50's fold-back sunshine roof was now optional. Inside the car, more rear seat legroom had been found by re-jigging cushion positions.

These were the last Heralds of all to be produced, the final saloon being built in December 1970, the other types five months later.

Vitesse 1600 1962-66

Only when the Vitesse appeared in mid-1962 did the ingenious Webster/Michelotti stratagem of providing an almost infinitely flexible combination of engines and body styles on one basic chassis frame become clear. The Vitesse name, incidentally, had been used on Triumphs in the 1930s.

The new Vitesse had a beefier chassis frame (the Herald would pick up the improvements too), and a more robust rear axle, and there was a 1596cc six-cylinder engine up front, with twin semi-downdraught Solex carburettors; this was a smaller derivative of the Standard Vanguard Six unit. The engine was mated to a close-ratio gearbox (still lacking synchromesh on first gear) with optional overdrive. This amounted to an intriguing combination, though the car could not quite reach 90mph.

SPECIFICATION

BODY STYLES: saloon, drophead

PRODUCTION: 31,278

ENGINE & TRANSMISSION: 1596cc, 6cyl ohv, 4sp man, or o/d, f/r

POWER: 70bhp @ 5000rpm

MAX SPEED (MPH): 89

0-60MPH (SEC): 17.6

SUSPENSION & BRAKES: coil ifs, leaf irs, disc f/drum r

LENGTH (IN)/WEIGHT (LB): 153/2004

LAUNCH PRICE: £839

Triumph Vitesse, 1962, with 1.6-litre six-cylinder engine.

Apart from having a four-headlamp nose in a modified front-end assembly, with duotone colour schemes on most cars, the bodies – saloon or convertible – looked just like those of contemporary Heralds. Front disc brakes were standard, but the rest of the chassis was like that of the Herald.

Development changes included a new fascia style with more instruments including a rev-counter in September 1963, and SU carburettors replacing the Solex units from mid-1965. This gave more power, but Triumph never told us how much ! Officially, no estate cars were ever built, but a few were created at Standard-Triumph's London service centre on Hanger Lane, in west London.

Faster and much smoother than the Herald, this Vitesse had all the same handling failings but sold very well. The 1600 was displaced by the 2-litre Vitesse in October 1966.

Vitesse 2 Litre Mk I/Mk II 1966-71

Although the original 2-litre Vitesse of October 1966 was a near-100mph car, it ran into media trouble because its handling was still tail-happy; the Mk II version, intoduced in October 1968, was a much more capable machine.

The original Vitesse 2-Litre (we called it Mk I after it had gone), shared many components with the new GT6 sports

SPECIFICATION

BODY STYLES: saloon, drophead

PRODUCTION: 19,952

ENGINE & TRANSMISSION: 1998cc, 6cyl ohv, 4sp man, or o/d, f/r

POWER: 95bhp @ 5000rpm/104bhp @ 5300rpm

MAX SPEED (MPH): 97/101

0-60MPH (SEC): 12.6/11.3

SUSPENSION & BRAKES: coil ifs, leaf irs, disc f/drum r

LENGTH (IN)/WEIGHT (LB): 153/2085

LAUNCH PRICE: £839/£951

Power was up to 95bhp in the Vitesse 2-litre. This is a Mk II of 1968.

coupé (described below), including the twin Zenith-Stromberg carburetted 95bhp 1998cc engine, and the all-synchromesh gearbox, often with the optional Laycock overdrive bolted on

to the rear. Larger front discs and wider-rim wheels were added to improve the chassis, though radial ply tyres were still only optional. Apart from using a TR4A-type steering wheel, the interior was just like that of the 1600.

Two years later the Mk II appeared. Like the Mk II version of the GT6 it had 104bhp and much-improved rear suspension, incorporating lower wishbones, which succeeded in curing the tuck-under tendency completely. To allow the fixed-length drive shafts to work properly, there was now a rubber-based Rotoflex joint in each of them – these do tend to perish, crack and eventually tear in old age.

Visual changes included a new grille, new brightwork across the boot lid, pseudo Rostyle wheel covers, and changes to the instrument panel layout.

The Mk II was more costly than the Mk I at £951 instead of £839 but thought well worth the extra, and the chassis's reputation was saved. The Vitesse was now a genuine 100mph car, and it sold strongly until the last of all was produced in May 1971.

Spitfire Mk 1/Mk 2 1962-65/1965-67

Triumph's pretty little Spitfire, which terrified BMC because it was better-equipped than the Midget, relied heavily on tuned-up Herald running gear. Even so, much of the rest was new, with a totally different 83in-wheelbase chassis frame, and a one-piece Michelotti-styled body in which the sills were much more robust, stress-bearing, members than before. As on the Herald, the entire front end hinged upwards from the front to give access to the engine and front suspension.

The pure backbone frame supported modified Herald front and rear suspension and steering. The engine was a twin-SU 63bhp 1147cc version of the Herald power unit, with the same gearbox and rear axle (though with a modified gearchange). Disc front brakes were standard.

Marketing plus-points were the wind-up windows, the larger (TR4-type) windscreen, the cabin, which had more space than its rivals, and an even tighter (24 foot!) turning circle than the Herald. From late 1963, Laycock overdrive, wire-spoke wheels and a lift-off steel hardtop all became optional. In March

Triumph Spitfire Mk 1, 1962, with 1147cc and 63bhp.

1965 Mk 1 became Mk 2, with 67bhp, and carpets instead of moulded rubber mats on the floor.

Although Triumph proved, in a successful race and rally programme, how strong the basic car was, they couldn't hide the poor handling of standard cars: over-steer due to rear swing-axle habits was always a problem.

These were appealing cars, both for their looks and for their character; they always outsold the Sprite/Midget opposition too. Early Spitfires, always prone to rust, are quite rare today.

SPECIFICATION

BODY STYLES: sports car

PRODUCTION: 45,753/37,409

ENGINE & TRANSMISSION: 1147cc, 4cyl ohv, 4sp man, or o/d, f/r

POWER: 63bhp @ 5750rpm/67bhp @ 6000rpm

MAX SPEED (MPH): 91/92

0-60MPH (SEC): 15.4/15.5

SUSPENSION & BRAKES: coil ifs, leaf irs, disc f/drum r

LENGTH (IN)/WEIGHT (LB): 145/1568

LAUNCH PRICE: £730/£700

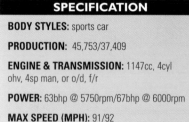

The team of works Spitfires, with fastback hardtops, on the 1965 Monte Carlo Rally.

Spitfire Mk 3 1967-70

In March 1967 the Spitfire became Mk 3, complete with more power (75bhp) and the revised "bone-in-the-teeth" front bumper position, though with no improvement on the somewhat difficult

The 1296cc Spitfire Mk 3 of 1967-70 had a raised front bumper.

SPECIFICATION

BODY STYLES: sports car

PRODUCTION: 65,320

ENGINE & TRANSMISSION: 1296cc, 4cyl ohv, 4sp man, or o/d, f/r

POWER: 75bhp @ 6000rpm

MAX SPEED (MPH): 95

0-60MPH (SEC): 14.5

SUSPENSION & BRAKES: coil ifs, leaf irs, disc f/drum r

LENGTH (IN)/WEIGHT (LB): 145/1652

LAUNCH PRICE: £717

handling characteristics of its forebears.

Bigger brakes, an eight-port cylinder head and a proper fold-away soft top all added to the equipment. With overdrive, and a bit of help from the wind, the Mk 3 could become a 100mph car – rather faster than the Midget of the day – and this showed up in the model's buoyant sales figures.

Until the 1500 came along in the mid-1970s, this car was the most desirable of the Spitfire family.

Spitfire Mk IV 1970-74

Big changes for the Spitfire arrived at the very end of 1970 – not only a comprehensive facelift of the body, but also a new and much more sanitary rear suspension. There was a change from English (Mk 3) to Latin (Mk IV) model notation; this move would be reversed in four years' time.

Michelotti's body style was much changed to provide a longer, flatter yet cut-off tail, and a re-skinned and neater bonnet with integrated front bumpers. Except for the doors, almost every exterior body panel was completely different. The optional hardtop now be came much more angular than before, with more volume and more glass. For the first time

there was a full-width fascia panel too.

There was Good News and Bad News under the skin. A new type of "swing-spring" rear suspension, and 4.5-inch wheel rims, eliminated all the old bad handling habits (no more vast camber changes, even in extremis), and a new all-synchromesh gearbox appeared (that would eventually be shared with other Triumphs and the MG Midget). On the other hand, and to meet encroaching exhaust emission rules in the USA, the engines were slightly less powerful than on the Mk 3.

From 1973, USA-market cars got 1493cc engines and different fascia styles, though neither of these would be

SPECIFICATION

BODY STYLES: sports car

PRODUCTION: 70,021

ENGINE & TRANSMISSION: 1296cc, 4cyl ohv, 4sp man, or o/d, f/r

POWER: 63bhp @ 6000rpm

MAX SPEED (MPH): 90

0-60MPH (SEC): 16.2

SUSPENSION & BRAKES: coil ifs, leaf irs, disc f/drum r

LENGTH (IN)/WEIGHT (LB): 149/1717

LAUNCH PRICE: £985

available at home until late 1974. At home, the car gained wider wheel tracks, a new front spoiler, a smaller steering wheel, a wood-panelled fascia, and other cosmetic improvements. The centre-lock wire-wheel option was dropped later in the year.

Once again, the sales figures tell their own story, for earlier Spitfire faults had mostly been eliminated; to Triumph's joy, too, the Austin-Healey Sprite had been abandoned. The Mk IV Spitfire would be replaced at the end of 1974 by the Spitfire 1500.

Revised styling for the 1970 Spitfire Mk IV.

Spitfire 1500 1974-80

The fifth, last, and longest-running of the Spitfire family was the 1500 model, which was introduced in October 1974 and finally discontinued in August 1980. Visually this car looked almost exactly like the previous Mk IV, though "1500" badges on the bonnet and boot lid gave the game away. Apart from frequent minor cosmetic updates, the 1500 looked much the same in 1980 as the Mk IV had done in 1970/71. The majority of cars were sold to the USA, where the engine specification was different, and where the

Spitfire 1500.

SPECIFICATION

BODY STYLES: sports car

PRODUCTION: 91,137

ENGINE & TRANSMISSION: 1493cc, 4cyl ohv, 4sp man, or o/d, f/r

POWER: 71bhp @ 5500rpm

MAX SPEED (MPH): 100

0-60MPH (SEC): 13.2

SUSPENSION & BRAKES : coil ifs, leaf irs, disc f/drum r

LENGTH (IN)/WEIGHT (LB): 149/1750

LAUNCH PRICE: £1360

bumpers were eventually lumbered with large, lumpy black over-riders to meet crash-test requirements.

The big mechanical change was the adoption of the biggest possible SC engine, which had been enlarged to 1493cc, its 71bhp giving the Spitfire the 100mph top speed it had deserved for so long. Except in small details, this engine and its associated single-rail gearbox were also used in the MG Midget 1500 of 1974-79, though the Midget never came with overdrive. Compared with the Mk IV, the gearbox selector mechanism was

new, and the final drive ratio (3.63:1) was the highest ever fitted to a Spitfire. Development changes over the years included fitment of TR7-type steering column switchgear from March 1977, and wider wheel rims for the 1979 and 1980 model years.

Although it was a significantly faster car than the Mk IV, the 1500 had a very similar character. Like the Mk IV, many 1500s were sold with the angular hardtop and overdrive options, these being fittings which have survived into modern times on many collectors' cars.

2000 Mk I 1963-69

Fifteen years after the Standard Vanguard went on sale, the Standard brand was dumped, and a new model, the Triumph 2000, replaced the Vanguard. The new car's engine was an up-rated version of the Vanguard Six power unit,

SPECIFICATION

BODY STYLES: saloon, estate

PRODUCTION: 115,242

ENGINE & TRANSMISSION: 1998cc, 6cyl ohv, 4sp man, o/d or auto, f/r

POWER: 90bhp @ 5000rpm

MAX SPEED (MPH): 93

0-60MPH (SEC): 14.1

SUSPENSION & BRAKES: coil ifs, coil irs, disc f/drum r

LENGTH (IN)/WEIGHT (LB): 174/2576

LAUNCH PRICE: £1094

Triumph 2000 Mk 1, competitor to the Rover P6 2000.

but everything else was fresh. It was a package which would remain on sale until 1977.

The basis was a 106in-wheelbase four-door monocoque structure (supplied by Pressed Steel), styled by Michelotti, with

a smart four-headlamp nose and a cut-off tail. McPherson strut front suspension, unassisted rack-and-pinion steering and coil spring semi-trailing link independent rear suspension were all new to Triumph – and would eventually be modified for use in the Stag sports car of the 1970s.

The 90bhp 1998cc engine, canted at a slight angle to provide more engine bay clearance, had twin Zenith-Stromberg carburettors. The all-synchromesh gearbox was related to that of the TR4, as was the optional overdrive. Borg Warner automatic transmission was an optional extra; deliveries began in 1964.

The interior trim and equipment were of a much superior grade to those of the Vanguard, with well padded seats (the fronts reclined and leather was an option), wood veneer on the fascia and door cappings, and good-looking carpets.

Plans to offer a 1600cc version of this car, incidentally, had been abandoned at a late stage.

A smart estate car (body by Carbodies) followed from late 1965, and from 1966 the range effectively became "Mk 1½", with an up-rated interior and a new instrument display (white numerals on black dials, instead of the black-on-white of the original).

This was always a very successful model (especially when joined by the fuel-injected version, described next), and was still selling fast when replaced by the Mk 2 in October 1969. It was brisk, smooth

and well-furnished, with a soft ride and good road-holding. Rust prevention, too, seemed to have improved, with the result that many 2000s lasted well into the final years of the 20th century.

The estate version of the 2000 came in 1965.

2.5PI Mk I 1968-69

Two events in 1967 seemed to make the launch of a fuel-injected Triumph saloon inevitable – one being the introduction of the TR5 sports car, the other being the appearance of prototypes on the (cancelled before the start) RAC rally. Both showed that the larger engine and its neat new manifolding would easily fit into the 2000's body.

The engine was a slightly de-tuned 132bhp version of the TR5's Lucas-injected 2498cc six-cylinder unit, backed by the usual three transmission option. There were actually few other mechanical changes, though as the road wheels had false "Rostyle" covers it looked as if the wheels were fresh.

Only the saloon as available at first, but an estate car version was added in March 1969; by the end only 223 of these had been built making them rare

The 132bhp Triumph 2500 PI Mk 1, 1968.

SPECIFICATION

BODY STYLES: saloon, estate

PRODUCTION: 6742

ENGINE & TRANSMISSION: 2498cc, 6cyl ohv, 4sp man, o/d or auto, f/r

POWER: 132bhp @ 5500rpm

MAX SPEED (MPH): 106

0-60MPH (SEC): 10.4

SUSPENSION & BRAKES: coil ifs, coil irs, disc f/drum r

LENGTH (IN)/WEIGHT (LB): 174/2632

LAUNCH PRICE: £1450

and desirable today. The 2500 PI was by no means as fuel-efficient as Triumph had hoped, but it was a fast and capable car. Only the high selling prices, and the inability of Lucas to supply more injection systems, held sales back.

Because these cars only had a one-year career they were relatively rare, and in later years most of them disappeared. The fact that some fuel-injected cars suffered unexplained engine bay fires didn't help. Like the carburetted cars, they were replaced by the facelifted Mk 2s in October 1969.

Paddy Hopkirk in a works 2.5 PI Mk 1 on the 1969 RAC Rally, where the three-car team took first, second and third in class.

2000 Mk 2 1969-77

The Mk 2 was a clever facelift of the original range, effected without disturbing the main platform or the cabin. All cars had a lengthened nose with a full-width grille which embraced the four headlamps, while saloons also had a lengthened tail; estate cars retained the original sheet metal structure at the rear.

Running gear was initially much as

Triumph 2000 Mk 2 was introduced in 1969.

before, though the quoted power was now DIN-rated and the latest "full-width" cylinder head, previously fitted only to injected engines, was standard. A larger brake servo and wider-rim wheels made up the principal chassis changes.

The big up-date was to the interior, where a very smart full-width wood-veneered dashboard replaced the old type. As before, there was a saloon and an estate car, with manual, overdrive, or automatic transmission all available.

Changes over the years would be limited. In May 1974 an additional (2000TC) "interim" model would appear, and from 1975 the power would increased to 91bhp, at which point the model name changed to 2000TC; the last saloons had optional power-assisted steering.

Estate cars were discontinued in 1975 but production of the saloon carried on until mid-1977. The 2000 was a fine car, which fully deserved its long and successful career.

SPECIFICATION

BODY STYLES: saloon, estate

PRODUCTION: 104,580

ENGINE & TRANSMISSION: 1998cc, 6cyl ohv, 4sp man, o/d or auto, f/r

POWER: 84bhp @ 5000rpm/91bhp @ 4750rpm

MAX SPEED (MPH): 96

0-60MPH (SEC): 14.9

SUSPENSION & BRAKES: coil ifs, coil irs, disc f/drum r

LENGTH (IN)/WEIGHT (LB): 182/2620

LAUNCH PRICE: £1412

2.5PI Mk 2 1969-75

Like the 2000, the fuel-injected 2.5 PI became Mk 2 in October 1969, with a facelifted body covering a largely unchanged platform, chassis and running gear. In particular, the 132bhp 2498cc engine was not altered, nor were the three transmission options or the choice of saloon and estate car bodies. The fascia was like

The 2.5 PI Mk 2, 1969.

that of the latest 2000, though a rev-counter was now standard. Trim, seating and car-peting were to a higher standard than on the 2000, which seemed to justify the higher pricing.

Power-assisted rack-and-pinion steering was now optional (and increasingly chosen), and overdrive would become

standard from late 1972, but few other changes were ever made. Due to the imminent launch of the 2500S (a carburetted version of the same car, see entry below)) the last PI saloon was built in May 1974, and the last estate car followed a year later. Like the Mk 1 PI, this was a fast, capable car.

SPECIFICATION

BODY STYLES: saloon, estate

PRODUCTION: 49,742

ENGINE & TRANSMISSION: 2498cc, 6cyl ohv, 4sp man, o/d or auto, f/r

POWER: 132bhp @ 5500rpm

MAX SPEED (MPH): 106

0-60MPH (SEC): 11.5

SUSPENSION & BRAKES: coil ifs, coil irs, disc f/drum r

LENGTH (IN)/WEIGHT (LB): 182/2760

LAUNCH PRICE: £1595

1300/1300TC/1500 1965-70/1970-73

Triumph's one and only front wheel drive car appeared in 1965. Based on a completely new four-door monocoque body, it had an four-cylinder Herald-based engine, with a four-speed transmission under/behind the engine. It was aimed at a very different market than the BMC 1100 range, and had a much higher standard of trim, instrumentation and equipment.

The engine/transmission assembly sat quite high in the chassis and there were Rotoflex inner joints on the drive shafts to the front wheels. The rest of the running gear was conventional enough, with coil spring and wishbone front suspension (the spring damper units were atop the upper wishbone), a coil spring and semi-trailing arm rear end, and front disc brakes.

This, in fact, was the first Triumph to use the 1296cc eight-port cylinder head package, rated at 61bhp. The new gearbox was all-synchromesh. No overdrive or automatic transmission options were available.

Although the seat coverings were in

The 1965 front wheel drive Triumph 1300.

plastic, there was much carpet and wood veneer in view, including a full-width veneered fascia. When *Autocar* magazine tested this car, they summarised it as "the best small car currently available".

In September 1967 Triumph added the 1300TC, which had a Spitfire-tune 75bhp engine and servo-assisted brakes, but both cars gave way to the 1500 model in August 1970. This car used the same basic platform and four-door body but had a four-headlamp nose and a single-carburettor 1493cc 61bhp version of the engine; a year later power was pushed up to 65bhp. Servo brakes were standard, but on the 1500 there was a simple "dead" rear axle in place of the independent rear end of the 1300. This series finally disappeared in October 1973 when the identical looking but very different rear wheel drive 1500TC took over.

All these cars had rather soft suspension but were endowed with very good front wheel drive handling. Although never exciting to drive, they

The 1300TC, introduced in 1967, could do 90mph.

Triumph 1500, 1970-73.

sold very well, and it was only boredom and neglect which caused many to fade away.

SPECIFICATION

BODY STYLES: saloon

PRODUCTION: 148,350/66,353

ENGINE & TRANSMISSION: 1296cc/1493cc, 4cyl ohv, 4sp man, f/f

POWER: 61bhp @ 5000rpm/75bhp @ 6000rpm/61bhp @ 5000rpm/65bhp @ 5000rpm

MAX SPEED (MPH): 84/93/85

0-60MPH (SEC): 19.0/15.9/17.1

SUSPENSION & BRAKES : coil ifs, coil irs (coil rear on 1500), disc f/drum r

LENGTH (IN)/WEIGHT (LB): 155/2016 - 2128

LAUNCH PRICE: £797/£874/£1113

1500TC 1973-76

In the early 1970s Triumph gradually shed the front wheel drive configuration first seen on the 1300 in 1965. In October 1973, therefore, the rear wheel drive 1500TC took over from the front wheel drive 1500,

though visually there was nothing except badging to make this clear.

Under the skin, the basic layout of the engine, driveline, rear axle and suspension was now exactly the same as that of the Toledo, though in 64bhp

1493cc form, the style being the four-door, four-headlamp, long-tail version of the well-established monocoque body. One important advance was that an automatic transmission could be made available (it had never been possible, of course, with the front wheel drive layout). In the spring of 1975 the engine was up-rated to 71bhp, this being near-identical with the contemporary Spitfire power unit.

Carrying forward the high-quality trim and furnishings of the 1500, which included a wooden fascia and door cappings, in marketing terms this car was above the Toledo and below the Dolomite 1850, sharing most of their handling and road behaviour habits. The 1500TC had a short career, for in early 1976 both it and the Toledo were re-vamped and re-named Dolomites.

SPECIFICATION

BODY STYLES: saloon

PRODUCTION: 25,549

ENGINE & TRANSMISSION: 1493cc, 4cyl ohv, 4sp man, or auto, f/r

POWER: 64bhp @ 5000rpm/71bhp @ 5500rpm

MAX SPEED (MPH): 91/91

0-60MPH (SEC): 13.2/not measured

SUSPENSION & BRAKES: coil ifs, coil rear, disc f/drum r

LENGTH (IN)/WEIGHT (LB): 162/2061

LAUNCH PRICE: £1295

Triumph 1500TC, 1973, had conventional rear-wheel drive.

GT6 Mk I 1966-68

Because of the separate chassis layout used, Triumph could employ a mix-and-match philosophy to all their Herald, Vitesse, Spitfire and, from 1966, GT6 models. In effect, therefore, the GT6 could be described as a Spitfire chassis and basic body, but with a Vitesse 2-litre engine and transmission, and a fastback hatchback style. Sometimes described as a "miniature E-Type", it was stylish, smooth and fast, though rather let down by the usual Herald/Vitesse handling problems.

Like the contemporary Vitesse 2-litre models, the original cars had a 95bhp

Triumph GT6 Mk 1, 1966.

SPECIFICATION

BODY STYLES: sports coupé

PRODUCTION: 15,818

ENGINE & TRANSMISSION: 1998cc, 6cyl ohv, 4sp man, or o/d, f/r

POWER: 95bhp @ 5000rpm

MAX SPEED (MPH): 106

0-60MPH (SEC): 12.0

SUSPENSION & BRAKES: coil ifs, leaf irs, disc f/drum r

LENGTH (IN)/WEIGHT (LB): 145/1904

LAUNCH PRICE: £985

1998cc engine, a new all-synchromesh gearbox, and optional overdrive (but no automatic option). The chassis and suspension were much the same as the contemporary Spitfire's (centre-lock wire wheels were optional extras), but felt softer, with serious understeer at lower speeds, then flick oversteer (very discon-certing) as cornering forces built up.

This was strictly a two-seater, not a 2+2. The interior was snug – cramped, even – and was well-equipped, with a full-width wooden fascia and special squashy seats. Like the E-Type, the GT6 had an enormous rear window which also doubled as a hatchback, opening upwards when required.

Because this was a 106mph car it almost qualified as being "too fast for chassis", though the Americans, who bought most of them, didn't seem to care. Triumph, however, reacted as soon as customers' feelings about the handling characteristics were known – and the Mk 2 of 1968 would be a much better car.

GT6 Mk 2/Mk 3 1968-73

Only two years after the GT6 Mk 1 went on sale, the Mk 2 model took over in October 1968. As well as having more power than before – 104bhp instead of 95bhp – the chassis was much improved, and the car's handling was quite transformed.

Like the contemporaneous Vitesse 2-litre Mk II (already described), the latest GT6 used a little-changed chassis frame, but had a different type of rear suspension, with reversed-wishbone geometry, this time controlled by telescopic rear dampers. The new suspension greatly reduced rear-wheel camber change and killed off the previous model's on-the-limit oversteer.

The new car inherited the Spitfire Mk 3's "bone-in-the-teeth" front end, but otherwise the styling was not changed, though inside the cabin there was now a matt finish on the wood fascia instead of the gloss finish on the Mk 1 fascia. There were face-level fresh air vents and

GT6 Mk 2, 1968, had improved rear suspension.

a padded-spoke steering wheel. The then-fashionable dummy Rostyle wheel covers were fitted, and centre-lock wires were still optional.

Motor magazine thought this one was "much improved", and the Americans (who got it badged as the "GT6 +") were equally impressed.

Two years later, in November 1970, the Mk 3 version took over, with all the same re-style features as the Spitfire Mk IV, namely the squared-off tail, re-skinned nose and integrated front bumper, There were no major chassis changes, but through-flow ventilation in the cabin, and an alloy-spoked steering wheel, all helped, along with different road wheels (no more sham Rostyles!). When fitted, the overdrive was controlled by a slide switch in the top of the gear-lever knob, which was a British motor industry "first".

The top speed was now up to 112mph

(so the aerodynamic shape must have been better ....), and the handling didn't suffer in 1973 when the Spitfire-type "swing-spring" rear suspension took over. Production ran out at the end of 1973 when Triumph rationalised its sales to the USA.

Predictably enough, the Mk 3s were the best of all the GT6s – not only because they were fastest, but because they handled best and had the best ventilation and packaging in the cabin. Well thought of in later years, these cars collected a following, which has persisted.

GT6 Mk 3, 1970-73

SPECIFICATION

BODY STYLES: sports coupé

PRODUCTION: 12,066/13,042 – of which 4218 with final rear suspension

ENGINE & TRANSMISSION: 1998cc, 6cyl ohv, 4sp man, or o/d, f/r

POWER: 104bhp @ 5300rpm

MAX SPEED (MPH): 112

0-60MPH (SEC): 10.1

SUSPENSION & BRAKES: coil ifs, leaf irs, disc f/drum r

LENGTH (IN)/WEIGHT (LB): 145 – 149/2030

LAUNCH PRICE: £1125/£1287

Toledo 1970-76

Triumph's intended replacement for the long-running Herald was the Toledo of 1970. Apart from the engine and gearbox there were no links between the two cars. However, there were very strong links with the 1300 and 1300TC, which were just coming to the end of their lives. This car, incidentally, was the first and only Triumph family car to be

totally assembled at the labour-torn factory at Speke, near Liverpool.

While the 1300 had had front-wheel drive, the Toledo had a rear wheel drive layout. It used a modified version of the 1300 body shell, but with a different floorpan, nose, and a two-door style at first (four-doors would follow).

Sounds complicated, for sure, but

Triumph somehow pulled it off, later donating the much-modified platform to 1500TC, Dolomite and Dolomite Sprint types too.

The original Michelotti profile and proportions were maintained, along with the cut-off tail, but most other details were different, and the interior specification was much simplified.

For the Toledo the 1296cc engine was in 58bhp tune, very similar to the old FWD 1300 engine. A 1493cc 65bhp version later went into some export models. The corporate all-synchromesh four-speed gearbox was fitted, though there were only drum brakes all round (unless you paid for the disc brake option), and a simple beam rear axle suspended on coil springs.

Changes followed: the four-door saloon option arrived in autumn 1971, disc brakes were standardised in autumn 1972, and the two-door saloon was dropped in March 1975. From that point, every car got reclining front seats and enhanced equipment, but in March 1976 the Toledo died away, to be replaced by a similar car known as the Dolomite 1300.

At one time we would have classed the Toledo as "grey porridge", for it was a boring car which did nothing outstandingly well, though it had no major vices either. Triumph sold loads because they were well-equipped, presentable, and appealed to customers who wanted something with a bit more class than a Ford. But pundits always preferred the front wheel drive cars.

The Triumph Toledo enjoyed healthy sales.

BODY STYLES: saloon

PRODUCTION: 119,182

ENGINE & TRANSMISSION: 1296cc/1493cc, 4cyl ohv, 4sp man, f/r

POWER: 58bhp @ 5300rpm/65bhp @ 5000rpm

MAX SPEED (MPH): 85/88 (E)

0-60MPH (SEC): 17.1/not measured

SUSPENSION & BRAKES: coil ifs, coil rear, drums f&r (disc f/drum rear from late 1972)

LENGTH (IN)/WEIGHT (LB): 157/1905

LAUNCH PRICE : £889

Stag | 1970-77

If only the now well-known engine problems had been sorted out before the Stag was launched, it would certainly have sold better and kept its reputation. In truth, the problems were sorted out by the mid-1970s, but the "give-a-dog-a-bad-name" syndrome persisted.

The Stag was based on a shortened version of the 2000's platform. It shared the same front suspension, steering (though power-assistance was standard), rear suspension, gearbox, rear axle,

The handsome 1970 Triumph Stag. The T-bar gave extra rigidity.

SPECIFICATION

BODY STYLES: sports car

PRODUCTION: 25,939

ENGINE & TRANSMISSION: 2997cc, V8cyl ohc, 4sp man, or o/d or auto, f/r

POWER: 145bhp @ 5500rpm

MAX SPEED (MPH): 117

0-60MPH (SEC): 9.7

SUSPENSION & BRAKES: coil ifs, coil irs, disc f/drum r

LENGTH (IN)/WEIGHT (LB): 174/2807

LAUNCH PRICE: £1996

brakes (larger) and general proportions, though the Stag's wheelbase was 100in instead of 106in. It carried a very smart two-door 2+2 sports drophead body, the front and rear ends of which were almost identical with those of the 2000 and 2.5PI Mk II models.

Sold either as a convertible with fold-back soft-top or as a coupé with a massive (and heavy!) lift-off hardtop, which was fully glazed, it had wind-up windows in

the doors, and the cabin was trimmed up to and beyond the 2000 Mk II's level. Disc wheels were standard at first, with optional wires, though cast alloy wheels would become available from 1973; they would be standard from 1976.

Under the bonnet was a new 2997cc 90-degree V8, with a single overhead camshaft on each aluminium cylinder head and an iron block. Elements of this engine were already being used in a four-cylinder unit being supplied to Saab for its 99 model and being readied for the Dolomite 1850 of 1972. Backing this was a beefed-up TR6 gearbox, with or without overdrive, and Borg Warner automatic transmission was optional.

The Stag was smooth, fast (120mph in overdrive form), and endowed with good handling, but it was badly let down from the start by recurring cooling problems and cylinder head gasket failures. It took ages to sort out the problems, but by then the car had been withdrawn from the USA, and sales dropped: although 5500 cars had been built in 1973, less than 5,000 cars were produced in the last two years. Assembly finally ended in June 1977.

The Stag's look were not spoilt by the heavy, lift-off hardtop.

Dolomite 1850 1972-80

It was sometimes difficult to get one's head round what Triumph was doing in the early 1970s. Although the Dolomite 1850 looked like the 1500 of the period (it shared the same four-door shell, the four-headlamp nose, though with a different grille, and the same long tail), it had rear-wheel instead of front-wheel drive, and the engine was a new overhead-cam four-cylinder which was related to the Stag V8 !

Like other cars built on this much-developed platform, the 1850 had a 96.6in wheelbase and used basically the same coil spring front and rear suspension layout as the Toledo. Its 91bhp

Dolomite 1850.

SPECIFICATION
BODY STYLES: saloon
PRODUCTION: 79,010
ENGINE & TRANSMISSION: 1854cc, 4cyl ohc, 4sp man, o/d or auto, f/r
POWER: 91bhp @ 5200rpm
MAX SPEED (MPH): 100
0-60MPH (SEC): 11.6
SUSPENSION & BRAKES: coil ifs, leaf rear, disc f/drum r
LENGTH (IN)/WEIGHT (LB): 162/2127
LAUNCH PRICE: £1399

engine drove through a close-ratio gearbox which was closely related to the GT6, Spitfire and Morris Marina unit. Overdrive and automatic transmission were both optional extras.

The engine itself (already being supplied to Saab for use in the 99), would soon, in enlarged form, go into the Triumph TR7: product planning within British Leyland was very complex at this time.

With an interior rather like that of the latest 2000s – an alloy-spoked steering wheel, generous instrumentation and satin-finish wood on the fascia and door cappings – this was an appealing little sports saloon. It was in production for eight years and there were few major development changes, so the 1850 ended its career looking the same as in 1972, though it became the 1850HL in March 1976, with tinted glass as standard. The last car was produced in November 1980.

Although it featured a 100mph top speed and good handling, there were some early engine problems (overheating and gasket failures) which took time to resolve. The Dolomite Sprint was a further development of this design.

Dolomite Sprint 1973-80

Yet another variation on a theme: to get a handle on it, think of a Dolomite 1850 but with a different engine – and a lot more performance, for the Dolomite Sprint was the fastest of all the derivatives of this long-running design. Annnounced in July 1973, it had an enlarged and complex-looking 16-valve version of the 1850's engine, and this unit proved to be reliable and (in motorsport) formidably tuneable. The capacity was 1998cc and power output a creditable 127bhp. It was linked to the sturdy TR6-type gearbox (a larger 'box than the 1850 unit), with optional overdrive or optional automatic transmission. Almost all the early cars were painted in the same shade of yellow.

With a genuine top speed of 115mph in standard form, and with good handling, the Dolomite Sprint was a very successful sports saloon which, incidentally, easily outsold the more glamorous 16-valve "sports saloons" from Ford and Vauxhall! The style was almost identical with that of the contemporary Dolomite 1850, as were the interior trim and furnishings.

Few important development changes were made – or needed – in this car's seven-year life. On manual gearbox cars, overdrive was standardised from

May 1975, as was tinted glass all round. Like the Dolomite 1850, the last of these cars rolled off the production line in November 1980.

The 16-valve Dolomite Sprint, 1973, had 127bhp and alloy wheels.

SPECIFICATION

BODY STYLES: saloon

PRODUCTION: 22,941

ENGINE & TRANSMISSION: 1998cc, 4cyl ohc, 4sp man, o/d or auto, f/r

POWER: 127bhp @ 5700rpm

MAX SPEED (MPH): 115

0-60MPH (SEC): 8.7

SUSPENSION & BRAKES: coil ifs, coil rear, disc f/drum r

LENGTH (IN)/WEIGHT (LB): 162/2214

LAUNCH PRICE: £1740

Dolomite 1300/1500 1976-80

In March 1976 Triumph rationalised the complex Toledo, 1500TC, Dolomite and Dolomite Sprint range. All cars shared the same basic four-door saloon body with the longer of the tails.

The old short-tail Toledo was dropped in favour of a new Dolomite 1300. This car retained the original two-rectangular-headlamp grille style, and the 1296cc engine of the Toledo.

The old 1500TC was dropped in favour of a new Dolomite 1500, there also being a 1500HL version. This car always had the four-circular-headlamp nose style.

The Dolomite 1850 became the 1850HL (this has already been described).

The Dolomite Sprint carried on virtually unchanged, though a laminated windscreen was standard.

The new Dolomite 1300 was a better car than the old Toledo, for it now had pile carpets, wider-rim wheels and a front anti-roll bar, plus a larger boot, larger fuel tank and a better-equipped dashboard. It was and would remain the entry-level car in this range.

The Dolomite 1500 was better than the old 1500TC in that it was fitted with Dolomite-type suspension and (for the first time) optional overdrive, but it retained a two-rectangular-headlamp nose.

Dolomite 1500SE, 1979.

The new Dolomite 1500HL was really a halfway house towards the Dolomite 1850, with the same running gear as the 1500 but the 1850s four-headlamp nose, trim, equipment and instrumentation. In early 1976, customers had to pay an extra £235 for that package, and many of them chose to do so.

The Dolomite 1300s and 1500s then carried on, virtually unchanged, for more than four years, running out of production in November 1980, when all assembly at the Canley plant finally closed down.

SPECIFICATION

BODY STYLES: saloon

PRODUCTION: 32,031/43,235

ENGINE & TRANSMISSION: 1296/1493cc, 4cyl ohv, 4sp man, or auto, f/r

POWER: 58bhp @ 5300rpm/71bhp @ 5500rpm

MAX SPEED (MPH): 83/91

0-60MPH (SEC): 20.1/14.2

SUSPENSION & BRAKES: coil ifs, coil rear, disc f/drum r

LENGTH (IN)/WEIGHT (LB): 162/2079-2161

LAUNCH PRICE: £2070/£2205/(1500HL) £2441

2500TC/2500S 1974-77/1975-77

In 1974 and 1975, Triumph extended the life of the big Mk 2 saloons and estate cars. With the fuel-injected 2.5 PI soon due to be dropped (there had been continual trouble with the Lucas fuel injection, and it was also too costly) two mechanically different cars eventually took its place. The 2500TC appeared in May 1974 (while the 2.5PI was still on the market), the 2500S following in May 1975 as a replacement for the PI.

Except for badging and a few trim details, these cars were virtually indistinguishable from the PIs.

The 2500TC was effectively a 2498cc-engined derivative of the 2000, fitted with two SU carburettors and producing 99bhp. The final drive ratio

Triumph 2500TC, 1974. Twin carburettors replaced the 2.5 PI's injection system.

SPECIFICATION

BODY STYLES: saloon, estate

PRODUCTION: 32,492/8164

ENGINE & TRANSMISSION: 2498cc, 6cyl ohv, 4sp man, o/d or auto, f/r

POWER: 99bhp @ 4750rpm/106bhp @ 4700rpm

MAX SPEED (MPH): 104/105

0-60MPH (SEC): 11.8/10.4

SUSPENSION & BRAKES: coil ifs, coil irs, disc f/drum r

LENGTH (IN)/WEIGHT (LB): 182/2609-2760

LAUNCH PRICE: £2166/£3271

was raised to 3.45:1, and overdrive was standard.

The 2500S of 1975 also used a carburetted 2498cc engine, but was fitted with larger SUs and produced 106bhp; overdrive was standard. At the same time, 14in Stag-style cast alloy road wheels were standardised, as was power-assisted steering. For the first time under this body a front anti-roll bar was fitted, this also fitted to the 2500TC from that moment.

As you might expect, these two models were the nicest, best-handling and best-balanced of all the range, but they arrived when their effective replacement

2500S, 1975, with 106bhp and Stag-style alloy wheels.

models (the Rover 2300 and Rover 2600) were well on the way to being introduced, so they were not in production for long. The last of these cars, therefore, were built in May 1977.

TR7 1975-81

Developed to meet the requested specification of Triumph's North American workforce, the TR7 went on sale there in January 1975 but not in the UK until May 1976. It became the best-selling of all Triumph TRs, but for five years it struggled against labour relations crises, criticisms of its styling, and two moves of final assembly plant.

It had no connection with any previous TR, for every part – mechanical, body and trim – was different. It was built on an 85in-wheelbase platform, and was originally sold as a two-seater fixed-head coupé; the convertible, held back because of doubts over USA legislation,

Triumph TR7 fixed-head coupé.

did not appear until early 1979, but the drop-top car became the better seller.

The style, which came from BL's studios at Longbridge, had a wedge nose with pop-up headlamps, and early cars seemed to have a tail-high attitude. The underpinnings were conventional, with MacPherson strut front suspension, rack-and-pinion steering, and a beam rear axle suspended on coil springs with trailing and semi-trailing links for location. The 1998cc overhead-cam engine was an enlarged version of the one fitted to the Dolomite 1850, and on early cars the gearbox was the four-speeder used in the Dolomite 1850 and the Spitfire 1500. USA cars had only 92bhp, UK-market cars 105bhp.

Development changes were often held up by supply and labour relations problems. It was also no help that the cars were built at Speke until early 1978, at Coventry from late 1978 to mid-1980, and at Rover's Solihull factory from 1980 to late 1981.

A five-speed gearbox was optionally available from late 1976 (but soon withdrawn), as was Borg Warner automatic. The five-speed option came back at the end of 1977, and from late 1978 all Coventry-built cars had five-speed gearboxes, the four-speed 'box being dropped; all these types had a more robust rear axle than the original.

The TR7 falls easily into the "give a dog a bad name" category, for the later convertibles, riding lower at the rear, with five-speed 'boxes and the better build quality of the Solihull-erected models, were considerably better cars than the original Speke-built variety.

Fast but mechanically simple, the TR7 handled well and fitted its market better than the old TR6 had ever done. The sales figures – more than 112,000 in five years – bear that out.

A 'homologation special' TR7 V8 driven by Tony Pond on the 1980 Manx Stages Rally.

SPECIFICATION

BODY STYLES: sports coupé, sports car

PRODUCTION: 112,368

ENGINE & TRANSMISSION: 1998cc, 4cyl ohc, 4sp man, 5sp man, or auto, f/r

POWER: 105bhp @ 5500rpm

MAX SPEED (MPH): 109

0-60MPH (SEC): 9.1

SUSPENSION & BRAKES: coil ifs, coil beam rear, disc f/drum r

LENGTH (IN)/WEIGHT (LB): 160/2205

LAUNCH PRICE: £3000

The convertible TR7 did not arrive until 1979.

TR8 1979-81

The TR8 was never officially sold in the UK but was built exclusively for sale in North America (the USA and Canada) between 1979 and 1981. UK sales were originally planned, but a series of strikes, and British Leyland's deteriorating financial position, caused the entire TR7/TR8 programme to be cancelled before UK-market TR8s could go on sale.

A limited number of fixed-head coupé TR8s were produced in 1978 and 1979, but the TR8 was officially only sold in convertible form. Visually there was

The TR8. A few right hand drive examples were built, like this one.

virtually no way of picking a US-market TR8 from a USA-market TR7 – only the twin exhaust tail pipes and the badging giving the game away.

It was powered by a de-toxed version of the Rover V8 engine. 1980 models had 133bhp with carburettors and 137bhp with fuel injection, while all 1981 models used fuel injection. It had the same five-speed gearbox and "medium duty" rear axle as the later-model TR7, and Borg Warner automatic transmission was optional. Air conditioning was also available, and power-assisted steering was standard.

Unhappily for British Leyland, the TR8 had to struggle against the effects of the second energy crisis and the oil price rises which followed, against British price inflation pressures, and against the TR7's still doubtful quality reputation in the USA. Even though this was a very fast sports car, with good roadholding and light steering, it sold very slowly indeed. Along with the TR7, the last TR8 was produced in October 1981.

This were to be no more Triumph TR sports cars.

TURNER

Jack Turner was a Wolverhampton-based enthusiast, racer and engineer who produced an unsuccessful four-cylinder 500cc Formula Three engine before designing a simple little two-seater sports car which sold slowly, but steadily, from 1955 to 1966. Like most such enterprises of the time, the Turner sports car relied on a steel tubular chassis, GRP (glass-fibre) bodywork, and proprietary engines, for Turner had neither the resources nor the premises to be any more ambitious than that.

His mistake, perhaps, was to go further up-market with the

GT model of 1961, for although this looked smart and modern, it had crept up to the MGA/MGB market sector, and struggled to find any buyers.

Though most UK-market Turners were sold as kits (which means that there is really no such thing as a "standard" car), the majority of these cars were exported as completely built-up machines. By the mid-1960s Turner's market had virtually disappeared, and since the GT was a commercial failure, and his own health was not what it had been, Jack Turner closed down the business.

803cc/948cc Sports 1955-57/1957-59

The original Turner two-seater was a simple little machine, built up around a sturdy tubular chassis – with parallel main tubular members and outriggers under the sills, and substantial sub-structures to carry the front

Turner 950 Sports.

and rear suspension. For the first two years, much of the running gear was from the Austin A30 803cc chassis, which explains the hydro-mechanical brakes and the wishbone front suspension, yet the performance was almost on a par with the Austin-Healey Sprite, which was still in the future.

These cars had clever coil spring and trailing arm suspension of the A-Series rear axle (some cars had transverse torsion bars), with a Panhard rod for transverse location. The simple two-seater body, in glass-fibre, was light and barchetta-like, with an AC Ace-like grille shape, and the cockpit was small. There were lift-off sidescreens.

Once the Austin A30 became the A35, the Turner was up-dated and given the

948cc engine, better gear ratios, full hydraulic brakes, and a modified body with rear fins. It was an appealing though quite expensive machine, let down by its too basic trim and fittings.

Some were fitted with Coventry Climax engines (see the Turner-Climax entry below). Cars could be sold as kits or fully built-up. Quite a number were exported, to North America.

Mk I Sports 1959-60

What Turner called the Mk I sports was, illogically, not the company's first sports car design, but the first one to combine the latest rolling chassis of the earlier car with a revised body shell, a

Turner Mk I Sports, 1959.

slightly longer wheelbase, more cockpit space, and a revised front end style.

The wheelbase was quoted at one inch longer than before, but the overall length (138in) was not changed, and this time the rear suspension always seems to have used coil-over-shocks as the springing medium.

The cockpit was now three inches longer and five inches wider, which seemed to make all the difference, and now there was a full-width (almost TR3A-type) grille, and no rear fins. Many options were available, including wire spoke wheels.

SPECIFICATION

BODY STYLES: sports car

PRODUCTION: c.160 including Climax-engined cars

ENGINE & TRANSMISSION: 948cc, 4cyl ohv, 4sp man, f/r

POWER: 34bhp @ 4750rpm/43bhp @ 5000rpm

MAX SPEED (MPH): up to 90mph

0-60MPH (SEC): not measured

SUSPENSION & BRAKES: coil ifs, coil beam rear, drums f&r (optional disc f/drum r)

LENGTH (IN)/WEIGHT (LB): 138/1288

LAUNCH PRICE : £840, built up

Mk II/MK III Sports 1960-63/1963-66

Yet more variations on the theme, this time by combining the latest Mk I style (wide-mouth grille, no rear fins) with one or other of Ford's new breed of oversquare four-cylinder engines. Anglia, Classic and Cortina GT power units, with appropriate gearboxes, were fitted over the years, though the chassis and basic suspension layout of the car were not changed. Like many other limited-

SPECIFICATION

BODY STYLES: sports car

PRODUCTION: c.150/c.90, including Climax-engined cars

ENGINE & TRANSMISSION: 997cc/1340cc/1498cc, 4cyl ohv, 4sp man, f/r

POWER: 45bhp @ 5000rpm/61bhp @ 4900rpm/78bhp @ 5200rpm

MAX SPEED (MPH): 95-100mph

0-60MPH (SEC): not measured

SUSPENSION & BRAKES: coil ifs, coil beam rear, disc f/drum r

LENGTH (IN)/WEIGHT (LB): 138/1288

LAUNCH PRICE: £878, complete, with 997cc engine

The Turner Mk II Sports.

production cars of the period, these Turners used Triumph Herald front suspension and steering.

Mk II turned into Mk III in 1963, the obvious difference being to add a large scoop in the bonnet moulding – this being needed to help keep the more powerful engines cool.

The 1498cc-engined Mk III was the last Turner to be sold, in 1966, as the GT (see below) had already dropped out of production by then).

The Mk III Sports had a large scoop moulded into the bonnet.

Turner-Climax 1959-66

Once Turner had proven its rigid tubular chassis, it always offered the serious club-racer the chance of buying a Coventry-Climax-engined version of the car. Structurally and visually there were no changes, except that these cars were usually supplied with centre-lock wire-spoke wheels.

In "standard" form (which means the

Turner-Climax.

least powerful, least specialised type) the engine gave 75bhp, and was matched to a BMC A-Series gearbox including close-ratio gears; there was a wide choice of final drive ratios too.

Production was always very limited, but most of these cars had the Mk I/II/III body style, complete with the larger more spacious cockpit, and the

full-width grille style. Front wheel discs were standard equipment and some cars used the laminated torsion bar type of rear suspension.

Such Turners were built for function, not refinement, and did not bear their age gracefully. A few have been preserved, mainly for use in historic motorsport.

SPECIFICATION

BODY STYLES: sports car

PRODUCTION: included in other Turner totals

ENGINE & TRANSMISSION: 1098cc/1216cc, 4cyl ohc, 4sp man, f/r

POWER: 75bhp @ 6000rpm (more power to special order)

MAX SPEED (MPH): 99

0-60MPH (SEC): 12.8

SUSPENSION & BRAKES: coil ifs, tor beam rear, disc f/drum r

LENGTH (IN)/WEIGHT (LB): 138/1372

LAUNCH PRICE: special order

GT 1962-65

The Turner GT was first shown at the Racing Car Show in January 1962. Totally different from the original open-top model, it was also rather larger – 154in long instead of 138in – with a brand new chassis and a smoothly-styled two-seater closed coupé body. Pre-dating the MGB by almost a year, the new car also had the semi-recessed headlamps which were so fashionable at the time.

As you would expect in a Turner, the GT had a tubular chassis frame, using square-section tubes, though extra steel fabrications were welded to this to make a very solid platform. The GRP body shell was then moulded to this structure on assembly, the result was a very sturdy monocoque. Front suspension and steering were lifted from the Triumph Herald/Vitesse, and BMC provided the A-Series rear axle, as fitted to the earlier types.

The car was originally released with a

tuned-up Ford 109E (Classic) three-main-bearing 1340cc engine, mated to the latest all-synchromesh Ford gearbox. At the time Turner suggested that they could also supply cars with the Lotus Elite's Coventry-Climax FEW engine. Turners fitted with this unit were ultra-rare (were any actually sold?), and in later years the bigger five-bearing 1498cc Cortina GT engine took over instead.

The interior was simply but completely trimmed, with drop-windows in the doors, the rev counter and speedometer in a nacelle ahead of the driver's eyes, and a light alloy rimmed steering wheel. Turner claimed that if they supplied a kit car it would only take 25 hours of "unskilled labour to assemble the car".

Unhappily, the GT was a commercial failure. It was no faster than the MGB, it was more costly, and it was not backed by a dealer network.

Turner GT.

SPECIFICATION

BODY STYLES: sports coupé

PRODUCTION: 9

ENGINE & TRANSMISSION: 1340cc/1498cc, 4cyl ohv, 4sp man, f/r

POWER: 70bhp @ 5500rpm/78bhp @ 5200rpm

MAX SPEED (MPH): 100 (E)

0-60MPH (SEC): not measured

SUSPENSION & BRAKES: coil ifs, coil rear, disc f/drum r

LENGTH (IN)/WEIGHT (LB): 154/1568

LAUNCH PRICE: £850 (as kit), £1277 (complete car)

TVR

Engineer Trevor Wilkinson set up shop in Blackpool in 1947, and soon got into the specialist sports car business. At first he supplied chassis, then began making the first tubular-chassis TVR in 1958. For the next few years, glass-fibre bodied Granturas matured slowly, with a variety of engines and changes to the body style, but the company ran through several pots of capital before the Lilley family (father and son) rescued it in 1965.

Progress thereafter was steady and successful, though production never reached ten cars a week. The first MG-engined coil-sprung TVR had appeared in 1962, the first Ford-USA V8 types followed, the switch was made to Ford-UK and (later) Triumph engines in 1967, and a brand-new M-Type chassis followed in 1972. A disastrous fire at the Blackpool factory in January 1975 held back production for half of the

year, but the company bounced back, and sold even more cars thereafter.

During the 1970s, not only did TVR produce a smart hatchback Taimar, but a Convertible and Britain's first turbocharged road car (the Turbo), all of them evolving from the same basic body style, and sales boomed to almost 400 cars a year.

Very neatly for our story, the next-generation TVR, the Tasmin, would be all-new, and would not appear until January 1980. In later years TVR built on that basis, first by developing new body styles, later by inserting Rover V8 engines and boosting performance. Model after model followed in the 1980s and 1990s, boosting demand and the company's reputation. Entrepreneur Peter Wheeler bought the company in 1982 and was in sole control until 2004.

Grantura I 1958-60

The original Grantura road car set the TVR pattern for the next fifty years by using a tubular steel backbone chassis frame and a two-seater glass-fibre body shell. Over time, every detail would change, but the basic layout of a modern TVR is much the same as ever.

The design of the original backbone chassis revolved around the use of VW Beetle-type trailing link suspension at front and rear, with very stiff transverse torsion bars providing the springing. Steering was by VW worm-and-sector. The frame, fabricated by TVR itself, was

The 1958 TVR Grantura.

SPECIFICATION

BODY STYLES: sports coupé

PRODUCTION: c.100

ENGINE & TRANSMISSION: 1216cc, 4cyl ohc, 4sp man, f/r

POWER: 83bhp @ 6000rpm

MAX SPEED (MPH): 101 (E)

0-60MPH (SEC): 11.0 (E)

SUSPENSION & BRAKES: tor ifs, tor irs, drums f&r

LENGTH (IN)/WEIGHT (LB): 138/1455

LAUNCH PRICE: £1426

arranged so that four tubes surrounded the engine, transmission and rear axle.

Although TVR engineered this car to take the Lotus Elite's Coventry-Climax FEW engine (backed by an MG MGA gearbox), they were also ready to supply alternative engines, the least powerful being the 997cc Ford Anglia power unit. Amazingly, and even with the 83bhp of the Climax engine, drum brakes were still fitted. Centre-lock wire wheels were standard.

The body, which was moulded to the frame, was a tightly dimensioned two-

seater fastback coupé, with a front-hinged front end. The tail, which featured a huge Perspex rear window, was stubby in the extreme, and there was no exterior access to the luggage space. The spare wheel, and any baggage, had to come through a passenger door.

Although build quality improved as TVR gradually gained experience, these original cars offered little more than high performance, good (though hard-sprung) roadholding, and the exclusivity which came with limited production. Later Granturas would be much better cars.

Grantura II/IIA 1960-61/1961-62

In mid-1960 the Grantura became the Mk II, with a change of marketing emphasis. From this point, the MGA

1600 engine of 1588cc became standard equipment, and the price was reduced considerably. As before, however, there were several other engine options,

were several other engine options, though sidevalve Ford engines, however tuned, were no longer on offer.

TVR Grantura II, 1960, used mostly MGA engines.

BODY STYLES: sports coupé

PRODUCTION: c.400

ENGINE & TRANSMISSION: 1588cc/1622cc, 4cyl ohv, 4sp man, f/r

POWER: 80bhp @ 5600rpm/86bhp @ 5500rpm

MAX SPEED (MPH): 96/98 (E)

0-60MPH (SEC): 12.5/12.0 (E)

SUSPENSION & BRAKES: tor ifs, tor irs, drums f&r (disc f/drum r on Mk IIA)

LENGTH (IN)/WEIGHT (LB): 138/1570

LAUNCH PRICE: £1183/£1291

NOTE: 39bhp/997cc, 54bhp/1340cc, 72bhp/1489cc or 83bhp/1216cc engines also available)

Chassis changes were limited, but Coventry Climax-engined cars got rack-and-pinion steering, and there were minor style changes including the use of rear wheelarch flares.

The Mk II was available for less than a year, as from early 1961 it evolved into the Mk IIA. This was the definitive version of the original chassis, for the MGA engine was pushed up to 1622cc, front-wheel disc brakes were standardised, and the Ford Classic 1340cc engine also became optional. On the Coventry Climax-engined cars (rare, by this time) a ZF four-speed gearbox was optional.

Grantura IIA gained front disc brakes.

Grantura III/IV/1800S 1962-67

The Grantura III introduced a brand new chassis frame and suspension layout, under essentially the same GRP body style, this making the TVR a more generally attractive package.

With a slightly longer wheelbase than before – 85.5in instead of 84in – the new frame continued the original four-tube backbone layout, but had coil spring and wishbone independent suspension at

Grantura III had redesigned frame and suspension.

BODY STYLES: sports coupé

PRODUCTION: c.90 Mk III, c.128 1800S, 78 Mk IV

ENGINE & TRANSMISSION: 1622cc/1798cc, 4cyl ohv, 4sp man, (or o/d with 1798cc), f/r

POWER: 86bhp @ 5500rpm/95bhp @ 5400rpm

MAX SPEED (MPH): 100/108 (E)

0-60MPH (SEC): not measured/10.9

SUSPENSION & BRAKES: coil ifs, coil irs, disc f/drum r

LENGTH (IN)/WEIGHT (LB): 138/1625 - 1790

LAUNCH PRICE: £1183/£1043

front and rear, with twinned rear dampers on each side of the rear suspension. Triumph rack-and-pinion steering was fitted, and the brakes were enlarged. The new chassis was so sturdy, and so versatile, that it would feature under all new TVRs built in the next ten years (up to the launch of the M-Type, which was different). Compared with the old chassis, the frame was much stiffer than before, in both bending and torsion.

Mk IIIs had MG engines – 1622cc in a few cars, 1798cc as standard – and there may have been a handful of cars with other engines. By this time TVR had decided to standardise its model, this being the last to be offered with options of any sort. From early 1963 the option of an overdrive for the MGB-type gearbox was a novelty. Prices were down once again, which ensured that more cars were sold.

From early 1964, the Mk III became 1800S, which heralded the arrival of a longer, squared-off "Manx" tail, Ford Cortina MK 1 tail lamps and an even larger rear window, though the relocated spare wheel still had to be extracted through one of the passenger doors.

Following yet another management upheaval, the 1800S dropped out of production for a time in 1965, and was then revived in July 1966 as the Mk IV 1800S. This then carried on until October 1967, when the Ford-powered Vixen took over. The last cars had a 15-

gallon fuel tank, up from 10 gallons.

These were the best TVRs so far, though they still had a hard ride and there seemed to be a rather casual attitude to build quality. The steel tube frames do rust, but a fair proportion of the cars have been preserved.

Vixen S1/S2/S3/S4 1967-72

Under Martin Lilley's management, TVR re-designed the 1800S/Mk IV model, ditched the MGB engines, and replaced them with Ford Cortina GT power units and transmissions, this being the essence of a new breed of TVR, known as Vixens.

Visually, the change was signalled by a new engine-bay air intake in the centre of the bonnet, but there was much more to come in the Vixen's five-year life.

The Vixen S1 appeared in October 1967, and had an 88bhp 1599cc engine. The Vixen S2 took over in October 1968, having a 90in wheelbase (which meant a longer and more roomy cabin and larger doors), a modified bonnet with a bulge instead of an air-scoop, and wrap-around tail lamps replacing the

TVR Vixen S2, 1969, now with 1.6-litre Ford engine.

SPECIFICATION

BODY STYLES: sports coupé

PRODUCTION: 117/438/168/23

ENGINE & TRANSMISSION: 1599cc, 4cyl ohv, 4sp man, f/r

POWER: 88bhp @ 5400rpm

MAX SPEED (MPH): 109

0-60MPH (SEC): 10.5

SUSPENSION & BRAKES: coil ifs, coil irs, disc f/drum r

LENGTH (IN)/WEIGHT (LB): 138-145/1680-1735

LAUNCH PRICE: £1387

Cortina units. From 1969, two air scoops were reinstated, close to the nose. For the first time, the bodyshell was bolted on, rather than moulded into place.

The Vixen S3 took over in late 1970, featuring cast alloy road wheels instead of centre-lock wires, and more delicately detailed air outlets in the front wings, behind the wheel arches. A minor engine re-tune was introduced, though the quoted figures do not make this clear.

The Vixen S4 appeared in April 1972, this effectively being a Vixen S3 but with a new M-Type chassis frame, which is described in the 2500M entry.

Throughout its career the Vixen did

much to build up TVR's reputation. It was a likeable car from what was now perceived as a stable business. Each version seemed to be genuinely better than the previous one, and many were well enough liked to be preserved for later years.

Vixen S4, 1972.

Griffith 200/400 1963-65

Jack Griffith, an American motor trader, had the idea of mating the Ford V8 engine with TVR's new Grantura Mark III (after all, if Carroll Shelby could do it with the AC Ace...?), and persuaded TVR to supply him with "empty" cars on which he would carry

out engine and transmission transplants in the USA.

The first TVR Griffiths (subsequently known as 200s) of 1963 were built on Mk III chassis which were stiffened around the suspension pick-up points. They had twin rear spring/damper

installations on each side, a sizeable bonnet bulge to clear the much more bulky V8 engine and fatter-section (185) radial ply tyres on 5-inch wire wheels. The rear axle was the robust Salisbury 4HU unit. Although these cars were undoubtedly very fast, they were also very under-developed. Brakes, though servo-assisted, were the same size as those of the Grantura Mk III.

The Griffith 400s which followed in 1964 (the launch came in April), were better, for they had much more effective engine cooling and were better-built. These, too, were the first TVRs to have the cut-off Manx tail with the circular

tail lamps. The best that can be said of these cars is that while they were ferociously accelerative they were still by no means fully developed, even after two

years of production. Most customers, or second owners, or third owners, had to do much dedicated work to turn them into reliable transport.

The 4.7-litre V8-powered TVR Griffith, with characteristic bonnet bulge.

SPECIFICATION

BODY STYLES: sports coupé

PRODUCTION: c.300

ENGINE & TRANSMISSION: 4727cc, V8cyl ohv, 4sp man, f/r

POWER: 195bhp @ 4400rpm/271bhp @ 6500rpm

MAX SPEED (MPH): 140 (E) -155 (E)

0-60MPH (SEC): not measured

SUSPENSION & BRAKES: coil ifs, coil irs, disc f/drum r

LENGTH (IN)/WEIGHT (LB): 138-145/1905

LAUNCH PRICE: £1620

Tuscan V8/V8SE 1967-70

Once Martin Lilley had taken control of TVR at the end of 1965 he set about sanitising the Griffith-type chassis, the result being launched as the Tuscan V8 in 1967.

The original Tuscan of 1967 was a direct development of the Griffith 400 and had a highly polished wooden fascia, different in layout from that of the 1800S or Vixen. It also used the "soft" tune 195bhp engine, which made the car more tractable. Just 28 were

SPECIFICATION

BODY STYLES: sports coupé

PRODUCTION: 28 V8, 24 lwb Tuscan SE, 21 "wide body"

ENGINE & TRANSMISSION: 4727cc, V8cyl ohv, 4sp man, f/r

POWER: 195bhp @ 4400rpm/271bhp @ 6500rpm

MAX SPEED (MPH): 140 (E) -155 (E)

0-60MPH (SEC): not measured/7.5

SUSPENSION & BRAKES: coil ifs, coil irs, disc f/drum r

LENGTH (IN)/WEIGHT (LB): 145/1905

LAUNCH PRICE: £1967

TVR Tuscan V8. Attractive young women – not always completely undressed – were a frequent feature of TVR showstands.

built during the year. Only four were built with right-hand drive.

The Tuscan V8 SE of 1967 and 1968 had the longer-wheelbase (90in) chassis

frame, which allowed the passenger doors to be lengthened, and the cabin increased in volume. It also had the wrap-around tail lamps. It was related, therefore, to the

Vixen S2. Mechanically, though, it was like the original Tuscan V8, and had 6in wheel rims. Only 24 of these cars were produced in 1967-68 – 12 each with left- and right-hand drive.

The Tuscan V8 SE "wide body" was an even rarer beast. Although it used the SE LWB's rolling chassis, with a similar GRP style, the body was widened by a full four inches, with new and rather smoother lines around the nose and the tail. 21 such cars were produced from 1968 to 1970, all but two with left-hand-drive.

Although commercially unsuccessful (TVR made all its money from four-cylinder and V6-engined cars at this time), these Tuscans set performance trends which did great things for the company's image. Rare at the time, and even rarer today, they have become collectors' pieces.

Tuscan V6 1969-71

Mixing-and-matching in the best USA "product planning" manner, TVR's Martin Lilley tried yet another engine and chassis combination in 1969. This was the Tuscan V6, effectively a Vixen which had been given more power.

This car had the 90in-wheelbase Mk III-type chassis, and the longer-door, longer-cabin, Manx tail body of the current Vixen, but it was powered by a Ford Zodiac/Capri 3-litre V6 engine,

Tuscan V6.

SPECIFICATION

BODY STYLES: sports coupé

PRODUCTION: 101

ENGINE & TRANSMISSION: 2994cc, V6cyl ohv, 4sp man, or o/d, f/r

POWER: 128bhp @ 4750rpm

MAX SPEED (MPH): 125 (E)

0-60MPH (SEC): 8.3

SUSPENSION & BRAKES: coil ifs, coil irs, disc f/drum r

LENGTH (IN)/WEIGHT (LB): 145/2000

LAUNCH PRICE: £1930

and also used the Zodiac/Capri gearbox. Overdrive was an optional extra. The Tuscan V8-type rear axle was retained.

To balance the chassis, the brakes were from the servo-assisted Tuscan V8, and there were cast alloy road wheels with 5.5in rims. All this made the car a very attractive proposition, but the V6 engine was not cleared for use in emissions-conscious North America, so sales were mainly restricted to the home market.

In production from mid-1969 until the end of 1971, the Tuscan V6 had an unspectacular career, though at least it got TVR used to the V6 engine, which would feature very strongly in their models in the 1970s and 1980s.

2500 1970-73

SPECIFICATION

BODY STYLES: sports coupé

PRODUCTION: 385

ENGINE & TRANSMISSION: 2498cc, 6cyl ohv, 4sp man, and o/d, f/r

POWER: 106bhp @ 4900rpm

MAX SPEED (MPH): 111

0-60MPH (SEC): 10.6

SUSPENSION & BRAKES : coil ifs, coil irs, disc f/drum r

LENGTH (IN)/WEIGHT (LB): 145/1960

LAUNCH PRICE: £1927

The Triumph-engined TVR 2500.

The key to this car's success was its engine. To secure its market in the USA, TVR needed an engine which would meet all the burgeoning exhaust emission rules. They found it in the form of the 2498cc Triumph six-cylinder unit, as used in the TR6. The result was the 2500, launched in October 1970, with UK deliveries beginning in April 1971.

This model, essentially, was a re-engined Tuscan V6. The Triumph engine featured twin Zenith-Stromberg carburettors, and produced 106bhp. It was backed by the sturdy TR6 gearbox, and Laycock overdrive was optional. It was not as fast as the Tuscan V6 – its top speed was only 111mph compared with an estimated 125mph for the Tuscan.

For TVR, it was a huge success. In just over two years 385 cars were produced, 289 of them with the old Vixen/Tuscan chassis, and the final 96 cars with new M-Type chassis (but the same style). Most cars were exported to North America, and sales in the UK were limited.

More refined than the Tuscan, the 2500 had all the same rugged simplicity, and the corrosion-resistant bodywork. Maybe not as extrovert as a V-engined TVR, it was still a smart and brisk machine.

1300 1971-72

This Triumph Spitfire-engined model was, frankly, an aberration which TVR would rather forget. The clientele, in any case, never took much notice of it as an offering, for only 15 examples were sold.

Built at a time when TVR was also producing the 2500 (which had a much larger Triumph engine), the 1300 was effectively a re-engined Vixen of the period, and looked identical to the Vixen

TVR 1300 of 1971, using the Triumph Spitfire power unit.

SPECIFICATION

BODY STYLES: sports coupé

PRODUCTION: 15

ENGINE & TRANSMISSION: 1296cc, 4cyl ohv, 4sp man, f/r

POWER: 63bhp @ 6000rpm

MAX SPEED (MPH): 90 (E)

0-60MPH (SEC): 16.0 (E)

SUSPENSION & BRAKES: coil ifs, coil irs, disc f/drum r

LENGTH (IN)/WEIGHT (LB): 145/1625

LAUNCH PRICE: £1558

S3, with the same chassis, suspension, steering, body and equipment. The first nine cars had Vixen-type chassis ("Grantura Mk III" types), while the last six had M-Type frames.

This was almost the slowest of all TVRs, and has long since became a forgotten model.

2500M 1972-77

The very first TVR to carry a new-type chassis frame, the 2500M, was unveiled at the London Motor Show of October 1971, though deliveries did not begin until 1972. Almost immediately this new frame took over from the older Grantura III-based design which had served for the previous nine years, and it would be used on 1600M, 3000M, Taimar and Convertibles, as well as providing interim support for change-over models at this period.

Still with a classic four-tube backbone layout, the new frame was more robust than before (thicker-section tubing was used in certain areas, and there was square-section tubing in others), and had its own design of independent suspension (front and rear) by coil springs and wishbones. The GRP body was really an evolution of the "wide-body" Tuscan V8 shape, still with only two seats, and still with no exterior access to the luggage area. The wheel-base, at 90 inches, was as before, though the track was marginally wider. This was the first TVR in which the spare wheel was mounted up front, under the bonnet and ahead of the engine.

Like the 2500 before it (for which this new car was a replacement), the 2500M used a USA-specification Triumph TR6 2498cc six-cylinder engine, with its related gearbox and chassis-mounted final drive unit, for this was a car which TVR intended to sell mostly in the

USA. The sales figures – 947 cars in five years – give an indication that TVR had produced a successful recipe.

Like the 2500 this was a brisk but not very fast TVR since the engine only had an output of 106bhp – so perhaps the top speed of 109mph counts as slightly disappointing. It was for this reason that the 3000M outsold the 2500M by a considerable margin in the UK market. Over time there were a number of small, but significant style changes, including the deletion of front wing vents when production re-started after the factory fire of 1975, and a revised bonnet moulding for the final (1977) model year. The alloy wheel pattern changed in late 1973, with tyres changed from 165-15in to 185HR-14in.

SPECIFICATION

BODY STYLES: sports coupé

PRODUCTION: 947

ENGINE & TRANSMISSION: 2498cc, 6cyl ohv, 4sp man, or o/d, f/r

POWER: 106bhp @ 4900rpm

MAX SPEED (MPH): 109

0-60MPH (SEC): 9.3

SUSPENSION & BRAKES: coil ifs, coil irs, discs f&r

LENGTH (IN)/WEIGHT (LB): 154/2240

LAUNCH PRICE: £2170

The 2500M had a new frame, a longer body and all-round independent suspension.

1600M 1972-73-1975-77

The model name tells it all, for here was the 2500M/3000M chassis and body style, with a Ford Cortina GT/Capri GT 1599cc "Kent" engine giving 86bhp. In effect, this was a direct replacement for the Vixen S4.

The 1600M had a Triumph GT6-type chassis-mounted final drive assembly, but the rest of its chassis, suspension, running gear and structure was much like that of the larger-engined M types.

SPECIFICATION

BODY STYLES: sports coupé

PRODUCTION: 68/80

ENGINE & TRANSMISSION: 1599cc, 4cyl ohv, 4sp man, f/r

POWER: 86bhp @ 5500rpm

MAX SPEED (MPH): 105

0-60MPH (SEC): 10.4

SUSPENSION & BRAKES: coil ifs, coil irs, discs f&r

LENGTH (IN)/WEIGHT (LB): 154/2000

LAUNCH PRICE: £1886

TVR 1600, with Cortina GT engine.

Because TVR's own market aspirations had changed – it was moving further up-market, with more powerful cars – the 1600M was no more than a partial success, certainly never selling as well as the Vixen had done. The first production run covered mid-1972 to mid-1973 (only 68 cars sold), but the model was then re-introduced after the factory fire, and was built from May 1975 until mid-1977 (80 cars produced). The second tranche of 1600Ms used 14in road wheels, had no wing vents from later in 1975, and had a restyled bonnet from 1977.

In earlier years the 1600M would no doubt have been a success, but with more powerful models now available TVR's customers tended to go for them instead.

3000M 1972-79

The 3000M, produced from 1972 to 1979, was one of TVR's most successful cars of the 1970s. Even so, the British, who did not see many 2500Ms (most went to the USA), tend not to realise that it was outsold by the Triumph-engined car.

Once again, the model name tells its own story. The chassis, suspension, steering, running gear and two-seater body shell were all like other M-type cars, but this time the engine was the 138bhp 2994cc V6 power unit of the Ford Capri/Granada of the day, allied to the Capri gearbox and (until 1977) a TR6-type final drive. After that the final

3000M had the138bhp Ford Capri engine.

SPECIFICATION

BODY STYLES: sports coupé

PRODUCTION: 654

ENGINE & TRANSMISSION: 2994cc, V6cyl ohv, 4sp man, or o/d, f/r

POWER: 138bhp @ 5000rpm

MAX SPEED (MPH): 121

0-60MPH (SEC): 7.7

SUSPENSION & BRAKES: coil ifs, coil irs, discs f&r

LENGTH (IN)/WEIGHT (LB): 154/2240

LAUNCH PRICE: £2170

drive unit became a Salisbury 4HU as used by Jaguar.

On the 3000M, the two-seater body was exactly the same as on the 1600M and 2500M, while the rolling chassis would also find use in the Taimar (hatchback) and Convertible models which were to follow. The Ford V6 was not as smooth in character as either of its stablemates – it was never the most vibration-free of motors – but it was an immensely torquey beast, and delivered top speeds of more than 120mph.

As with other M-types, there were several detail changes in equipment and styling in nine years. Laycock overdrive became optional from late 1975. Other changes were made at the same time as they were adopted by the 1600M and 2500M. Amazingly, TVR was able to have the Ford V6 engine de-toxed for sale in the USA (Ford themselves did not achieve this, but TVR's consultants did) so from 1977 the 3000M also went on sale in North America.

The last 3000M was produced at the very end of 1979, before the totally new Tasmin took over.

Taimar 1976-79

Although TVR's history is sometimes difficult to unravel, that of the Taimar was simple enough. To

SPECIFICATION

BODY STYLES: sports hatchback

PRODUCTION: 395

ENGINE & TRANSMISSION: 2994cc, V6cyl ohv, 4sp man, or o/d, f/r

POWER: 142bhp @ 5000rpm

MAX SPEED (MPH): 121

0-60MPH (SEC): 7.7

SUSPENSION & BRAKES: coil ifs, coil irs, discs f&r

LENGTH (IN)/WEIGHT (LB): 154/2260

LAUNCH PRICE: £4260

TVR Taimar, 1976-79, had a full hatchback.

satisfy the demand for easier access to the luggage area of the 3000M, TVR produced a hatchback version, calling it the Taimar.

Mechanically, and in most of its body style and structure, the Taimar was closely based on the 3000M (the weight penalty was only about 20lb), and first deliveries were made at the end of 1976. From that point, Taimars and 3000Ms were produced together at Blackpool until both cars were discontinued at the very end of 1979. Like other late-model Ford V6-engined cars, the Taimar was sold in Europe and in North America.

The rear hatch itself was bulky, rather than heavy, and was hinged in the roof, therefore opening upwards. Unlatching was internal, by operating a release in the driver's side door jamb. In some ways the Taimar competed with the Reliant Scimitar GTE of the day, and fulfilled a similar marketing function. But there was no loss of performance, and the Taimar was a great success.

Taimar dash and controls.

Convertible 1978-79

By the later 1970s TVRs were selling strongly in North America. The Convertible, whose body shell was different in many ways from that of the 3000M and Taimar, was aimed especially at that market.

The running gear was almost exactly the same as that of the other contemporary mainstream TVRs, as was much of the floorpan, and the entire front end moulding, though the windscreen was unique. This was a simply-equipped drop-top two-seater, and was the very first TVR

The 1978 TVR Convertible was the company's first.

to have a separate boot compartment.

The doors had detachable sidescreens (all previous TVRs had had glass drop windows), while the soft-top was a simple fold-back assembly, permanently attached to the shell. The fascia/instrument panel was new, and much criticised at the time, for the rev counter and speedometer had been moved to a central position (in other words, not in front of the driver's eyes).

In character, in performance, and in general behaviour, this Convertible was just like that of other TVRs of the period, but its drop-top feature made it unique, and very popular.

Even though it was only on sale for less than two years – early 1978 to late 1979 – no fewer than 258 cars (and a further 13 fitted with turbocharged engines) were produced.

SPECIFICATION

BODY STYLES: sports convertible

PRODUCTION: 258

ENGINE & TRANSMISSION: 2994cc, V6cyl ohv, 4sp man, or o/d, f/r

POWER: 142bhp @ 5000rpm

MAX SPEED (MPH): (E) 125

0-60MPH (SEC): 7.7

SUSPENSION & BRAKES: coil ifs, coil irs, discs f&r

LENGTH (IN)/WEIGHT (LB): 154/2420

LAUNCH PRICE: £6390

Turbo 1975-79

Strictly speaking, the TVR Turbo was not a model, but a conversion of other models. Launched in 1975, it was the first British example of turbocharging for a production road car, using a factory-approved conversion of the 2994cc Ford V6 engine which was then available in the 3000M and would soon appear in the Taimar and Convertible.

Except that the turbocharged engine would be fitted on initial assembly, in almost all other respects the cars involved would be like their normally-aspirated parent models.

Broadspeed did the engineering of the turbocharged engine for TVR. It delivered 230bhp at 5500rpm instead of the normal 142bhp at 5000rpm – a 67 per cent increase, no less. To make sure everything worked well, TVR included a front-mounted oil cooler as

standard, and fitted the hefty Salisbury 4HU final drive assembly. This axle was of Jaguar E-Type/XJ-S type, so could certainly deal with the torque.

When the first cars were delivered in 1976, the 3000M Turbo cost £6903, which compared with just £3990 for the normally aspirated car – a 73 per cent price hike, broadly in line with the extra power!

Naturally this was not a car for

everybody – it was not even a car for every TVR customer – for it delivered rip-roaring, extrovert performance without much refinement, all at a high cost. Upkeep and maintenance costs, too, were high.

TVR never expected many such cars to be sold – nor were they. In four years just 63 cars – 20 3000Ms, 30 Taimars and 13 Convertibles – got the turbocharging treatment.

A Broadspeed turbocharged V6 engine gave the Turbo 230bhp.

Tasmin S1 1980-88

Launched in January 1980, the Tasmin started a family of new-type TVRs which would keep the Blackpool-based company busy for more than a decade. Although they do not fall into our period, it is worth noting that the Tasmin name would disappear in 1988; cars like the 350i, 390SE, and 420SEAC would all carry the engineering forward into the 1990s.

Though the Tasmin retained much established TVR "DNA" in its layout – a multi-tube backbone chassis, all-coil-spring independent suspension, a GRP body shell and (soon) a choice of closed or open styles – it was different in every detail. The wheelbase was a touch longer

The 1980 Tasmin, first of the wedge-shaped TVRs.

than before, at 94in, while the styling, by Oliver Winterbottom, was much sharper in theme than that of the obsolete 3000M/Taimar/Convertible family, with a long angular tail and a vertical span of glass close to bumper level, plus flip-up headlamps, Triumph TR7-style, behind the front bumper.

The engine was Ford-Germany's 160bhp 2.8-litre Bosch-injected V6, backed by the Capri 3000-type gearbox (automatic transmission followed as optional from October 1980). Salisbury provided the chassis-mounted axle, while Ford provided the steering and some front suspension pieces. The fascia panel featured much polished wood and conventional circular instruments, and the seats were quite plushy.

The original Tasmin was a two-seater hatchback coupé, but within a year it was joined by a Convertible and the Tasmin +2. From nose to windscreen, the Convertible shared the two-seater's body mouldings, but then had unique doors and tail section; the doors, incidentally, had wind-up windows. The +2 might have looked the same as the two-seater fixed-head, but was entirely different, with a larger cabin and just enough space for two extra seats to be squeezed into place.

This model then evolved, over time. The original Tasmin would become S2 in late 1981, the "+2" would only survive until 1983, and the Convertible would be renamed 280i in 1983. This was only the beginning, for there would be 200s, 350is, 390SEs and more.

The original Tasmin was not a total success. Though it handled well, and was faster than the 3000M family that it replaced, its sharp looks were not to everyone's taste. When Peter Wheeler took control at the end of 1981, one of his first decisions was to instal Rover engines in future models, and to begin softening the contours of the car.

Tasmin interior, with wood dash.

U N I P O W E R

Universal Power Drives of Perivale in Middlesex was a company which specialised in building forestry tractors. In the mid-1960s, BMC racing enthusiasts Andrew Hedges and Tim Powell encouraged the company to take an interest in building specialist sports cars. The result was the tiny but attractive mid-engined Unipower GT, which relied on Mini-Cooper running gear.

The problem, as with so many other limited-production vehicles, was in building an image. Although UPD found about 50 customers for the car – either in 998cc or 1275cc guise – when a separate company (Unipower Cars) was set up in 1968 there was no surge in demand. Sensibly, therefore, the project was wound up in 1970 after around 75 had been manufactured.

The Unipower was a well-engineered and reputedly well-built machine, and a number have survived. They come as a surprise to onlookers because of their road manners and their tiny stature.

GT 1966-70

Andrew Hedges, a successful BMC works race driver in Midgets and MGBs, together with Tim Powell inspired the birth of the Unipower GT, a Mini-powered machine so small that it was only 40 inches high, its floor pan a mere six inches off the deck.

It was engineered around the special builder's usual Meccano set of square-section tubes laid out in a sturdy three-dimensional multi-tube layout (the under-door sills were particularly strong). It had a transversely-mounted Mini-Cooper engine and transmission

The mid-engined Unipower GT, 1966.

SPECIFICATION

BODY STYLES: sports coupé

PRODUCTION: 75

ENGINE & TRANSMISSION: 998cc/1275cc, 4cyl ohv, 4sp man, m/r

POWER: 55bhp @ 5800rpm/76bhp @ 5800rpm

MAX SPEED (MPH): 101/125 (E)

0-60MPH (SEC): 12.6/9.0 (E)

SUSPENSION & BRAKES: coil ifs, coil irs, disc f/drum r

LENGTH (IN)/WEIGHT (LB): 164/1254

LAUNCH PRICE: £900 (in kit form)

installed behind the seats and driving the rear wheels. Front and rear suspension was by coil-over-shock absorbers, with (for obvious reasons) Mini-like front suspension geometry at the rear. The bodywork, manufactured from glass-fibre, was so low that semi-racing seats were considerably reclined, the driver's eye being no more than three feet off the ground.

Once one got used to the tiny dimensions, the rather uneasy sense of vulnerability – compared with a London bus the Unipower felt absolutely mini-scule – and the race car ambience, this was an extremely effective car. Conventional car niceties like luggage space and creature comforts were distinctly limited, but for the enthusiastic driver who liked to press on this didn't seem to matter at all.

Unhappily, of course, there were too few such people, which explains why the project eventually died away.

VANDEN PLAS

Although VDP began way back as a respected Belgian independent coachbuilder, it set up shop in Kingsbury, North London in 1923, after which many vintage Bentleys came to have Vanden Plas bodies. Austin absorbed this business in 1946, and set it to building Princess body shells and completing the assembly of those massive cars.

From 1959, BMC, which controlled Austin, promoted Vanden Plas to separate marque status. Apart from the 4-Litre limousine (which carried on until 1968), every VDP was no more than a reworked Austin model, though the cars always carried special trim and equipment, and were completed at Kingsbury. In the 1960s, VDP also completed assembly of the huge Jaguar-based Daimler DS420 limousine.

The majority of sales were of small Austin-based front wheel drive cars: the Austin 1100-based Princess 1100 of the 1960s was well regarded, but the slide from credibility came in the 1970s when its successor, the 1500, was based on the dreadful Austin Allegro.

Under British Leyland, factory rationalisation led to the closure of Kingsbury in 1979, after which the marque speedily died out. Thereafter the name was only used as a top-of-the-range trim level for other British models.

Princess 4-Litre 1957-68

Except for its new badging, and for the final technical changes, this car has already been described, because the VDP 4-Litre Limousine was no more than a slightly improved version of the Austin Princess long-wheelbase limousine which had first appeared in 1952. That car had always been assembled by Vanden Plas at Kingsbury, and so was this later machine. Officially it became a Princess from 1957, and a Vanden Plas Princess from June 1960.

To summarise, here was a vast car with a 132in wheelbase, a coachbuilt body shell comprising a wooden skeleton with steel and aluminium reinforcement, and steel skin panels. The limousine division was a permanent fixture, and because fold-away seats were provided in the rear compartment, the car could easily carry six people, some in more comfort than others. Because it was much cheaper than similar Daimlers or Rolls-Royces it was an ideal vehicle for the weddings and funerals market, or for mayors of councils who would not pay up for more expensive official cars. Hearse conversions were often made.

Technically this remained a 1950s car, for it had drum brakes to the very end, and the engine was closely related to those used in BMC trucks (and in Jensen 541 cars). GM Hydramatic automatic transmission was optional, and power assisted steering helped the poor chauffeur stave off heart attacks. During the 1960s the only real technical advances came in late 1962, when Selectaride rear dampers and servo-assisted brakes were added.

Like the Austin-badged types, these limousines were often used for decades after production ended, but as body parts are no longer available, not many have survived.

SPECIFICATION

BODY STYLES: limousine

PRODUCTION: 3344, all types 1952-68

ENGINE & TRANSMISSION: 3993cc, 6cyl ohv, 4sp man, auto, f/r

POWER: 120bhp @ 4000rpm

MAX SPEED (MPH): 75

0-60MPH (SEC): 26

SUSPENSION & BRAKES: coil ifs, leaf rear, drums f&r

LENGTH (IN)/WEIGHT (LB): 215/4810

LAUNCH PRICE: £3047

Vanden Plas Princess 4-litre limousine.

3-Litre/3-Litre Mk II 1959-64

Although Rootes already knew a lot about badge engineering, BMC went several stages better in the 1960s. The Princess 3-Litre, badged officially as a Vanden Plas from mid-1960, was part-manufactured at Cowley, then shipped to North London for completion at Kingsbury. It was really little more than an up-market derivative of the Austin A99/A110/Wolseley 6/99 family, though with a special front-end style, duotone paintwork, and nicely thought-out interior trim featuring lots of walnut veneer, leather and high-grade carpet.

Like the A99 (already described), this car took shape around a Farina-styled four-door saloon with front-wheel disc brakes, soft suspension and ponderous handling. Until 1961 the 3-Litre had a 103bhp engine, a column-change three-speed manual gearbox with overdrive, or Borg Warner automatic transmission as an option. In 1961 they became Mk IIs, with floor change and with power increased to 120bhp. Power-assisted steering became an option in mid-1962. Mk IIs also had a slightly longer wheelbase (no bodywork changes though) and handled somewhat better.

BMC clearly got its marketing right, for no fewer than 12,703 VDP 3-Litres were sold in five years, a figure which was limited not by demand but by the capacity of Kingsbury to churn out the product. For once the ambience was

Princess 3-Litre, 1959, based on the Austin Westminster.

right. Although the engineering was mundane, the cabin was very nicely finished, and the car seemed to offer good value for money. It was perhaps best not to ask about fuel economy though – but customers for these cars rarely cared anyway.

The 3-Litre was replaced by the very different Rolls-Royce-engined 4-Litre R in late 1964.

Being chauffeur-driven came naturally to the dignified Princess.

SPECIFICATION

BODY STYLES : saloon

PRODUCTION TOTAL: 4719/7984

ENGINE & TRANSMISSION : 2912cc, 6cyl ohv, 3sp man, o/d or auto, f/r

POWER : 103bhp @ 4750rpm/120bhp @ 4750rpm

MAX SPEED (MPH) : 97/105

0-60MPH (SEC) : 17.9/16.9

SUSPENSION & BRAKES : coil ifs, leaf rear, disc f/drum r

LENGTH (IN)/WEIGHT (LB) : 188/3465 - 3660

LAUNCH PRICE : £1396/£1626

Six Princess 3-Litre estate cars were built, one of them for the Queen.

Princess 1100/Princess 1300 1963-74

Although it was the fourth ADO 16 derivative to be announced (the parent models being the Austin-Morris 1100s), the Princess was always the best trimmed and the most highly priced. Only four-door saloons were produced, and (except for a short period in 1966-67) all were finally assembled at the Kingsbury factory in North London.

In all but its grille, paintwork and interior furnishings, the Princess was virtually identical to the MG 1100/1300 which had already been announced – it took on alternative engines at the same time in 1967, became Mk II later that year, got an AP automatic transmission option at the same time, and inherited an all-synchromesh gearbox during 1968. The Princess 1300, on the other

The Princess 1300 arrived in 1967.

hand, never got more than a 65bhp engine, and had a special 60bhp 1275cc engine tune to suit automatic transmission.

All the USPs (Unique Selling Points) were in the cabin, where the Princess had high-quality leather seating, a polished wooden fascia with a special instrument display, and was obviously put together and finished off with care.

Although no one would call a Princess sporting, it was a brisk performer with a good ride and pin-accurate steering. Apparently it sold in large numbers to retired people who wanted a touch of

luxury for their old age and who were careful with their cars, which explains why a goodly number survived without rusting away.

The Princess was opulently trimmed.

SPECIFICATION

BODY STYLES: saloon

PRODUCTION: 16,007/27,734

ENGINE & TRANSMISSION: 1098cc/1275cc, 4cyl ohv, 4sp man, or auto, f/f

POWER: 55bhp @ 5500rpm/58bhp @ 5250rpm/60bhp @ 5250rpm/65bhp @ 5750rpm

MAX SPEED (MPH): (1100) 85, (1275) 88

0-60MPH (SEC): (1100) 21.1 (58bhp 1275) 17.3

SUSPENSION & BRAKES: Hydro ifs, Hydro irs, disc f/drum r

LENGTH (IN)/WEIGHT (LB): 147/1950

LAUNCH PRICE: £895/£1000

4-Litre R 1964-68

BMC had big plans for this car, and for the models which might, just might, have followed it – but the public thought otherwise, and saw it destined for early retirement little more than three years after launch,

Structurally the 4-Litre was an Austin A110/Princess 3-Litre four-door shell with style changes and power by Rolls-Royce. Automatic transmission and power steering were both standard, as was a duotone colour scheme. We were never told what the "R" stood for.

BMC got together with Rolls-Royce to

use the latter's alloy-block FB60 engine, which had overhead inlet and side exhaust valves. It was loosely related both to the obsolete Rolls-Royce Silver Cloud I's six-cylinder engine, and to R-R military units of the period. It was rated officially at 175bhp, but the performance figures show that this must have been a major overstatement of the truth. Along with the Borg Warner automatic transmission, however, it provided suitably silky power, even if the fuel consumption could be as low as 15mpg, even on long runs.

SPECIFICATION

BODY STYLES: saloon

PRODUCTION: 6999

ENGINE & TRANSMISSION: 3909cc, 6cyl ioe, auto, f/r

POWER: 175bhp @ 4800rpm

MAX SPEED (MPH): 106

0-60MPH (SEC): 12.7

SUSPENSION & BRAKES: coil ifs, leaf rear, disc f/drum r

LENGTH (IN)/WEIGHT (LB): 188/3530

LAUNCH PRICE: £1994

Compared with the Princess 3-Litre, which it replaced, the roof line was flattened out, the tail fins were removed, and at the front the extra driving lamps were now built in. Smaller wheels brought the body a touch closer to the ground. Curiously the 4-Litre was slightly lighter than the old model.

Although there was talk of production exceeding 100 cars a week, and rumours of waiting lists building up, the gloss soon wore off this new car's image. It was, after all, more expensive than the well-liked old 3-Litre and in many customers' eyes no more desirable. Before long factory car parks were full of unsold stock, and the new bosses at British Leyland pulled the plug as soon as they had control.

Princess 4-Litre R, 1964, dispensed with the 3-Litre's tail fins.

Princess 1500/Princess 1750 1974-80

It was asking too much for Vanden Plas to make a good little Princess on the basis of the Austin Allegro, and they could not. Announced in September 1974, the new Princess 1500 followed the usual formula of melding a new grille, and a more up-market interior, on to the basis of an otherwise standard saloon. This had worked well on the earlier (1100/1300) model, but in this case it just looked awkward.

The base car was the Allegro 1500, complete with 69bhp/1485cc over-head-cam four-cylinder engine, and its related five-speed transmission, plus the Hydragas suspension, but with fatter – 155-section – radial ply tyres.

Some might agree that the Vanden Plas version of the Allegro was an unhappy concept.

AP automatic transmission was an optional extra. At least the steering wheel was circular (not 'Quartic', as on early Allegros).

Because VDP had to graft a vertical-type radiator grille to an already high bonnet line, the style looked awkward, though VDP then did their best with the interior. The original Allegro interior trim was gutted, in its place being thick carpets, leather-covered seats (the fronts reclined), a slab of real tree wood on the fascia, and wood cappings on the doors. Build and assembly quality was higher – and so it should have been, when the high price (£1951) was considered.

Though the ride was rather soft and bouncy, the interior ambience felt right, and the 90mph top speed was enough for the type of person who bought such cars. From 1979, final assembly was moved from the original VDP works in London, to the MG factory at Abingdon. From late 1979, too, the specification was changed, so that manual transmission cars had a 77bhp twin-carb 1485cc engine, while automatics were fitted with an 84bhp 1748cc overhead-cam engine instead.

Though the Allegro itself still had two years to run, the Princess 1500 was killed off when its adopted assembly factory – Abingdon – was closed at the end of 1980.

SPECIFICATION

BODY STYLES: saloon

PRODUCTION: 11,84

ENGINE & TRANSMISSION: 1485cc/1748cc, 4cyl ohv, 5sp man, or auto, f/f

POWER: 69bhp @ 5600rpm/77bhp @ 5750rpm/84bhp @ 5000rpm

MAX SPEED (MPH): 90/ - /(E) 97

0-60MPH (SEC): 16.7/ - /Not measured

SUSPENSION & BRAKES: HydraG ifs, HydraG irs, disc f/drum r

LENGTH (IN)/WEIGHT (LB): 154/2000

LAUNCH PRICE: £1951/£5265/£5706

VAUXHALL

Founded in 1904, and established at Luton soon afterwards, Vauxhall was absorbed by America's General Motors in 1925. The transformation from a maker of thoroughbreds to a mass-market car-maker took a decade, but by 1939 Vauxhall had become one of Britain's "Big Six".

After a War spent making military machinery, including Churchill tanks and thousands of Bedford trucks, Vauxhall greeted 1946 with three revived 1939-40 models. New-generation Wyvern and Velox models arrived in 1948, 1951 and 1957, but the smaller (and controversial) Victor also appeared in 1957 and Vauxhall's first really small saloon, the Viva, followed in 1963.

Throughout this time production expanded mightily, a new assembly plant was opened up on Merseyside, and in true American "product planning" style the number of models became positively byzantine. Long before this, GM had also absorbed Opel of Germany, and from the end of the 1960s their policy was to merge the new-model development of the two, and to turn Vauxhall into a junior partner of the German marque.

Opel mechanical elements had already been hidden inside the Viva and late 1960s Victor models, but once the Cavalier appeared in 1975, and the first of the front wheel drive Astras arrived in 1979, the process was virtually complete. Although Vauxhall would never again have any technical independence, the marque at least persisted, especially in the UK market.

Even so, by the early 2000s, there were signs that Vauxhall might not have a secure long-term future, and after the centenary had been celebrated it began to look as if the marque might disappear before long.

10hp/12hp 1946-48

Re-introduced in 1946, the H-type Vauxhall had been Britain's first monocoque-structured car when new in 1937. It set the pattern for post-war years. The 1203cc engine (new in 1937) was retained for the 10hp, and for the 1947 12hp the 1442cc unit from the previous I-type 12-4 (see entry below) was used.

Both 10hp and 12hp H-types had a four-door four-light steel saloon body. The fixed-head coupés built before the War were not revived. Dubonnet-type torsion bar independent front suspension was a feature – with this system, when one hit the brakes the nose rose instead of diving. The rest of the chassis was conventional enough – overhead-valve engine, three-speed floor gearchange, hydraulic brakes. The interior trim and equipment were built down to a price,

The Vauxhall Ten was re-introduced in 1946. A pre-war example is shown – the post-war version had horizontal grille bars.

SPECIFICATION

BODY STYLES: saloon

PRODUCTION: 44,047

ENGINE & TRANSMISSION: 1203cc/1442cc, 4cyl ohv, 3sp man, f/r

POWER: 31bhp @ 3600rpm/35bhp @ 3600rpm

MAX SPEED (MPH): 60 (E)/63

0-60MPH (SEC): not available/39.2

SUSPENSION & BRAKES: tor ifs, leaf rear, drums f&r

LENGTH (IN)/WEIGHT (LB): 159/2016-2072

LAUNCH PRICE: £371/£403

rather than up to a standard.

Nothing to get excited about (especially with the original 31bhp 1203cc engine, with which this 2000lb car struggled even to reach 60mph), and not even the engine transplant of 1947 could do much about that. Vauxhall didn't mind, as their major competition came from the Ford Prefect, which was even less soul-stirring.

With an apology to all Vauxhall fanatics, this was a car which sold well at the time but did not deserve to retain much of a reputation. Slow, soft handling, and with awfully rust-prone bodywork, it has virtually disappeared .

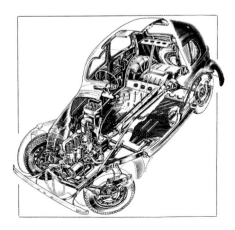

The Ten was of monocoque construction.

12-4 (I-type) 1945-46

Why re-introduce this model in 1945, if only six (that's right, 6) were to be made? We can only think that Vauxhall discovered spare body shells when the factory was re-converted to peacetime production, and decided to turn them into a bit of useful cash. Vauxhall certainly didn't need three different shells at this time, so to drop this one made sense.

The I-Type had appeared in 1938, and more than 10,000 had already been sold when civilian production closed down for the duration. Though sharing

SPECIFICATION

BODY STYLES : saloon

PRODUCTION: 6

ENGINE & TRANSMISSION: 1442cc, 4cyl ohv, 3sp man, f/r

POWER: 35bhp @ 3600rpm

MAX SPEED (MPH): 60 (E)

0-60MPH (SEC): not available

SUSPENSION & BRAKES: tor ifs, leaf rear, drums f&r

LENGTH (IN)/WEIGHT (LB): 163/2050

LAUNCH PRICE: £403

Vauxhall Twelve, 1945-46. This is the six-light I-type, replaced by the four-light HIX model using the Ten's hull.

some of its monocoque structure with the H-type (described above), this was a six-light saloon, with an eight-inch longer wheelbase and more cabin space. The Dubonnet torsion bar front suspension, the three-speed gearbox and the rear suspension were all shared, but in this case the only engine to be offered was the 35bhp/1442cc "four",

and the top speed was still no more than 60mph.

This is not quite the forgotten Vauxhall (the brief pre-war success made that impossible), but it is hardly worth recalling here. Like other late 1940s Vauxhalls, in any case, it was a rust trap, and all six have surely gone to the great scrapyard in the sky?

14-6 (J-type) 1939-48

GM's product planners must have been proud of the way they milked so many body derivatives from one basic monocoque, platform and Dubonnet suspension design. Here was

SPECIFICATION

BODY STYLES: saloon

PRODUCTION: 30,511 post-war

ENGINE & TRANSMISSION: 1781cc, 6cyl ohv, 3sp man, f/r

POWER: 48bhp @ 3600rpm

MAX SPEED (MPH): 67

0-60MPH (SEC): 38.6

SUSPENSION & BRAKES: tor ifs, leaf rear, drums f&r

LENGTH (IN)/WEIGHT (LB): 169/2374

LAUNCH PRICE : £480

Vauxhall J-type 14-6.

the largest of the trio (only two really – see I-type, above), this time with a smooth and durable 48bhp 1781cc long-stroke six-cylinder engine which Vauxhall had first introduced in 1933. This was linked to a three-speed all-synchromesh gearbox with a floor change. The cabin was the same as the

short-lived I-type's, but there was a projecting boot offering more luggage space. The car was a sure-fire winner.

It had been new in 1938, and sold like mad before the war broke out, selling particularly well in export markets. From late 1945 to 1948 Vauxhall built more than 30,000 cars –

successful by any of their existing standards – even if they were not very nice cars to drive and tended to rust away before your very eyes.

Don't knock it though, the balance sheets were positive, and it all helped Vauxhall plan for their next generation of cars.

Wyvern/Velox (L-type) 1948-51

For its first true post-war model, Vauxhall chose the "quick and dirty" method by giving a thorough overhaul to the H-type, which had started life in 1937. By keeping the same basic platform, cabin and mechanical layout, the company could spend most of its time on style changes while also introducing a new engine derivative. The marketing master-stroke was to label the two cars Wyvern (4-cylinder) and Velox (6-cylinder), both of these being old Vauxhall names from the 1920s.

One careful look at the body revealed its H-Type origins, though there was a longer and more modern nose with built-in headlamps, an extended tail, and a bonnet which opened up, alligator-style, for access. Interestingly, counterbalanced quick-lift window glass took over from conventional winding-handle types.

Under the skin, the platform and chassis were like those of the H-type, complete with Dubonnet torsion bar independent front suspension and a three-speed gearbox. The choice of engines, however, was now different.

The L-type Wyvern: 35bhp and 60mph were not impressive even in 1948.

Wyverns had the 1442cc four-cylinder engine from the 12hp, while the Velox had a closely related long-stroke 2275cc six-cylinder engine instead.

These were less than wonderful cars in many ways: the style was controversial, the handling was poor, and the Wyvern was dreadfully slow. Other minuses included the bench front seat, the

absence of synchromesh on first gear, the steering-column gearchange, and (we now know) the rust-prone bodies. Yet in sales terms they hit the spot. The Velox sold best, proving that export markets needed the extra performance, and both cars kept Vauxhall's pot boiling until the next-generation Wyvern and Velox appeared in 1951.

SPECIFICATION

BODY STYLES: saloon

PRODUCTION: 55,409/76,919

ENGINE & TRANSMISSION: 1442cc, 4cyl/2275cc, 6cyl ohv, 3sp man f/r

POWER: 35bhp @ 3600rpm/55bhp @ 3300rpm

MAX SPEED (MPH): 60/74

0-60MPH (SEC): not available/22.7

SUSPENSION & BRAKES: tor ifs, leaf rear, drums f&r

LENGTH (IN)/WEIGHT (LB): 165/2184-2380

LAUNCH PRICE: £448/£550

With six cylinders and 2275cc the L-type Velox went a lot better.

Wyvern/Velox (E-type) 1951-57

Here was Vauxhall's first true post-war car, which is to say that there was a brand-new monocoque, much larger but surprisingly lighter than the interim Wyvern/Velox cars of 1948-51. This new style would dominate the scene at Luton for the next six years.

The new models were launched in August 1951 with a 103in wheelbase and a four-door saloon style clearly influenced by GM in Detroit. Once again two engines were offered, the same 35bhp 1442cc and 54bhp 2275cc units as the previous Wyvern and Velox. The old three-speed gearbox with column change was also carried over, but the rest of the running gear was new. This was the first Vauxhall for many years to have coil spring independent front sus-pension.

The balance of the specification was as expected – full hydraulic brakes (though the handbrake lever was now alongside the driver's seat), a bench front seat, a cavernous boot, and a full-width grille.

Totally new short-stroke engines – a 40bhp 1508cc four-cylinder and a 64bhp 2262cc six-cylinder – took over during 1952, there was recirculating-ball steering from 1953, a new grille in 1955, and wind-up windows reappeared at the same time. There was another and rather more restrained grille, and a wrap-

The E-type Wyvern had a livelier engine from 1952, and room for six inside.

around rear screen, in August 1956, along with electric rather than engine-driven wipers (which would rather frustratingly slow down when you changed up).

At the very end of the run, from June 1957, Vauxhall up-graded the 2262cc engine to 83bhp and introduced an all-synchromesh gearbox, both of these changes being made ahead of the launch of the next (P-type) Velox/Cresta.

One of Vauxhall's favoured coach-builders, Grosvenor, finally produced an estate car conversion of the Velox (not the Wyvern or the Cresta, though) in

August 1956, which meant that it was on sale for only a year, costing £1126. That car gained factory approval, while a Martin Walter conversion apparently did no. Both were very rare.

These cars were hugely successful, and more than 500,000 of all types were eventually produced. They were not considered good drivers' cars, they felt cheap inside and out, and they rusted very fast, but the short-stroke engines were good, there was room and comfort for six inside, and the Velox would cruise all day at 70mph. Neglect is the reason why very few examples survived.

E-type Velox ran smoothly to nearly 80mph with the 1952-on short-stroke 2262cc engine. Its direct rival was the Ford Zephyr, whose engine was of the same capacity.

The E-type Velox had a front end re-style in 1955 and got rear wheel spats.

Last of the E-type Veloxes, with horizontal grille bars.

Velox estate car by Martin Walter, 1957.

Cresta (E-type) 1954-57

Although Ford started this trend in 1953 with the Zephyr Zodiac, Vauxhall followed suit only a year later with the new E-type Cresta. Effectively, this was a 2262cc-engined Velox with every bell-and-whistle that Vauxhall could add to the specification.

Mechanically the Cresta was nearly identical with the Velox, though cosmetic changes included a different grille, a two-tone colour scheme (a three-tone scheme would be available from late 1955), whitewall tyres, leather upholstery and a heater as standard, plus a redesigned fascia with circular instruments. Like the Velox, the Cresta gained enlarged front and rear glass from late 1955, with the more powerful 83bhp engine and all-synchromesh gearbox from June 1957.

Vauxhall's stance was that for all this

The E-type Cresta of 1955, ritzy version of the Velox.

extra glitz one only had to pay an extra £85. The public, it seems, found this a reasonable bargain, and would buy shed loads of them in just three years. So what

if it wasn't classy, and so what if it didn't handle that well – it did make the neighbours look twice, and to Vauxhall buyers, it seemed, that was everything.

Cresta specification included two-tone paint and trim, leather, a heater and a clock.

Victor (Type FA) 1957-61

Motoring pundits gave the original Victor a very hard time. Almost everyone hated the styling, no one liked the build quality or specifications and there was no praise for the handling or performance either. Yet the car was another great success for Vauxhall. Nearly 400,000 were sold in four years, and no accountant was ever heard to complain about that.

Because the Wyvern/Velox range was physically large, Vauxhall needed a smaller car to attack what was then called the Ford Consul class. Although it used an up-dated Wyvern engine and gearbox, the F-Type had an all-new four-door saloon body on a 98-inch wheelbase. The set-up was strictly conventional: 1508cc, 48bhp, three-speed all-synchromesh gearbox with column change, coil spring independent front suspension and fully hydraulic brakes. But the body was something else.

The styling, complete with wraparound windscreen and dog-leg front pillars, Vauxhall flutes along the flanks and a weird kink in the rear door skin, was bizarre, while the interior, with its bench front seat and GM-USA-type

The first Vauxhall Victor sold nearly 400,000 examples.

instrument layout, looked awful. Even so, prices started at £729 and people queued up to buy it.

A five-door estate car and two-pedal "Newtondrive" transmission became optional in March 1958. Then, thank goodness, some of the oddities were stripped away in February 1959 with the Series II, when the chrome side strips disappeared, as did the rear door pressing kink, and there was a new grille. At the same time, conventional bumpers and rear wings were specified, and the power was eased up to 55bhp. A De Luxe version, with separate front seats and leather upholstery, was added – and range prices started at £748. This was a better car, but still an acquired taste.

One either liked the Victor's value, or hated its styling and strongly Transatlantic character, there being few halfmeasures. If you didn't look at it, and if

you didn't mind the steering-column change, this was a sturdy but very ordinary car – until, of course, the body rusted away, as it very speedily did.

The Victor Estate, introduced in 1958, was Vauxhall's first ever factory-produced estate car.

SPECIFICATION

BODY STYLES: saloon, estate

PRODUCTION: 390,745

ENGINE & TRANSMISSION: 1508cc, 4cyl ohv, 3sp man, semi-auto, f/r

POWER: 48bhp @ 4200rpm/55bhp @ 4200rpm

MAX SPEED (MPH): 74

0-60MPH (SEC): 28.1

SUSPENSION & BRAKES: coil ifs, leaf rear, drums f&r

LENGTH (IN)/WEIGHT (LB): 166/2150

LAUNCH PRICE: £729

Victor FB 1961-64

What a relief! The second-generation Victor of 1961, coded FB, was a much better car than the original type. It was built on a new, longer-wheelbase platform, with some

platform and body pressings shortly due to be shared with a new-generation Velox/Cresta (the PB of 1962). This was a more conventional Victor, its looks much less offensive than before.

Powered by basically the same the 1508cc engine, with the column-change three-speed gearbox as before, the new car had a 100in-wheelbase platform. In this case, the coil spring independent front suspension worked from a cross-member which was welded to the shell, rather than detachable. The FB was also the first post-war Vauxhall to offer an optional all-synchromesh four-speed gearbox with floor change, but there was no automatic transmission yet.

Lower, wider, and looking altogether more restrained than before, this car dumped the unpopular dog-leg front pillars and wrap-around screen of the original, and was the first Vauxhall for many years not to have "signature" chrome spear decorations at the front end. An altogether more tasteful fascia layout, with circular dials, added to the

Victor FB, 1961, comfortable and roomy.

effect. Separate front seats with leather facings were standard on De Luxe versions, and optional on less specified models.

Two years later, in September 1963, the engine was enlarged, to 1594cc, giving 59bhp. Front-wheel disc brakes became optional extras (they came with 14in in place of 13in wheels), and on

De Luxe models there was a walnut veneer fascia.

Along with the more powerful VX4/90s, these were much better cars than the early Victors, more attuned to both home and export markets. Even so, they would only be on sale for three years before yet another type of Victor, the FC, was launched.

SPECIFICATION

BODY STYLES: saloon, estate

PRODUCTION: 328,640

ENGINE & TRANSMISSION: 1508cc/1594cc, 4cyl ohv, 3sp man, 4sp man, f/r

POWER: 50bhp @ 4600rpm/59bhp @ 4600rpm

MAX SPEED (MPH): 76/80

0-60MPH (SEC): 22.6/18.2

SUSPENSION & BRAKES: coil ifs, leaf rear, drums f&r (disc f/drum r from late 1963)

LENGTH (IN)/WEIGHT (LB): 173/2100 - 2128

LAUNCH PRICE: £745/£635

Victor VX4/90 FB 1961-64

The original VX4/90 was Vauxhall's very first attempt at building high-performance saloon, and it was a great success. Based on the mainstream FB saloon (no estate car version was ever available), it was faster, better equipped, and had improved handling.

Compared with the mainstream FB, the engine got a considerable makeover involving a light alloy cylinder head and twin downdraught Zenith carburettors. It gave 71bhp. The new all-synchromesh four-speed gearbox with floor change was standard, as were front-wheel disc brakes and 14in wheels. There was a walnut veneer instrument panel and a rev-counter was standard. The body was brightened up by a bright colour flash along the flanks.

Like the other FBs, in September 1963

Victor FB VX4/90 had 71bhp and could hit nearly 90mph.

the VX4/90 was up-gunned, this time with a 75bhp 1594cc engine, which did little for the top speed but improved the acceleration.

As a direct competitor to Ford's Cortina GT, the VX4/90 sold well, though its early-rusting problem was never solved.

SPECIFICATION

BODY STYLES: saloon

PRODUCTION: included in FB total, above

ENGINE & TRANSMISSION: 1508cc/1594cc, 4cyl ohv, 4sp man, f/r

POWER: 71bhp @ 5200rpm/75bhp @ 5200rpm

MAX SPEED (MPH): 88/88

0-60MPH (SEC): 16.4/15.4

SUSPENSION & BRAKES: coil ifs, leaf rear, disc f/drum r

LENGTH (IN)/WEIGHT (LB): 173/2184-2198

LAUNCH PRICE: £984/£840

VX4/90 on the 1962 RAC Rally.

Victor FC (101) 1964-67

Announced on the very eve of the 1964 London Motor Show, in October, what became known as the "101" (a project code) came as a real surprise, for the previous model had only been on sale for three years. As before, there was a four-door saloon, a five-door estate car and a VX4/90.

Cleverly based on the platform, suspension and all the basic running gear of the Victor FB, the FC/101 was effectively a new and much roomier body on the same footprint.

The familiar 1594cc engine had been

SPECIFICATION

BODY STYLES: saloon, estate

PRODUCTION: 219,814

ENGINE & TRANSMISSION: 1594cc, 4cyl ohv, 3sp man,4sp man, or auto, f/r

POWER: 61bhp @ 4800rpm

MAX SPEED (MPH): 81/84

0-60MPH (SEC): 20.4/17.1

SUSPENSION & BRAKES: coil ifs, leaf rear, drums f&r (optional disc f/drum r)

LENGTH (IN)/WEIGHT (LB): 173/2150-2194

LAUNCH PRICE: £678/£702

Vauxhall Victor FC 101 estate.

slightly improved, to give 61bhp and as before there was a choice of three-speed column-change gearbox, or four-speed floor-change unit. Eight months later, from June 1965, GM's own Powerglide automatic transmission became the third transmission option. Front-wheel disc brakes were still an optional extra, and though drums were standard, they were at least self-adjusting. This time around,

13in wheels were standard on all models.

The body was smoother than before, with slightly convex sides. Along with the use of curved window glass, this made the interior four inches wider, without having to alter the platform or the monocoque. The fascia featured a combined strip instrument. Neat, no doubt, but the circular dials of the VX4/90 were better-liked.

As usual, there were three trim levels – Basic, Super and De Luxe, with prices spanning £678 to £763. Two different trim levels of estate car, at £775 and £859, completed the range.

As time passed the Victor gradually lost all the idiosyncrasies of the original model, and by the mid-1960s it was thoroughly conventional, well developed and commercially successful. Unlike Ford, though, Vauxhall did not seem to inject much character into these cars, so they are not as well-remembered as the Cortinas which were their major rivals.

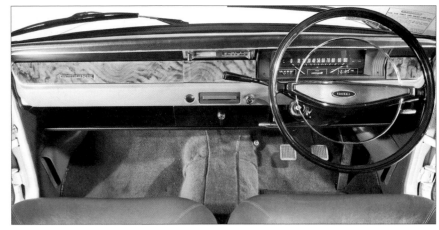

101 De Luxe dashboard. The steering column change was standard, but four-on-the-floor was available as an option

VX4/90 FC (101) 1964-67

The third-generation VX4/90 was launched at exactly the same time as the other Type 101 models, having the same basic body style, but of course only as a four-door saloon. The 75bhp 1594cc engine and the four-on-the-floor gearbox were not changed, but when GM Powerglide automatic appeared on other Victors, it was also made available on the

Vauxhall FC VX4/90 .

SPECIFICATION

BODY STYLES: saloon

PRODUCTION: 13,449

ENGINE & TRANSMISSION: 1594cc, 4cyl ohv, 4sp man, or auto, f/r

POWER: 75bhp @ 5200rpm

MAX SPEED (MPH): 93

0-60MPH (SEC): 16.0

SUSPENSION & BRAKES: coil ifs, leaf rear, disc f/drum r

LENGTH (IN)/WEIGHT (LB): 173/2254

LAUNCH PRICE: £872

VX4/90. Disc front brakes were standard. This was the first VX4/90 to use 13in road wheels, with radial ply optional. In 1966 and 1967 there was also the option of a limited-slip differential, which was standardised from October 1965.

The VX4/90 had its own special instrument panel, with four same-size dials ahead of the driver's eyes, and it also had separate front seats.

Quicker than before, but still not sensationally fast, the VX4/90 was a success, but it never built up a motorsport reputation to help sprinkle itself with stardust.

Victor FD 1967-72

Here was a new beginning for the Victor – a new platform, new style, and a new family of overhead-camshaft engines which were laid over at an angle of 45 degrees in the engine bay. Introduced as four-door saloons, with 1599cc and 1975cc engines, they were joined by a five-door estate from May 1968.

The platform featured a 102in wheelbase, with Viva HB-inspired coil spring independent front suspension, and a coil-sprung rear axle located by twinned trailing arms and a Panhard rod. Rack-and-pinion steering was a real advance over the older type.

Product planning was intense. The driveline choice was complex – engines of 72bhp/1599cc or 88bhp/1975cc came with a three-speed column change, four-speed floor change, four-speed plus overdrive, or Borg Warner automatic transmission. Front-wheel disc brakes were standard on 2-litres but an optional extra on 1.6-litres.

This was a much more spacious car than the Victor 101 which it replaced and the styling introduced the "Coke bottle" waistline to the British market. Cars with the three-speed column change had a bench front seat, while four-speed 1.6-litre customers could buy separate seats as an option. Separate seats

SPECIFICATION

BODY STYLES: saloon, estate

PRODUCTION TOTAL: 198,085, including Ventora

ENGINE & TRANSMISSION: 1599cc/1975cc, 4cyl ohc, 3sp man, 4sp man, or auto, f/r

POWER : 72bhp @ 5600rpm/88bhp @ 5500rpm

MAX SPEED (MPH): 90/95

0-60MPH (SEC): 19.3/14.0

SUSPENSION & BRAKES : coil ifs, coil rear, drums f&r, or disc f/drum r

LENGTH (IN)/WEIGHT (LB): 177/2321 - 2350

LAUNCH PRICE: £819/£910

The Victor FD was available as a 1600 or a 2000. This is a 1972 Victor Super.

were always standard on 2-litre types.

In more than four years, the only significant mechanical up-date came in January 1970, when a new "small" GM automatic transmission took over from the earlier Borg Warner type. Faster, better handling and altogether more capable than the Type 101 Victors, these were successful cars, but were often let down by doubtful build quality and a lack of refinement. The six-cylinder Ventora (see below) was a better bet, but much more costly. These Victors, like the ones before, are nearly all gone.

VX4/90 FD 1969-72

After the new-generation overhead-cam Victors went on sale, there was a two-year gap before the expected high-performance VX4/90 was revealed – actually in October 1969 – which meant that it would only be only on sale for a little over two years.

Developed from the Victor series of the day, the 1970-model VX4/90 shared the same four-door "Coke bottle" style of saloon body, and the same basic suspension. Externally, the only obvious

SPECIFICATION

BODY STYLES: saloon

PRODUCTION: 14,277

ENGINE & TRANSMISSION: 1975cc, 4cyl ohc, 4sp man, o/d or auto, f/r

POWER: 104bhp @ 5600rpm

MAX SPEED (MPH): 98

0-60MPH (SEC): 13.2

SUSPENSION & BRAKES: coil ifs, coil rear, disc f/drum r

LENGTH (IN)/WEIGHT (LB): 177/2396

LAUNCH PRICE: £1203

The FD VX4/90 offered 104bhp, overdrive and Rostyle wheels.

recognition points were the fitment of Rostyle road wheels with radial ply tyres, and a different grille, while inside the car there was a fully equipped fascia with rev-counter and matching speedometer placed ahead of the driver's eyes.

By using twin Zenith-Stromberg carburettors (as in the Viva GT), the 1975cc overhead-camshaft engine was boosted to 104bhp. An overdrive gearbox was standard and GM automatic transmission was an optional extra. One interesting touch, a first for Vauxhall, was that the overdrive switch was located in the gearlever knob.

This was a brisk, almost-100mph car which handled well. Somehow or other, it never built the same sort of sporty reputation as did, say, the Ford Cortina GT. Though build quality was never better than average, we might call this car a worthy "sleeper".

Velox/Cresta PA 1957-62

Six years after the E-typeVelox had gone on sale, Vauxhall finally replaced it, introducing a much larger, much more stylish and altogether more appealing package. The new PA-type Velox and Cresta had lots to offer, and were worthy competition for Ford's Zephyrs and Zodiacs. Now that the Victor had appeared there was no longer an entry-level Wyvern version of the big Vauxhall.

These were big and impressive four-door saloons built on a 105in wheelbase. The Friary estate, which followed from April 1959, was a conversion of the same shell, and rare. The styling was obviously influenced by GM in Detroit, and featured a large panoramic windscreen with dog-leg screen pillars. At the rear there was three-piece window, although a one-piece wrap-around rear window came in August 1959. Inside the car there was a bench front seat, a column gearchange, and a twin-dial fascia which also reflected

1957 Cresta PA with the straight-top grille.

what GM was offering in the USA at the time.

Under the skin, the latest version of the 2262cc "six" had a new cylinder head with individual inlet and exhaust ports and produced 83bhp, enough to deliver a top speed of 87mph. The independent front suspension, by coil springs and wishbones, was closely related to that of the newly-launched Victor. Velox and Cresta were mechanically identical, the differences being the higher level of trim and equipment of the Cresta..

In five years, there was much improvement to the range. From summer 1960 servo-assisted brakes become optional and in August of that year the engine was enlarged to 2651cc (once again with a different cylinder head casting), now giving 95bhp. The 14in wheels hid larger drum brakes, and Laycock overdrive or GM Hydramatic transmission were options. The fascia was now much smarter and less Americanised than before, with a revolving-drum type of strip speedometer.

In September 1961 these cars were offered with power-assisted front disc brakes and separate front seats as optional extras. The PAs have enjoyed a devoted following for some time.

In 1959 the PA's grille and rear window were revised and a new 2.6-litre engine was fitted in 1960. This is a 1961 Velox.

PA Friary estate was not often seen.

SPECIFICATION

BODY STYLES: saloon, estate

PRODUCTION: 173,759

ENGINE & TRANSMISSION: 2262cc/2651cc, 6cyl ohv, 3sp man, o/d or auto, f/r

POWER: 83bhp @ 4400rpm/95bhp @ 4600rpm

MAX SPEED (MPH): 87/95

0-60MPH (SEC): 18.0/15.2

SUSPENSION & BRAKES: coil ifs, leaf rear, drums f&r (disc f/drum r optional)

LENGTH (IN)/WEIGHT (LB): 178/2520-2688

LAUNCH PRICE: £984/£929

Velox/Cresta PB 1962-65

The third-generation Velox/Cresta had more conventional looks than the PA models but did not sell quite as well. Even so, the formula – a spacious five/six-seater car powered by a lazy six-cylinder engine – was well established, and carried the big Vauxhalls on for three more years.

Vauxhall initially built only four-door saloons, though Martin Walter were then encouraged to add officially-approved estate cars to the range. For the PB cars there was a totally new platform and body shell. The wheelbase, at 107.5in, was longer than before. The 2.6-litre six-cylinder engine of the PA was retained, as were the coil spring independent front suspension and the transmission choices (three-speed manual, overdrive, or automatic). On the PB front-wheel disc brakes were standardised.

A1965 3.3-litre Cresta PB.

The styling theme was totally different from that of the PA, being more angular, visually similar to the Victor FB of the period. This meant that Vauxhall had abandoned the exaggerated wrap-around screen and chosen a much more conservative rear window style.

Inside the car, the cabin was rather more spacious than before. Vauxhall claimed an extra six inches, front to rear bulkheads. A bench front seat was normal in the Velox and Cresta (individual front seats were not available), and as ever there was a steering-column gear change. By comparison with the earlier Velox/Cresta, this was a more refined and less glitzy car than before, with leather upholstery and walnut veneer fascias featuring on the Cresta.

From October 1964 the engine was enlarged to 3294cc, giving 115bhp (this was its final stretch), and an all-synchromesh four-speed gearbox with floor change became optional, though overdrive was not available with it. Also from this point, Cresta customers could once again specify separate leather-covered front seats. With the torquey 3.3-litre engine and the four-speed 'box the PB had quite surprising performance.

Finally, from April 1965, power-assisted steering became optional, which was good, but the automatic option became the GM Powerglide unit, which had only two speeds: Sluggish and Dead Slow, some dubbed them. It can only have been top-level GM policy that inflicted this awful system on British Vauxhall drivers.

Another family of Crestas was in the wings, however, this duly following later in 1965.

SPECIFICATION

BODY STYLES: saloon, estate

PRODUCTION: 87,044 produced)

ENGINE & TRANSMISSION: 2651cc/3294cc, 6cyl ohv, 3sp man, 4sp man, o/d or auto, f/r

POWER: 95bhp @ 4600rpm/115bhp @ 4200rpm

MAX SPEED (MPH): 93/99

0-60MPH (SEC): 13.8/11.6

SUSPENSION & BRAKES: coil ifs, leaf rear, disc f/drum r

LENGTH (IN)/WEIGHT (LB): 182/2744

LAUNCH PRICE: £1046/£849

Cresta PC 1965-72

The simple way to describe the Cresta PC is as a PB in a fresh, new-fashion party frock. The platform, many inner panels, the suspension, brakes, steering, engine and transmission were all developed versions of those used in the last of the Cresta PBs. There was no Velox version of the new model range.

While still using the 107.5in-wheelbase platform, the PC had much smoother lines than its predecessor. There was just one four-door style at first, though De Luxe Crestas had four headlamps, ordinary Crestas only two. An estate car

conversion, once again by Martin Walter, went on sale in January 1967.

Because the door glass was curved, and the body profiled accordingly, the cabin was even larger than before. Crestas had bench front seats, Cresta De Luxes had individual front seats (though a bench was still optional). The strip speedometer of earlier types had been abandoned in favour of conventional circular dials set in a walnut veneer fascia panel.

The engine was still the same size as before, at 3294cc, but its peak power had been increased to 123bhp. The gearbox

choices were three-speed with column change and optional overdrive, four-speed floor change and two-speed Powerglide automatic. In spite of the shortcomings of the GM automatic, a greater proportion of cars were to be fitted with it in future years. Rear suspension location was improved by a pair of semi-trailing radius arms, servo-assisted front-wheel disc brakes were standard, and power steering was optional.

This car would be on sale until July 1972, though sales fell away significantly after 1970. The estate car derivative was only available from January 1967 until February 1968. The three-speed (with or without overdrive) option disappeared in mid-1970, and at the same time GM-Europe's new automatic transmission took over from the Powerglide.

Vauxhall kept this model going for years, knowing that it would never be replaced. Like its predecessors, it was big, comfortable, and good value for money. While the PC was not particularly fast or sporting, its large engine did not need revs to give its pleasingly effortless brand of performance. Once the model was dead, survivors disappeared rapidly and few have been preserved.

SPECIFICATION

BODY STYLES: saloon, estate

PRODUCTION: 53,912

ENGINE & TRANSMISSION: 3294cc, 6cyl ohv, 3sp man, 4sp man, o/d or auto, f/r

POWER: 123bhp @ 4600rpm

MAX SPEED (MPH): 103

0-60MPH (SEC): 12.6

SUSPENSION & BRAKES: coil ifs, leaf rear, disc f/drum r

LENGTH (IN)/WEIGHT (LB): 187/2796

LAUNCH PRICE: £956

The Cresta PC arrived in 1965. There was no Velox version.

Viscount 1966-72

Introduced in June 1966, the Viscount was effectively a Cresta PC, mechanically unchanged but with even more up-market trim and equipment. It was on sale alongside the Cresta PC until both cars were withdrawn in 1972.

Under the skin the only difference from the Cresta PC was that the Powerglide automatic transmission was standard, whereas the four-speed all-synchromesh manual gearbox was actually a reduced-cost option. Power-assisted steering was now standard and larger-section tyres were specified. As on the Cresta PC,

Where the Cresta had been the luxury version of the Velox, the Viscount became the luxury version of the Cresta. A 1971 Viscount is shown.

SPECIFICATION

BODY STYLES: saloon

PRODUCTION: 7025

ENGINE & TRANSMISSION: 3294cc, 6cyl ohv, 4sp man, or auto, f/r

POWER: 123bhp @ 4600rpm

MAX SPEED (MPH): 103

0-60MPH (SEC): 12.5

SUSPENSION & BRAKES: coil ifs, leaf rear, disc f/drum r

LENGTH (IN)/WEIGHT (LB): 187/3070

LAUNCH PRICE: £1680 (automatic transmission), £1611 (manual transmission)

GM-Europe automatic transmission replaced Powerglide in mid-1970.

All the novelty was inside the cabin, where there was a distinctive wood-veneer instrument panel which was matched by wood cappings on the doors and drop-down picnic tables in the rear compartment. The seats (separate at the front) were leather-covered, and there was much more sound-deadening equip-ment to further reduce cabin noise.

Externally, there was a vinyl roof covering, a die-cast front grille and special wheel trims. All cars were saloons, there being no estate car alternative.

The Viscount was an impressively large, luxurious, squashily-sprung "executive" car which offered no more than a Cresta except for the additional fixtures and fittings.

Ventora/Victor 3300 1968-72

Soon after the all-new Victor FD generation went on sale, Vauxhall introduced a six-cylinder version, which was originally known as the Ventora (saloon) or Victor 3300 (estate car).

Launched in February 1968, these cars essentially used the same unit-construction body, suspension and steering as the Victor FDs. The latest 123bhp 3294cc engine, as fitted to the contemporary Cresta PC, was squeezed into the engine bay, and the Cresta-type four-speed gearbox with floor change was standard. Laycock overdrive was an optional extra (£43), as was Powerglide automatic transmission (£98). Front-wheel disc brakes were standard.

Externally there was a different grille,

With the 123bhp 3.3-litre engine and plenty of torque, the 1968-72 Ventora was an effortless cruiser.

SPECIFICATION

BODY STYLES: saloon, estate

PRODUCTION: included in Victor FD

ENGINE & TRANSMISSION: 3294cc, 6cyl ohv, 4sp man, o/d or auto, f/r

POWER: 123bhp @ 4600rpm

MAX SPEED (MPH): 103

0-60MPH (SEC): 11.8

SUSPENSION & BRAKES: coil ifs, coil rear, disc f/drum r

LENGTH (IN)/WEIGHT (LB): 177/2553

LAUNCH PRICE: £1102

and most early cars had a vinyl roof covering (which was made standard from September 1968). From August 1969 the Ventora became Ventora II, with a new fascia and instrument display and with the reclining front seats which the first cars so desperately needed.

As with all other Victor/Cresta types of this period, GM-Europe automatic transmission replaced the Powerglide, this time from January 1970. From

February 1971 power-assisted steering became standard on automatic transmission models.

Significantly faster than other Victors, this was a well-received car, though its relatively high price put off many prospective customers. Its handling was still too soft, but its performance delivery was seamless, and with over-drive it was a very long-legged car.

Yet again, we have to say, there are few survivors.

Viva HA 1963-66

When the original Viva was revealed in September 1963, it was the smallest ever post-war Vauxhall, by any measure. Vauxhall did not like to admit it at the time, but even though it was British-built (at Ellesmere Port, on Merseyside) it was virtually a mechanical clone of the Opel Kadett of the period.

Opel, of course, was also a GM subsidiary, and these two cars shared the same basic platform, front and rear suspension, engine and transmission, though the all-steel unit-construction shell of the Viva had its own two-door body style. The styling was simple and

First of the Vauxhall Vivas, the 1-litre HA of 1963.

slab sided, for this car only had a 91.5in wheelbase and had to accommodate four passenger seats.

There was nothing fancy about the running gear. The 1057cc engine had pushrod overhead valves. (The Kadett engine, in a car not imported to the UK, was slightly smaller at 993cc.) There was a small new all-synchromesh four-speed gearbox, with a diaphragm clutch. But there were no more complications – no overdrive or automatic transmission options.

Independent front suspension was by Opel-type transverse leaf spring (rather old-fashioned, but cheap to build), but at least there was rack-and-pinion steering. The rear axle was partly located by a short torque tube and rode on half-elliptic springs. Four-wheel drum brakes were standard, but front-wheel discs were optional extras.

Priced to sell (as they say in the auction

business), at £527 the Viva competed head on with the Ford Anglia at £514, so there were no frills, either in the equipment or in the character and performance.

Even so, it was a car which Vauxhall dealers sold in huge numbers at the time, though there was never much justification for keeping one going after the inevitable body rot had set in. Vauxhalls, at the time, were famous for their rusting tendencies.

The Viva was spacious and modern inside. This De Luxe model has carpets.

SPECIFICATION

BODY STYLES: saloon

PRODUCTION: 309,538

ENGINE & TRANSMISSION: 1057cc, 4cyl ohv, 4sp man, f/r

POWER: 44bhp @ 5000rpm

MAX SPEED (MPH): 77

0-60MPH (SEC): 22.1

SUSPENSION & BRAKES: leaf ifs, leaf rear, drums f&r

LENGTH (IN)/WEIGHT (LB): 155/1564

LAUNCH PRICE: £527

Three of the six privately-entered Vivas that took the first six places in their class in Australia's "Armstrong 500", the longest motor race in the world for standard production cars.

Viva HA 90 | 1965-66

SPECIFICATION

BODY STYLES: saloon

PRODUCTION: 11,794

ENGINE & TRANSMISSION: 1057cc, 4cyl ohv, 4sp man, f/r

POWER: 54bhp @ 5600rpm

MAX SPEED (MPH): 81

0-60MPH (SEC): 18.2

SUSPENSION & BRAKES: coil ifs, leaf rear, disc f/drum r

LENGTH (IN)/WEIGHT (LB): 155/1750

LAUNCH PRICE: £607

The performance version of the Viva was the 60bhp HA 90.

The Viva HA 90 was a one-season wonder. It was announced in October 1965, but was quickly rendered obsolete by the launch of the new style HB precisely one year later.

Compared with the mainstream Viva, the HA 90 had a tuned version of the 1057cc engine with a higher compression ratio, revised manifolding and a side-draught Zenith-Stromberg carbu-

rettor in place of the standard car's downdraught Solex unit. Combined, these modifications pushed the power output up to 54bhp (instead of 44bhp), and gave the car a top speed of 81mph, with a 0-50mph time of 18 seconds Why was it dubbed "90"? No one now knows, for that was certainly not its top speed!

Servo-boosted front-wheel disc brakes

were standard (they were optional on other Vivas), and there was a decorative stripe along the flanks, but this was the sum total of the changes, for which Vauxhall only charged an extra £28.

No more attractive to look at, and certainly no better-handling, the HA 90 still sold well – nearly 12,000 sales in a year must have made the company happy.

Viva HB 1966-70

Only three years after the Viva name was coined, Vauxhall brought in the second-generation model, which was an altogether more satisfactory proposition. From HA to HB, was a big step forward, not only in looks, but also in accommodation, in equipment, and in available options.

The first Viva HBs were two-door saloons riding on a new platform, this one having a 96-inch wheelbase, with coil spring suspension front and rear, and with the HA's engine enlarged to 1159cc, giving 47bhp..

The HB was available in Base, De Luxe and SL trim packs, and modifications and additions followed thick and fast,

The Viva HB arrived in 1966. This is a 1600 De Luxe of 1968. In August that year the Viva took its highest ever share of the UK market, at 10.7 per cent.

SPECIFICATION

BODY STYLES: saloon, estate

PRODUCTION: 569,908

ENGINE & TRANSMISSION: 1159cc, 4cyl ohv/1599cc, 4cyl ohc, 4sp man, auto, f/r

POWER: 47bhp @ 5200rpm/83bhp @ 5800rpm

MAX SPEED (MPH): 78/88

0-60MPH (SEC): 19.7/15.1

SUSPENSION & BRAKES: coil ifs, coil rear, drums f&r, or disc f/drum r

LENGTH (IN)/WEIGHT (LB): 162/1778 - 1955

LAUNCH PRICE: £579/£663/£789

including an automatic transmission option from January 1967, three-door estate cars from June 1967, and the option of an 83bhp 1599cc overhead-camshaft (FD Victor-type) engine from June 1968 (with this engine front-wheel disc brakes came as standard).

From September 1968 a four-door saloon version was made available with both engines and after January 1970 the new (optional) GM automatic transmission replaced the original Borg Warner type.

Equipped with a more up-market and

more stylish interior than the HA, the HB Viva was an altogether more aspirational car than before, and would also spawn off successful derivatives such as the HB90 and Viva GT (described separately). It also provided the platform for the next-generation Viva HC. By the end of the HB's run, in August 1970, there were no fewer than 20 different Vivas of all types in the line-up. Up to this time it was Vauxhall's best-selling and most successful car.

These were good, practical cars, not exciting but giving reliable service.

Viva HB 90 1966-70

The second-generation Viva 90, announced in September 1966, was a much better car than the original type. Not only did it share the vastly more modern style and structure of the Viva HB, but its all-round coil spring

suspension too. With a 60hp 1159cc engine it delivered an 83mph top speed and sold by the bucket load.

Structurally and mechanically, the HB 90 was really an HB which had been given a 9:1 compression ratio and

Zenith-Stromberg carburettor in place of the Solex. The engine revved higher than the standard unit and was thus linked to a lower final drive ratio, further improving acceleration. Servo assisted front-wheel disc brakes were standard, and there were two trim packs, De Luxe' and SL.

Development changes included optional Borg Warner automatic transmission (from February 1967), an estate car version (June 1967), a four-door saloon version (October 1968), with GM-Europe automatic transmission replacing Borg Warner from January 1970.

SPECIFICATION

BODY STYLES: saloon, estate

PRODUCTION: 78,296

ENGINE & TRANSMISSION: 1159cc, 4cyl ohv, 4sp man, or auto, f/r

POWER: 60bhp @ 5600rpm

MAX SPEED (MPH): 83

0-60MPH (SEC): 17.6

SUSPENSION & BRAKES: coil ifs, coil rear, disc f/drum r

LENGTH (IN)/WEIGHT (LB): 162/1778

LAUNCH PRICE: £663

Viva HB 90. Not 90bhp but 60, and not quite 90mph.

Brabham Viva HB 1967-68

Double F1 World Champion Jack Brabham's garage business joined forces with Vauxhall to offer a bright, but not sensationally so, conversion for Viva 90s and SL90s from February 1967. Sales, however, were poor, and since by that time they had already trumped their own ace with the Viva GT, Vauxhall lost courage and dropped it by mid-1968.

This was a modest conversion, with twin Zenith Stromberg carburettors,

SPECIFICATION

BODY STYLES: saloon

PRODUCTION: not known

ENGINE & TRANSMISSION: 1159cc, 4cyl ohv, 4sp man, f/r

POWER: 69bhp @ 5800rpm

MAX SPEED (MPH): 90

0-60MPH (SEC): 15.1

SUSPENSION & BRAKES: coil ifs, coil rear, disc f/drum r

LENGTH (IN)/WEIGHT (LB): 162/1778

LAUNCH PRICE: £773

Brabham Viva GT had some more horsepower and a go-faster stripe around its nose.

which pushed up peak power from 60bhp to 69bhp (only 12 per cent improvement), and which delivered a top speed of 90mph, but none of this was any big deal and we can see where the apathy came from.

Visually there was little change to the Viva 90 model chosen (a "go faster" stripe kit was provided, but was not affixed by the dealer until the customer asked him to do so). Under the skin the twin-carb engine was joined by servo-assisted front disc brakes and wider-rim wheels. The handling was as good as every other Viva HB's.

Although it certainly delivered what was promised and the upgrade was not expensive, the car costing £773 instead of £736, the Brabham GT never captured the public's imagination. The Viva GT was a more obviously attractive machine.

Viva (HB) GT 1968-70

Although it was planned before Ford's Escort Twin-Cam appeared, the Viva GT was much the same sort of concept, with lots of power somehow squeezed into a compact body. Public launch came in March 1968, and deliveries began almost at once.

The GT was based on the up-market versions of other Vivas, and was only sold in two-door saloon form, No one ever got to ignore a Viva GT, which was given a matt black bonnet with air scoops, and special wheels. The fascia got a comprehensive display of dials and controls, there was a centre console, and a leather-rimmed steering wheel was standard.

The secret was under the bonnet, where a twin-Stromberg 104bhp version of the overhead-camshaft Victor 2000 engine and a close-ratio

The 1968 Viva GT replaced the Brabham version. This time there were two litres under the bonnet, with 104bhp and a genuine 100mph.

SPECIFICATION

BODY STYLES: saloon

PRODUCTION: 4606

ENGINE & TRANSMISSION: 1975cc, 4cyl ohc, 4sp man, f/r

POWER: 104bhp @ 5600rpm

MAX SPEED (MPH): 100

0-60MPH (SEC): 10.7

SUSPENSION & BRAKES: coil ifs, coil rear, disc f/drum r

LENGTH (IN)/WEIGHT (LB): 161/2070

LAUNCH PRICE: £1022

Cresta-type gearbox, were somehow squeezed in. Victor-type front-wheel disc brakes were standard, and the more robust Victor rear axle was also fitted.

Vauxhall always made it clear that this was not intended to be a competition car, and it soon built up a "boy racer" image instead. The running gear was all standard Vauxhall (though used in a different combination) so there were no complications for the owner to

fear, and the GT sold very well indeed.

From September 1968 a larger (12-gallon) fuel tank was fitted, and from January 1970 there were revised axle and gear ratios, reworked suspension settings and Rostyle road wheels as standard.

When the Viva HB was dropped in favour of the new HC, the Viva GT had to go as well. There would be a successor, though not until 1972, and without the GT badge.

Viva HC 1970-79

The third-generation Viva appeared in October 1970 and would be on sale until 1979, when the front wheel drive Astra took over. Not even General Motors could afford yet another brand-new platform, so the new Viva (Type HC, in GM-speak) used the old HB's platform and running gear, covered by a new and rather blandly styled body, with a more roomy cabin. As before, there would be two-door and four-door saloons, and an estate car, this one having a very raked tail.

The 1159cc engines were a touch more powerful than before – 49bhp instead of 47bhp - and the 1599cc engine was unchanged. This was the first Vauxhall on which a new type of GM automatic transmission (not Borg Warner) was optional.

Drum brakes were standard on 1159cc models, but front-wheel discs were optional, and were standard when the larger 1599cc engine was specified. 13in wheels were used (instead of 12in on the HB), and there was now an energy-

absorbing steering column, but the rest of the chassis was much as before

This was the just the start of an HC range which would evolve during the 1970s, the process including enlarged and more powerful engines of both families – overhead-valve and overhead-camshaft. There were also to be two-door coupé versions and a Magnum model range on top of that.

Evolution was complex for this was, after all, a product planned GM car. A 1256cc engine replaced the 1159cc unit from August 1971, and a 1759cc engine replaced the 1599cc unit from early 1972. A 2300SL model appeared in March 1972. The HC range included Base, L, DL, SL, GLS and (from 1976) E (for Economy) versions. Sometimes the larger-engined types crossed over with Magnum models (described separately),

for the chassis and running gear were very similar.

Like the previous Vivas, these were all worthy, though never inspiring, cars to drive and own. Although straight-line

speed was not lacking, especially in the larger-engined versions, any sporting character usually was. Like other Vivas, too, they were still distressingly rust-prone, and they did not survive for long.

SPECIFICATION

BODY STYLES: saloon, estate

PRODUCTION: 640,863

ENGINE & TRANSMISSION: 1159cc/1256cc, 4cyl ohv/1599cc/1759cc/2279cc, 4cyl ohc, 4sp man, or auto, f/r

POWER: 49bhp @ 5300rpm-110bhp @ 5200rpm

MAX SPEED (MPH): 78-99

0-60MPH (SEC): 20.6-11.5

SUSPENSION & BRAKES: coil ifs, coil rear, drums f/r (1159cc and 1256cc), or disc f/drum r (with larger engines)

LENGTH (IN)/WEIGHT (LB): 162/1859 - 2273

LAUNCH PRICE: £783 upwards

Viva HC was introduced in 1970. This is the two-door.

Firenza Coupé 1971-73

Vauxhall never really had the bravery to turn this "Viva Coupé" (for that is what the Firenza really was) into a properly sorted sports coupé, so it did not sell as well as hoped. In the end, Firenzas of this type were on sale for less then three years, as the body style was subsumed into the Magnum range at the end of 1973.

Structurally, and in its engineering, the

SPECIFICATION

BODY STYLES: coupé

PRODUCTION: 18,352

ENGINE & TRANSMISSION: 1159cc/1265cc, 4cyl ohv/1599cc/1759cc/19975cc/2279cc, 4cyl ohc, 4sp man, auto, f/r

POWER: 62bhp @ 5500rpm - 110bhp @ 5200rpm

MAX SPEED (MPH): 83 (E)-103

0-60MPH (SEC): not measured-11.4

SUSPENSION & BRAKES: coil ifs, coil beam rear, disc f/drum r

LENGTH (IN)/WEIGHT (LB): 162/1821 - 2130

LAUNCH PRICE: £1017

The 1972 1256cc Firenza.

Firenza was no more and no less than a two-door Viva HC with a different roof and tail, for the platform, front end, screen, doors, front and rear suspension, and the ever-widening choice of engines were just the same. Small-engined basic-spec cars kept their twin rectangular headlamps, but SLs always had four circular headlamps. From August 1971

there was a more stylish instrument layout, with circular instruments, in place of the original rectangular arrangement. 2300SLs (March 1972 on) had a yet more special fascia, with seven dials, which would be carried forward to the Magnums.

The engine choice needs sorting out. The 1159cc engine was available only for a few months, until August 1971, when the enlarged 1256cc engine took over. Right from the start there were 1599cc and 1975cc slant-four overhead-camshaft Viva GT-type engines and their related transmissions, these being up-rated to 1759cc and 2279cc from March 1972.

The Firenzas did not look as special as the Ford Capris with which they had to compete, and their lack of style held them back. Even so, the big-engined types were fast and interesting machines to drive (though tending to oversteer when pushed hard). They would be even better when turned into Magnums from late 1973.

Firenza Sport SL, with 110bhp engine.

Firenza Droopsnoot 1973-75

Here was an interesting special edition of the Firenza which was built in very limited numbers between the death of the mainstream Firenza and the build-up of Magnum Coupés. It was based on the running gear of the Firenza 2300SL, but with much novel engineering, was one of the quickest and (by definition) most expensive Vauxhalls produced so far.

Compared with the last of the Firenzas, the Droopsnoot had a dramatically different nose, with a wedge profile, a big spoiler under the bumper and rectangular Perspex covers over four halogen headlamps. Sports road wheels and fat radial ply tyres all added to the effect.

The 2279cc engine had been tuned up to 131bhp by using twin Zenith-

The 131bhp Firenza droopsnoot coupé came in one colour only – Silver Starfire.

Stromberg carbs and a different camshaft profile, and was backed by a rugged but none too refined five-speed ZF gearbox. There was a full seven-dial array of circular instruments (this was the more-or-less standard display on Magnums of the same period), and the trim was all well up to Magnum standards.

In some ways the performance was a disappointment, for 131bhp should surely have delivered a higher top speed, which must have meant that the aerodynamic performance of the special nose was not up to its visual promise, but the handling was very satisfactory.

The car was previewed at the Motor Show in October 1973, but deliveries

did not begin until mid-1974, when the after-effects of the first Energy Crisis were still apparent. Price was always a problem – in October 1973, when the Droopsnoot was previewed, a Magnum 2300 Coupé cost only £1465, but by the time Droopsnoot deliveries began it was priced at a preposterous £2625. No amount of good publicity, or even favourable reports of the performance or handling, could overcome that. Vauxhall was disappointed, but refused to reduce prices. After this car had gone, by the way, development of the Chevette HS followed.

Later this near-unique nose found itself fitted to a run of Magnum Sports Hatches in 1975.

SPECIFICATION

BODY STYLES: sports coupé

PRODUCTION: 204

ENGINE & TRANSMISSION: 2279cc, 4cyl ohc, 5sp man, f/r

POWER: 131bhp @ 5500rpm

MAX SPEED (MPH): 117

0-60MPH (SEC): 8.5

SUSPENSION & BRAKES: coil ifs, coil beam rear, disc f/drum r

LENGTH (IN)/WEIGHT (LB): 169/2296

LAUNCH PRICE: £2625

Magnum 1973-77

In late 1973 Vauxhall rationalised its product planning and the naming of its Viva-based cars. From that time, the large-engined Viva and the Firenza coupés were all amalgamated, up-rated in many respects, and renamed as Magnums. All four body types – two-door saloon, four-door saloon, three-door estate car, and two-door coupé – carried on with the same bodies as before, but with four-circular-headlamp noses.

For 1974 Magnums had 77bhp 1759cc and twin-carb 110bhp 2279cc engines, and all the larger-engined versions had Vauxhall's new seven-dial instrument panel. All cars had optional GM automatic transmission, individual reclining front seats, split propshafts, a

Vauxhall Magnum 2300 saloon, 1974.

rear anti-roll bar which helped trim the handling and radial ply tyres on 5-inch rims.

Two years later, in October 1975, the coupé was dropped, and the larger engine reverted to a single carburettor, producing 88bhp in that form. At the same time the seven-dial dashboard was fitted to 1800 models.

In April 1976 there was also a special edition Magnum Sports Hatch. This consisted of the 2279cc engine in the estate car body, with the droopsnoot nose previously seen on late Firenzas. At

£2918, this machine also had alloy wheels, a rear spoiler, and special paint and trim. Interestingly, from May to October 1976 the Magnum was taken out of production, though it came back strongly before finally dropping away in May 1977.

There is no doubt that these cars did not sell as well as Vauxhall hoped – two reasons being that they were always seen as being close relatives of the Viva and were also seen as expensive. Even so, the 2300s in particular were rapid and well-balanced machines.

SPECIFICATION

BODY STYLES: saloon, coupé, estate

PRODUCTION: 20,300

ENGINE & TRANSMISSION : 1759cc/2279cc, 4cyl ohc, 4sp man, or auto, f/r

POWER: 77bhp @ 5200rpm/88bhp @ 5800rpm/110bhp @ 5000rpm

MAX SPEED (MPH): 93/99/103

0-60MPH (SEC): 15.6/11.7/10.0

SUSPENSION & BRAKES: coil ifs, coil rear, disc f/drum r

LENGTH (IN)/WEIGHT (LB): 163/2135

LAUNCH PRICE: £1305

Magnum 1800 estate.

Magnum 2300 coupé, 1974.

Victor (FE) 1972-76

SPECIFICATION

BODY STYLES: saloon, estate

PRODUCTION: 44,771

ENGINE & TRANSMISSION: 1759cc/2279cc, 4cyl ohc, 4sp man, o/d or auto, f/r

POWER: 77bhp @ 5200rpm/100bhp @ 5200rpm

MAX SPEED (MPH): 92/96

0-60MPH (SEC): 15.9/12.4

SUSPENSION & BRAKES: coil ifs, coil rear, disc f/drum r

LENGTH (IN)/WEIGHT (LB): 179/2495

LAUNCH PRICE: £1186

The fifth-generation Victor, often known as the FE type, was launched in March 1972. A direct replacement for the FD series (described earlier), it had an all-new monocoque structure, but used the same family of engines and transmissions as before.

This Victor, in fact, was built on the same platform and suspension as the new Opel Rekord, for General Motors was already on the way to rationalising the engineering of its two European subsidiaries. The new body style featured rectangular headlamps and front-wheel

disc brakes were standard on all types. As before, there were two versions of the slant-four overhead-camshaft engine, but both had been enlarged, to 1759cc and 2279cc. The old three-speed gearbox had been dropped and all cars were supplied with four-speed all-synchromesh 'boxes with floor change. As on the FD, overdrive was optional, as was the modern GM-Europe automatic transmission.

The FE was larger than the FD, the wheelbase being three inches longer, giving a roomier cabin. It was also 137lb heavier. It was sold in De Luxe or SL trim

Vauxhall Victor FE was introduced in 1972. This is a 1974 2300 saloon.

as a four door saloon or five-door estate car. De Luxe cars had a front bench seat as standard – individual front seats were optional at first, but standardised after only six months. Overdrive was withdrawn from 2300 models after late 1973, but there were no other major technical changes before this model gave way to the VX series early in 1976.

Perhaps these Victors had now grown too large, for they certainly did not sell as well as the previous types. Vauxhall assured everyone that these were better built and had been given better anti-corrosion protection than before, but not everyone was impressed. Their rather anonymous character left no mark on the motoring scene.

Victor VX4/90 (FE) 1972-76/1977-78

Announced in the same week as the mainstream FE types, in March 1972, Vauxhall's FE VX4/90 was a thoroughly competent sporting saloon and it sold surprisingly well. It was evolved from the Victor 2300SL and had a 2279cc twin-carburettor 110bhp engine. A four-speed gearbox with overdrive was standard, and automatic transmission was optional but rarely specified.

With a near-100mph top speed, top of the range trim and equipment, a unique nose style which featured four headlamps and Rostyle road wheels with radial ply tyres, this was the fastest VX4/90 so far. Surprisingly, overdrive was withdrawn from the specification in late 1973 (just as it

Victor FE VX4/90 had unique front-end styling with four headlamps.

SPECIFICATION

BODY STYLES: saloon

PRODUCTION: 18,042/900

ENGINE & TRANSMISSION: 2279cc, 4cyl ohc, 4sp man, 5sp man, o/d or auto, f/r

POWER: 110bhp @ 5200rpm/116bhp @ 5000rpm

MAX SPEED (MPH): 99/102

0-60MPH (SEC): 12.0/11.1

SUSPENSION & BRAKES : coil ifs, coil beam rear, disc f/drum r

LENGTH (IN)/WEIGHT (LB): 179/2590-2765

LAUNCH PRICE: £1479/£2115

was on FE 2300s), but this was the only important technical change before the first-phase models were dropped in January 1976.

There was then a hiatus, with no VX4/90 on the market, until a final derivative of the VX1800/VX2300 cars appeared in March 1977 (export) and mid-summer 1977 (UK market). Compared with the earlier type, the new VX4/90 now had single rectangular headlamps, more power (116bhp instead of 110bhp), and a five-speed Getrag gearbox. In addition there were

built-in front fog lamps and an under-bumper front spoiler. This was a better car than before, but not sensationally so. The five-speed transmission was a good marketing novelty, and the top speed was now a genuine 102mph.

Like the previous VX4/90, though, this car was always in a cleft stick, for those wanting a high-performance Vauxhall usually chose a Magnum, or a Cavalier Coupé, while those wanting a fast Victor often chose the Ventora instead. Yet this was a good car which deserved a better reputation.

Ventora/Victor 3300 (FE) 1972-76

The biggest, heaviest and fastest of all the FE derivatives was the second-generation Ventora, which appeared in March 1972 and ran through until January 1976. When the VX series took over from the Victor there was no Ventora in the range.

Like the previous Ventora (of 1968-72) the new car blended the Victor body with the six-cylinder engine of the Cresta, which produced 124bhp and guaranteed a top speed of 104mph. In spite of having high overall gearing, with this engine the

Ventora FE was the last model to use the 3.3-litre six-cylinder engine .

SPECIFICATION

BODY STYLES: saloon, estate

PRODUCTION: 7291

ENGINE & TRANSMISSION: 3294cc, 6cyl ohv, 4sp man, o/d or auto, f/r

POWER: 124bhp @ 4600rpm

MAX SPEED (MPH): 104

0-60MPH (SEC): 12.6

SUSPENSION & BRAKES: coil ifs, coil beam rear, disc f/drum r

LENGTH (IN)/WEIGHT (LB): 179/2651

LAUNCH PRICE: £1763

Ventora felt as if it could do everything in top gear. Overdrive and GM automatic transmission were both optional, the interior was the plushiest of all this generation of cars, and power-assisted steering and radial ply tyres were standard.

The five-door estate car version originally carried the name of Victor 3300SL, and had two rectangular head-lamps. Power-assisted steering was only standardised on this model from late

1972. In September 1973 a reshuffle of trim saw the Victor 3300SL estate disappear in favour of a Ventora-based equivalent.

The exterior styling of the Ventora was almost identical to the Victor FE's, though with four headlamps and a unique type of cross-hatched grille. Inside the car, the fascia layout was based on that of the VX4/90 but had extra dials and controls, with a full-length centre console.

VX1800/2300 (FE) 1976-1978

For the final two years of the Victor FE's life the Victor name was dropped, trim and equipment levels were enhanced (though there were few mechanical changes) and the VX cars

The FE Victors were renamed VX1800 and VX2300 in 1976.

SPECIFICATION

BODY STYLES: saloon, estate

PRODUCTION: 25,815

ENGINE & TRANSMISSION: 1759cc/2279cc, 4cyl ohc, 4sp man, f/r

POWER: 88bhp @ 5800rpm/108bhp @ 5000rpm

MAX SPEED (MPH): 100/104

0-60MPH (SEC): 13.7/11.3

SUSPENSION & BRAKES: coil ifs, coil beam rear, disc f/drum r

LENGTH (IN)/WEIGHT (LB): 180/2569

LAUNCH PRICE: £2592/£2709

were produced from 1976 to 1978. This move was mainly marketing-led, to push these large saloons further up-market from the new Cavalier.

Compared with the last of the Victor FEs, there were no sheet-metal changes,

no new body types (four-door saloon and five-door estate were on offer), though each of the overhead cam engines was made more powerful. VXs had 88bhp and 108bhp, compared with the 77bhp and 100bhp of the obsolete Victor FE.

Chevette 1975-84

This was a best-selling Vauxhall by any measure – by the end of 1970s only the Viva HC had sold more – but the Chevette was neither pure Vauxhall nor even pure-bred Opel. It was an intriguing and altogether successful variation on a theme, for at this time GM was promoting the complex "T-Car" programme over the world.

The Chevette was a conventional front engine/rear drive machine which took shape around the current 94in-wheelbase Opel Kadett platform but was fitted with the Vauxhall Viva HC's 1256cc engine and its four-speed gearbox. Much of the internal structure of the engine bay, bulkhead and cabin was Opel Kadett, but there was a unique wedge nose (including part-recessed rectangular headlamps), and a stubby three-door hatchback body. The hatchback was Vauxhall's first, and would not appear on an Opel for some time yet.

The Chevette was not a replacement for the Viva HC, for the two cars would run on, side by side, for four years. It was

The 1256cc Vauxhall Chevette GL hatchback, 1976.

smaller, more elegant and more nimble than the Viva. The all-round coil spring suspension, including torque-tube axle location at the rear, was pure Kadett, while the engine was pure Viva and was rated the same.

From mid-1976, a conventional four-door saloon body like that of the Kadett was offered, and from this point there were E, L, GL and GLS trim packs. A three-door estate car (also Kadett-derived) was added before the end of 1976. From that point, technical

changes were minimal, though there were gradual improvements to the trim. From August 1979 the nose was re-styled to feature flush headlamps, but after that the model carried on virtually unchanged until April 1984.

The Chevette was never meant to be exciting to drive or to own (Vauxhall absolutely did not want it to be either of those things), but it was a very useful – and very successful – small runabout, though very few examples seemed to survive the inevitable corrosion.

SPECIFICATION

BODY STYLES: saloon, hatchback, estate, commercials

PRODUCTION: 415,608

ENGINE & TRANSMISSION: 1256cc, 4cyl ohv, 4sp man, f/r

POWER: 59bhp @ 5600rpm

MAX SPEED (MPH): 91

0-60MPH (SEC): 14.5

SUSPENSION & BRAKES: coil ifs, coil beam rear, disc f/drum r

LENGTH (IN)/WEIGHT (LB): 157/1879

LAUNCH PRICE: £1650

Chevette Special four-door saloon, 1980.

Chevette HS 1976-79

This was Vauxhall's homologation special, intended to be used in rallying and to compete with the Ford Escort RS1800. Launched prematurely at the end of 1976, it did not become available in numbers until 1978. Like Ford with the RS1800, Vauxhall always

struggled to sell the road cars, which were very specialised and rather rough and ready. Vauxhall claim that 400 were built, but it seems that only about 350 were sold, the balance becoming HSRs.

Based on the Chevette hatchback, the HS (High Specification?) used a 16-

valve twin-overhead-cam version of the familiar Vauxhall slant-four power unit, with a Getrag five-speed gearbox and an Opel Kadett GT/E rear axle. The suspension was reinforced and stiffened up, brakes were enlarged, and there were special alloy wheels. The Magnum-type fascia was used, and there was a special paint job (all cars, it seems, were in silver with red striping). An under-bumper front spoiler was fitted and there was a big spoiler on the tail too.

This was an effective machine whose main purpose was to be modified for use in international rallies. Early scandal surrounded the DTV works cars, which were found to be running non-homologated parts, but they proved to be very strong and very tuneable, which was also good for the reputation of the road cars.

The Chevette HS was never meant to be a series-production model, and its obvious appeal was to the rally-following fraternity. As a consequence it seen gained its own mystique, and a high proportion of the cars were preserved, becoming classics as that movement developed.

SPECIFICATION

BODY STYLES: sports hatchback

PRODUCTION: 400

ENGINE & TRANSMISSION: 2279cc, 4cyl 2ohc, 5sp man, f/r

POWER: 135bhp @ 5500rpm

MAX SPEED (MPH): 115

0-60MPH (SEC): 8.5

SUSPENSION & BRAKES: coil ifs, coil beam rear, disc f/drum r

LENGTH (IN)/WEIGHT (LB): 157/2235

LAUNCH PRICE: £5107

Chevette HS, 1976-79, was a "homologation special" with 16-valve twin-cam cylinder head and 135bhp.

Chevette HSR 1979-80

The Chevette HS was rare enough, but the HSR of 1979-80 was even less known, and in later years it achieved near-unicorn status. Built officially to extend the potential of the HS for rallying, it was also apparently a desperate measure to get rid of unsold HS types. Although 50 HSRs were officially made, the true figure is apparently lower, for 34 were converted from unsold Chevette HSs, the balance being "created" as out-and-out rally cars.

SPECIFICATION

BODY STYLES: sports hatchback

PRODUCTION: 50

ENGINE & TRANSMISSION: 2279cc, 4cyl 2ohc, 5sp man, f/r

POWER: 150bhp @ 6000rpm

MAX SPEED (MPH): 125 (E)

0-60MPH (SEC): not measured

SUSPENSION & BRAKES: coil ifs, coil rear, disc f/drum r

LENGTH (IN)/WEIGHT (LB): 157/2235

LAUNCH PRICE: £7146

Tony Pond on his way to winning the 1981 Rothmans Manx International Trophy Rally in a Chevette HSR.

Compared with the HS, the HSR (R= Rally?) had flared front and rear wheel-arches, a plastic bonnet with a bulge to clear the engine, extra plastic sills under the doors, the possibility (not all cars) of a 150bhp engine with twin dual-choke Dell'Orto carbs, a twin-plate clutch, revised rear suspension location and even wider (7in) wheel rims.

Once again, this was all done to make an established rally car even better, and the HSR did that job (Tony Pond, in 1981, was sensationally successful), but the very very few road cars were even rougher and readier than ever.

Virtually no one wanted to pay £7146 for a new one in 1979, but the cars are worth good money today.

Cavalier 1975-81

This was the very first Vauxhall to be an absolute clone of a new-model Opel (the earlier Chevette was not, since it used Vauxhall engines). The new-generation Opel Ascona appeared in 1975 and was almost immediately followed in October 1975 by the equivalent Vauxhall Cavalier, whose principal visual difference was its wedge nose with rectangular headlamps.

Assembly was always at Vauxhall's Luton factory, there being two-door and four-door saloons and a two-door coupé (described below). Interestingly, there was no estate car version. Cavaliers

Vauxhall Cavalier 1600L two-door, 1976.

SPECIFICATION

BODY STYLES: saloon

PRODUCTION: 238,980, inc. Coupés

ENGINE & TRANSMISSION: 1256cc, 4cyl ohv/1584cc/1897cc/1979cc, 4cyl ohv, 4sp man, or auto, f/r

POWER: 58bhp @ 5400rpm/75bhp @ 5000rpm/89bhp @ 4800rpm/100bhp @ 5400rpm

MAX SPEED (MPH): 87-111

0-60MPH (SEC): 17.8-9.2

SUSPENSION & BRAKES: coil ifs, coil beam rear, disc f/drum r

LENGTH (IN)/WEIGHT (LB): 174/2005 - 2144

LAUNCH PRICE: £1975

would be sold with four different engines, and in L, GL and LS trim packs. This was a typical GM product-planned model, with many different trim options and accessories, the specs being up-rated and shuffled around, year on year, until a new-generation Cavalier took over at the end of 1981.

Early cars had 1584cc and 1897cc Opel cam-in-head engines, with manual or optional automatic transmission. Then, in August 1977, a new entry-level model appeared, with the 58bhp 1256cc Viva engine and no automatic transmission option. From January 1979 the 1979cc Opel engine was progressively added, the

1897cc engine therefore dropping away. The last of these cars was produced in July 1981

The Cavalier's chassis was strictly conventional GM of the period – coil spring independent front suspension being matched by coil spring/torque tube location at the rear. The ride was soft, the handling safe but uninspiring, the whole character of the car being unassuming, ultra-reliable, something-for-everyone transportation.

Like many Vauxhalls of the period, the Cavalier rusted away rapidly if ignored, which means that almost all of them rotted out within a decade or so.

Cavalier Coupé and Sports Hatch 1975-81

Though it was not as specialised as its obvious competitor, the Ford Capri of the period, the two-door Cavalier Coupé was a very successful and somewhat trendy alternative to the Cavalier saloon. Whereas the saloon was a "rep's delight", the coupé was fast enough, stylish enough and handled well enough to build its own image. Once again, this was a Vauxhall-ised version of an Opel, that being the new-generation Opel Manta.

The Coupé was based on the 98in platform of the Cavalier, with the same front end and many common inner panels. It was a close-coupled four-seater which, in original form, featured a

Cavalier GL Coupé, 1975.

separate boot compartment. The cabin was surprisingly roomy, the fascia was neat, and there was a remote-control gearchange.

The first cars had an 89bhp 1897cc engine which delivered a top speed of 106mph. Regular development changes updated this model. From September 1978 an alternative rear-end style, a hatchback coupé, with 75bhp 1584cc or 100bhp 1979cc engine, was added, after which the conventional coupé disappeared in mid-1979.

Although the 1584cc-engined car was always available as an entry-level coupé, the vast majority of these machines were sold with the 1979cc engine, which offered a top speed of 111mph. The Cavalier Coupé then dropped out of production at the end of 1981, while the "parent" car – the Opel Manta (soon with new-type petrol engines) – carried on until 1988.

Bigger, more roomy and, some say, more attractive than the rival Capri, this Coupé was successful, but when the next-generation Cavalier (a front wheel-drive car) came along, there was no replacement model.

The Cavalier Sports Hatch arrived in 1978. The cars in the background were design studies.

SPECIFICATION

BODY STYLES: coupé/hatchback coupé

PRODUCTION: see Cavalier, above

ENGINE & TRANSMISSION: 1584cc/1897cc/1979cc, 4cyl ohv, 4sp man, or auto, f/r

POWER: 75bhp @ 5000rpm/89bhp @ 4800rpm/100bhp @ 5400rpm

MAX SPEED (MPH): 98/106/111

0-60MPH (SEC): 14.8/11.2/9.2

SUSPENSION & BRAKES: coil ifs, coil beam rear, disc f/drum r

LENGTH (IN)/WEIGHT (LB): 174/2092-2144

LAUNCH PRICE: £2707

Carlton 1978-86

By the late 1970s General Motors had almost completed the integration of Vauxhall engineering with that of Opel. Accordingly the Carlton of 1978, which was effectively a Vauxhall VX replacement, was no more than a re-badged and re-trimmed new-type Opel Rekord, though it was assembled in the UK.

Like its little brother the Cavalier, the Carlton was a conventional front-engine/rear-drive car, available as a four-door saloon or a five-door estate car, with wedge-nose styling and rectangular headlamps. Original cars came with a 1979cc Opel cam-in-head engine and a choice of manual or automatic transmission.

In the autumn of 1982 a front-end facelift coincided with the introduction of a new 1796cc overhead-camshaft engine, along with a lumpy 65bhp diesel unit. Two years later a 2197cc cam-in-head engine with fuel injection was

Vauxhall Carlton.

added, by which time a five-speed manual gearbox had been standardised.

Like all such cars from Vauxhall and Ford, the Carlton was offered with several trim packages, including L, GL and CDi, and with an impressive options and accessories list. It was, in fact, specifically designed as a car for business, and it sold well to fleet purchasers. The Carlton did everything well, but nothing outstandingly so, and was almost instantly forgotten when a replacement Carlton came along in 1986.

The Vauxhall Royale of 1978 and the Viceroy of 1980 were six-cylinder derivatives of this Carlton. Both used the same 105in-wheelbase structure, both were re-badged Opels, and both were assembled in Germany.

SPECIFICATION

BODY STYLES: saloon, estate, coupé

PRODUCTION: 87,119

ENGINE & TRANSMISSION: 1796cc, 4cyl ohc/1979cc/2197cc, 4cyl ohv/2784cc/2969cc, 6cyl ohc petrol/2260cc, 4cyl ohc diesel, 4sp man, 5sp man, or auto, f/r

POWER: 90bhp @ 5400rpm-180bhp @ 5800rpm (petrol)/65bhp @ 4200rpm (diesel)

MAX SPEED (MPH) : 104-117

0-60MPH (SEC) : not measured-10.3

SUSPENSION & BRAKES : coil ifs, coil beam rear, disc f/drum r

LENGTH (IN)/WEIGHT (LB) : 187/2430 - 2745

LAUNCH PRICE : £4600

The Royale Coupé, equivalent to the Opel Monza.

The 2.8-litre Vauxhall Royale saloon of 1978, a rebadged Opel Senator

Astra I | 1980-84

When Opel announced its new front wheel drive Kadett in 1979, it seemed to be inevitable that Vauxhall would follow suit with a clone. In early 1980, therefore, the first

SPECIFICATION

BODY STYLES: saloon, hatchback, estate, commercials

PRODUCTION: 1,117,662, including next-generation Astras

ENGINE & TRANSMISSION: 1196cc, 4cyl ohv/1297cc/1598cc/1796cc, 4cyl ohc/1598 cc, 4cyl ohc Diesel, 4sp man, 5sp man (1796cc only), or auto, f/f

POWER: 60bhp @ 5800rpm-113bhp @ 5800rpm (petrol/54bhp @ 4600rpm

MAX SPEED (MPH): 91-116

0-60MPH (SEC): 15.5-8.5

SUSPENSION & BRAKES : coil ifs, coil irs, disc f/drum r

LENGTH (IN)/WEIGHT (LB) : 157/1814 - 2175

LAUNCH PRICE: £3404

The front wheel drive Vauxhall Astra, 1980. This is the 5-door GL hatchback.

Vauxhall Astra appeared, as a very lightly modified version of the new Kadett. This was also Vauxhall's first front wheel drive car, and although it was assembled in the UK it was Opel through and through, with Opel-engineered four-cylinder overhead-valve, overhead-camshaft and diesel engines.

Kadetts and Astras were all built around a new 99in-wheelbase platform, with transversely mounted engine. The suspension arrangements were conventional, by MacPherson struts at the front, with a "semi-independent" twist-beam rear end. This combination gave safe and predictable handling, with no fireworks and no quirks.

The style was crisp if rather angular, and in the five years that this car was on sale there would be a truly bewildering number of styles – two-door and four-door saloons, three-door and five-door hatchbacks, three-door and five-door estate cars – all of them with different trim and equipment packages.

Early Astras had 1196cc overhead-valve or 1297cc overhead-camshaft engines, but a 1598cc ohc option arrived at the end of 1981, and a 54bhp 1.6-litre diesel from September 1982. Then, in April 1983, came the 100bhp 1798cc GT/E, a three-door sports hatchback which competed with Ford's Escort XR3i and which had fuel injection, a five-speed gearbox, alloy wheels, low-profile 14in tyres and Recaro front seats.

The mainstream Astras – mainly the 1.3-litre and 1.6-litre types – gradually took on enhanced trim and fittings during the 1980s, though an 'E' (for Economy) type also appeared in January 1982, while an up-market 1.6 SR with alloy wheels came along in January 1983. Modern cars, with the range of engines and trim options offered, and the number of different body derivatives, were becoming more complex all the time. The next-generation Astra, which took over in October 1984, would offer much more of the same.

WARWICK

No sooner had the finances of the Peerless project collapsed in 1960 than one of the original founders, Bernie Rodger, set up another company (Bernard Rodger Developments Ltd), with R H Ham as chairman, to start building a modified version of the same car. This time, assembly was to be at Colnbrook, a few miles away from the Peerless works at Slough and even closer to Heathrow airport. The car was renamed Warwick: this was because one of the co-directors was Jimmy Byrnes, a restaurateur from the Warwick area. .News of the re-launch came in August 1960.

As ever with such enterprises, the money available to float the business was limited, suppliers were not about to offer extended credit, and as the new car sold no more quickly than the previous Peerless there was scant chance of making profits.

Since Rodger was now operating on his own (John Gordon had gone off to promote his own Gordon GT project, which became the Gordon-Keeble, already described) this was more than he could be expected to handle. Not even an attempt to please the potential Transatlantic market with a Buick V8-engined version of the car was viable. Warwick therefore closed its doors in 1962.

2-Litre GT 1960-62

Although the Warwick GT was essentially the same car as the Peerless GT, but further developed, the company claimed that it was more refined and better built than before. The James Whitson company still produced the glass-fibre bodies but claimed to have saved 80lb in the transformation. Structurally, the important change was that the Warwick now had a one-piece

SPECIFICATION

BODY STYLES: sports coupé

PRODUCTION: not known

ENGINE & TRANSMISSION: 1991cc, 4cyl ohv, 4sp man, o/d, f/r

POWER: 100bhp @ 5000rpm

MAX SPEED (MPH): 103

0-60MPH (SEC): 12.8

SUSPENSION & BRAKES: coil ifs, DD leaf rear, disc f/drum r

LENGTH (IN)/WEIGHT (LB): 162/2160

LAUNCH PRICE: £1666

The Warwick GT, a revival of the Peerless and using the same TR3 engine and 'box.

lift-up front end, hinged at the nose.

As before, the basis of the car was a multi-tube chassis frame, Triumph TR3A running gear and own-brand De Dion rear suspension. Laycock overdrive was still standard but (unlike the Peerless) the centre-lock wire-spoke wheels were optional extras.

In spite of Warwick's claims that this car was better built than its predecessor, there were continuous rumblings about quality and reliability. Accordingly, because this was such an expensive machine, sales soon dried up.

3½-Litre 1961-62

In a brave attempt to make the Warwick more acceptable to the USA market, in August 1961 the company built a prototype powered by the modern light-alloy Buick V8 engine. This very engine, incidentally, would eventually become the famous and long-running Rover unit as seen in Range Rovers and the like, but that was still years away.

News of Warwick's ambitious project was always sparse, no full technical description was ever sent to the press, and apparently only two such cars were produced. The engine, however, was reputedly capable of 240bhp, which would have made for an exciting drive. The original car supposedly had a Jaguar-type Moss four-speed gearbox, though a ZF gearbox was fitted to the second car. Laycock overdrive was fitted in both cases.

All in all this was an intriguing project, but nothing came of it.

The 3.5-litre Warwick had the Buick V8 engine later used in Rovers.

BODY STYLES: sports coupé

PRODUCTION: 2

ENGINE & TRANSMISSION: 3528cc, V8cyl ohv, 4sp man, o/d, f/r

POWER: 185bhp (claimed)

MAX SPEED (MPH): 130 (E)

0-60MPH (SEC): not measured

SUSPENSION & BRAKES: coil ifs, DD leaf rear, disc f/drum r

LENGTH (IN)/WEIGHT (LB): 162/not known

LAUNCH PRICE: no British price released

WOLSELEY

Wolseley was one of the pioneers of British motoring and sold many thousands of cars in the 1910s and 1920s, but it hit hard times and was eventually acquired by William Morris (later Lord Nuffield) in 1927. By 1939 the Birmingham-based concern was making more and more up-market Morris-based saloons and limousines.

After the War, Wolseleys were late-1930s Nuffield designs and were built at Ward End in Birmingham, but from late 1948 the first new post-war models, the 4/50 and 6/80, went into production, originally at Ward End but from early 1949 at Cowley (the Morris Motors plant). As with Riley, this was the start of a process which ensured that all future Wolseleys would be closely based on Morris (later BMC) products, though they would retain their own grille treatment and be endowed with a higher level of trim and equipment.

By the late 1950s, Wolseleys were effectively twinned with Rileys, the basic difference being that Rileys were often given a more powerful version of the engines, or a more sporty specification. The 15/50 was a better Austin A55, the 6/99 a better Austin A99, the Hornet a better Mini, and the 1100 a better Austin-Morris 1100.

The last new-model Wolseley of the 1945-70 period was the 18/85 of 1967, which was based closely on the front wheel drive Austin-Morris 1800, but there was a further fling in the early 1970s when a six-cylinder engined 2200 was produced. The last Wolseley of all – the top-of-the-range Austin-Morris 18-22 saloon – was built in 1975 and was replaced by the Princess.

8hp 1946-48

Ready for launch as a 1940 model, and previewed just as war broke out, the little 8hp Wolseley finally went on sale in 1946. So typical of the "Nuffield-generation" Wolseleys of the day, it was based on a contemporary Morris, the 8hp Series E, but with a unique nose and overhead valves. The later MG YA/YB saloons were also close relatives.

The engine was an overhead-valve version of the Morris 8 E's, with 33bhp instead of 30bhp (and Alec Issigonis briefly thought of using it in the still-secret Morris Minor). Much of the chassis was shared with the Series E, though the grille, bonnet and exposed headlamps were all specially designed for this car.

Out of sight there was half-elliptic leaf spring suspension at front and rear, with full hydraulic drum braking and a four-speed gearbox, controlled by the long and spindly central lever of the Series E. Only available as an all-steel four-door saloon, the Wolseley struggled to reach 60mph, and at £416 it was significantly more expensive than the £301 Morris.

Not that the clientele seemed to mind, for there was just enough up-market equipment – leather-trimmed seats, a wood veneer fascia panel, for instance, and an openable windscreen, but no question of a heater – to satisfy them. Then, of course, there was the overall post-war shortage of new cars, so buyers were not terribly fussy.

Small, neat by 1946 standards, meek and unobjectionable, the 8hp was not a car to leave anything but a tinge of memory behind.

SPECIFICATION

BODY STYLES: saloon

PRODUCTION: 5344

ENGINE & TRANSMISSION: 918cc, 4cyl ohv, 4sp man, f/r

POWER: 33bhp @ 4400rpm

MAX SPEED (MPH): 60 (E)

0-60MPH (SEC): not available

SUSPENSION & BRAKES: beam leaf front, leaf rear, drums f&r

LENGTH (IN)/WEIGHT (LB): 145/1904

LAUNCH PRICE: £416

A Wolseley 8hp on a hill climb in the early 1950s.

10hp 1939-48

The Wolseley Ten had originally appeared in February 1939, effectively as an up-market version of the new Morris Ten Series M of the period. It was re-introduced in 1946. Apart from having a Wolseley radiator grille, it shared almost all its steel body pressings with the Morris, and was a typically Nuffield-ised Wolseley.

However, it did not have the same structure as the Morris. Strangely enough, while the Morris version had a monocoque body/chassis structure, the Wolseley still had a separate traditional chassis frame, with channel-section

Wolseley 10, 1946. The model had been launched in 1939.

side members and drilled cruciform cross-bracing. The rest of the running gear was almost pure Morris Ten – a 40bhp 1140cc overhead-valve engine (the Morris had 37bhp), half-elliptic front and rear suspension, hydraulic brakes and pressed-steel road wheels.

Wolseley justified the higher post-war price - £474 instead of £378 for the Morris (a considerable increase) – by providing a steel sliding roof, leather seat coverings and a telescopically adjustable steering column. There was real walnut for the door cappings and trim fillets.

Made at Ward End, Birmingham, throughout its life, the Ten's relatively high price made it a slow seller, and the drophead coupé version which had been offered in 1939 did not re-appear after the War. Like the related Morris, in any case, this was a slow and staid car (69mph maximum speed) with a relatively hard ride and not a lot of character, which endeared itself to very few people.

SPECIFICATION

BODY STYLES: saloon

PRODUCTION: 2715, post-war

ENGINE & TRANSMISSION: 1140cc, 4cyl ohv, 4sp man, f/r

POWER: 40bhp @ 4400rpm

MAX SPEED (MPH): 69

0-60MPH (SEC): 38.1

SUSPENSION & BRAKES: beam leaf front, leaf rear, drums f&r

LENGTH (IN)/WEIGHT (LB): 147/2061

LAUNCH PRICE: £474

12/48 1938-48

Along with the 14/60 and the 18/85, this was one of a trio of pre-war Wolseleys which were reintroduced in 1945. Never meant to be other than interim models, they stayed in production until 1948, when the first post-war Nuffield Wolseleys replaced them. There had been a fixed-head coupé, too, in 1939, but that never came back.

The 12/48, mechanically an up-market relative of the Morris 12 of the period, had been launched in 1938, when Wolseley's Birmingham-based fortunes were booming. Like all such late-1930s Wolseleys, it

The four-cylinder Wolseley 12/48 dated back to 1938.

SPECIFICATION

BODY STYLES: saloon

PRODUCTION: 5602, post-war

ENGINE & TRANSMISSION: 1548cc, 4cyl ohv, 4sp man, f/r

POWER: 44bhp @ 4400rpm

MAX SPEED (MPH): 63

0-60MPH (SEC): not measured

SUSPENSION & BRAKES: beam leaf front, leaf rear, drums f&r

LENGTH (IN)/WEIGHT (LB): 163/2968

LAUNCH PRICE: £569

had a separate chassis frame, half-elliptic leaf front and rear suspension, an all-steel four-door body, and a high standard of trim and equipment.

With only 44bhp from a long-stroke engine of ancient lineage, hauling a very large body, this was neither a fast nor an interesting car for the driver, but at least he could enjoy features such as on-board Jackall jacks, a sliding steel sun-roof, an openable front windscreen and leather trim.

The special Wolseley nose made sure that

his neighbours knew he had paid £569 for it immediately after the war – and in this case he also knew that there was no equivalent post-war Morris (nothing bigger than a Morris Ten at this point).

If new cars had not been in such short supply at this time there would surely not have been much demand for a car like this, yet between 1945-48 Wolseley managed to sell 5602 examples to those who could procure a licence to buy them. They were buying status, not modern engineering, and that seemed to be enough at the time.

14/60 1938-48

Here was Wolseley, and Nuffield, at their product planning best. Essentially, the 14/60 was a longer-wheelbase 12/48, with the same four-door passenger cabin but a longer and heavier 58bhp

SPECIFICATION

BODY STYLES: saloon

PRODUCTION: 5731, post-war

ENGINE & TRANSMISSION: 1818cc, 6cyl ohv, 4sp man, f/r

POWER: 58bhp @ 4200rpm

MAX SPEED (MPH): 70

0-60MPH (SEC): 36.2

SUSPENSION & BRAKES: beam leaf front, leaf rear, drums f&r

LENGTH (IN)/WEIGHT (LB): 172/3080

LAUNCH PRICE: £614

Wolseley 14/60 managed 70mph on 1.8 litres.

1818cc six-cylinder engine. This model had originally appeared in 1938, with a range of bodies, but only the four-door

saloon re-appeared in 1945.

The chassis design – half-elliptic leaf springs and beam axles at both ends – was much the same as that of the 12/48, but the wheelbase was up from 98in to 104.5in, the increase all needed to accommodate the longer engine.

More power was unhappily matched by a bit more weight – an extra 14bhp, but 112lb – yet this car was quite a bit faster than the 12/48. It would cruise at more than 60mph, but by later "classic" standards took an age to get there. The usual middle-class Wolseley equipment, and a £614 price tag (only £45 more than the 12/48) meant that it sold well.

Yet this was never a car about which anyone got excited. There are a few still in existence, and loved rather like faithful old Labradors, but they are never likely to bring on any heart attacks.

18/85 1938-48

The third car of the immediate post-war Wolseley range was the 18/85, which had set several hearts aflutter in 1938 and 1939, when it was new. It had the 104.5in wheelbase of the 14/60 but boasted an 85bhp 2322cc of the six-cylinder engine.

In its short pre-war heyday it had been thought to be a quick car, though by late 1940s standards maybe one shouldn't get too excited over the 75mph top speed. Even so, the cars were quick enough, and robust enough, for a number of British police forces to buy fleets of them – we probably remember more 18/85s with Police signs and strident bells than without.

A 2.3-litre Wolseley 18/85 in familiar guise as a Police car.

SPECIFICATION

BODY STYLES: saloon

PRODUCTION: 8213, post-war

ENGINE & TRANSMISSION: 2322cc, 6cyl ohv, 4sp man, f/r

POWER: 85bhp @ 4000rpm

MAX SPEED (MPH): 75

0-60MPH (SEC): 25.4

SUSPENSION & BRAKES: beam leaf front, leaf rear, drums f&r

LENGTH (IN)/WEIGHT (LB): 172/3108

LAUNCH PRICE: £680

Technically, therefore, the 18/85 was like the 14/60, with the same chassis, suspension, four-speed gearbox, and four-door body. None of the pre-war special coachwork returned in 1945, or later. Except in detail, by the way, the engine and gearbox were shared with the pre-war MG SA saloon, though that car had entirely different coachwork and did not come back after 1945.

The 18/85 was naturally the best-equipped of all the 12/48, 14/60 and 18/85 generation. In addition to the fittings on the 12/48 amd 14/60 there were twin Windtone horns and a built-in radio aerial to whisper the word "luxury", but this model didn't handle any better, or stop any better, than the others. Because it cost £680 – only £66 more than the 14/60 – it always outsold that car. In 1948 its natural successor was the all-new Morris-based 6/80.

25hp 1937-39/1947-48

Here was a real oddity. Wolseley had produced several different 3485cc 25hp models in the late 1930s – saloons, drophead coupés and limousines – all of them with this Morris engine and gearbox, but none were re-introduced immediately after the War.

Until September 1947, that is, when the 25hp Limousine re-appeared, at a very high price, and only to be built in very limited quantities. Suggestions that a surplus pre-war stock of running gear had been found in store were never denied, since could be no economic justification for laying down new tooling and new components for a production run of only 75 vehicles!

All 25hp models, therefore, ran on a massive 141in-wheelbase chassis, with a 104bhp 3485cc six-cylinder engine (which found its way into Nuffield trucks too), half-elliptic springs, and Lockheed hydraulic brakes. All the attention, though, was directed at the bodywork, for this car was sold only as a seven-seater limousine, complete with glass division and two foldaway jump seats.

Coachbuilt at Ward End, Birmingham, with a great deal of wood in the construction, this was a formal beast meant only for formal use. The poor driver had no seat adjustment, but at least there were separate heaters in front and rear compartments. Wolseley publicists spoke of "quiet good taste", which meant that the style was strictly late-1930s, with big exposed headlamps and a very upright stance (the 25hp was 72in high). One fascinating detail was the provision of a front-to-rear driver's telephone.

When introduced, the 25hp cost £2568, which was not up at Rolls-Royce levels, of course, but left the car having to compete with Austin Sheerlines, Princesses and Humber Pullmans. Always old-fashioned in style, the 25hp was a surprisingly brisk performer, though it took ages even to shift the sanction of 75 machines. There was to be no successor of any type.

The Wolseley 25hp was only available as a limousine after the War.

SPECIFICATION	
BODY STYLES: limousine	
PRODUCTION: 75, post-war	
ENGINE & TRANSMISSION: 3485cc, 6cyl ohv, 4sp man, f/r	
POWER: 104bhp @ 3600rpm	
MAX SPEED (MPH): 85 (E)	
0-60MPH (SEC): 20.4	
SUSPENSION & BRAKES: beam leaf front, leaf rear, drums f&r	
LENGTH (IN)/WEIGHT (LB): 212/4816	
LAUNCH PRICE: £2568	

4/50 1948-53

The first true post-war Wolseleys – actually modified versions of new Morris models, as usual at this period of history – came along in October 1948. The two new cars, 4/50 and 6/80, were closely related to each other, and to the new Morris Oxford MO and Morris Six models launched in the same year. For the first few months they were built at Ward End, but assembly moved to Cowley during 1949.

Based closely on the four-door monocoque body of the Morris Oxford MO, which had a vee-screen, the 4/50

The 1.5-litre Wolseley 4/50, made 1948-53.

SPECIFICATION	
BODY STYLES: saloon	
PRODUCTION: 8925, only 99 of them at Ward End	
ENGINE & TRANSMISSION: 1476cc, 4cyl ohc, 4sp man, f/r	
POWER: 51bhp @ 4400rpm	
MAX SPEED (MPH): 74	
0-60MPH (SEC): 31.6	
SUSPENSION & BRAKES: tor ifs, leaf rear, drums f&r	
LENGTH (IN)/WEIGHT (LB): 169/2576	
LAUNCH PRICE: £704	

had a five-inch longer wheelbase (the stretch was at the front), with a characteristic Wolseley radiator grille and a 51bhp overhead-camshaft version of the MO's sidevalve engine. The torsion bar independent front end was shared with all other cars in this model range. Up-grades were later shared with the 6/80.

Inside the car, the trim and fittings were of higher quality than the Oxford MO's, with wood fascia and door cappings and a well-equipped dash, but being a Nuffield car it had the then-fashionable steering-column gear change.

The 4/50's problem was that it wasn't much cheaper than the faster and more charismatic 6/80. It had very pedestrian performance and was no great shakes as a driver's car. Yet it did a reasonable sales job for the Wolseley dealer chain. In 1953, its replacement was the more elegant 4/44, which had a smaller engine and less power but was an altogether nicer car. The 4/50 didn't keep many long-term fans.

6/80 1948-54

To understand the 6/80, all any historian has to write is "Police car", for thousands were bought by police forces all round the country – and in "Empire" countries too, for that matter. If you have seen any British cops-and-robbers films of the 1950s, a 6/80 is bound to have been in shot at times.

Looking exactly like the 4/50 at the front, it carried on that well-known Wolseley grille, this time with extra driving lamps. The 6/80 was the fastest and best-specified of all this Morris and Wolseley range. It had the same long-wheelbase monocoque as the cheaper

A Mitchell and J Roberts's lightly biffed Wolseley 6/80 passes the gravely wounded Bristol of Bill Banks and M Porter on the 1955 Monte Carlo Rally.

Morris Six and shared the same four-door saloon cabin as the rest of the family. It was the only one, however, to put 72bhp at the driver's disposal, courtesy of the twin-SU version of the 2215cc overhead-camshaft engine. This was an eager, revvy unit which made all the right noises but was rumoured to suffer burnt valves. The four-speed gearbox, the steering-column gearchange, and the torsion bar independent front suspension were all corporate fittings, but the 6/80 featured the up-market Wolseley fascia, and leather seats and a heater/demister were standard.

Technical upgrades included the fitment of telescopic dampers to the rear suspension from January 1950, and twin telescopic dampers on each side of the front suspension from May 1950. The change from separate bucket seats to a divided front bench (spring 1952) was seen as a retrograde step by many.

By later standards the 6/80 didn't look all that fast, or handle all that well, but because of its police connections it built up a strong following and a surprising number were preserved. In the autumn of 1954 it was replaced by the all-new 6/90 model.

SPECIFICATION

BODY STYLES: saloon

PRODUCTION: 25,281, of which just 19 at Ward End

ENGINE & TRANSMISSION: 2215cc, 6cyl ohc, 4sp man, f/r

POWER: 72bhp @ 4600rpm

MAX SPEED (MPH): 77

0-60MPH (SEC): 27.8

SUSPENSION & BRAKES: tor ifs, leaf rear, drums f&r

LENGTH (IN)/WEIGHT (LB): 177/2688

LAUNCH PRICE: £767

4/44 1953-56

Although the 4/44 was a Nuffield-sponsored project, and intended to replace the 4/50, it appeared soon after

SPECIFICATION

BODY STYLES: saloon

PRODUCTION: 29,845

ENGINE & TRANSMISSION: 1250cc, 4cyl ohv, 4sp man, f/r

POWER: 46bhp @ 4800rpm

MAX SPEED (MPH): 73

0-60MPH (SEC): 29.9

SUSPENSION & BRAKES: coil ifs, leaf rear, drums f&r

LENGTH (IN)/WEIGHT (LB): 173/2445

LAUNCH PRICE: £997

The Wolseley 4/44, 1953-56, was nicely fitted out but had to manage on 1250cc.

the formation of BMC. With much of its engineering and the basic layout of its four-door monocoque shell shared with the yet-to-appear MG Magnette ZA, the 4/44 was actually the last new model to be powered by the pushrod overhead-valve Morris/MG engine, known as the XPAG, which had been fitted to T-Series MGs and to the YA/YB saloons.

The 4/44 was four inches longer than the 4/50 and while looking smaller was equally spacious. Beneath the elegant body was a brand-new monocoque, with coil spring independent front suspension and rack-and-pinion steering. The 1250cc engine produced 46bhp – so it had to work quite hard – the gear change was on the steering column, and there was a split-bench front seat.

Features like the traditional Wolseley radiator grille, with its badge illuminated at night, the circular instruments and (from 1954) a wood veneer fascia, plus leather seat coverings, were all what Wolseley customers had come to expect, so there was little resistance to the £997 selling price.

Compared with the lumpy Morris Oxford-based 4/50, the 4/44 was a great marketing success, with nearly 30,000 cars sold in less than four years. This was down to a combination of appealing looks, good road manners, and visual links with only one other car – the equally striking MG Magnette ZA of the same period.

6/90 Series I/II/III 1954-59

Launched In the autumn of 1954, the 6/90 was the very first BMC-Wolseley – the first Wolseley-badged car to be engineered after the BMC merger, and to use a BMC instead of a Nuffield engine. Although it was not an exact clone of the Riley Pathfinder, the 6/90 shared many chassis components and the same basic body shell proportions, but by no means all the same pressings.

As a direct replacement for the Nuffield-type 6/80, the 6/90 was a big car which almost automatically attracted much attention from the nation's police forces. With 95bhp instead of 72bhp, it was much more powerful and a lot faster than its predecessor. A four-speed manual gearbox with steering-column gearchange was standard and Borg Warner overdrive was an option.

Like the Pathfinder, the 6/90 ran on a perimeter-like separate chassis frame, with torsion bar front suspension, and with its back axle sprung on coils, but located by radius arms and a Panhard

The 1954-57 Wolseley 6/90, with 2.6 litres, was also a police favourite.

rod. The four-door saloon body (there were no alternatives) naturally featured the traditional Wolseley grille, and there was a sloping tail. The front seat was a divided bench, and the circular instruments were positioned ahead of the driver's eyes.

Although many 6/90s were sold to police forces as "chase" cars, their handling was clearly not good enough. From October 1956, therefore, the 6/90 became Series II, looking the same as before but with conventional half-elliptic leaf spring rear suspension. There was also a change to a right-hand floor gear change, the lever being alongside the driver's seat, close to the door.

Engine power rose to 97bhp, and Borg Warner automatic transmission became optional. By this time a real wood fascia had already been adopted.

From mid-1957 the car moved up to Series III, with servo-assisted Lockheed brakes and an enlarged rear window. This type, in fact, was almost identical in every way with the Riley 2.6 model, which went on sale at the same time. In mid-1059, the 6/90 gave way to the entirely different Farina-styled 6/99.

Big, impressive and roomy, these cars did not quite hit the spot, as they were too heavy and were not nimble enough to match their performance. Survivors are very rare.

SPECIFICATION

BODY STYLES: saloon

PRODUCTION: 5776/1024/5052

ENGINE & TRANSMISSION: 2639cc, 6cyl ohv, 4sp man, o/d or auto, f/r

POWER: 95bhp @ 4500rpm/97bhp @ 4750rpm

MAX SPEED (MPH): 94

0-60MPH (SEC): 18.1

SUSPENSION & BRAKES: tor ifs, coil rear (leaf rear on Series II), drums f&r

LENGTH (IN)/WEIGHT (LB): 188/3220

LAUNCH PRICE : £1064

15/50 1956-58

When the MG TF dropped out of production the Wolseley 4/44, being the only BMC model still using the old Nuffield XP-series engine, was in danger. To replace and improve on the 4/44, the near identical-looking 15/50 appeared in June 1956.

Visually and structurally there was virtually no change from the older model, the big advance being the use of a 50bhp 1489cc BMC B-Series engine, and its related gearbox. This time round there was a centre-floor gear change – a great improvement over the steering-column change of the 4/44. Traditionalists

In 1956 the 4/44 received a 1.5-litre engine and became the 15/50.

SPECIFICATION

BODY STYLES: saloon

PRODUCTION: 12,352

ENGINE & TRANSMISSION: 1489cc, 4cyl ohv, 4sp man, or semi-auto, f/r

POWER: 50bhp @ 4200rpm

MAX SPEED (MPH): 78

0-60MPH (SEC): 24.3

SUSPENSION & BRAKES: coil ifs, leaf rear, drums f&r

LENGTH (IN)/WEIGHT (LB): 173/2490

LAUNCH PRICE: £961

complained, of course (they always did), but the fact was that this was a more powerful, more torquey and slightly cheaper car than the 4/44 it replaced. From late 1956 Manumatic two-pedal transmission became optional. This was no more successful or reliable than on any other BMC model.

The 15/50. in effect, was a less powerful version of its sister car, the MG Magnette ZA/ZB series, though it retained the Wolseley grille and front end. Minor style and equipment changes included the use

of a dished steering wheel, and a full-width wood veneer fascia panel with glove boxes at each side, outboard of the instrument panel

All in all, the 15/50 was a better car than the 4/44, but no enthusiastic motorist ever chose one, for the MG Magnette ZB of the period was considerably more desirable and more satisfying to drive. At the end of 1958 this model would be replaced by the Farina-styled 15/60, the first of five different BMC brands to share that new body style.

1500 1957-65

Although the 1500 had a rather tortured development period, once it went on sale it was a surprisingly successful compact four-door saloon.

SPECIFICATION

BODY STYLES: saloon

PRODUCTION: 46,438/22,295/31,989

ENGINE & TRANSMISSION: 1489cc, 4cyl ohv, 4sp man, f/r

POWER: 43bhp @ 4200rpm

MAX SPEED (MPH): 78

0-60MPH (SEC): 24.4

SUSPENSION & BRAKES: tor ifs, leaf rear, drums f&r

LENGTH (IN)/WEIGHT (LB): 152/2060

LAUNCH PRICE: £759

Wolseley 1500, sister of the Riley 1.5. This is a 1961 Series III, distinguished by its wide radiator side grilles.

In the beginning this monocoque shell had been considered as a Morris Minor replacement, then there were Australian cars (Austin Lancer and Morris Major) to be made out of it, but the resulting Wolseley was a surprisingly integrated little car.

It was built on the Morris Minor platform and thus had torsion bar independent front suspension and rack-and-pinion steering. It was, incidentally, always built at Longbridge, which was not traditionally a Wolseley assembly plant.

The 1500, effectively, was the less-powerful sister of the Riley 1.5 (already described). It had near-identical body, suspension, steering, accommodation and basic engine/driveline package. The Wolseley, though, had its own front-end design, a 43bhp instead of a 62bhp 1489cc B-Series engine, and different trim and seating decoration. The fascia had a walnut veneer finish, and the gearchange was on the floor, with MGA-type remote control.

Minor changes over time included the Mk II of 1960, which had hidden bonnet and boot hinges (originals were exposed), while the Mk III of October 1961 had a new grille and sat lower on its suspension (it was commonised with the Riley 1.5). It also sported new tail-lamp clusters, like those of the Asutin A40, and wider radiator side grilles. Production ran out, unheralded, in mid-1965.

Since nearly 110,000 1500s were sold in eight years, BMC would have counted it as a commercial success, but it was a car which somehow lacked a bit of glamour. With more power, and with firmer roadholding, that could have been very different – but one could say that of the Riley 1.5 too. Like the Riley, the bodies were sadly rust-prone, so few examples seem to have survived.

15/60 and 16/60 | 1959-71 |

The 15/60 holds the crown as the first of the five near-identical Farina-styled B-Series BMC saloons which appeared during 1958-59; this Wolseley, in fact, came out in December 1958. It shared the same basic platform and four-door saloon body – not forgetting the fins – as the other cars in the family, but in true BMC style it had all the expected Wolseley touches.

Like the others – Austin A55, Morris Oxford V, MG Magnette III and Riley 4/68 – the 15/60 had a rather narrow track, vague steering and floppy roadholding. It also had the same 52bhp engine as the Austin and Morris types. Though other derivatives had an estate car option, this was never offered behind the Wolseley badge.

At least, though, it had a centre-floor gear lever and was nicely trimmed, with

The Wolseley 16/60 of 1961, another of the BMC Farina family.

leather, wood and reasonable carpeting much in evidence. Two-tone paintwork was optional, and bumper over-riders were standard.

Three years later BMC tried again, improving all five of these B-Series Farinas at the same time. By giving the Wolseley a longer wheelbase, wider track, stiffened-up suspension and a larger, more powerful engine, the 15/60 became 16/60 and was a more satisfying package. Disc brakes were not available, however.

The engine was now of 1622cc, producing 61bhp, and there was the option of Borg Warner Type 35 automatic transmission. At the same time, the rear

tail fins were cropped back, which improved the balance of the styling, and there was a deeply dished steering wheel, along with a more integrated fascia layout. All in all, this was a better car, which BMC could seemingly afford to ignore (in marketing terms) throughout the 1960s. The last car was built in April 1971.

No one ever got excited about the 15/60 or 16/60 models (except, perhaps, to complain about the roadholding, in the early days), which was exactly what the planners had hoped. Aimed at the uncomplaining, slightly status-conscious middle classes, the cars did their job very well indeed.

SPECIFICATION

BODY STYLES: saloon

PRODUCTION: 24,579/63,082

ENGINE & TRANSMISSION: 1489cc/1622cc, 4cyl ohv, 4sp man, or auto, f/r

POWER: 52bhp @ 4350rpm/61bhp @ 4500rpm

MAX SPEED (MPH): 77/81

0-60MPH (SEC): 24.3/21.4

SUSPENSION & BRAKES: coil ifs, leaf rear, drums f&r

LENGTH (IN)/WEIGHT (LB): 178/2473

LAUNCH PRICE: £991/£993

6/99 1959-61

Taking over from the Nuffield-inspired 6/90 of the 1950s, the Farina-styled 6/99 saloon appeared in mid-1959 and, appropriately revised, would stay on the market until the newly-formed British Leyland killed it off in March 1968. Throughout this period it was produced at Cowley.

As was to be expected by industry watchers, the 6/99 had to share almost all its four-door monocoque, and its running gear, with the Austin A99

which was introduced at the same time. This big and heavy structure hid a lusty 103bhp 2912cc pushrod overhead-valve six-cylinder engine, which was backed by a brand-new three-speed all-synchromesh gearbox with Borg Warner overdrive; Borg Warner automatic transmission was an optional extra. The gear lever of both types was on the steering column.

The suspension was utterly conventional, with coil springs at the front and

semi-elliptic leaf springs at the rear. Power-assisted steering was not offered but servo-assisted front-wheel disc brakes were standard. Up front was the usual Wolseley grille, with recessed auxiliary lamps on each side of it. Duo-tone paint was standard as were, a polished wood veneer fascia, plushy leather seats and up-market furnishings.

This big car, it seems, was exactly what the Wolseley dealers wanted. It was handsome and could get very close to 100mph. It would be further improved, as the 6/110, in future years. Guess what? The police bought lots of them!

Wolseley 6/99, 1959, 2.9 litres and 103bhp, replaced the 6/90.

SPECIFICATION

BODY STYLES: saloon

PRODUCTION: 13,108

ENGINE & TRANSMISSION: 2912cc, 6cyl ohv, 3sp man, o/d or auto, f/r

POWER: 103bhp @ 4500rpm

MAX SPEED (MPH): 98

0-60MPH (SEC): 14.4

SUSPENSION & BRAKES: coil ifs, leaf rear, disc f/drum r

LENGTH (IN)/WEIGHT (LB): 188/3415

LAUNCH PRICE: £1255

6/110 Mk I/II 1961-68

From the autumn of 1961, in a general up-grade of its mass-market medium and large saloons, BMC changed the 6/99 into the

SPECIFICATION

BODY STYLES: saloon

PRODUCTION: 10,800/13,301

ENGINE & TRANSMISSION: 2912cc, 6yl ohv, 3sp man, 4sp man, o/d or auto, f/r

POWER: 120bhp @ 4750rpm

MAX SPEED (MPH): 102

0-60MPH (SEC): 13.3

SUSPENSION & BRAKES: coil ifs, leaf rear, disc f/drum r

LENGTH (IN)/WEIGHT (LB): 188/3470

LAUNCH PRICE: £1343

Last police Wolseley was the 6/110, with output increased to 120bhp.

6/110, with significant but not major differences to the body or the performance (the Austin A99 became A110 at the same time).

The package of changes included a slightly longer wheelbase, modified rear suspension linkage and (from July 1962) the option of power-assisted steering and air conditioning. The engine had been improved to give 120bhp, which guaranteed a top speed of more than 100mph – the first time ever for a Wolseley. At last there was a centre-floor gearchange instead of the unpopular steering-column location.

Less than three years later, though, the 6/110 progressed to 6/110 Mk II, with revisions which included a four-speed manual gearbox, with overdrive now a £51 extra-cost option instead of being standard. The road wheels were smaller (13-inch instead of 14-inch), the suspension was firmed up to make it identical with the latest Austin A110's, while inside the car the front seats now had reclining backs, and fold-out picnic tables for the use of the rear seat passengers.

The last version of the 6/110 was was the most satisfactory of this family of big Wolseleys, and would carry on selling until March 1968.

Hornet 1961-69

In all except tiny details, the Hornet was the same car as the Riley Elf (already described) – which is to say that it was a long-tailed version of the front wheel drive Mini, offering more refined interior appointments and more luggage space. The Hornet had a Wolseley grille and its fascia was based on that of the Mini-Cooper, but with wood veneer surrounding the instruments. It was launched with the Mini's 848cc engine and rubber suspension

The 1963 Wolseley Hornet.

SPECIFICATION

BODY STYLES: saloon

PRODUCTION: 3166/16,785/8504

ENGINE & TRANSMISSION: 848cc/998cc, 4cyl ohv, 4sp man, or auto (from late 1967), f/f

POWER: 34bhp @ 5500rpm/38bhp @ 5250rpm

MAX SPEED (MPH): 71/77

0-60MPH (SEC): 32.3/24.1

SUSPENSION & BRAKES: rubber ifs, rubber irs (Hydrolastic from late 1964), drums f&r

LENGTH (IN)/WEIGHT (LB): 129/1435

LAUNCH PRICE: £672

Changes came along at the same time as with the Elf, the Mk II of late 1963 having a 998cc engine. Hydrolastic suspension followed in late 1964, while wind-up windows and a remote gearchange came with the Mk III. There was optional automatic transmission from late 1967 and an all-synchromesh gearbox from mid-1968.

Mk III Hornet with concealed door hinges and Hydrolastic suspension.

1100/1300 1965-73

BMC watchers of the 1960s could take one look at the badging and work this one out for themselves, for the Wolseley 1100 of 1965 was yet another version of the ubiquitous front wheel drive Austin-Morris 1100 range, and so were all its evolutions. Available only as four-door saloons, these cars were always based on the MG1100/1300 types, though with their own archetypal Wolseley front end. The Riley Kestrel (already described) was a very close relation.

Like all other 1100/1300s, the cars had crisp Pininfarina styling, and the Wolseley's fascia was similar to the Austin/MG versions, complete with a strip speedometer and wood veneer, while duotone paintwork was a popular option.

Changes and up-dates were mainly mechanical. Original types had a 55bhp 1098cc A-Series engine and a four-speed manual gearbox. In summer 1967 a 58 bhp 1275cc engine became optional.

In late 1967 the Mk II model was introduced, this having chopped-off tail fins. A few 1100s were made, some with AP automatic transmission, but most of the cars sold were 58bhp 1300s, also with an automatic option.

The 1100 was finally discontinued in February 1968. After this the 1300s got 65bhp with the manual gearbox (all synchromesh from mid-1968), or 60bhp with automatic transmission.

Although they were just as fast as the Riley Kestrels, the Wolseleys were never marketed as sporty cars, but more as miniature "gentlemen's carriages". They sold well, and steadily, until they were dropped in 1973 to make way for the Austin Allegro range.

Wolseley 1300 was introduced in 1967.

SPECIFICATION

BODY STYLES: saloon

PRODUCTION: 17,397/27,470

ENGINE & TRANSMISSION: 1098cc/1275cc, 4cyl ohv, 4sp man, or auto, f/f

POWER: 55bhp @ 5500rpm/58bhp @ 5250rpm/60bhp @ 5250rpm/65bhp @ 5750rpm

MAX SPEED (MPH): 85-97

0-60MPH (SEC): 18.4-14.1

SUSPENSION & BRAKES: Hydro ifs, Hydro irs, disc f/drum r

LENGTH (IN)/WEIGHT (LB): 147/1820

LAUNCH PRICE: £754/£825

18/85 1967-72

The last badge-engineered Wolseley of the 1960s was the 18/85, which was revealed in March 1967. It was a lightly re-engineered and better-trimmed version of the front wheel drive Austin 1800. As one might expect, the basic structure and mechanical layout were not changed, except for the usual Wolseley grille up front, and unique tail lamps.

Inside the car, there were optional reclining front seats, pile carpets, leather facings for all the seats plus a special instrument panel layout. The only technical novelties were power-assisted steering as standard, with Borg

Wolseley 18/85, a close relative of the Austin/Morris 1800.

Warner automatic transmission as an optional extra.

Only two years after launch, in 1969 the 18/85 became Mk II, with minor technical changes, reclining front seats as standard, revised switchgear and a significant price increase (to £1224). At the same time, the 18/85S was launched, this effectively being a 96bhp version of the 18/85 – the same engine tune as already described under Austin 1800 and Morris 1800 S types.

Like other late 1960s Wolseleys, the emphasis was on quality, refinement and superior equipment, which put the 18/85 on a par with smaller Wolseley models of the period. The customer did not buy such a car to boast about its performance, but rather to indulge his taste in in-car furnishings.

The 18/85 was dropped in 1972, when a 2.2-litre six-cylinder version of the same car – the Wolseley Six – was introduced.

SPECIFICATION

BODY STYLES: saloon

PRODUCTION: 35,597

ENGINE & TRANSMISSION: 1798cc, 4cyl ohv, 4sp man, or auto, f/f

POWER: 85bhp @ 5300rpm/86bhp @ 5300rpm/96bhp @ 5700rpm

MAX SPEED (MPH): 90/99

0-60MPH (SEC): 17.1/13.7

SUSPENSION & BRAKES: Hydro ifs, Hydro irs, disc f/drum r

LENGTH (IN)/WEIGHT (LB): 166/2576

LAUNCH PRICE: £1040

Six 1972-75

SPECIFICATION

BODY STYLES: saloon

PRODUCTION: 25,214

ENGINE & TRANSMISSION: 2227cc, 6cyl ohc, 4sp man, or auto, f/f

POWER: 110bhp @ 5250rpm

MAX SPEED (MPH): 104

0-60MPH (SEC): 13.1

SUSPENSION & BRAKES: Hydro ifs, Hydro irs, disc f/drum r

LENGTH (IN)/WEIGHT (LB): 1567/2620

LAUNCH PRICE: £1470

The 1972-75 Wolseley Six was wide enough to accommodate a transverse six-cylinder engine under the bonnet.

The original Six was the third of the near-identical E6-engined front-drive cars launched by British Leyland in March 1972. It would remain in production, little changed, for just three years before being replaced by the new-generation wedge-shaped Six.

Technically identical to the Austin and Morris 2200s of the period (see above), the Six was a direct replacement for the 18/85S, and was closely linked to the existing 18/85, both visually and structurally.

Because it was Wolseley-badged, the Six wore that marque's usual unique grille, the fascia featured circular dials set in a wide expanse of highly polished walnut veneer, and the car's occupants lounged in cosseted luxury. For all other details, see the Austin 2200 1972-75 entry.

Six (18-22 type) 1975

Like its Austin and Morris 18-22 equivalents, this was a very short-lived model indeed, for after only one sales season (March to August 1975), it was dropped in favour of re-badged cars called Princess.

Technically this car was the same as the

SPECIFICATION

BODY STYLES: saloon

PRODUCTION: see Austin/Morris 18-22

ENGINE & TRANSMISSION: 2227cc, 6cyl ohc, 4sp man, or auto, f/f

POWER: 110bhp @ 5250rpm

MAX SPEED (MPH): 104

0-60MPH (SEC): 13.5

SUSPENSION & BRAKES: HydraG ifs, HydraG irs, disc f/drum r

LENGTH (IN)/WEIGHT (LB): 175/2638

LAUNCH PRICE: £2838

Wolseley version of the British Leyland 18/22 family was the Six, made in 1975 only.

contemporary six-cylinder Austin and Morris models, though there were certain unique trim and decoration features. The Wolseley version had a different front grille (by no means the same shape as before, though), along with nylon velours upholstery, a wood veneer instrument panel with circular instruments, and several items of extra equipment.

For all further technical details, see the Austin 18-22 entry.